Jacques Derrida's famously challenging book *Glas* puts the practice of philosophy and the very acts of writing and reading to the test. Formatted with parallel texts, its left column discusses G. W. F. Hegel and its right column engages Jean Genet, with numerous notes and interpolations in the margins. The resulting work, published for the first time in French in 1974, is a collage that practices theoretical thinking as a form of grafting.

Presented here in an entirely new translation as *Clang*—its title resonating like the sound of an alarm or death knell—this book brilliantly juxtaposes Hegel's totalizing, hierarchical system of thought with Genet's autobiographical, carceral erotics. It innovatively forces two incompatible discourses into dialogue with each other: philosophical and literary, familial and perverse, logical and sensory.

In both content and structure, *Clang* heightens the significance of all encounters across ruptures of thought or experience and vibrates with the impact of discordant languages colliding.

Clang

CARY WOLFE, SERIES EDITOR

Jacques Derrida

Clang

Translated by Geoffrey Bennington and David Wills

posthumanities 62

MINNESOTA

University of Minnesota Press
Minneapolis
London

The University of Minnesota Press gratefully acknowledges financial support for the publication of this book from the Centre national du livre.

Originally published in French as *Glas*. Copyright Editions Galilée 1974.

Published by the University of Minnesota Press
111 Third Avenue South, Suite 290
Minneapolis, MN 55401-2520
http://www.upress.umn.edu

ISBN 978-0-8166-9150-0 (hc)
ISBN 978-0-8166-9152-4 (pb)

Library of Congress record available at https://lccn.loc.gov/2020023719

Printed in Canada on acid-free paper

27 26 25 24 23 22 21 10 9 8 7 6 5 4 3 2 1

Contents

French Edition Insert

First: two columns. Truncated, at top and bottom, and carved out in their flanks: incisions, tattoos, incrustations. A first reading could act as though two texts, standing one against the other or one without the other, did not communicate with each other. And in a certain deliberate way that remains true, as to pretext, object, language, style, rhythm, law. A *dialectics* on the one hand, a *galactics* on the other, heterogeneous and yet indiscernible in their effects, sometimes to the point of hallucination. Between the two, the clapper of another text, one might say of another "logic": nicknamed *obsequence, penitrate, stricture, lock, antherection, bit*, etc.

For whomever is attached to the signature, to the corpus, to what is proper, let us declare that putting my name, my body, my signet into play (or rather into pieces), in one and the same blow I elaborate, literally, those of a certain Hegel in one column, those of a certain Genet in the other. You'll see why—by chance and necessity—it's those two. The thing, then, rises up, details and detaches itself, turning into two towers, and the incessant acceleration of a turn by turn. In their double solitude, the colossi exchange an infinite number of overlaps, of winks, double each other up at every opportunity, interpenetrate each other, stick and unstick, passing the one into the other, between the one and into the other. Each column here figures a colossus [*colossos*], the name given to the dead man's double, to his erection's substitute. More than one, before all.

Colossal writing outplays quite differently mourning's calculations. It surprises and unsounds *the economy of death* in all its reverberations. *Glas* in decomposition, its double bind, its double getting hard, hardbind against hardbind, is first the analysis of the word *glas* in all the twisted and retrenched virtualities of its "meaning" (staves, peal of any and every bell, burial, funeral rites, legacy, last will and testament, contract, signature, proper name, forename, nickname, classification and class struggle, the labor of mourning in the relations of production, fetishism, transvestism, preparation of the dead body, incorporation or introjection of the corpse, idealization, sublimation, sublation, rejection, remainder, etc.) and of its "signifier" (theft and deportation of all the forms of *Glas*—acoustic and graphic, musical and rhythmic—choreography of *Glas* in its letters and polyglottic fecundations). But this opposition (*signified/signifier*), moreover like all oppositions—in particular sexual opposition—is by regular chance compromised, each term divided in two agglutinating with the other. A *gl* effect (glue, birdlime, spit, sperm, balm, unguent, etc.) forms the identity-less conglomerate of this ceremonial. It replays mimesis and the arbitrariness of the signature in a wild coupling (fake, signet, milk), drunk like a bellringer hanging from his rope.

What remains of absolute knowledge? Of history, of philosophy, of political economy, of psychoanalysis, of semiotics, of linguistics, of poetics? Of labor, of language, of sexuality, of the family, of religion, of the State, etc.? What remains, to be detailed, of the remainder? Why these questions in the form of colossi and phallic flowers? Why exult in thanatopraxis? What's the enjoyment in celebrating, me, here, now, at a given time, baptism or circumcision, marriage or death, of father or mother, Hegel's father, Genet's mother? Remains to know—what has failed to be thought: the detail cut in a *coup*.

J. D.

Translators' Preface

Hegel and Genet, poles apart. Seemingly, as far apart as the scent of a rose and the fetid odor of a reformatory latrine, putatively as different as the sexuality one might associate with one or the other. Apart—you immediately see the empty space—but contiguous or adjacent enough to produce an echo chamber, to allow sound and smell, whether welcome or unwelcome, joyous clamor or death knell, perfume or fart, to waft across, producing something we would struggle, but nevertheless be required to, call knowledge. Poles—you immediately see a certain erect verticality—but the interruptions are also evident, the softoffs as inevitable as the hardons, indeed a whole industrious fabrication of feminization is woven through the literature that Derrida foregrounds, a wholesale queering and *transing* of virile (homo)sexuality takes place, to the extent that we would struggle to know, in spite of the familiar, even stereotypical practices, what constitutes (a) sex and (a) sexuality.

The Genet column of *Clang* was born from a conjunction of professional and personal interests, as recounted in the biographies of one and the other writer by Edmund White on one side, and Benoît Peeters on the other. It began with Derrida's 1965 *Tel quel* article on Artaud ("La parole soufflé"), which attracted the attention of a mutual acquaintance, Paule Thévenin, who hosted a dinner where Genet and Derrida met and immediately formed a close friendship. That friendship flourished in particular over a period of about five years, with notable manifestations such as a series of tête-à-têtes in the uncanny calm and agitation of May 1968 Paris, Derrida's support of Genet's activism in favor of Angela Davis and the Soledad brothers, and a touching letter contributed by Genet to an issue of *Les Lettres françaises* devoted to Derrida's work in March 1972, in which he compares the philosopher's writing to that of Proust, and advises a slow reading that accepts "what is offered to us with good grace, namely poetry. Then, sense will be proffered in recompense, very simply, as in a garden." They were still in contact following Derrida's brief incarceration in Prague in 1982, with Genet wanting to know, precisely, whether Derrida had recognized the odor of that other garden, the prison.

Genet's response to *Clang* in 1974 was friendly, if muted. The book's righthand column was mostly composed in summer of 1973, written at a feverish pace on a portable Olivetti typewriter. Derrida had earlier begun writing a double-column work on Condillac, which had perhaps been inspired by Genet's "What Remains of a Rembrandt," a text that had appeared in *Tel quel* in 1967. But we should remember that Derrida flirted more than once with such manufactured formal interventions during the same period, for example in his "Double Session" of 1970, one of whose most explicit subjects was Mallarmé's obsession with white, blank, and black spacings, especially the latter's "Un Coup de dés [Throw of the Dice]"; or the twin columns of "Tympan," which Derrida wrote in 1972 as the Preface to *Margins of Philosophy*. Countless hours of artisanal, manual cutting, pasting and typesetting were required to produce the marriage of dialectics and galactics, or the treatise on organology, that the book engineers. It appeared with Éditions Galilée in September 1974. The stakes of the experiment were very high for Derrida, who recognized the book's "scandalous, or obscene" provocation, but also saw it as reviving an old tradition of embedding text within commentary unfettered by current academic norms, providing "another space, another practice of reading, of writing, of exegesis" (*Points*).

*

At first sight, the exuberance of the Genet column, with its proliferating neologisms and its bold claims to have seen off most, if not all, the "archeologists, philosophers, hermeneuts, semioticians, semanticians, psychoanalysts, rhetoricians, poeticians, perhaps even all those readers who still believe, in literature or anything at all," stands in quite stark contrast to the manifest pedagogical patience of the Hegel column, with its careful exposition of a number of difficult moments in Hegel's thought, gathered around the motif of the family. And indeed the basis for that column is provided by a seminar first taught at the École normale supérieure in 1971-2 under the title "La famille de Hegel," which explicitly presents itself as an "introduction" to Hegel (something of this gesture is still to be found in *Clang*). The first 225 or so pages of the Hegel column correspond quite closely to the fourteen typed sessions of the seminar, the session divisions of which can sometimes (though not systematically) be detected in *Clang* itself (larger gaps in the text correspond at certain points to breaks between sessions). Although almost every sentence of the seminar text has been somewhat edited or rewritten for *Clang* (but not to an unusual extent for Derrida texts based on seminar materials), and some quite substantial additions have been made (most obviously the developments on *pleroma* and on John the Baptist, and the lengthy inserted quotations from Hegel's correspondence), the text follows quite recognizably the general shape of the seminar, which ends its fourteenth and final session on the question of the prohibition of incest. Even some of the inserts into the body of the text correspond to asides or (sometimes handwritten) marginal annotations to the seminar, and certain more striking "inventions" of the text, such as the neologistic deployment of the usually feminine noun *pénombre* in the masculine are to be found in annotations to the seminar (in this case some dense, difficult to decipher handwritten marginal additions to session 9). The final 70-odd pages of *Clang,* including the discussions of Feuerbach, Marx, the long excursus on fetishism, and the reconstruction of the passage in Hegel from religion to philosophy as presented especially in the *Phenomenology of Spirit,* do not correspond to anything in "La famille de Hegel," but they certainly do not break with the pedagogical commitments of the earlier part, and indeed archival research confirms that they too are in fact largely based on seminar materials (this time from the seminar given the very next year at the Ecole Normale Supérieure, under the title "Religion et philosophie") and may have already been incorporated into the presentations Derrida gave of this material in Berlin in 1973, which he subsequently described as a presentation of *Clang* itself.

This pedagogical quality of the Hegel column (which can, and indeed should therefore be read—a first time at least—as an "Introduction to Hegel") displays all the qualities of Derrida's expository writing, familiar from, for example, the second part of *Of Grammatology*, or texts on Husserl and Heidegger. The meticulous and generous quality of the writing should disallow any hasty sense, which some readers have had, that Derrida, in seeking "a staircase that would not be Hegelian," is simply *critiquing* Hegel. This could also be demonstrated by placing the Hegel column of *Clang* into the series of other substantial engagements with Hegel, most notably "The Pit and the Pyramid" in *Margins.*

Derrida's choice of the motif of the family as a guiding thread for his "introduction into Hegel" can seem surprising or capricious, but in fact it allows him to range widely over the whole of Hegel's vast corpus from very early to very late, to address many concepts and arguments that would be widely accepted as central to Hegel's thought, and in many cases to contrast their articulation in Hegel with the way they are thought by others, especially Kant. Throughout the text, Derrida is concerned to appreciate the strength and resilience of Hegel's thinking, and indeed its almost invincible quality, the way it anticipates and incorporates opposition to it as part of its imposing and somewhat intimidating logical advance. The crux of the reading, we might reasonably suppose, concerns the way that the Hegelian dialectic, and especially its major operator, that is the movement of *Aufhebung* [sublation], appears able to process and overcome—without insuperable sticking points or erratic remainders—difference in general. Hegel's dialectic relies on the claim that difference must, logically, resolve into opposition and thereby contradiction, with contradiction necessarily sublating to an ever higher, more spiritual level of thought, finally culminating in philosophy itself as Absolute Knowing, which "knowing" includes the knowledge of all the steps in the complex process leading to that culminating stage, in which spirit sums itself up, finally sublates sublation itself and cancels the temporal dimension that allowed for its progress, and comes to the endless enjoyment of itself in its absolute and assured possession of itself.

Like some other French thinkers of his generation, Derrida is suspicious of this treatment of difference: as he had trenchantly stated in the "Positions," which dates from the same time as the "Hegel's Family" seminar, "if there were a definition of *différance*, it would be precisely the limit, the interruption, the destruction of Hegelian sublation *everywhere* it operates." As Hegelian sublation indeed operates everywhere, this is an ambitious claim that might find parallels in Deleuze, Lyotard, or Michel Serres: but Derrida's way of developing that interruption involves a process of *reading* unlike that of any of his contemporaries: *Clang* is the enactment and record, the *signature* of that reading.

Along the complex dialectical path that defines Hegel's system as encyclopedic, Derrida pays particular attention to a number of difficult moments and makes a number of "methodological" points that are of the greatest interest and importance in understanding the relationship of deconstruction and dialectic. Thematically, all the while following the guiding thread of the family, this involves detailed reconstruction of, for example, the following: the philosophical status of language as it emerges from mere sound (*Klang*); the relationship between Christianity and Judaism (with the striking suggestion that from a Hegelian point of view, Kant is, structurally speaking, Jewish); the relation between the sexes and its import for the relationship of individual to family to civil society and the state (with memorable and fascinated focus on Antigone); the relationship between religion and philosophy more generally, which engages with a lengthy discussion of fetishism, and the suggestion that Hegel's treatment of "inner Africa" in his philosophy of history perhaps secretes a negativity that cannot strictly be dialectized as Hegel claims it must. Methodologically speaking, none of this is presented as a *refutation* of Hegel (the concept of refutation falling readily within Hegelian schemas): and in the insert on fetishism this very situation is schematized, such that "inner Africa,"

> *if we extract the logical schema* of the analysis, [belongs] to an unconscious which cannot be dialectized as such, has no history, stands stubbornly on the threshold of the historico-dialectical process. But this non-dialecticity, this ahistoricity can always be interpreted as negativity, the resistance proper to the dialectical economy, and thenceforth interned in the speculative process.

> A certain undecidability of the fetish leaves us oscillating between a dialectic (of the undecidable and the dialectic) or an undecidability (between the dialectic and the undecidable).

But that oscillation is, as it were, all that Derrida needs: what "*can* always be interpreted as negativity" perhaps *need* not always be interpreted as (dialectical) negativity, and once the necessity of the dialectic is questioned in this way, then the prospect of some radically *other* understanding of history, religion, and philosophy in general opens within the absolutizing embrace of the Hegelian system. That "other understanding" is then regularly enacted in the process of reading that deconstruction is: and that process here involves both the as it were internal infecting of the Hegelian encyclopedia with the virus of *différance,* and the opening of that system to all the forces of subversion unleashed by the work of Genet over in the other column, itself assertively and provocatively read according to no philosophically or theoretically recognizable "method."

*

The formal innovation of *Clang* is visibly one of the book's most significant features, something most relevant to the volume's republication at a date that is rushing toward a half century after its initial appearance. That is to say, the *parenthetic prosthetizing*, or *prosthetic parenthesizing* of *Clang* represents a level of technological—might we say "genetic"—engineering of the textual body that obviously points forward to the hypertextual possibilities of the information age. For we should not forget the distance traveled from 1965, when the word "hypertext" first appeared in print, through Douglas Engelbart's demonstration of a hypertext interface in 1968, to the development of more complex systems through the 1970s and 1980s, up to the first internet browsers of the early 1990s. Of such contemporary technological innovations Derrida was no doubt blissfully unaware as he toiled in 1973-74 with scissors and glue à la William Burroughs to graft, cultivate and bring to bloom this striking textual hybrid.

On the other hand, he was patently cognizant, to the extent of having made it a constitutive quasi-transcendental postulate of deconstruction, of the very idea of grafting as the very idea of textuality as writing. Here are three moments of exposition of that postulate, sowing the proverbial seeds that would sprout into *Clang*: "To write means to graft. It's the same word" ("Dissemination," 1969); "One ought to explore systematically not only what appears to be a simple etymological coincidence uniting the graft and the graph (both from *graphion*: writing implement, stylus), but also the analogy between the forms of textual grafting and so-called vegetal grafting, or even, more and more commonly today, animal grafting. . . . one must elaborate a systematic treatise on the textual graft" ("Double Session," 1970); "And this is the possibility on which I want to insist: the possibility of sampling [*prélèvement*] and citational graft which belongs to the structure of every mark, spoken or written, and which constitutes every mark in writing before and outside of every horizon of semio-linguistic communication" ("Signature Event Context," 1971). Every inscription, therefore, pierces and rends the presumed homogeneous purity of the text, from the "moment" one puts stylus to papyrus, and conceptually speaking before that, in the trace that gives rise to such a material possibility.

Derrida's linking of inscribing and hybridizing within the sense of the graft underscores the extent to which *Clang*'s biological and floral emphasis, the wordflowers it strews, the botanic ontology it hypothesizes, is as artificially constructed as are its columns. Its discourse of fertilization, germination, generation, vegetation, pullulation, luxuriation, and attendant sensorialization, sensualization and sexualization, is at the same time a discourse of technologization. For that reason, by means of grafting, the book speaks to us precisely of the bioengineering to which we just referred. As much as it evokes, or reverts to a type of plant or flower ontology—as if promoting a botanical animism, rehabilitating the innocent religion or primitive vitalism disparaged by Hegel—it also promotes or allows for a *culture* of the flower that is an interventionist transformation, and potentially an adulteration, of the *nature* in it: nature's hybridization, cross-fertilization as trans-fertilization, implanting as mechanized reproducibility, splicing and cloning, originary miscegenation or "vegetal incest."

Consistently, in the Genet that Derrida lays out in his righthand column, one finds side by side the natural mingling of "flowers and odors" of "a wisteria vine and a rose-bush," and, in the first place, a frank, transgressive sexuality ("a vegetal incest would waft its fragrance toward a band of youngsters . . . who, with a hand in a torn pocket, were stroking themselves"), coupled with, in the second place, a complex array of "confabulations" (*Miracle of the Rose*). Just as no floral perfume is ever far from a fart (roses do indeed fart in Genet), neither is any natural flower ever far from a fake flower. The whole thematics of the artificial, *ersatz*, *toc*, *postiche* that is explicitly developed in Genet—emblematized by the bunch of artificial grapes Stilitano uses for a codpiece in *The Thief's Journal*—is both underscored by Derrida and staged in the contrivances of his column, by means of its subdivisions, its incisions or incrustations, its decontextualizations and recontextualizations, its catachreses (*bande*, *cloche*), its anagrams, its interrupted syntagma (*cou . . . p*, *gl . . . obal*, *moi . . . gnon*). Some jar, or come across as more disingenuous than others, but all of them are undeniably theatrical: never just some grand dramatization of nature without also being nature gone to the theatre.

For those reasons, as we find ourselves some seventy years after the major texts by Genet, some forty-five years after *Clang*, at the dawning of a whole new age of manipulations of life, these fragmentary remnants speak to us perhaps more contemporaneously still. They speak to us of what is born from bodies that couple—as used to be said—*with* and *against* nature. They speak to us in a language of flowers, as if speaking flower: uttering beauty and disconsolation, sensuality and pollinose overload, outpouring, abundance. Yet also, of course, uttering ephemerality and extinction. From the remains in its first words—those of a Hegel, those of Genet's Rembrandt, whichever first catches your readerly glance—to the piece of debris that is its final vocable, *Clang* tolls in the littered space of a type of species extinction; decay, disappearance and death inhabit it. It speaks vanishing.

Bits remain, archival jetsam, more or less sedimented tatters of various textual fabrics, but there is little to help us understand some operative law of survival any more than some logic of natural or artificial selection. What has a better chance of survival: the thoroughbred stallion or the broom, the plant or the human? Or even: what is the chance that the sound of clapper against bell rim, not to mention the forged iron itself—its integrity, shape, and fissures—have a future existence or resonance once they are consigned to the accumulations of geological time? On Genet's side, there is first the etiolated condition of the monochrome carceral universe, which is conversely enhanced by the colorful characters who inhabit it, by the florid language that describes it, and by the natural beauty of wisteria, tea-rose and hawthorn that abounds in its rural ambience. His comrade inmates represent the abject detritus of respectable society, but the fetid quarantine of their lives comes alternately to be celebrated or redeemed as a type of religion, and indulged as the site of overwhelming dejection and nostalgic desire. If Genet's fiction finds no contradiction in a farting rose it is because the prison is its most familiar world—indeed where family is found—and the overgrown outhouse is its most familiar abode. His narrators pine after that world and after their comrades and lovers in it, from poem to poem and from volume to volume. They worship most those who pay the supreme sacrifice—Our Lady, Pilorge, Harcamone—revering them for having embraced the cult of abjection all the way to the guillotine, to the extent of decapitation or decollation, self-*abjecting* all the way to *rejecting* the head itself.

*

Between the columns of *Clang*, then, one hears echoing the death knell of various pasts reduced to ruins, a tolling that either mourns them or celebrates their demise: Hegel's encyclopedic philosophical system, Genet's strange faith in a redemptive literature beyond or through his execration of it. Similarly, Derrida's own inflammatory and flamboyant construction of the columns and knotted insets that constitute this book represent a spectacular raising of the stakes—albeit two bizarrely skewed stakes—for any future project of philosophy on one side, and the reading of literature on the other. Both in its explicit thematic gestures and more massively in the typographical fact of the ongoing juxtaposition of its two very different columns, *Clang* insists on asking more or less explicit questions about how Hegel or Genet might be read, but also about how *Clang* itself is to be read, and indeed whether it is readable at all in any recognizable sense, once the horizon of meaning has been breached and the academic professionals have left the "theoretical agora."

Unsettling, sometimes incongruous, shocking, or simply aleatory echoes and resonances emerge across and between the columns, often as enigmatic as the unavoidable but not obviously meaningful parallelism of the "proper" names hEgEl and gEnEt, as indecipherable as the more or less discreet or insistent signatures and counter-signatures that disturb the order of the concept, that stage and displace the old quarrel between philosophy and literature in a way that will continue to challenge all our available reading strategies. The problem that has been obvious from beginning to end of *Clang*, from its first lower case q, or cue—*quoi du reste . . .*—or its first fragmentary quote about a (presumably reproduced) masterpiece torn into fragments—*ce qui est resté d'un Rembrandt déchiré*—is the enormous problem of how to take, receive, or read it, let alone comment on it, translate it, critique it. For the student of literature as much as for the philosopher, Derrida's columns remain as hard to process forty-five years after the event as they were in 1974, as fascinating as they are confounding. What, then, remains, and what, moreover, is to be done with these leftovers? How will this knell now be heard, having somehow survived its own tolling, its own entropic drift? The answer is very different, no doubt, the hearing that *Clang* now receives will be very different from the intonations and detonations that accompanied, perhaps even provoked its writing. We can understand elements of that original context: a type of exhaustion of or from the pace of Derrida's breathless output during the five-year period 1967-1972, a desire to strike out in a new direction that might have been as much a strategy of not letting deconstruction settle into a predictable mold as an urgency dictated by the approach of middle age; or a form of outbidding or raising of the stakes [*surenchère*] such as will come to be thematized in the other formally audacious text of this decade of Derrida's work, namely his 1980 "Envois" (*The Post Card*). But whatever cause or motive we ascribe to *Clang*, staying attuned to various instantiations of now or then, there is no avoiding its clamor for attention, no pretending it doesn't exist or that it speaks too softly to be heard. For that reason we can hope, perhaps even presume, that the translation undertaken here, for all that it inevitably leaves unattended of the rich network of resonances that Derrida produces, will nevertheless transfer something of that clamor, as translation in its etymological sense is given to perform, transferring or carrying across, *transing* it, some operative remainder of what, from utterance to utterance, from column to column, and between those columns, among them, in this knell, still sounds out.

*

Clang translates the French *glas* [glɑ], a masculine noun referring to the fact, event and performance of a bell ringing: a clang, knell, peal, toll, or chime. The word conveys the initial violence of the sounding of the bell, its echoing or resounding effects, and its fade to silence; and it speaks to the short life of that sound, whereby its ringing—like every such sound—is also its own death knell. Like the event it refers to, when the word *glas* is pronounced it begins as a guttural, quasi-metallic, perhaps even industrial clamor or pure noise, and ends in a type of crystalline vocalic sonority or music.

In that way, the French word can be heard as having two parts to it (*gl-as*), like the two columns of Derrida's text; two parts that are in tension or opposition to each other, but that are nevertheless made to function as a unit. The first part of the word *glas*—its *gl*—is all phonemic stress. The English *clang* repeats something of that stress. *Gl* or *Cl* is a vocal contortion, requiring the rapid articulation of two very different phonemes (in phonetic terms a velar plosive [g/k] and an alveolar lateral approximant [l]), to activate the back of the throat and the tongue as it were on the edge of physiological capacity (although, of course, languages other than French or English seamlessly produce sounds that would for us be far more challenging). One gags or chokes somewhat as one pronounces *gl/cl*, as though one's speech were impaired by a clot of saliva, mucus, milk or sperm, which sets in motion some of the semantic networking that *Clang* exploits, particularly in its Genet column.

The second part of the word *glas*, its vocalic but banal purity [a], fades easily to silence. To subvert that, emphasizing now not the oral but the written form of the word, Derrida sets about reversing, inverting or *palindromizing*, and *consonantizing* it. The semi-silent final two letters of *Glas* become *sa*, and its pure sonority mobilizes instead a massive semantic system. *Sa* is first of all the third person feminine singular possessive adjective ("his," "her," or "its" followed by a feminine noun). *Sa* is also, by homonymic extension, *ça*: a demonstrative pronoun, the indefinite "that"; and, when used as a noun (*le ça*), is French for Freud's miasma of driven energy, the "Id." But more importantly in *Clang*, *sa* is the acronym or signature for Hegel's "Absolute Knowing [s*avoir* a*bsolu*]," to which Derrida wants to take some sort of blunt instrument, such as the clapper of a bell—or which he wants to face down with something as distasteful (for a Hegel) as the literature of a Genet—or whose death knell he wants to sound even as, readers will find, he painstakingly or surgically analyzes it.

The 1986 translation of *Glas* by John P. Leavey, Jr. and Richard Rand was an extraordinary labor of erudition, for which Derrida himself expressed his own "demonstrations of friendship and gratitude" in his Preface to *Glassary*. Now, approaching thirty-five years later, and more than fifteen years since Derrida's death, we believe that his 1974 work is able to function differently within that corpus and philosophy: that is to say, while remaining one of the most complex and formidable texts he ever produced, *Glas* is now able to function more "freely" within the broader context of his work, and, we wager, able to perform its tightrope act without the support apparatus that Leavey and Rand provided. That said, we wish to pay formal homage to their work here.

In 1986, the translators' attention to signifying play and networks, and cross-referencing within Derrida's existing corpus and philosophical thinking, seemed indispensable to the extent of Leavey's producing a type of concordance to accompany the translation itself. And indeed, our own translation continues to rely on *Glassary*'s identification of extensive quoted material, mainly from Hegel and Genet, that Derrida decided not to acknowledge in formal academic terms, no doubt because of the general non-respect for norms that *Glas* demonstrates. For all quotations, then, the reader is referred to John P. Leavey, Jr. (ed.), *Glassary* (Lincoln and London: University of Nebraska Press, 1986), pp. 137-81, which is all but impeccable in identifying excerpted quotes page by page and line by line. For quotations from Hegel's *Philosophy of Right, Science of Logic,* and *Phenomenology of Spirit,* we have referred to the more recent translations by H. B. Nisbet (Cambridge: Cambridge University Press, 1991), George Di Giovanni (Cambridge: Cambridge University Press, 2010), and Terry Pinkard (Cambridge: Cambridge University Press, 2019) respectively.

Clang obviously presents many challenges for the translator. We have silently modified existing translations where inaccuracies exist or where Derrida's commentary draws attention to a particular word or nuance. Wherever no English translation exists, translations are our own.

This new translation and edition preserves the pagination of the Galilée edition, which will allow readers of French to locate elements of the original text in the English translation. We have tried to avoid having the reading of *Clang* interrupted by an undue number of glosses, Gallicisms, or linguistic contrivances. Some, however, we found impossible to avoid. The following list is a minimal set of words used repeatedly by Derrida, and which, in our opinion, require explanation for a non-French speaker:

bander: both "to get/have an erection," and "to bind" or "to bandage." We have often used the portmanteau neologism "hardbind" to combine the two senses of the word.

déjà: "already," but used repeatedly by Derrida as a signet or signature through play on, and inversion of, his own initials [ʒide].

je m'ec: a fragment Derrida extracts from Genet, it could be the beginning of various reflexive verbal clauses, such as *je m'écris* [I write myself], *je m'écœure* [I make myself sick] or *je m'écoule* [I flow out]. *Mec* is a common slang word for "guy," but with more masculinist force than the English word; it is derived from *maquereau*, argot for "pimp."

recouper: literally "to recut," but also "match up," "crossrefer," "overlap," "cut across."

seing: "signet" (traditionally a wax seal with a stamped signatory impression, or the stamp or finger ring used to make that impression). *Seing* is pronounced the same as *sein* ("breast"), and it evokes *sang* ("blood"). It is also an anagram of *signe* ("sign"), which keys into Derrida's rewriting of signification as a function of signature effects.

tomber: "to fall," but in the third person of the present tense (*tombe*) it becomes a homonym for "tomb." We have opted for the portmanteau neologism "tombfall" where both those senses are mobilized.

voire: most literally translatable as "verily," as it is derived from Lat. *verus*, but that sense has fallen into disuse. It is currently used in French to reinforce a contrast, comparable to English "or even . . ." In *Clang*, Derrida uses it sometimes in isolation, reverting to its antiquated usage, but also suggesting an ironic touch ("oh, really?"). *Voire* is of course a homonym for *voir*, "to see," suggesting something like "we'll see about that," perhaps also "go see for yourself."

*

We wish to express our heartfelt gratitude for the invaluable assistance of a group of students and colleagues at various stages in the preparation of *Clang*. The translation has benefitted greatly from the efforts of Rébecca Ausseil, Katie Chenoweth, and Rodrigo Therezo. Special thanks to Andrew Kingston for his meticulous reading of the final draft and scrupulous attention to the proofs.

Geoffrey Bennington
David Wills

what remains today, for us, here, now, of a Hegel?

For us, here, now: that's what will not, henceforth, have been thinkable without him.

For us, here, now: these words are quotations, already, always, we will have learned that from him.

Who, him?

His name is so strange. From the eagle it gets imperial or historical power. Those who still pronounce it *à la française* [*aigle*], and there are some, are ridiculous only up to a point: the restitution—semantically infallible for anyone who's read him a little, only a little—of magisterial coldness and imperturbable seriousness, the eagle caught in ice and frost.

Let the emblemed philosopher be thus fixed.

Who, him? The leaden or golden eagle, white or black, did not sign the text of absolute knowing [*savoir absolu*]. Still less the red eagle. What's more, we don't yet know if *Sa* is a text, gave rise to a text, if it was written or if it wrote, caused to write, allowed to write.

Sa will henceforth be the acronym of *savoir absolu* [Absolute Knowing]. And *IC*, let us note already since the two staves represent each other, short for the Immaculate Conception. A properly singular tachygraphy: it's not there primarily, as one might think, to dislocate a code, i.e. what people bank on too much. But perhaps, much later and slowly this time, to exhibit its edges

We don't yet know if it let itself be taught, signed, ensigned. Perhaps there is an incompatibility, more than a dialectical contradiction, between teaching and the signature, a magister and a signatory. Letting oneself think and letting oneself sign—perhaps these two operations can never ever overlap.

His signature, like the thought of the remainder, will envelop this corpus but will no doubt not be comprehended in it.

remains to be thought: that's not emphasized here now but will already have proven itself on the other side. Meaning must respond, more or less, to the calculations of what in terms of engraving is called counterproof

This is—a legend.

Not a fable: a legend. Not a romance, a family romance as Hegel's family is in play here, but a legend.

It does not claim to give the whole corpus to be read, texts and drawings of Hegel, only two figures. More precisely two figures in the process of effacement: two passages.

"*what remained of a Rembrandt torn into small quite regular squares and tossed in the shitcan*" divides in two.

Like the rest.

Two unequal columns, they say, each of which—envelope or sheath—incalculably overturns, turns inside out, replaces, remarks, cuts across [*recoupe*] the other.

What is incalculable in *what remained* makes its own calculation, elaborates every blow, twists or scaffolds them in silence, you'd wear yourself out faster by counting them. Each little square is delimited, each column cut out with impassive smugness, and yet the element of contagion, the infinite circulation of general equivalence brings each phrase, each word, each stump of writing (for example "*je m'éc . . .*") back to each of the others, within each column and from one column to the other of the infinitely calculable *what remained*.

Just about.

Of the remainder moreover, there are always, overlapping, two functions.

The one assures, guards, assimilates, interiorizes, idealizes, sublates the fall in the monument. The fall is maintained there, it embalms and mummifies, monumemorizes, is named there—tombfall [*tombe*]; so then, but as fall, is erected there.

Two very determinate, partial, particular passages, two examples. But of the essence the example perhaps makes play.

First passage: the religion of flowers. In the *Phenomenology of Spirit,* the development of natural religion has as always the form of a syllogism: the mediate moment, "plant and animal" includes a religion of flowers. It isn't even a moment: a station. It is almost exhausted in a passage (*Übergehen*), a vanishing movement, the effluvium floating above a procession, the march from innocence to guilt. The religion of flowers is supposedly innocent, the religion of animals guilty. The religion of flowers (the factual example of it supposedly comes from Africa, but especially from India) does not remain, or scarcely, it proceeds to its own culpabilization, its own animalization, to the becoming guilty, and therefore serious, of innocence. And this to the extent that the same, the self-same (*Selbst*), does not yet take place in it, still gives itself only (in) its representation (*Vorstellung*). "The innocence of the *flower religion,* which is merely a selfless representation of the self, passes over into the seriousness of warring life, into the guilt of *animal religion*; the motionless being and the impotence of intuiting individuality passes over into destructive being-for-itself."

"Die Unschuld der Blumenreligion, die nur selbstlose Vorstellung des Selbsts ist, geht in den Ernst des kämpfenden Lebens, in die Schuld der *Tierreligion*, die Ruhe und Ohnmacht der anschauenden Individualität in das zerstörende Fürsichsein über."

Second passage: the phallic column of India.

The *Aesthetics* describes its form in the chapter on "Independent or Symbolic Architecture." It supposedly spread to Phrygia, Syria, Greece, where during the Dionysian festivities, according to Herodotus quoted by Hegel, women pulled the thread attached to a phallus, making it stand erect in the air, "almost as big as the rest of the body." In the beginning, then, the phallic columns of India, enormous formations, pillars, towers, broader

always look sideways toward India to follow this enigmatic passage, that passes very poorly, between the Far West and the Far East. India, neither Europe nor China. A sort of historical bottleneck. Tightly gathered like Gibraltar "sterile and costly rock," columns of Hercules the history of which belongs to that of the route to the Indies. In these slightly shady straits, the east-west-Eurafrican panorama shrinks infinitely. Point of no becoming. The rocky point has often changed names, however. The promontory has been called Mons Calpe, Notre-Dame-du-Roc, Djebel Tarik (Gibraltar)

The other—lets fall the rest. Risking coming down to the same thing. Tombfall—two times columns, waterspouts—remains.

Perhaps the case (*Fall*) of the signet [*seing*].

If *Fall* marks case, fall, decadence, failure or slit, *Falle* equals snare, trap, noose, machine that grabs you by the neck.

The signet tombfalls.

The remainder is unutterable, or almost: not through empirical approximation but rigorously undecidable.

"*Catachresis,* n. 1. Trope by which a word that has been diverted from its proper sense is accepted into everyday usage to designate something else that retains an analogical relation with the first object. For example, tongue, because the tongue is the principal organ of articulated speech; an ice (-cream) . . . a leaf of paper. It is also by means of catachresis that one says: decked out in silver [*ferré d'argent*]; to ride on a stick . . . 2. Musical term. Harsh and uncommon dissonance. [Gr. Καταχρησις, misuse, from κατα, against, and χρησις, usage].

Catafalque, n. Raised ceremonial stage in the middle of a church for the coffin or representation of a dead person . . . [It. *catafalco;* LL. *catafaltus, cadafaldus, cadafalle, cadapallus, cadaphallus, chafallus.* According to Du Cange *cata* is from LL. *catus,* war-machine called a *cat,* after the animal; and according to Diez, *catare,* see, look at; moreover, finally, those two etymologies overlap, given that *catus,* cat, and *catare,* to look at, have the same root. It remains to explain *falco,* which, given the Low Latin variants that use a *p,* can only be the Germanic word *balk* (vide "balcony"). *Catafalque* is the same word as *scaffold* (vide that word)

Cataglottism, n. Term from ancient literature. Use of mannered words. [Καταγλωττισμος, from κατα, indicating a search, and γλωσσα, word, tongue (vide glose)." (*Littré*)

The ALCs echo, clang, burst, reflect and overlap in every sense, count and discount, opening—here—in the stone of each column sorts of inlaid peepholes [*judas*], crenels, slats [*jalousies*], loopholes [*meurtrières*], for seeing so as not to let oneself be imprisoned in the colossus, tattoos in the folded skin of a phallic body, given to read

at the base than at the summit. Now at the outset—but as an outset already setting out away from itself—these columns were intact, untouched, smooth. And it is only later (*erst später*) that in their flank, if one can call it that, notches, excavations, openings (*Öffnungen und Aushöhlungen*) were made. These hollowings, these holes, these deep lateral marks supposedly supervened, as it were, on phallic columns that were first of all not pierced or apparently unpierceable. Images of the gods [*Götterbilder*] were placed, nested, inserted, embedded, sunken, tattooed there. These little lateral caves or pockets on the flank of the phallus heralded the Greeks' little portable and hermetic temples, as they also cut into the model of the pagoda which is not quite yet a dwelling and which is distinguished by the separation between shell and kernel (*Schale und Kern*). A scarcely determinable middle between column and house, sculpture and architecture.

So no lodging there. For anything whatever, dead or alive. It is neither a house nor a burial place. Who contemplates such a structure, who can, one wonders. And how in an altar, a habitat or a funerary monument, an urban landscape or a mausoleum, the family and the state can find their origin.

Let's bet—throw of the dice—that I have already chosen

there, behind the absolute of an *already* [*déjà*], what is there

"Hauptsächlich in Indien nun gingen von dieser Art der Verehrung der Zeugungskraft in der Form der Zeugungsglieder auch Bauwerke in dieser Gestalt und Bedeutung aus; ungeheure säulenartige Gebilde, aus Stein, wie Türme massiv aufgerichtet, unten breiter als oben. Sie Waren ursprünglich für sich selber Zweck, Gegenstände der Verehrung, und erst später fing man an, Öffnungen und Aushöhlungen darin zu machen und Götterbilder hineinzustellen; was sich noch in den griechischen Hermen portativen Tempelhäuschen, erhalten hat. Den Ausgangspunkt aber bilden in Indien die ausgeholten Phallus-säulen, die sich später erst in Schale und Kern teilten und zu Pagoden wurden."

Correspondences: the moment that follows immediately both the religion of flowers and the phallic columns, as it were sublating them immediately, is the Memnon, the colossal resounding statue (*kolossale Klangstatue*) that produces a *Klang* when struck by the sun's rays. The *Klang* announces the end of the religion of flowers and of the phallic columns, but it is not yet a voice or a language. This vibrating, sonorous light, reverberating as though on a stone bell, is already no longer mute, but not yet speaking (*nur Klang und nicht Sprache*). One can verify the structural correspondences among all the descriptions of the *Klang* in the *Aesthetics*, the *Phenomenology of Spirit*, the *Philosophy of Nature*, etc.

Cause to pass between the words, within the word itself dividing into two (noun and verb, cadence or erection, hole and stone), the very fine, barely visible stem, something that can't be sensed in a cold lever, a scalpel or *style*, in order to irritate then ruin enormous discourses that, even as they disclaim it more or less, always finish by attributing an author's copyright: "that comes back to me," the signet is mine.

Stakes of the signature—does it take place? which place? how? why? for whom?—that will be dealt with practically, *en passant*: indispensable preamble for explaining formality ("literary" formality, for example) with all the pumped-up judges who question it on the basis of apparently extrinsic standpoints (the

only ever upon erection, legends also for the stones of *The Balcony* or the brothel. Irma tells the Chief of Police that his "image does not yet conform to the liturgies of the brothel." He protests: "My image is growing bigger and bigger, I assure you. It's becoming colossal. [Like the "gigantic phallus," the "prick of great stature" whose form this head cop will later be advised to take.] You've got secret peepholes in every wall. Every partition, every mirror is rigged. . . . You don't need me to tell you that brothel tricks are mainly mirror tricks." If you were able to go right round this column you would come back toward *The Balcony*, reading in it ("The Envoy: History was lived so that a glorious page might be written, and then read. It's reading or the Image that counts." Further along, Roger repeats the sentence, adding again: "It's reading that counts." . . . "Carmen: The truth: that you're dead, or rather that you don't stop dying and that your image, like your name, reverberates to infinity") through the "stones" that "say," that "venerate [*tutoient*]," death standing tall, the knockingshop, the ringing of bells, apotheosis, tomb as pedestal, mausoleum, the neck of a prelate, the great comedown of the Immaculate Conception, etc., the letters and stairways of "glory." Concerning what clangs here—and decomposes the corpse of the word (balc, talc, alga, brilliance [*éclat*], ice [*glace*], etc.) in all senses—this is the first and last time that, to make an example, you are here as if *forewarned* by this text. You'll have to do the rest of the work alone and blame yourself, like him, like one who writes, in your tongue. At least. "Perhaps I wanted to accuse myself in my own tongue." You will also have to work with the word "tongue" as does an organist

these two narrow passages, this angle or this strange strait in order to introduce, strictly, to Hegel's name.

Einführung, as the German philosophers say, introduction *into* Hegel. *Einführung* takes the accusative and thus marks the active movement of penetration. Do not stay here on the edge of the Hegelian thicket. Do not stop immediately at all the difficulties, intrinsic or extrinsic, intrinsically extrinsic—and supplementary—that the decision of such a dice-throw opens up. There have been many introductions into Hegel, you can buy them in bookstores; and the problem of the introduction to Hegel's philosophy is *the whole* of Hegel's philosophy: *already* posed everywhere, in particular in his prefaces and forewords, introductions and preliminary concepts. So one would find oneself, already, drawn into the circle of the Hegelian beginning and set skating or sliding endlessly in it. I mark the decision and interrupt the vertigo with a fictive rule: this operation—the knell of *Sa,* the knell as *Sa*—is addressed to someone who has not yet read or understood Hegel, which is perhaps the most usual situation, in any case mine here now.

To work in Hegel's name, to raise it up for the duration of a ceremony, I have decided to pull on one thread. It will appear too thin, strange and fragile. It is the law of the family, Hegel's family, the family in Hegel, the concept of the family according to Hegel.

In the great expositions in the *Encyclopedia* or the *Principles of the Philosophy of Right*, "objective spirit" is developed in three moments, abstract right (*Recht*), morality (*Moralität*), and *Sittlichkeit,* which is variously translated (ethics, objective morality, good customs) and which I will not try to translate in my turn. (One day, elsewhere, I'll say why I love this German word.) Now within *Sittlichkeit,* the third term and moment of synthesis between the formal objectivity of law and the abstract subjectivity of morality, a syllogism develops in its turn.

Its first term is the family.

Its second, civil or bourgeois society (*bürgerliche Gesellschaft*).

Its third, the State or the constitution of the State (*Stadtsverfassung*).

Even before analyzing these dialectical syllogisms and the architectonic to which they give rise, one can see the stakes and the interest of this familial moment. The interpretation of it immediately engages with Hegel's entire determination of right on one side, politics on the other. Its place

question of the subject classified biographically, historically, economically, politically, etc.). As for general textuality, the signet perhaps represents the case, the place of (topical and tropical) overlapping, of intrinsic by extrinsic.

Initialling [*émarger*], an incessant operation: sign in the margins, exchange the name for revenue, whittle down, try to reduce the margin and let oneself precipitate in the angles—labyrinthine frame.

Case and offcut. What remains of a signature?

First case: the signature belongs within what it is presumed to sign (painting, relief, discourse, etc.). It is in the text, it signs no more, it operates as an effect within the object, plays as a part in what it claims to appropriate for itself or deport back to the origin. Filiation is lost. The signet is deducted [*se défalque*].

Second case: it stands, as is usually thought, outside the text. By the same token it emancipates the product that does without it, without the name of the father or mother, no longer needing that to function. Filiation is still denounced, it is always betrayed by what remarks it.

In this double case the secreted loss of the remainder crossrefers. There is supposedly only excrement. If we were to push it, the whole text (for example when it is signed "Genet") would gather inside some "vertical coffin" (*Miracle of the Rose*) like the erection of a signet. The text is remaining [*r(est)e*]—tomb, the signature is

is such in the structure and the development of the system, in Hegel's encyclopedia, logic and onto-theologics that the displacements or disimplications it will be subjected to cannot have a simply local character.

Before attempting an active interpretation or even a critical displacement, supposing that to be rigorously possible, we still have to decipher patiently this difficult and obscure passage. However preliminary it be, such a deciphering cannot be neutral and passive. It intervenes violently, at least minimally so: the choice of this place and this moment, the family, in Hegel's systematics.

This choice is far from innocent. It does not just depend on theoretical ulterior motives; no doubt also on unconscious motivations, which must be put into play and put to work, without any prior theorization of them being possible.

The concept of the family is very rigorously inscribed in the system: in those final forms, later than the *Greater Logic*, constituted by the *Encyclopedia* and the *Principles of the Philosophy of Right*. Must we limit the analysis to this final, systematic place?

It can be limited in two ways. By being content to have these last texts do the work, or by considering that everything preceding them can be read as a development teleologically oriented, without break, without essential displacement, toward this final fulfilment.

One can dream of a strait between these two limits which in truth are only one. But there is no pure solution, no solution in principle to such a problem.

What in it remains always irresolute, impracticable, non-normal or non-normalizable is what interests and constrains us here. Without paralyzing us, but forcing us to adopt a *way of proceeding* [*démarche*]: zigzagging, oblique what's more, buffeted by the shore the point is to avoid, like a ship in a difficult maneuver.

by jerks, jolts, little successive tremors, touching the banks

We cannot pretend to begin with the chronological beginning, pretty much *The Life of Jesus*: there is no sense in privileging here the law of temporal or narrative unfolding which has, precisely, no inner conceptual sense. That's already a resonance of Hegel's teaching. And at the limit, even if we did agree to proceed in that way, somewhere we would

remaining—tombfall—the text. The signature remains abode [*demeure*] and tomb. The text works to get over mourning it. And reciprocally. Endless crosscutting of noun and verb, of proper name and common noun in the case of the castoff [*rebut*].

The grand stakes of literary discourse—I indeed say discourse: the patient, cunning, almost animal or vegetal, tireless, monumental—laughable also but making itself a laughingstock rather—transformation of its proper name, *rebus*, into things, into the name of things. The thing, here, would be the glass in which is captured the chant or heat of an appellation bandaged [*qui se bande*] in the name.

Genet often pretended to define the "magnifying" operation of his writing by the act of nomination. That claim appears frequent enough for us to suspect some hackneyed refrain.

What is a refrain?

What does the act of "magnifying" nomination consist in? Giving to a proper name the form of a common noun? Or the opposite? In both cases one denominates, but in each case is it appropriating, expropriating, or reappropriating? What?

What is a thing? What is the name of a thing?

have to anticipate, if only the end of the first sentence of the first text.

Genealogy cannot begin with the father.

Anticipation or precipitation (risk of precipice and fall) is an irreducible structure of reading. And teleology does not only and always have the appeasing character people like to ascribe to it. One can interrogate it, denounce it as a lure or an effect, but one cannot reduce the threat it poses.

With the *telos* one can also find a cliff. On which to stand firm or fall.

In positing teleological necessity *in effect* we are already in Hegel. All he did was powerfully deploy the consequence of this proposition.

So we cannot either avoid or accept in principle teleological anticipation, and nor can we accept or avoid in principle the empirico-chronological delay of narrative.

A bastard way to proceed?

Is there a place for the bastard in onto-theology or in Hegel's family? That's a question to leave on one side, to keep in the margin or on a leash when we enter into a true family or into the family of truth. No doubt it is not so external to the question of the *Klang*; at least its exteriority pushes toward the center of the question another exteriority, without corresponding to the Hegelian concept of exteriority.

A bastard path, then, which will have to pretend to follow naturally the circle of the family, either to enter into it, or to share it: either to share it as one partakes in a community, a supper, or to share it out as one does by dividing up.

I won't say any more about the procession or the method. As Hegel would say, it will speak of itself as it goes along.

I begin with love.

This concept does not leave much room for gossip, in spite of appearances, nor for declaration.

It is constructed in the third part of the *Philosophy of Right*, the one that deals with *Sittlichkeit*, after the first two parts have dealt with abstract right and morality, respectively. *Sittlichkeit* sublates *Moralität* as it separates itself from it. These two words are difficult to translate and even, *qua* words if not *qua* concepts, to distinguish. Hegel explains himself here as to some arbitrariness. And he explains himself in order to show: 1. that he was concerned to distinguish the signifier from the concept; 2. that he was not entrusting

Let's drop for now his personal case. When Genet gives names, he baptizes and denounces at the same time. He gives the most: the name is not, or so it seems at first glance, a thing that one encounters in nature or that one acquires in commerce. It appears produced, once only, by an act without a past. There is no more pure present, no generosity more inaugural. But such a gift of nothing [*don de rien*], of no thing, such a gift violently appropriates, it collars, accosts what it seems to engender, it penetrates and paralyzes at one fell swoop the donee hallowed thus. The latter is magnified, becoming somewhat the thing of the one who names or nicknames it, especially if it is the name of a thing.

"I was chaste.
Armand was away on a trip. Although I heard that he was sometimes called by other names, we shall keep this one. Am I myself not up to my fifteenth or sixteenth name, including Jean Gallien, my current one?"
One would have to dig into what is arbitrary about this name—Gallien—not to mention these initials, J.G. And if this chance pseudonym were to form the first name matrix of the text?
As for initials, in *Funeral Rites* it is J.D. Jean D. "The escutcheon with a capital D embroidered in silver had been, for a day, the family's coat of arms." "My contact with the concrete wounds my sensibility cruelly: the black escutcheon adorned with the silver-embroidered 'D' that I saw on the hearse . . ." The capital D to which falls the representation of the family name doesn't necessarily come back to the father. In any case, it concerns the mother and she is the one who benefits from the title, "the mother was ennobled by the escutcheon on which a capital D was embroidered in silver." As for the one who organizes the *Funeral Rites*—literary, that is—of J.D., shall we say he is the author, the narrator, the narratee, the reader, but then of what? He is both the dead man's double (*colossos*) who remains living after him, his son, but also his father and his mother. "The star of my friendship rose up larger and rounder into my sky. I was pregnant with a feeling that could, without my being surprised, make me give birth to a strange but viable and certainly beautiful being, Jean's being its father [*la paternité de Jean*] vouched for that." He was always afraid of his death being stolen from him, and since that couldn't fail to happen to someone who has only one, he has occupied ahead of time all the places where there is dying. Well played? Who can do better, who can say better, the dead one

to etymology the right to regulate the content of a concept. One cannot find out what a word properly means by referring to some supposed primitivity or authentic originarity. Which didn't prevent him from playing, productively and genetically, poetically even, with dictionaries. The proof that a word is never a concept is that the same word or two words with an analogous root can have two different, even opposed, conceptual significations. Which immediately disqualifies the authority of etymology, at least as a philosophical, logical, conceptual recourse. Hegel says so at the end of the *Introduction*, when, following the procedure of all his systematic expositions, he presents the schema of internal division, of auto-differentiation as auto-determination and auto-production of the concept. The moment when the *Einleitung* (introduction) becomes *Einteilung* (division). He then explains the passage from *Moralität* to *Sittlichkeit* and tries to justify the all but arbitrary choice of these two words. It is because this choice is arbitrary that the translations waver. "*Moralität* and *Sittlichkeit*, which are usually regarded as roughly synonymous (*die gewöhnlich etwa als gleichbedeutend gelten*), are taken here in essentially distinct senses (*sind hier in wesentlich verschiedenem Sinn genommen*). Yet even representational thought [*Vorstellung*] seems to distinguish them; Kantian usage prefers the expression *Moralität*, as indeed the practical principles of Kant's philosophy are confined throughout to this concept, even rendering the point of view of *Sittlichkeit* impossible and in fact expressly (*ausdrücklich*, strictly) infringing and destroying it. But even if *Moralität* and *Sittlichkeit* were etymologically synonymous (*gleichbedeutend ihrer Etymologie nach*), this would not prevent them, since they are now different words, from being used for different concepts." [PhR §33]

the critique of Kant's practical philosophy organizes the whole of the *Philosophy of Right*: it secures the passage from *Moralität* to *Sittlichkeit*. Kant cannot—in Hegel's eyes does not want to—think the possibility of *Sittlichkeit* and therefore neither can nor wants to, for reasons to be analyzed (with or without Hegel) think this essential moment of *Sittlichkeit* that is the family. There is supposedly no Kantian concept of the family, no philosophical, logically deducible and rigorously assignable concept that escapes the chatter of an empirical anthropology. There is no Kant family in the sense that there is a Hegel family; what this latter implies—love, (monogamous) marriage and above all the child—would be inconceivable for Kant. Except through an empirical and extrinsic accident: like a bastard.

At the end of his life, Hegel replies to a natural son come to get himself recognized: I know I had something to do with your birth, but previously I was in the accidental and now I'm in the essential

The thing: magnificent and classified, both raised above every taxonomy or nomenclature, and already identifiable within some order. To give a name is always, like every birth decree [*acte de naissance*], to sublimate a singularity and finger it, hand it over to the police. All the police in the world can be put to rout by a nickname, but even before they know it a secret computer will have kept them up to date at the moment of baptism.

To accost [*arraisonner*] is to ask for identity papers, an origin and a destination. It means claiming to recognize a proper name. How to name without accosting? Is it possible?

When Genet gives his characters proper names, kinds of singularities that are capitalized common nouns, what is he doing? What is he offering to be read under the visible scar of a capitalizing emajusculation [*émajusculation*] that always threatens to reopen? If he calls Mimosa, Querelle, Divine, Yeux-Verts, Culafroy, Notre-Dame-des-Fleurs, Divers,

sibylline effect of arbitrariness in the immaculate choice, in the conception of syllables that name and open glory. Convention dethrones and crowns at the same time. The ablation of the forename, with the nickname alone doing the task, concentrates the powers of crosscutting, remarks and suppresses ad infinitum the uniqueness in what is common, scattering it in the namelessness of what is variable and diversifiable given that the singular individual—

Is the question of vocabulary marginal here?

Hegel did not skirt the problem of philosophical language. Is it a natural language or a formal language?

It matters here that Hegel did not separate this question from a family question.

I begin by summing up the results of his analysis: the family speaks and does not speak; it is a family from the moment it speaks—passing from *Klang*, if you will, to *Sprache*, from resonance to language—but it destroys itself *qua* family as soon as it speaks and abandons the *Klang*. Like natural language, like language in general, it stops being what it is as soon as it posits itself as such, it denies itself as nature in becoming what it is naturally, just like nature itself moreover [*du reste*].

The Jena texts describe the development of the family within the *Volksgeist*, the spirit of a people. The family is essentially spiritual. Language too: "Only as the work of a people is *speech* the ideal *existence of the spirit*." Spiritual language is therefore also natural. Belonging to the people, the family is therefore always speaking; there is no biological family; but the language it speaks is not, or so it seems, formal or arbitrary. And yet, by reason of the structure of the internal development of language, what is elaborated in it is destroyed itself by that very fact, or rather subjects itself to the process of the *Aufhebung*, is sublated. By positing itself as a system of natural signs, existing in exteriority, language rises to the concept (internal ideal signification) and from then on denies itself as a system of natural signs.

there is no family without *Geist*, no *Geist* without family. *Geist*, spirit: both the possibility of repetition (tradition, history) and of breath holding itself in in sonorous vibration (inhalation/exhalation). *Geist* also concords with death according to Hegel, spiritual life with natural death. To understand something about spirit, sniff out some exhalation, some expiring repetition.

Let that not prevent the same words being used for different concepts, and, in order to betray the language, homonyms and false etymologies for analogous concepts.

Words are therefore unleashed. They enrage the dictionary. Language has no place, no safe place. Discourse gives meaning, but like an informer comes to betray a network. *Traditio* delivers (*überliefert*) meaning but only to lose the institution in repetition. The scene of language must always be calibrated on one too many. The opposition (language/discourse) denounces itself, itself and all the others

The thing (the referent) is sublated (*aufgehobene*) in the sign: raised up, spiritualized, magnified, embalmed, interiorized, idealized, named, since the name accomplishes

prisoner of common law—is named Divers. The nomination is more solemn, more inaugural, more instituting also, when the thesis of the name erects the attribute, the epithet, the adjective, which is not even yet the name of the thing but the accident that occurs, adding itself without necessity to the substance and being always capable of detaching itself in order to fall. What is the epithet? What is its status? In other words, how does one confer on it its status? And what if, conversely, every status were that of an epithet? "The fact that his name was Divers endowed him with an earthly and nocturnal dream quality sufficient to enchant me. For one isn't called George Divers, or Jules or Joseph Divers, and that nominal singleness set him on a throne as if glory had recognized him when he was still in the children's hell. The name was almost a royal nickname, in short, haughty, a convention. And so he galloped in and took possession of the world, that is, of me. Henceforth I enjoy it as though pregnant with it" (*Miracle of the Rose*). The "nominal singleness" stiffens, stretching out the name as a single piece toward the point or toward infinity. It reduces the classifying gap between last and first name. The body proper, sublime, glorious, gathers in an utterance, without organ. And signs itself in a monogram. "The black escutcheon adorned with the silver-embroidered 'D'" and the "ivy monograms" of *Funeral Rites* form the ideal of the signet. Querelle of Brest "took his knife and cut a highly stylized design of his initials into the humid bark of an acacia. . . . Querelle kept a double watch on himself . . . thoughts offered up to the Holy Virgin. Around his own altar, Querelle embroidered a protective veil, with his own monogram on it, equivalent to the gold-thread on blue altar cloths, the celebrated: M."

etc.,

is he violently snatching a social identity, an absolute property right? Is that the most effective political operation, the most significant revolutionary practice? Or rather—but here we have the refrain of contraries that continuously overlap—is he baptizing them with the pomp and ceremony (glory

the word *glory* is one he uses, proportionally, about as often as the translator of the Gospels, of which he is in the end the most destructive parodying

the sign. In the sign, the (external) signifier is sublated by the signification, by the (ideal) signified meaning, the *Bedeutung,* the concept. The concept sublates the sign, which sublates the thing. The signified sublates the signifier which sublates the referent. "Speech, then, is reconstructed [*rekonstruiert*] in a people, in that although it is the ideal nullification [*Vernichten*] of the external, it is itself *an exterior* [ein Äusseres] that must be nullified [*vernichtet*], sublated [*aufgehoben werden*], in order to become meaningful language [*um zur bedeutenden Sprache zu werden*], i.e. to become what it implicitly is according to its concept [*zu dem, was sie an sich, ihrem Begriffe nach ist*]; thus language is in the people like a total other [*als ein total Anderes*], and becomes totality when it is sublated [*aufgehoben*] as an other, and comes to fruition in its concept."

Language accomplishes itself, therefore, becomes meaningful only by sublating into itself the signifier (sensible, external), traversing it and denying it in view of the concept. In view too of its own concept of language. It becomes language only by canceling/conserving itself in the concept. *Traditio* is *Aufhebung.* Language rejoins its own concept only by getting to the end of what induces it, to the end of its own internal negativity, following a schema of essence as negativity that ceaselessly verifies and elaborates itself.

This becoming (*traditio*) of language, or rather of the linguistic, happens, then, in the heart of a people, of a spirit of a people that would not posit itself without it. Linguistic negativity is reduced neither to a rooting nor an uprooting of a language with respect to the ground of the historical community. The uprooting, denaturalization, explantation of a language completes the enracinating essence of language. This language belongs to a people *qua* finite totality: it is then a "natural language," a finite, particular, determinate language. But it stops being that as soon as it posits itself as such; it completes its essence as "natural" language only by sublating itself, by sublating the natural limits of its system, by de-limiting itself, by overflowing itself toward the universality of the concept. It is thus immediately a universal language that destroys the natural language in it.

The dialectic of language is dialectophagous.

Without this overflow of language that swallows and eats itself, which also vomits up a natural remainder—its

double. I see him working on the Gospels, along with all the mythological texts of which he is a connoisseur, and which he inhabits in name, like a miner who isn't sure that he will emerge alive from the depths of the earth, and who, in his tunnel, experiments with explosions and caving. "Tunnel [*galerie*]," however, needs to be deciphered: it speaks, writes. On legendary partitions. It writes to him, says many things to him. Why does he like galleries so much (what was he planning to do there?)? Not only those that protect, direct or threaten you under the earth, but also those for whom one exposes oneself at the theatre, those that architecture associates with loges, lodgings, balconies, all the galleries of language, all the constructions of simulacra off to one side, all the shelters, more or less fake, hidden away in corners: "the most meager shelter became habitable. I would sometimes adorn it with an artful comfort drawn from what was peculiar to it: a box in the theater, the chapel of a cemetery, a cave, an abandoned quarry, a freight car and so on. Obsessed by the idea of a home, I would embellish, in thought, and in keeping with its own architecture, the one I had just chosen. While everything was denied me, I would wish I were meant for the fluting of the fake columns that ornament façades, for the caryatids, the balconies, the stone, for the heavy bourgeois assurance which these things express" (*Thief's Journal*).

is his word) that he always confers on nomination?

"I wanted them to have the right to the honors of the Name." That statement multiplies, metamorphoses endlessly, to the point of obsessing the totality of the corpus. The proper (nick)name that is given lifts the head that falls on the scaffold but simultaneously doubles what is arbitrary in the sentence by means of its nominating decision;

own—that it can neither assimilate nor equate with the universal potency of the concept, language would not be language—living language, that is—it would not be what it is in itself, in conformity with its concept (*Begriff*), with what in it can be conceived, grasped, taken and comprehended, raised up, what in it leaves with a wing-beat the native soil, carrying off its natural body.

without the conception of the concept, we have dead language, writing and defunct speech, or resonance without signification (*Klang* and not *Sprache*). Affinity here between *Klang* and writing. Insofar as it resists conception, the *Klingen* of the *Klang* plays for the Hegelian logos the role of its mute or its fool, a sort of machinal automat that starts up and acts without meaning to say anything.

Fall, in this case, of language

The natural language of a people becomes what it is, thinks itself, expounds itself as what it was to be, what it will have to have been, by becoming other than itself, making itself artificial, rational, universal, at the moment when the people dies as a natural people. It dies as a natural people by universalizing its products through language and labor. Language and labor, in the Jena field of analysis, sound the end of the natural people by positing it as such, by allowing it to be recognized and named as such.

Now this passage within the language of a people had already opened the path from family to people. The movement whereby the family posits itself as such, gives itself a head, groups itself into a family of families, a sort of hierarchized clan that becomes a people—this movement is also an *Aufhebung*, the retention of what flows away, inasmuch as it flows away. A sort of historical grating or sluice-gate prevents what passes from passing or lets pass what does not pass.

So in order to explain Hegel's disqualification of etymology and assumption of a certain arbitrariness in the use of words, we must thus accordingly take on board his whole theory of language and, in this theory, the whole procession of the negative (the *Aufhebung*). At that point no opposition holds up, there is no longer a choice to be made between natural language and formal language. Natural language carries and touches within itself the sign of its death; it pertains to its body to resound and in so doing to raise up its natural cadaver to the height of the concept, to universalize it and rationalize it in the very time of its decomposition.

This dialectical law folds and reflects itself, it applies itself to its own statements, to its own metalinguistic effects, for example to this apparently singular signifier that in German is called *Aufhebung* and that allows the designation—Hegel

it consecrates and glorifies the fall, cuts one more time, and engraves—on a literary monument. Crashing down like a capital sentence and last judgment the nickname sounds all the louder, bursting your tympanum with its tocsin. All that will have echoed in the striking of a signature.

Ascension of the glorious body, after forty days.

"Tocsin, n. 1. Sound of a bell that is chimed by being struck quickly and repeatedly . . . 'One says "sound the tocsin" . . . but one were better to write *tocquesin;* and then again, if by addition of a "g" one were to write *toquesing,* one would come closer to the etymology. For it is a Gascon word, composed of *toquer,* for which we would now say "touch" or "strike," and *sing,* which signifies "bell," notably a large bell, since in taking fright one sounds more willingly the biggest such.' *H. Est,* Précellence, p. 186. Etym. *Toquer,* and Lat. *signum,* taken, in the Middle Ages, in the sense of bell." (*Littré*)

"It uttered for the first time, following the name Baillon, the words: 'Known as Our Lady of the Flowers.' Our Lady was given the death penalty. The jury was standing. It was the apotheosis. It's all over. When Our Lady of the Flowers was given back to the guards, he seemed to them invested with a sacred character, like the kind that expiatory victims, whether goat, ox, or child, had in olden times and which kings and Jews still have today. The guards spoke to him and served him as if, knowing he was laden with the weight of the sins of the world, they had wanted to bring down upon themselves the benediction of the Redeemer. Forty days later, on a spring evening, the machine was set up in the prison yard. At dawn, it was ready to cut. Our Lady of the Flowers had his head cut off by a real knife. And nothing happened. What would be the point? There is no need for the veil of the temple to be ripped from top to bottom because a god gives up the ghost. All that this can prove is the bad quality of the cloth and its deterioration.

is thrilled—of a law of essential and speculative universality within a natural language, the language of a people. The people that has *Aufhebung* in its throat denies itself as a particular people, chokes and de-peoples itself but this is the better to extend its imperium and infinitely deploy its scope.

Aufhebung is not the only example of this law. Is it even an example?

There remains, then, the general question: how can the idiom of a familial generation be thought, i.e. denied by erecting itself into speculative-type universality?

It supposedly starts with love.

Love is an essential predicate of the concept of family, i.e. an essential moment of *Sittlichkeit.*

How is the passage (*Übergang*) from *Moralität* to *Sittlichkeit* brought about? In *Moralität,* a Kantian-type subjective area, the Good, universal substance of freedom (no freedom without relation to the Good and vice versa) still retains its abstract form. Reciprocally, moral consciousness, the demand for universal objectivity, remains formal and virtual, and therefore immoral. It does not overflow its own unilateral subjectivity. It becomes the contrary of what it is (immoral) to the very extent that it remains closed in on its own side. So Kant holds *Moralität* within a certain unilateral abstraction. The Good on one side, moral consciousness on the other remain separate, facing one another but inaccessible to each other. They are therefore not yet what they are. They are not "explicitly posited" (*gesetzt*) as what they nevertheless are in themselves. They attain to this positing, this being-posited (*gesetztwerden*) only in their negativity, "They become posited in their negativity, for as they one-sidedly (*einseitig*) constitute themselves as independent totalities, both refusing to accept what is present in itself within them—the good lacking subjectivity and determination, and the determinant, i.e. subjectivity, lacking what has being in itself—they sublate themselves [*sich aufheben*] and are thereby deposed (*herabsetzen*), reduced to moments, to moments of the *concept* which becomes manifest as their unity."

The two sides face each other without being able to come together or complete each other, like the two halves or the two abstract walls of one and the same spiritual body. They must negate their unilaterality in the concept, reconstitute in it their menaced or morselled integrality.

The first synthesis that allows them to be linked or read

Though it behooves me to be indifferent, still I would not mind if an irreverent scapegrace kicked through it and ran off shouting, 'A miracle!' It's flashy and would make a very good framework for the Legend."

He who nominates de-nominates—the grand denominator officiates right next to the scaffold, at the moment when *it* [ça] *tombfalls.*

This institution, the law that imposes the name while de-posing the head, goes not without a neck in a single blow.

Division is barely more complicated when the denominator (the Cratylic nomothete) institutes itself or erects itself in its own signature.

Colossal habitat: the masterpiece.

Glory again, whose syllabary initiates—in the future perfect, in the publisher's contract, signed with the institution (family and municipality), that is to say with funeral rites—the organization of the sepulcher. Tear up the contract; the literary operation comes down henceforth to no more than confirming it, indefatigably, in the margin, by means of initials. "There is a book entitled *I'll Have a Fine Funeral.* We are acting with a view to a fine funeral, to formal obsequies. They will be the masterpiece, in the strict sense of the word, the

[*de les lier ou de les lire*] together, to think of them as the flanks of one and the same piece, their first integration (*Integration*), is *Sittlichkeit.* In it the Idea of freedom becomes actually present, it is not merely in the heads of subjective individuals. "That this Idea is the *truth* of the concept of freedom cannot be assumed or derived from feeling or from any other source, but, in philosophy, can only be proved [an object of demonstration, *ein Bewiesenes*]. Its deduction consists solely in the fact that right and the moral self-consciousness [the first two moments of the philosophy of right] can be seen in themselves to return to this Idea as their own result.—Those who think they can dispense with proofs and deductions in philosophy show that they are still far from forming the least idea of what philosophy is; they may well speak (*reden*) on other matters, but those who wish to speak without the concept have no right to participate in philosophical discourse."

the beginning—before it the *already*—supervenes, as always, as the result. The rebounding of the *already* should leave no remainder. In speculative dialectics, the result is not a remainder, the remainder does not result. *Qua* remainder at least. If it could result, it would sublate its remaining. That is no doubt the inevitable consequence of an *already* conceived as origin, beginning, foundation in the sense of presentation

Sittlichkeit, of which the family constitutes the first moment, is the idea of freedom, then, but of freedom as living, present and concrete Good in the present (*vorhandenen*) world, which implies actual elaboration (*Wirklichkeit*), action, operation (*Handeln*). At that moment, the concrete substance of mores (*Sittlichkeit*), such as it is produced and remains in the *Vorhandensein* of the world, exceeds *Meinen* (according to Hegel's play on words between the subjective vacillation of the opining I and what is "mine"); it constrains subjective caprice and vague intention (*Belieben*). It finds its consistency in laws, enduring organizations (*Einrichtungen*), *institutions.*

The consistency, the permanence of the trans-subjective institution goes beyond the individual, imposes itself upon him, binds him, yes, but with the force and dignity of the rational. It erects the individual's freedom and holds it upright. The individual subject is not subjected to it as he is to the empirical force of the natural elements, sun, moon, mountains and rivers. In *Sittlichkeit,* the authority of the laws is "infinitely higher, because natural things display rationality only in a completely external and

It gets erect in its signet but also occupies it like a sarcophagus.

The form of the name—place of reclusion—eats the body and keeps it upright.

Then, sampling in "what remained . . . ," let's not forget that the "vertical coffin" was describing a prison cell ("I entered one of the narrow cells, a vertical coffin"): "nothing tender, no affection. Neither in regard to that form assumed by the other—or its prison. Or its tomb? On the contrary, I tended to show myself as pitiless with it as I was

major work, quite rightly the crowning glory of our life. I must die in an apotheosis, and it doesn't matter whether I know glory before or after my death *as long as I know* that I'll have it, and I shall have it if I sign a contract with a firm of undertakers that will attend to fulfilling my destiny, to rounding it off." At the moment of the "theatrical stunt" in *Funeral Rites,* when the coffin was "slid" into the catafalque—"the conjuring away of the coffin"—prior to its reduction, like the casket of "*Sainte-Osmose*" (fictitious letter about the Golden Legend, published in Italian), to a box of matches—"Jean's death was duplicating itself in another death." The dead Jean, whose corpse is being wrapped [*dont on bande le cadavre*] so that it then takes "the shape and consistency of a milk-almond in its cloths and wrappings," "a soft, compact almond," is watched over, written, hardbound [*bandé*] by the other, by the headstrong friendship of the other ("my friendship went to my head [*m'entêtait*] (as one says: reseda goes to my head)" of him who "love[s] the executioner," wants to make "love with him, at dawn!" And also gets hard. The other gets hard too. In front of him, in front of the flowers, in front of nothing at all. "In the presence of the flowers I got a hard-on, and it made me feel ashamed, but I felt that I could oppose the stiffness of the corpse only with the stiffness of my prick. I had a hard-on and desired nobody." The other gets hard too, such is the question of the noun (of every gender) and of the verb. Getting hard in front of the flower and corpse of his double, a colossal homonym itself erected in its theatrical adversity, that is something that can be observed only from a certain angle, also from a gap in language, which we must now recognize. All writing is perhaps caught, walled in [*enceinte*] in this scene that we could still try to name. For the first name is not enough to classify it. Nor is the second name. One must hardbind the other

singularized manner and conceal it under the form of contingency." This rationality is no longer hidden, but on the contrary unveils itself in the institution.

In the family, love forms the first moment of this rationality. There is no love or family in physical or biological nature. The *logos*, reason, freedom are the milieu of love. The *Encyclopedia* makes this more specific: in the animal realm, generation, sexual relation, the process of copulation which, like the copula of a syllogism, gathers the species together, swallow up individuals in a death without phrase. Contrary to what happens in the human and rational family, animal copulation gives rise to no superior determination. It leaves behind no monument, no burial place, no institution, no law to open and secure a history. It names nothing. "The genus preserves itself only through the destruction of the individuals who, in the process of generation, fulfil their destiny [determination, *Bestimmung*] and, in so far as they have no higher destiny, in this process meet their death."

But death does not appear as such to animals. On the contrary, the limit that *Sittlichkeit* imposes on empirical subjectivity, ultimately its very death, opens up the relation of subjectivity to its substantial freedom. Mortality is experienced in *Sittlichkeit* as an effect of freedom. Individual subjectivity finds in the apparently repressive objectivity of *Sittlichkeit* (its laws, its police, its prisons, its prison colonies) the condition of its freedom, its truth, its essentiality. What negates and cuts subjectivity from itself is also what raises it up and fulfills it.

"The right of individuals to their subjective determination to freedom is fulfilled (*hat seine Erfüllung*) in so far as they belong to ethical actuality (*sittlichen Wirklichkeit*); for their certainty of their own freedom has its truth in such objectivity (*Objecktivität*), and it is in the ethical realm (*Sittlichen*) that they actually (*wirklich*) possess (*besitzen*) their own essence (*ihr eigenes Wesen*) and their inner universality."

Far from being simply restricted and strangled in it, the proper essence, the propriety of individual subjectivity appropriates itself, becomes what it is, possesses itself in the form of its contrary or its negation. It possesses itself: *besitzen* is very strong and one must not erase this sense of possession, of private property, of goods or possessions that constructs the whole problematic of the family. The subjective appropriates itself in the objectivity of *Sittlichkeit*, the individual possesses himself in the generality of

with that form that answered to my name and wrote these lines."

Must we decide between the two effects of this so-called literature of theft, betrayal, denunciation? Expropriation or reappropriation? Decapitation or recapitation? Dissemination or recapitulation, recapitalization? Which way to slice it?

To all appearances, giving in to the Passion of Scripture, Genet has made himself a flower. And he has planted in the earth—with great pomp, but also like a flower, tolling the knell—his proper name, common law names, language, truth, sense, literature, rhetoric and, if possible, the remainder.

At least that is how it appears. And it supposedly began by poisoning the flowers of rhetoric or poetics. The latter, parodied, altered, transplanted, very quickly begin to rot, resembling funerary wreaths thrown over the walls of the cemetery. These flowers are neither artificial nor totally natural. Why does

"The hangman follows close behind. He's whispering sweet nothings in her ear. Claire! The hangman's by my side! . . . They'll all be wearing crowns, flowers, streamers, banners. They'll toll the bell. The funeral will unfold its pomp. It's beautiful, isn't it? . . . The hangman's cradling me. I'm being acclaimed. I'm pale and I'm about to die."

At the moment the knell sounds, allow oneself to be cradled. By an executioner. Having oneself cradled, being given the breast even, by an executioner; by him who, don't forget, allows you to have a name. The name is given next to the scaffold. Whoever gives your name and seal bares your neck to his blade. To divide you. And, in the same gesture, transforms you into a god. But one has only one executioner—as one has only one mother—and so it is your first. And what comes near to the blade, never castrating in the present to elaborate decapitation, will or would have had to be, like the mother, like a child, a virgin. Like Solange in *The Maids*, Our Lady of the Flowers "loved his executioner, his first executioner. . . . Exactly what is an executioner? A child dressed as a fatal sister, an innocent . . . a poor, a humble fellow."

the institution, freedom in the obligatory regularity of a law. This appropriation that means that in order to stand upright, to have consistency, essence, existence, substance, one must rise up into one's opposite, is also an interiorization and an idealization: a magnification since the ideal here causes one to grow. Negativity erects the one in the other. Dialecticity is marked here in the fact that the objectivity (*Objectivität*) of *Sittlichkeit* is at the same time the inner universality (*innere Allgemeinheit*) of the individual subject, of the proper name that posits itself and thus recognizes itself in it.

We have not yet arrived at the family. Only at the general concept of *Sittlichkeit* that defines the general field in which something like a family arises.

Is it by chance that in the paragraphs from the *Philosophy of Right* that present the concept of *Sittlichkeit*, even before there is any question of the family, a quasi-proverbial or legendary quotation should appeal to the father and the education of the son? It is a Remark at the end of a paragraph. Education is also an operation that constitutes/deconstitutes the family, an *Aufhebung* through which the family fulfills itself, *raises itself up* by destroying itself or by falling as a family. *As* a family: once the *as*, the *as such* of essentiality, of essential property raises only by barring, is itself the *as* only as other than what it is, it phenomenalizes the phenomenalization that it discovers only by pulling it down or by having it go under. It appropriates itself only in expropriation.

That's how the father loses the son: by winning him, by educating him, by raising him, by drawing him into the circle of the family, which, according to the logic of *Aufhebung*, comes down to helping him leave it, pushing him out while holding him back. The father gives the son a hand in destroying the family by fulfilling it in what destroys it: civil or bourgeois society (*bürgerliche Gesellschaft*) first of all, and then the State which fulfills *Sittlichkeit* by "sublating the family and civil society," magnifying it.

Here's the remark: an hors-d'oeuvre that is out of place: first as a quotational example, then as an addition to a philosophical and speculative paragraph, finally because its content is "familial," borrowed from a particular determination of *Sittlichkeit*. And for now, this latter is defined only in a preliminary and general way. This anticipation cannot be insignificant.

"When a father asked him for advice about the best way

one say "flowers of rhetoric?" And what would the flower be when it becomes merely one of the "flowers of rhetoric?"

In *Saint Genet* the question of the flower, the anthological question, among others, is unfailingly avoided. Along with those of "psychoanalysis" and "literature," avoided by the most agile and intelligent of lessons in French-style phenomenological ontology of the time. One passage, however, only just misses it. Note that it begins like this: "There remains the simple possibility of *not* reading him. That is the only risk he runs, and it is a big one. But, in the last analysis, whether he is read depends *on him*, on him alone." Indeed [*voire*]. Two figures of the flower are then reduced to the most conventional semantic content, crushed, in the course of the dissertation, between an ontological reading and a poetico-rhetorical reading, each confirming its homology

of educating his son in ethical matters (*seinen Sohn sittlich zu erziehen*), a Pythagorean replied: 'Make him the citizen of a state with good laws (*eines Staats von guten Gesetzen*).' (This saying has also been attributed to others.)"

in the manuscript, Hegel adds this by hand, which will not be found in the French translations: "that of Socrates." Under the heading of the legend, but taking account of the system, I am, then, working here with autographic or oral remarks added by Hegel as though in the margins of his main text. I am working *mit Hegels eigenhändigen Notizen und den mündlichen Zusätzen* that are inaccessible in French. The reader concerned with philological and editorial authentications will always be able to protest or consider them fictions. The onus of the demonstration falls on him

This remark illustrates the general law, the law of the law: individual subjectivity fulfills in truth its freedom in the universality of the *Sittlichkeit* that negates it.

The family is the first moment of this process. The first of the three moments of the syllogism (family, civil society, State) is itself articulated in three moments or three instances that will fulfill it by negating it: marriage, family property, education of the children. But the dialectical unity of these three moments, what makes the family what it is in its being carried away, the unity of its syllogistic self-destruction, is love. A unity that is felt, or rather is feeling, to be felt, a unity of feeling (*sich empfindende Einheit*), a unity that feels itself.

To know what love is, we must therefore find out what it is to *feel*, or feel oneself.

But we won't really know this before we know what love, i.e. the family, is. One feels oneself only *en famille.*

What is the family?

"The ethical (*sittliche*) substance, as containing self-consciousness which has being for itself and is united with its concept, is the *actual spirit* (*wirkliche Geist*) of a family and a people."

Spirit can achieve its actuality only in the family and the people. It would remain abstract, it would choke in singularity. The Remark to this paragraph adds that one must not raise oneself "atomistically" on the basis of singularity considered as a ground (non-spiritual point of view) but proceed from spirit as synthesis of the singular and the universal. The concept of the Idea is spirit, but spirit insofar as it knows itself and insofar as it is actual (*als sich wissendes und wirkliches*). Now it can know itself and become actual only to the extent that it objectivates itself. This objectivation (*Objekti-*

with the other: "The structure of the poetic sentence accurately reflects the ontological structure of saintliness." Whether we are concerned with flowers covering the poor old woman ("perhaps my mother") or with a "logical" paradox of the type "the gardener is the most beautiful rose in her garden," the question of knowing why the flower is, as Sartre says, "the poetic object par excellence" disappears between a pre-Heideggerean meontologism and some vague Mallarméism. One evokes a "vibratory disappearance" and the flower absent from every bouquet, "[w]herein lies all the poetry of Genet."

"Such a flower always bears its double within itself, whether it be seed or type . . . and by virtue of the repetition in which it endlessly puts itself into *abyme*, no language can reduce into itself the stricture of an anthology. This supplement of a code which traverses its own field, endlessly displaces its closure, blurs its line, opens its circle, and no ontology will have been able to reduce it." (Offered for grafting, white mythology

But what is poetry once the flower is "the poetic object par excellence?" What is rhetoric if the flower (of rhetoric) is the figure among figures and the place among places? How are we to read this *effect* of transcendental excellence, how is it elaborated? Why does the flower dominate all the fields to which it nevertheless belongs? Why does it stop belonging to the series of bodies or objects of which it is a part?

The flower is (de)*part*(ed). It derives from its being-part the force of transcendental excrescence that makes it only seem such (transcendental), and that no longer needs to be deflowered. The practical deconstruction of the transcendental effect is at work in

vierung) happens through "the form of its moments" (*durch die Form seiner Momente*). Becoming an object for itself, spirit departs from itself. But it does so in order to remain (to) itself, return to and equal itself. This very general procession of Hegelian spirit here has *Sittlichkeit* as its principal stage or station.

But since any departure of spirit from itself has the general form of its opposite, namely nature, since nature is spirit outside itself but also a moment of the return to self of spirit, *Sittlichkeit* will involve this naturality. It will be a nature-spirit. Its naturality will be absorbed, will be spiritualized as *Sittlichkeit* develops through the form of its moments, exhausts the inner negativity working on it, produces itself by negating itself as nature. Each of its three moments will mark a step forward in this sublation of naturality. *Wirklichkeit,* actuality, the *Wirken* of *Wirklichkeit* will be the operation of negativity reappropriating spirit, bringing it back home, close to itself, through its ethical objectivation. Having negated itself by naturalizing and objectivizing itself, spirit will negate its negation by coming back to itself via the less and less abstract form (*Form*) of its moments. Being at home for spirit in its generality is not the same as being at home for the family. But this latter is nonetheless a determinate representation of it, and such a representative relation opens the question, precisely.

why is the reconstitution of a Hegelian process easier to write in the future? Narrative, pedagogical facility? Why does a philosopher so stern about narrative, which he always opposes to the concept, encourage a sort of conceptual narrative? When one explicates Hegel, one is always in a seminar and one recounts to pupils [*élèves*]: the history of the concept, the concept of history.
Élève: that's the word I'm dealing with here, as with the thing, in all senses.
Élève. What is raising [*élever*] in general (breeding [*élevage*], elevation, r(a)ising up [*élèvement*])? Against what does one practice a r(a)ising? What does it come under? What does it sublate [*De quoi relève-t-elle? Que relève-t-elle?*]? What is it to sublate an *élève*?
There is a levity in all this. The eagle's dream is to lighten. Wherever it falls. And to sublimate.
When one uses a future faced with the *élève*, it is a grammatical cunning of reason: the meaning that it will have meant to say is, in truth, the future perfect. The encyclopedic version of the greater *Logic* (circular pedagogy, for the *élève*) is narrated in the future perfect

Love is in view: one will not be able to think it in its concept (the concept of feeling-oneself that does not itself feel itself) without taking account of this sublating negativity. If *Sittlichkeit* is a sublating naturalization of spirit, and if each of its moments participates in this process, the first moment will also be the most natural. It will be the most natural form of spirit as *Sittlichkeit*: the family, love in

the structure of the flower, as of every *part*, inasmuch as it *appears* or grows *as such*.

The question of the plant, of *phuein*, of nature and what is elsewhere called—reference being made to a certain taboo—*verg*inity. How can a part be something taking? So it could have begun with a parodic poisoning—altering, rotting, in anthological dosage—of the ground of ontological truth on which rhemes and poems have grown. Moreover the taste and handling of the poison are explicit throughout the text. It feeds on them. And if I tell you right now that clang is a sort of poisoned milk you will find the dose too strong and the image dissonant. So it's not yet time.

"This century is certainly the century of poison . . . and my fondness for poisons, the appeal they have for me . . . . but the doctors gave me an emetic and, after analyzing my vomit . . ." He is therefore sentenced for bringing poison into a prison, for "having smuggled a dangerous drug into the prison." Can this clang be read as the interminable analysis of vomiting, of a retching rather that I have affected and that makes me write myself: "*Je m'ec*."

Let's keep it limited: the clang rising and echoing on the surface of some page—already [*déjà*]—between "lilacs" and "explosions," also announces, covering it with flowers, the death of every code, *The Man Condemned to Death*

the circle or, what comes to the same thing, the symbolic triangle of the family. In the objectivating movement of actual spirit, Hegel indeed discerns three moments:

"A. immediate or natural (*natürliche) ethical* (*sittliche*) spirit—the *family*.

This substantiality passes over into loss of unity (*geht in den Verlust ihrer Einheit . . . über*), division (*Entzweiung*), and the point of view of relativity, and is thus

B. civil society, i.e. an association of members as *self-sufficient individuals* in what is therefore a *formal universality*, occasioned by their *needs* and by the *legal constitution* as a means of security for persons and property (*Eigentums*), and by an *external order* for their particular and common interests. This *external state*

C. withdraws and comes to a focus in the end (*Zweck*) and actuality (*Wirklichkeit*) of the substantial universal and of the public life which is dedicated to this—i.e. in the *constitution of the state* (Staatsverfassung)."

These are the three, dialectically linked moments through which *Sittlichkeit* penetrates and gathers itself, returns into its proper substance. People are most often interested in the two final phases of the movement (civil society and State), for good reason. The problems of right, politics and political economy appear in them in a thematic form that can be readily recognized. But such a privilege has no philosophical foundation. If, in order to compensate for this, we dwell at greater length on the family, this will be simply to bring out a problematic pertinence for the whole field. And not, obviously, to displace a privilege.

In the additional Remark in the margin of the preceding paragraph, Hegel enumerates, in the form of scarcely written out notes, the lines of opposition between the family and the State. The most general opposition, the law of opposition, is the opposition between law and its other. In the State, attention is given to the law, to the universal—the State is a universal (*ein Allgemeines*)—which, *qua* law, is the same for all (*das Gleiche für alle*), indifferent to subjective desire. For the family as such, inasmuch as it is not yet proceeding toward civil society and the State, the equal and the universal (*das Gleiche, das Allgemeine*) of the law count less than the subjective difference between "love and fear."

How does the egality of legality come to the family?

"Your mouth is the mouth of a dead woman, your eyes are her roses,

. . .

The glittering frost . . .

. . .

That crowned your forehead with thorns of the rosebush

. . .

Despite your frozen tears

. . .

. . . will you steal the keys

. . .

From where you sow, regal one, the white enchantments,
This snow on my page, in my silent prison:
The dread of it, the dead in violet blossoms
Death with her roosters!

. . .

A dazzling pimp carved from an archangel,
Working it up over the bouquets of carnations and jasmine

. . .

Be the young girl with the pure radiant neck,
Or, if you have no fear, be the melodious child
Dead within me long before the axe slices me in two.

Fair child of honor crowned with lilac!
Bend over my bed, let my rising cock
Smack your golden cheek. Listen, your killer lover
Is telling you his story in a thousand explosions!

He's singing that he once had your body and your face,
Your heart that a massive rider's spurs
Will never open."

In other words to what feels itself? In other words to nature? Immediacy?

Following paragraph: "The family, as the *immediate substantiality* of spirit, has as its determination the spirit's feeling [feeling, feeling itself, sensitive to itself, as feeling of self, *seine sich* empfindende *Einheit*] of its own unity, which is *love*. Thus, the disposition (consciousness, *Gesinnung*) [appropriate to the family] is destined (*Bestimmung*) to have self-consciousness of one's individuality *within this unity* as essentiality which has being in and for itself, so that one is present in it not as an independent person [*eine Person für sich*] but as a *member* [Mitgleid]."

Love—the relation of the *Mitgleid*, of the articulated member to the family body—therefore determines the unity of the feeling-itself as self-adherence of the family. But what allows the family to constitute itself, to hold to itself, is also what holds it back in naturality and would prevent it, on its own, from proceeding towards civil society and towards the State. On its own, affect would prevent it from negating itself *qua* family and thus from sublating itself; by the same token affect would itself negate the family. As is always the case, the choice happens only between two self-negations. Economy—the law of the house—has to get organized to pay for it.

For love, *qua* affect (*Empfindung*), still belongs to nature. It is what is natural in spirit. From this point of view, Hegel always limits its value: love *remains* in the being-outside-itself of spirit. It comes back to it, comes back up to it, of course, but as such, in its proper instance, as though in a staircase. It is like a step. Or rather a banister, the rising coil of a movement, because love always already carries itself beyond each station. It is only ascension and thus has no proper instance on which it could be stopped in order to consider itself in itself. This figure of the banister has a general bearing for the whole speculative dialectic. Whence the impossibility of finalizing the determining limit of a concept.

Staircase: one step against another.

What is being sought out here is a staircase that would not be Hegelian, a slightly silly way of saying another staircase of spirit on the basis of which to understand, mount and unmount the Hegelian process.

So one can no longer even say "it starts or it ends with love." "I begin with" or "I end with" equals: "the I begins where it did not begin or where it did begin before the I thought" and "the I ends where it keeps on starting again," already.

Remark to the previous paragraph: "Love means

Always cover with flowers, culled with the dead, the coffin, the rigid body of the verge, also of the virgin and the mother. Theft of flowers in the place of verginity. Theft of keys, exploding in pieces, exploding in splatters, pealing bells [*voler les clés, voler en éclats, voler en éclaboussures, volée de cloches*].

> "To fly, to fly through your blood-splashed heaven
> And make a single masterpiece with the gathered dead
> Here and there, in the meadows, the hedgerows . . ."

Such seemingly conventional flowers, damaged pearls from funeral wreaths, are already worth their weight in sperm and phallus. Death cuts them from nature, whence—already—the signature that engraves or grafts the artificial flower. Pastiche and fake [*postiche*], inversion of values for fucking up. The flower the penis always for cutting—guilty [*coupables*]—and derive erection from faking.

> "Oh come, my roseate heaven! Oh my blonde basket!
> . . .
> Come, trickle into my mouth a bit of heavy sperm."

> "Who carved a windrose in the plaster?
> . . .
> A consoling hell peopled with handsome soldiers
> Naked to the waist, and from their reseda pants
> Pull up those heavy flowers whose odor strikes me like thunder."

(What I must let fall, with each cut, from all the letters of the text—from the law that is thereby verified—should echo after the fact, if not be resumed, bursting, into clanging. I cut from the "complete works," I carve out another text, a little like his pimp graven in an archangel with a hard-on. But why an archangel? Which one? What is he announcing?)

in general the consciousness of my unity with another, so that I am not isolated on my own [*für mich*], but gain my self-consciousness only through the sublation of [*Aufgebung*, the giving up of] my being-for-me and through knowing myself (*Mich-Wissen*) as the unity of myself with another and of the other with me."

"... sondern mein Selbstbewußtsein nur als Aufgebung meines Fürsichseins gewinne."

The movement described is, then, the sublation of a giving up, the *Aufhebung* of an *Aufgebung* through which I recover in the other what I *lose of myself*. But this gaining back has already begun to have love go beyond itself, and the family go into the law, etc. The remark immediately turns on itself (*sondern, aber*, but, but): "But love is a feeling [*Empfindung*], that is, ethical life in its natural form. In the state, it is no longer present [in natural form]. There, one is conscious of unity as law; there, the content must be rational, and I must know it. The first moment in love is that I do not wish to be an independent person in my own right and that, if I were, I would feel deficient and incomplete (*mangelhaft und unvollständig*). The second moment is that I find myself in another person, that I gain recognition in this person, who in turn gains recognition in me."

"Die liebe ist aber Empfindung ..."

So these two moments divide *the* moment of love, they divide, split, work over the inside of the essential nucleus of the family. Contradiction: I do not want to be independent, I do not want to be what I am, I experience autarchy as a lack; but what I am worth in love, the price of what I dispossess myself of, is fixed by what the other finds in me. I am only inasmuch as I am worth (*ich gelte*). *I am worth (something for) the other [je vaux pour l'autre]*, a formula on which we'd need to spend some time before concluding any deal at all, good or bad. I speculate here, like the other, to gain some profit from a contract between love as narcissism and the speculative dialectic.

This contradiction is unintelligible, its economy passes the understanding, no formal logic can master it or resolve it. Its actual solution does not fall within intellectuality (*Verstand*), within the instrument of a formal analysis.

That does not pull love into irrationality, on the contrary. It plays on the contrary in the gap between understanding and reason. The dialectical contradiction of

That can already be checked against the "lofty foremast" of *A Song of Love*, above the "O my black continent, my gown of deep mourning" enjoining "clusters" and "gloves" whose becoming-fake will be developed, a "windflower" as "scarf" or tie knotted over a tree, an "angel of ivy" or "little girl curled up" like a creeper and all the wisteria of the corpus, around a tree erected, the pink

the text is composed of ivy and creepers. It is first of all gleaned. Gleaning ("Norm. *lianne;* Berry, *glene;* Genev. *glenne*") is to be rolled, woven, plaited like a creeper ("Norm. *liaune,* name for the clematis; *lianne,* gleaning. The word seems to come from 'to bind [*lier*],' and to be a form of 'link'") around a column that is already upright; it gives its form to all the textual enchainings, all the sexual couplings. "A few days later, Divers did the very same thing and thus tugged at all my nerves, which wound about him and climbed lovingly over his body." "I wanted to give my body the suppleness of osier so as to twine round him, though I wanted to warp, to bend over him." (Stilitano is the column here). "The boy I was at fifteen twined in his hammock around a friend." Entangled texte [*texte torsé*]. Always one, at least, or even one torso twist to describe.
In the *Littré* etymology again, gleaning [*glaner*] (playing, at poetics): "Etym. Genev. *gléner, glainer;* Picard. *glainer;* Berry, *glainer, glener;* Provenç. *grenar* . . . LL. *glenare* . . . Diez notes the etymology indicated by Leibniz: Cymric, *glain, glân,* clean; to which he adds the Scandinavian *glana,* sunny spell; such that *gleaning* would properly be cleaning. That is possible without being very satisfying; one shouldn't lose from sight the LL. *geliba, gelima, gelina,* bouquet, handful; Anglo-Saxon, *gelm, gilm,* handful. The sense here is satisfying, and the variations in the consonant open the way to transformation. Uncertainty remains, then, between an etymology whose form is strong but whose sense is less so; another whose sense is strong but form less so. The Provençal *grenar* seems to be an accidental form, and in no way relates to *granum,* grain."

[*le rose*], the rose [*la rose*], the "petals"

love—and thus here of the family—passes the understanding only to resolve itself in effective rationality. ". . . I am worth what in its turn it attains in me. Love is therefore the most immense contradiction [unheard-of, extraordinary, prodigious, monstrous: *ungeheuerste Widerspruch*]; the understanding cannot resolve it, because there is nothing more intractable (*härteres*) than this punctiliousness of the self-consciousness which is negated and which I ought nevertheless to possess as affirmative (*affirmativ*). Love is both the production (*Hervorbringen*) and at the same time (*zugleich*) the resolution (*Auflösung*) of this contradiction. As its resolution, it is ethical unity [*die sittliche Einigkeit*]."

In the *simul*, the *zugleich*, the at-the-same-stroke, the production and the solution of the contradiction do not remain together in the stroke. The *zugleich* is immediately divided, unbalanced, its symmetry broken, the *same-stroke* worked on by two unequal forces: the solution—also the dissolution—wins out over the production. But only to announce or prepare another stroke: the solution is already busy producing another unheard-of contradiction whose *zugleich* will come apart of its own accord in order to reason against the understanding.

I'll stop on this step. I won't follow for now the deduction of the concept of the family, with its three moments: monogamous marriage, property of goods, education of the children or dissolution of the family.

Leaving the completed system (*Philosophy of Right*) to its own devices, I'm going back down to the first stories of its constitution, the texts from Frankfurt, Jena, the *Phenomenology of Spirit*. But I will also try not to transform love and the contradiction of familial affect into a privileged guiding thread, still less a *telos* or regulative ideal. It is the trial that interests me, not success or failure. The circle is not practicable; nor avoidable. To the question "what is

especially ("hemmed petal", "pearly petal") whose name displaces the letters, condenses and loses its leaves, decomposes endlessly, is analyzed: everywhere, in the play of this or that 'p,' farts [*pets*], fags [*pédales*]; enjoins a gel, a collar, a neck also, a "hand that hastens in vain, hacked off," and you can follow interminably, beyond the "first poems," what might be called an elaboration. One would of course have to reread all these words at least once.

He who signs *A Man Condemned to Death* offers himself, already

read *already* [déjà] as initials. When I sign I am already dead. I hardly have time to sign before already being dead. I have to abridge the writing, whence the initials, because the structure of the "signature" event carries my death within itself. In that way it isn't an "event," and perhaps means nothing, written from a past that has never been present and from a death of someone who has never been living. Write for the dead—from where they are—who have never been living: that desire (formulated for example in *The Studio of Giacometti,* but repeatedly taken up again) questions and resounds here as clang to finally have heard the unheard of, what is illegible in an *already* that doesn't revert to anything present, even though it be past. "I am therefore dead. I am a dead man who sees his skeleton in a mirror" in *Miracle of the Rose* is not one proposition among others. Wherever it is repeated, exchanged, detailed, it strikes a written blow [*un coup d'écriture*] (or an *already* one) against all the forces that cling to the present, to truth as presence. The past is not a past present, nor is the future a present to come. And all the values that depend on this axiom are ruled out by the initials. They no longer function already, they are defunct in advance. Right here one must indeed

under his own name—his knell—an antho-

called thinking?" "what calls itself thinking?" [*"qu'appelle-t-on penser?" "qu'est-ce qui s'appelle penser?"*] one can reply only by an impracticable and unavoidable circle once one does not displace in its literality the statement of the question.

To think is to be called.

How to think, i.e. to be called outside the family name? And how to think the family outside the circle or trinitary triangle?

The question of the method that is working on your reading already inscribes the family name. It is a family question.

The family is a *party* to the system of spirit: it is a part and the whole of the system.

The system repeats itself in it. *Geist* is always, in the very production of its essence, a sort of repetition. Coming round to itself after having lost itself in nature and in its other, spirit constitutes itself as absolute spirit through the negative process of a syllogism the three moments of which are *subjective spirit* (anthropology, phenomenology of spirit, psychology), *objective spirit* (right, morals, *Sittlichkeit*) and absolute spirit (art, religion, philosophy). Each of the three moments of the three moments itself involves three syllogistic moments. So the family is the first moment of the third moment of objective spirit, the first moment of *Sittlichkeit*. It forms *Sittlichkeit*'s still most natural instance and fulfills itself by destroying itself in three stages: marriage, estate, education.

At the stage of this initial sluicegate, a first methodological temptation: after having recognized love in its dialectical contradiction as the "hardest" rational nucleus of the family structure, if one can risk this metaphor of metaphor, one could work back towards the works of the young Hegel, the so-called early works, towards the philosophy of love and life in the texts

As is well known, this can only be said in this way in French. The question is exactly there. "*Was heisst Denken*" gives rise to another literal chain: neither closed nor simply open to this one. The relation of the one to the other is not a relation of translation but of transformation. Of work, sluicing, winnowing. It never takes place right here, but elsewhere.
Another form of the same question: can a family name be translated? Strangulation: the singularity of the general, the classification of the unique, the shrinking structure of an embrace in which the concept is conceived, limited and delimited. The bottleneck (grasping/ungrasping) is called in the concept.
The passion of the proper name: never let itself be translated—according to its desire; but suffer translation—which is intolerable to it. To want to reappropriate itself, take back into its belly all the languages in the world that came to lick its surface when, exposed, pronounced, it has commonly engaged in the concept or the class

logical basket. Already—watch out—doesn't signify that the signature will always be gathered, summed up, announced in advance in its initials [*sigle*]. This already marks something quite different. Tocsin:

> "Let the sky awaken, the stars blossom,
> Even if the flowers sigh, and in the fields the black grass
> Greets the dew that morning will drink,
> Let the bell ring: I alone go to my death.
>
> Oh come, my rosy sky! Oh come my blond basket!
> Come visit in his night your man sentenced to death.
>
> . . .
>
> The dairyman's cans, a bell in the air,
>
> . . .
>
> My God, I'm going to croak without once being able
> To hold you close to my heart and to my cock!"

What does the knell of the proper name signify? Before that: does that [*ça*] signify?

The phallic flower is guilty [*coupable*]. It cuts itself, castrates itself, guillotines itself, decapitates

on Christianity. What one finds in them does indeed present itself both as a seed and as a set of invariant features of the system. A seed that one could legitimately consider Hegel to have allowed to grow, develop, raise itself, teach itself, run through its cycle and accomplish its *Bestimmung*, the destination or determination that was calling it, in which it was calling itself, thus giving itself to be thought, from itself to itself. A complex of invariant features because between the seed and the adult concept something does not change, and allows itself to be identified with no possible doubt. The early works on Christianity—and especially on the Last Supper—would for example be read as the teleological preformation of the completed system. Nothing in the author would forbid this. On the contrary, he produced many propositions on teleology, on the system as development of a seed.

So we can operate according to his rule. We will. But we'll make the price of this obedience to the rule a detour the cost of which it is still too early to calculate.

The family is marked twice over.

It is a determinate, very narrowly particular moment. Its place is inscribed in the encyclopedia and in history as history of spirit. It is a finite moment and one never goes through it more than once.

But simultaneously one must keep another account of it, in another register, another charter. This determinate moment of the family, this finity *figures* (for now I'll leave this word very open) the totality of the system. A certain family scheme, a certain family scene *befits* the infinite totality of the system. The infinite totality of the system is thought, produced and reflected in it.

Will we say hastily that the finite family furnishes a metaphorical model or a convenient figuration for the language of philosophical exposition? An easy pedagogical option? A good way of speaking to the student of abstract things while playing on the familiarity of family significations? We'd still have to know what the absolute familiarity of a signification is. Whether it can be thought and named without the family. And then be sure that the finite family in question is not already infinite, in which case what this supposed metaphor was coming to figure would be already in the metaphor.

How is the family remarked?

A very late text analyzes *the determination of spirit.* Spirit thinks and at the same time is conscious of itself. I know the object only to the extent that I know myself

itself. Before that: it *appears* only on the scaffold, it is what is deducted, reduced and let fall. That appearance, that luminous—*debodied*—phenomenon of the flower, was glory:

> heed the attack of the word "glory." A calculating machine for reading would no doubt confirm that it is, along with "gallery," "galley [*galère*]," and a few others, one of the author's favorite words. For example, it falls three times on a page that explains that "death on the scaffold . . . is our glory," why we "secretly choose decapitation." Glory is always born from a "severed head" (that is why it "is not human" but "heavenly," making you divine): "Each of them knew that the moment his head fell into the basket of sawdust and was taken out (by the ears) by an assistant whose role seems to me strange indeed, his heart would be garnered by fingers gloved with modesty and be carried off in a youngster's bosom that was adorned like a spring festival. I thus aspired to heavenly glory." It is lodged not far from the chest, from the heart, of course, but also the breast and throat. That risks explaining already—its reasoning will come later—the adjacency of *milkman* and *bell* in *The Man Condemned to Death*

Our Lady of the Flowers opens with the archive of all the heads that have just fallen, condemned to death. "Weidmann appeared before you," as virgin as a suckling infant or nun, head enveloped in flannel or a wedding veil, newborn, royal mummy, "his head swathed in white bands, a nun and yet a wounded pilot fallen into the rye." Notice everything, in particular the rye. "His handsome face, multiplied by the presses, swept down upon Paris." But in being let fall the head has already raised itself. It emerges, erects itself precisely, decidedly in this case. To be decapitated is to appear—hardbound [*bandé*]: like the "swathed head" (Weidmann, the nun, the aviator, the mummy, the infant)

in it, I think it also in thinking myself thinking it. In which respect I am human and not animal: "in other words, I only know an object in so far as I know myself and my own determination through it, for whatever I am is also an object of my consciousness, and I am not just this, that or the other, but only what I know myself to be. I know my object, and I know myself; the two are inseparable." Given which, inasmuch as it knows itself knowing something else, the content of spirit is spiritual. Its content never simply resides outside itself, does not impose itself on it from outside. To know is to appropriate, to produce or reproduce the known. One must not even say that spirit does not have a content outside itself, an object of which it would be merely the knowing form. One must say: what cannot have a content outside itself, what interiorizes all content—even infinite, or rather by infinitizing it in advance, is what is called spirit, conceives itself or grasps itself as spirit. *Geist* repeats itself. So only spirit can conceive spirit. As such, it has no outer limit, it is therefore the free and the infinite.

Infinite freedom, the other name of spirit inasmuch as it gives itself its proper element and thus dwells "at home." It can be only close to itself, gathered with itself, bound to itself by itself, huddled right up against itself by itself. It is free, infinitely, only by remaining close to itself, as though standing vigil over itself while murmuring its proper name to itself. "Thus by nature the spirit is self-sufficient [*bei sich*] or free."

How is this "at homeness" of spirit represented? Why does it stand out in the family hearth itself, at the center of its circle? Why would being at home come down to "being *en famille*," infinitely or indefinitely *en famille*?

Let us proceed slowly.

Free and infinite in itself, spirit has no absolute opposite. At least its opposite cannot be absolute. Absolute, it would be spirit. Habitually, says Hegel in the same passage, matter is posited as the opposite of spirit. Matter is not free. It weighs down, it goes downwards.

It falls.

But there is a law to its weight. If we analyze weight and the dispersion of matter in exteriority, we have to recognize in it a tendency, an effort tending towards unity and

and the phallus, the erectile stalk—the style—of a flower.

When a flower opens or "blossoms," the petals spread, and so there stands what is called the *style*. The stigma designates its highest part, the *summit* of the style.

Following the appeal to those condemned to death—Weidmann, Angel Sun, Pilorge—still on the first pages: "I learned only in bits and pieces of that wonderful blossoming of dark and lovely flowers: one was revealed to me by a scrap of newspaper; another was casually alluded to by my lawyer; another was mentioned, almost sung, by the prisoners—their song became fantastic and funereal (a *De Profundis*), as much as the plaints which they sing in the evening, as the voice which crosses the cells."

But this voice reaches only at the instant in which it "breaks," when it carries the trace of a "crack," perhaps like a bell, the "bell" that is "unleashed" for a child on the same page.

self-gathering. As a tendency towards the center and unity, matter is therefore the opposite of spirit only inasmuch as it remains resistant to this tendency, inasmuch as it opposes its own tendency. But in order to oppose its own—matter's—tendency, it must be spirit. And if it gives in to its tendency, it is again spirit. It is spirit in any case; its only essence is spiritual. The only essence is spiritual. Matter is therefore weight inasmuch as it is seeking the center, dispersion inasmuch as it is seeking unity. Its essence is its non-essence: if it answers to that essence, it comes back to center and unity, it is no longer matter and begins to become spirit, for spirit is the center, unity bound to itself, wrapped up by and around itself. And if it does not rejoin its essence, it remains (matter) but no longer has any essence: it does not remain (what it is).

one can attempt to displace this necessity only by thinking—but what is called thinking?—the remainder [*le reste*] outside the horizon of essence, outside the thinking of being. The *reste n'este pas* as they translate [into French], getting help from a crutch, an *ersatz* or a prosthesis (*west nicht*).
You still have to take the dialectical leap.

"Speculative philosophy has shown that freedom is the one authentic property of spirit. Matter [*Materie*] possesses gravity in so far as it is impelled [it has a *Trieb*] to move towards a central point [the middle: *Mittelpunkt*]; It is essentially composite [*zusammengesetzt:* gathered], and consists entirely of discrete parts which all tend (*streben*) towards a center (*Mittelpunkt*); thus matter has no unity. It is made up of separate elements [*Aussereinander*] and aspires to (*sucht*) a condition of unity; it thus endeavors to overcome itself [*sich selbst aufzuheben*] and seeks its own opposite [*Gegenteil*]. If it were to succeed, it would no longer be matter, but would have ceased to exist as such [*untergegangen als solche*]; it strives towards ideality, for unity is its ideal existence. Spirit, on the other hand, is such that its center is within itself; it too strives (*strebt*) towards its center, but it has its

here is confirmed the essential—and not merely figurative—affinity between the movement of sublation (*Aufhebung*) and what rises [*l'élève*] in general: elevation, rising, raising. Aerial ascension of the concept. The *Begriff* grasps and carries off upwards, opposes its force to all that falls. It is necessarily victorious. Victory does not fall to it, it is what wins. Whence its imperial character. It wins against matter which can stand up to it only by sublating itself, negating itself in rising to spirit. It also wins against death: by erecting all the way to the tomb. The sepulcher rises.
Let's not close in too quickly on Hegel's sepulcher that we'll need to busy ourselves around later

The flower opens, achieves, consecrates the phenomenon of death in an instant of *trance*. The trance is the sort of limit (trance/partition), of unique case, of singular experience in which nothing comes to pass, where what emerges collapses "at the same time," where one can't slice between more and less. Flower, trance: the *simul* of erection and castration. Where one gets hard for no reason, where nothing gets hard, where it is nothing that "gets hard."

Not that nothing is.

Perhaps one could say that *there is* the nothing (that gets hard).

Transe, n. Great apprehension concerning an evil thought to be about to occur. . . . Etym. Walloon, *transs*, knell that announces death; Span. and Por., *trance*, hour of death, decisive moment; Ital. *transito*, passage from life to death [*trépas*]; from Lat. *transitus*, passage. In French, *transe*, which signifies any strong painful emotion, derives from *transir* (vide that word)." (*Littré*)

Earlier than *there is not* [il n'y a], it gets hardbound [*il y bande*] (impersonal form) in a past that was never present (the signature—already—always denied it [*le nia*]): it *got hardbound* [il banda] (impersonal

bander is always to tighten, to gird (*bandé*: girded), to stretch, with a band, a corset, a cord, into a binding [*lien*] (creeper, ivy or strap). "*Bande*, n. Etym. Walloon, *baine*; Namurois, *bainde*; Rouchi, *béne*, Provinçal and Ital. *benda*; Span. *venda;* from Old High German, *binda*; Ger. *binden*, to bind; Sans. *bandh*, to bind. Compare the Gaelic *bann*, strap, tie [*lien*]." Earlier: "They fed their children without swaddling them, or strapping them with blankets" (*Amyot. Littré*). One should read that entire article, in order to note at least that in relation to printing "bands" are "iron parts attached to the two tongues in the middle of the press cradle, upon which the train rolls." Double countersense, at least, of the word *bandé*. What does one call bandaging

regime) equals *it tied up* [il lia]. Locked in.

A certain nothing, a certain void, therefore, erects.

center within itself. Its unity is not something external; it always finds it within itself, and exists in itself and with itself (*bei sich*). Matter has its substance outside itself; spirit, on the other hand, is self-sufficient being (*das Beisichselbstsein*), which is the same thing as freedom. For if I am dependent, I am beholden to something other than myself, and cannot exist without this external point of reference. If, however, I am self-sufficient (*bei mir selbst bin*), I am also free."

So: spirit is. Alone. Its contrary, matter, is only inasmuch as it is not what it is, inasmuch as in order to be what it is (falling weight and dispersion's tendency to unity), it becomes what it is not: spirit. Spirit is. Alone. To be, is to be at home with oneself [*être auprès de soi*]. Weight and dispersion, the essence of matter, cannot qualify an essence. Matter has no essence, its essence is its opposite, its essence is to have no essence. Dispersion, like weight (non-unity and non-ideality) has no essence. *Therefore* is not. Being is idea.

So: in being, matter will-already-have-become spirit. And as it will have been nothing before becoming spirit, it is always spirit that will have preceded or accompanied itself to the end of the procession. Matter precedes itself or remains (first and last) only as spirit: by raising or erecting what falls.

What is the relation between this being-at-home-with-oneself (another way of saying being) and the family?

When one says that spirit is—alone—that it has its own essence, its own center and its own unity in itself, this is not a simple and tautological assertion. This proposition is speculative in the Hegelian sense of the word, it states the dialectical identity of identity and non-identity. The being-at-home of spirit is produced actively through a negativity without limit. Spirit becomes for-itself, at home with itself, only by actively negating everything that limits its freedom from the outside. Its essence is active,

Geist can therefore only repeat itself, repeat its own breath, aspirate/expirate itself. Effluvium or sublimate, the repetition of a breath maintains itself above what falls, above matter. Such a repetition unfolds the infinite freedom of an auto-affection. Between self and self, in being-at-home-with-oneself, what can prevent spirit from repeating? Tie the hands and cut out the tongue, limit all possibilities of action and auto-affection: how could one prevent *Geist* from repeating? This operation, about which it can never be decided if it is internal or external, spontaneous or accidental, is the ultimate refuge of spirit—its supreme irony—against all repressive constraints. But it is almost nothing and it still needs matter to ferment (all of this is waiting for us around the sepulcher): but is not ferment, the warmth that decomposes matter, still, already, spirit preparing a beautiful repetition? For that it must first forget itself

The bells were unleashed just a moment ago.

Now reconstitute the chain that sets in motion the clang machines (you can link all of their parts together further along), its rings, its links. The erection (of the guilty flower), the undulation of the creepers (or ivy; here, straps), the rhetorical reading of the fleur-de-lis and the bed [*des lis et du lit*] (here the coffin laid over the virgin mother), the unsheathed bell that strikes a seal; and everything streams out like milky sperm, "in little continuous jerks" [*par petites secousses continues*] (that is how it is written).

Simul of orgasm:

"I approach, my heart racing wildly, and discover nothing, nothing but looming emptiness, sensitive and proud like a tall foxglove!" And immediately following the embalming emblem, exclamation point: "I do not know, as I have said, whether the heads there are really those of my guillotined friends, but I have recognized by certain signs that they—those on the wall—are thoroughly supple, like the lashes of whips, and rigid as glass knives, precocious as child pundits and fresh as forget-me-nots, bodies chosen because they are possessed by terrible souls.

The newspapers are tattered by the time they reach my cell, and the finest pages have been looted of their finest flowers, those pimps, like gardens in May. The big, inflexible, strict pimps,

dynamic, negative: "When the spirit strives (*strebt*) towards its center, it strives to perfect (*vervollkommen*) its own freedom. . . . To say that spirit exists would at first seem to imply that it is a completed entity (*etwas Fertiges*). On the contrary, it is by nature active (*Tätiges*), and activity (*Tätigkeit*) is its essence; it is its own product (*Produkt*), and is therefore its own beginning and its own end. Its freedom does not consist in static being (*ruhende Sein*), but in a constant negation of all that threatens to destroy freedom. The business of spirit is to produce itself, to make itself its own object, and to gain knowledge of itself; in this way, it exists for itself. Natural objects do not exist for themselves; for this reason, they are not free. The spirit produces and realizes itself in the light of its knowledge of itself; it acts in such a way that all its knowledge of itself is also realized. Thus everything depends on the spirit's self-awareness; if the spirit knows that it is free, it is altogether different from what it would be without this knowledge. For if it does not know that it is free, it is in the position of a slave who is content with his slavery and does not know that his condition is an improper one. It is the sensation (*Empfindung*) of freedom alone which makes the spirit free, although it is in fact always free in and for itself."

Spirit is always—already—free *qua* spirit, but it remains to it to be what it will have been: to have the phenomenal experience of its freedom, to appear to itself as such, to liberate itself, to liberate its liberty. There is nothing more painful, in spite of appearances—but the pain is here that of appearance—than this return to self and this liberation of liberty. This happens first in the becoming-alive, becoming-life of matter. In life, spirit which had lost itself, scattered itself in the exteriority of matter, begins to relate itself to itself. First in the form of *self-feeling*. This instance of self-feeling, which predicates love too, first gives itself—immediately, naturally and externally—(feeling) in animality. Human feeling is still animal. *Qua* spirit, I feel the animal limitation as a negative constraint I am trying to free myself from, a lack I am trying to

activity: the place of man (*vir*). The pure activity of spirit—it produces itself—induces a little later the assimilation of spirit to the father who produces himself or, by doubling himself up, gives himself a son. I am my father my son and me. I call (myself) my father. But the giving-oneself-producing-doubling insinuates into pure activity an internal division, a passivity, an affect that obscurely breaches the paternity of the father and begins to ruin all the determinations and oppositions that form a system with it. All the familial meanings then begin to pass into each other and nothing can stop them. Such is the play of spirit with itself, as soon as it begins to extend itself. For *Streben* (tending), as we have just seen, forms its essence. Its play ruins and relaxes it immediately

their members in full bloom—I no longer know whether they are lilies or whether lilies and members are not totally they, so much so that in the evening, on my knees, in thought, I encircle their legs with my arms—all that rigidity floors me and makes me confuse them, and the memory which I gladly give as food for my nights is of yours, you who, as I caressed you, remained inert, stretched out; only your verge, unsheathed and brandished, went through my mouth with the suddenly cruel sharpness of a steeple puncturing a cloud of ink, a hatpin a breast. You did not move, you were not asleep, you were not dreaming, you were in flight, motionless and pale, frozen, straight, stretched out stiff on the flat bed, like a coffin on the sea, and I know that we were chaste, while I, all attention, felt you flow into me, warm and white, in little continuous jerks. Perhaps you were playing at coming. At the climax, you were lit up with a quiet ecstasy, which enveloped your blessed body in a supernatural nimbus, like a cloak that you pierced with your head and feet."

one does not know, in the strict sense, which figure to recognize

In little continuous jerks the sequences are enjoined, induced, sliding silently. No category exterior to the text may allow one to define the form or allure of these passages,

fill. I share this tension, this tendency to free myself from feeling, with every living being. Hegel calls this *Trieb*. One cannot translate *Trieb* here, as has been done, by *desire* or by *drive*. Let's say *impulse* [*poussée*] so as not to decide anything yet.

Man passes from feeling to conceiving only by repressing the impulse, which the animal, according to Hegel, cannot do. Ideality, *qua* thought of the universal, is born of, and then bears the mark of, a repression of the impulse: a violent interruption between impulse and satisfaction, between the animal and the spiritual moment of life, death in natural life, natural death as life of the spirit. The family is looming.

"The most immediate knowledge spirit can have of itself when it assumes the shape of a human individual is that it is *capable of feeling* [fühlend]. It does not as yet have an object [*Hier ist noch keine Gegenständlichkeit vorhanden*], and the individual simply feels himself determined in some particular way. He then tries to distinguish between himself and this determinate quality [*Bestimmtheit*], and sets about creating an internal division within himself. Thus, my feelings are split up into an external and an internal world. My determinate nature thereby enters a new phase, in that I have a feeling of deficiency [of being *mangelhaft*] or negativity; I encounter a contradiction within myself which threatens to destroy [*auzulösen*] me. But I nevertheless exist [*ich bin aber*]; this much I know, and I balance this knowledge against my feeling of negation or deficiency. I survive and seek to overcome [*aufzuheben*] the deficiency, so that I am at the same time an *impulse* [Trieb]. The object towards which my impulse is directed is accordingly the means by which I can attain satisfaction and the restoration [*Wiederherstellung*] of my unity. All living things are endowed with impulses. We are therefore natural beings, and all our impulses are of a sensuous character. Objects, in so far as I am drawn to them by impulse, are means of integration, and this is the entire basis of theory and practice alike. But in our intuitions of the objects to which our impulses are drawn, we are dealing directly with externals and are ourselves external. Our intuitions are discrete units of a sensuous nature, and so also are our impulses, irrespective of their content. By this definition [*Bestimmung*], man would be no different from the animals; for impulses are not conscious of themselves. But man has knowledge of himself, and this distinguishes him from the animals."

some would be tempted to keep the inversion: *je suis mais* [ich bin aber, I am but]. But what? *je suis cependant* [I am however] is more seductive.

The leap from animality to humanity, as leap from

these writing trances. There are only ever sections of flowers, from paragraph to paragraph, such that the anthological specimens inflict only the violence necessary to take account of the rest. Keep count of the crosscutting effects and you will see that the tissue keeps reforming over the gash.

a paraph is the abbreviation of a paragraph: what is written to the side, in the margin

What was elaborating as it rotted, under the foxgloves, lilies or forget-me-nots, was a burial: that of Divine, which won't therefore have surprised us, two pages later. "Decaying flowers," violets, in a bouquet that—don't forget—becomes an umbrella, and vice versa: umbrellas are *like* bouquets, then bouquets are *like* umbrellas. A stairway also—don't forget—shows the way to death. That of Divine. Monumentalized in stone, against which the explosion of names resounds. The theory of queens—"girl-queens and boy-queens, the aunties, fags, and nellies"—proceeds, a crowd of flowers, with a similar movement.

the umbrella [*parapluie*], like all figures of *para-* (lightning conductor [*paratonnerre*], parachute, screen [*paravent*]) is an absolutely threatening figure for warding off [*apotrope*]. Protection and aggression blend into each other, replace one another in their veiled relation to truth. Always reversible function of the supplement. *The Screens* are full of umbrellas. Tableau 6: "An open umbrella is resting upside down in front of the screen. A blazing sun is painted on a very blue sky."

"The stairway leading up to it [Divine's

feeling to thinking, gets its impetus from a repression of the impulse. Man has impulses, like the animal, but he can inhibit, suppress, hold back, brake, contain them. This negative power—which we are in no hurry to call repression [*refoulement*]—is what is proper to him. It is in it that he becomes conscious and thinking. The process of idealization, the constitution of ideality as the milieu of thought, of the universal, of the infinite, is the suppression of the impulse. *Aufhebung* is thus also a suppressive counter-impulse, a counter-force, a *Hemmung*, an inhibition, a sort of anti-erection.

Hegel goes on: idealization, inseparable from suppression, is just as inseparable from the relation of spirit to itself as the relation of father to son in a trinitarian structure

"But man has knowledge of himself, and this distinguishes him from the animals. He is a *thinking* being [denkend]. Thought, however, is knowledge of universals, and it simplifies the content of experience, so that man too is simplified by it so as to become something inward and ideal. Or, to be more precise, this inwardness and simplicity is inherent in man, and the content of our experience only becomes universal and ideal if we proceed to simplify it. What man is in reality [*reell*], he *must* also be in ideality [*ideell*]. Since he possesses knowledge of reality [*Real*] as ideal [*Ideell*], he ceases to be merely a natural being at the mercy of immediate intuitions and impulses which he must satisfy and perpetuate. This knowledge leads him to control [*hemmt*] his impulses; he places the ideal, the realm of thought, between the demands [*Drängen*] of the impulse and their satisfaction. In the animal, the two coincide; it cannot sever their connection by its own efforts—only pain or fear can do so. In man, the impulse is present before it is satisfied and independently of its satisfaction; in controlling or giving rein to his impulses, man acts in accordance with *ends* and determines himself in the light of a general principle. It is up to him to decide what end to follow; he can even make his end a completely universal one. In so doing, he is determined by whatever conceptions he has formed of his own nature and volitions. It is this which constitutes man's independence: for he knows what it is that determines him. Thus he can take a simple concept as his end—for example, that of his own positive freedom. The conceptions of the animal are not ideal and have no true reality; it therefore lacks this inner independence. As a living creature, the animal too has its source of movement within itself. But it can only respond to those external stimuli to which it is already inwardly susceptible; anything that does not match

garret] plays an important role today. It is the ante-chamber, sinuous as the corridors of the Pyramids, of Divine's temporary tomb. This cavernous hypogeum looms up, pure as the bare marble arm in the darkness, which is devouring the queen to whom it belongs. Coming from the street, the stairway mounts to death. It ushers one to the final resting place. It smells of decaying flowers and already of the odor of candles and incense. It rises into the shadow. From floor to floor it dwindles and darkens until, at the top, it is no more than an illusion blending with the azure. This is Divine's landing. While in the street, beneath the black haloes of the tiny flat umbrellas which they are holding in one hand like bouquets, Mimosa I, Mimosa II, Mimosa the half-IV, First Communion, Angela, Milord, Castagnette, Régine—in short, a host, a still long litany of creatures who are flittering names—are waiting, and in the other hand are carrying, like umbrellas, little bouquets of violets which makes one of them lose herself, for example, in a reverie from which she will emerge bewildered and quite dumbfounded with nobility for she (let us say First Communion) remembers the article, thrilling as a song come from the other world, from our world too, in which an evening paper, thereby embalmed, stated: 'The black velvet rug of the Hotel Crillon, where lay the silver and ebony coffin containing the embalmed body of the Princess of Monaco, was strewn with Parma violets.'"

Follow interminably the cortege and you will

its inner being simply does not exist for it. The animal is divided [*sich entzweit*] from itself and within itself. It cannot interpose anything between its impulse and the satisfaction of its impulse; it has no will, and knows nothing of inhibition [*Hemmung*]. Its activating impulses come from within itself, and their operation presupposes that they contain the means of their own fulfilment. Man, however, is not independent because he is the initiator of his own movement, but because he can restrain this movement and thereby master his spontaneity and natural constitution."

The automobility of the animal is absolute only to the extent that it remains an external or sensory automaticity, a pure constraint as far as spirit is concerned. Inhibiting animal automobility in himself, man liberates the automobility of spirit, freedom.

This is explained—the style is pretty much that of a seminar—by semen. Or seed. Which intervenes immediately after the analysis of the impulse. The seed (*der Same*) is also in seed form the onto-theological figure of the family.

This seed-concept (*Same*, semen, seed, sperm, grain) regularly takes the stage in the speculative dialectic, in places and regions of the encyclopedic discourse that are at one and the same time homologous and distinct, whether we are dealing with the vegetable, biological, anthropological or onto-logical order in general. Among all these orders, it ensures a system of figurative correspondences.

Whence are these figures supposed to be exported? What would be their proper place?

The figure of seeding (let's provisionally call it that) is immediately determined: 1. As the best representation of the self-relation of spirit; 2. As the circular path of a return to self. And in the description of spirit that returns to itself via its own product, after losing itself in it, there is more than mere rhetorical convenience in giving spirit the name "father." In the same way the advent of the Christian trinity is more than an empirical event in the history of spirit.

". . . thereby master his spontaneity and natural constitution.

powerful and extensive chain, from Aristotle at least to our own day, links onto-theological metaphysics to humanism. The essential opposition of man and animal—or rather animality, a univocal, homogeneous, obscurantist concept of animality—always serves the same interest here. The Animal supposedly does not have Reason, Society, Laughter, Desire, Language, Law, Repression. Of the three wounds to anthropic narcissism, the one Freud uses Darwin's name to point out seems more intolerable than the one Freud signed himself. It will have been resisted longer

see "magnified" all the accidents, "trail of slime," "the weighty magnificence of the barbarian who tramples choice furs beneath his muddy boots. . . . Merely to have mentioned him is enough for my left hand in my torn pocket to. . . . the plaster cast that Divine herself made of his cock, which was gigantic when erect. . . . I can't stop praising him until my hand is smeared with my liberated pleasure. . . . in short, all the queens, imparted a tendril-like movement to their bodies and fancied they were enlacing this handsome man, were twining about him. Indifferent and bright as a slaughterhouse knife, he passed by, cleaving them all into two slices which came noiselessly together again."

The thyrsus, thyrsanthus, which was first of all a sharp, penetrating weapon, here informs both the text and its "object."

Are you going to fall precipitately into the trap?

The root characteristic [*Wurzel*] of human nature is that man can think of himself as an ego [*Ich*]. As a spirit, man does not have an immediate existence but is essentially turned in on himself [*in sich zurückgekehrtes*]. This function of mediation [*Vermittelung*] is an essential moment of the spirit. Its activity consists in transcending and negating its immediate existence so as to turn in again upon itself [*Rückkehr in sich*]; it has therefore made itself what it is by means of its own activity. Only if it is turned in upon itself can a subject have true reality. Spirit exists only as its own product. The example of the seed may serve [*die Vorstellung des Samens dienen*] to illustrate [or as clarification of: *zur Erlaüterung*] this point. The plant begins with the seed, but the seed is also the product of the plant's entire life, for it develops only in order to produce [*hervorzubringen*] the seed. We can see from this how impotent life is [*die Ohnmacht des Lebens*], for the seed is both the origin and the product of the individual; as the starting point and the end result, it is different and yet the same, the product of one individual and the beginning of another. Its two sides fall asunder like the simple form [*Form*] within the grain [of wheat: *Korn*] and the whole course of the plant's development.

mediation: the return to self that overcomes division and loss. The sublation of the two in the three, return to the self of unity. The father divides himself, goes outside himself in the son, recognizes himself in him and finds himself again, counts himself again in his revenue

Every individual has an example [*Beispiel*] even closer to hand in the shape of his own person. Man can only fulfil himself through education [formation, culture: *Bildung*] and discipline [*Zucht*]; his immediate existence contains merely the possibility of self-realization (i.e. of becoming rational and free) and simply imposes on him a vocation [*Bestimmung*] and obligation which he must himself fulfil. The animal's education is soon complete [*fertig*]; but this should not be seen as a blessing bestowed on the animal by nature. Its growth [*Wachstum*] is merely a quantitative increase [*Erstarken*] in strength. Man, on the other hand, must realize his potential through his own efforts, and must first acquire everything for himself, precisely because he is a spiritual being; in short, he must throw off all that is natural in him. Spirit, therefore, is the product of itself."

Dialectical paradox: the natural living being, life *qua* nature develops of itself without freedom insofar as its automobility is finite. It does not get outside itself, all it does is develop the seed: quantitative growth without any break,

And translate that The Flower, which signifies (symbolizes, metaphorizes, metonymizes, etc.) the phallus, once it is caught in the syntax of cutting, signifies death, decapitation, decollation? Anthologos signifying the signifier signifying castration?

That would be to bring to a halt once more, and in the name of the law, of truth, of the symbolic order, the working of an unknown: its clanging, what is in action here.

Try to arrest him, once more, as in 1952, while leaving prison, where the ontophenomenologist of liberation

liberation—under this title one has to think, first of all and at least, the bypassing of psychoanalysis and Marxism in the name of freedom, of the "original choice" and existential "project." "Such is the case of the child Genet. . . . It was, I think, Genet's optimism that kept him from adopting this conclusion in reality [killing himself like "the punished child who chastises his mother by depriving himself of dessert"]. I mean thereby to designate the very orientation of his freedom. . . . He has chosen to live; he has said, in defiance of all, I will be the Thief. I deeply admire this child who grimly *willed* himself at an age when we were merely playing the servile buffoon. So fierce a will to survive, such pure courage, such mad confidence within despair will bear their fruit. Twenty years later, this absurd determination will produce the poet Jean Genet. . . . But when a systematized, hardened sulking holds out for ten years, thirty years, when it is at the root of the most singular, the most beautiful poetic work, when it changes into a world system, into an occult religion, then it must singularly transcend the level of a simple childish reaction, a man's freedom must be thoroughly involved in it. . . . If we want to understand what he is today and what he writes, we must go back to this original choice and try to give a phenomenological description of it."

insisted on handing over,

without relation to the outside and the absolute other. *Qua* natural necessity following its own bent, without freedom, its automobility is therefore the result of something other than itself. It is the result of something other precisely because it remains closed up in itself and has no relation to itself as to the other. Doubtless, the natural living being divides into two; but as this division is not absolute, the animal does not have an absolute relation to itself. Nor to the other. Neither self nor other. This is why there is no natural family, no father/son relation in nature.

The qualitative leap is supposedly made with the human individual: dividing himself radically, he is conscious of himself as of the other. No longer, by reason of this division, having his natural movement within him, he constitutes himself by his *Bildung*, his culture, his discipline, his symbolic formation. Paradoxically he is, more than the plant or the animal, his own product, his own son, the son of his works. More than the plant or the animal, he issues from his own seed. He conceives himself. It is because he has interrupted the natural impulse and deprived himself of automobility that he has given himself the law. He has called himself, autonomously.

But the human individual, the particular, finite, individual, as such, is only an *example* of this autoproduction, as inhibitory negation of natural automobility. And the (human) father/son relation is only a (finite) example of the infinite father/son relation, of the relation of infinite spirit freely relating to itself as its own rebound, its own resource. Just as there was a leap into negativity, between the negativity of natural *Entzweiung* (plant, animal) and that of spiritual or human *Entzweiung*, between sublation *in* nature and the sublation *of* nature in *finite* spirit, so there is a dialectical leap which is the absolute rebound *of* the result, between the *Aufhebung* of finite spirit and that of infinite spirit. Just as—just so: the analogy or the proportion depends on the fact that the finite *is qua* passage to the infinite.

Whence Hegel's exemplary rhetoric, the exemplarist proceeding of his rhetoric: of his rhetoric as figural technique and as form of argumentation.

After giving its due to the human individual as an example (*Beispiel*) of the movement of infinite spirit and the rebound of the result, Hegel moves to the infinite movement of the re-bound [*ressaut*] itself, to infinite spirit which for its part can no longer be an example since it is not finite. At least it can no longer play the role of an example if the example is a particular case in a homogenous set or series. It can play

into your own hands, into a safe place, the "keys" of the complete-man-and-work, their ultimate psychoanalytico-existential meaning.

The echo was heard for a long time ("This is the key to his conduct and his disorders" . . . "The Other than self. Here we have the key to Genet. This is what must be understood first: Genet is a child who has been convinced that he is, in his very depths, *Another than Self*. . . . Our certainty of ourself finds its truth in the Other").

The fence was at that time as blind to the sexual figure of the key as he was to his own capacity to be careful as a screw [*faire gâfe*] not to let it fall into the wrong hands. General enough to introduce the transcendental structures of the ego, as effective and undifferentiated as a master key, a skeleton key sliding into every signifying space.

A note in Jacques Lacan's *Écrits* (Genet is one of the rare "French writers," modern or not, not to figure in the Index of Proper Names) names the object that "I could no better designate than by calling it the universal phallus (as one says, master key)."

so what signs Genet will be there only to provide an example, the case of a universal structure, which will give us the key. When one speaks of a *case*, the doctor, the judge, the prof, the screw, and the lawyer are already consulting. You can see the robes, uniforms and starched shirts all getting busy. And the ties. Several years earlier François Mauriac wrote "The Genet case." Several years later, Bataille's sentence: "Genet's Failure."

What signs is also interested—but literally, which is something else entirely—in the case of the key. How it is linked, how it opens up, how it falls and rings. And how the case can falsify, force rather a dialectical law, a lock that should however open onto everything. Attacked from a certain angle

that role if the example is the exemplary ideal, the absolute meaning of which the finite examples are, precisely, merely approximating exemplars. This passage from the example to the exemplarity of the example, this passage from the finite to the infinite can sometimes look like rhetoric or a mode of exposition. It is *in truth* the ontologic of the passage, the reason of the finite that posits itself as such only by passing into the infinite. In the finite the examples (*Beispielen*) can substitute for each other and that's why they are examples, particular cases classified according to the general law. This substitution is the freedom of play, of the play among the examples. This freedom is finite. The play is here made possible by finitude; but finitude sublates itself.

In the—unclassifiable—case of absolute spirit (God), no more play in this sense.

The case of God—can one say that? Can one classify the name of God?

If there were a case of God, if God could be taken as an example, that would mean that one takes him as a finite body, that one makes the mistake of having him fall out of what he is, that one takes him for another. God, if he is God, if one thinks what one says when one names him, can no longer be an example of *Aufhebung*. He is the infinite, exemplary, infinitely high *Aufhebung*. He is no longer an example and the play of substitution can no longer operate.

But can not God—of himself—fall into the finite, become incarnate, become his own example, play with himself as infinite becoming finite (dead) in order to reappropriate his infinity, repeat the spirit, i.e. have a man-son who would be his own seed, his own product, his own result, his best return?

Only the figure of Christ can, therefore, regulate the productive exchange—amortization and profit—between rhetoric and onto-logic. Investment of the Holy Family, or rather of the Trinity:

"The most sublime example [lofty, high up, eminent: *das erhabenste Beispiel*] is to be found in the nature of God himself; strictly speaking [*eigentlich*], this is not a genuine example in the sense of one casual instance among others [*ein Beispiel* (*Bei-her-spiel*)], but rather the universal truth itself, of which all other things are examples [*Beispiel*]. It is true that the older religions also referred to God as a spirit; but this was no more than a name which was not yet understood [grasped: *gefaßt*] in such a way as to explain the nature of spirit. In

"untranslatable play on words," as the [French] translators duly point out. This play on words is not one play on words among other possible plays on words. It is the play that makes possible all plays: the play of

That transcendental key, condition for all determinate signifiers and concatenation of the chain, was prescribed and inscribed—but as a working part and effect in the text—enchained and pulled into *Miracle of the Rose*. It therefore falls, owning up as a pen. "All burglars will understand the dignity with which I was arrayed when I held my jimmy, my 'pen.' From its weight, material, and shape, and from its function too, emanated an authority that made me a man. I had always needed that steel penis. . . . The two wedges . . . lightened it and gave it that air of a winged prick by which I was haunted. I slept beside it, for the warrior sleeps armed."

Let's cut to the chase, very quickly: this cock I sleep next to is less that of the father, as one might think, than the Virgin Mary *herself*. I *don't* say that it *isn't* that of the father; I say "less than." But if one is to know how that of the father is written there would need to be still more elaborating, inducing, the better to slide.

So, instead of the flower, the anthographic, marginal, initializing text, which signifies no more.

the infinite with itself, the exemplary play that plays more—or less—than any other. It plays less by playing more. It plays with itself without limit and with no rule that it does not give itself. Which by the same token infinitely limits the play

the Jewish religion too, the spirit was at first represented [*vorgestellt*] only in an abstract way. In Christianity, however, God is revealed [*offenbart*] as Spirit. In the first place, he is the Father, a power [*Macht*] which is universal but abstract [*abstrakt Allgemeines*] as yet veiled [*eingehüllt*]. Secondly, he is his own object, another version of himself, dividing himself in two [*ein sich Entzweiendes*] so as to produce the Son [*der Sohn*]."

The Christian God manifests concrete spirit, which remained still veiled and abstract in Judaism; but he manifests it only by becoming a father. The father—the Jewish God was of course one—remains an abstract universal form so long as he has no recognized son. A father without a son is not a father. He manifests himself as concrete spirit—and not only anticipated, represented, *vorgestellt*—only by dividing himself in his seed which is *his* other, or rather which is itself like an object for itself, another for him and which therefore returns to him, in which he returns to himself: his son.

As this son is infinite—son of God—he is not the other of God. He gives God his image. But as this son of God is human—finite—he is God separated from himself and appearing to himself as passage from the infinite to the finite, from the finite to the infinite. God knows and recognizes himself in his son. He attends (to) his death, his burial, his magnification, his resurrection. The knowledge-relation that organizes this whole scene is a third, a third term, the element of the relation of the infinite to itself: this is the holy spirit. This medium procures the element of *familiarity*: familiarity of God with his own seed, the element of the play of God with himself. The (infinite) exemplar gives himself and has come back to him the (finite) exemplar. The infinite father, by auto-fellatio, auto-insemination and auto-conception, gives himself a finite son, who, by the fact of positing himself, and incarnating himself as son of God becomes infinite, dies *qua* finite son, allows himself to be buried, bound in bands that he will soon undo to be reborn an infinite son.

"But this other version is just as immediate an expression of him as he is himself; he knows himself and contemplates himself in it—and it is this self-knowledge and self-contemplation which constitutes the third element, the Spirit as such."

The spirit is neither the father nor the son, but filiation, the relation of father to son, of son to father, of father to father by the mediation of the son, of the son to the son by

The knells, as we will have heard them, sound the end of signification, of sense and of the signifier. Outside of that—not to oppose it, even less to appose it—we remark the signature that, through its name, despite what is called thus, signifies no more.

Signifying *no more*, the signature

what is a signature? And what does the language of flowers become in it? The question must find a form capable of, for example, the following propositions: 1. *Miracle of the Rose*—"the flowers were spoke"; 2. "I do not think they [flowers] symbolize anything" (*Funeral Rites*).

In these conditions, then, what is a "book laden with flowers" (*Our Lady of the Flowers*)? A bed of course, that is to say, as will later be seen, pages, the skeleton of J.D. who "had been laid out on a bed of roses and gladioli" (*Funeral Rites*) and whom one wants to eat with dialectophagous words: "I am his tomb." "I was hungry for Jean." "I shall never keep close enough to the conditions under which I am writing this book. Though its avowed aim is to tell of the glory of Jean D., it perhaps has more unforeseeable secondary aims."

I am fit only for embalming.

If, then, there is no language of flowers, if the flower is in the place of zero signification, how does this symbolic

the mediation of the father. The spirit is the element of the *Aufhebung* through which the seed returns to the father.

"In other words, the Spirit is the whole, and not just one or other of the elements in isolation. Or, put [defined, expressed, *ausgesprochene*] in terms of feeling [*Empfindung*], God is eternal love, whose nature is to treat the other as its own [*das Andere als sein Eigenes zu haben*]. It is this doctrine of the Trinity [this triplicity, *Dreifaltigkeit*] which raises Christianity above the other religions. If it did not have this doctrine, the other religions might well provide more material for thought than it does. The Trinity is the speculative part [*das Spekulative*] of Christianity, and it is through it that philosophy can discover the Idea of reason in the Christian religion too."

But just as Christianity is only represented and anticipated in Judaism which is its *Vorstellung*, so the absolute religion that Christianity is remains the *Vorstellung* of *Sa* as philosophy. The structure of *Vorstellung* opens the scene of the Holy Family onto *Sa*.

Christianity thus offers the example of a *naturally speculative* religion. Philosophy—speculative dialectics—will have been the truth of this religious representation of the speculative. Just as German, a naturally speculative language in some of its features, sublates itself in order to become a universal language, so a historically determinate religion becomes an absolute religion and an absolute religion sublates its status as representation (*Vorstellung*) in order to become absolute truth. That explains why people were able to read Hegel's philosophy—which is through and through a philosophy *of* religion—as an effect of Christianity as well as an implacable atheism. Religion fulfills itself and dies in philosophy which is its truth, as truth of past religion, of the essence as the past in thought (*Gewesenheit*) of the Christian religion.

The truth—the thought-past—is always the death (raised up, erected, buried, unveiled, dis-banded [*débandée*]) of that of which it is the truth.

The position of the father, filiation as we have just read it, is also interpreted *in truth* as position of the dead father.

corner of the Supper and judas. *Totem and Taboo* has just inscribed the Orphic origin of the doctrine of original sin, the relation between Christ and Dionysos-Sagreus cut in two: "There can be no doubt that in the Christian myth the original sin was one against God the Father. If, however, Christ redeemed mankind from the burden of original sin by the sacrifice of his own life, we are driven to conclude that the sin was a murder. The law of

zero *take* in a jungle of signs and figures belonging to natural language, to nature, to the physical, to physical language as mother tongue that is necessarily foreign to it? Question again of *physis* qua *mimesis*. It also comes down to knowing how to have done with what one eats. The work of mourning as work of the tongue, teeth and saliva, of swallowing also, assimilation and belching. Jean's end is related to the Last Supper. "... the tomb. He needs light, for two thousand years! ... and food for two thousand years.... (*She shrugs her shoulders.*) Oh well, everything's in working order, and dishes have been prepared. Glory means descending into the grave with tons of victuals!" (*The Balcony*)

If flowers represent "infernal props" it is because, signifying nothing, they are nevertheless the forever withdrawn support of the whole text, of every determination. "... they were beginning to exist for me with their own existence, with less and less the help of a support: the flowers" (*Miracle of the Rose*). Such is the relation between miracle and text. That is to say the relation to a leftover [*reste*] that remains from nothing, that doesn't rest in peace; that is certainly not a result in the sense of the speculative dialectic.

"THE QUEEN: But it was I who did everything, who organized everything.... Stay.... What will....
(*Suddenly a burst of machine-gun fire*)"
(*The Balcony*)

You see, but you can't see, you are necessarily blind to the fact that flowers—not even shown, hardly even promised—are constantly stolen, swiped, poached from you. In the *Journal*: "The burial. We need flowers." "Go swipe some flowers with his pals." "At night, with two friends, he pilfered some flowers from the Montparnasse Cemetery.... They went looking for roses with a flashlight.... A joyous intoxication made them steal, run and joke among the monuments. 'Now I've seen everything,' he said to me."

is no longer to the order of, or of the order of signification, of signified or signifier.

Hence—what is emitted by a toll of the knell [*un coup de glas*] is that the flower, for example, inasmuch as it signs, no longer signifies anything.

talion, which is so deeply rooted in human feelings, lays it down that a murder [*ein Mord*] can only be expiated by the sacrifice of another life: self-sacrifice points back to [*weist zurück*] blood-guilt. And if this sacrifice of one's own life brought about reconciliation with God the Father, the crime to be expiated can only have been the murder of the father [*der Mord am* Vater].

"In the Christian doctrine, therefore, men were acknowledging in the most undisguised manner [*am unverhülltesten*] the guilty primaeval deed [*zu der schuldvollen Tat der Urzeit*], since they found the fullest atonement for it in the sacrifice of this one son. Reconciliation with the father was all the more complete (*um so gründlicher*) since the sacrifice was simultaneously accompanied by a total renunciation of the women on whose account the rebellion against the father was started. But at that point the psychological fatality of ambivalence demanded its rights. The very deed in which the son offered the greatest possible atonement to the father brought him at the same time to the attainment of his wishes against the father. He himself became God, beside, or, more properly, in place of, the father [*neben, eigentlich an Stelle des Vaters*]. A son-religion displaced the father-religion (*die Sohnesreligion löst die Vaterreligion ab*). As a sign of this substitution [of this ersatz, *zum Zeichen dieser Ersetzung*] the ancient totem meal was revived in the form of communion, in which the company of brothers ate the flesh and blood of the son—no longer the father—obtained sanctity thereby and identified themselves with him. . . . The Christian communion, however, is at bottom a new setting-aside (*Beseitigung*) of the father, a repetition of the deed that must be expiated." What difference between this point of view (gaze through the judas) and that of the speculative dialectic, as to the most unveiled truth? When seated at table, what is the gap between Judas and the one who is the truth? Who holds the truer discourse here? So what place is due to a Judas? But can the discourse of truth leave the table?

Verily.

The life of spirit as history is the death of the father in his son. The sublation of that death always has the sense of a reconciliation: death can only have been a free and violent act. History is a murder trial. But this murder is a sacrifice: the victim offered himself up. This is a scandal which a finite tribunal cannot understand at all: a victim will have held out to the murderers, along with his body, the instrument of the crime.

What is the function of this Christian model? In what sense is it exemplary for speculative onto-theology? Can it

Tombfall, remains.

Neither a noun nor a verb in any case.

The signet doesn't suffer from being illegible in this respect. To the extent that reading means deciphering a sense or referring to something. But this illegibility that forms by falling (for example from my hand), that confuses and cuts into signification, is that without which there would be no text. A text "exists," resists or consists, pushes back, allows itself to be read or written only if it is worked on by the illegibility of a proper name. I haven't said—not yet—that the proper name exists and becomes illegible once it falls into the signature. The proper name resounds, losing itself immediately, only at the instant of its *debris*, once it breaks, gets mixed up, jammed by touching the signet.

You are still *in the stairway*, heading towards

be circumscribed and displaced as a finite and particular structure, linked to given historical conditions? Can one interrogate a history other than the one represented here? Can one change one's horizon? One's logic?

which can be done notably on the basis of *The Origin of the Family, Private Property, and the State*. Engels's title reproduces the first and last moments of Hegelian *Sittlichkeit* and takes the analysis outside the Western Christian center on the basis of research in the ethnology of the family by Bachofen and Morgan

Inside the system, the program of the so-called early texts on Christianity will have laid down the law. With a significance as powerful and invariable as the opening words of the gospel of John for the history of the West.

As for the family, one can follow a very precise homology between the early schemas and those of the final period of the system. The passage from Judaism to Christianity is interpreted as the advent of love, in other words of the family, as sublation of formal and abstract morality (*Moralität*) (in this respect Kantianism is, structurally, a Judaism). It puts to work a theory of the figure, an ontotheological rhetoric and semiotics that belong by rights to the very content of the discourse.

So was there no family before Christianity? Before Christianity, the family had not yet posited itself as such. It was announced, represented, anticipated. Love was not yet at the heart of the family. The true father/son relation was waiting for Christianity, and also monogamy, as the latter will be defined in the *Philosophy of Right*. Dating from Christ, love is put in place of law and abstract right: in general and not just in relations between spouses.

The Spirit of Christianity: "over against *dutiful* fidelity in marriage and the *right* to divorce a wife, Jesus sets *love*. Love precludes the lust not forbidden by that duty and, except in one eventuality, cancels this leave to divorce." [ETW, 216–17]

Jesus suspends, lifts the authorization, except in one case. The German word for suspend or lift is here *aufheben*. Jesus suspends the authorization only inasmuch as it still belongs to abstract right. In truth he suspends and lifts abstract right into love.

We are not going to ask ourselves here *what* this operation *is*. Once the ontological question (what is? what is it? what does being mean?, etc.) deploys itself here only according to the process and structure of *Aufhebung*, is one with the absolute of *Aufhebung*, one can no longer ask: what is

a crypt that still waits for you having preceded the very thing that it appears to conceal. "It was then that we began to exchange the love letters in which we spoke of ourselves, of plans for robberies, of prodigious jobs and, above all, of Mettray. He signed his first letter 'Illegible,' as a matter of caution, and I began my reply with 'Dear Illegible.' Pierre Bulkaen will remain for me the indecipherable. It was always on the stairs, where he waited for me, that we handed each other the slips of paper."

Miracle of the Rose began (at Fontevrault, with cells in the form of "vertical coffin[s]" among the "ivy") by staging anthotropically—although indirectly and as if to leave it sitting like a seedling [*en plant*], as if one had to be as careful as a screw not to hinder it in any way (that's how it's always written: the grand style of the flower comes up giving the appearance of not affecting it at the moment when it is most elaborated)—the grafting of the proper name. A graft does not supervene on what is proper. The proper begins by finding its blossoming in the graft: its appearing or its blooming, but also its fragmenting.

The name of the one who appears to appose

Aufhebung? as one might ask what is this or that? or what is the determination of this or that particular concept? Being is *Aufhebung*. *Aufhebung* is being, not as a determinate state or the determinable totality of beings, but as the "active," productive essence of being. So it cannot be the *object* of any determinate question. We are ceaselessly referred to it, but that referral refers to nothing determinable.

Impossible, for example—but the example sublates too—to understand the advent of the *true* family (love and monogamy), of the Christian family, without taking into account the *Aufhebung* of abstract right. The loving being reconciles himself in spite of the insult, without taking account of right, of the judge and of the one who judges right (*nicht von Richter ihr Recht zumessen*), without respect and without regard [*sans égard et sans regard*] for right (*ohne alle Rücksicht auf Recht*). A manuscript note adds: "Love demands even the *Aufhebung* of the right born of a separation (*Trennung*), a lesion (*Beleidigung*), it (love) demands reconciliation [*Versöhnung*]."

The schema of the *Philosophy of Right* is in place: love as sublation of right and abstract morality, i.e. of a split between objectivity and subjectivity.

The manuscript note has been crossed out but it is in accord with the whole context that constantly confirms it. Immediately afterwards is the proposition on love as the *Aufhebung* of conjugal rights and duties as such.

In the (Judaic) order of abstract right and duty, of objective law, the duty of fidelity, fidelity as duty went along with the right to separate from one's wife. But duty as such does not forbid the desire for infidelity, it merely forbids, in objectivity, the act of infidelity. The love that Jesus opposes to this objective law suspends even the unfaithful desire. At least it excludes (*ausschließt*) this desire at the same time as it suspends (*aufhebt*) the authorization (to separate from one's wife) inasmuch as it is contrary to fidelity. The interdiction weighing on infidelity is maintained, but simultaneously abolished: it is no longer an interdiction weighing from outside, in heteronomic fashion. It belongs to the spontaneity of love, it is assumed in the freedom of desire, in the autonomy of a desire that no longer desires what it cannot have or which desires only what it can have, which desires what it has. Vulgar translation of *Aufhebung*: nothing external any

his signet here (Genet) is known as that—but how and from where does this knowledge come?—of his mother. Who would therefore have produced a child by means of a sort of immaculate conception.

The name of the mother is supposedly—commonly—that of a plant or flower, with a difference of one letter, a fallen s, or a circumflex, to scar over the fall. Covering what is between the two opened lips or letters—in the place of s—with a stretched, pointed cloth, a tent or pyramidal *monumiss* [monumanque].

Genêt names a plant with yellow flowers (*sarothamnus scoparius*, *genista*, common or Scotch broom [*genêt-à-balais*]; it is poisonous and medicinal, distinct from the dyer's broom, *genista tinctoria*, *genestrolle*, yellowing herb); *genet* names a species of horse. From Spain, an important country throughout the text.

If all of his literature sings and weaves a funereal hymen for nomination, Genet, noblesse oblige, only ever attaches importance to naming himself.

He is mounted astride his proper name. He holds on to its bit. Like a grand Spanish knight or a circumflex. But also like a child on his father's stool [*selle*].

longer forbids you from cheating on your wife, but you no longer want to since you love her. So the authorization to separate from her, an authorization contrary to the duty of fidelity, remains suspended (*aufgehoben*) as it was in the past, but you won't notice any longer since you no longer want to stray.

here of course, discourse of the man, for the man

The interiorization of the interdiction, the interiorization of objective law (right and duty) by love, the assimilation that digests objective debt and abstract exchange, the devouring of the limit is thus the *economic* effect of the *Aufhebung*. Economic: once subjectivated, the interdiction is in a certain way lifted; I am freer because I am no longer subjected to any external interdiction. Economic: my satisfaction is, in conscience at least, regulated by my desire; I do what I desire, I am faithful because I desire to be so and nothing other than that.

But maybe the economy is simply interiorizing an interdiction? Domesticating it in the at-homeness of freedom?

The economic effect is more complex. If one is to say that the interdicting limit has simply passed from outside to inside, without being transformed by that passage, desire in the Christian marriage would have to be limited, and limited first of all to a finite being. But this is not at all the case. The finite is being traversed toward the infinite. One is no longer limited to loving a finite being: one loves a finite being as infinite. In moving to the inside, the limit becomes infinite: so there is no longer any finite limit, therefore no longer any limit or, what comes to the same thing, an infinite limit. Conjugal desire is free because it is subjected to an infinite law.

The family according to (Christian) love is infinite. It is already what one could call the speculative family. And the speculative family follows the infinitely circular trajectory of the father/son filiation: the infinity of desire, of marriage and the inner law is situated between father and son. With the exception of one brief detour, the insignificant exception of an inessentiality (the woman is here like matter), the essence of speculative marriage consecrates the union of father and son, with all the systematic consequences that can be induced from this.

One column in the other.

The exception, the only case (*Fall*) in which the right to separate from one's wife is maintained, in which the suspense is suspended, the *Aufhebung* sublated, is when the

The horseman's fantasy presides over the grand interior scene and takes over all the senses. Pretending perhaps to offer for reading "my" "illegible name." Illegible, hence positively legible name.

Miracle of the Rose: "'You're going by? Where are you going? . . . And besides, I don't like your tone. Take your hands out of your belt.'

I was on a horse.

Even when I am very calm, I feel as if I am being swept by a storm. This may be due to my mind's stumbling over every unevenness of surface because of its rapid pace, or to my desires, which are violent because they are almost always repressed, and when I live my inner scenes, I have the exhilaration that comes from always living them on horseback, on a rearing and galloping steed. I am a horseman. It is since I have known Bulkaen that I live on horseback, and I enter the lives of others on horseback as a Spanish grandee enters the Cathedral of Seville. My things grip the flanks. I spur my mount, my hands tighten on the reins.

Not that it happens quite that way, I mean not that I really know I'm on horseback, but rather I make the gestures and have the spirit of a man on horseback: my hand tightens, I toss back my head, my voice is arrogant. The sensation of riding a noble, whinnying animal overflowed into my daily life and gave me what is called a cavalier look and what I considered a victorious tone and bearing.

"Your heart that a massive rider's spurs / Will never open," my gashed paraph wandering at liberty like a wild animal, "A curious creature would appear if each of my emotions became the animal it evokes: anger rumbles within my cobra neck; the same cobra swells up what I don't dare name; my steeds and merry-go-rounds are born of my insolence."

woman *took the initiative*, when "the wife has bestowed her love on another." According to Jesus, "the husband may not continue a slave to her."

Doubtless, the speculative family fulfills its destination only with Christ. But this proposition is not simple. To fulfill one's destination is to raise oneself and leave oneself. Christianity itself fulfills itself only by sublating itself into its philosophical truth. So we need to specify that with Christianity the speculative family makes a start, begins to come to itself, to love and to the true marriage that constitutes the family as family. The first moment of *Sittlichkeit* is supposedly inaugurated by Christ. This does not form a simple proposition either: the emergence of Christianity has announced itself. There is *some family* before *the* (Christian) *family*. So we must interrogate this circular and teleological structure of the before and the after, this speculative reading of the future perfect that places the family before itself.

Immediately before Christianity, there is Judaism: simultaneously family and non-family, non-family as not-yet-there of the already-there, the being-there of the family *not consisting*, consisting only in dissolving in its passage.

The Christian thesis, the axial thesis that replaces the Jewish thesis by opposing it, overturns mastery. By substituting love for mastery, for the Jewish relations of violence and slavery, Jesus founded the family. The family constituted itself through him: "To the Jewish idea of God as their Lord [*Herrs*] and Governor [*Gebieter*], Jesus opposes a relationship of God to men like that of a father to his children." Such is the "exact antithesis" that gives the family its infinite foundation.

Before the antithesis that comes to take the place of the thesis, there was nonetheless family. Judaism was not only what preceded the advent of the speculative family, what resisted it up to a point. It had constituted a certain natural family by sublating already a still more natural family. The value of nature must be handled very cautiously. Nature is not a determinate essence, a single moment. It covers all forms of self-externality of spirit. It therefore appears—progressively disappearing—at every stage of the becoming of spirit. For example, for all its having broken with the natural-biological group, the family is nonetheless the natural moment, the most natural moment of *Sittlichkeit,* etc. In this sense the family is always natural, even the Christian family. But this latter sublates a natural family, the Jewish

The guard reported me, and I was brought up before the warden . . ."

Don't interrupt the course of a Genet. This is the first time that I am afraid, in writing, as one says, "on" someone, of being read by him. Don't stop him, don't hold him back, don't bridle him. He let me know yesterday that he was in Beirut, with the Palestinians at war, the encircled excluded ones. I know that what interests me takes (its) place there, but how to show that? He practically doesn't write anymore, he has buried literature like no other, he parachutes in everywhere the world is coming apart, everywhere European absolute knowing is taking a hit, and all this talk of knell, signet, flower and horse must bore him shitless [*le faire chier*].

Concerning the "fear of metamorphoses" and especially of animals, *The Thief's Journal* specifies that "it is not mere rhetoric which requires the comparison."
So start getting closer to the unnamable crypt and to Alberto Giacometti's studio; that wound of a paraph there takes on an animal form. You'll already suspect that if it is all that at once the signature is neither a thing, nor a flower, nor an animal. Remains to be known if there is any

How right he is. That's what I wanted to show by carrying you off as quickly as possible to the edges of a pool, a sea, where the Greek, Jew, Arab and Hispano-Moorish all find their moorings for an interminable war. On the trace of which I too am following.

family, which itself sublates a more natural family. And each sublation breaks with what it sublates, leaves between that and itself a sort of margin that constitutes the truth of the other as (past) essence, the truth of which it gives to be read, from its side.

There was—then—a Jewish family deprived of love, and it had itself broken with a more primitive and natural family.

Here begins the legendary discourse of the eagle and the two columns.

On castration and dissemination, a question that goes back to the flood.

Like Condillac, like Rousseau, Kant and others, Hegel resorts to a sort of theoretical fiction: the narrative of a catastrophic event reconstitutes the ideal-historical origin of human society. And he reinscribes the biblical narration with his eyes fixed on a network of philosophemes. For that to work, somewhere the two texts really must be homogenous.

The flood is the loss of the state of nature (*Verlust des Naturzustandes*). Before the flood (*Flut*) man lived in natural harmony with nature. The flood tears at man, drags him away from nature, destroys the beautiful unity. From that point on, man nurses an infinite, monstrous distrust (*ungeheuerste Unglaube*) of nature. It is no longer his mother, she has taken back or poisoned all the resources of protective belief (*Glauben*) that she had given or promised. Of this mother we have kept only a few obscure traces (*sind uns nur wenige dunkle Spuren aufbehalten worden*). Up until that point, she had been "friendly or calm (*freundlich oder ruhig*)" in "the equal equilibrium (*Gleichgewicht*) of her element"; now here she is responding to humanity's faith (*Glauben*) with "the most destructive, the most invincible, the most irresistible hatred." The mother turns against man, loses it, rages.

In the flood, man then conceives the project of dominating in turn what had sheltered, protected and nourished him. When we say that he conceives the project of mastering, of defending himself by an apotropaic gesture from what had falsely promised him symbiosis, putting to sleep, cradling his belief with an equal and regular movement, that is saying too much: one could be content to say that he began to conceive—period.

If all this eloquence over the signature in the form of a horse bores him shitless, too bad. The signet also falls like an excrement under seal.

Magnify the *turd* [étron], glorify what falls cut (*stronzo, stronzare, strunzen*) sealed as a stool [*sous la selle*], erect the standard [*étalon*] of his signature, or make fall a horse's erection, the king from his throne, all that would be equivalent.

Remains—to be known—what makes one (bored) shit(less).

Now—the horseriding scene ("I was on a horse") draws into its procession, in little continuous jerks, at a trot, the two pages that follow, where, by chance, there stands, in the "center of the circle" at Fontevrault (whose roots "are to be found in the vegetal world of our children's hell"), "the can into which the men shit."

It's a thoroughbred, Arab this time, a sort of hole erected there that one mounts like a horse, a throne, the cone of a volcano. Erection *en abyme*,

In all senses of this word. Noah [*Noé*] is the concept. In a bad play on words, Jewgreek, like in Joyce, with a pinch of Gallicism thrown in, one might say Noesis.

For indeed, in order to dominate the hostility of maternal nature in her unleashed waters, she had to be thought, conceived, grasped. Being thought is being dominated. The concept marks the interruption of a first state of love. Her son says to nature: you don't love me, you don't want me to love you, I'm going to think you, conceive of you, dominate you. The concept gets busy around a wound. "If man was to hold out against the outbursts of a nature now hostile, nature had to be mastered [*behersscht*]; and since the whole divided in two [*des entzweite Ganze*] can be divided only into idea and reality [*in Idee und Wirklichkeit*], so also the supreme unity of mastery [*Beherrschung*] lies either in something thought [*Gedachten*] or in something real [*Wirklichen*]."

Noah chose to gather the torn world, in sum to reconstitute the *Gleichgewicht* in being-thought. He chose to have his thought-ideal (*gedachtes Ideal*) come to being, to divinize it as it were and to oppose to it all the rest of nature as nature thought, i.e. mastered (*als Gedachtes, d.h. als Beherrschtes*). The thought ideal (God) then "promised" Noah that he would place the elements at his service, to hold them within their limits, such that no flood could come to submerge humanity. This sort of covenant with the father reinstates by contract the natural *Gleichgewicht* that nature had broken by unleashing her waters. The ark could float, bearing in its flanks, up on deck or down in its holds, the exemplary living beings.

The noetic response to the murderous aggression of the mother is thenceforth accompanied—this is what is odd about it—by a cult of life (*Zoe*). Man was forbidden to kill man. Breaking this rule means you lose your own life. Such is the contract of thought with itself, i.e. with God. As a recompense, God gives man mastery (*Herrschaft*) over the plants and the animals. Killing them, the only authorized destruction of the living, validates the exchange. But in return the living must be honored, and it remains forbidden to consume the blood of animals, which still contains their soul or their life (the same thing in Hebrew, and *The Spirit of Christianity* here follows Genesis 9:4 very closely).

To the breaking of the maternal *Gleichgewicht*, another response was possible.

that is how it signs and gets into the saddle to make a stool, and how it reigns, how it jams, how it signs and reigns. Broom also grows close to volcanoes. "At the centre of the circle is the can into which the men shit, a recipient three feet high in the form of a truncated cone. It has two ears, one on each side, on which you place your feet after sitting down, and a very low back-rest, like that of an Arab saddle, so that when you drop a load you have the majesty of a barbaric king on a metal throne. When you have to go, you raise your hand, without saying anything; the assistant makes a sign, and you leave the line, unbuttoning your trousers, which stay up without a belt. You sit on top of the cone with your feet on the ears and your balls hanging. The others continue their silent round, perhaps without noticing you. They hear your shit drop into the urine, which splashes your bare behind. You piss and get off. The odour rises up. When I entered the room, what struck me most was the silence of the thirty inmates and, immediately, the solitary, imperial can, centre of the moving circle. . . . 'One . . . two! One . . . Two!'

It is still the same guttural voice, a big shot's voice, that issues from a throat encumbered with oysters which he can still spit violently in the face of a jerk. It is the same cry and voice he had at Mettray."

The "punished" one, the "round" of the "punished," standing strictly upright, resembling

Not the appeased flanks of a floating dwelling but the erection of a war-tower.

Like Noah, Nimrod retaliates against natural violence by making be what is thought, the *Gedachtes*. Like Noah, he also imposes the law of the living. But contrary to Noah, he does not proceed under the sign of peace: he unleashes in his turn a tyrannical violence, distrust, war; he founds a society united by force, and the law of the living is the law of the strongest. Instead of opposing the sea with the very thing that it carries still posed upon it, rocked by it, the Ark, he confronts it, collides with it and splits it with a huge tower. Hegel here follows what Moses points out, which agrees with Josephus's *Jewish Antiquities*: "'For [Nimrod] had resolved to build a tower [*Turm*] which was to be far higher than the waves and streams [*Wasserwogen und Wellen*] could ever rise [*sich auftürmen*] and in this way to avenge the downfall [*Untergang*] of his forefathers (according to another tale—Eupolemos in Eusebius, *Praeparatio evangelica,* ix, 17—the tower was to have been built by the very survivors of the flood)."

By the device of a contract, Noah had delegated mastery to one more powerful; Nimrod himself repulsed, bound and tamed the hostile power (*daß er selbst sie bändigte*). But in both cases we are dealing with a "forced peace" with the sea. The split is consummated by a war and it reproduces the cleavage whereby nature separated herself from herself, promising maternal protection and in truth deploying the worst threat.

To this warlike, rigid, revengeful apotropaic, Hegel already opposes the Greek response to the flood: not a forced peace but a peace of harmonious friendship, of reconciliation. And it is not concluded or imposed by a chief, but by a happy couple: neither Noah nor Nimrod reconciled with nature the enemy the way a very beautiful couple (*eine schöneres Paar*), Deucalion and Pyrrha did, when after the flood they invited humankind to renew its friendship with the world, with nature, made it forget need and hatred in joy and enjoyment, concluded a peace of love, became the stock of a fine nation and made their times into the mother of a newly born nature, which would conserve the flower of its youth (*und ihre Zeit zur*

the fact remains that all this is done with stones: Nimrod's tower and the insemination of a new stock: ["After the flood, which left them at the summit of Parnassus, both Deucalion and Pyrrha created human beings by throwing stones over their shoulders. While Pyrrha created women,

and substituting for each other in silence like letters on a page, one in the place of the other, one counting for the other, the glob that echoes in cadence against the walls of the grotto like a moist and guttural clang, coated and hard, the glory of solid excrement that rises in an incorporeal odiferous song while everything "falls," collapses, hangs, causing the liquid rod to splatter upwards toward the bare behind, you have there a whole mobile glossary, more active in the missing words, in everything it steals from your pocket at the moment you are strolling through the text like a tourist, eyes fixed on what the native is happy to show you, nonchalantly, about his operation. Once it hits [*après le coup*] it will be too late.

Miracle of the Rose thus cultivates graftings of the proper name. Struggle, labor, ploughing, backlashes, waves of repression, against the desire to reconstitute, from the virgin's signet, the genealogical force. In fragmenting, dissociating it, making it unrecognizable as it bursts and shatters, one extends the name, having it gain territory like a clandestine occupying force. At the extreme there would remain no more of the text or world than an enormous signature, big with everything that it would have swallowed up in advance but pregnant with itself alone.

Necessarily undecidable if not contradictory movement. Economy of loss (→ breast [*sein*] ↔ child ↔ excrement ↔ penis →). The signature keeps nothing of the everything it signs.

Plant there the *genêt*, the horseriding inscrip-

Deucalion created men."]. How does stone become a child? A flower become an animal? Innocence guilt? *Phenomenology of Spirit:* "Hence, innocence amounts to non-action (*Nichttun*), like the being of a stone (*das Sein eines Steines*) and not even like that of a child."

Mutter einer neuegeboren, ihre Judendblüte erhaltenden Natur machten).

So the Jew remains rigid, clenched, tense in opposition to maternal nature. He is ugly, makes a spectacle of ugliness, he "lacks the spirit of beauty" (*Geist der Schönheit).* He remains cut in two and the even the tragedy of his cut is ugly, abominable. "The great tragedy [*Trauerspiel*] of the Jewish people is no Greek tragedy; it can rouse neither terror nor pity, for both of these arise only out of the fate which follows from the inevitable slip of a beautiful character [*schönen Wesens*]; it can arouse horror [*Abscheu*] alone. The fate of the Jewish people is the fate of Macbeth who stepped out of nature itself, clung to alien beings, and so in their service had to trample and slay everything holy in human nature, had at last to be forsaken by his gods (since these were objects and he their slave) and be dashed to pieces on his faith itself."

As interpreted by Hegel, the Greek flood has greater affinity than does the Jewish one with the spirit of Christianity: reconciliation, love, and founding of a family. The opposition between the Jew and the Greek continues, precisely as concerns the family. The contrast between Abraham on the one hand, Cadmos and Danaos on the other, reproduces in its meaning the contrast between Noah or Nimrod on the one hand, Deucalion and Pyrrha on the other.

Abraham abandons Chaldea, his native land, in the company of his father. Then in the flat plain of Mesopotamia (*in den Ebenen Mesopotamiens*), he repeats and aggravates the break. He wants to become a chief and make himself absolutely independent. He breaks with his family (*riß er sich auch vollends von seiner Familie los*). And he does so decisively, almost arbitrarily, without having been offended or thrown out, without having suffered the slightest of those pains that go along with some injustice or cruelty; such pains would still bear witness to a love that was wounded but alive, trying to find a new homeland in order to "flourish" in it. No: it is without the slightest affection, without the slightest affect that Abraham tore *die Bande*, the ties of communal life, thus setting in train his story and engendering that of the Jewish people. "The first act which made Abraham the progenitor of a nation (*Stammvater einer Nation*) is a disseverance (*Trennung*) which snaps the bonds of communal life and love (*die Bande*

tion tombfalls from it, the funerary monument is a *genêt* plant; one that writes, that is to say speaks without accent.

"Some moments later, likewise muffled, but remote, a voice, which sounded to me like that of an inmate, cried out:

'Regards to your fanny from my dick!'

The guards in the office heard it too but didn't bat an eyelash. Thus, as soon as I arrived I realized that no convict's voice would be clear. It is either a murmur low enough for the guards not to hear, or else a cry muffled by a thickness of walls and anguish.

As soon as each of us gave his name, age, occupation, and distinguishing marks and signed with the print of his forefinger, he was taken by a guard to the wardrobe. It was my turn:

'Name?'

'Genet.'

'Plantagenet?'

'I said Genet.'

'What if I felt like saying Plantagenet? Do you mind?'

'. . .'

'Christian name?'

'Jean.'

'Age?'

'Thirty.'

'Occupation?'

'No occupation.'

The guard gave me a dirty look. Perhaps he despised me for not knowing that the Plantagenets were buried in Fontevrault, that their coat of arms—leopards and the Maltese Cross—is still on the stained-glass windows of the chapel."

des Zusammenlebens und der Liebe). The entirety of the relationships in which he had hitherto lived with men and nature, these beautiful relationships of his youth (Joshua 24:2-3), he spurned."

The Jew does not love beauty. Suffice it to say that he does not love, period.

Of course, Abraham raises: a genealogical tree, a family, a people, a nation. But things whose lineage, as it were, never touches the earth. It is rooted nowhere, never reconciles with nature, remains foreign everywhere. Cadmos and Danaos too had abandoned their fatherland, but their departure had been motivated—it had taken the form of a combat. After which they had sought another land, there to be "free" and to "love." Abraham, for his part, "wanted *not* to love, wanted to be free by not loving."

He does not take his household gods with him, like the Greeks; he gives up hearth, home, all residence, all domiciliary sedentarity. He does not dwell, not even with himself. Desert, nomadism, wandering with flocks in an arid land "without limit" (*Grenzenlosen*). No proper place. Conflict with nature, wrestling with it to take its water, warring with foreign nations that he penetrates and tries to dominate. "The same spirit which had carried Abraham away from his kin led him through his encounters with foreign peoples during the rest of his life; this was the spirit of self-maintenance in strict opposition to everything—the product of his thought (*Gedachte*) raised to be the unity dominant over the nature which he regarded as infinite and hostile (for the only relationship possible between hostile entities is mastery (*Herrschaft*) of one by the other)."

What comes to be consigned in the Abrahamic cut? Two remarks about this:

1. Wandering, war with nature and nations, ruse, domination, violence, do not dissolve the Jewish family. This latter is on the contrary constituted in isolation, in a closure jealous of its identity, in the ferocity of its endogamy. Abraham will have cut the ties with his family and with his father only to become the stronger father of a more determinate family. What remains from the cut becomes stronger.

To remark the isolation, reinforce the identification, call itself a family (a family less natural than the preceding one but still too natural by the very fact that it opposes nature): circumcision.

Second crowd movement in the theoretical agora.

Gone are those who thought that the flower signified, symbolized, metaphorized, metonymized, that we were involved in making a list of anthic figures and signifiers, classifying flowers of rhetoric, combining and ordering them, binding them in a spray or bouquet around the phallic arch (*arcus*, *arca*, *αρχη*, it matters little if one gets caught there).

All gone, then, with some exceptions and as such, archeologists, philosophers, hermeneuts, semioticians, semanticians, psychoanalysts, rhetoricians, poeticians, perhaps even all those readers who still believe, in literature or anything at all.

Waiting a moment longer those still in a hurry to recognize: as long as it's anagrams, anamorphoses, semantic insinuations that are a little more complex, deferred, diverted, capitalized at the bottom of a crypt, cleverly hidden in the play of letters and forms. Genet would thus join the powerful occult tradition that has long been preparing its move, its leap backward, obscuring

Circumcision is a determining cut. It allows one to cut but by the same token to remain attached to the cut. The Jew finds a way to have the one who is cut remain attached to the cut. Jewish wandering limited by adherence to the counter-cut. The Jew cuts only by dealing thus, by having the cut contract with itself. "He [Abraham] steadily persisted in cutting himself off from others, and he made this conspicuous by a physical peculiarity imposed on himself and his posterity." Abraham associates endogamy with this symbolic castration that Hegel's discourse slides over: "Even his son he forbade to marry any Canaanite woman but made him take a wife from his kinsfolk, and they lived at a great distance from him."

Er hielt an seiner Absonderung fest, die er auch durch eine sich und seinen Nachkommen auferlegte körperliche Eigenheit auffallend machte.

2. Opposing hostile, infinitely aggressive nature and humanity, Abraham behaves like a master. Through his infinite opposition he accedes to that thought of the infinite that the Greek lacks. In this sense the spirit of Judaism elaborates a negativity or an abstraction that is indispensable to the production of Christianity. Desert, nomadism and circumcision delimit the finite. In them, the finite overflows and un-bounds itself. But by the same token, founding Jewish law by this passage to the abstract infinite of mastery, Abraham (a historical, finite, determinate being) submits to infinite domination. He becomes a slave to it. He can tame nature only by contracting a relation with the infinite mastery of an all-powerful, jealous, violent, transcendent master, the God of the Jews. Abraham is not the master that he is, because he also has a master; he is not the mastery that he possesses by contract. *Qua* finite subject, he suffers the infinite force that is lent to him, entrusted to him. Constructed, raised up on this slave-relation, "he could love nothing," he could only fear and be feared.

He could not even love his son. Just as he imposes on himself the sign (or the simulacrum) of castration, he forces himself to cut himself from his son, or at least to start out on the operation that itself remained a simulacrum of sacrifice. His son was his only love (*einzige Liebe*), the only kind of immortality he knew. His disquiet was calmed only once he undertook to make sure he could overcome this love and slaughter his son "with his own hand."

Circumcision and the sacrifice of Isaac are analogous gestures.

Reading problems we have to keep a tally of here.

its work by itself, anagrammatizing proper names, anamorphosing signatures and everything that follows. By means of one of those *ana* movements, whether he knows it or not—I have my own opinion on that but never mind—Genet supposedly places his signatures as replacements for all the lacking objects, silently, laboriously, minutely, obsessively, compulsively, with all the gestures of a thief in the night. Next morning, expecting to recognize familiar things, you find his name everywhere, in large letters, small letters, whole or in pieces, deformed or recomposed. He is no longer there but you inhabit his mausoleum or his shithouse. You thought you were deciphering, tracking down, following, but you fell into it. He has touched everything with his signature. He has affected his signature. He has affected it with everything. He has affected himself with it (later he will even deck himself out with a circumflex). He has tried to write, yes he has, properly, what occurs between the affect and the signet.

How to give the signet [*donner le seing*] to an affect? How to do that without simulacrum where everything is flaunted? By means of fakes, fetishes, pastiches? And in the end, will one ever know whether he managed to sign, whether the signature arrived at his text, whether the latter arrived at a proper name? Visibly dreaming of

The two operations that are conjugated under the concept "simulacrum of castration" appear on the same page. Although it is not by chance that they are picked out by Hegel from among the set of features and events forming the Abrahamic *gestus*, it must be recognized that

1. The two operations are not placed immediately in relation with one another. But following a short meditation, they are, in one jolt, related to one another by Hegel's interpretation. Both signify retrenchment, cutting, transcendence, absence or subordination of love. All of that comes to fill up the concept of castration. Is one saying anything more or other than this when one uses the word "castration"? A question that is the more acute because castration here has an essential economic relation with the simulacrum and cannot be thought of as a real "event," in the usual sense of these words.

2. Hegel puts forward neither the concept nor the word "castration." Given everything that has happened since Hegel in that domain, are we reading in the text that he is reading, and the one he is writing, something that he himself, let alone Abraham, could not read? Apparently and in many respects this can scarcely be contested. The word "castration," the very rapidly reconstituted chain, the style of decipherment, the selection of lexemes—all that decides [*tranche*]. If Hegel had thought that, he would have said and done it like that.

But however important these differences, they do not suffice to confer any rigorous status on the separation between the two readings. They might be secondary, external, non-conceptual. From the conceptual point of view, what is a difference of style or rhythm, or even of narrative space?

It is not insignificant that the concept reduces that difference to nothing.

Once it is reduced, are we adding anything, something else to Hegel's discourse in referring the Abrahamic figure to castration, or even to auto-castration, supposing any such thing exists? Are we doing anything other or anything more than placing them, like Hegel, in relation to the process of *Aufhebung,* truth, law? One cannot fail to see that Hegel is proposing a powerful systematic articulation of them. I've always said so, Hegel would reply to the doctors of castration. And anyway, what do you mean by castration? We're not dealing here with a real event but with an economic simulacrum: propriety is constituted by what is truly feigned in castration (circumcision and interrupted sacrifice of Isaac). The doctors concur.

becoming, by resounding, his own (knell), of being present at *his own* burial after giving birth to himself or executing his own decapitation, he appears vigilant in blocking everything he writes into the forms of a tomb. A tomb that is summarized by his name, whose stony mass no longer even encroaches on the letters, yellow like gold or like treachery, like broom. Letters without a pedestal, a contract with writing as funeral rite.

More precisely, the contract doesn't have the sepulcher for object. The sepulcher isn't an event to come, foreseen by the contracting act. It is the signature of the contract. So that in determinate places—those that here seem to interest us—this so-called literature of treachery would apparently betray itself; the theft of the signature would have its squealer in the text.

Verily [*voire*].

This word will henceforth come down to say what is true (*verus*, verily), but also the undecided suspense of what remains on the way or in the margins within the true, not for all that being false in no longer being reducible to the true.

Defined elsewhere: the truly feigned.

What remained of a Rembrandt develops

Hegel: if we are not dealing with a real event, you have to elaborate a whole discourse to describe or fill out the conceptual structure of what you call castration, you have to recount a legend, bring in a whole network of significations, truth be told the whole world of signification, beginning with sublation, truth, being, law, etc. Which is what I've been doing from the work on Judaism and Christianity to the philosophy of right, via the encyclopedia and the greater logic. And you cannot even understand what you mean by castration if you do not take on board the whole idealism of the speculative dialectic.

And it's true.

So it is not certain that one is saying more or anything different from Hegel, that one is reading more and something different than he was reading himself when one foregrounds the word "castration" and other such things. It is not certain that one is intervening conceptually in his logic. To do so, one would need to displace conceptually the conceptual articulation—manifest in Hegel—between *Aufhebung*, castration, truth, law, etc. One has to bring out forces of resistance to *Aufhebung,* the process of truth, speculative negativity, without those forces of resistance constituting in their turn sublatable or sublating negativities.

In sum a remainder that *is* not, without being nothing: a remainder that not be.

It is not easy. From the *point of view* of the concept, it is predictably impossible.

The question is *of the order of the concept.* We must question the order of the concept or else still question the question-form, which is ordered according to conceptual authority in general.

So at stake here is the relation or non-relation between castration and concept, castration and truth.

A desert question that must be given the time for parched wandering.

Abraham could love nothing. His heart was cut from everything (*sein von allem sich absonderndes Gemüt*)—"circumcised heart." Hegel makes no allusion to the fact that the sacrifice of Isaac was interrupted—by the one who was going to bestow the benefit of the operation. But he does note the economic advantage, the amortization of the sacrifice embarked upon: more than the beloved son of a father to whom he offered his son, Abraham becomes the *Gunst,* the *Günstling,* the only favorite of God, and this favor is hereditary. Abraham reconstitutes a family—become stronger—and a nation that is infinitely privileged, raised above the other, separated from the others. But the privilege of this

across its two columns a theory or an event of general equivalence: subjects ("every man *is worth as much as* every other"), terms, opposites that endlessly swap sides, the *je m'éc* fragment ("I flowed out" into my body, into the other's body). To flow out: syntagm relayed through the "disgust [*écoeurement*]," the "exchanged [*échangé*] look," "feeling himself flow out [*s'écouler*]," "I had flowed [*écoulé*]," "I wrote [*j'écrivais*]," I wrote "with so much disgust [*écoeurement*]," with "sadness" (the word returns six times in fewer than ten pages), infinite exchange of two columns that face off back to front.

X, almost perfect, more than perfect chiasmus between two texts arranged in each other's sight: a gallery and a *graphy* that keep each other and lose each other from view. But the paintings are written and who or what writes or is written sees itself looked at by the painter.

The word "gaze" that opens the righthand column stares back at you again at the end of the lefthand column. You think you are looking and it is the text of the painting (Rembrandt) that is surveilling, pointing you out, denouncing you—for what moreover? "The rest, all the rest, seemed to me the effect of an optical error provoked by my appearance, itself tampered with. Rembrandt was the first to denounce me. Rembrandt! That severe finger that spreads open the rags and shows . . . what? An infinite, an infernal transparency."

mastery remains abstract, and thus simultaneously collapses back into its opposite: it implies an absolute slavery with respect to God, an infinite heteronomy. The Jewish realm is a realm of death, it destroys the life of the other national families, commands on the basis of its own death, symbolized by submission to a transcendent, jealous, exclusive, miserly god, presentless. The Jew is dead, castrated: by his father who is therefore not a good father, therefore not a father. On the basis of this position he kills, transforms into death, in other words materializes everything he touches and everything that is not him. He plays on his death or his castration in order to enslave (always the question—who plays dead best). He castrates on the basis of his own castration. He petrifies, makes everything ugly, transforms everything into matter. His castration is a materialist weapon. A materialist and warlike people with a petrifying power:

"How could they have an inkling of beauty who saw in everything only matter?"

"Mastery (*Beherrschung*) was the only possible relationship in which Abraham could stand to the infinite world opposed to him; but he was unable himself to make this mastery actual, and it therefore remained ceded to his Ideal (God). He himself also stood under his Ideal's domination (*Herrschaft*), but the Idea was present in his mind, he served the Idea, and so he enjoyed his Ideal's favor (*Gunst*); and since its divinity was rooted in his contempt for the whole world, he remained its only favorite (*ganz allein der Günstling*). Hence Abraham's God is essentially different from the Lares and the national gods. A family which reverences its Lares, and a nation which reverences its national god, has admittedly also isolated itself, partitioned (*geteilt*) what is unitary (i.e. human life), and shut others out of its god's share (*Teile*). But, while doing so, it has conceded the existence of other shares; instead of reserving the immeasurable to itself and banishing others therefrom, it grants to others equal rights with itself; it recognizes the Lares and gods of others as Lares and gods. On the other hand, in the jealous God of Abraham and his posterity there lay the horrible claim that He alone was God and that this nation was the only one to have a god.

But when it was granted to his descendants to attain a condition less sundered from their ideal—when they themselves were powerful enough to actualize their idea of unity—then they exercised their dominion (*herrschten*) mercilessly with the most revolting and harshest tyranny, and utterly extirpated all life; for it is only over death that unity hovers. Thus the sons of Jacob avenged with satanic atrocity

In order to see you have then to reverse the perspective along with the rest, to provide some distance [*recul*]. "You don't have much room to stand back in the Cologne museum. You have to position yourself diagonally, at an angle. It's from there I looked at him, but the head—mine—lowered, turned sort of upside down. The blood rushed to my head, but how sad this laughing face was!"

Now this double theory (or double column keeping a ledger of the general equivalence of subjects and opposites) describes the text, describes itself while pretending to narrate the paintings, "works of art," as suspending the truly seen [*voire*]: remainder beyond the true and the false, neither completely true nor completely false. That is stretched out between two subjects absolutely independent in their distress and nevertheless intertwined, interwoven, entangled like two vines orphaned from their tree.

At the top on the left: "It's only those kinds of truths, the ones that are not demonstrable and even '*false*,' the ones that one cannot without absurdity lead to their extremity, without going as far as to negate them and oneself—those are the ones that must be exalted by the work of art. They will never have the good—or bad—luck to be applied someday. May they live by the song that they have become and that they give rise to."

the outraging of their sister even though the Shechemites had tried to make amends with unexampled generosity. Something alien had been mingled (*gemischt*) with their family, had put itself into connection (*Verbindung*) with them, and so willed to disturb their segregation. Outside the infinite unity in which nothing but they, the favorites (*Leiblingen*), can share, everything is matter (the Gorgon's head turned everything to stone), stuff, loveless, with no rights, something accursed which, as soon as they have power enough, they treat as accursed and then assign to its proper place (death) if it attempts to raise anything [a finger, a voice, a protest]."

"... ist alles Materie—das Haupt der Gorgo verwandelte alles in Stein—, ein lieb- und rechtloser Stoff; ein Verfluchtes, das denn, sobald die Kraft dazu da ist, auch so behandelt, ihm, das sich regen wollte, seine Stelle angewiesen wird."

The head of Medusa, one of the three gorgons, is between dashes. Like the gorgon, the Jew materializes, petrifies everything he sees and everything regarding him, everything that raises—eyes for example—toward him. An analogous accusation had been made against Socrates and the analogy gives much to be read.

Hegel does not exploit further this little phrase between dashes. It seems on the surface to perform a sort of conventional, illustrative and pedagogical function. And no more. A Greek mytheme seems nonetheless relevant to him to describe a figure of Judaism. One could ask oneself, in Hegel's terms, or differently, about the general, prephilosophical power of a mytheme derived from a highly determined culture, one that is even opposed—if needs be—to Judaic culture.

So Hegel has the gorgon rise up and then holds her between dashes, as though in parentheses or brackets. In the same manner as he had situated in passing circumcision and the sacrifice of Isaac.

Jawdropping effect. Convergence: the Jew operates (on) himself a simulacrum of castration in order to mark what is proper to him, his propriety, his name, to found the law he will submit to in order to impose it on the others and make himself the favorite

"But *what is* the stone, the stoniness of the stone? Stone is the phallus. Is this any answer? Is this saying anything if the phallus is the stealing away of the thing? And what if, occupying no center, having no natural place, following *no path of its own*, the phallus has no meaning, eludes any dialectical sublimation (*Aufhebung*), tears the very movement of signification, the signifier/signified relation, away from any *Aufhebung*, in one direction or the other, both amounting ultimately to the same? And what if the 'assumption' or denial of castration should also, strangely enough, amount to the same, as one can *affirm*? In that case, apotropaics would always have more than one surprise up its sleeve. Remarks for rereading as a block Freud and the scene of writing, the procedure that

On the right, toward the middle: "It goes without saying that everything I've just said hasn't the least importance unless you accept that the whole of it is more or less false. . . . Now I've played that game too."

Remainder—the more or less? Further down, at the end of the right column: "And it goes without saying that Rembrandt's entire oeuvre has no meaning—at least for me—unless I know that what I have just written is false." But if I only know it. Remains to be known.

It was a matter of what can be uncovered, even shielded "under the skirts," "under the fur-lined cloaks," "under the painter's extravagant robe," where "the bodies dutifully carry out their functions."

Double anatomy lesson in the margins, and on the margins of the margins.

It is thus true that the flower signifies, symbolizes, figures and rhetoricizes his own proper, which Genet then anagrammatizes, sowing more

opens and closes it, the signification of the phallus, the short analysis of *Das Medusenhaupt* ('To decapitate = to castrate. The terror of Medusa is thus a terror of castration that is linked to the sight of something.' Freud goes on to explain that what in the end turns to stone does so for and in front of the Medusa's severed head, for and in front of the mother insofar as she reveals her genitals. 'The hair upon Medusa's head is frequently represented in works of art in the form of snakes, and these once again are derived from the castration complex. It is a remarkable fact that, however frightening they may be in themselves, they nevertheless serve actually as a mitigation of the horror, for they replace the penis, the absence of which is the cause of the horror (*dessen Fehlen die Ursache des Grauens ist*). This is a confirmation of the technical rule according which a multiplication of penis symbols signifies castration (*Verfielfältigung der Penissymbole bedeutet Kastration*). The sight of Medusa's head makes the spectator stiff with terror, turns him to stone. Observe that we have here once again the same origin from the castration complex and the same transformation of affect! For becoming stiff [*das Starrweden*] means an erection. Thus in the original situation it offers consolation to the spectator: he is still in possession of a penis, and the stiffening reassures him of the fact. . . . If Medusa's head takes the place of a representation (*Darstellung*) of the female genitals, or rather if it isolates their horrifying effect from their pleasure-giving ones, it may be recalled that displaying the genitals is familiar in other connections as an apotropaic act. What arouses horror in oneself will produce the same effect upon the enemy against whom one is seeking to defend oneself. We read in Rabelais of how the Devil took to flight when the woman showed him her vulva. The erect male organ also has an apotropaic effect, but thanks to another mechanism. To display the penis (or any of its surrogates) is to say: 'I am not afraid of you. I defy you. I have a penis.' Here, then, is another way of intimidating the Evil Spirit.'), and the rest. In lapidary fashion, one could lay out the infinitely opened and turned-back series of these equivalents: stone–tomb–erect–stiff–dead, etc. Dissemination would always arrive on the scene to threaten signification."

slave of the infinite power. By cutting into his glans, he defends himself in advance against the infinite threat, castrates the enemy in turn, elaborates a sort of immeasurable apotropaic. He exhibits his castration like an erection defying the other.

Paradoxical logic of the apotropaic: castrate oneself *already*, always already, to be able to castrate and repress the threat of castration, give up on life and mastery to make sure of them; put in play, by ruse, simulacrum and violence, the very thing that one wishes to preserve; lose in advance what one wants to erect; suspend what one raises: *aufheben*. Sublation is indeed the apotropaic essence of life, life as apotrope. Now, being is life, being is *Aufhebung*. Medusa affords no off-stage. She sees, gives to be seen, only stony columns.

The Judaic destiny is however only one example on the stage.

But the example sublates itself into ontologic.

The Jew was able to ensure mastery and bring death everywhere all over the world only by petrifying the other and himself turning to stone. Playing more or less well in this way, he petrified himself. But he does not exist, him (he), the Jew, before turning himself to stone.

than any other and gleaning his name on whatever he happens upon. Gleaning equals reading.

Really, because that's not all. If this (double) operation—signifying and anagrammatical—were possible, absolutely practicable or central, if the irrepressible desire that activates it (with death or life, it comes down to the same thing) were to take effect, there would be neither text nor remainder. Still less this one. The summing up would be absolute, it would carry itself off, whisk itself away in a wingbeat.

Objection: where do you get that *there is* text, and remainder, for example this text, or this remainder?

There is [il y a] doesn't mean there *exists*, *remains* doesn't mean *is*. The objection belongs to ontology. It is irrefutable. But you can always let it drop. And not take account in the least of this remainder. That is moreover your lookout [*cela vous regarde d'ailleurs*].

There is what counts: the operation in question involves several proper names. And *glas*, myriad names sleep in those letters.

This time the theoreticians of the *ana-* are going to be discouraged because the proper names crossrefer when they sow [*sèment*], just as the semes invert when they crossrefer.

So it [*ça*] got turned to stone before him.

The Jew is a heart of stone. He is insensitive. Now sentiment, feeling (*Empfinden*) has been determined to be the focus, the living unity of life in the family. There is no true family where *feeling* has allowed itself to become anaesthetized, cut, denied or petrified: no true Jewish family, and first of all because no relation of familiarity was possible between the Jew and his God.

This insensitivity, this incapacity to form a true family is not an empirical trait, it is a structural law that organizes the figure of the Jew in all the forms and all the places of its manifestation. For example, contrary to what one might expect, the sedentarization of Joseph and Jacob does not interrupt the effects of this law. In it, mastery remains slavery. This relation persists right up to the way the Jews subsequently experience their liberation, when Moses comes to propose it to them.

Hegel comments further: this is unintelligible to us. We cannot grasp with our understanding (*mit unserem Verstand*) this becoming-free of the Jew. This is due to the overflowing of the intellectual order. The irruption of the infinite, and therefore of reason, rages in Jewish destiny. But it remains abstract and desert-like, it does not become incarnate, does not unite concretely and effectively with the forms of the understanding, imagination or sensibility.

Such is the insensitivity of the Jews. It holds fast, as if in ice, their entire history, their political practice, their juridical and familial organization, their ritual and religious procedures, their very language and rhetoric.

For example, given that the liberation of the Jews by Moses is inaccessible to the understanding (*Verstand*) if not to reason (*Vernunft*), one might think that, failing rational discourse, some form of imagination (*Phantasie*) was able, would have been able adequately to represent the phenomenon. Impossible adequation: when Moses comes to apprise the Elders of his project of liberation, he cannot talk to them in the language of the intellect, but neither can he talk in the language of sensibility. If the Jews rebelled, this is not because their heart (*Gemüt*) was rebelling against oppression

Thus the flower (which equals castration, phallus, etc.) "signifies"—still!—or at least cross-refers to virginity in general, the vagina, clitoris, "feminine sexuality," matrilinear genealogy, the mother's signet [*seing*], the integral signet, i.e. the Immaculate Conception. That is why flowers no longer have anything symbolic about them. "They symbolize nothing."

Demonstration. For castration to overlap with virginity, for the phallus to be reversed into a vagina, for apparent opposites to be equivalent and reflect each other, the flower has to turn inside out like a glove, and its style like a sheath. *The maids* spend their time reflecting or replacing one sex by another. Yet they stuff their whole "ceremony" into the structure of the glove, mirror, or flower. The opening is organized by the signifier "glove [*gant*]." *Gant* is held out like a contrived signifier. First words: "Those gloves! Those eternal gloves!" They will have been preceded only by the stage directions indicating "flowers in profusion" and a dressing table mirror that Claire has her back to. But these gloves are not only artificial and reversible signifiers, they are almost false gloves, kitchen gloves, "rubber gloves" with which, at the end of the ceremony, they will mime strangling Madame, and which will in short circulate between two places (the kitchen and Madame's bedroom). *The maids* are gloves, Madame's gloves; they are also called "angels." Both

(*Unterdrückung*), because they were homesick for fresh air and freedom. They did not liberate themselves in order to be free, but to proceed from one place of reclusion to another. They have no sense of freedom. How did they let themselves be convinced? Neither by intelligence, nor by sensibility.

By imagination? Yes and no.

Yes, because Moses, still in the grip of enthusiasm, indeed acts on their imagination (*Phantasie*). No, because by reason of the cut between infinite reason and the determinate orders of the understanding, imagination and sensibility, the appeal to imagination remains abstract, loose, artificial, inadequate. The intermediate schema of an incarnation is lacking.

This inadequation explains that the Jew would be incapable of understanding a concrete symbol and that he would be insensitive to art. The *Aesthetics* makes a place for Hebrew poetry, but under the category of the *negative* sublime: an impotent, crushed, dashed attempt to express the infinite in phenomenal representation.

When Moses proposes to the Jews that they liberate themselves, his rhetoric is necessarily cold and artificial. He resorts to artifices, to ruses (*Künsten*) of eloquence. He dazzles more than he touches or convinces. As a stranger to the symbol, to the concrete felt unity of the infinite and the finite, the Jew has access only to an abstract, empty rhetoric. That is why he writes very badly, as though in a foreign language. The split between the infinite and the finite blinds him, deprives him of any power to give himself a concrete representation of the infinite. His very iconoclasm signifies the aridity of his heart: seeing in sensory representations only wood and stone—matter—he easily rejects them as idols.

It's always the same law: they are dealing only with stone and they have only a negative relation to stone. They don't even think death as such, although they have a relation to it alone. They are preoccupied only with the invisible (the infinite subject is necessarily invisible, non-sensory), but as they cannot see the invisible, they remain by the same token riveted to the visible, to the stone that is only stone. They have dealings only with the invisible and the visible, with the non-sensory and the sensory, but they are incapable of seeing the invisible, of sensing the non-sensory, of feeling (such is the mediating, agglutinating function of feeling) the invisible in the visible, the insensible in the sensible, of letting themselves be affected by their unity: love and beauty, the love of beauty open to this unity of the sensory and the

castrated and castrating (spider or umbrella case), full and emptied of Madame's phallus that Madame doesn't have, they exchange first names and transform them endlessly into adjectives or common nouns:

"CLAIRE [*calmly*]: I beg your pardon, but I know what I'm saying. I'm Claire. I'm ready. I'm tired of it all. Tired of being the spider, the umbrella-case, the shabby, godless nun, without a family! I'm tired of having a stove for an altar."

The ceremony is maintained, therefore, between two pairs of gloves turning inside out endlessly in front of a mirror. "I'm tired of . . . this frightful mirror."

But between these pairs of gloves are flowers, only flowers, too many flowers. Their movement is like the law, the metronome also, almost inaudible, the lateral, dissimulated cadence of each gesture. Madame's openings—the one mimicked by Claire at the beginning of the play, then, in the middle, Madame's "real" entrance—work through flowers. In both cases flowers forewarn of death. Announced once more by a *je m'éc*:

1. "CLAIRE [*she primps in front of the mirror.*]: You hate me, don't you? You crush me with your attentions and your humbleness; you smother me with gladioli and mimosa. [*She stands up and, lowering her tone*] There are too many flowers. It's overbearing [*mortel*]. [*She looks at herself again in the glass.*]"

2. "MADAME: There's no end to it! Such horrible gladioli, such a sickly pink, and mimosa! . . . one fine day I'll collapse, dead beneath your

non-sensory, of the finite and the infinite. "The infinite subject had to be invisible, since everything visible is something restricted (*ein Beschränktes*). Before Moses had his tabernacle, he showed to the Israelites only fire and clouds which kept the eye busy on a vague play of continually changing shapes without fixing it on a specific form." Free play without form, a play both natural and sublime but without formal determination, infinite play but without art, pure spirit and pure matter. "An idol (*ein Götterbild*) was just stone or wood to them; it sees not, it hears not, etc.—with this litany they fancy themselves wonderfully wise; they despise the idol because it does not manage them, and they have no inkling of its deification (*Vergöttlichung*) in the enjoyment of beauty or in a lover's intuition."

during the exodus from Egypt, Yahweh went before the Jews and showed them the way. Two columns: a column of fire during the night, a column of clouds during the day. "Neither the pillar of cloud by day nor the pillar of fire by night left its place in front of the people." (Exodus 13:22)]

Christianity will precisely have operated this sublation of the idol and of sensory representation into the infinity of love and beauty.

Such a blind secession paralyzes art, speech, rhetoric. But first it fractured the structure of the tabernacle.

The tabernacle gives its name and place to the Jewish family dwelling. This is where the Jewish nation is established. In it, that nation deposits and adores the sign of God and his covenant. At least that's what one would think.

But the tabernacle (a texture of "bands" the excess of which must be constantly re-used, *Exodus* 26) remains a signifier without a signified. The Jewish home forms an empty house. Of course, sensing the absence of all sensory forms, the Jews tried to produce an object that would, as it were, give a place and a figure to the infinite. But this place, this figure, has an odd structure: it encloses its void within itself, it shelters only its own interiorized desert. It opens onto nothing, encloses nothing, contains as its treasure only (the) nothing: a hole, an empty spacing, a death. A death or a dead one, because according to Hegel space is death and this space is also absolutely vacuous. Nothing behind the curtains; whence the ingenuous surprise of the non-Jew when one allows him to open the tabernacle or when he violates it, when he enters the dwelling or the temple and after so many ritual detours to gain access to the secret center, he discovers nothing—nothing but the nothing.

No center, no heart, an empty space, nothing.

flowers. Because it is my tomb that you are preparing, because for some days now you've been piling up funeral flowers in my room!"

In both cases the gladiolus, small sword [*glaive*], from the iris family (Provençal *glaviol*; the common gladiolus has often had other therapeutic and nutritional properties attributed to it; the harvest gladiolus

extract from Walther von Wartburg, *Französisches Etymologisches Wörterbuch,* following the entry on *glacées* and before *glans, glarea,* which can also be consulted to good advantage:

gladiolus schwertlilie

I. Fr. *glaïeul,* "gladiolus" (seit 13. jh., R 16, 600), afr. *jagleux* (pl., 13. jh., Gdf; Galeran), *jaglol* Antid Nic, afr. mfr. *glagol* (Esc; Cotgr 1611), afr. *glagel* HMond, mfr. *glageul* Modus, *glageur* Modus, *jageul* Modus, *glagou* Cotgr 1611, aflandr. *glagiot* (15. jh.), apr. *glaujol* (hap.), *glaugel* (pr. 14. jh.), *glongol* (1397, Pans), Colembert *glazœ Viez* 55, pik. boul. *glajeu,* Formerie id. G 17, Noyon *glaju,* Dém. "id.; iris pseudacorus," norm. *glajeul* "glaïeul," Bray. yèr. havr. *glageux,* Thaon *glodyœ* "iris pseudocarus," *gladyœ,* Vire *liageu,* hag. *glazœ* (pl.–œr) "glaïeul," Guern. *glazœr* "marsh iris," Jers. *gliageu* "glaïeul," *glajeur* Z 13, 391, *bliagieu,* Canc. *glageu,* nant. *glajou,* saint. *liajou.*

. . .

Agen *graoujol, glaoujol;* Péz. "cornet, edible mollusk"; cogl. *glaizœ* "horse necklace made from dried aquatic grasses" ABret 18, 473.

Ablt.—Afr. glaioloi m. "site planted with gladioli" (13. jh., Gdf; R 11, 143).—Apik. *glaiollat* (ca. 1330).—Mfr. *glaioleure* f. "iris tincture" (Reims 1340).—Afr. *jagolé* "having the color of an iris" (1260), *glagolé* (Douai 1400).—Apik. *glaiolé* "strewn with gladioli, greenery, flowers in general (as in a room)" Bueve 2; *englaiolé* (ca. 1200—15. jh., Gdf; Bueve 3 b).

II. Nfr. *gladiole* f. "glaïeul" (Boiste 1829—Besch 1858.—Ablt. Nfr. *gladiolé* "arranged in the manner of gladioli (as of another plant)" (seit Besch 1845, auch 1901, Huysm); *gladiolage* "quirk of writing that

Undo the bands, move the fabrics, pull back the veils, open the curtains: nothing but a black hole or a deep gaze, without color, without form and without life. That was the experience of Pompey the powerful at the end of his avid exploration: "Though there was no concrete shape (*Gestalt*) to be an object of religious feeling (*Empfindung*), devotion and reverence for an invisible object had nonetheless to be given direction (*Richtung*) and a boundary (*Umgrenzung*) inclusive of the object. This, Moses provided in the Holy of Holies of the tabernacle and the subsequent temple. After Pompey had approached the heart of the temple, the center (*Mittelpunkt*) of adoration, and had hoped to discover in it the root of the national spirit, to find indeed in one central point the life-giving soul of this remarkable people, to gaze on a Being [an essence, *Wesen*] as an object of his devotion, on something full of meaning (*sinnvolles*) for his veneration, he might well have been astonished on entering the arcanum [the familiar and secret intimacy, *Geheimnis*] to find himself deceived [*getäuscht*] so far as some of his expectations were concerned, and, for the rest, to find himself in an empty space [*in einem leeren Raume*]."

The Jewish *Geheimnis,* the hearth whose center is being sought under the sensory envelope—the tent of the tabernacle, the stone of the temple, the robe clothing the text of the covenant—finally shows itself as an empty space, does not uncover itself, never finishes uncovering itself, having nothing to show.

That the absolute familiarity of the proper *Geheimnis* be thus emptied of all proper content in its vacant center signifies, according to Hegel, that the Jewish essence is totally alienated. What is proper to it is infinitely foreign to it.

So he cannot enjoy (it). As everything is obtained by favor of a transcendent and separated God, what the Jew enjoys is sealed up in expropriation. What I enjoy does not belong to me. My life and my body are not mine. Hegel recalls that every first-born could be put to death: "Sanctify unto me all the firstborn, whatsoever openeth the womb . . ." (*Exodus,* 13:2). Because the human body belongs to God, it had to be kept clean, but like a disguise, like the livery of a servant. The Jew wears everything like a gift, or rather a loan: clothing, livery, name. Because the Jews identified with one of their tribes from which they received their denomination, they were God's classified property, the managers or the servants of this domain. They administered God's possessions and property, defended his rights, organized themselves into a hierarchy going from the most humble servant up to the minister. This latter was not considered to be the guardian of

has the letters reduce in height from the beginning to the end of a word" (seit Lar 1930; Bonn).

. . .

Der ersatz von–*a*– durch–*au*– findet sich auch bei *gladius.* Es liegt wohl einfluss eines andern wortes zugrunde. In lt. handschriften und glossaren, die vor dem 11. jh. liegen, finden sich mehrfach schreibungen wie *glavdius, claudius, gaudio,* welche offenbar die ältesten belege für diese formen mit –au– sind. Vgl. Birt, Der Hiatus bei Plautus; Marburg 1901, s. 279.

gladius schwert

I. 1. a. Awald. *glai* "sword," *glay* "lance," Chayt, alyon. *glaio* R 30, 224.—Ablt. Apr. *esglaiar* "kill using a weapon" Gir Born, *desglaiar* Gir Born.

b. Apr. *glai* m. "dread" (13. jh.).—Ablt. Apr. *esglaiar* "frighten, intimidate" Kolsen 171, hdauph. *eiglayé* "v. a. astonish, delight; v. r. be astonished, burst out laughing," mdauph. *eyglayá,* bdauph. *esglayá,* Queyr. *esgalayar* "frighten," lang. *esglajá.* Bdauph. *esglayá* "frightened," Alais *esglaiat.* Apr. *esglai* "dread, pain, din," "fear" SHon, Queyr. "fright," castr. *eglach,* Carlat *esglach* "agitation" Delh 155, Teste *esglady* "fright taken to the point of madness." Mdauph. *eyglayá* f. "astonishment, spontaneous laughter," bdauph. *esglayado.* Mdauph. *eyglayáyre* "one who astonishes, causes laughter"; *eyglayamen* "astonishment, outburst of laughter."

c. Apr. *glai* m. "ice" (hap.).—Ablt. Dauph. *eiglayé* "slip, take a slide" Ch, hdauph. *eyglayé; eiglayada* "slide."

2. Fr. *glai* m. "glaïeul" (Ben SMaure—1709, s. Trév; Gdf; Chrestien; Gace; Escoufle; Mon Guill; Enf Guill; Molin; JLemaire; Tristan H), judfr. *glaid* Rs, anam. *glare* Haust Méd. Cherb. *gliai* "iris faetidissima" Joret Fl, Troyes *glas* "glaïeul" Gr, Esternay *glai* "iris", HMarne *gye* ALF 1599 p 28, *gla* ALFSuppl p 128, Marne *gle* "reed" ALF 1166 p 135, Vouth. *diâ* "glaieul," Brillon, Dombras *glâ,* Cum. gaum. "iris," Metz *gya* "glaïeul," Isle *gyo,* saun. *dya,* Brotte "marsh iris," Gruey *dye,* bress. *diê,* Plancher *hya, gya,* Châten. *iâ, iaî,* fourg. *ła,* Schweiz *glé,* rhod. *glai* "glaïeul," St-André V. *glays* ALLo 332, périg. *glai;* afr. *lai* "place where gladioli grow" Gerbert, *glai* Gloss Douai 244, alütt. *glay* (ca.

the secret (*Bewahrer des Geheimnisses*) but merely of secret or familiar things (*nur der geheimen Dinge*), things detached from the inaccessible secret in order to represent it. The *Geheimnis* is not even available to the chief who remains a minister of God.

What is proper to them remains foreign to them, their secret, secret: separated, cut, infinitely distanced, terrifying. "The arcanum itself was something wholly alien (*Das Geheimnis selbst war etwas durchaus Fremdes*), something into which a man could not be initiated; he could only be dependent on it. And the concealment (*Verborgenheit*) of God in the Holy of Holies had a significance quite different from the arcanum (*Geheimnis*) of the Eleusinian gods. From the pictures, feelings, inspiration, and devotion of Eleusis, from these revelations of god, no one was excluded; but they might not be spoken of, since words would have desecrated them. But of *their* objects and actions, of the laws of *their* service, the Israelites might well chatter (Deuteronomy 30:11), for in these there is nothing holy. The holy was always outside them, unseen and unfelt (*ungesehen und ungefühlt*)."

How could one have a secret?

Absolute expropriation renders the secret of the sacred inaccessible to the very one who has the privilege of it. In this absolute alienation, the keeper of the inaccessible can just as well calmly manage its effects or its phenomena, chat about them, manipulate them. The invisible remains invisible, out of reach, the visible is merely the visible. Simultaneously the most familiar, secret, proper, proximate, the *Heimliche* of the *Geheimnis* presents itself as the most foreign, the most worrying (*unheimliche*).

One cannot even decide as to the expropriation, cut one way or the other as to castration, run after its truth. The undecidability of a system is here more powerful than the value of truth. Like this text of Hegel's, *Das Unheimliche* ought to overflow, ought to have overflowed the opposition or even the dialectic of (the) true/not true.

Having this problematic chain borne by a political discourse—does that limit its extent? Does it shrink the field of a general question that was in any case elaborated in other places?

Hegel, for example, and his discourse, is attached to the truth; whence the political accusation he makes against the Jew.

The Jew cannot, as such, become a citizen, cannot have true State laws. Why?

Hegel is in dialogue with Mendelsohn—author of *Jerusalem oder über religiöse Macht und Judentum* (1783)—an Enlightenment philosopher, a Jewish Enlightenment philos-

1380), nfr. *glai* "mass of gladioli forming an islet in a pond" NM rust 2, 582—Besch 1858. . . .

Ablt.—Afr. *glaie* f. "glaïeul" (lothr. ca. 1220), *glalie* Gl Vat 1020, mfr. *glage* Baïf, *glaye* "iris" (Cotgr 1611; Oud 1660), Esternay *glaje* "glaïeul, iris, etc. (t. coll.)," Reims *glages* "tall grasses on the edge of trenches and rivers" S, Rethel "cluster of gladioli," Guign. *glage* "rush," périg. *glèio* "reed," M, Chabrac *glayē*, Puyb. *głoyē* RPGR 5, 263.—Rhod. *glaujo* f. "iris," périg. *glauso* "glaïeul."—Maug. *głavart* "marsh iris."—Mfr. *glaitel* "glaïeul" (Cotgr 1611; Oud 1660). . . . Afr. *glageure* "strewn" Ruteb, Cum. Chatt. "any greenery spread before the path of a distinguished person, in particular along the route of the Corpus Christi procession," Brillon *glaïures*.—Agn. *deglagier* "cut down" Edm.—Afr. *sorglaigier* "overwhelm" (hap.)

II. 1. Apr. *glazi* m. "sword; any sharp weapon" (13.-14. jh.), Cantal *glasi* "sword," lim. *glaize*. Übertragen apr. *glazi* "slaughter, carnage"; *mort de glazi* "sudden death," *glazi* (Lv; SFR 7, 168); périg. *glase* "glaïeul."—Ablt. Apr. *glazier* adj. "one who takes up arms; cruel, bloodthirsty; m. slaughter"; *glazios* adj. "murderous."

2. Bigorre, Gers *glasì* "frighten." Pr. *glàri* m. "grief."—Apr. *esglasiat* "devil-possessed" Jaufre, "terrible (as in a blow)" (hap.), pr. *eigleriá* "possessed, demonic; enraged, alarmed," mars. *esglariat* "frightened, hot-tempered, beside oneself, disturbed" A, *aiglariat* A, St-Simon *eglosiat* "terrified." Gers. bearn. *esglasiá* "frighten." BAlpes *eiglári* m. "anxiety suddenly mixed with fear," Alais *esglari* "dread." Barc. *esglarir* "frighten."—Apr. *deglaziar* "kill using a weapon."—Apr. *aglaziar; aglaziador* "murderer."—Apr. *englasiat* "devil-possessed" Jaufre. Ariège *englasi* "frighten" Am. Toulouse *englázi* m. "dread" G, Tarn, castr. id.; Puiss. *englas* "fright."

III. 1. Afr. mfr. *glaive* m. f. "lance, javelin" (12.-14. jh., Gdf; Gay; Chrestien; R 21, 292; Beneit Th; Arch 97, 441; Edm; Huon Abc; Perc; Fille Ponth; Tournai 1280, RF 25, 132; Eust; Beaum Cout; Ibn Ezra; Perl), *glavie* Brendan 1713, *claive* Perl, *glave* Veng Rag, *clave* Veng Rag, judfr. *groibe* (1100, RSt 1, 186), mfr. *gleve* "short pike" (St-Quentin 1340), *glave* "lance" (14. jh.), apr. *glavi* (lang. 14. jh., Lv; Bonis), *clavi* CCons Albi. Über-

opher for whom Judaism was not a revealed *religion* but a revealed *law*; it prescribes laws but in no way enriches our knowledge. Hegel seems to agree: (the) Jewish religious laws bring us no knowledge, no consciousness, no eternal truth: "Mendelssohn reckons it a high merit in his faith that it proffers no eternal truths. 'There is one God' is an assertion which stands on the summit of the state's laws. . . ." One cannot call those things truths, except to say that there is no deeper truth for the slave than the fact that he has a master. But Mendelsohn is right not to call that truth. Because God does not manifest himself, he is not truth for the Jews, (not) total presence or parousia. He gives orders without appearing. "Hence the existence of God (*Dasein Gottes*) appears to the Jews not as a truth but as a command (*Befehl*)." The Jews were slaves and one cannot be slave to a truth or a beauty: "how could they have an inkling of beauty who saw in everything only matter? How could they exercise reason and freedom who were only either mastered or masters?"

Foreign to reason and freedom, the Jews did not have rational laws either. The absence of obligation is not a sign of freedom, quite the contrary. The Jews have no political obligation because they have no concept of freedom and political rationality. Violence reigns. This unleashing does not correspond to a liberation or to any political progress: would Eskimos have the right to consider themselves superior to Europeans because they do not pay excise duty on wine or taxes on agriculture?

Once more the analogy between (the) Greek and (the) Jew is only apparent. As to property rights and family possessions (the second moment of the family syllogism in the *Philosophy of Right*), the early texts on the spirit of Christianity compare some of the measures of Mosaic law to some of the rules established by Solon and Lycurgus. In both cases the point is to put an end to inequality of wealth. "Socialist" laws tend to neutralize a disproportion that threatens political freedom. Both legislations put in place a whole juridical process to stop the theft that allows a family to grow rich beyond certain limits.

But the Greek process founds right and politics, it constitutes family subjects as citizens. The Jewish process on the

tragen mfr. *glaive* m. "soldier armed with a lance" (14. jh., Gdf; Runk), apr. *glavi* (14. jh., Lv; Millau 1359, Doc 113).—Mfr. nfr. *glaive* "sword" (seit 15. jh.), mfr. *glave* (Molin; Mist). Bellau *glievo* "sharp"; faria *gliâve* "knife," bellau *diâvo*. . . .

Ablt.—Mfr. *glavelot* "short pike" (14. jh.).—Mfr. *glaviot* "sort of dagger (or pike?)" (15. jh., Gay).—Nfr. *glaivataire* "sword-bearing angel" (1891, Huysm). . . . Mfr. *glavieur* "gladiator" (1531, Mir. hystorial XIV, 36, Db).—Afr. *glavoier* "pierce with a sword" (13. jh.).—Afr. mfr. *deglaiver* v. a. "put to death by the sword" (13.-15. jh., Gdf; TL; Gaimar 3000); afr. *deglaveis* "slaughter" Wace. Afr. mfr. *desglavier* "put to death by the sword" . . .

2. Afr. *glaive* m. "slaughter, carnage" (norm., 12. jh.); "epidemic, calamity" (ca. 1210–1380, Gdf; Ilvonen), St-Omer mourir *à glave* "to die en masse (during an epidemic)" (1790), pic. St-Pol id. (dazu pic. *aglaver de soif* "be very thirsty"; Manche *églavé* "dying of hunger" Dm); Lille il pleut *à glave* "raining buckets," Metz e *gläf*; flandr. Tourc. *a glafe* "in profusion, a great deal."

. . .

2. Fr. *gladiateur* "man who is made to fight in a circus for the amusement of the people (in ancient Rome)" (seit 13. jh.); nfr. "duelist, swordsman" (Retz 1646—Lar 1872); "type of dolphin" (Boiste 1829—Lar1872).—Nfr. *gladiatrice* "woman who fights with a sword" (Balzac G; Prévost, s. Trév 1771).

. . .

5. Nfr. *gladié* "having the form of a sword, with sharp edges (botanical term)" (seit Boiste 1803)."

The sword or glans in the phoneme, the clang in the phenomenon. Panglossia. Is there *gl* in every *natural* tongue? *gl* . . . *ph* . . . It shines and shatters

passed for an aphrodisiac and emmenagogue.)

In only a single case is it the reseda, a yellow flower (*reseda lutea, luteola*), source of the color

contrary flouts right and politics: in order to limit property rights and therefore rights of expropriation/appropriation, it indeed stipulates that the possessions of a family belong to it forever. Whoever had to sell his property or his person because he was in need "was to enter on his property rights again in the great jubilee year, and in other cases on his personal rights in the seventh year." That is indeed laid down in *Leviticus*. In the same way, he who had inherited surplus fields was not their owner, merely their manager, and had to return the supplement on a given date. This system of compensation, in spite of appearances, negates civil right as Hegel interprets it. Civil right presupposes family property. As the *Philosophy of Right* will confirm, there can only be internal public right if property of goods and the right of inheritance are untouchable. Yet Mosaic law limits the right of inheritance and property rights by subjecting them to an *external* rule. The proper is determined from outside, equalized, leveled by extrinsic measures. The family name becomes secondary, it falls to the rank of subjugated accident, "Thus to belong to a family depended for him rather on something acquired than on what of all he had was most peculiarly his own (*Eigentlichsten*), on a characteristic otherwise indelible, i.e. on his descent from certain parents." The problem is therefore a radical expropriation that turns property into management or husbandry, possession into loan, and therefore the name into a fake name [*un prête-nom*: a front].

Hegel's interpretation here concerns a certain "spirit" of the Mosaic law. In its letter, it is hard to see what really distinguishes it from the arrangements thought up by Solon and Lycurgus. But the same literality has according to Hegel a quite different spirit with the Greeks: and that means first of all having a spirit at all, an inner sense animating the law from within. The limitation of property is destined to forbid violence, to guarantee the freedom of the citizen, to make every subject feel at home and not a foreigner in the city. For that, he needs his own property.

In this sense all Greeks are citizens, but no Jew has a true right to citizenship. Hegel quotes Leviticus: "The land shall not be sold (*veräussern*) for ever: for the land is mine, for ye are strangers and sojourners with me (*Einheimische von fremder Nation*)."

If we follow this value of property (*Eigen, Eigenheit, Eigentum*), we have to conclude that the independence and the quality of free citizen go together with private property.

yellow and credited with medicinal and preventive qualities. The pants, those in *The Man Condemned to Death* especially, are "reseda." In both cases the threat is also a defense, forewarning; the flower that kills embalms, the weapon barricades (*gladiolus*, *reseda morbos*): "I had a terrible decision to make, for it meant breaking the barrier of flowers, fighting my way into the realm of the fabulous. . . . I stood . . . looking perfectly natural so that neither the guard nor the flowers would suspect what I was up to" (*Miracle of the Rose*). *The Maids*: "CLAIRE: . . . I act from below, camouflaged by my flowers, but you can't do anything to me. . . . SOLANGE: Madame thought she was protected by her barricades of flowers. . . . I'm going back to my kitchen. I'll find there again my gloves and the smell of my teeth. The silent belch

according to Pliny, the reseda ought to reduce the swelling of the tumor, and prevent it from getting bigger or fatter, so long as its application was accompanied by a formula: *reseda morbos*

in order to really hear this "silent belch" one has to remember that she who here pronounces the word and claims the thing is Solange: later she will ask that they "toll the bell" for her, and that the hangman cradle her. Certainly, none of that is very far from the Holy Virgin's furnace, but it first attempts to go through a bell, a glottis, a throat. Like toxic milk if you wish, and the milkman is never very far from the tocsin, he who poisons the desire of all three. What is so unusual about him, the very rarity of the association (milkman-tocsin, morning-tocsin, arousal-tocsin) confirms the distant but powerful constraint of agglutination ("her morning milkman, her messenger of dawn, her delicious tocsin, her pale and charming lover. That's over. Take your place for the ball.")
Like a spermatic pharmakon that one spits back out. This room stuffed with gladioli is also a stage for spitting. "Everything, yes, everything that comes out of the kitchen is spit! Get out. And take your spit with you. . . . I've told you, Claire, without spit. Let it sleep in you my child. . . .

"Among the Jews, [the source of these laws lay] in the fact that they had no freedom and no rights, since they held their possessions on loan and not as property (*nicht als Eigentum*), since as citizens they were all nothing. The Greeks were to be equal because they were *all* free, independent; the Jews equal because *all* were incapable of independence."

So there is no Jewish "for itself," no Jewish being-at-home-with-oneself.

Question of the letter. Hegel refers to the spirit of the law and recognizes that the only thing that matters to him is the intention of the legislator. If "in the soul" of the Jewish legislator, in his "intention" (*Absicht*), the point were really, as with the Greeks, to limit the inequality of wealth and ensure the freedom of the citizen, there would be a whole system of other convergent measures. Hegel says he can't find any in the Mosaic law. The Jews, then, are all slaves of an invisible sovereign: between them and their sovereign, there is no legal and rational mediation, only tribal chiefs appearing and disappearing according to the state of forces on the ground. The powers are real, not juridical. There are indeed empirical powers, functionaries or "scribes" (*Schreiber*). But the scribes are not guided by the spirit of a law. They obey empirical rules, precepts and commands (*Befehle*). Their writing is heteronomic. And as this literality remains empirical, one can always contravene the prescription when the situation of forces allows or requires. Indictment of Phariseeism. "In the event of the Israelites having a notion to be ruled by a king like other peoples, Moses issued only a few orders (*Befehle*), some so fashioned that the monarchical power could abide by them or not as it pleased, others with no bearing whatsoever (not even only in general) on the founding of a constitution or of any popular rights against the kings. Of the rights which a nation has had to fear might be jeopardized, the Jewish nation had none; and among the Jews there was nothing left to oppress."

So there is an abyss between divine all-powerfulness and the empirical unleashing of forces. No law comes to schematize the abyss that leaves the dead letter to the scribes.

Whence Moses's failure. Double failure: he died unjustly for having disobeyed a single time, for having marked his independence "when he struck one single unbidden blow

Do you think I find it pleasant to know that my foot is shrouded by the veils of your saliva?" That foot induces—the whole text. "SOLANGE: Will we even be able to go on with it [the game]? And if I have to stop spitting on someone who calls me Claire, I'll simply choke on it! My spurt of saliva is my spray of diamonds! . . . CLAIRE: Spit in my face! Cover me with mud and filth. . . . Cover me with hate! With insults! With spit!" Whom or what does one want to "cover" thus, with a "veil," with a sheet or shroud, of flowers or spit? And what, in *glas*, is induced by spit? What else

of the sink. You have your flowers, I have my sink."

The flower thus plays as a sort of poison-counterpoison. One negative works against the other.

Madame's exit also marks, as does her entrance, a return of the flower: a gala poison to be immediately vomited up. "MADAME: You're trying to kill me with your [phenobarbital] tea and your flowers, your suggestions. . . . Tea! Served in the gala tea set. . . . Take away those flowers. Take them home with you. . . . Madame is leaving. Get rid of those flowers!"

Reciprocally, specularly, Madame, each of whose maids [*bonne*] has successively taken her place, poisons them [*les bonnes*] with her flowers. Madame is a very good [*bonne*] poisoner. "The apartment is poisoned." "CLAIRE [*alone*]: For Madame is good! . . . Madame poisons us with her goodness. For Madame is good. . . . She overwhelms us with faded flowers. Madame prepares our tea."

In both cases the pharmakon is a hymen, that is to say also its contrary: "MADAME: . . . And those flowers which are there for the very opposite of a [wedding] celebration!"

(*in einem einzigen unbefohlenen Schlag*)." And the structure in question left room only for a *Schlag*. And then, Moses did not succeed in *raising* the Jew, in grasping and dragging him above his literal and servile down-to-earthness, carrying him towards the heights of freedom. The Mosaic *Aufhebung* did not take to the air.

This failure, this fall, has nothing accidental about it; the Jewish figure does not suffer weight as a contingent event. It does not fall, it has fallen. That is its essential mark. Moses' failure did not happen to the Jews. Judaism is constituted on the basis of it, as Moses' incapacity to lift his people up, to educate them and raise them (*erheben* and *aufheben*).

To raise the Pharisee letter of the Jew would also be to constitute a symbolic language in which the literal body allowed itself to be animated, aerated, lifted, pervaded by the spiritual intention. But the Jew is incapable of this in his family, his politics, his religion, his rhetoric. If he became capable of it, he would no longer be a Jew. When he becomes capable of it, he will have become Christian.

Moses, the dead Jew, the Jew whose death comes to fix at a stroke the figure of Judaism. Moses was conscious, or pre-conscious, of this limit. And to say so, he has, Hegel recalls, a "comparison" (*Vergleichung*).

The *Vergleichung* has more than one import: in itself, in the correction or complement that Hegel brings to it, and finally because it remarks the rhetoric or rather the rhetorical impotence of Judaism, the figural failure of a people incapable of appropriating and raising the letter.

The *Vergleichung* explains failure, fall or precipice. It is to be found in *Deuteronomy* 32: "In the survey of his political life, he [Moses] compares (*vergleicht*) the way in which God has led the Jews, through his instrumentality, with the behavior of the eagle (*des Adlers*) which wishes to train its young to fly—it continually flutters its wings over the nest, takes the young on its wings, and bears them forth thereon."

This is how the eagle is spoken in Moses's *Vergleichung*. Hegel begins by reproducing the statement. He transcribes *Deuteronomy* more or less faithfully. Then he complements it and corrects it to throw the stone again. Logically speaking one must be stone in order to transform the other into stone. Like the Gorgon, the Jew petrifies the other. Hegel has already said this: now he points out that the Jew is himself stone. His discourse is not only rhetorical, but *of* rhetoric, on the subject of rhetoric: "Only the Israelites did not complete

In both cases—wherein one never knows "who's threatening whom? Eh? You're hesitating?"—the most natural flowers are the most artificial, like the Holy Virgin's virginity, her altar, hearth, stove and sheath watching over the whole scene. "CLAIRE: It *is* right, isn't it? Let's skip the devotions to the plaster Holy Virgin, the kneeling. I won't even mention the paper flowers. . . . [*She laughs.*] Paper flowers! And the branch of holy boxwood! [*She points to the flowers in the room.*] Just look at these flowers open in my honor! Claire, am I not a lovelier Virgin?"

Much further along, it is still a matter of Madame's belly, stove and sheath: "Never will we be able to replace Madame. . . . Madame's armoire is for us like the Chapel of the Holy Virgin. When we open it . . . SOLANGE [*dryly*]: The tea will get cold. CLAIRE: We open both doors on our holidays. . . . Madame's armoire is sacred. It's her grand hanging closet!"

And each maid asks the other to carry her inside her, like Madame's penis.

Naturally the author of these paper flowers insists for this play [*pièce*] (the room [*pièce*], the bedroom, in the play) and for this ceremony (performance, "evening," in the performance)

they would have liked to strangle her. They mimed strangling Madame, it was about binding her to give her a hard-on, about finally getting into her grand hanging closet, or, which comes down to the same thing, by getting rid of her to get to the other, Monsieur (or) the Milkman. So many figures of the cradler executioner representing one another, detaching themselves one from the other next to what makes the text pant out of breath, chasing after a signet that it can't touch. The invisible lover of *The Maids*, who makes Madame drool, the man of the "delicious clarion" couldn't have any other livelihood. A galactic law exists there;

this fine image (*Bild*); these young never became eagles. In relation to their God they rather afford the image of an eagle which by mistake warmed stones, showed them how to fly and took them on its wings into the clouds, but never raised their weight into flight or fanned (*aufschlug*) their borrowed warmth into the flame of life." [ETW, 199]

The logic of the concept is that of the eagle, the remainder of stone. The eagle grasps the stone in its talons and tries to raise it.

The Jew falls back down, he signifies what cannot be raised—sublated perhaps but then negated *qua* Jew—to the height of the *Begriff*. He holds back, pulls the *Aufhebung* towards the earth. The case of the Jew does not refer to a past event. It indicates the system of a figure in the synchrony of spirit. He is even what as such resists history, paradigmatic remainder: "The subsequent circumstances of the Jewish people up to the mean, abject, wretched circumstances in which they are still today, have all of them been simply consequences and elaborations of their original fate. By this fate—an infinite power which they set over against themselves and could never conquer—they have been maltreated and will be continually maltreated until they appease it by the spirit of beauty and so sublate [*aufheben*] it by reconciliation."

For the sublation of this destiny, of this stone of death, we have to wait for Our Lady, the Messiah, another supper [*une autre Cène*], another stone, a living one this time, Pierre [Peter], the Church built upon it, a certain Holy Family.

The difficulty of making progress is getting more serious.

More clearly still, we are entering into the analyses of Christianity and the Christian family worked out by the young Hegel as the conceptual matrix of the whole systematic scene to come. It is not only the whole philosophy of religion, the description of revealed religion in *The Phenomenology of Spirit*, some fundamental interpretations of the *Philosophy of Right*, etc. that are engendered here. The zig-zag we announced will be necessary but the indispensable anticipation will be as rare as possible. Precipitation is too easy.

But the question of the procedure, of the teleology or not of the reading, cannot be avoided. And it is *already* posed, within the "earliest" elaborations, precisely as an ontological question, a question of the ontological.

It is the question of the *Wesen* (essence) and of the copula "is" as a question, relation or name of the father-to-son.

Knowing for example whether one can treat the "later" texts as the descendent and resembling consequence, the

that the flowers be "real flowers." Here, from "How to play *The Maids*": "fake trains, fake frills, [but] the flowers will be real flowers, the bed a real bed. The producer must understand, for I can't explain everything, why the bedroom must be the almost exact copy of a woman's bedroom, the flowers real, but the dresses monstrous."

henceforth we'll see it applied, from a certain angle, to every case. It initiates into the mother bearing that name. What must be tightened here is the angle from which a neck and peniclitoris come to be bandaged together. Which a strangulation hardbinds—

The cradler executioner—the one who feeds Solange her poisoned breast, that is to say, by means of a belching round or circular spitting, also feeding it to Claire and Madame who spend their time catching themselves in the mirror—that executioner is represented only by each term of the identificatory and specular trio. Which shouldn't overhastily be defined as homosexual: the excluded fourth, uncounted, decapitated, always invisible but never absent, always absent but never without effect, represented by the acorn that falls from the tree, by gloves, gladioli or spitting, the executioner cut from the scene, Monsieur or the Milkman (phallic homologues) appear within what they seem to put into motion only in a species-less writing, almost anonymous, without signature. A writing that will never return, by some proper or circular trajectory, to its place. For it has no place and its nonplace has no determinable contour. It relates to the machination of the letter that denounces Monsieur, in which the maids hope and fear that their handwriting will be recognized. "Your denunciations, your letters, it's working out beautifully.

filiation, the product, the son of the youthful elaborations that would be the paternal seed of the system, knowing whether the later, consequent and consecutive texts are or are not the same, the development of the same text—this question is posed in advance, reflected in advance in the analysis of Christianity. It is the very question of Christianity put on stage at the Last Supper [*mise en cène*].

The Father *is* the Son, the Son *is* the Father; and the *Wesen,* the essential energy of this copulation, its unity, the *Weseneinheit* of the first and the second, is the essence of the Christian supper. The Spirit of Christianity is, rather, the revelation of the essentiality of the essence that permits in general to copulate in the *is,* to say *is.* Unification, conciliation (*Vereinigung*) and being (*Sein*) have the same meaning, are equivalent in their signification (*gleichbedeutend*). And in every proposition (*Satz*), the binding, agglutinating, ligamental position of the copula (*Bindewort*) "is" reconciles the subject and the predicate, enlaces the one around the other to make of them one single being (*Sein*). The *Sein* is constituted, reconstituted on the basis of its originary division (*Urteil*) by allowing itself to be thought in a *Bindewort.*

Now this conciliation which—already—presupposes a reconciliation, which as it were produces the ontological proposition in general, is also the reconciliation of the infinite with itself, of God with himself, of man with man, of man with God as unity of father-to-son. All the "early works" elaborate the demonstration of the presence of the father in the son, the end of opposition in the bosom of the divine, the necessity of the copula in the following proposition that speaks the possibility of the speculative family, as it will be maintained in its concept, up to the *Philosophy of Right*: "The child is the parents themselves," or "After their union the lovers separate again, but in the child their union [*Vereinigung*] has become unseparated [*ungetrennt*]."

In this way the space is opened and determined in which the ontological (the possibility of *Wesen,* of *Sein,* of *Urteilen*) can no longer be detached from the familial; and, par excellence, from the question of the father-to-son, where the figural value of "par excellence" emphasizes what it is excluding.

Given this, before even wondering whether the ontological project was first a Greek event from out of which Christianity supposedly developed an external graft, we must be sure that, for Hegel at least, no ontology is possible before the Gospels or outside them.

And then the link that is looming between the question

And if they recognize your handwriting, it'll be perfect. . . . Even the game is dangerous. I'm sure we've left traces. . . . I see a host of traces I'll never be able to cover up. And her, she walks about in her tamed menagerie. She unravels the clues. She points to our traces with the tip of her pink toe." "MADAME: . . . who has been playing again with the key to the secretary ? . . . Who could have sent those letters? . . . Monsieur will be able to figure out the mystery. I want them to analyze the handwriting and to find out who could have concocted such a machination. . . . Someone phoned?"

What would the Immaculate Conception have to do with these little letters?

The work of art, the unattainable flower, more natural and more artificial than any other, is *The Miracle of the Rose.*

of the copula and the question of the family also bears this consequence: if we try to articulate an apparently "regional" (sociological, psychological, economico-political, linguistic) problematic of the family with an ontological problematic, the place we have just recognized cannot be avoided.

If *Sein* cannot be what it is, posit itself, become and deploy itself, manifest itself without traversing the fate of Christianity, this is first of all because it must determine itself as subjectivity. Being perhaps lets itself be covered over and hidden, bound or determined by subjectivity (Heidegger), but this is, according to Hegel, in order to think itself. First of all in Christ.

Jesus' revolution consisted in opposing the subjective principle, which means the principle of freedom, to the enslavement of objective laws or, more precisely, of objective commands. Each time Jesus transgresses one of those commands, for instance a prescription of Jewish ritual, he does so in the name of man, subjectivity, and the heart. So, it is on

the miracle of the hand: Jesus gives back to a man the use he had lost of a hand: "On the same [Sabbath] day Jesus healed a withered hand (*ein verdorrte Hand*)."
"For the Son of man is Lord even of the sabbath day. And when he was departed thence, he went into their synagogue: And, behold, there was a man which had his hand withered. And they asked him, saying, Is it lawful to heal on the sabbath days? that they might accuse him. And he said unto them, What man shall there be among you, that shall have one sheep, and if it fall into a pit on the sabbath day, will he not lay hold on it, and lift it out? How much then is a man better than a sheep? Wherefore it is lawful to do well on the sabbath days. Then saith he to the man, Stretch forth thine hand. And he stretched it forth; and it was restored whole, like as the other. Then the Pharisees went out, and held a council against him, how they might destroy him."

a Sabbath day that he heals a man's withered hand.

Not that Jesus opposes the heterogeneous and heteronomous objectivity of the commands with the formal universality of the law or of a *thou shalt* in the Kantian sense. In that case, the Jewish cut would be merely displaced and interiorized. The outer tyrant would become a domestic tyrant. (Kantian) autonomy would remain apparent, and would have its truth in a severe and implacable heteronomy.

Hegel does not doubt the possibility of autonomy. Parodying Kant and *Religion Within the Boundaries of Mere Reason*, turning Kant's phrase back against him, he displaces the difference: the profound heteronomy of the Kantian *thou shalt* would mean that between the Tunguska shaman,

Harcamone's knell is this time strewn among wisteria and eglantine. Harcamone is going to die. You remember the "eglantine bush," next to which he "fell on top of [the young girl]" and ended up cutting her throat after speaking "into [her] neck." And the wisteria that invades the places of a mimed crucifixion. It—the wisteria—becomes Christ's body.

eglantine: one of the popular names for the sweetbriar, also called Our Lady's seal, or Our Lady's glove. It is presumed that the plant received its Latin name (*aquilegia, aquilea*) from the fact that its nectaries have the curved profile of an eagle's beak, or else from its capacity to render sight as piercing as that of the eagle (*aquila*).
An eagle, white eagle, black eagle, Ganymede's eagle especially, dominates the whole corpus, swooping down on it regularly, from behind, gripping and tightening it in its claws, fucking it with a beak in the neck. One can say a she-eagle [*une aigle*].

Touched by grace under the eye of one Perdoux. "I was suddenly moved [*touché*] by the smell of roses, and my eyes were filled with the sight of the wisteria at Mettray. As you know, it was at the end of the Big Square, toward the lane, against the wall of the custodian's office, and was entangled in the thorns of a bush of tea-roses. The trunk of the wisteria was enormous, twisted with suffering. It was fastened to the wall by a wire network. Some of the overgrown branches were supported by a forked post. The rose-bush

Flight without reference, textual fiction, pure letters in the ear or throat. Eagle: tattoo in *The Miracle of the Rose*. Eagle: chimera—associated with the unicorn when it has two heads, in *The Balcony*. Eagle: absence of content and heaviness, sublime elevation, flight [*vol*] of the thief [*voleur*] become light, dreaming of being called—a little—Ganymede: "I shall be light. I shall have no further responsibility. I shall gaze over the world with the clear gaze that the eagle imparted to Ganymede." (*The Thief's Journal*)
The flight of his empire—polysemy

the prelates of the European Church, the Mongol or Puritan on the one hand, and the man of formal duty on the other, the difference would not be between slavery and freedom. Simply the former have their master outside them and the latter has it within him, as his own death, as a love that is "pathological" in the strict sense this word has in Kant. Kantian autonomy is pathological.

Now in preaching love, Jesus is proposing neither laws nor a transgression of the laws: he is recommending a sublation, an *Aufhebung* of the law, of the formal legality of the law. However, legality suppresses and fulfills itself at one blow: "This spirit of Jesus, a spirit raised above morality (*über Moralität erhabene Geist*), is visible, directly attacking laws, in the Sermon on the Mount, which is an attempt, elaborated in numerous examples, to strip the laws of legality [*das Gesetzliche*], their legal form (*Form von Gesetzen*). The Sermon does not teach reverence for the laws; on the contrary, it exhibits that which fulfils (*erfüllt*) the law but sublates (*aufhebt*) it as law and so is something higher than obedience to law and makes law superfluous." Jesus is not preaching the dissolution (*Auflösung*) of the laws but on the contrary the fulfillment of what is lacking in them (*Ausfüllung des Mangelhaften der Gesetzte*). Rising above cold formal universality, living love thus describes the great syllogistic movement of the *Philosophy of Right*: objective morality (*Sittlichkeit*), the third moment that begins with the family, and in it with love, emerges with the sublation of abstract right and of formal subjective morality. The schema is very quickly put into place: one can understand the principles of the philosophy of right and grasp its conceptuality only in the echo of the historico-speculative event constituted by the Sermon on the Mount.

"Think not that I am come to destroy the law, or the prophets: I am not come to destroy, but to fulfil. For verily I say unto you, Till heaven and earth pass, one jot or one tittle shall in no wise pass from the law, till all be fulfilled."

That sermon seems to proceed by "paradoxes": in truth the "reconciliation" that forms its central motif comes to overcome all the oppositions fixed by Judaism. In the light of the logic of Judaism, reconciliation appears unthinkable: "another genius," "another world," in which opposites are no longer opposed (law and nature, the universal and the particular, duty and inclination, subject and object, etc.) or in any case are no longer opposed in that sort of indifference and positive immorality that characterizes the Jew or the

was attached to the wall with rusty nails. Its leaves were gleaming and

"A girl may be a Maid, but she nevertheless gets her period. . . . Joan of Arc mounted the stake . . . and stood exposed with that rusty rose at cunt level." Elsewhere, again in *The Miracle of the Rose,* the game ends thus with the chain of roses and the chain of steel tying Harcamone's hands: "I put the rose in the false pocket that was cut in my jacket." The rose is always more or less fake, as is the pocket, a false pocket: they are cut one and the other out of fabric. We will speak more of trimming the rose and of cutting in general. Rose, which isn't simply a noun, nor an adjective, its masculine or feminine gender by no means assured, one can play with it as though it were a proper name. For example, hidden in a foreign language, that of Warda (Warda means rose), who is always working on her mouth. Warda picks her teeth, all day long, with a hatpin that she calls her style. She is the one who doesn't believe in truth. The play takes place in a sort of rose garden full of nettles, whose owner tries to increase in size by means of a fake belly and ass (cushions, padding). "THE VOICE: . . . . Madame, I love only your belly, where for nine months I took the pink [*rose*] shape that the rose of your womb dropped on the floor . . ."

the flowers had all the tints of flesh. . . . it was in front of the mingled wisteria and rose-bush that M. Perdoux, the head of the shop, used to make us halt. The roses shot at our faces whiff

the essence of the rose is its non-essence: its perfume inasmuch as it evaporates. Whence its effluvial affinity with the fart or belch: these excrements neither stay, nor even form. The remainder doesn't remain. Whence its interest, its absence of interest. How could ontology take hold of a fart? It can always get its hands on what stays in the shitcan, never on the air biscuits released by roses. One must therefore read the anthropy of a text that makes roses fart.

Kantian subject. Jesus opposes the opposition that is formal and therefore indeterminate, indifferent. He thus opposes one "or" (*das Oder*) to another: for example the opposition between virtue and vice was opposed to the opposition between rights or duties and nature. "In love all thought of duty vanishes (*wegfällt*)." At the same time the old opposition is fulfilled, filled up, overrun by a richer principle. *Pleroma* (πληρωμα) will have been the name of this overflowing fulfillment of the synthesis.

The living, conceptual meaning of life as love is pleroma.

The superabundance of the pleroma unbalances the principle of equivalence, commerce, the exchange economy that regulates *justice*: I give you what you give me, I take from you what you take from me, I exchange blow for blow. Castration, according to justice, is justice. Castration is not simply something one exchanges (eye for eye, tooth for tooth). It is the very principle of exchange. It castrates, equalizes or prunes the pleroma, it tends to maintain two forces, two erections, two impulses at the same height. Somewhere it is failing, as is justice, whenever an inequality appears. But it takes its revenge by the same token: is not inequality of height castration itself? Castration is indifference, castration is difference. By opposing positive justice does Christ suspend or aggravate castration? Does he permit or forbid erection? No doubt both—both operations must be read at the same time—because he sublates. He castrates on the one hand, and thinks the end of castration on the other.

"An eye for an eye, a tooth for a tooth say the laws. Retribution (*Wiedervergeltung*) and its equivalence (*Gleichheit*) with crime is the sacred principle of all justice, the principle on which any political order must rest. But Jesus makes a general demand on his hearers to surrender (*aufgeben*) their rights, to lift (*erheben*) themselves above the whole sphere of justice or injustice by love, for in love there vanish not only rights but also the feeling of inequality and the hatred of enemies which this feeling's imperative demand for equality implies."

Pleroma, break with the principle of equivalence, at least apparent unbalancing of exchange economy, dissymmetry between opposables. The two Xs must not take account of each other, reflect each other, record each other, inscribe each other equally the one in the other. This is how Hegel interprets "Let not the left hand know what the right hand doeth" (*Laß die linke Hand nicht wissen, was die*

And yet the text itself doesn't disappear entirely, not quite as fast as the farts that blow through it. *The Screens*, which can be experienced as the enormous parade of a fart produced from the first word ("Rose!"), remain, are reread, repeated. That suspense between remainder and the non-remainder of the remainder moreover, that suspension of the text that delays absolute dissipation a little—one mustn't exaggerate anything—could be called effluvium. Effluvium designates in general organic substances in the process of decomposition, or rather their product floating in the air, the sort of *gas* that hovers for a time over swamps, magnetic fluid also. The text is thus a gas; concerning the origin and stakes of the word one hesitates—but it comes down to the same thing—between spirit (*Geest, Geist*) and fermentation (*gäschen*).

If there is a sense to the problem of repetition, then it is that. And in order to read it you have to sniff out the expiration

after whiff. No sooner was I visited by the memory of the flowers than there rushed to my mind's eye the scenes I am about to relate.

Someone opened Harcamone's door."

What is going on here with the eyes? Is it a question of worn out metaphors? "My eyes were filled with the sight of the wisteria," "there rushed to my mind's eye the scenes I am about to relate."

Although they open suddenly the scenes have nevertheless been elaborated way back. From a long time ago, expert, loving, diligent hands have been caressing the surface of the fabric, undoing the folds, slipping under the lining, unhooking, unbuttoning. While all the time speaking, telling you stories. With eyes closed or turned elsewhere.

rechte tut). This does not mean, as is usually thought: do not try to get yourself applauded when you act according to duty, ignore what you do so as to leave it unknown, in the shadows and without publicity. No more does it mean: be content with being conscious of what good you do without seeking recognition from others. In fact the simple consciousness of doing good is already an inner applause and a sort of economic recompense, an equivalence for myself of the benefit I pretend to renounce when it comes from others. Good conscience (*gute Gewissen*) maintains the circle of exchange. I take back with one hand what I give with the other, each hand keeps a tally of the other, masters and annuls the difference between the two operations. A superior, remainderless calculus: what consciousness wants to be.

Being somewhere unconscious, on the one hand, of what is going on on the other, dissociating absolutely one hand from the other, that's the condition for breaking exchange in the pleroma and exposing the fraud, the simulation, the totalizing lure of good conscience. That is Hegel's interpretation of "let not the left hand know what the right hand doeth."

But what makes this interpretation specifically Christian is not only the promise of a sublation that will come to compensate for the dissymmetry, not only the expectation of an infinite reconciliation that will again appease the inequality. The fact is that the break in equivalence here, at this particular moment, takes the form of a consciousness that is essentially guilty, guilty and self-accusatory, self-mutilating at every stroke. To the good conscience of the Pharisee satisfied with duty done, holding in one hand what he gives with the other, Hegel opposes the look of the publican who beats his breast: "The consciousness of the Pharisee (a consciousness of duty done), like the consciousness

the gift without counterpart, or even without profit, is apparently resolved in the very speech Jesus makes to the young man, and that Hegel nonetheless opposes to the miserly logic of exchange. The spiritual or symbolic profit reconstitutes the ring and makes the prodigal into a profound miser. Is the sequence unstitched? A little after the discourse on the eunuchs ("All men cannot receive this saying, save they to whom it is given. For there are some eunuchs, which were so born from their mother's womb: and there are some eunuchs, which were made eunuchs of men: and there be eunuchs, which have made themselves eunuchs for the kingdom of heaven's sake. He that is able to receive it, let him receive it"), having laid his hands on the little children one should suffer to come to him because the kingdom of heaven belongs to them, Jesus addresses the Young Man who asks him what he is failing to do, once he has observed all the commandments: "If thou wilt be perfect, go and sell that thou hast, and give to the poor, and thou shalt have treasure in heaven" (Matthew 19).

This manipulation of the fabric gives nothing to be seen in the manner of a perception or hallucination. If one had a good definition of the phantasm at one's disposal, perhaps one could say if this writing were that of a phantasm. In everyday language [*langue*] one would say a dream. But the text requires us to draw [*la tirer*] it out: this dream is a dream within another dream, and within another's dream. That, the miracle of the rose, which can take place only within a text, as text, implies a certain linking of the critical body.

Point of view. Scenes that *fill* one's view violently or are *thrust* into the mind's eye produce the blinding that is necessary for theatre. The point of view envelops or blinds itself. There is first the point of view of the one pretending to be the narrator: "Someone opened Harcamone's door. He was sleeping on his back. First, four men entered his dream. Then he awoke. Without getting up, without even raising his torso, he turned his head to the door. He saw the black men and understood immediately, but he also realized very quickly that, in order to die in his sleep, he must not disrupt or destroy the state of dreaming in which he was entangled. He decided to maintain the dream."

The one seeming to pretend to be the narrator sees Harcamone's point of view only by following the four black men as they break and enter and penetrate Harcamone in contraband, insinuating

of the young man (the consciousness of having truly observed all the laws—Matthew 19:20), this clear conscience, is a hypocrisy (*Heuchelei*) because (a) even if it is bound up with the intention of the action, it is a reflection on itself and on the action, is something impure [*ein Unreines*] not belonging to the action; and (b) if it is an idea [*Vorstellung*] of the agent's self as a moral man, as in the case of the Pharisee and the young man, it is an idea whose content is made up of the virtues, i.e. of restricted things whose sphere is given, whose matter is limited, and which therefore are one and all incomplete, while the good conscience, the consciousness of having done one's duty, hypocritically claims to be the whole (*sich zum Ganzen heuchelt*)."

Beating one's breast, breaking by guilt every economy of equivalence, dividing the good conscience that reappropriates the whole: to this pleroma, to this revolution in the circle of restricted economy, to this humiliation without *quid pro quo*, will correspond a dissymmetry on the other side. Pardoning sins also rises above the law, i.e. the principle of reciprocity.

An example on which Hegel dwells at length: that of the "beautiful and famous sinner Mary Magdalene."

The details of the narration are taken from several gospels. An opportunity to recall that the factuality of the

Mary Magdalene was the first name of the mother (Maria Magdalena Louisa, née Fromm), Maria that of the daughter (Susanna Maria) and of the wife (Maria Helena Susanna). Hegel's daughter dies almost immediately after birth (1812). On a trip to Dresden (1821), he writes to his wife. As usual, he talks to her about the art galleries he systematically visits on every trip. In particular about a painting by Holbein the Younger, *The Madonna of the Burgermeister Meyer*. He always took the original—which he saw regularly in Berlin—to be a copy, and the copy, which he had just seen in Dresden, to be the original. "I went of course to the gallery and among the paintings inspected dear old friends. Above all I was anxious to see the painting by Holbein of which we saw a copy in Berlin, and I paid special attention to the particulars which I had already noted in Berlin, namely the complexion of the middle figure among the three female figures, the nose of the mayor, and the child on Mary's arm. Considering these particulars, it was immediately clear to me that the figures in the Berlin painting, as beautiful as it is, taken for itself, were made by an understudy. Visibly, the child in the painting here is sickly. It is obviously—and I in this am completely convinced of the correctness of what was indicated by the local inspector—supposed to be a dead child of the female donor which they see in the Heavenly Mother's arm, and which in this embrace

themselves clandestinely into his "dream," thus multiplying the point of view to infinity.

Who is dreaming? Who? Who is writing? What? Who signs the miracle of the red rose? Who signs at the bottom of this text that gets its period according to the same rules [*qui n'en a pas moins ses règles*]?

Will it manage to bleed?

One can leave the question suspended at least for a time. The risk is that of dying before finishing writing one's knell.

Remains to be known—refuse to die asleep in the name of what, of whom.

"He decided to maintain the dream." Let's let the miracle of the rose wait, since it's the very object of the detour, and will be produced from the dream of the other: golden Harcamone

sends down to them [a message of] consolation and resignation [to the divine will]. The accuracy of this interpretation is confirmed by the child in the middle at the bottom, who is almost standing and which who here is most beautiful. I have no doubt at all that the painting in Berlin is a skillfully made copy, but one in which there is above all a lack of spirit."

And the following year, the very day he writes to Goethe the great letter about colors (15 September 1822): "Good morning, dear Maria, from the sunshine of Marianburg, i.e. Mag deburg, whose maid *[Magd]* is Holy Mary, to whom the Cathedral is—or was—dedicated. [. . .] it is more difficult to get out of Magdeburg than into it."

narratives (*Erzählungen*), the variations as to places, times and circumstances change nothing as to the conceptual aim (*Ansicht*), and that "nothing is to be said [judged, decided [*gesprochen*] about the actual facts (*Wirklichkeit*)," as to the factual reality of the events. The point for Hegel is not to "put all the facts aside," as Rousseau proposed to do in the narrative of the origin: rather, after the fashion of *Religion Within the Boundaries of Mere Reason*, to seek in the Biblical text a semantic weave of philosophemes or prephilosophemes. The facts were or were not as they are told; what counts is the interpretation one draws from them from the vantage of what they will have become: philosophy. The truth of Christianity is philosophy.

The "fine example" is, then, that of Mary the sinner who comes to Jesus during a meal with the Pharisees. She throws herself at his feet, sobbing, bathes his feet in tears, dries them with her hair, kisses them and rubs them with a pomade, anoints them with an ointment, a balm (*salbet sie mit Salben*), a "pure and costly spikenard" (*mit unverfalschten und köstlichen Nardenwasser*). When the virtuous Simon sees her drowning her faults and drinking reconciliation, he concludes that she is a sinner and that if Jesus were a seer (*Seher*) he would know that. Jesus forgives her. Because she loved much, of course. But above all, says Hegel, because she did something "beautiful" for Jesus: "this is the only thing in the whole story of Jesus which goes by the name of 'beautiful.'"

To what beauty was Jesus sensitive? To that of the outpouring of love, of course, to the kisses, to the tears of affection, but above all, if we are to believe Hegel, to that perfumed oil, that cream with which she anointed his foot. It is as though in advance she were taking care of his dead body, adoring it, pressing it gently with her hands, soothing

sleeps [*Harcamone d'or*].

As always, the pealing of the narrative echoed out in advance; within itself, hence as close to silence—through citing of self or the other—as snow brushing a sensitive golden bell. From earlier on: "The magnificence of my tale springs naturally (as a result of my modesty too and of my shame at having been so unhappy) from the pitiable moments of my entire life. Just as the Golden Legend flowered from a banal sentence to torture pronounced two thousand years ago, just as Botchako's singsong voice blossomed into the velvet corollae of his rich rippling voice, so my tale, which issues from my shame, becomes glorious and dazzles me."

From the moment he is condemned to die, Harcamone the Christ flees into slumber; he sleeps wakened, cared for, and fattened by society like a pharmakos or scapegoat. "Each day the trusty took better care of him than the day before. His face grew a little fuller. He was acquiring the majesty of glutted dictators.

As the fatal moment approached, I felt Harcamone getting more and more tense, carrying on an inner struggle, seeking to escape from himself so as to escape from here. To break loose, to leave, to flee through the fissures, like a golden vapour! But he had to transform himself into a golden powder. Harcamone clung to me. He urged me to find the secret. And I raked up all my memories of miracles, known or unknown, those of the Bible, of mythologies, and I sought the likely explanation, the kind of simple trick . . ."

it with a holy pomade, wrapping it in little bands just as it is beginning to go stiff. This whore who behaves like a virgin

equivalences: "And one of the Pharisees desired him that he would eat with him. And he went into the Pharisee's house, and sat down to meat. And, behold, a woman in the city, which was a sinner, when she knew that Jesus sat at meat in the Pharisee's house, brought an alabaster box of ointment, And stood at his feet behind him weeping, and began to wash his feet with tears, and did wipe them with the hairs of her head, and kissed his feet, and anointed them with the ointment.
Now when the Pharisee which had bidden him saw it, he spake within himself, saying, This man, if he were a prophet, would have known who and what manner of woman this is that toucheth him: for she is a sinner. And Jesus answering said unto him, Simon, I have somewhat to say unto thee. And he saith, Master, say on. There was a certain creditor which had two debtors: the one owed five hundred pence, and the other fifty. And when they had nothing to pay, he frankly forgave them both. Tell me therefore, which of them will love him most? Simon answered and said, I suppose that he, to whom he forgave most. And he said unto him, Thou hast rightly judged. And he turned to the woman, and said unto Simon, Seest thou this woman? I entered into thine house, thou gavest me no water for my feet: but she hath washed my feet with tears, and wiped them with the hairs of her head. Thou gavest me no kiss: but this woman since the time I came in hath not ceased to kiss my feet. My head with oil thou didst not anoint: but this woman hath anointed my feet with ointment. Wherefore I say unto thee, Her sins, which are many, are forgiven; for she loved much: but to whom little is forgiven, the same loveth little."
This passage of the Gospel According to Saint Luke is followed, as is well known, by a description of the women in Jesus and the disciples' entourage, then the parable of the four seeds. In Matthew, the story of the anointment at Bethany ("For in that she hath poured this ointment on my body, she did it for my burial.") immediately precedes Judas' betrayal

(*Die schüchterne, sich selbst genügende stolze Jungfräulichkeit*) "has anointed me for my burial" (*Sie hat mich, sagt Jesus, im voraus auf mein Begräbnis gesalbt*). The unctuous balm makes Christ's body glisten, he is caressed by a sort of funerary glory. A brilliant, yellow, waxy patch in a very dark picture. Promised to virginity, the prostitute stands by the Son of God. The weeping woman also melts on him like a candle.

The extreme of love inundates, pleroma always gives rise to unction.

Love is the pleroma of the law. But the logic of pleroma leaves nothing at rest. What is accomplished with

Everything happens then while Harcamone sleeps. And near the heart of the dream, read the caption [*légende*], there shines the Golden Fleece. Around the collar, the neck, is a necklace. The latter—owing to the privilege, in a word, that it derives from providing for decollation, from assigning to the executioner a dividing line (circumcision or castration)—represents the most menacing adornment or parade, one that portends taking part in the body it takes apart [*celle qui d'avance fait, du corps, partie*].

Writing, for Genet: knowing how to have it consist [*comporter*], how to carry the neck,

"And when he was on his feet, upright in the middle of the cell, his head, neck and entire body emerged from the lace and silk which are worn, in the most trying moments, only by diabolical masters of the world, and with which he was suddenly adorned. Without growing an inch, he became huge, overtopping and splitting the cell, filling the universe, and the four black men shrank until they were no bigger than four bedbugs. The reader has realized that Harcamone was invested with such majesty that his clothes themselves were ennobled and turned to silk and brocade. He was clad in patent leather boots, breeches of soft blue silk and a shirt of old blond-lace, the collar of which was open on his splendid neck that supported the collar of the Order of the Golden Fleece. Truly, he came in a straight line, and by way of the sky, from between the legs of the captain of the galley."

What is it going to do in there, the little tom thumb of a toe that enlarges "without growing an inch" in its boots or "between the legs" of the galley captain? Which leads to the juvenile prison? To Guiana? In *The Journal*, "led by the ogre, Roger would drop little white pebbles."

love is still lacking something, is limping somewhere "Love itself is still incomplete in nature."

One can account for this only by putting back on stage the relation of father to son.

By recalling that this relation was instigated by Christianity, Hegel is appealing from love —still missing—to its—religious—pleroma. The religious restores to its rights an objectivity that love had suspended. The force of love that had succeeded in sublating opposition (subject/object for example) limits itself, encloses itself again, especially if love is happy, in a sort of natural subjectivity. The religious breaks into it with an infinite object.

All of this is consumed, it goes via the mouth. A long detour is necessary.

"To the Jewish idea of God as their Lord and Governor, Jesus opposes a relationship of God to men like that of a father to his children.

Morality (*Moralität*) sublates (*hebt auf*) domination (*Beherrschung*) within the sphere of consciousness; love sublates the barriers in the sphere of morality; but love itself is still incomplete in nature."

Anticipation of the *Philosophy of Right:* love (felt unity of the family) sublates subjective morality which had itself sublated abstract right or domination; but love (the family) is still nature, the first moment of an incomplete *Sittlichkeit*, and will therefore have in its turn to be sublated.

When Hegel says that Jesus opposes to the Jewish figure of God the relation of a father to his children, what discourse are we dealing with? A discourse of Jesus, of course, and one that Hegel takes on board or reproduces. But a discourse of what form? Symbol, figure, metaphor, comparison? Analogy of an infinite relation (implying God) with a finite relation (father/children)? But the "infinite" relation also implies finite terms, creatures. The very possibility of the question is therefore uncertain. To bring out its presuppositions, we must first take into account what Hegel himself says about this comparison in the Supper.

What is consumed on that occasion?

The opposition between (the) contraries (universality/particularity, objectivity/subjectivity, whole/part, etc.) is resolved in love.

Love has no other: love your neighbor as yourself,

But the galley captain is not the galley, which here carries over the ocean this giant little big toe, come to it "in a straight line, and by way of the sky," as if by immaculate conception. Would *galère* be the floating last name or forename borne by the holy mother? or placed on her? her initials at least that she might let us touch, summate, suck back, sound in the mouth?
Covered with algae ("velvet algae," "blue algae"), with runny [*glaireux*] "spit," with dripping "wet flowers," drenched in gold, in coffinless corpses or unadorned coffins, "La Galère" (Harcamone's poem, seen from *The Miracle of the Rose*) bears these lines on its flanks: "Clusters of poisoners hung high from the riggings / The prisoners jacking off mixing their ages. / From the Great Sleep a sleeping child came back / Stark naked and spotted all over with spewed sperm. / And the most agonizing of the trimmed sail's signs . . . a star . . . young guy's lips . . . damage."
The galley cradles like the executioner. Itself borne by the sea, it transports everywhere but also makes the condemned slave work endlessly. From the body of the galley that keeps him enclosed, in its flank, the galleyslave exhausts himself at his oar. He attacks the surface of the sea in cadence, the sea that shines, he makes a mark there, he leans on it, but the movement has no end, the element is equal to itself, reforms, impassive, swallowing up the wake or skimming off the initials, it shines, remains

carry off its final blo [*cou*] w [*p*]. To draw with a song the passage of a blade that, in erecting it, makes the text fall on the other side, casting down two inseparable heads, one exalted, brandished, haloed, the other, which resembles and reflects it within a slight margin that renders the tipping point undecidable and very soon announces the cost [*coût*] of the operation: a knell amortized no longer.

You can always keep the necklace. Believe in it in any case. Of that credence you have enough to sell on the market of what is called literature.

does not imply that you must love them as much as you love yourself. To love oneself is "a word without meaning" (*ein Wort ohne Sinn*). Love them rather as one (*als einen*) who is you or "that you are (*der du ist*)." The difference between the two statements is hard to pin down. If loving oneself had no sense, what would it mean to love the other as one that you are? Or who is you? One can only love them like another but in love there is no longer alterity, only *Vereinigung*. It is the value of *neighbor* (*Nächsten*) that here outplays the opposition of I to You as other.

If love has no other, it is infinite. To love is necessarily to love God. One can love only God. To love God is to *feel oneself* in the whole of life "without limit to infinity" (*schrankenlos im Unendlichen*).

Love, the sensory focal point of the family, is infinite or it is not.

One can no longer rigorously distinguish between a finite family and an infinite family. The human family is not *something other* than the Holy family. The human relation of father-to-son is not *something other* than God's relation of father-to-son. As these two relations cannot be distinguished, and above all cannot be opposed, one cannot pretend to see in one the figure or metaphor of the other. There is no way to compare the one to the other, to pretend to know what one term of the comparison can be before the other. One cannot know, outside Christianity, what the relation of a father to his son, or even (but let's keep this extension in reserve) to his children is. One cannot even know—we're coming to this—what the *is* in general is outside Christianity. Such is the Hegelian thesis on the spirit of Christianity, that is, on rhetoric.

The question of the figure thus appears very elusive.

Love is no longer opposed: therefore it has no object. Not even a religious object. The disappearance of the object poses the question—the question of rhetoric in particular—as a question of consuming. At Christ's table.

The farewell of Jesus to his friends, at the Supper, is a "feast of love" (*Feier eines Mahls der Liebe*). The most visible, closest, form of this is the position of the favorite disciple, John, on Jesus' breast.

Love is not yet the "properly religious" adoration that for its part addresses a determinate object, a form with contours, facing the adorer, without confusion. For an object to detach itself and for such a form to appear, for a finite representation of the infinite to stand out, opposition must intervene, of course, but also the

But you can be interested in what I am doing here only to the extent that you have some reason to believe that—*in some part*—I don't know what I am doing (I exclude something and exclude myself from it: something like "I put myself to one side [*je m'écarte*]," or "I crash [*je m'écrase*]"). Nor do I know what is in action here. Which is equal to constructing its scaffold.

Why have a knife pass between two texts? Why, at least, write two texts at once? What scene is being played out? What is being desired? In other words what is being feared? Who? Whom? Wanting to make writing impregnable, of course. When your head is in this one you'll be reminded that the law of the text is found in the other, and so on ad infinitum. By impregnating the margin—(no) more margin, (no) more frame—one annuls it, one smudges the line, one deprives you of the straight line that would allow you to delimit, cut out, dominate. One no longer lets you know where the head or body of this discourse is, one hides its neck so you can no longer strike your blow.

So don't trust the proper name that is always worn like a chain or necklace. Genet has attached the necklace of the Golden Fleece all over his text, but never far from "between the legs of the captain of the galley [*galère*]." (*Galère* is moreover a strange word that takes you literally everywhere.) Diabolical master of the world, he has arranged the necklace

imagination (*Einbildungskraft*). It produces a finite object, an image of the infinite. Religion is adoration of this image (*Bild*). But love does not yet accede to religion because this opposition between the finite and the infinite does not take place in it, does not yet or no longer take place. The Supper, the feast of love, therefore does not belong to a religious space. All actions in it manifest love, love itself is present (*vorhanden*) in it, to hand, but only *qua* feeling (*Empfindung*). No image (*Bild*), no figure, no schema detaches from it in order to unite feeling with representation, sensibility to the concept. "The feeling (*Gefühl*) and the representation (*Vorstellung*) of the feeling are not unified (*vereinigt*) by the productive imagination (*Phantasie*). Yet in the love-feast there is also something objective in evidence, to which feeling is linked but with which it is not yet united into *one* image (ein *Bild*). Hence this eating (*dies Essen*) hovers (*schwebt*, floats) between a common table (*Zusammenessen*) of friendship and a religious act, and this hovering makes difficult the clear understanding of its spirit."

So what is Jesus doing when he says, breaking the bread: take this, this is my body which is given for you, do this in remembrance of me? Why memory already in present feeling? Why does he present himself, in the present, before the time, as if cut off from his own body and following his funeral procession? What is he doing when he says, taking the cup: drink, this is my blood, the blood of the New Covenant, of the new contract made with religious pomp, spilled for you and for many others in remission of their sins, do this in remembrance of me? Memory is here *Gedächtnis*: Hegel often insisted on the family relation between memory and thought (*Denken*). Think me, says Jesus to his friends, saddling them in advance with a bloody corpse. Prepare shrouds, bandages, the unctuous substance.

What is he doing, the anointed of the Lord? Is he using a signifier? A symbol? An image? What about the *this* when he holds out the bread and the wine? When he talks about intaking and undertaking [*mangeaille et funéraille*] in the place of his body, his individuality, his finity?

We are not dealing here with a sign, nor a comparison, nor an allegory. In the sign, the relation between) signifier and signified, between sign (*Zeichen*) and designatum (*Bezeichnetes*) remains a relation of conventional externality. What ties the two members of the signification together still remains an objective ligament (*Verbindung, Band*).

with infinite cunning. That is to say necessarily finite.

It isn't enough to be cunning, there needs to be a general theory of cunning and the ruse *that takes part in it*. Which comes down to owning up to things, unconscious of course. The unconscious is something very theoretical.

If I write two texts at once you won't be able to castrate me. If I delinearize, I erect. But at the same time I divide my act and my desire. I—mark the division and, escaping you always, simulate all the time and don't come anywhere. I castrate myself—I remain(der) myself thus—and I "play at coming."

Well almost.

(Ah!) you are impregnable (well then) remain(s).

Obstruct two times, then.

For if my text is (were) impregnable it won't (wouldn't) be taken, nor kept. Who would be punished in that economy of the undecidable? But if I linearize—if I keep myself straight and believe—stupidity—that I am writing only one text at a time, it amounts to the same thing and one still has to account for the cost of the margin. In every case I win and lose my sting.

Under the sign of Plato the pharmacy had distilled this effect, labeled "glyph" or *coup de glyphe*. This remarking, a gash in

double posture. Double postulation. Self-contradiction of two irreconcilable desires. Taken on my tongue I give to it here the title DOUBLE HARDBIND, putting it (him, her, them) practically into form and into play. A text is girded bleeding [*sangle*] in two senses. Twice breastboundsigned [*ceint*]. Hardbind against hardbind

For example, when an Arab drinks a cup of coffee with a stranger, he enters into a contract of friendship with him. This act in common "binds" the Arab and this bond commits him to being loyal and helpful. "The common eating and drinking here is not what is called a sign. The connection (*Verbindung*) between sign and designatum is not itself spiritual, is not life, but an objective bond (*ein objektives Band*): sign and designatum are strangers to one another, and their connection lies outside them in a third thing; their connection is only a connection in thought. To eat and drink with someone is an act of communion [*Vereinigung*] and is itself a felt communion, not a conventional sign." In communion, the third term disappears, it is properly consum(mat)ed. The sign is swallowed up.

That is already true of the Arab. But something extra happens in transubstantiation. This extra, to put it briefly, is a judicative proposition of the type *S is P* (this is my body, the wine is blood, the blood is spirit) and a certain intervention of the father in the discourse.

The banquet, of course, is an act of friendship. The disciples bind themselves to him and among themselves, think themselves together. This is not a "simple sign" but a felt experience (*Empfindung*). Religion has not yet appeared since there is no object as such. But religion is looming, gives a glimpse of itself, when Jesus adds something to this communal consumption. What? What is this extra (*das Weitere*)? A declaration, a clarification, a discursive manifestation, an *Erklärung* that explains, is stated in the form *S is P*, and thence constitutes an objective judgment, an objectivity that opens, although still incompletely, the space of religion. He says: "*Dies ist* (this is) my body (*mein Leib*). *Hoc est enim corpus meum, toutô estin to sôma mou to uper umôn didomenon*, this is my body given for you." The appearance of the ligament, of the copula (couple) and *the pair,* produces an object that exceeds the interiority of feeling. This judicative declaration, plus the fact of *sharing* (*Austeilung*), of dividing the bread and wine to consume them together, expels feeling outside itself and renders it "in part objective" (*zum Teil objetiv*). Hegel is no doubt playing here on *Austeilung* and *Teil* as he does elsewhere on *Ur-teil* (judgment and originary division: judgment corresponds to an originary division of being, of *Sein*, into subject and predicate, the copula couples, mates

the writing, overflowing the piece on both sides, remained totally tautological, because *glyphe* means *coup*. And scalps.

What is the fleece? Golden fleece. Outside of common broom, of course.

It surrounds the neck, the cunt, the cock, apparition or appearance of a hole erect, of a hole and an erection at the same time, an erection in the hole or a hole in the erection: it surrounds a volcano.

The edges of the hole that it hides or delimits are indeed those of a pit, and what the four black men find at the heart of Harcamone's heart, at the heart of the rose, is "a shadowy pit" ("At the very edge of this pit, which was as murky and deep as an eye, they leaned forward and were seized with a kind of dizziness"), but also the edges of the capital erection, the trunk, pyramid, or cone of a volcano.

it is said that the broom also lives on the edge of volcanoes. Leopardi's *ginestra,* the *odorata ginestra* grows "su l'arida schiena / Del formidabili monte / Sterminator Vesevo." The epigraph is from St. John. And one finds there a broom flower that is "content with the desert," with "fields sown / with infertile ashes and covered with petrified lava / that crackles under the feet of the traveler." The burning lava flows like milk "dell'inesauto grembo," from the inexhaustible breast. The "supple broom" that bends its "innocent head" will have chosen neither "abode" nor "birthplace." "Fortune" alone decided that.

"SAID: The woman the birds in the sky shitting on her so you become a stone statue. Leopardi Square in Verona, I saw you one day around four o'clock in the morning, beneath the shit from the doves, and naked. Magnificent in the daylight." To Roger Blin, "For a few seconds, he has been known to wander off to Leopardi Square in Verona, or to the Rue Saint Benoît."

the pair, ties in the same ligament (*Band*) the thing and the attribute that then becomes an active part of *Sein*). At the moment when through this sharing and this predication *(das Weitere, die Erklärung Jesu)*, the disciples are dealing with definite objects (this is that), their friendship, the union in the one they recognize as their midpoint and their master (*in ihrem Mittelpunkte, ihrem Lehrer*) becomes more than sensory, more than internal. It is visible, obvious on the outside (*sichtbar*), objectivated, as the thing itself that it is. It is no longer merely "represented" (*vorgestellt*) in an "image" (*Bild*) or in an "allegorical figure."

And yet this object is not an object like any other. This thing itself does not give itself "in person" like any other. On one hand the feeling becomes objective but on the other hand the wine, the bread and the sharing are not "purely objective." There is in them something more than what is seen. This is a "mystical operation" which can be understood only from the inside. From the outside, one sees only bread and wine. In the same way, when two friends part and break a ring of which each keeps a piece, the third party who isn't part of their contract sees only two bits of metal without symbolic power. The ring does not come back together.

So what is the nature of this surplus, of this more (*dieses Mehr*)? Presupposed everywhere, this *Mehr* cannot be counted, cannot give rise to an objective calculation, to a discursive explanation. It does not refer to "objects." No analysis can account, via the ways of comparison or analogy, for the relation it enters into without ever belonging to it. No explanatory statement (*Erklärung*) can say here "this equals that," "this does not equal that." The *Mehr* in question is neither equal nor unequal to any object; it is *like* nothing, it does not resemble, does not get assembled with anything in the mode of the *like* (*Gleichwie*) (*Dieses Mert hängt nicht mit den Objekten, als eine Erklärung, durch ein bloßes Gleichwie zusammen*"). The point here is not to say "in the same way as"; the *same as* cannot envelop and think love. It is not as if one were saying: just like the particular, divided, singular pieces (*vereinzelten Stücke*) that you are eating are from *one and the same* loaf, just as the wine you are drinking, you are drinking from *one and the same* cup, so you are divided or separated, particular (*Besondere*), cut from each other but in love, in spirit, you are *one* (*eins*), one and the same *being* (*Sein*), together; just as you have your share of this bread and this wine, so you

Around the spitting abyss, the inexhaustible belching of letters in fusion, the fleece (*εριον*), the pubic fleece [*la toison pubien*]

the text is the golden fleece: precious object, detached like a sort of scalp. The galley's name here would be Argo.

Writing remains modest [*pudique*] because it is caught in a fleece. Concerning modesty, "plaiting," weaving," and "matting," Freud applies a natural model to the feminine technique of the text: the hair that hides the genitals and especially, for the woman, the lack of a penis. And he says he is defenseless should his hypothesis be taken for a fantasy or obsession.

Coat over the hair, make it shine, make it sticky with saliva, spit, or milk, and you'll have a sort of textual veil. *The Thief's Journal,* for example, envelops everything there: "I barely recognized him . . . but hardly had he opened his mouth for a more softly uttered phrase when there again, veiling it, was the white blob of spit, and through the strange mucosity which formed it, though remaining intact, I recognized, between his teeth, the Stilitano of old." Worm and cocoon, apotrope for the guilty: "Within his shame, in his own spittle, he envelops himself; he spins a silk which is his pride. This is not a natural garment. The guilty man has woven it to protect himself, woven it crimson to embellish himself."

Fleet of floating screens with purple veils, ready to attack, to defend, protecting itself prow and stern, golden spurs for the parade.

all participate in my sacrifice. Same thing for all the *likes*, each *Gleichwie*.

In this case, the question is indeed that of the participating part(y). What is a *morsel*—literally, what do you get to bite into—once you can no longer count on anything?

Except some incalculable enjoyment.

The ligament, the synthesis, the *Zusammenhang*, the tension that holds together the objective bit [*mors*] and the subjective bit, the bread and the people, for example, is not the ligament "of the compared with a comparison (*des Verglichenen mit einem Gleichnis*)." We do not have here a "parable" in which "the compared (*Verglichene*) is posited as dissociated, separated (*als geschieden, als getrennt*)"; nor a comparison (*Vergleichung*) which requires that one think the equality of diverse things (*das Denken der Gleichheit Verschiedener*). In this copulation, in this ligature (*Verbindung*), on the contrary, diversity falls (*fällt die Verschiedenheit weg*) and with it the very possibility of a comparison, an equating. The equal disappears, but this end of the equal is not reasoned as the subsistence of the unequal. The heterogeneous terms remain, yes, but knotted, attached, enveloped (the) one in the other in the most intimate way. "*Die Heterogenen sind aufs innigste verknüpft*." The act of *verbinden* thus does not signify simply the emergence of an objectivity through the operation of the holy copula, it also annuls the opposition of the diverse, erases what is discontinuous in all objectivity. All the difficulties of transubstantiation and the Eucharist, as they torment for example Cartesian rationalism and the logic of Port-Royal, are here given to be read indirectly [*par la bande*].

A feeling, an enjoyment (*Genuß*), even, are induced by this copulation without proper object. More precisely, by (a) penetration (*Durchdringen*).

This is where the father comes in.

Jesus does not say merely "wine is blood," he also says "blood is spirit." The common cup, the fact of drinking together, of swallowing in one gulp the same liquid substance, is in spirit a new binding (*der Geist eines neuen Bundes*). This spirit is thus proffered in the alliance and penetrates (*durchdringt*) "many men." Many come to drink of it, parched, to gain height and raise themselves (*zur Erhebung*) above their sins. The present of the cup that makes possible the copulation in the alliance—this present is not given, it is not present. It presents itself only in the expectation of another coupling that will come to fill, accomplish (*vollenden*) the one who

The parade always stays behind.

Behind [*Derrière*]: whenever the word comes first, if it is written following a full stop, with a capital, something in me begins to recognize in it the name of my father, in gilded letters on his tomb, before he was even in it.

All the more so when I read *Behind the curtain* [Derrière le rideau].

Is behind not always already behind a curtain, a veil, a woven fabric. A text abounding in fleece: "One other of my lovers adorns his bush with ribbons. Another once wove a tiny wreath of daisies for the tip of his friend's prick. A phallic cult is fervently celebrated in private, behind the curtain of buttoned flies. If a rich imagination, availing itself of the disturbance, should turn it to account, just imagine the revels—to which plants and animals would be invited—that will ensue and the spirituality that will emanate from them and hover about them! I arrange in Java's bush the feathers that escape at night from the crushed pillow. The word balls is a roundness in my mouth." (*Thief's Journal*)

[*ne*] weaves, braids, slicks, *tricks* its writing. In it everything is sewn, set up, giving place, on the edges, to all the flowers. The chasm hides its borders there. In the weave of that dissimulation erection is produced only *en abyme*.

The entangled tracing of his threads [*fils*] assures *both* (impossible castration decision) sewing *and* cutting: of the crowd of flowers as phallic

is announced or broached here. One day we will drink—we already have a taste for it—to the father himself, in his realm: "when I drink it new with you in my Father's kingdom."

That is why this operation is not a useful sacrifice—of objective utility at least—exchanging some thing against another in the form of an object. It comes down to allowing oneself to be penetrated (the word *durchdringen* occurs three times) and identified. The identificatory penetration of Jesus into his disciples—first John, the cherished disciple—of the Father into Jesus and through him into his disciples—John first—first subjectivates, then objectivates, then becomes subjective again by ingestion. Consummation interiorizes, idealizes, sublates.

In a noteworthy reflection, Hegel *compares* this resubjectivating penetration to the very movement of language. More precisely, he proposes to read in it something like the hearing-oneself-speak of language in reading. More precisely still, its absolute murmur in silent reading [*à voix basse*]. The silenced voice, the absolutely withheld voice abolishes the objective exteriority of the signifier. The letter and the word disappear at the moment they are heard within, and first of all simply grasped, comprehended. As long as it names, starts a discourse, the movement of language is analogous to copulation in the Supper.

This whole analogon gets formed, stands and lets itself be grasped only under the category of the categories. It sublates itself all the time. It is an *Aufhebung*.

Of blood.

"Not only is the wine blood but the blood is spirit. . . . The blood is the tie between them and the wine which they all drink out of the same cup and which is for all and the same for all. All drink together; a like emotion (*ein gleiches Gefühl*) is in them all; all are permeated (*durchdrungen*) by the like spirit (*vom gleichen Geiste*) of love. If they are made alike simply as recipients of an advantage, a benefit, accruing from a sacrifice of body and an outpouring of blood, then they would only be united in a like concept (*im gleichen Begriff*). But because they eat the bread and drink the wine, because his body and his blood pass over into them, Jesus is in them all, and his essence (*sein Wesen*), 'as love,' has divinely permeated (*durchdrungen*) them. Hence the bread and the wine are not just an object, something for the intellect. The action of eating and drinking is not just a self-unification brought about through the destruction of food and drink, nor is it just the sensation of merely tasting food and drink.

upsurge *and* vaginal concavity (little *glas* that has grown, summated between the two, at the bottom of the glottis), intact virginity *and* bloody castration, cutting of a rose, of "the red rose of monstrous size and beauty" that will open in a moment as a "shadowy pit."

Erion—fabric of writing and pubic fleece—is the maddening, atopical place of *voire*: more or less (*than the*) truth, more or less (*than the*) veil. It covers with derision everything said in the name of truth or of the phallus. It plays erection in the naked hairy [*à poil*] being of its writing. Derision doesn't simply cause erection to fall, it keeps it but by submitting it to what it protects it from, already, the crack in the non-proper. Apotropaic incantation of the reseda, derisory erection of the gladiolus.

The author laughs his ass off [*se poile*] seriously, imperturbably. He slogs as well, with the application of a galleysl [*galé*]

you don't yet perceive the word "galleyslave [*galérien*]." What must be avoided is underlining, rapping out the words and letters, picking them out of a text whose style slides along the important syllables, brushes against each part of its body, buries down, erases the essences, which end up being equal, muffling the sounds in the back of the tongue, in the crypt of the palate. Everything must float, suspended, then moreover echo after the event for the first time. As if coming from an almost closed grotto: ". . . the collar of which was open on his splendid neck that supported the collar of the Order of the Golden Fleece. Truly, he came in a straight line, and by way of the sky, from between the legs of the captain of the galley.

The spirit of Jesus, in which his disciples (*seiner Jünger*) are one (*eins*), has become a present object, a reality, for external feeling. Yet the love made objective, this subjective element become a *thing*, reverts once more to its nature, becomes subjective again in the eating. This return may perhaps in this respect be compared (*verglichen*) with the thought which in the written word becomes a thing and which recaptures its subjectivity out of an object, out of something lifeless (*aus einem Toten*), when we read. The simile (*Vergleichung*) would be more striking if the written word were read away, if by being understood it vanished as a thing, just as (*so wie*) in the enjoyment (*Genuß*) of bread and wine not only is a feeling (*Empfindung*) for these mystical objects aroused, not only is the spirit made alive, but the objects vanish as objects. Thus the action seems purer, more appropriate to its end, in so far as it affords spirit only, feeling only, and robs the intellect of its own (*das Seinige*), i.e. destroys the matter (*Materie*), the soulless (*das Seelenlose*)."

The proper (*das Seinige*) of the understanding disappears only *qua* finite object, i.e. *qua* object, *qua* insufficiently reappropriable (inanimate matter).

Hegel defines the return to subjectivity in the act of consumption by means of a comparison. The comparison with reading must here define the very thing that escapes from the comparative structure, as he told us just a little earlier. The necessity of comparison perhaps provokes the constant fall back of what ought to escape it, but this fatality is itself sublated: the comparison receives its possibility from a spiritual analogy that always pulls upward.

Once again, give stone its due. In the present sublation of the Supper, sublimation (idealization-interiorization-animation-subjectivation, etc.) works right on stone.

Stone twice over, love fixed in stone.

But this time stone, the stone of love that is opposed to Christian sublation, the stone that cannot be sublated is Greek and not Jewish.

The movement is necessarily complicated here by the fact that stone always falls back down. Remains.

The Supper does of course accomplish a consummation of love to which Greek plastic art cannot attain: split again, with the Greek, between the stony matter and the interiority of love. But Christian consumption will also divide.

Perhaps because of the miracle of which he was the place and object, or for some other reason—to give thanks to God his Father—he put his right knee on the floor. The four men quickly took advantage and climbed up his leg and sloping thigh. They had great difficulty, for the silk was slippery. Halfway up the thigh, forgoing his inaccessible and tumultuous fly, they encountered his hand, which was lying in repose. They climbed on to it, and from there to the arm, and then to the lace sleeve. And finally to the right shoulder, the bowed neck, the left shoulder and, as lightly as possible, the face. Harcamone had not moved, except that he was breathing through his parted lips. The judge and the lawyer wormed their way into the ear and the chaplain and executioner dared enter his mouth. They moved forward a little along the edge of the lower lip and fell into the gulf. And then, almost as soon as they had passed the gullet, they came to a lane of trees that descended in a gentle, almost voluptuous slope. All the foliage was very high and formed the sky of the landscape. They were unable to recognize the scents, for in states like theirs one can no longer distinguish particular features: one passes through forests, tramples down flowers, climbs over stones. What surprised them most was the silence."

[*rien*]

ave forced to write by orders received from behind, threatened with the whip if he pauses.

The miracle is that it sings, it cocks, it stiffens like a lyre.

Erion will therefore have been able to open out like a flower. In botany, erianthus designates an organism having shaggy or woolly flowers. One can no longer decide, then—that's the whole *interest* of writing—if there is a style or not under the fleece. One also says εριον της αραχνης,

A new split will disappoint it with itself to call it to another sublation, an *Aufhebung* at the heart of Christianity first, then an *Aufhebung* of Christianity, of revealed absolute religion into philosophy which will have been its truth.

Here are the Greek stones, other stones than those of Epimetheus or Pyrrha, but always on the track of a delay: "... the soulless (*das Seelenlose*). When lovers sacrifice before the altar of the goddess of love and the prayerful breath of their emotion fans [or spiritualizes, *begeistert*] their emotion to a white-hot flame, the goddess herself has entered their hearts, yet the marble statue remains standing in front of them (*das Bild von Stein bleibt immer vor ihnen stehen*). In the love-feast, on the other hand, the corporeal vanishes and only living feeling is present (*vorhanden*)."

But the spirituality of the Christian Supper consumes its signs, does not let them fall outside, loves without remainder. This assimilation without leftover [*relief*] has a price too. The destruction of the object maintains love in view of the religion to which that destruction denies it access. Religion is always linked to an object. Love is still too subjective, it still marks Christianity, in the moment of the Supper, with an internal split. Then when religion is born, the existence of the object, the institution, the stone of the Church will provoke another split, will call for another reconciliation, beyond religion and the religious family.

Love—remains inside. Speaking of the sublation of objectivity and the superiority of the Christian feast, Hegel names neither Plato's symposium nor a certain feast of stone. "But what prevents the action [of eating and drinking] from becoming a religious one is just the fact that the kind of objectivity (*diese Art von Objektivität*) here in question is totally sublated (*ganz aufgehoben wird*), while feeling remains (*bleibt*), the fact that there is a sort of confusion between object and subject rather than a unification, the fact that love here becomes visible in and attached to something which is to be destroyed."

Consumed without remainder, the mystical object becomes subjective again but ceases by that very fact to be an object of religious adoration. Once inside, the bread and wine are doubtless subjectivated, but they immediately become bread and wine again, digested food, naturalized anew; they lose their divine quality. It is true that they would lose it just as much if they were not digested. Their divinity stands

thread and web of the spider,phallic or castrating mother, tarantula or large spider

before the appearance of the fleece, the lecture on femininity stages the spider in its web ("in some classes of animals the females are stronger and more aggressive and the male is active only in the single act of sexual union. This is so, for instance, with the spiders." Karl Abraham, who weaves the thing around the phallic mother—"the spider's web represents the pubic hair"—and around the *Unheimliche,* also recalls the suction by means of which the spider, or incestuous mother, kills its victim) and poses the problem of the pharmakon in galactic terms. "The fear of being poisoned is also probably connected with the withdrawal of the breast. Poison is nourishment that makes one ill." Milk, poison against poison, is also treated as the source of jealousy. Which would amount to our question: what is the excess of zeal around the signature? Can one be jealous of anything other than a seal [*seing*]? Such a question galvanizes and vulcanizes everything.
The clang is also that of a war over the signature, a war to the death—the only possible one—in view of the text, then, that finally, funerally, remains for nobody. The text is written neither on this side nor that, one counting for the other to show up the failure in the doubling, the colossus the column, the column the colossus. It strikes between the two. We can name *colpos* the place that will have, necessarily, preoccupied what is alternating [*le battant*]. In Greek it is the mother's breast but also the wet-nurse's, as well as a fold in clothing, the sea that falls back between two waves, the valley that hollows toward the interior [*sein*] of the earth

that eats its mate.

One of the two Erigones, the daughter of Icarius, slept with Dionysus who enjoyed her all the more with a goatskin of Icarius's wine. Some shepherds think they are poisoned by it and kill him. A barking dog, Maera, finds the place where the father's corpse lies deprived of a sepulcher. He leads Erigone there and she hangs herself from a nearby tree.

very precariously between swallowing and vomiting; and it is neither solid nor liquid, nether outside nor inside.

The moment the thing becomes thing again because it has been consumed—the thing is essentially consumed, the process of consumption constitutes it as a thing rather than broaching it as such—it can again once more be compared to Greek love statuary, the moment stone returns to dust. Hegel now takes up again the references to the statues of Apollo and Venus. So long as they have a form, one can forget their friable matter, the "fragile stone" (*zerbrechlichen Stein*); one is at that point addressing the immortal element in them, one is penetrated with love. But if the statue falls to ruin and one still says "this is Apollo," "this is Venus," the dust I have before me and the divine image in me can no longer be gathered together. The value of dust resided in form. After the form has disappeared, scattered dust becomes the main thing again. Meditating, adoring thought can no longer address it, but only, through it, the memory of self. Same thing for the mystic bread. Once eaten, even though this time the destruction is internal, it takes down with it the possibility of a properly religious adoration. Whence the mourning, the feeling of loss, of regret (*Bedauern*), of splitting (*Scheidung*) that comes over the young friends of Christ when the divine has melted in their mouths. Christians today still feel it. The imminent loss of Christ, the quasi-presence of his dead body can be felt precisely at the end of the meal, "after the enjoyment of the supper" (*nach dem Genuß des Abendmahls*).

The religious is not satisfied with this feeling of impotence and division after enjoyment. After an "authentic" religious operation, the soul should be appeased, i.e. continue to enjoy. The Supper is not yet religion. Its remains—i.e. a dead body—must be sublated. After the resurrection, building the church of stone will properly institute religion. But stone itself will give rise to another fracture, another ruin, another mourning, another sublation.

So we have to take an interest both in the immortality of Christ and in what goes via the mouth.

The immortality of the one who is God's anointed one, who is a being (*Wesen*) only as son of God—this immortality, the glorious resurrection of his body consists in allowing himself to be thought. To think is to think being; and to think being as immortal is to think its life. To think being as life in one's mouth, is the *logos*. In the infinite unity

Dionysus's vengeance:

the scene of Christ, the sacrifice of the scapegoat, at the end of *The Miracle*, is preceded only slightly, almost accompanied, doubled, by a Dionysiac celebration. There, Harcamone is far from the Lord. The pharmakon suspends, apostrophizes the contraries, brings them together by de-separating [*é-loignant*] them. "The execution of Métayer was a revel, it began with immolation and continued with orgiastic frenzy. In short, I think that those children's joy was of a bacchic order, a kind of drunkenness caused by certain cruelties so intense that the joy could be expressed only by a hoarse but also musical laugh. . . . Flowers are gaiety and some are sadness become flowers. . . . And the whole colony composed one enormous Harcamone. . . . Can it be that that monstrous thicket of vipers which has enticed so many boys withered in its prime?" And if you follow the tentacular and dumbfounding [*médusants*] movements of the writing up to the execution of Harcamone, you'll never get to the end of it. As this is the writing of decapitation it has no center. And it would be a mistake, a supplementary decapitation, to see everything agglutinate, agglomerate around a central suction point, be it virgin/castrated like a flower ("metamorphoses into flowers," "flowers condemned mirthlessly by notorious councils," "a huge, ridiculous water-lily" of a life—sister Zoe, the "virgin"—who, "utterly astounded [*le souffle coupé*] . . . toppled into the water": "And from their flowery mouths the big shots spat smacking gobs of spit . . ." "the thought of being the mystic betrothed of the murderer who had let me have the rose that had come directly from a supernatural garden") or the whole familial structure of the maternal tongue properly and lovingly sliced through, deglotted, erected/excreted deep in a grotto or a forge (sound of "sobs," of "*cloches*," of a "bugle" ringing out one page; then the next: ". . . a huge crucifix. All the kids who were being punished that day were waiting at the door for their turn to be sentenced . . ."; then the next, ". . . their unwashed asses. They would say of a youngster whose toenails were too long: 'His nails are curling.' They would also say: 'Your crap basket [*panier à crotte*]' (hearing the word *crotte* the child would add its infamous 's').")
Why would the 's' be a mark of infamy? What is at stake in this story of infamy

drive the young

of the *logos* being, life, father, and son become equal.

As Hegel recalls, Jesus often says that what speaks through his mouth is both in him and greater and higher than he. He thus calls himself—the Son of God. His Father traverses him and goes beyond him. And this filiation, which constitutes his *Sein,* his *Wesen,* can be revealed, attested, declared only by the Father. When Peter recognizes the one in whose favor God bore witness, the son of Life, Jesus said to him: it is not your finitude, it is my father who revealed it to you. Only the infinite—the Father—can name the bond between the finite and the infinite. Here, Hegel determines what binds as life. It is the bond (*Band*) that holds together God and Jesus, the infinite and the finite; and of this life Jesus is a part, a member (*Glied*) but a member in which the infinite whole is re-membered, is recalled entirely. Such is the secret (*Geheimnis*) of life, remembrance, the inner recollection of the whole in the part, such is the mysterious and incalculable operation that the Jews could not understand. To grasp the strange unity that keeps this unity standing, you have to stop thinking human nature and divine nature separately: bring the father into the son and think them together, gather them in one and the same elevation. Such is the essence of life as reconciliation, and the essence of being, the essence itself as life. To be is measured by thinking-together in the inner ligature, to be is to be equal to oneself in infinite reconciliation.

What thus stands upright and remains inaccessible to the Jew, is not, then, a column, of stone, or fire or of clouds—of matter—nor even a *colossus*, the double of the dead man, but a tree, a vegetable being, a tree of life. The whole circulates in it, from the root up to the top, through all its parts. It already inhabits the acorn [*le gland*].

Is this a comparison, a metaphor, a phallocentric figure? Phallogocentric? It has been said that the tree is essentially feminine. Is that contradictory?

Remark in a sort of appendix: "This relationship of a man to God in which stands the son of God, like the relation of the branches, leaves and fruit to the tree-trunk their father, had to arouse the most profound indignation of the Jews, who had maintained an impassable abyss between human and divine being and had granted our nature no participation in the divine."

This apparent metaphoricity is the essence of life or rather life as the essence of being. When one is Jewish, when one does not understand life, when one is cut from it

women of Athens mad and induce them to hang themselves.

The name of Erigone was given to the Virgin, celestial constellation and Mother of Christ.

What the four black men find in penetrating Harcamone's body through his ear and mouth: the Immaculate Conception and the Mystical Rose.

Like the executioners, like Our Lady of the Flowers threatened by the feminine "sword" of justice (multiplied by "bayonets" when the hour of his death is tolled, which will be signaled to him by the Presiding Judge de Sainte-Marie), Harcamone is a virgin.

At least that is what he is when he cuts a little girl's throat while deflowering her next to an eglantine bush: "At the age of sixteen, he was frightened by women, and yet he could not keep his flower any longer. He was not afraid of the girl. When they were near an eglantine bush, he stroked her hair. The shuddering little bitch let him do it. He must have whispered something trivial, but when he put his hand

and no longer feels it, one sees in it only an accessory metaphor, a rhetorical auxiliary without truth of its own. When one feels it from inside, one knows that life is metaphoricity, the living and infinite bond of the whole thought in its parts.

The language of the Jews does not accede to this. It is both capable and incapable of metaphor. The evaluation of its powers will therefore be ambiguous. The Jew is capable of metaphor, of stating metaphors, but he is incapable inasmuch as he sees here a metaphor, precisely, only a metaphor, a finite image leaving the finite and the infinite separated. But because language, the historical state of a language is conceived by Hegel in teleological fashion, as the becoming of a sort of acorn, as a dynamic preparation for the fulfillment of the *logos* that will fill the mouth of the Christian, the Jew's very incapacity is merely an infancy. The Jewish tongue speaks without yet knowing how to speak, without being able to develop fully the sperm of the *logos*. It is the infancy of language.

Here it consists in a certain sort of analysis: dissociate, oppose, allow the opposites to become stubborn in reflection, to enclose themselves in the limits of the understanding, without comprehending the living unity that circulates among the terms—that's infancy. It is not, as is too facilely thought, sensory and imaginative confusion that cannot rise to the level of the intellect. Infancy here is the state of the intellect (*Verstand*), but as under-development of Reason (*Vernunft*). The Jews do not understand the metaphor of the tree that they take as a mere metaphor because their language or their culture still has something of the acorn about it.

The Evangelists, constrained, restrained by the laws of the Jewish language, felt hemmed in. They had to fix, harden, petrify oppositions where they should have let flow the unity of the divine sap, of the infinite life swallowing these oppositions. They had in spite of themselves to speak the language of infancy.

This is the case in the gospel of John. Hegel pays it particular attention: "Pure life is *being* (*Sein*). . . . This pure life is the source (*Quelle*) of all separate lives, impulses, and deeds. . . . In the determinate situation in which he appears, the man can appeal only to his origin (*Ursprung*), to the source (*Quelle*) from which every shape of restricted life flows to him (*ihm fließt*); he cannot appeal to the whole, which he now is, as to an absolute. He must call on something higher, on the Father (*an das Höhere, an den Vater*

under her skirt, she defended herself and blushed [*rougir*], out of coquettry—or perhaps fear. Her blushing made Harcamone blush, and he became disturbed. He fell on top of her." The red is insistent, it will flow through the text until the four black men also fall on the red rose at the heart of the tabernacle body of Harcamone, also spreading wide his skirts.

The scene of the Mystic Rose is cut out, like the rest (of a Rembrandt for example), facing a painting without our ever knowing (no more illustration, legend, margin, signature) whether the gallery is looking at the text or whether I don't have in front of me anything other than a voice *off* describing or illuminating a painting like some invisible nightlight. All of that is in any case wrapped up deep inside a cradle: "When we were in our shirts, we embraced again. The mattress was warm. We pulled the brown woolen blankets over our heads, and for a moment we lay still, as in cradles where Byzantine painters often confine the Virgin and Child. And after we had taken our pleasure twice, Divers kissed me and fell asleep in my arms. What I had feared occurred: I was left alone." That's the end.

Then begins the elaboration of Harcamone's

appellieren) who lives immutable in all mutability. Since the divine is pure life, anything and everything said of it must be free from any [implication of] opposition. And all reflection's expressions about the relations of the objective being or about that being's activity in objective action must be avoided, since the activity of the divine is only a unification of spirits. Only spirit grasps and comprehends spirit. Expressions such as 'command, teach, learn, see, recognize, make, will, come into the Kingdom of Heaven, go,' express only the relations of an objective being . . . . Hence it is only in inspired terms (*Begeisterung*) that the divine can [properly] be spoken of. . . . John is the Evangelist who has the most to say about God and the bond (*Verbindung*) between God and Jesus. But the Jewish culture, which was so poor in spiritual relationships, forced him to avail himself of objective ties and matter-of-fact phraseology (*Wirklichkeitssprache*) for expressing the highest spiritual realities, and this language thus often sounds harsher than when feelings are supposed to be expressed in commercial style. 'The Kingdom of Heaven; entry into the Kingdom; I am the door; I am the true bread (*rechte Speise*), who eats my flesh, etc. (*wer mein Fleisch ißt usw.*)'—into such matter-of-fact and everyday ties is the spiritual forced (*ist das Geistige hineingezwängt*)."

John is thus induced, compelled to force open the entrance of Jewish culture, to make do with its form, indeed, but to do it violence so as to slip in—at risk of wounding it—the Christian semanteme. Can one say that in so doing he violated infancy?

Yes and no. Jewish culture does indeed have something of under-developed infancy about it. But it is, however, perverse enough to have lost the profound charm of infancy. It has neither maturity nor innocence. It was never formed, only deformed. Neither culture nor lack of culture: misculture (*Mißbildung*). It is a monstrous acorn: "The state of Jewish culture cannot be called the state of childhood, nor can its phraseology be called an undeveloped, childlike phraseology. There are a few deep, childlike, tones (*Laute*) retained in it, or rather reintroduced into it, but the remainder, with its forced (*gezwungene*) and difficult mode of expression, is rather the consequence of the supreme miseducation (*Mißbildung*) of the people. A purer being (*ein reineres Wesen*) has to fight against this mode of speaking, and he suffers under it when he has to reveal himself (*sich darstellen*) in forms (*Formen*) of that kind; and he cannot dispense with them, since he himself belongs to this people."

dream. Like the executioners, like Our Lady of the Flowers, like any flower, Harcamone is a virgin. And his dream, on the eve of his death, repeats the process of Our Lady threatened by the feminine "sword" of justice. It is also a question of a miracle: "In a hamlet, the name of the flower known as 'queen of the fields' made a little girl who was thinking of Our Lady of the Flowers ask:

'Mommy, is she someone who had a miracle?'

There were other miracles that I haven't time to report."

In the spacing of writing, during the process of the narrative, the vertical lines (tie, rain, sword, cane, or point of an umbrella) cut the horizontal lines of the newspaper or book, the wings or ribs of the umbrella. Language cuts, decollates, decapitates. The sentences roll around an axis like creepers along a truncated column. The direction—backwards, everything has to be read backwards—leads us back to a cradle: what I am (following) is always the Immaculate Conception. "Thus, the newspapers were disturbing, as if they had been filled only with columns of crime news, columns as bloody and mutilated as torture stakes. And though the press has very parsimoniously given to the trial, which

Where does John take place? Who signed his text? On the one hand, he was born of the Jewish people, he is Jewish, he forms part of what "*zu diesem Volke gehört.*" He suffers its cultural and linguistic constraints, he is *formed* as a Jew. It is a Jew writing, accusing himself in his language.

Because simultaneously he also represents the *reineres Wesen*, the purer being who breaks into the Jewish world. He must "combat" his own belonging.

Now he can combat it only by using the weapons it has placed at his disposal. He must steal its categories, its values, in order to annul them or turn them against their own nature, against their congenital essence. Are these stolen categories categories of language or of thought?

John writes in Greek. The gospel undersigned by John is that of a Greek Jew. How were these Jewish categorical constraints able to ligature, age in advance the writing of the good news?

In the beginning was the *logos* [*Au commencement était le* logos]. I write here in French the translation of a Greek text whose apparent signatory, transcribing it from an inspiration that was neither Greek nor Jewish, had to continue to a certain extent to think in the language of his childhood while imprinting it in the foreign tongue.

Im Anfang war der logos, that's what interests Hegel. Of the four gospels, the one he spends most time on—the most philosophically, the most dialectically—remains apart. The original written text, the only one we possess, with its marks of Hellenism (of Philonism or Hermeticism), poses all sorts of problems for philologists and exegetes. Are these Hellenic features accidental, prophetic or essential?

This reading problem can be deployed only on a family stage.

What interests Hegel is that the most Greek of the gospels still holds back the revelation of the *logos* within the Judaic limit and yet already begins to free it from that limit. The beginning of the Gospel of John does certainly happen "in a more proper language" (*in eigentlicherer Sprache*), both because it is later and because it is Greek. But it remains still tied up in analytic and intellectualist—schismatic—formality. So one must distinguish between the essential content of the meaning and the formal appearance through which one has to take aim at it. *Im Anfang war der Logos* only appears to be a thetic proposition, a judicative statement positing both an existence and a copulated relation of subject to predicate. One must not, one should not have analyzed into several terms the true sense, the whole *Anfang-Logos*—archeology or logoarchy—the spiritual and luminous life that traverses

we shall read about tomorrow, only ten lines, widely enough spaced to let the air circulate between the overviolent words, these ten lines—more hypnotic than the fly of a hanged man, than the words 'hempen collar,' than the word 'Zouave'—these ten lines quickened the hearts of the old women and jealous children. Paris did not sleep. She hoped that the following day Our Lady would be sentenced to death; she desired it."

It? What? Whom? *What* she desires is *him*, *and that* he be condemned to death. She desires *him as* one condemned to death and condemns him to death by desiring him. In a word she makes *him* desirable and decapitable.

Let's space it out. The art of this text is the air that it has circulate among its screens. The links are invisible, everything seems improvised or juxtaposed. It draws one in by agglutinating rather than by demonstrating, by apposing and unsticking rather than by exhibiting the necessity—continuous and analogical, pedagogical, stifling—of a discursive rhetoric.

"The hearing. . . . The courtroom is not majestic, but it is very high, so that it gives a general impression of vertical lines, like lines of quiet rain.

and assembles it. One should not have divided, judged (*urteilen*), distributed into subject and predicate, temporal modes modifying pure presence. It is both by naivety and by reflexivity, those two accomplices, that one uses the imperfect; by thingism that one says of the *logos* that it *was in God* (*war bei Gott*), that God *was* the *logos*, that in him *was* life. The crudeness of these statements depends on the fact that division, and the relation of inherence also, introduces finitude (as though something could be *in* God) and abstraction (as though being and living could be universal predicates). Predicative division, mere judicative copulation, is here going the wrong way, it is *widersinnig*. If one puts into relation true sense and inadequate judgment, one has the feeling of a contradiction: one must immediately cancel what one posits, what is in God is not in God, what was, was not but still is, etc. This disorder, this contradiction (*Widerspruch*) exist as such only for formal, finite understanding: and for the one who is content to read, or rather who reads badly because he is content to read, because he does not animate the objectivity of (the) dead language. Hegel takes into account the textual fact but also the need to sublate it: if the reader receives the gospel text passively, without spiritual activity, without living repetition, he will see only formal contradictions, but if on the contrary he knows how to read, no longer being content to read, things will go quite differently. Everything depends on the reader's spirit: "This always objective language hence attains sense and weight only in the spirit of the reader." The variations, the diversity depend here on the reader's level of consciousness and on what he is able to think of the living relations, and of "the opposition of the living and the dead."

The family theatre organizes this theory of judgment, the schema of which is already fixed for the entire future of Hegelian logic. It is dominated by the Johannine values of life (*zôè*) and light (*phôs*), i.e. of truth. For there are two ways of conceiving the *logos* in the Gospel of John. Both are inadequate and unilateral. The way Hegel qualifies as "more objective" consists in making the *logos* into something, an individual effectivity; the other way, the "subjectivist" one, determines *logos* as reason, universality, being-thought. But this division represents the "Jewish principle" of opposition between thought and effectivity, rationality and the sensory, the division of life, a relation of death between God and

Upon entering, one sees on the wall a big painting with a figure of justice, who is a woman, wearing big red drapings. She is leaning with all her weight upon a saber, called here a 'glaive,' which does not bend. Below are the platform and table where the jurors and the presiding judge, in ermine and red robe, will come to sit in judgment on the child. The name of the presiding judge is 'Mr. Presiding Judge Vase de Sainte-Marie.'"

At this table (*The Miracle of the Rose* also stages a "Holy Table" scene prior to Harcamone's execution), the presiding judge who, under his red robe, is stiff as justice (a woman "wearing big red drapings. . . . leaning . . . upon a saber, here called a 'glaive'") and has the name of the Virgin, simultaneously takes the place of God and, like Our Lady, of the thirteenth one: "The twelve jurors are twelve decent men suddenly become sovereign judges. So the courtroom has been filling up since noon. A banquet hall. The table was set."

They are going to drink and eat the pharmakos, but it is already clear that each figure occupies all the places at once, circulates from one to the other, like the tie later on.

the world. Such a schismatic operation presupposes, as its unthought or its unreflected, the very thing to which it gives reflexive form: the one, the unique (*das Einige*) in which no division (*Teilung*) and so no objectivating judgment (*Urteil*) could take place. Simultaneously it needs to presuppose the possibility of division, of the infinite separation of the one, and therefore the unity of unity and separation, of reality and thought, etc. God and the *logos* are one. But they are different inasmuch as God is the content (*Stoff*) in the form (*Form*) of the *logos.* Only the understanding requires such a distinction and so it alone can oppose them. "The Logos itself is with God [*bei Gott*]; both are one."

By the *logos*: the mediation of the *logos* interrupts any emanationism. If effectivity were an emanation of God, it would be through and through and immediately divine. Hegel vigorously excludes this possibility. And yet, he adds immediately, *qua* effectivity, it is an "emanation," a part, a piece (*Teil*) of the infinite dividing (*Teilung*).

This apparent contradiction is thinkable only via the familial determination of the concept of emanation. Emanation is not here what its name seems to indicate: continuous production flowing from the source. As relation of living to living, it lets itself be troubled [*travailler*] by discontinuity, division, negativity. Life and division go together, and with them vision, the dehiscence of the living being the very thing that opens it to light and therefore to truth (*phôs, alethéia*).

Hegel follows John literally: "Yet, as real, it *is* an emanation, a part of the infinite partitioning, though at the same time (*zugleich*) in the part (*hen auto* is much better taken with the immediately preceding *oude hen o gegonen*), or in the one who partitions ad infinitum (if *hen auto* is taken as referring to logos), there is life." Life is therefore both part and parting, the piece and the whole, its own difference, its own opposition to itself. Each living part is the whole. Life is that strange division that produces wholes.

Here the "metaphor" of the tree comes up again: a genealogical tree in a radical sense.

The individual, the singular, the limited, inasmuch as it is opposed to the originary unity of the living, *qua* dead, is therefore a piece of life, a branch in the tree of life. Branch is *Zweig*. Like the two, the bough is produced from division,

But to see it you need a peephole [*judas*]. "At the edge of a gulf bristling with bayonets, Our Lady is dancing a perilous dance. . . . The public comes here only insofar as a word may result in a beheading and as it may return, like Saint Denis, carrying its severed head in its hands. . . . Here death is only a black wing without a body, a wing made with some remnants of black muslin [*étamine*] and supported by a thin framework of umbrella ribs . . ."

Étamine: if you were in a hurry to use the remnant, in order to sew it in somewhere else, like each piece of cloth or each flower of the text, you would find it in *The Thief's Journal*, on a Spanish whore's cunt.

But the erecting has to be elaborated very slowly, the cutting and sewing proceed on their own, without any visible application: ". . . umbrella ribs, a pirate banner without a staff. This muslin wing floated over the Court, which you are not to confuse with any other, for it is the Court of Law [*Palais de Justice*]."

Indeed, if you were to move the tongue the palate [*palais*] would no longer be the same.

this dead thing (*Totes*) is at the same time (*zugleich*) "a branch of the infinite tree of life (*ein Zweig des unendlichen Lebensbaumes*). Each part, to which the whole is external, is yet a whole, a life." What is incomprehensible, what the understanding does not understand, what the Jew is deaf to, is this *zugleich*, the structural *simul* of the living whole and piece. Reflected and divided, considered from the point of view of the dividing (*Teilung*) that both divides and makes possible the object of a judgment (*Urteil*), life is both subject and predicate, synthesis of existence and thought universality: both life (*zoē*) and life thought, grasped (*ausgefaßtes*), light (*phōs*), truth (*Wahrheit*). Life is life, life is light, life is truth.

Hegel translates John into German but also, according to a dialectical law, into a family syllogism. The new coming of light into the world, the coming of life into the light of truth, follows a process such that recognition, consciousness of a revelation that is already there, bringing light to light, the truth of light in the light of truth, the truth of truth, comes down to recognizing God and recognizing ourselves (*sich erkennen*) as children of God (*als Kinder Gottes*). This process is a process of familial reappropriation. The point is to recognize what comes back to the father.

Light is in the world, in the ordered beauty of the *kosmos*. "Although John was not himself the light," the light was, in all men entering the world of men, equivalent. The *kosmos,* a notion narrower than that of *panta*, designates the totality of human relations. Light does not supervene on the *kosmos*, the *kosmos* is in the light inasmuch as it is human and is the work of *anthropou phôtos* or *anthropos phôtizomenos*. The light of truth never flourishes and nothing flourishes in it—before the anthrope. But there is in man something from before man, and in his light something that refuses (itself to) the light. Man began by closing himself off from what was, however, the most proper and proximate to him (*sein Eigenste* (*idion*)), the most related. He treated what is proper to him as a stranger (*als fremd*). As proper light is also the light of life, not to receive it is to cut oneself off from life. Those who receive it on the other hand, those who recognize

"Muslin wing [*elle/aile d'etamine*] . . . enveloped it in its folds and had detached a green crepe de Chine tie to represent It in the courtroom. The tie, which lay on the Judges' table, was the only piece of evidence. Death, visible here, was a tie, and this fact pleases me: it was a light Death."

It is too early to consider *étamine*.

But the wing she is, Death who hovers over the Court is *represented* by a tie. "[It/*Elle*] had detached a green crepe de Chine tie to represent It . . ." A fabric is represented by a fabric. The tie sliding around the neck is the murder weapon and, in a moment, it will become—in the hands of God, the Virgin Mary, the Apostles, Judas—what it will have always been in the hands of Our Lady, the Christ, Christ himself, a phallus. It is too obvious, there would be no need to insist on it. Thus, it isn't at all what interests us in the representation of a text by a text. What interests us is that the textile that always represents never represents anything. And we like it to be thus: the simulacrum of the represented is the lightness of Death. There are only representatives. Death is nothing. But its representatives even less than nothing. And yet everything is written for Death, from the vantage of Death, addressing the Dead. I write for the dead, he says everywhere. Read the letters to Roger Blin, *The Studio of Giacometti*, read it all. But he specifies: for the dead

themselves in it as though they were at home, give themselves a power (*Macht*) which is not a new force (*neue Kraft*) but an extra level (*Grad*) in the equality or inequality (*Gleichheit oder Ungleichheit*) of life.

In so doing, they do not become different, "but they know God and recognize themselves as children of God, as weaker than he, yet of a like nature (*von gleicher Natur*) in so far as they have become conscious of that spiritual relation [*Beziehung*] suggested by his name [*onoma*] as the *anthropos* who is *photizomenon photi alethino*. They find their essence (*Wesen*) in no stranger, but in God."

What Hegel translates as relation, rapport, is the name. What man discovers as most proper in him, in his proper name, is God and God as his father. The truth thus comes to the world, or rather reveals itself as the structure of the *kosmos* in the nomination of the filial relation. The name, the relation, the spirit (Hegel sometimes translates *onoma* as *spirit*) is the structure of what comes back to the father.

This nomination is not an event. Not simply. It is an event insofar as it is new, the absolutely new. But this newness lights only light, brings the day to daylight.

The sign that this nomination of truth as filiation is not absolutely new, that it *already* repeats, and that spirit always repeats, is the sign. This sign—of novelty as repetition—is a linguistic sign. The familial or filial syntagm did not arise with the good news. As if by chance, contingently, *zufällig*, he says, the Jewish language had it at its disposal. It was one of those rare naturally felicitous expressions that were awaiting their fecundation, their true fulfillment, their full reference.

John is not without a hand in this. He introduced concrete, individual, existential reference into the discourse of truth. "John bore witness, not of the *phos* alone (verse 7), but also of the individual (verse 15)." This is how the generic relation replaced the discourse on man in general and truth in general. "The most commonly cited and the most striking [*bezeichnendste*] expression of Jesus' relation to God is his calling himself the 'son of God' and contrasting himself as

who have never been living. The knell is nobody's [*le glas n'est de personne*]. Nobody. It neither announces nor recalls anything. It barely sounds, echoes rather, before having ever touched the matter of any sign. It [*ça*] resounds. Why call that death? Because that *already* took place [*ça a* déjà *eu lieu*].

This strange *déjà* must be deciphered.

What gets represented (wing, hovering death) is nothing, but like a past that has never been present, never taken place. We wait for death, desire it only as a past that we haven't yet lived, that we have forgotten but with a forgetting that hasn't come to cover over an experience, with a more ample memory, more capable and older than all perception. That is why there are only traces here, traces of traces without tracing, or if you wish tracings that track and retrace only

already. Death has already taken place, before everything. How to decipher this strange anteriority of a *déjà* that always lands you with a cadaver? You will have noticed that he is always unloading his corpse on you. He wants you never to be able to get rid of the very stiff body that his literature, his funeral rites, has hardbound for you. How can one seduce, how can one be loved without telling you *I am dead?* Not only—for this would have only a provisional and relative effect—"careful, I am going to die," "I am mortal," but also "I am *already* dead," before even living. Who could do better? Who could say it better? And if, as I have shown elsewhere (*Speech and Phenomena, Glas in phenomen* in Slovenian translation), *I am* and *I am dead* are two indistinguishable statements sensewise, the *déjà* that I am clangs its own knell, signs its own death warrant, looks at you in advance, sees you coming in its direction without understanding anything to do with what you love, following, in column, the funeral march of an erection that the whole world will henceforth have at its disposal.

More or less slang translation of the *cogito:* "I am therefore dead." That can only be written. After calling up his friends, "friends new and old, those to whom I am 'Jeannot with the Pretty Ties,'" it is written "I am therefore dead. I am a dead man who sees his skeleton in a mirror, or a dream character who knows that he lives only in the darkest region of a being whose face he will not know when the dreamer is awake."

son of God with himself as the 'son of man'. The designation (*Bezeichnung*) of this relation is one of the few natural expressions [*Naturlaute*] left by accident (*zufällig übriggeblieben war*) in the Jewish speech of that time, and therefore it has to be counted among their happy expressions (*glücklichen Ausdrücke*)."

This remark belongs to the whole Hegelian system of felicity of expression in naturally speculative language-effects.

Why does the Jew not understand, in sum, what he is saying, what his language is already saying for him? More precisely, why does he not say what he can say?

Literally speaking, one cannot say that the Jew does not understand, does not grasp what he is saying. On the contrary, he conceives what he proffers, what his language puts in his mouth. That is his limit: he conceives. He stays at the level of the concept. But the relation of father to son is inconceivable, at least in terms of universal generalities, "thoughts." The unity of the son and the father is not conceptual because every conceptual unity lives on opposition; it is finite. Yet life is infinite. If the living relation of father to son is life as non-conceptual unity, every conceptual unity presupposes it, implies this non-concept as production of the concept, non-conceptual conception of the concept. Living conception is the relation of father to son. It forms a contradiction in the logic of the understanding, here that of the Jew, who cannot master it—precisely because he intends to master. One masters only finite life—or death.

"The relation of a son to his father is not a conceptual unity (as, for instance, unity or harmony of disposition, similarity of principles, etc.), a unity which is only a unity in thought and is abstracted from life. On the contrary, it is a living relation of living beings, a likeness of life (*gleiches Leben*). Father and son are simply modifications of the same life, not opposite essences, not a plurality of absolute substantialities. Thus the son of God is the same essence (*Wesen*) as the father . . ."

This unity cannot be stated in the analytic and finite logic of the understanding. In the almost unconceivable judgment "the son is the father," "the father is the son," there is neither formal tautology nor empirical heterology. This infinite *a priori* synthesis is the condition of all synthetic judgments *a priori.*

Given that it cannot be stated in the abstract language of the understanding, it requires a sort of

other texts, wing/tie again, hymen and screen in the end torn [*qu'on crève*] "for nothing." That's all it was and they make such a fuss. The Mother croaks [*crève*] last. There is a whole "theory" of the event there—by "theory" I of course mean *theater*—sewn with the same threads, a whole theory of the immemorial also. But the theory—always blind to this point—seduces us less than the event that parades past, in the studio, in the text, in the scene. You'd find this other logic of the event and of time spelled out in his letter (to Roger Blin), even though the signatory "doesn't have the time to tell you at greater length," or elsewhere, everywhere else. For example in *The Studio*: "I don't quite understand what in art is called an innovator. Should a work be understood by future generations? But why? And what would that mean? That they could use it? For what purpose? I don't see it. But I see much better—though still very obscurely—that every work of art, if it wants to reach the most spectacular proportions, must with infinite patience and care from the moment of its production onward, come down through the millennia, reach if it can the immemorial night peopled with the dead, who will recognize themselves in this work.

No, no, the work of art is not destined for unborn generations. It is offered to the innumerable populace of the dead. Who recognize it. Or refuse it. But these dead of whom I spoke have never been alive. Or I am forgetting."

I don't see it. But I see much better—though still very obscurely . . . The whole of *The Studio* describes the point of view of Oedipus.

metaphoricity. Beyond the concept, this metaphoricity also delivers the condition of possibility of every determinate concept.

The metaphor remains still natural, physical, apparently vegetal. Again the tree, a tree with three branches: "It is true only of objects, of things lifeless, that the whole is other than the parts; in the living thing, on the other hand, the part of the whole is one and the same as the whole. If particular [separate, cut, *besondere*] objects, as substances, are linked together while each of them yet [*zugleich*] retains its character as an individual (as numerically one), then their common characteristic, their unity, is only a concept, not an essence (*Wesen*), not something being (*Seiendes*). Living things, however, are essences, even if they are separate (*Abgesonderte*), and their unity is still a unity of essence. What is a contradiction (*Widerspruch*) in the realm of the dead (*im Reich des Toten*) is not one in the realm of life. "A tree which has three branches makes up with them *one* tree (einen *Baum*); but every 'son' of the tree, every branch (and also its other 'children,' leaves and blossoms) is itself a tree. The fibers bringing sap to the branch from the stem are of the same nature (*gleichen Natur*) as the roots. If a tree is set in the ground upside down it will put forth leaves out of the roots in the air, and the boughs (*Zweige*) will root themselves in the ground. And it is just as true to say that there is *only one* tree here as to say that there are three."

on the same page, the example of the Arab: among the Arabs, a son of the Korech tribe is the whole tribe. Whence the form of warfare that "natural and undivided people" (*natürlichen ungeteilten Volke*) wage on each other: individuals do not count; they are massacred with the utmost cruelty. In Europe on the contrary—and this time Hegel seems to see a falling-off here—the individual does not have an organic bond (*Band*) with the whole, but merely a bond of abstract thought. War is then a relation between State totalities. "As with any genuinely free people (*wie bei jedem echt freien Volk*), so among the Arabs, the individual is a part and the same as the whole (*ein Teil, aber zugleich das Ganze*)."

The possibility of turning upside down, of inverse erection, is inscribed in the cycle of the family stance. The son is the son only in being able to become a father, being able to supplement or sublate the father, to occupy his place, becoming the father's father, i.e. the son's son. A father is always his grandfather and a son his own grandson.

For whom does one write, who approves or refuses? For whom is this gift that never becomes present?

The Studio and the remainder. It *describes* the point of view of Oedipus, skims its surface of blindness from the tip of a style about which you can never know whether or not it belongs to the surface described. Of course it touches on it. But one must be able to read this point of contact.

It isn't only true of *The Studio* that we are in and which we'll come back to (it is precisely contemporaneous with the "event" recounted in "What remains . . ."), but of all the rest. It is always written not *within* [dans] the story of Oedipus but in [*en*] Oedipus, like a piece of music composed *in*, a book written in such and such a script. More precisely, given the importance of the syncategoremes, all the rest is written *on* Oedipus, mounted onto Oedipus, as on a setting, a sawhorse, a plinth or a ring. A slab [*dalle*]. And the one who mounts—listen for the laughs from the avant-garde and trailblazers—knows well that this cavalier operation, of the painter, sculptor or goldsmith, is no more for Oedipus than against Oedipus, no more inside than outside him. And if the Oedipal event were something, it would be what here gives it the strength to mount Oedipus, to say fuck you, to trip you up when you want to interpret, judge, decide. You are still in the

The movement of inverse erection describes the structure of the non-conceptual conception of the concept.

This "metaphor" is marked twice and occupies two places at once. By its semantic tenor, it stands, like life, beyond the concept—understand by this beyond the dead concept, the finite analysis of the understanding, or objectivating determination. But this life is not the life designated by the metaphorical "vehicle"; the life of spirit is named via the natural life in which it vegetates. But between the two lives, analogy makes the metaphor possible. Between the two, there are the concept and death. This double mark can be found throughout the whole of history and the whole system, describing even the structure of the whole of life, the living organization of the Hegelian system.

One index, among many others, but in a privileged place—at the end of the *Greater Logic.* In the last section of Subjective Logic ("The Idea"), life is inscribed both as a syllogism and as one moment of a syllogism. The first of the three chapters about the Idea deals, precisely, with life. The first determination of the Idea is life; the second, knowledge and the will (the idea of the true and of the good); the third, the absolute Idea in which (the) spirit recognizes itself in its "absolute truth", infinite, in and for itself. In this syllogism of the Idea, life appears first as a natural and immediate determination: spirit outside itself, lost in naturality, natural life that itself constitutes a "smaller" syllogism. The immediate Idea has the form of life. But the absolute Idea in its infinite truth is still determined as Life, true life, absolute life, life without death, imperishable life, the life of truth.

Between the two lives, like their hyphen, their contract or their contraction: death. But also the space for the metaphorical play and the analogy that interests us here under the heading of filiation.

Does "life" have here or there its proper sense? There is no choice to be made. Life does not have what is proper to it here or there, it is produced as the circle of its reappropriation, return to self before which there is no proper self. Nothing precedes the return. "The absolute idea, as

Palais. In the mother tongue. You still have the tie in your hands and you're not too sure what to do with it.

The other paragraph: Our Lady enters the courtroom: "Nevertheless, I shall make so bold as to say that all eyes could read, graven in the aura of Our Lady of the Flowers, the following words: 'I am the Immaculate Conception.'"

Who will get the tie?

Our Lady, virgin virgin-born, who announces himself —he's an archangel—and who says to us in short "I conceive myself without a father, I am born from myself or by the operation of the Holy Spirit," I am my father, my mother, my son, and myself—Our Lady has killed. With a big stick [*verge*]. He has put a tie into play, but he didn't even possess that tie in the beginning. And nobody wants it, nobody can even hold on to it.

Word for word: "Have I mentioned the fact that the audience was made up mostly of men? But all of them, darkly dressed, with umbrellas on their arms and newspapers in their pockets, were shakier than a bower of wisteria, than the lace curtain of a crib. Our Lady of the Flowers was the reason . . ."

the rational concept that in its reality only rejoins itself, is by virtue of this immediacy of its objective identity, on the one hand, a turning back to *life* (*die Rückkehr zum* Leben); on the other hand, it has equally sublated [*aufgehoben*] this form of its immediacy and harbors the most extreme opposition within." The Idea, immediate natural life, sublates itself, cancels and preserves itself, dies in raising itself up to spiritual life. So life develops in contradiction and negativity; the metaphor between the two lives is simply this movement of sublating negativity. "The concept is not only *soul* [*Seele*], but free subjective concept that exists for itself and therefore has *personality*—the practical objective concept that is determined in and for itself and is as person impenetrable, atomic subjectivity—but which is not, just the same, exclusive singularity; it is rather explicitly *universality* and *cognition*, and in its other has *its own* objectivity for its object (*seine eigene Objektivität zum Gegenstande*). All the rest is error, confusion, opinion (*Meinung*), striving, arbitrariness, and transitoriness [*Vergänglichkeit*]; the absolute idea alone is *being* (Sein), imperishable *life* (*unvergangliches* Leben), *self-knowing truth*, and is *all truth*."

"*in seinem Anderen*": "Its other" is the very syntagm of the Hegelian proper; it constitutes negativity in the service of the proper meaning. When life becomes its proper object for itself, the objectivity of natural life dies and takes a position "over against" the Idea, as a particular thing, about which one can speak. In truth, it is life that always speaks of itself, of its life and its death, still of its life

Same movement in the *Encyclopedia*, at the end, as to *Sa*. As the third term comes back to immediacy, and as this return operates by the sublation of difference and mediation, natural life occupies both the beginning and the end. In their ontological meaning, metaphors are always metaphors of life, they give rhythm to the imperturbable equality of life, of being, of truth, of filiation: *physis*.

The Hegelian system thus demands that it be read as a book of life. The reading categories first must comply with that. To speak of several states of Hegelian thought, of a young Hegel or an accomplished Hegel, is both Hegelian and anti-Hegelian. Thus the book by Bourgeois about Hegel in Frankfurt applies to its subject Hegel's most preformationist categories. It does, it is true, oppose "the advent of mature Hegelianism" to "budding Hegelianism," but specifies that this latter "sets out on the path of Hegelianism properly speaking, whose genius intuition he will formulate at Jena when he writes that

I don't have the right to operate in this way, but let's select all the same, let's cut sections out from the two pages that follow to join the tie that's dragging ("Punch . . . glory . . . lovely crevice . . . Our Lady's thousand forerunners, an annunciatory angel of this virgin,

"Our Lady . . . annunciatory angel of this virgin": Our Lady is thus not only another name for the Virgin Mary, for the Presiding Judge, for Christ and the whole Holy Family, he is also the annunciating angel of the virgin, like another *forename* of the mother.
In *Our Lady of the Flowers*, Divine loves Gabriel, nicknamed the Archangel. To make him love her, she puts a little of her urine in what she gives him to eat or drink. That is the way they keep dogs attached to one another, she'd heard it said. She lures him into her attic, and organizes there a funereal ambience (darkness, incense, bells): "She was bound to have Gabriel up sooner or later. As the curtains are drawn, he finds himself in a darkness the more massive for having been mildewed for years (as by a scent of chilled incense) by the subtle essence of the farts that had blossomed there." When Gabriel penetrates her he "make[s] his tool quiver like a shying horse." It is true that in penetrating her, presuming that he bears somewhere the same forename as this whore of a mother, he merely reassumes her form and place. Divine had told him: "I love you as if you were in my belly," or again:
"'You're not my sweetheart, you're myself. My heart or my sex. A branch of me.'
And Gabriel, thrilled, though smiling with pride, replies:
'Oh, you little hussy!'"

a blond young boy ('Girls blond as boys' . . . I shall, indeed, never weary of this phrase, which has the seductive charm of the expression: 'a French guardswoman') whom I used to watch in gymnasium groups. He depended upon the figures that he helped to form and, thus, was only a sign. . . . on the earth. . . . nun pushing aside her veil. . . . poem (or fable) that was born of it (recurring miracle of Anne

the absolute must be conceived as 'the identity of identity and non-identity.'" We see Hegel "anticipating future themes," "the philosophy of the concept; i.e. of Hegelianism," "Hegelianism itself," "Hegelianism," title of the third chapter of the book being presented as the conclusion of a syllogism of which "Judaism" and "Christianity" (the two other titles) are supposed to be the first two terms. "First Hegelianism," "budding Hegelianism," "mature Hegelianism," "accomplished Hegelianism," "Hegelian philosophy properly speaking," "Hegel become fully adult as a speculative philosopher," realizing what "he was aspiring to from his adolescence on," etc., all these categories reflect and double Hegel's teleological discourse. It is to be expected, given that the truth of Hegelianism is conceived only at the end of the journey, that (the) philosophical narration (should) be done in the future tense. Bourgeois's book says all the time: Hegel will think, Hegel will have to, Hegel will come to, etc. Frankfurt is nothing but the to-come of the completed system. It is (only) to be expected too that the logical reading (should) be constantly accompanied by a biographical narrative (young Hegel, adult Hegel, etc.).

Nothing could be more Hegelian. But nothing could be less Hegelian: in distinguishing the old from the young, the systematic chains of the "early" texts are sometimes hidden; and above all a dissociating, formal analysis, the point of view of the understanding, is applied in a narration that runs the risk of missing the living unity of the discourse; how can one distinguish philosophically a before from an after if the circularity of the movement makes the beginning into the end of the end? And vice versa? The Hegelian tree is also inverted, the old Hegel is the father of the young only by having been his son, his great grandson.

So the risk is the Jewish reading.

What do the Jews make of Hegel? What do they do when they hear it said that the son is one with the father? When they are presented with the unity of essence (*Weseneinheit*) of (the) father and (the) son? Or else the inverse erection?

They count, they do accounts. And they cry scandal. How can Jesus identify with God, equal him and think that's possible when he calls him his father. They understand this unity in terms of numerical equality, which Hegel never stops denouncing, even when it has to do with the Trinity.

before Jena, the *Systemfragment* (1800) takes up again the essential aspects of the theses on Christianity: "*Das Leben sei die Verbindung der Verbindung und der Nichtverbindung*," i.e. the copula or the ligament of the ligament and the non-ligament in which life at the same stroke bands and disbands itself. Now life is being

Boleyn: from the steaming blood sprang a bush of roses, that might have been white, but were certainly fragrant), the necessary sifting was done in order to disengage the truth beneath the marble. . . . With a stab of the knife, he had put out Alberto's eye. . . . On the table, the lithe little Death lay inert and looked quite dead. . . . The Court entered by a door that was cut out of the wallpaper behind the jurors' table. . . . just as, on Palm Sunday, the clergy, who usually leave the sacristy by a side door near the choir, surprise the faithful by appearing from behind them [the rooms open like that—from behind and in the text—onto their structure, almost always; see the opening of the maids]. . . . Our Lady had a foreboding that the whole session would be faked and that at the end of the performance his head would be cut off by means of a mirror trick. . . . M. Vase de Sainte-Marie was wearing a monocle . . .").

There is, then, the tie on stage at the Last Supper. Left hanging [*cependant*], who gets it.

"The judge had the soft tie in his fingers, a tie like a piece of ectoplasm,

everything is always attacked from the back, inscribed, described from behind. *A tergo*. I am already [*déjà*] dead means that I am behind [*derrière*]. Absolutely behind, the Behind that will never have been seen face on, the Already that nothing will have preceded, which has therefore conceived and given birth to itself, but as cadaver or glorious body. To be behind is to be before everything—breaking all symmetry. I take refuge—behind—I bleed at the bottom of my text. "The author of a beautiful poem is always dead." (*Miracle of the Rose*) At the same time, in taking refuge, in subtracting my presence, in dying, I escape the blows in advance. Behind and Already protect me, make me illegible, shelter me on the other side of the text. I am accessible, legible, visible only in a rearview mirror. All the flowers of rhetoric within which I disperse my signature, within which I apostrophize and *apotropize*, are to be read also as forms of repression. It is a matter of pushing back the worst threat, and in order to do so, to take refuge from oneself, in advance: the broom is thus a sort of *reseda morbos*, an incantation by one as it hides itself behind the other, enclosing itself in its protected interior.

Given this, the father/son relation becomes impossible, unthinkable for them. They consider the familial nomination of the relation of God to man or to Jesus as images (*Bilde*), in the most external sense, turns of speech or imagination. They thus disqualify what the advent of Christianity might involve that is essential in the history of spirit. Understanding the father/son relation both as purely conceptual and as purely imaginative, they miss its schema and are wrong twice over. "Jesus continually appealed, especially in John, to his oneness [*Einigkeit*] with God, who has granted to the son to have life in himself, just as the father has life in himself. He and the father are one; he is Brod come down from heaven, and so forth. These are hard words (σκλεροὶ λόγοὶ) and they are not softened [*milder*] by being interpreted (or explicated: *erklärt*) as imagery (*für bildliche*) or misinterpreted as the uniting of concepts instead of being taken spiritually as life. Of course, as soon as intellectual concepts are opposed to imagery (*Bildlichem*) and taken as dominant, every image must be set aside as only play (*Spiel*), as a by-product (*Beiwesen*) of the imagination (*Einbildungskraft*) and without truth; and, instead of the life of the image, nothing remains but objects."

The Jew sticks with this objectivism that, incapable of departing from the understanding or the imagination in their finite closure, also remains a subjectivism. Closed up in this non-dialectical double unilaterality, he gains access neither to the divine nor to the spiritual meaning of filiation. This is because the spirit has not yet spoken in him. It has not become adult in him. At bottom the Jew may well be a sort of executioner, but he is also a child. And what characterizes childhood is that it cannot think childhood as such, filiation as such. So long as he is a child, the son is blind to the father/son relation. To see it, he has to become an adult. He becomes the son for himself only by becoming an adult, and therefore by identifying with the father. Only a father can become a son and a son can think himself as such only by identifying with the father. This strange indifferent difference opens spiritual filiation, sublates the genealogy of the natural family. Hegel says so in a play on words that must not be considered an imaginal *Beiwesen*. The Jew is not filial (*kindlich*) because he is puerile (*kindisch*). Not childlike but childish. If he accuses Jesus of blasphemy when he says that his father has entered into him, this is because he understands neither the finite nor

a tie that had to be looked at while there was time, for it might disappear at any moment or stiffen in the dry hand of the judge, who felt that if it did actually become erect or disappear, he would be covered with ridicule. He therefore hastened to pass the instrument of the crime to the first juror, who passed it to his neighbor, and so on, without anyone's daring to linger over recognizing it, for each of them seemed to be running the risk of being metamorphosed before his own eyes into a Spanish dancer."

In silence fallen into the prison of the other.

"And I, having only the name Divers as a visible, prehensile asperity for grasping the invisible, contorted it so as to make it enter mine, mingling the letters of both. Prison, particularly a state prison, is a place which makes things both heavier and lighter. Everything that pertains to it, people and things alike, has the weight of lead and the sickening lightness of cork. Everything is ponderous because everything seems to sink, with very slow movements, into an opaque element. One has 'fallen,' because too heavy. The horror of being cut off from the living precipitates us—the word calls for precipice (note the number of words relating to prison that evoke falling, 'fall' itself, etc.)."

The "and so on" in this circulation of the fatal phallus—further attack suddenly of one and the same neck, tighten the tie—always comes back to the movement of the virginal flower (*varginal*: between prick [*verge*] and vagina of the virgin, small stone or clitoral hood), of the phallus taken from the Holy Mother, belonging no more to the Presiding Judge de Sainte-Marie than to Our Lady of the Flowers ("I am the Immaculate Conception").

the infinite, neither the measured nor the immense, neither the part nor the whole. More precisely, what he does not understand is not this or that, but the commensurability or the passage between the two—the presence of the immense in the determinate, the beauty and the immanence of the infinite in the finite.

Castration and prison: "The Jewish multitude was bound to wreck his attempt to give them the consciousness of something divine, for faith (*Glaube*) in something divine, something great, cannot make its home in a dunghill (filth, mud, *Kote*). The lion has no room in a nest, the infinite spirit none in the prison (*Kerker*) of a Jewish soul, the whole of life none in a withering leaf. The hill and the eye which sees it are object and subject, but between man and God, between spirit and spirit, there is no such cleft (*Kluft*) of objectivity and subjectivity; one is to the other an other only in that one recognizes the other; both are one. One branch [one corollary: *Zweig*] of taking the relation of son to father objectively, or rather the consequence which this interpretation has for the will, is (a) the discovery of a connection (*Zusammenhang*) between ourselves and God in the connection between the separate human and divine natures thus conceived and reverenced in Jesus, and (b) the hope for a love between two total dissimilars (*Ungleichen*), a love of God for man which might at best be a form of sympathy. Jesus' relation to God, as the relation of son to father, is a childlike (*kindliches*) relation, since in essence, in spirit, the son feels himself one with the father who lives in him. This has no resemblance to that puerile (*kindischen*) relation in which a man might put himself with the rich overlord of the world whose life he feels wholly alien to him and with whom he connects himself only through presents showered on him, only through the crumbs falling from the rich man's table."

One does not bind oneself to the father with leftovers, by calculating exchanges. The bond with the father is incalculable. The being, the essence (*Wesen*) of Jesus, inasmuch as it couples him with his Father, "can be truly grasped only by Glauben"; *Glauben,* the act of faith, has here an infinite ontological force. This hangs on the fact that contrary to finite knowledge relating a spirit to a determinate object that remains heterogeneous to it, *Glauben* is of a spirit for a spirit. Whence the "metaphor" of harmony: "The relation of spirit to spirit is a feeling of harmony, is their unification (*Vereinigung*); how could heterogeneity be unified?"

The homogeneous, then, what is born of the same in the self-same—that is the harmonious element of *Glauben.* One who believes in this element of the same does not believe

It might seem to belong to the victim (of the theft or murder) since it is his own tie. But it has to say goodbye [*faire son deuil*] to what should have come back to it like the phallus to the virgin mother.

Indignation of Vase de Sainte-Marie precisely when Our Lady—himself—reveals to him that it is the murder victim—himself—who gave him the weapon and the idea for the crime ("[he] was wearing a tie that was too tight. He was all red.")

The effort to *render* the flower cannot but fail. No circular and proper trajectory: signet [*seing*] letter of the Mother hiding and losing itself among all the proper names of the erianthus. The flower is nothing, never takes place because it is never either natural or artificial. It has no assignable edge, no fixed perianthus, no being-girded [*être-ceint*]. That is how proper names, which are always nicknames of *classification*, violently imposed, operations of class, ringing out to call to the work of mourning, to expropriation, always come back down to (Our Lady of the) flowers.

Is the work of mourning work, a kind of work? And thanatopraxy, the technique of funeral rites taught today in special institutes, leading to recognized

as strictly determined by psychoanalysis, as such, the work-of-mourning would simply gulp down more quickly, in the course of a single meal, the gathered time of a Last Supper [*Cène*], a bigger bite

in some other thing, he finds himself again in his *Glauben,* he "rediscovers his own nature" (*seine eigene Natur wiederfindet*). The musical metaphor of the homogeneous has its analog in the anthropo-photological metaphor. The proper nature of light-bearing man becomes clearer. Man does not bring light the way one bears a torch. Light and life are in him. He is in light and in life, carried by them rather. In all senses of this word, he belongs to light, "he is the property of the light" (*er ist das Eigentum des Lichts*). If man is the proper of light (of truth, of being, etc.), he does not receive it from outside, he burns in it, he catches fire in the homogeneity of his element and in the act of *Glauben*. The gleam (*Glanz*) of light is not foreign to him, it imbues his whole substance and the whole glory of his body. "He is the property of the light. He is not illumined by a light in the way a dark body is when it borrows a brightness not its own (*nur fremden Glanz*); on the contrary, his own inflammability (*sein eigener Feuerstoff*) takes fire and he burns with a flame that is his own (*eine eigene Flamme*)."

This is what Jesus explains to Simon: the divine that is in you recognized me as divine. We are the same, born of the same. My essence "has re-echoed in thine" (*in dem deinigen wiedergetönt*). And then from Simon, son of Jonah, he makes Peter, he transforms him into "the rock [*zum Felsen*] on which his community was to be founded." The power that is granted him is essentially that of "binding and loosing (*binden und lösen*)."

Peter's faith still represents only the first step (*die erste Stufe*) of this procession towards the light in light. John: "Until ye have light, believe in the light, that ye may be the children of light." To believe in the light, to bear witness in favor of it, like John the Baptist, is not yet to be, as was Jesus, an "individualized light." No doubt his disciples are united in Jesus, in his flame, like the vine shoots (*Ranken*) are united with the vine (*Weinstock*). But they will have a life of their own and will at the same time be fully penetrated by the divine spirit only after the death of Jesus, of their master, of the one who still occupied the individual place of a center or a vine. When the vine is as it were cut, there will fall with it what still separates them from God, the wall, the diaphragm (*Scheidewand*) between the Father and his children. Jesus is the diaphragm of divine light. His body subtly blocks its passage. So his death is indispensable. John pointed this out: the waters can flow from the

diplomas—is that to be limited to one corporation among others, within a social economy? Isn't all work a work of mourning? and at the same time a work of appropriation of more or less loss, a *classical* operation? a violent operation of class and classification? a decollation of what holds the singular to itself? This work of mourning is *called*—clang. It always concerns the proper name. The clang is first of all (*clas*, *chiasso*, *classum*, *classicum*) the blast from a trumpet used to call (*calare*), convoke, gather together as such a *class* of Roman people. There is therefore clanging in classical literature, but also in class struggle: class

"**classicus** bürger der ersten klasse (in Rom).

Daraus entlehnt nfr. *classique* adj. "(author) who is in the ranks of the most esteemed, who merits most being imitated" (1548), "man of the highest rank, whose example should be followed" (ca. 1550), nfr. "(author) taught in schooling" (seit Cotgr 1611): "relating to the teaching of Greek and Latin languages and literatures" (seit Ac 1798).
Ablt.—Nfr. *classicisme* "system of exclusive partisans of writers of antiquity or classic writers of the 17th century" (seit Besch 1845).
Lt. Classicus "bürger der ersten klasse" wird einmal, von Gellius, als adj. gebraucht: *vel oratorum aliquis vel poetarum, id est classicus assiduusque aliquis scriptor, non proletarius*. Es wird im 16. jh., bei der übernahme ins fr., zum adj. gemacht. Zuerst erscheint es bei Th. Sebillet. Art poétique (1548): *the reading of good classic French poets such as, among the elders, Alain Chartier and Jean de Meun*. Es wird also mit bezug auf französische Dichter verwendet. Da die Pleiade die ältere französische literatur verleugnet, macht ihr sieg die anwendung des wortes auf die französische literatur unmöglich. Sein sinn wird nun umgebogen zu einer ablt. von *classe* "schulklasse": *classique* bedeutet jetzt "(autor) der in der schule gelesen und interpretiert

body only *after* the vine itself is cut. In the future. "When Jesus says (John 7:38-9): 'He that believeth in me, out of his belly *shall* flow rivers of life (werden *Ströme des Lebens quellen*),' John remarks that this was spoken of the thorough animation which was still to come." Jesus has not yet been transfigured, he will be only by death. In the interval, he is a man among men, he opposes and is individualized only faced with the Jewish character. "John says (2:25) of Jesus that he knew what was in man; and the truest mirror (*Spiegel*) of his beautiful *Glauben* in nature is his discourse at the sight of uncorrupted beings." Not to sully this nature or become a child ("in my name," *in meinem Namen*) is the same thing. What will be done to (the) one who sullies immaculate nature? He will be drowned "in the deepest sea (*im tiefsten Meere*)." After having a stone, "a millstone (*Mühlstein*) tied around his neck." He will be like a hanged man at the bottom of the sea.

One is punished for no longer being enough of a child.

What is the difference between this immersion and that of baptism?

John is the only one able to explain this to us. It was his "habit" to "immerse" (*unterzutauchen*) in water those who had risen to his spirit. "Nothing similar is known to have been done by Jesus." Now this habit of John's has a "symbolic signification (*ist eine bedeutende Symbolische*)." To understand anything of this Johannine symbol, you need to know what "to be immersed [*être plongé*]" means.

That is, what a child is and what an angel does.

The angels contemplate the face of my father in heaven. This proposition is very rich: "Unconsciousness (*das Bewußtlose*), undeveloped unity, being (*Sein*) and life in God, are here severed from God because they are supposed to be represented, as modifications of divinity, in existing children; yet the being (*Sein*) and doing (*Tun*) of the angels is an eternal sight of God." Bound to God and unbound from him, the angels are not Platonic souls that, initially plunged in the intuition of the divine, have later, in their "later life on earth," only a darkened consciousness of the divinity. Jesus binds and unbinds otherwise. A man must not be purely and simply "immersed in the intuition of the sun" (*ganz in die Anschauung der Sonne versunken*): he would then become confused with a mere luminous feeling. A man plunged in the contemplation of another man would be only this other, etc. Division, *Entzweiung*, is therefore necessary. But what is divided in two (*entzweit*)

wird"; die einschränkung auf die literatur des Altertums hängt unmittelbar damit zusammen. Erst im 18. jh. wurde das adj. auch auf die nun als vorbilder betrachteten autoren des 17. jhs. ausgedehnt (erster beleg Voltaire 1761), gegen ende des 18. jhs. auch auf andere dinge, die in ihrer art als vorbild, als vornehmster vertreter gelten können (*classic land of liberty*). Zur zeit der Romantik wird *classique* zum kennzeichen des literarischen programms der gegner der neuen bewegung. Im einzelnen müssen diese entw. noch an hand der texte untersucht werden.

classis abteilung

1. Mfr. *clas* m. "fleet" (1530); *classe* f. (1560, Pold. d'Albenas, Antiquités de Nîmes 205, Db—Mon 1636)
2. a. Mfr. nfr. *classe* "category of Roman citizens within the civil, political order" (seit Bersuire); übertragen nfr. "rank in which persons of the same profession are placed, according to their merit" (seit Rich 1680); "category of ships that can be called into service for the State navy" (seit 1670): nfr. "category of citizens distinguished by their social condition" (seit 1792, Frey).—Ablt. Nfr. *classer* un matelot [*sailor*] "register in the class of his military sign-up" (seit 1767, Brunot 6).

Nfr. *déclasser* "be removed from the class in which one was classed; strike from the class register" (seit Boiste 1829); *déclassé* "individual fallen from a certain social class into an inferior class" (seit Lar 1869); *déclassement* "act of removal from a class" (seit 1863).—Nfr. *enclasser* "register (sailors) in their class" (Voltaire Siècle de Louis XIV; 1761, Brunot 6).

b. Nfr. *classe* "each of the large groups of animals, plants" (seit Enc 1753).—Ablt. Nfr. *classer* "distribute (animals, plants) by class; organize within a certain class; organize in a category" (seit Trév 1771); *classeur* "folder or chest with compartments used for classifying documents" (seit Besch 1845);

reunifies, comes back to itself and this is true childhood. Communion, which is granted by the father, consists neither in being plunged in the elementary, nor in being dragged away from it. It plunges back in.

The plunging back in *consounds*. It consounds with consonance and with the name. Onomastic symphony: "Jesus explains this unity (*Einigkeit*) in another way: 'If two or three of you shall agree as touching anything that ye shall ask (*bitten*), it shall be done for you of my father'. The expressions 'ask' (*bitten*) and 'vouchsafe' (*gewähren*))are relative strictly to a unification [*Vereinigung*] in respect of objects (πράγματα); it was only for a unification of this kind that the matter-of-fact language (*Wirklichkeitssprache*) of the Jews had words. But here the object in question can be nothing but the reflected unity (συμφονία τῶν δυοῖν ἒ τριῶν); regarded as an object, this is a beautiful relationship, but subjectively it is unification (*Vereinigung*); spirits cannot be one in objects proper. The beautiful relationship, a unity of two or three of you, is repeated in the harmony of the whole (*in der Harmonie des Ganzen*), is a sound (*Laut*), a consonance (*Einklang*) with the same harmony and is produced thereby. It *is* because it is in the harmony, because it is something divine. In this association (*Gemeinschaft*) with the divine, those who are at one are also (*zugleich*) in association with Jesus. Where two or three are united in my spirit (εἰς τὸ ὄνομά μου), as in Matthew 10:41), in that respect in which being (*Sein*) and eternal life fall to my lot, in which I *am*, then I am in the midst of them (*in ihrer Mitte*), and so is my spirit."

When Jesus explains to his disciples that he must die, that his death will not leave them orphaned but on the contrary will give them back filiation, that they will receive as much as what they think they are losing, they are frightened. In Peter's fright (*Erschrecken*) in particular, one understands what separates faith from its fulfillment (*der Abstand des Glaubens von der Vollendung*). They are scared like abandoned children but this is because they are not yet true children. Their faith is still addressed to an external God. "Everything lives in the Godhead, every living thing is its child, but the child carries the unity, the connection, the concord (*Einklang*) with the entire harmony, undisturbed though undeveloped, in itself. It begins with faith in gods outside itself." Through new splits and new reconciliations, it must form again the "circle" through which, in becoming a child again, it reestablishes the whole "God, the Son, the Holy Spirit!"

classement "act of classifying" (seit 1798); *inclassable* "unable to be classified" (seit 1890, Journ Gonc). Nfr. *classifier* "divide up according to a classification" (seit Raym 1832); *déclassifier* v. r. "remove from a classification" (1876).—Nfr. *classification* "methodical distribution of individuals by species, genus, class, etc." (seit Fér 1787); *classificatoire* adj. "relating to classification" (seit

1874); *classificateur* "one who makes classifications" (Besch 1845–1863, so Ste-Beuve. Lundis 14, 120).

3. a. Nfr. *classe* "category of students who follow each level of a course of study" (seit Est 1549); "teaching given to a class" (seit Ac 1740); "room where such teaching takes place" (seit Mon 1635, s. auch ALF 441 école; ALLo 1778); neuch. "company of pastors"; Paris "place where porters of a particular quarter wait to be employed" Rich 1680–1863).—Ablt. Ménades *quiasseux* "school pupil."

b. Nfr. *classe* "category of young men called up each year for military service" (seit 1863). Übertragen *être de la classe* "to be in one's second year of service; to have experience" (seit 1888, Daud).

Mfr. *clacyfier* "establish (a text) following classifications" (ca. 1500).

Lt. Classis, ursprünglich "aufgebot in militärischem Sinn" erhält durch die von Servius Tullius getroffene einteilung der bürger in sechs gruppen die bed. "volksklasse," sodann "landheer" und "flotte," endlich, zu Augustus zeit, auch "gruppe von knaben, die gemeinsam unterrichtet werden." In verschiedenen dieser bed. ist es vom fr. entlehnt worden: 1 aus der bed. "flotte" (wohl nur mit bezug auf das Altertum); 2 a aus der bed. "volksklasse," zuerst auch mit bezug auf das alte Rom, dann aber auf moderne verhältnisse übertragen; dabei ist b eine sekundäre verwendung dieser bed. In der naturwissenschaftlichen terminologie. 3 a aus der bed. "schulklasse"; b ist daraus übertragen, weil auch die jahresklasse der soldaten aus gleichaltrigen besteht.

In ausdrücken wie *faire ses classes, faire la classe* usw.

This is how he plunges back in. When Matthew talks of "plunging" (*tauchen*), he is not talking about immersion in water, about what is called baptism (*Taufe*). The name (ὄνομα) is the relation between the split and the reconciliation. In Matthew, Jesus asks where John's baptism comes from: from heaven or from man? In the consecration of spirit and character, (the) immersion must never be considered to be other than an accessory thing (*Nebensache*). John himself, at least according to Luke, presents water as the supplement. Of fire. It's when the people are wondering if *he* is not the Christ. "I indeed baptize you with water; but one mightier than I cometh, the latchet of whose shoes I am not worthy to unloose: he shall baptize you with the Holy Ghost and with fire." During the same scene, in the Gospel of John and in that of Mark, the fire disappears. But not the sandal straps. John still feels unworthy of undressing Christ and even of kneeling to undo the straps fastened around his feet.

But why does John like plunging bodies into water, even as an *ersatz*? Why did he baptize Jesus in the Jordan? John's desire carries him neither into the water nor out of the water. He negotiates with the liquid, engulfs the body in it to enjoy the dripping, gleaming, slippery emergence. He wants the plentitude of the aqueous universe but in order to look at it, which is possible only by regularly withdrawing the body from it, interrupting the effusion, the self-forgetting, returning to walking, to being upright. "John's habit . . . is an important and symbolical one. No feeling is so homogeneous (*homogen*) with the desire for the infinite, the longing to merge into the infinite, as the desire to immerse one's self (*sich begraben*) in a liquid plenitude (*Wasserfülle*). To plunge into it is to be confronted by an alien element (*ein Fremdes*) which at once (*sogleich*) flows round us on every side and which is felt at every point of the body. We are taken away from the world and the world from us. We are nothing but felt water which touches us where we are, and we are only where we feel it. In the liquid plenitude there is no gap, no restriction, no multiplicity, nothing specific. The feeling of it is the simplest, the least broken up [dissipated, unbound, *unzerstreuteste*]. After immersion a man comes up into the air again, separates himself from the water, is at once free from it and yet it still drips from him everywhere. So soon as the water leaves him, the world takes on specific characteristics again, and he comes back strengthened (*gestärkt*) to the consciousness of multiplicity.

classum lärm

1. Afr. *glas* "echoing sound, wailing" (12.-13. jh., BenS-Maure; Perl), *glais* (12. jh.), afr. mfr. *glai* (12.-15. jh.), pik. *glay* (Th 1564—Voult 1613). mfr. *mener grand glas* "make a lot of noise" (Th 1564—Mon 1636), mfr. *clas* "repercussion" D'Aubigné, apr. "cry, clamor"; afr. *a (un) glais* "with one voice, all together," apr. *a un clas;* mfr. *glai* "chirping of birds" (15. jh.); afr. *glas* "sort of trumpet" (Veng Al, R 56, 131), *glai* (1285), mfr. id. (1612); mfr. *claz* "summoning trumpet sound" (1530); mfr. *glai* "honor, happiness" Eust Desch.

2. Afr. *glas* "peel of all the bells of a church" (13. jh., Gdf; Guernes S Thomas), *glais* Chrestien, mfr. *claz* (poit. 1456), abress. *clars* pl. (Châtillon D. 1483, Ann Ain 1927), apr. *clar* (Hérault 15. jh. AM 18, 204), mfr. *glay* (1382), *clax* pl. (Rochelle 1465).

Afr. *glais* "slow tolling of the churchbell to announce someone's death throes, death, or burial" Florence, mfr. *glay* Guill Mach, Paris *glais* (1488, Gdf; Mén 1650), mfr. nfr. *glas* (seit Th 1564, doch bis Voult 1613 als speziell orl.), nfr. *glais* (Mon 1635—Trév 1771), Bonneval *glas* MAnt 2, 428, hbret. *gla*, Landujan *y a* ABret 15, 390, Loire I. *klā*, ang. *clâs*, poit. *kła*, Vendée *cliâ* (1807), bgât. *clas*, saint. *kyā*, kanad. *glas* pl., centr. *clas*, Allier *klā*, Varennes *clairs*, morv. *iâs*, Mâcon *clar*, verdch. *glia*, Côte d'Or *gyā*, Yonne *glais*, Vassy P. *guiais*, Créancey *ghiai* F 279, Gr Combe *kyas*, Jura *gya*, Vaudioux *(ë)gliés* pl., Thônes *glié*, Vaux *tyår*, Lyon *clior*, Mornant *glió*, St-Genis *lyôr*, Loire *klar*, stéph. *clo*, Cr. *gya*, Estr. *głā*, voir. *clias*, Cordéac *klēr*, Trem. *tšyer*, mdauph. *klē*, Die *clers*, HAlpes, Lallé, Barc. *klars* pl., pr. id., *kla, klas*, Nice *clar*, lang. *classes* pl., Aniane *klar* Zaun 95, Ariège, H Gar. *klases* pl., Tarn, aveyr. *klas*, Lozère id. (nordwesten), *klases* pl., vel. *clas, gla*, Aurillac *clar* Verm 317, Ytrac, St-Simon *clar*, Puy D. *xya*, Vinz. Chav. *kłyar*, lim. *clhar* DD. gask. *glas*. ALF 650; G de Guer 74—87; ALLo 2087.—Übertragen nfr. *glas* "cannon shots fired at intervals during military funerals" (Boiste 1803—DG), "sound of a bomb, or of fireworks" BL 1808.

When we look out into a cloudless sky and into the simple, shapeless, plain of an eastern horizon, we have no sense of the surrounding air, and the play of our thoughts is something different from mere gazing. In immersion there is *only one* feeling, there is only forgetfulness of the world, a solitude which has repelled everything, withdrawn itself from everything."

Such is the experience of Jesus after John has plunged him into the waters of the Jordan. The sky has split open, the spirit has descended on him in the form of a dove and the voice recognizes him as his son. After the forty days in the desert and the temptation of Satan, the work of splitting is done. But this splitting, like the death of Jesus, which is analogous to it, allows the return to childhood and to the liquid element. By dying, by leaving his disciples, by emerging, Jesus returns to his father who is greater than he is (*Heimkehr zu seinem Vater, der größer ist als er*). He leaves the water to allow himself to be penetrated by the spirit of the one who is greater than he. But by the same token, he allows his young disciples to plunge into spirit as into water and let themselves in turn be penetrated by it: "'All power is given unto me in heaven and upon earth. Go ye therefore unto all nations and make them your disciples so that ye consecrate them into connection with the Father, Son, and Holy Ghost, so that that united spirit may flow round them and be felt round them just as the water touches every part of the body of those immersed in it, and lo, I am with you always, even unto the end of the world.' . . . He is with them and their essence is permeated (*pénétré, durchdrungen*) by the Holy Spirit . . ."

In this movement that Mark, locked up in the "Jewish language," rendered poorly according to Hegel, emergence drags the body from the natural element, water or the mother, only to plunge the spirit in the paternal element. The father penetrates the spirit—the metaphor of the father is therefore the metaphor of the mother—on condition that the body has broken with the mother, i.e. on the condition of its death. I.e. of its birth, its erection, its resurrection. Birth only emerges *as such* in resurrection. Death is therefore this equal inequality of the father and the mother—the spiritual metaphor, Christianity, nomination, baptism, etc. In the chain of these values, no term can be decided on as accident, the predicate, the narrowing determination of another.

At least narrowness regularly gives its form to the relation of one to the other, without the slightest conceptual privilege. Each is narrower than the other, none is

Ablt.—Apr. *clasejar* "to ring the bells; convoke by ringing the *clas,*" Tarn *classexá* "toll the bells for a long time."
Zuss.—Apr. *aclassar* "to make a noise" (12. jh.).—Boussac *glas d'emprunt* "tolling for someone having died outside the parish." Trans *glas à bouillie* "tolling for a baptism."
Von lt. Classicum "trompetenstoss; trompete" ist früh ein Classum zurückgebildet worden, das durch die frühmlt. ablt. *conclassare* (= klt. *convocare classico*) bezeugt ist. Classum lebt in it. *chiasso* "lärm," emil. *stšas* (z. b. Firenzuola d'Arda, Casella 19), Rovigno *stšaso* Ive 35, sowie im gallorom., wo die klt. bed. zum teil noch erkennbar ist. Aus dem fr. entlehnt me. *glase* "trompetenstoss" Arch 109, 331. Im gallorom. wird es auf den klang der glocken eingeschränkt, so auch piem. *tšas* AGI 14, 363. Aus dem fr. entlehnt bret. *glâz*. Im fr. gibt es, in allen bed., neben der form mit *a* eine mit *ai;* die entstehung dieses vokals ist noch nicht abgeklärt.—Gröber ALL 1, 547; Z 15, 497; ML 1965." *Von Wartburg*

Glas fleshes out a grammatological reading of Saussure, yet again, precisely, on the page of the *Course* that establishes the patronage of linguistics ("It can be said, then, that signs that are wholly arbitrary realize better than others the ideal of the semiological process; that is why language, the most complex and universal of all systems of expression, is also the most characteristic; in this sense linguistics can become the master-pattern [*le patron general*] for all branches of semiology, *although* language is only one particular semiological system"). I underlined "although": violent instituting of patronage. After that comes the opposition between signifier and symbol: the latter is not arbitrary, it isn't empty, "there is the rudiment of a natural bond between the signifier and the signified. The symbol of justice, a pair of scales, could not be replaced by just another symbol, such as a chariot." But it can always be

broader than all the others—that's enough to force, wound, oblige one to think—reason.

In glory, with the erection of the stillborn anointed one, the equal inequality of the father and the mother has just appeared. It appears, it is therefore in the phenomenon, in the light, in glory. But what appears is stated, in the voice, as a play of liquid and solid. It's all said via the slipping of a step, the surrection of a dripping limit, always unequal to itself.

Hegel's reading of Christianity seems to describe a reconciliation, to say it all in a word: between faith and being, *Glauben* and *Sein*. "Faith presupposes a being (*Glauben setzt ein Sein voraus*)." Union, communion, reconciliation are one with *Sein*. We're touching the same sign here. Communion and being have the same signification: "*Vereinigung und Sein sind gleichbedeutend*."

Yet the fate of Christianity starts a new fragmenting. The word *fate* already has this meaning in the Hegelian context. Splitting and unilaterality in love, which *is not yet* religion, then in religion itself and in the rock of the church which cannot resolve in this world the painful opposition between living and dead, the divine and the real. The Christian religion remains sublime. Jesus has left, separated himself from the world, leaving his disciples without present, suspended between memory and hope. The accusation against Jesus' political passivity, against his idealism, now gets louder: he preferred to reconstitute with his father, in ideality, a life otherwise disappointed. He was not able to struggle in the world against the Jewish reality. And so, paradoxically, he had to repeat Judaism. Like Abraham, he separated from his family; what is more, he loved no woman, engendered no child. He even left his mother. In order to flee warfare and announce love, he brought the sword to earth, pitting the son against his father, the daughter against her mother, the daughter-in-law against her parents-in-law. His abandoned disciples, like the Jews, could only speak of their "absent master," pray together, fail in their political efforts. When their enemies accused some of their societies of practicing "community of women," they were "neither courageous enough nor pure enough to merit this accusation nor to be ashamed of it." They often lived in emigration, in expectation, in the sign. It all happens around a sepulcher. No doubt the memory of the rotting body was first of all erased in the intuition of glory, but it returned, it insisted, to the same extent that the splitting continued its work. Because the dead body

replaced, by a sword, by a woman, etc. And its naturality is thus always already cut into. And the flower, is it a symbol or sign?

But that isn't yet the case involving *glas* in the strict sense. The same page of the *Course* includes a *remark* and responds to two objections. And it is then, as if by chance, that the example of *glas* comes up, treated by Saussure as a word ("Words like French *fouet* ('whip') or *glas* ('knell') . . ."). The remark concerns arbitrariness, the word "arbitrary": "The word 'arbitrary' also calls for comment. The term should not imply that the choice of the signifier is left entirely to the speaker (we shall see below that the individual does not have the power to change a sign in any way once it has become established in the linguistic community); I mean that it is *unmotivated,* i.e. arbitrary in relation to the signified, with which it has no natural attachment [*attache*] in reality." The signifier (flower or knell, for example) is constraining for the subject ("the individual") but is presumed to be "unmotivated" with respect to the signified (which? where? when?), to the referent (which? where? when?). What is the individual? reality? nature? And especially attachment? The whole work of clang could at least provide material for the re-elaboration of those questions: upstream from the word (and from linguistics, then, which remains that of the word, indeed of the noun, even when it denies that), from the opposition between *physis* and its other (where to place the flower?) and in particular in another, practico-theoretical, tied and knotted [*cravatée*] logic of the bit(e), of what remains from the detachment of the attachment and always comes to add to it.

Following the remark, Saussure's response to two objections. They concern *onomatopoeias* and *interjections,* and they shouldn't come close to "refuting our thesis [*ne sont pas . . . dangereuses pour notre thèse*]." One may first wonder how a thesis can be put in danger (that is responded to elsewhere). Here in any case is the response to the objection regarding onomatopoeia: "In concluding let us consider two objections that might be raised to the establishment of Principle I:

stays there, in the interminable decomposition of relics, the spirit never rises high enough, it is held back like a sort of effluvium, a sort of gas fermenting above the cadaver. A sort of heaviness "draws it towards the earth" (*ihn zur Erde zieht*) and "the God was thus supposed to hover [*schweben*] midway between heaven's infinity, and earth, this collection of plain restrictions." Spirit is again like a kind of eagle that would like to rise up whereas "lead" (*Blei*) weighs down its wings or its feet. Now Jesus looks like Moses. He is decidedly too Jewish. One might think he was a bit Greek: "like Hercules" who rose from his pyre, he "soared" up from the "tomb." But the shrines and (the) prayers of the Greeks are for the benefit of a god who does not carry on fighting on earth, who no longer remains in his body. In his wandering and in his teaching Christ remains nailed or rotting: "monstrous liaison" (*ungeheure Verbindung*).

The accusation keeps getting harsher, and above all becomes political. Encouraging utopia led to the unleashing of fanatical violence. Escape into the void produces atrocity and devastation. Flight is impossible. The too-powerful fate of the world not only weighs on the Church, it acts within it. Even if it is not provoked by them, this situation is exploited by "the great hypocrites" (*große Heuchler*), the falsely sanctimonious, actors, powerful priests. The structure of their ruse is analyzed: "They devised for every civil action (*bürgerliche Handlung*) or for every expression of desire and passion a hiding place (*einen Schlupfwinkel,* a corner, a retreat) in the unity in order by this fraud (*Betrug*) to retain at once (*zugleich*) possession and enjoyment of every restriction and yet at one and the same time (*zugleich*) to renounce it."

Such is the very great calculus to which the anointed of the Lord has given rise in history. In his very passivity, in the *actio in distans* of the miracle and the scission, in his false starts. Hegel speaks often, expressly, of the unconscious, or let's say at least the unconsciousness in which this fate operates. His reading is thus double: on the one hand Christianity succeeded in lifting the Jewish limitation; and the death of Christ allowed the sons to be sons; baptism took place. On the other, Christianity repeats, at a slightly higher level, the Jewish cut: the disciples remained like sheep without a shepherd, the name unrecognized. Failure of filiation, of the family, of the city, hypocrisy, calculation, violence, appropriation. Stones (*Pierres*).

It is not the reading that is double, but Christianity, and

1) Onomatopoeia might be used to prove that the choice of the signifier is not always arbitrary. But onomatopoeic formations are never organic elements of a linguistic system. Besides, their number is much smaller than is generally supposed. Words like French *fouet* ('whip') or *glas* ('knell') may strike certain ears with suggestive sonority, but to see that they have not always had this property we need only examine their Latin forms (*fouet* is derived from *fagus,* 'beech-tree,' *glas* from *classicum,* 'sound of a trumpet'). The quality of their present sounds, or rather the quality that is attributed to them, is a fortuitous result of phonetic evolution.
As for authentic onomatopoeic words (e.g. glug-glug [*glou-glou*], tick-tock [*tic-tac*], etc.) not only are they limited in number, but they are also chosen arbitrarily, for they are only approximate and more or less conventional imitations of certain sounds (cf. English 'bow-wow' and French *ouaoua*). In addition, once these words have been introduced into the language, they are to a certain extent drawn [*entraînées*] into the same evolution—phonetic, morphological, etc.—that other words undergo (cf. pigeon, from Vulgar Latin *pīpīo,* derived in turn from an onomatopoeic formation): obvious proof that they lose something of their original character in order to assume that of the linguistic sign in general, which is unmotivated."

We'll leave these strange agglutinations of examples with inaudible consonance to work all on their own: the supreme question of the beech and the knell, beech as becoming-whip, the seemingly quite random association (we'll talk more about that) of *glou-glou* and *tic-tac,* those "authentic onomatopoeic words."

Saussure thus seems to know what "authentic onomatopoeic words" are. But that knowledge presumes that one can seize the original instant at which they hadn't yet been "drawn into . . . evolution." Where to recognize that pure instant, alone capable of drawing the dividing line here? Further recourse to a pure origin, etymological this time: the extent of their etymological filiation allows one to demonstrate

the structure of sublation. The analysand is unconscious of the truth of his process. That truth appears to him only in philosophy, in the future perfect of absolute religion.

The Christian religion is already posited as the absolute religion. So it is in the absolute religion that the split remains; and it remains for all times and all the figures of Christianity: "In all the forms of the Christian religion which have been developed in the advancing fate of the ages, there lies this fundamental characteristic of opposition in the divine, which is supposed to be present in consciousness only, never in life." The representative nature of the presence of the divine which stands *before* consciousness and keeps one waiting for it in life, which leaves religion in an anticipatory posture—these are already, from these early texts on, features that the *Phenomenology of Spirit* will recognize, will have recognized, in absolute religion, i.e. in Christianity. Jesus in the end chose, elected (*wählte*) the scission, but this gesture cannot be simple. By cutting and running, he declared war in the name of reconciliation, he divided himself in his own scission, braced against the division itself, multiplying it and thus raising it to infinity. What happened, like an accident, to Christianity as it ought to (have) be(en) is therefore not an accident at all. This is the very definition of fate and can be recognized by the fact that Jesus did not hallucinate, nor even love his death. Or if he did hallucinate or was hallucinated, this was not for himself. "To every dreamer who dreams for himself alone, death is welcome: but the man who dreams for the fulfilment of a great plan can feel nothing but grief in leaving the stage [*Schauplatz*] on which his plan was to have been worked out. Jesus died in the confidence that his plan would not miscarry."

This scission has effects the political analysis of which is scarcely begun. It is developed in fragments from the same period, in particular in *The German Constitution*. Hegel begins to study more closely the problems of political economy, he reads Stewart's *Inquiry into*

that *glas* and *fouet* haven't retained onomatopoeic value. Will one trust etymology, and even a historicist and unilinear concept of etymology in order to analyze the functioning of a linguistic signifier and recognize its belonging "organic[ally]" to the "linguistic system?" Does an element leave language when it doesn't conform to its presumed semantic origin?

What are the "organic elements of a linguistic system?" Words? But "words" can become onomatopoeic, by means of functional grafting, in part or in whole, through decomposition or recomposition, detachment or reattachment. But onomatopoeias can become words, and since their being "drawn"—neither an accident nor coming from outside the system—has always already begun, the judges, those supposedly in possession of the criteria of systematicity no longer know what belongs to whom or to what.

The "authentic onomatopoeia" is fleeting, and with it all the preceding or subsequent oppositions. Moreover, the concept of onomatopoeia presumes, in the manipulation being made of it here, a very simplified structure of imitation (between noise made by the thing and sound in the language). In this respect the resemblance between *glas*—and what in fact? the sound of a bell?—between *fouet* and the swishing sound of lashes, is weak, even nonexistent. One wonders why Saussure chose these "words" as examples of presumed *onoma*topoeias. He must remove all rigor from his empirical statements: these words "may strike" (what luck: like the whip and knell, words "strike"; like the whip and knell words make a noise, and it is the ear that they strike. As though there were something like bits of whip and knell in every word), they "may"—potentially—"strike with suggestive sonority," but only "certain ears." In other words these examples are too badly or too well chosen: no one can consider

the Principles of Political Economy. But even if the politico-economic consequences of the early essays are not developed, they are conceptually marked. In particular as to the place of the family. Is that to say that a saturation to come will fill out a space whose edges and inner limits will remain untouched? Doubtful. The almost total silence on woman, the daughter, the sister, the mother probably signals something other than a gap to be filled within a field left intact. What happens when this silence is broken, for example in the *Phenomenology*?

The most general question would now take the following form: how does the sublation of religion into philosophy happen? How on the other hand does the sublation of the family structure into the structure of civil (bourgeois) society happen? In other words, within *Sittlichkeit* (the notion of which begins to be elaborated in *The Difference between Fichte's and Schelling's System of Philosophy*, in *Faith and Knowledge* and in the article on *Natural Law)*, how is the passage from the family syllogism to the syllogism of civil society effected? These two problems intersect at a point to be determined. It is indicated in an essential way in the penultimate chapter of the *Phenomenology*: absolute religion which immediately precedes its own truth, *Sa*. At the end of the syllogism (natural religion, aesthetic religion, revealed-manifest religion), Christianity, the absolute religion, is itself developed according to the following syllogism: 1. Spirit within itself: the Trinity; 2. Spirit in its alienation: the Kingdom of the Son; 3. Spirit in its plenitude: the Kingdom of Spirit. Through the death of the mediating term, the reconciliation still remains affected by the competing opposition of a beyond (*Gegensatze eines Jenseits*); it remains far distant, in the distance of a future (the Last Judgment for the religious community) and in the distance of a past (the Incarnation of God). It is not present. Present in the heart, it is cut from consciousness, divided in two (*entzweit*). Its effectivity is broken. What enters into consciousness as the in-itself is reconciliation inasmuch as it stands beyond; but what enters into it as presence is the world that awaits its transfiguration; whence the division between the spiritual and the political.

Now this ultimate scission between presence and representation, between the for-itself and the in-itself, takes the form of an inequality between father and mother, in the

fouet and *glas* as authentic onomatopoeic words. Moreover, no one has done so, and moreover, there is no authentic onomatopoeia. But instead of concluding from that that neither is there any longer, therefore, any authentic arbitrariness, instead of being interested in *contaminated* effects of onomatopoeia and arbitrariness, of language's being drawn (toward the whip or toward the knell), he runs ahead of the "danger" to save the thesis of the arbitrariness of the sign.
If arbitrariness and un-motivation can happen to the claimed "original character" of such "authentic onomatopoeic words," why would a re-motivation not be able to re-draw the supposed arbitrariness? If arbitrariness were pure, that wouldn't be possible. Yet it is possible, attested to at least by what Saussure wants to keep within the status of artificial, illusory, and chance *attribution:* "The quality of their present sounds, or rather the quality that is attributed to them, is a fortuitous result of phonetic evolution."

What will remain of the internal system of language—these "organic elements of a linguistic system"—once one has purified it, stripped it of all these qualities, of these attributions, of this evolution? What will remain of it and where will it be found? And on the basis of what are these attributed "qualities" and these "result[s] of the phonetic evolution" to be considered "fortuitous?" The latter word is moreover surprising: it's all as if the processes of re-motivation and re-naturalization escaped all necessity, whereas arbitrariness, for its part, would have nothing fortuitous in its functioning. Re-motivating arbitrary signs would be fortuitous—and hence arbitrary. And, on top of that, the choice of examples of alleged onomatopoeias is supposedly "arbitrary" (Saussure's word). One could follow at length the effects of this opposition between arbitrariness and motivation inside a logic that, permanently presupposing knowledge of what constitutes freedom, consciousness, nature, necessity, runs out of breath trying to delimit the inside and outside of a linguistic system, to frame it, with all the assurances that are invested in such a frame.

relation to the father and the relation to the mother. The passage from absolute religion to *Sa* is prepared as the sublation of that inequality.

Is it an analogy? Let's leave the analogy hanging a few lines before *Absolute Knowing*: "Just as (*So wie*) the *individual* [*einzelne* is emphasized: it's Jesus, the historic individual] divine man has a father existing-*in-itself* (ansich*seienden Vater*) and merely an *actual* mother (wirkliche *Mutter*), so too (*so*) the universal divine man, the religious community (*die Gemeinde*), has as its father its *own activity* (*ihr* eigenes Tun) and *knowledge* (*Wissen*), but for its mother it has *eternal love*, which it merely *feels* (*die sie nur* fühlt) but does not intuit in its consciousness as an actual immediate *object*."

It is too soon to read this passage. Let's hold on to just one indication of it and a program: what is at stake in the passage to *Sa* resembles a transformation of the familial relation. Even if it is by figure or formality that one calls it a family relation, its ontological import is undeniable. In the constitution of an absolute onto-logic, the family discourse cannot be relegated to the subordinate realms of a rhetoric, an anthropology or a psychology. Such a familial dehiscence, once it appeals to *Sa*—to philosophy—is an essential stake in the history of the meaning of being. The appeal to absolute knowing is inscribed in it. The place of this inscription is also an un-consciousness rigorously situated between *The Phenomenology of Spirit* and the *Greater Logic*, at the articulation of *Sa*.

What does the family still need? And why does it need philosophy? Why does one need *Sa* only *en famille*?

The split—which reaches its absolute in the absolute religion—is the need for philosophy. Philosophy issued, as its proper object, from Christianity whose truth it is, from the Holy Family (out of) which it sublates. *The Need for Philosophy* (*Befürdnis der Philosophie*) (the subtitle of a text roughly contemporaneous with *The Spirit of Christianity*) emerges in the *between,* in the narrow gap of a scission, a split, a separation, a division into two. One divides into two, such is the painful source of philosophy: "*Entzweiung ist der Quell des Bedürfnisses der Philosophie*." Reason then proceeds, busies itself in thinking the wound, reducing the division, returning back before the source, back with infinite unity. To sublate the terms of the opposition, the effects of the division, such would be "the interest of reason," the only interest of

And what if *mimesis* no longer allowed itself to be audited [*arraisonner*], required to provide accounts and reasons, to submit to an identity-check within such a frame? What if it operated along lines and necessities whose laws are interwoven and determined otherwise? With resources that would lead inside the system of language, importing *into* linguistics all the questions and all the questioning codes that are being developed here, around "proper name" and "signature" effects, carrying off in the course of this breaking and entering all the rigorous criteria of framing—between inside and out—taking away the frame along with the inside and out, the picture or the thing (imagine the damage resulting from a theft that would deprive you of frames alone, and of any possibility of reframing your objects of value or objects of art). And if *mimesis* were to cause the internal system of language not to exist or to make it so that one never uses it, or at least that one uses it only by contaminating it, and to make that contamination inevitable, thus regular and "normal," taking part in the system and its functioning, taking part in it, that is to say also making of it, the whole, part of a whole that is bigger than it? Saussure's conclusion: "Onomatopoeic formations and interjections are of secondary importance, and their symbolic origin is in part open to dispute." (Arbitrariness too, then. As for the so-called "symbolic" origin, in part open to dispute, thus in part symbolic, it derives from the logic of the bit(e) and of antherection. Follow the consequences.)

Immediately following that conclusion, there's section 3: "*Principle II: The Linear Nature of the Signifier.*"

Once again, what is being read here is objections or questions addressed not to "Saussure," but to two pillars of the *Course* that oppose each other by leaning on each other in order to hold up a powerful edification. As we know, on the other hand, Saussure himself elsewhere takes account of the "relative motivation" of the sign. He mistrusts everything that could imply the reduction of lan-

philosophy (*Solche festgewordene Gegensätze aufzuheben, ist das einzige Interesse der Vernunft*). The progress of culture has brought oppositions such as spirit/matter, soul/body, faith/understanding, freedom/necessity and all those that derive from them back towards the great couple reason/sensibility or intelligence/nature, i.e. "with respect to the universal concept, of absolute subjectivity and absolute objectivity." Now these oppositions are posited as such by the understanding which "imitates" (*ahmt*) reason. This enigmatic relation, this rational *mimesis* thus organizes the whole history of philosophy as history of need, history of the interest of reason in sublating the two. Reason is another name for the power of unification (*Macht der Vereinigung*). When this force weakens or disappears, the need for philosophy makes itself felt.

All the finite syntheses that, in art and religion, give themselves out as absolute syntheses, are therefore merely going to imitate the absolute operation of reason. In this respect they are still so many "amusing games."

The need for philosophy is not yet philosophy. There is a *not yet* of philosophy. Philosophy—already—announces itself in it. Now—and this is an essential proposition of reason and hence of Hegelian philosophy—philosophy has its beginning only in itself. It is the beginning, as beginning of itself, self-positing of the beginning. How are we to reconcile these two axioms: philosophy proceeds only from itself and yet is the daughter of a need or an interest that is not yet philosophy?

In its own positing, philosophy *presupposes*. It precedes and replaces itself in its own thesis. It comes before itself and substitutes itself for itself. A *pro-* movement: one might be tempted to translate the fundamental concept of *Voraussetzung* as pro-position or pros-thesis rather than as presupposition, as is usually done.

The need for philosophy stands as a limen, a forecourt, a vestibule, a step, a stair, a threshold (*Vorhof*), a pre-emption: "The need of philosophy can be called the *presupposition* [*Voraussetzung*] of philosophy if philosophy, which begins with itself, has to be furnished with some sort of vestibule (*Vorhof . . . gemacht werden soll*)."

The question of the family, and therefore of religion, is thus posed in the preamble; the family is at home only in time—where reason has not absolutely

guage to a "nomenclature" (*nomenclature—calare nomen*—calls names, classifies by name, honors and gives renown to names, but by the same token, by inscribing them in taxonomic networks and intersections among generalities, sets them decomposing, destroying the singular integrity of their being proper names). In *Anagrams* he even attempted a "re-motivating" reading that is barely forgiven him, as a reverie, a learned one granted, and practiced at a superior degree, but in essence, within the existing framework of the scientific institution, crazy [*dingue*]. (Let's forewarn those who would be mad enough to remotivate this last word that it has no attested etymological filiation with *dinguer.* A real pity but it can be repaired.

For poetics: "*Dingo,* adj[ective] and n[oun], m[asculine]. (Dingot, end 19th century; from *dingue*). Fam[iliar], "mad." Vide *Cinglé, dingue . . .*" "*Dingue,* adj. et n. (1915, unknown origin, perhaps from *dengue**, cf. slang la dingue, "yellow fever" (1890); or from *dinguer*). Pop[ular]. Mad, dingbat. He is a little whacky. You should be sent to the crazies." *Dinguer,* i[ntransitive] v[erb] (1833; from an onomat[opoeic] rad[ical] *din-, ding-,* expressing the side-to-side movement (of bells, etc.). Fam. (from a verb), to fall. "*J'eus un éblouissement et m'en allai dinguer au pied d'un marronnier* [I felt faint and went and fell down at the foot of a chestnut tree]" (Gide). *Envoyer dinguer:* repel violently, and fig[uratively] "show out unceremoniously." "*Si c'était moi qui avais voulu les lui presenter, ce qu'il m'aurait envoyé dinguer* [If it were I who wanted to introduce them, he would have thrown me out in no time]" (Proust). *Dengue, n[oun], f[eminine] (1866, Spanish word, "simpering"). Endemo-epidemic disease from equatorial regions, caused by a filterable virus and characterized by pain in the muscles and joints, producing a rigid gait that seems affected. Hom[onym] *Dingue.*" *Dictionnaire Robert* this time.)

But isn't re-motivation, whether naïve or subtle, always a little crazy? Isn't that what a theoretician of motivation might think: "The constraint of demotivation—or rather the incapacity to demotivate—is one of the characteristic symptoms of aphasia. Patients interpret compound words as if they obeyed the rules of charades: *chiendent* [couchgrass] = *chien* [dog] + *dent* [tooth] (Goldstein).

reappropriated itself, has not got back with itself in its absolute familiarity, where it does not yet dwell. The crossing of the vestibule—the family, religion—is the passage from the pro-position to the philosophical position that is its truth. Philosophical truth says: I am always following [*je suis toujours*] the family and religion.

Given this, the death of God, the Christian advent, infinite pain, unction, the trinity, Calvary, and resurrection are played out on the forecourt, even form a sort of *representation*—like the elliptical glory of a tympan—*before* the erected edifice of philosophy.

The limen of the "speculative Good Friday": "But the pure concept or infinity as the abyss of nothingness (*Abgrund des Nichts*) in which all being is engulfed (*versinkt*), must signify the infinite grief [of the finite] purely as a moment (*rein als Moment*) of the supreme Idea, and no more than a moment. Formerly, the infinite grief only existed historically (*geschichtlich*) in the formative process of culture. It existed as the feeling (*Gefühl*) that 'God Himself is dead,' upon which the religion of more recent times rests; the same feeling that Pascal expressed in so to speak sheerly empirical form: 'la nature est telle qu'elle *marque* partout un Dieu *perdu* et dans l'homme et hors de l'homme.' [Nature is such that it *signifies* everywhere a *lost* God both within and outside man.] By marking this feeling as a moment of the supreme Idea, the pure concept must give philosophical existence to what used to be either the moral precept (*Vorschrift*) that we must sacrifice the empirical being (*Wesens*), or the concept of formal abstraction. Thereby it must re-establish for philosophy the Idea of absolute freedom and along with it the absolute Passion, the speculative Good Friday in place of the historic (*historisch*) Good Friday. Good Friday must be speculatively re-established in the whole truth and harshness of its Godforsakenness (*Ungründlichere*). Since the more serene, less well grounded, and more individual style of the dogmatic philosophies and of the natural religions must vanish, the highest totality can and must achieve its resurrection solely from this harsh consciousness of loss, encompassing everything, and ascending in all its earnestness and out of its deepest ground to the most serene freedom of its shape."

The family never stops occupying the scene and yet one has the impression that it is never talked about. The philosophical object called "family" seems to withdraw ceaselessly. It is true that the onto-theological premises, the infinite nucleus of the family structure, of nomination, certainly of filiation,

Remotivation accompanies every chronic mental regression. . . . Recovery is accompanied by the progressive return of demotivated expressions.
The frenzied ideas of schizophrenics can be interpreted as *lived metaphors*." (Fonagy, "*Motivation et remotivation, Comment se dépasser?*" in *Poétique* 11)

That is no doubt true. But what relevant conceptual grasp can the motivation/demotivation-unmotivation opposition deliver to us once one escapes the "chronic mental regression" of remotivation only to risk the "verbal regression" of demotivation? Six pages further along: "It is interesting to see that the tendency toward demotivation—one of the principal forces of linguistic evolution—can be found at the source of a profound verbal regression." No doubt "verbal regression" is not to be confused simply with "mental regression" (even though in that outdated code one has difficulty distinguishing them): no doubt also that the author is here aiming at "mathematical language" as the example of perfect demotivation. But if mathematical language (is it a language?) alone can "bring to an end" the process of demotivation, then all "natural" language has something to do with "chronic mental regression" and "schizophrenia."

That is no doubt true and why not? But the author also counts the activity of "schizophrenic patients" as demotivation! The concept of motivation is therefore too loose and its presuppositions too obscure. They lead one to conclude, following the schemas of Condillac, Rousseau, and others, that progress is a regression (a good and/or bad recession toward the origin, or even on the other side of the origin): "The genesis

are visible. But the whole fundamental syllogistic is dominated by the father/son relation about which we might wonder whether it opens or closes the possibility of the family. It seems that this domination belongs to the essence of the Holy Family. Now it is in moving on to *Gottlosigkeit* and harsh impiety that one accomplishes the Supper; in so doing one develops speculatively what was merely historical in it. So long as we remain with the Holy Family, it looks as though there is not yet a problematic of the family properly speaking. Unless the Holy Family is the family properly speaking, the sole essential paradigm of any authentic family.

For what indeed is lacking in the Holy Family? What can be *absent* in it and what does *absent* mean in this case? Is it the father who is absent? Is it the mother? Since Joseph is absent and Mary is a virgin, the son is the son of the Father: what is lacking are the father and the mother, the one from the finite "point of view," the other from the infinite "point of view." But this dissociation between the two points of view is the very thing that is criticized by the speculative dialectic. The relation of the Holy Family to the earthly family is played out in this strange game or musical score [*partie ou partition*] for two, three, and four players, that works over the early texts and "develops" throughout the later system. In still speaking of development, we are simply naming, without resolving, a difficulty we have now recognized.

The problematic of the "earthly" family has *Sittlichkeit* as its conceptual space. Now this space is *not yet* opened, defined, determined in *The Spirit of Christianity*. That does not mean that Hegel had not yet discovered or developed the concept of *Sittlichkeit*: rather it shows that it could not be effectively, historically deployed in Christianity as such. Christianity makes the family both possible and impossible. The political limit (divorce between spiritual action and "worldly action," scission between the beyond and this world, unfinished reconciliation between the father and the Son, etc.), compromises the totality and reintroduces a new schism. This must be overcome: one thus moves on to the syllogism of *Sittlichkeit* which is developed in the State, following the stages of the family and civil society. *Sittlichkeit* has its *departure* here: both its origin and what takes it away from its origin. It *issues* from Christianity, the offspring of the Holy Family. Development, then, and break: response to the question of method.

The essential features of *Sittlichkeit* are apparent in the *Difference. . .*, *Faith and Knowledge,* and the article on

and evolution of language is a permanent struggle between tendencies that push toward demotivation and those that favor remotivation. Language owes its birth to motivation but would not be able to evolve without permanently having recourse to the remotivation of signs and structures." But what does one say, then, and what are the stakes, forms and forces of that struggle? Why does it immobilize its representation of itself in a duel between constraint and freedom, motivation and arbitrariness, nature and *thesis*.

It is not *a* thesis that is structurally in danger here but *the* thesis, being motivated to demotivate. At this precise point, if de-motivation is motivated, if indeed "theory *thesei* . . . the categorical disavowal of all motivation . . . is a defence, a protection against the attraction exercised by this too weakly disguised content," then the simple alternative of two opposing forces (motivation/non-motivation) within a homogeneous field cannot account for the internal and uneven division of each force: re-motivation is also apotropaic.

No doubt a certain logic of repression is indispensable and irreducible here, and it is very much lacking in modern reflection on the problem of "motivation." But it is not sufficient to fall back on "notions" from psychoanalysis to resolve the problem on the basis of principle and to start a systematic classification of the elements in play. For example, concluding precisely that "each sound of language is a set of distinctive articulating and acoustic traits, as a result lending itself to representation of several drives at once," the author of "*Bases pulsionnelles de la phonation*" complicates all the previous propositions retroactively and even risks contradicting or compromising them. And what would happen if the drives (what is that about?) were not content to compete by means of economy within a single acoustic or phonic "representation," but divided themselves rather, or even undecided one by one in their internal contradiction?

What interest

against class, clang of classes, right here, right here and now. Fate of the same name always in play. It's written with detachment.

Natural Law. But the great syllogism of the *Philosophy of Right* is not as such visible in them.

The point here is to impose a speculative science of right, a speculative concept of *Sittlichkeit*; and in order to do so to criticize simultaneously empiricism and formalism. These two demarcations are always inseparable, for essential reasons. In the course of this double critique, the question of the family seems to intervene only as an example. If one wishes to find out, for example, in what marriage consists, that structured totality of conjugal union, how should one proceed? The empiricist never wants to anticipate: he claims to proceed passively, faithfully, to recount, recite (*erzählen*) what he believes he sees, to enumerate a certain number of predicates that come to meet him. He says "marriage is this, and then that, and again that." This supposed concrete content is already in a situation of formal abstraction with regard to the total unity that the narrator wishes to explore. But as he cannot fail to presuppose a principle of unity—what is called marriage—he uncritically picks out a predicate and, through the "exclusion" of others, places it in a dominant situation. He makes of it "the essence and the goal." He says for example that the essence of the "conjugal relation" resides in the education of the children or else in the community of property. Which limits the concrete unity of conjugal development (its total syllogism), and affects the "organic relation," affects it with violent abstraction, indeed, but also with a stain: *das ganze organische Verhältnis bestimmt und verunreinigt*, it determines and sullies the whole organic relation. Why would the empiricist procedure sully the essence of marriage by situating it in the education of children or the community of property? Perhaps in overlooking love. *Verunreinigt* could just as well be *veruneinigt,* a synonym of *entzweit*: divides, disunites, cuts.

This example only takes up three lines but it comes very quickly, as soon as the project of a philosophical science of *Sittlichkeit* is formulated. Starting from the "absolute idea" one must consider "the nature and relation of the sciences of the *Sittlichen* as philosophical sciences, and to their relation with what is called the positive science of law." Now when this science is constituted, when *Sittlichkeit* is defined from the speculative point of view, the family will form its first moment. So here it is not merely an example and its place is not fortuitous.

The two features invoked (community of property and education of children) will never be disqualified as

For if proper nicknames come back down to (Our Lady of the) flowers, the latter are cut from the mother.

Detached rather.

Detach.

Can one do without that word here? Detached: like the grandest style.

Cutting, de-liaison, certainly, but also representative delegation, the sending of a detachment, on a mission to the other, to oneself: "The wing [muslin wing, "she," Death] . . . had detached a . . . tie to represent It . . ."

And as with all fabrics, when one wants to restore the text of the Immaculate Conception, the tie detaches.

With this detachment, re-elaborate—as a problem of the signet, of the signature and the mother's name—the alternative between formalism and biographism, the unnarratable and oh so classic question of the subject in literature. "Thus, in the eyes of Our bewildered Lady, the little faggots from Pigalle to Place Blanche lost their loveliest adornment, their names lost their corolla, like the paper flower that the dancer holds at his finger tips and which, when the ballet is over is a mere wire stem.

such. The critique here bears on the way the empiricist operates the deduction. Later, in the family syllogism, first circle of the grand syllogism of *Sittlichkeit,* these two predicates will be ordered as the second and third in a historical totality of which marriage ("immediate ethical relation," natural unity of the sexes transformed into a spiritual unity) will be the first moment.

What is more, and above all, the division, scission, and dissolution will be conceived. It will appear in actuality and will be consummated with the education of the children, having been prepared by marriage and the community of property. But then it will no longer be a question of dissolving the family *theoretically*, by an empirical knowledge-procedure, by a scientific failing. We will have to understand and conceive how the family *dissolves itself really, actually,* in the education of children and the passage to civil society.

As internal principle of destruction, domestic negativity intervenes not only at this precise point, within the family moment. Exposure to death is the condition of every ethical totality in general, here that of the *people*.

For it is the doctrine of the death penalty that ensures the passage from the critique of formalism to the positing of absolute *Sittlichkeit*. In an interpretation that is uniquely his own, Hegel takes up again an argument that was quite current at the time, common to Rousseau and Kant, for example: the death penalty is the condition of freedom. The criminal is distinguished from the animal, posits himself as a free subject, assumes the identity of his name, etc., by rising above life. The penalty is not a constraining or repressive punishment. As application of the universal law, it manifests the freedom of those who apply it and of those who suffer it. By accepting his penalty, or even in demanding it, glorifying it, the criminal recognizes the law and is therefore free. The death penalty takes to the absolute this manifestation of freedom. The article on *Natural Law,* as does the *Phenomenology* in the chapter on "Self-sufficiency and non-self-sufficiency of self-consciousness; mastery and servitude," makes of putting natural life at stake the condition of a free subjectivity.

At the center of this demonstration, a couple of concepts designating legal operations. By accepting the principle of a penalty whose purpose is not to punish, chastise or mutilate him, but on the contrary to raise him to the freedom of the ethical community, the singular individual becomes free, has himself recognized as such by society, and

here the wire tendered, by the fingertips, holds up the paper flower: in its erection and its appearance, for the time of the ballet. But it is also what remains when the flower falls, reduced, without adornment or natural color, to its real twig. And to its "proper name." The queens lose their adornment, the names their corolla, once the clerk shouts out the official "proper names," calling, classifying according to the law, redistributing the genders: "When he called 'Antoine Berthollet,' First Communion appeared; at 'Eugène Marceau,' Lady-Apple appeared. Thus, in the eyes of Our bewildered Lady, the little faggots from Pigalle to Place Blanche lost their loveliest adornment." Return to natural naming, that is to say to the first classificatory violence, inversion of sex, reintroduction of the forename that comes second, in all taxonomic rigor. There no longer remains anything but wires.

But the role of wires can be inverted or show up the sense of engraving as counterproof. "The Tightrope Walker" is a hymn to the wire. This time the dancer doesn't hold the wire by the fingertips; he is held—like the text—on a wire. The wire—the subject of the text—supports him on the verge of a fall ("The wire will carry you better, more surely, than a road").

is at that point "be*zwungen aber nicht* ge*zwungen*." The French translators say that this play on words is untranslatable and no doubt they are not wrong. The two verbs are indeed very close in meaning, both referring to what I will call a movement of *striction*: embrace, constraint, restriction; the point is always to grip, contain, suppress, submit, compress, repress, tame, reduce, force, subjugate, enslave, encircle. But Hegel chooses to dissociate them and rigorously oppose one to the other, *zwingen* to *bezwingen*, in part taking up Fichte's terminology—Fichte who in his *Grundlage des Naturrechts*, speaks of a *Zwangsgesetz*. The striction of *bezwingen* is distinguished from a mere empirical constraint, it erects the empirical subject into a free subject. The highest point of this erection is called death: "This negatively absolute, pure freedom, appears as [has the appearance, *Erscheinung* of] death, and by his ability (*Fähigkeit*) to die the subject proves himself free and entirely above (*erhaben*) all *Zwang*. Death is the absolute *Bezwingung*." How to translate this? Death is the phenomenon (the brilliant appearing, the luster, the glory, the shining gleam, the *Erscheinung*) of the subject who frees himself to it by subjecting himself to the universality of the law. He then raises himself, stands up above a certain type of *striction* (*Zwang*); but he can stand up in this way only by suffering the absolute surfeit of a counter-striction that, by punishing him absolutely, totally frees him from the earlier striction, which is called natural, empirical, etc., and which is always weaker. *Bezwingung* erects freedom by lifting the *Zwang*. Absolute—or at least colossal—surfeit of a counter-erection. But what is an absolute surfeit? How to take account of it? How to take account of death in the calculus of everything one wishes to erect?

What is being raised here is not just being raised but first of all sublates (itself) (*aufhebt*). So calculation can no longer determine anything, for sublation suspends all determinacy, be it positive or negative, it suspends the *plus* and the *minus*. Death, freedom, are an "*Aufhebung sowohl des Plus als des Minus*," a sublation of the plus as of the minus. This sublation, the act of *aufheben* "can in itself be positively grasped by reflection." Before the infinite law that prescribes death, the equivalence of +A and –A nullifies both determinations. Death alone allows one to accede to this infinite that allows one to calculate the incalculable, in this way infallibly to annul calculation, without putting punishment on the market: "Thus the punishment is the restoration of freedom. . . . It issues from freedom and, even as subjugator (*als bezwingend*), remains in freedom.

The tightrope walker must love his wire as what carries him but first as what he will have carried, given birth to, or rather resuscitated, Oedipus or Jesus: "This love—almost desperate, but charged with tenderness—that you must show for the wire, will have as much strength as the metal wire has to carry you. I know objects, their malignancy, their cruelty, their gratitude, too. The wire was dead—or if you like, mute, blind—but here you are, it will live and speak." The places are going to be inverted, the wire dances and the dancer is blinded; glory returns to the real subject, the wire: "Your leaps, your somersaults, your dances—in acrobat slang, your pitter-patter, bows, midair somersaults, cartwheels, etc.—you will execute them successfully, not for you to shine [not so that she, the mother, will shine: "A gold sequin is a tiny disc of gilt metal, pierced with a hole" is how the text opens, its first sentence], but so that a steel wire that was dead and voiceless will finally sing. How grateful it will be to you if you are perfect in your performance, not for your glory, but its own!

May the audience applaud it:
—What a surprising wire! How it supports the dancer and how it loves him!

In its turn, the wire will make the most amazing dancer of you. . . . If your solitude, paradoxically, is spotlighted, and the darkness made up of thousands of eyes judging you, fearing and hoping for your fall ["She hoped that the following day Our Lady would be sentenced to death; she desired it."], it matters little: you will dance on in a desert solitude, blindfolded, if you can, eyelids fastened shut. But nothing—especially not applause or laughter—will keep you from dancing for your image. You are an artist—alas—you can no longer deny yourself the monstrous precipice of your eyes. . . . it is not you who will dance, it is the wire. But if it is the wire that dances motionless, and if it is your image that it makes leap, where, then, will you be?"

If, on the other hand, punishment is understood as coercion (*als Zwang*), it is posited merely as a specific determination and as something purely finite, carrying no rationality in itself. It falls wholly under the common concept of one specific thing contrasted with another, or as an item with which something else—the crime—can be purchased. The state as judicial power trades in specific wares, called crimes, for sale in exchange for other specific wares, and the legal code (*Gesetzbuch*) is its price-list (*Preiskourant*)."

As penalty *par excellence,* death escapes all juridical and repressive calculation that would seek to establish an equivalence between the register of the crime and that of the penalty, as if by adding up on the left the tally of infractions, on the right the tally of punishments, then subtracting one from the other on could annul a debt, acquit oneself of it. Death escapes the operation of finite death. Not that no equivalence happens here. Equivalence, reciprocity (*Wiedervergeltung*) is the rationality of every penalty. But in the death penalty, the equivalence becomes infinite, obeys an infinite law; it does not allow an empirical level to be determined in arithmetical columns. And precisely because the equivalence between debt and punishment is infinite, no resemblance, no commensurability, no determinable analogy can be grasped between their two registers, their two ranges. No relation can be understood here, no relation gives a purchase to finite concepts and the determinations of the understanding. The equivalence is infinite and null.

Such an analysis has already stopped treating the case of an individual subject to the death penalty. It was about the total functioning of an ethical community: infinite equivalence can be produced only in the relation between finite individuals or empirical groups. Hegel at this time calls the absolute ethical totality the *people*. Now the people itself accedes to *Sittlichkeit* and becomes free *qua* ethical totality (*sittliche*) only by putting its life at stake, rising up above its natural determinations in a strict movement. *Bezwingung,* the infinite and therefore non-constraining striction of death, produces the strict: what is called spirit, freedom, ethics, etc. The people must risk its life, not hesitate to allow itself to be destroyed *qua* empirical people in order to become a free people, i.e. a people *stricto sensu*. This is possible only in warfare. As condition of the ethical, war no longer belongs to the order of natural phenomena (as it does in Rousseau, for example):

"The Tightrope Walker" divides in two: paragraphs in italics, paragraphs in roman, narrative and apostrophe, *je-il, je-tu*. The textual thread disappears, reappears, stretches until it vibrates, becomes invisible by being too tight or having too many twists, is loaded with all names, carries Death and one who is dead. Already—vigil—the place of the dead one: "Death—the Death of which I speak to you—is not the one that will follow your fall, but the one that precedes your appearance on the wire. It is before climbing onto it that you die. . . . But be careful to die [*veille de mourir*] before appearing, and may a dead man dance on the wire."

The displacing echoes endlessly between keeping vigil [*veille*] and wire, reciprocally between tightrope walker and old woman [*vieille*], through a sort of alternating that is as regular as that between day and night: the tightrope walker becomes the old woman, an old tramp [*cloche*], rags, fake wig, which becomes the tightrope walker whose stretched wire she is as it were hiding under her tattered dresses: "*Must it be said? I would want the tightrope walker to live during the day disguised as an old, toothless female tramp, with a gray wig: seeing her, one would know what athlete reposes beneath the rags, and one would respect such a great distance of day from night. To appear in the evening! And he, the tightrope walker, no longer knowing who his privileged self might be: the seedy female tramp, or the gleaming loner? Or the perpetual movement from her to him?*"

The celebration is brief, it involves something other than "our world and its logic," leads us back to "this enormous canvas womb," "in the flanks of the monster" where "your brief tomb illuminates us."

it manifests consciousness, spirit, culture. A people afraid of war returns to animality, it wants to save its life, its natural biological health; but it adulterates its spiritual life and its ethical health.

Of course, if it loses the war—like the criminal *after* the blade's fall and the Eucharistic matter after consumption—it becomes empirical naturality again. Also if it wins, and what rises here therefore hangs by a mere thread, never lose sight of that.

War, then, supposedly prevents the people from rotting, it preserves "the ethical health of peoples," like the wind whipping up the seas purifies them, keeps them from decomposition, corruption, putrefaction (*Fäulnis*) with which a "permanent calm" (*dauernde Stille*) and *a fortiori* a "perpetual peace" would infect them. In this putrefaction, this return to inorganic nature, the people would lose its name and its face, its figure (*Gestalt*), its form. It would no longer be able to stand up. Hegel quotes Gibbon: peace and assured mastery acted on the Romans like a "slow and secret poison" (*langsames und geheimnes Gift*) in the vital forces of the empire, of the Roman eagle.

As all this is hanging by a thread, the ethical body must ceaselessly repeat the spiritual act of its emergence, it must always be born again, recall itself to its name and to its freedom. In this text, the name of what takes flight again is neither the owl nor the eagle, but the Phoenix: on the basis of its consumption, life, "like its own seed-corn (*als sein eigenes Samenkorn*)," "rises (*emporhebe*) eternally from its ashes to new youth." This is the representation, the execution, the interpretation (*Aufführung*), in the ethical world, of the "tragedy which the Absolute eternally enacts with itself": "by eternally giving birth to itself into objectivity, submitting in this objective form to suffering and death, and rising (*erhebt*) from its ashes into its glory [*Herrlichkeit*: its luster, its majesty, its sovereignty, its pomp]." In this radiance, the paradigmatic moment of the Phoenix, the absolute of this movement is tragic

Death takes the place of vigil, in other words of the Virgin. It is for her and in her name that the wire must stretch out and the tightrope walker fascinate ("you are not there to amuse the public, but to fascinate it"—the word "fascinate" is repeated three times), dance, get a hard-on, make others hard ("And dance! But with a hard-on. . . . Have a hard-on, and make others have one."). In the moment of absolute narcissism ("Have a hard-on, and make others have one. This heat that comes from you and shines, it is your desire for yourself—or for your image—never satisfied."). It is for death, and again for keeping vigil that the celebration is given—as present (vigil—already—in my place). Death taking the place of vigil, disavowal puts into the future that (what) will never have been present. "It goes without saying that I did not mean to say that an acrobat who works eight or ten meters above the ground must leave things to God (to the Virgin, tightrope walkers) and should pray and cross himself before entering the arena, for death is in the tent. As if to a poet, I was speaking to the solitary artist." Not to the artist alone but to the solitary artist. "If you danced one meter above the carpet, my injunction would be the same. It is a question, you understand, of deadly solitude, of that desperate and brilliant region where the artist operates. . . . Gothic legends speak of street acrobats who, having nothing else, offered their tricks to the Virgin. In front of the cathedral they danced. I do not know to what god you will address your games of skill, but you must have one. . . . God does not yet exist for anyone . . . Your gestures can be repeated."

Question of address, and of knowing *for whom* to sign still. In place and in view of whom, already, for whom a tightroper walks thus.

If you follow this thread, or another, of the tight-

because it is double, absolutely double: in it the Divine "is immediately double-natured (*gedoppelte*), and its life is the absolute unity (*Einssein*) of these natures."

"*Sein Leben ist das absolute Einssein dieser Naturen.*" *Einssein,* the radiant word of radiance, a word both double and one, literally the one and the other, the two in the heart of the one, the difference of the other bound in the one ("since its own life (*ihr eigenes Leben*) is only in connection (*Verbundensein*) with this other life"), *Einssein* is absolute tragedy because of this double ligature. Comedy, divine comedy and modern comedy, consists in untying the absolute, separating out its two members. Fate and combat become in it a shadow without essence, a farce assured of its enjoyment. What tenses the members of the *Einssein* in the "relation of a body proper (*in leibhafter Beziehung*)" has loosened. The two members have fallen back one next to the other.

Everything must be submitted to this regeneration, the highest instance of this flight: the world of work, of need, of enjoyment. Although it does not expressly place this world on the side of servility, the article on *Natural Law* clearly states the need to subordinate the "system of what is called political economy" and the science corresponding to it, to the mastery (*Herrschaft*) of the ethico-political totality consecrated by its exposure to death.

One must be vigilant to prevent this hierarchy being overturned. Hegel is in dialogue here with Plato and Aristotle. He distinguishes between classes or "estates" (*Stände*). The *System der Sittlichkeit* places the aristocratic (political and military) class at the summit of the hierarchy: that class confronts death and rises above needs. The commercial and industrial bourgeoisie, *die erwerbende Klasse*, the class of acquisition, forms wealth and locks itself up in the comfort of private life. It attains the universal only in formal abstraction and its right resembles the *pharmakon* in the *Republic,* quoted at length by Hegel: it engenders more varied and serious illnesses instead of restoring health. They are unaware that "in fact they are just cutting off a Hydra's head." (*sie in der Tat gleichsam die Hydra zerschneiden*: "Ὕδραν τέμνουσιν"). Finally, a third estate, a peasant class that has a relation to the concrete whole only in the sensory or sentimental form of confidence.

After possession (*Besitz*) has become property (*Eigentum*), after the institution of right and a formal ethical life, we come to the third stage, ethical life, absolute *Sittlichkeit*. The organizing schema of the *Principles of the Philosophy of Right* is legible, according to the problematic

rope walker to the *Ticktack des kleinen Glücks,* to the *Klang einer Glocke* and to the bitten piece of self, near the end, you have here, as if in contraband, everything necessary for an almost complete, literally literal reading of *Zarathustra.* You can check it out.

Remains to be detailed once more

Would it not have been better to have danced the entire dance with a simple wire? The question is worth examining. The faggots showed the framework that Darling discerned behind the silk and velvet of every armchair. They were reduced to nothing, and that's the best thing that's been done so far. They entered aggressively or shyly, perfumed, made up, expressed themselves with studied care. They were no longer the grove of crinkly paper that flowered on the terraces of cafés. They were misery in motley. (Where do the faggots get their *noms de guerre*? But first it should be noted that none of them were chosen by those who bore them. This, however, does not hold for me. I can hardly give the exact reasons why I chose such and such a name. Divine, First Communion, Mimosa, Our Lady of the Flowers and Milord the Prince did not occur to me by chance. There is a kinship among them, an odor of incense and melting taper, and I sometimes feel as if I had gathered them among the artificial or natural flowers of the chapel of the Virgin Mary, in the month of May, under and about the greedy plaster statue that Alberto was in love with and behind which, as a child, I used to hide the phial containing my spunk.)"

"This, however, does not hold for me," says

already we know about: abstract right that deals with property, formal subjective morality (*Moralität*), objective or ethical morality (*Sittlichkeit*), given its rhythm by the three totalities formed by the family, civil or bourgeois society, the State. "Above these two is the third, the Absolute or the ethical" . Everything that precedes it, possession, property, work, abstract right, formal justice "concerns the individual and thus does not include the danger of death."

This whole process is described through what Hegel considers to be natural "images." It is less that he is criticizing them than explaining their necessity: the regulated relation they entertain with their spiritual sense. The oriental animal figure of the Phoenix will be put back in its place by *Reason in History*. All references to natural life and death imitate and deform the process of spiritual life or death. Everywhere we see the relation of nature to spirit: spirit is (outside itself) in nature; nature is spirit outside itself. Finite metaphors, real organic life are impotent when it comes to taking in the whole spiritual divinity of *Sittlichkeit*; however it "already expresses in itself the absolute idea, but deformed." It has in it absolute infinity, "only as a counterfeit (*nachgeahmte*) negative independence." The same goes for the Platonic metaphor of the City as an immortal animal, for the perfection of the stone or the flowers of the heavenly system.

The perfect mineral seems indeed to represent the one-being (*Einssein*) of an absolute totality. In the outer form of its crystallization, in the inner form of its break (*Bruch*), each part seems to be "representative of the whole (*Repräsentant des Ganzen*)." In truth, that is an external association, of a compositional (*Außereinander*) and not penetrative reciprocity. No element is "penetrated" (*durchdrungen*) by the true identity of the infinite. The senses of the mineral have "no consciousness." Contrary to what happens with a spiritual sense, "its light is a singular color and does not see." It does not of itself emit the sound it makes when it is struck, like a voice, but it receives it as though from a foreign source (*Sein Ton tönt angeschlagen von einem Fremden, aber nicht aus sich*). Its taste does not taste, its smell smells nothing, its weight and hardness sense nothing.

The brittle and resistant rigidity of the mineral must be

the child with the greedy plaster.

Verily.

Throttle oneself with this tie [*se cravater*] of a text.

Our Lady—who strangles with the detachment of a phallus that his victim begins by offering him, tendering him (his neck, his tie)—is a virgin, conceived without sin, like his mother ("I am the Immaculate Conception") whose phallus he also is. Which she has given him. He is both his mother and himself, and his mother is his victim. He thus chokes while saying "I am the Immaculate Conception." He can say that only in the trance of a hiccup, close to vomiting. The mother's breast's spitting image. The child can only say "I am the Immaculate Conception" like he could give (himself) a fuck [*à vouloir se foutre de lui-même*]. And his mother, then. Whose phallus—however—(he) remains, the case according to Peter, like Christ and Dionysos.

Not far from the creche.

reduced. This is again an operation of *Bezwingung*: elementary fluidity must penetrate. This fluidity is first of all that of the ether, which announces the absolute indifference of spirit in a negative mode and which "espouses" the absolute infinity. Then come the "superior formations," "the fellowship of leaves in plants, of species, of the herdwise life and common labor of animals." In its absolute quantitative indifference, ether is what most resembles the indifference (*Indifferenz*) of ethical life. It has projected its absolute indifference outside, into "indifferences of light (*Lichtindifferenzen*)," it has placed its inner reason into expansion, given birth to it by expelling it (*in die Expansion herausgeboren hat*): these are the "blooms of the solar system" (*Blumen der Sonnensysteme*). These "individualizations of light (*Lichtindividuen*)" have scattered into multiplicity, whereas those which are arranged in a circle to form the "petals" of these flowers are set over against them, in a "rigid individuality," in a relation of exteriority. The flower of the celestial system thus resembles the unity of the ethical system, but its elements remain foreign to each other, in a sort of abstract ideality. The celestial flower forms a deployment without inner unity, a juxtaposition that is ordered but purely unfurled, unfolded, with neither secret nor relation to self: *die außereinandergefaltete Blume des himmlischen Systems*. In the analogy, difference remains essential: when one is speaking of the spirit, this flower gives a good image but its value is still rhetorical.

Potenz: this word appears sometimes in *Natural Law*. A few years later, it will furnish the most general organizing concept of the Jena philosophy of spirit. The analysis of consciousness will indeed there be divided or developed into three "potencies": 1. Memory and language; this is the "theoretical" potency: sensation, imagination, memory. 2. Instrument (*Werkzeug*), the "practical" potency: desire, labor, instrument. 3. Possession and family: family, struggle for recognition, passage to the spirit of a people.

What is *Potenz?* A moment of the moment, a moment of the Hegelian concept of the moment. The word and no doubt the concept were present in Schelling's philosophy

"And this fabulous impecuniousness [*dèche*] made for Our Lady a pedestal of cloud; he was as prodigiously glorious as the body of Christ rising aloft, to dwell there alone and fixed, in the noonday sky."

The virgin's son or phallus thus immediately sleeps with mother, the father being dead (or set aside by the Immaculate Conception, but also dispensing, as a result, with passing essentially through the mother, and so engendering his son all by himself, self-inseminating and calling himself in him: in the son who is mother and also father who is mother who is son, "and so on, without anyone's daring to linger over recognizing it," the tie, that is, and in the course of the proceedings, follow the detachment), pretends no longer to raise any objection.

Don't go thinking for a minute that I am here recounting—in back of Jesus' pharmacy—the story of a broomflower [*un genêt*] whose tincture, the pharmakon, interests me above all else. And it is true that I will have done nothing if I haven't managed to affect you with broom, coloring you, daubing you, pasting you, making you sensitive, transforming you, beyond everything concocted here, thanks to the most proper affect of this text.

But is there any such thing? And of which text, his, mine?

of nature. The *Ideas for a Philosophy of Nature* describes the going out of itself of the absolute into nature, as nature, according to the ternary rhythm of the "potencies." These are both a *dynamis* and an *energeia,* a virtuality and an act, an achieved totality on which is as it were suspended the totality to come. One potency bears the death of the other. The absolute goes out of itself into the finite, penetrates it with its infinity to have it come back to itself. It absorbs it, resorbs it after having entered into it. This movement of effusion/resorption manifests the absolute which differentiates itself, goes out of the night of its essence and appears in the daylight. This presentation happens in three acts, which Schelling names "potencies." *Nature,* the first unity which, penetrated by the infinite, transforms itself in its turn into the *ideal world*, which transforms itself again into *nature*. One finds the same schema in *The Ages of the World*; this time it's about *natura naturans* and God. The mark of Boehme is clear. The abyssal absolute (*Ungrund*) is without potency (*Potenzlos*). This im-potence is its primal germ. God comes out of this void and that is the being that is (*das Seiende*). Finally, the hierarchical union of being and non-being is the third potency. As in *Natural Law,* each totality, each potency proceeds to the striction of the previous one, strangles it and raises it to the following potency, following a circular process that goes as it were from seed to plant then from plant to seed.

So Hegel has more than a word in common with Schelling. But the whole critique of Schelling's triplicity can be seen, in particular in the substitution during the Jena period of the term *Moment* for the term *Potenz.* In the manuscript of the Jena *Realphilosophie,* a crossing-out keeps a trace of this; but elsewhere the word *Potenz* stayed in place for a long time.

What Hegel says about the structure of the *Potenz*—which will also be true of the dialectical moment—explains to us how he, Hegel, intended to be read. One can transpose what he states about each *Potenz* to each organized totality of his text, which both repeats and anticipates, and yet marks a leap, a jump, a rupture in repetition, all the while ensuring the continuity of the passage and the homogeneity of a development.

A plurality of continuous jolts, of uninterrupted jerks: such would be the rhythm. The last two pages of *Natural Law* indeed describe the life and death of the "potencies," for example those ethical totalities, "peoples." In each particular

I am placing this touch here only because of the color, a "corn mush" yellow that I no longer know where to put in my adoration.

See here. It's always during the proceedings, writing in an *annal* style. Divine comes to testify on Our Lady's behalf: ". . . I think he's being very naïve, very childlike. . . . He could be my son." Like the Archangel Gabriel, *remember*. The author or narrator (always between one signet or another) then explains to us how Culafroy became Divine, how his name was written Divine, transforming him thenceforth, him, the one named, the one nicknamed, into "a poem written only for himself, hermetic to whoever did not have the key to it."

by wanting to be Gabriel's mother also, she who is forenamed, nicknames him, denominates—Divine—announces in all the brilliance of his identity: I am my mother, my daughter, my son, and myself. The mother precedes and follows obstinately the cortege

It is therefore the moment to explain how the narrator, not the author—to be circumspect let's say *genêt*—has made himself a name, a flower, has carved out impressive renown in literature [*dans les lettres*]. He compares himself to Divine: "In short, this is his secret glory, like the one I have decreed upon myself so as to obtain peace at last." A palm-reader has in fact announced to *genêt* that he is a genius and will be famous one day. Against the background of this old "need for thinking I have genius," he ennobles his name, does up his genealogy with this virtual glory. He will achieve that glory, will possess it more sparkling than any other, will be crowned by it,

totality, as such, the absolute totality *arrests itself*, arrests its necessity. The particular totality then, *qua* part, takes on a certain independence, a certain subsistence. "Arresting itself" here is *sich hemmen*. *Hemmen* is often translated as inhibit, suppress. The infinite totality inhibits itself in the *Potenz*. It limits itself, gives itself a form, comes out of a certain *apeiron*, suspends itself, puts an end to itself, but the delay it thus takes on itself (*hemmen* also means to delay, to defer) is the positive condition of its appearing, its glory. Without it, without the suspensive and inhibitory striction, the absolute would not manifest itself. So the delay is also an advance, a progress, an anticipation of the absolute deployment of the absolute. Whence this double archeo-teleological movement: "The absolute totality restricts itself (*hemmt sich*) as necessity in each of its powers (*in jeder ihrer Potenzen*), produces itself out of them (*bringt sich hervor*) as a totality, and recapitulates (*wiederholt*) there the preceding powers just as it anticipates (*antizipiert*) the succeeding ones."

The powers form a chain: consequence from one to the next, and limitation which holds the absolute in its chains. The enchaining is not a serene and continuous deduction. In the conflict of forces, warfare, struggle to the death, the most potent potency suppresses the others. But as this war expresses absolute necessity, the greatest force is not constraining at the very moment when it imposes itself. *Qua* particular potency, it doubtless imposes a set of limitations; but inasmuch as it expresses the infinite potency held back in it, the limitation is no longer negative, it opens a set of conditions of possibility, of existence, of life, the best possible conditions at a given moment. Water is thus a determinate element that can be opposed to air or earth: for the fish, it is the only possible element and in no way constitutes a limit. Any more than does air for the bird. Any more than does an ethical totality for a man. The analogy stops there: the natural element has no history, the ethical element is historical through and through.

Now this history, although it deploys the divinity of the *telos*, happens in discontinuous and painful bounds. The penetration of the divine can obey only this rhythm. The passage from one potency to the next is dialectical, it proceeds by reversals and absolute oppositions. Such is the "misfortune (*Unglück*) of the period of transition": a sudden spurt (*Sprung*), then a dwelling (*Verweilen*) in which spirit "enjoys" (*geneißt*) the new form (*Gestalt*) it has just conquered. A metaphor, of course,

but while hiding it in some literal, ineffable crypt, completely illuminated from the inside. It is a "parchment that no one can decipher, an illustrious birth kept secret, a royal bar sinister, a mask or perhaps a divine filiation, the kind of thing that must have been felt . . ."

However, the divine filiation with which *genêt* is affected is an immaculate conception, allowing the son to take—and so to leave—each and every place, to sleep all alone, here with the father in itself, there with the actual mother (*ansichseiende Vater und nur eine wirkliche Mutter*, but *nur eine* is best) as in *absolute religion*, that is to say on the (representative) threshold of absolute knowing where *glas* finally turns back to itself, resounds, reflects itself for itself, admires its glory and is equal to itself. We are in Galilee, between 1810 and 1910 in our calendar. It is, as he wrote to Roger Blin, an event that is "gl

"Time. I know nothing very specific about time, but, if I acknowledge the existence and termination of an event, any event whatsoever. . . . The first Frenchmen bombarding Algiers in 1830, if you like, bombarded themselves from Algiers about 1800. . . . I haven't the time to go into the matter at greater length. . . . No sooner had Dey's fan stopped moving, no sooner had the first shot of cannon sounded, than 800,000 French settlers in Algeria were already fabricating Tixier-Vignancour. Everything was very rapid, rapid enough *to bring off an event* which has neither beginning nor end: global."

of the bomb, time of the explosive bomb: "Just as a bombshell starts suddenly [*Rück*: a stopping or recoiling movement, a jolt] towards its zenith and then rests for a moment in it; metal, when heated, does not turn soft like wax, but all at once (*auf einmal*) becomes liquid and remains so (*in den Fluß springt und auf ihm verweilt*)—for this phenomenon (*Erscheinung*) is the transition into the absolute opposite and so is infinite, and this emergence of the opposite out of infinity or out of it nothingness is a leap (*Sprung*). The shape, in its new-born strength, at first exists for itself alone, before it becomes conscious of its relation to an other. Just so, the growing individuality has both the delight (*Freudigkeit*) of the leap in entering a new form and also an enduring pleasure (*Genußes*) in its new form, until it gradually opens up to the negative, and in its decline (*Untergang*) too it is sudden and brittle (*brechend*)."

This structure—discontinuous bound, effraction and pacified dwelling in a form open to its own negativity—has no outer limit. Thanks to its inner limit, this squeezing or strangulation that it gives *itself*, it avoids getting lost in abstract indeterminacy (here, for example, "formless" cosmopolitanism or world republic, etc.). But its generality encounters no external obstacle. It regulates the relation between absolute spirit and all its "potencies" or determinate figures.

By the same token it organizes Hegel's text. Any commentary would disqualify itself that, *qua* commentary, did not follow its prescription or that dragged its feet hesitating between explication and rupture, within all the oppositional couples that sustain in general the history of the historians of philosophy. There is no possible displacement of this history without displacement—this word must itself be reinterpreted—of what in Hegel's text imposes this rule of reading, i.e. a displacement that itself would escape the dialectical law and its strict rhythm.

It seems like we are not there yet; and this can no more be done in one blow than by continuous approach. The

Like *classe, calende, glas,* calendar comes back to "call" (*appeler, calare*), name, convoke, assemble, commemorate, announce.

Clang is written here—uniquely—to celebrate, at the bottom of an absolute crypt, some *stroke of the calendar* [coup de calendrier] the chance of which marks a milestone [*aura fait date*]. And the blink of an eye in "That Strange Word . . ." or in "Plato's Pharmacy." One must always look for the place of who writes, even if it isn't fixed, if it doesn't allow itself to be taken any more than a replacement. Jean doesn't name himself but doesn't hesitate to point to himself, by his own pen, as Christ's preferred disciple. He sleeps with him, at least on his breast. Judas's betrayal: "Verily, verily, I say unto you that one of you shall betray me. Then the disciples looked one on another, doubting of whom he spake. Now there was leaning on Jesus' bosom one of his disciples, whom Jesus loved. Simon Peter therefore beckoned to him, that he should ask who it should be of whom he spake. He then lying on Jesus' breast saith unto him, Lord, who is it? Jesus answered, He it is, to whom I shall give a sop, when I have dipped it." Judas takes it but doesn't eat it. John replaces Jesus in relation to his mother and takes her to his home. After Pilate says "What I have written I have written" in the gospel signed John: "Now there stood by the cross of Jesus his mother, and his mother's sister, Mary the wife of Cleophas, and Mary Magdalene. When Jesus saw his mother, and the disciple standing by, whom he loved, he saith unto his mother, Woman, behold thy son! Then saith he to the disciple, Behold thy mother! And from that hour that disciple took her unto his own home."

Like the multitudinous multiplication of Johns (author, narrator, narratee, dead one), the play of wrapping [*bandes*] envelops the Gospel in *Funeral Rites* and mimes the resurrection: "Then she [Mary Mag-

event cannot be as noisy as a bomb, as flashy or burning hot as metal placed in the fire. Even if it were an event it would here be—stricture against stricture—unobtrusive and marginal.

Reading Hegel from within, the problematic of *Sittlichkeit,* and therefore of the family within that problematic, can henceforth be deployed only in a philosophy of spirit. The absolute ethical totality having been defined as "spirit of a people (*Volksgeist*)," its genealogy must be traced. That is the task of the first philosophy of spirit (Jena). The three "potencies" of consciousness (1. Memory, language. 2. Instrument. 3. Possession, family) constitute the spirit of a people at the end of their development. From an architectonic point of view, the third potency, the family, that marks the passage to *Sittlichkeit*, occupies by the same token the first phase, forms the first moment of ethical life, its most immediate and most natural one. This will be confirmed, if one could say that, fifteen years later, in the *Philosophy of Right*.

Indeed, immediately after expositing the third potency, the Jena philosophy of spirit describes the *transition* from the family to the people. A transition in the strong and active sense of this word: self-destructive passage. Via marriage, possession and education, the family destroys or sublates itself, "sacrifices itself," says Hegel. And then, in a struggle for recognition, it loses itself and reflects in another consciousness: the people. It exists in the people only "sublated" (*aufgehobene*), destroyed, preserved, abased, raised up.

What is consciousness, if its ultimate potency is achieved in the family?

Consciousness is the return to self of the Idea or of absolute being. This latter takes itself up again, it is *sich zurücknehmend,* it retracts, gathers itself, reassumes itself, resumes and reassembles itself, surrounds and envelops itself with itself after its death in nature, after having lost itself, having "fallen," Hegel says literally, out of itself into nature. The philosophy of nature is the system of this *fall* and this dissociation in exteriority. The philosophy of spirit is the system of the sublation of the idea that calls itself and thinks itself in the ideal element of universality.

The *transition* from nature to spirit is also a turning

dalene] runneth, and cometh to Simon Peter, and to the other disciple, whom Jesus loved, and saith unto them, They have taken away the Lord out of the sepulchre, and we know not where they have laid him. Peter therefore went forth, and that other disciple, and came to the sepulchre. So they ran both together: and the other disciple did outrun Peter, and came first to the sepulchre. And he stooping down, and looking in, saw the linen clothes lying; yet went he not in. Then cometh Simon Peter following him, and went into the sepulchre, and seeth the linen clothes lie, And the napkin, that was about his head, not lying with the linen clothes, but wrapped together in a place by itself." You see how he writes his *Funeral Rites,* and the rest: with the attentive gestures of a philologist, an archeologist, a mythologist determined to disperse, destroy, erase what he finds or reconstitutes. Most critical operation. But his application is strange, as if distracted by itself. He always gives the impression of in fact applying himself to something else, of being detached from what he is doing. He recounts another story, you carefully follow the narrative, he points with his finger to this or that, while however fucking your ass eyes elsewhere. In that way he gets off to the utmost, as in his paradigm, believing that in it he "recognize[s] a reminder of my childhood taste for tunnels. I bugger the world" (Funeral Rites). "He gets hard as a ramrod [il trique]. So hard and calmly that anuses and vaginas slip onto his member like rings on a finger. He gets hard as a ramrod. So hard and calmly that his virility, observed by the heavens, has the penetrating force of the battalions of blond warriors who on June 14, 1940, buggered us soberly and seriously, though their eyes were elsewhere as they marched in the dust and sun." (Our Lady of the Flowers).

Rings [*bagues*] don't only slip onto fingers like all the glottises standing erect in the text (I'll let you look for the "signifiers" if you wish, it's full of daggers [dagues], wisecracks [blagues], algae [algues], scabs [gales] being worked on behind his fly [braguette]), the rings are stolen from the fingers of the old man who stammers like a baby. "The old man undid his chain, from which the watch was hanging, and went forward to hand it to Stilitano, who took it.

inside out. At its highest point, it takes place in the *organic*, after the mechanical, the chemical and the physical. Because transition means violent self-destruction and passage to the opposite, the sublation of natural life into spiritual life necessarily happens through sickness and death. These latter are therefore the condition of spirit and of all its determinations, among others of the family.

Only among others?

The last chapters of the Jena *Philosophy of Nature*—more precisely the last paragraphs of the last chapter—concern the "process of disease." As dissolution of natural life, disease works for the transition toward spirit. The life of spirit then becomes the essence, the present truth of the past, the *Gewesenheit* of natural dissolution, of natural death. "With disease, the animal oversteps (*überschreitet*) the limits of nature; but the disease of the animal is the becoming of spirit." In the dissociation of natural organization, spirit reveals itself. It was working with its negativity on biological life, as on nature in general, and at the end reveals itself as such; it will always have been the essence of nature, nature is in it as its being-outside-itself. By freeing itself from the natural limits that were imprisoning it, it comes back to itself but without ever having left itself. Return procession. The limit was in it, it had enchained, restrained, imprisoned itself *in itself*. It always repeats itself. End of the analysis of animal disease: "Nature exists in spirit as in what is its essence."

In the circle of the *Encyclopedia,* this jointing will ensure the circle itself, the return to the philosophy of spirit. There too, the last paragraphs of the philosophy of nature deal with disease and death, having analyzed animal genus and the sexual relation. The point for Hegel is to fulfill here the teleology inaugurated by Aristotle, reawakened by Kant, the concept of inner purposiveness having been almost lost in between, in modern times. This inner purposiveness is not conscious, as would be the positing of an external end; it is of the order of the "instinct" (*Instinkt*) and remains "unconscious." Instinct is here a determination of the impulse (*Trieb*).

The normal fulfillment of the biological process and, within it, the generic process, is death. Death is natural. Violent by the same token: no contradiction there, no contradiction other than the contradiction internal to the process.

The genus designates the simple unity that remains with itself in each singular subject, in each representative or

'Your rings.'
'My rings . . .'
The old fellow was now stammering. Stilitano, standing motionless in the middle of the room, pointedly sharply to the objects he wanted. I was a little behind him, to his left, and I watched him in the mirror. I was sure that he would thus be, as he faced the trembling old queer, unnaturally cruel. In fact, when the old man told him that his knotted joints prevented him from removing the rings, he ordered me to turn on the water.
'Soap your fingers.'
Very conscientiously the old man soaped his hands. He tried to take off his two signet rings, but without success. Desperate, and fearing that his fingers might be cut off, he gave his hand to Stilitano with the timid anxiety of a bride at the foot of the altar. . . . Stilitano tried to pull the rings off. With one hand the old man held up the other which was being worked on. . . . As one does with babies, or as I myself would soap his one hand, Stilitano carefully soaped the old man's."
After calmly insisting Stilitano slaps the old man and gives up on the rings.

The ring [*anneau*] is too tight. Let's not give up. What I am trying to write—gl—isn't just any old structure, a system of signifier or signified, a thesis or a novel, a poem, a law, a desire or a machine, it's what passes, more or less well, through the rhythmed stricture of a ring.

example of that unity. But as this simple universality happens in judgment, in originary separation (*Urteil*), it tends to go outside itself in order to escape breaking-up or division and find itself again at home as subjective universality. This process of reassembling, of re-membering, negates natural universality that tends to get lost and divided. So the natural living being must perish. The necessary differentiation of the genus that determines itself in species provokes war. The species inflict violent death on each other. The genus produces itself naturally through its violent self-destruction. Lamarck and Cuvier—quoted at length—rightly chose the criteria of species differentiation: teeth, claws, etc., the "weapons" with which "in distinguishing itself from others, [the animal] establishes and preserves itself as a being-for-self."

Qua living being in nature, man does not escape this war of the species. This war is the negative face of the generic division. In its originary partition (*Urteil*), the genus divides or multiplies into specific pieces only to gather itself by itself. The bellicose and splitting operation of the generic process (*Gattungsprozeß*) is doubled by an affirmative reappropriation. The singularity joins up again, makes up with itself in the genus. The individual "is continued" in another, feels itself and experiences itself in it. This begins with need and the "feeling of that lack." The lack opens up with the inadequation of individual to genus. The genus is in the individual like a gapping, a tension (*Spannung*). Whence lack, need, the impulse: a movement to reduce the wound of the gap, close up the wound, bring its edges together. By the same token, the impulse tends to *fulfill* the very thing that it strictly reduces, the gap between the individual and the genus, of the genus in itself in the individual, *Urteil*, originary division and judgment. This operation that consists in filling the gap, uniting the one with the other by effecting the *Urteil* in the most accentuated way, is *copulation*. The word for copulation or coupling, for this general play of the copula, is *Begattung*, operation of the genus (*Gattung*), a generic and generating operation. In the same way what is, precisely, translated as sexual relation (*Geschlechtsverhältnis*) also designates the relation of the genus, the species or the race (family, lineage) or the relation of sex as masculine or feminine gender (*Geschlecht*).

As is often the case, the paragraph concerning the "sexual relation" and copulation is augmented with an

Try, on some anniversary, to push a ring around a style that is erected, swollen, stretched

obal."

". . . the kind of thing that must have been felt by Josephine, she who never forgot that she had given birth to the child who was to become the prettiest woman in the village, Marie, the mother of Solange—the goddess born in a hovel who had more blazons on her body than Mimosa had on her buttocks and in her gestures, and more nobility that a Chambure. This kind of consecration had kept the other women of her age (the others, mothers of men) away from Josephine. In the village, her situation was akin to that of the Mother of Jesus among the women of the Galilean village. Marie's beauty made the town more illustrious. To be the human mother of a divinity is a more disturbing state than that of divinity. The Mother of Jesus must have had incomparable emotions while carrying her son, and later, while living and sleeping side by side with a son who was God—that is, everything and herself as well—who could make the world not be, His Mother, Himself not be, a God for whom she had to prepare, as Josephine did for Marie, the yellow corn mush."

Then begins—it is the global event of this text—the elaboration of Harcamone's dream.

"appendix" precisely abridged from the classical *Encyclopedia of Philosophical Sciences in Basic Outline.* This addition (*Zusatz*) takes up again almost literally the end of the Jena *Philosophy of Nature*. Here Hegel deals with sexual difference. "The separateness of the two sexes" presents a very odd structure of separation. In each sex the organic individuals form a totality. But they don't relate to those of the other sex as to inorganic alterity. On both sides they belong to the genus, "they therefore exist only as *a single Geschlecht* (sex or gender)." "Their union is the disappearance of the sexes, in which the simple genus has come into being (*Ihre Vereinigung ist das Verschwinden der Geschlechter, worin die einfache Gattung geworden ist*)." When two individuals of the same species copulate, "the nature of each permeates both, and both find themselves within the sphere of this universality." Each one is, as participant, both a part and a whole; this general structure traverses them both, passes like bisexuality in each of them. What each is in itself (a single species), each posits effectively as such in copulation. "At this juncture, the idea of nature is actual in the male and female couple (pair: *Paare*); until now their identity and their being-for-self merely had being for us in our reflection, but they are now experienced by the sexes themselves in their infinite reflection into each other. This feeling of universality is the supreme moment of the animal's capabilities."

A "contradiction" inherent in the difference of the sexes: the generality of the genus as well as the identity of the individuals (belonging to the genus) are "different" from their separated, particular (*besonderen*) individuality. "The individual is only one of the two individuals, and exists merely as a singularity (*Einzelheit*), not as their unity (*Einheit*)." Sexual difference opposes unity to singularity and thus introduces contradiction into the genus or into the process of *Urteil*. This latter produces and allows itself to be constituted by this contradiction. In producing it, it resolves it: the process of copulation aims to preserve this difference while canceling it.

It sublates it: *Aufhebung* is very precisely the relation of copulation to sexual difference.

One cannot understand sublation in general without sexual copulation, nor the latter in general without sublation. In general: if we take into account the fact that the *Aufhebung* is described here at a strictly determined

Like Jean, Harcamone "wanted to keep a calendar" but he doesn't succeed, he "was unable to have a calendar. His dead life followed its course to infinity. He wanted to flee." He then kills a guard, repeating the murder of the little girl and so disguising his suicide. He behaves like the artist of his own life. He constructs his life like a column or like a tower, but he can see it, have it, know it only by putting an end to it. The structure of the tower is such that its construction reduces, stone by stone, to its destruction: one tower, two towers, one is (without) the other. "He had to erect his destiny, as one erects a tower, had to give this destiny tremendous importance, towering importance, unique and solitary, and had to build it of all his minutes. It seems to you impossible that I dare ascribe to a petty thief the act of building his life minute by minute, witnessing its construction, which is also a progressive destruction."

Like the executioners, like the galleyslaves, like Our Lady of the Flowers, as is true for all flowers, Harcamone is a virgin.

And his dream—the dream of him—repeats the same process.

Following a few *gl* strokes, as always, some tortuous detours in the "eglantine" and

(strangled) moment in the becoming of the idea (final moment of the philosophy of nature), but that this moment of life is re-marked at the end of the philosophy of spirit, then the *Aufhebung* of sexual difference is, manifests, expresses, *stricto sensu, Aufhebung* itself and in general.

Still in the appendix: "The activity of the animal consists in sublating this difference (*Die Tätigkeit des Tiers ist, diesen Unterschied aufzuheben*)." The process indeed has the form of a syllogism. And the "mediation, the milieu" of the syllogism is the gap (*Spannung*), the inadequation between the individual and the genus, the necessity for the singular to seek the "feeling of itself" in another.

What are the conditions of this sublating copulation? In describing what he calls the formation of sexual difference—or more precisely of the different sexes (*die Bildung der unterschiedenen Geschlechter*), Hegel subjects to the most traditional philosophical interpretation—Aristotelian in any case—what he considers to be the proven acquisitions of the anatomical science of the age. He finds in them the proof of a hierarchizing dissymmetry.

The formation of different sexes must be "different," differentiated. On account of the "original identity of their formation," the sexual parts of the male and the female must, it is true, belong to the "same type," but for the former and the latter it is this or that part that constitutes "the essential" (*das Wesentliche*). In the generality of the type, all the parts are thus present in each sex, but one is dominant here, another there, constituting the essence of the sex. The morphological type is bisexual in its profound, microscopic structure. Within this structure, the prevalence of one element provokes the hierarchy between the sexes.

But the difference is not so simple. It is not enough to say that one element is dominant here, another there: in the female, the essence consists in indifference—the indifferent, rather (*das Indifferente*); in the male the essence consists in difference—the divided-into-two, rather—opposition (*das Entzweite, der Gegensatz*). Male and female are not opposed as two differents, two terms of the opposition, but as indifference and difference (opposition, division). Sexual difference is the difference between indifference and difference. But each time, for it to *sublate*, *difference* must be determined as *opposition*.

It comes about, then, through the general identity of the anatomical type that is differentiating itself. In the lower

"wisteria [*glycine*]," the four black men, penetrating Harcamone's interior through his ear and mouth, get obsessively involved in a fervent and furious exploration, afraid, entranced, infinitely adventurous, exploring a body larger than theirs, that seems to have brought them inside it before they can ever think of breaking and entering, seeking rather its center or way out. Globally mimed, glossed, parodied, the whole worldwide literature of Oedipal crossroads, wanderings, odysseys, ordeals, descents into the underworld, through pyramids, labyrinths, mausoleums, wonderlands, subterranean crypts. We are in the element of the elements. It's sometimes a laborious trek, sometimes a flight without obstacle; a navigation also. I am controlling by resonance [*arrésonne*] only the mirror effect [*coup de glace*] within the labyrinth (which reflects, among other flashes, Rembrandt's gaze in the mirror and the coup of *je m'éc*, exchange, sicken, flow, write, listen [*échange, écoeure, écoule, écris, écoute*]) that organizes its shifts.

"Finally, all four met at a kind of crossroads which I cannot describe accurately. It led down, again to the left, into a luminous corridor lined with huge mirrors. . . .

'The heart—have you found the heart?'

And realizing at once that none of them had found it, they continued their way along the corridor, tapping and listening to the mirrors. They advanced slowly, cupping their ears and often flattening them against the wall. It was

animals, it is scarcely marked. Some locusts, for example the *Gryllus verrucivorus*, a sort of grasshopper, bear large testicles in convoluted fasciculi vessels, similar to large ovaries themselves, the oviducts being coiled in a similarly fasciculate manner. Same analogy between the testicles and the ovarian sacs of the gadfly.

"The most difficult": "the identification of the female uterus in the male parts." It was mistakenly thought to have been recognized in the testicular sac, the scrotum, since the testicles look exactly as though they correspond to the ovaries. But it is rather the prostate that fulfills in man a function like that of the uterus. In man, the uterus is demoted, falls to a glandular state, into a sort of undifferentiated generality. Hegel refers here to Ackermann's *Darstellung der Lebenskräfte*. Ackermann showed the place of the uterus on his hermaphrodite, in the "earlier male formations." But this uterus is not only in the place of the prostate: the ejaculatory conduits also traverse its substance and open onto the *crista galli*, in the urethra. The labia of the vulva are, moreover, testicular sacs; and testicular formations filled the hermaphrodite's labia. The median line of the scrotum opens finally in the woman and forms the vagina. "From this, it is quite understandable that one sex should change [undergo an *Umbildung*] into the other. On the one hand, the uterus in the male is reduced to a mere gland, while on the other, the male testicle in the female remains enclosed (*eingeschlossen*) within the ovary."

The description seems to be anatomical. But in its vocabulary and syntax, hierarchical evaluation mobilizes the object. The testicle "*bleibt eingeschlossen*", remains enclosed, enveloped. Development, rolling out, production has been insufficient, delayed, left behind. From this teleological interpretation is drawn a very marked speculative conclusion: "on the other hand, the male testicle in the female remains enclosed within the ovary, fails to emerge into opposition, and does not become an independent and active cerebrality. The clitoris moreover, is inactive feeling in general."

"The clitoris moreover, is inactive feeling in general," "*der Kitzler ist das untätige Gefühl überhaupt*," in general, absolutely, above all, above all else, principally. Who says *überhaupt* and what does *überhaupt* say? This

the executioner who first heard the beats. . . . The beats were nearer and louder. Finally, the four dark men came to a mirror on which was drawn (obviously carved with the diamond of a ring) a heart pierced by an arrow."

Past a first chamber, the emergence of a young drummer whose stick (cutting like the ring, inaccessible and tumultuous) falls down, there remains to be discovered the "mystery of the hidden chamber." By arriving at the heart of the heart, at the Mystic Rose, the four black men—each one of whom is as if in the other (judge, lawyer, chaplain, executioner in the same galley or palace)—repeat, in Harcamone's breast, the gesture of a virgin boy. Harcamone himself, not able to "keep his flower any longer" had fallen (they also fall) on a young girl near an eglantine bush and "put his hand under her skirt" before strangling her.

Dionysus Erigone Eriopetal Reseda.

"But no sooner did one of the four realize that they were not in the heart of the heart than a door opened by itself and we saw before us a red rose of monstrous size and beauty.

dissymmetry is not compensated for by the fall of the uterus in men. What does not yet emerge in women is sexual activity. Sexual difference reproduces the hierarchized opposition of passivity to activity, of matter to form. Hegel always expressly determines Reason as Activity. *Aufhebung*, the central concept of the sexual relation, articulates the most traditional phallocentrism with Hegelian onto-theo-teleology.

Production, differentiation, opposition, are linked to the value of activity. This is the system of virility. The clitoris, which resembles the penis, is passive: "in the male on the other hand, it has its counterpart in active sensibility (*haben wir dafür das tätige Gefühl*), the swelling of the heart (*das aufschwellende Herz*), the effusion of blood into the corpora cavernosa and the meshes of the spongy tissue of the urethra. The female counterpart of this effusion of blood in the male consists of the menstrual discharges." The same abundance of blood fills and rises on the one hand, spills and is lost on the other. The swelling of the heart also bespeaks erection; *aufschwellen* often signifies turgidity, tumescence.

who, we? Magisterial we, the we of *Sa*, we men? And what if it were always the same? And who-is-assisting-us here

The superiority of the man is compensated for by an inner division. By receiving passively, the woman remains one with herself; she works less but lets herself be worked on less by negativity. "Thus, the simple retention (*Empfangen*) of the conception in the uterus, is differentiated (*entzweit*) in the male into productive cerebrality and the external heart (*in das produzierende Gehirn und das äußerliche Herz*). On account of this difference therefore, the male is the active principle (*Der Mann ist also durch diesen Unterschied das Tätige*); as the female remains in her undeveloped unity (*weil sie in ihrer unentwickelten Einheit bleibt*), she constitutes the principle of conception (*das Empfangende*)."

Remaining enveloped in undifferentiated unity, the woman stays closer to the origin. The man is secondary, like the difference that moves into opposition. Paradoxical consequences of all phallocentrism: the working, determining sex enjoys its mastery only by losing it, enslaving itself to the feminine slave. The phallocentric hierarchy is a feminism, it subjects itself dialectically to Femininity and Truth, both capitalized, making man the *subject* of woman.

'The Mystic Rose,' murmured the chaplain.

The four men were staggered by the splendour. The rays of the rose dazzled them at first, but they quickly pulled themselves together, for such people never permit themselves to show signs of respect . . . Recovering from their agitation, they rushed in, pushing back the petals and crumpling them with their drunken hands, as a lecher who has been deprived of sex pushes back a whore's skirt. They were in the throes of a drunken profanation. With their temples throbbing and their brows beaded with sweat, they reached the heart of the rose. It was a kind of dark well. At the very edge of this pit, which was murky and deep as an eye, they leaned forward and were seized with a kind of dizziness. All four made gestures of people losing their balance, and they toppled into that deep gaze. I heard the clopping of horses that were bringing the wagon in which the victim was to be taken to the little cemetery. He had been executed eleven days after Bulkaen had been shot. Divers was still sleeping. He merely grunted a few times. He farted. An odd [*singulier*] fact: I had an erection all night long."

However, the

profound peephole gaze. This scene exposed to the multitude of people ("such people never permit themselves to show signs of respect . . . . gestures of people losing their balance", but what people? I have no means of knowing if they are gentile profaners, goyim, Christians or Jews, who divide or sign) falls into a profound gaze [regard]. The gaze is abyssal, it falls, and first of all for not coolly keeping its sense. A regard in painting is the arrangement of two figures who see each other. Example from Littré: "He has in his office a representation [regard] of Christ and Virgin." A regard is also the manhole through which one checks the flow of drainwater.

Double gaze. Cross-eyed reading. In keeping one eye on the corner column (contraband), read this as a new testament.

But also as a genesis. *The Thief's Journal*, which will soon disclaim its identity, as one disclaims responsibility, presents itself as "my book . . . become my

Subject and form: "Conception must not be regarded as consisting of nothing but the ovary and the male semen, as if the new formation were merely a composition of the forms or parts of both sides, for the female certainly contains the material element, while the male contains the subjectivity. Conception is the contraction of the whole individual into the simple self-abandoning unity of its representation (*in seine Vorstellung*)." The seed is this simple representation of itself, entirely reduced to a single "point," "as is its name and its entire self." "Consequently, conception consists of nothing but the unification of these opposed and abstract representations."

This discourse on sexual difference belongs to the philosophy of nature. It concerns the natural life of differentiated animals. It is silent on the lower animals and the limit defining them, and it excludes plants. There is supposedly no sexual difference in plants, the first *Potenz* of the organic process. The Jena philosophy of nature insists on this. The tuber, for example, may well divide (*sich entzweit*) into a "different opposition" (*differenten Gegensatz*) of masculine to feminine, but the difference remains "formal." It does not produce totalities, individual plants of which some would be male and others female: "The difference between male and female plants is only a difference of parts on the same plant, not the formation of two individuals." Hegel notes in passing that in cryptogams in general, it is supposed that the sexual parts are "infinitely small."

In this sense, the human female, who has not developed difference or opposition, is closer to the plant. The clitoris closer to the cryptogam.

There is no conceptual discrepancy in this respect between the *Encyclopedia* and the Jena philosophy. This latter describes the process of the genus as "the sublation of difference": the sublation of the difference opposed to the inorganic process becomes a difference of the sexes and the sublation of that first difference. And in a crossed-out note, we find again the figure of the circle and the point: the movement of genus is in itself and returns to itself; it is the "circle properly speaking"; but the movement of individuality moves like a bigger circle in the smaller peripheral circles and always touches them at one point.

This sublation is also the movement that makes us move on from nature to spirit. In both philosophies of nature, the paragraphs providing the articulation with the philosophy

decapitation of the other, divided in two.

"Singular fact," a fact as unsingular, however, as thinking—a paragraph further along, in the very place of Harcamone's suffering, in the weaning of the phallus fallen from the breast under the scaffold blade—of his rose, the one that carried him and that he carries in him, more or less well digested.

Genesis." Elsewhere, as "my nativity."

And if the reading of the Bible is not as familiar to you as to a slightly depraved altar boy, continuing is pointless, you won't follow, you won't be part of the cortege.

And if you protest against the squint being inflicted on you, you just need to ask yourself why. Querelle, who also uses his squint to his advantage, assumes his "incurable wound," and, like Stilitano, Giacometti, and the whole amputee, lame, and one-eyed class of characters, is thus loved, named, made sublime, magnified. He is not angered, on the contrary, when "I fixed my stare on him and told him: 'Do you have a slight quint?'" (*Querelle*).

Profound, stereoscopic gaze. See double. Two columns, two hillocks, two nipples. It is impossible. Between the one and the two, *colpos*. So you are split in two, nauseous, wanting to vomit, your head spins. You feel more than alone, more alone than ever. Without me. But, jealous of yourself, you make yourself erect, if you still can. You want it more than ever. It is precisely in Querelle, three lines in italics, without any apparent link with what precedes or follows, between two blank spaces: "*You are alone in the world, at night, in the solitude of an endless esplanade. . . . You are solitary and live in that double solitude of yours.*"

That's the end.

"In order not to suffer too much myself, I relaxed as much as possible [*me fis aussi souple que possible*]. For a moment, I was so flabby that it occurred to me that perhaps Harcamone had a mother—everyone knows that all men who are beheaded have a mother who comes to weep at the edge of the police cordon that guards the guillotine. I wanted to let my thoughts run on her and Harcamone, who was already divided in two.

of spirit analyze sexual difference, disease, and death. After naturally violent death, the negative face of generic inadequation, after copulation (positive relation of the genus to itself), another negativity works over the indefinite reproduction of the genus, the non-historicity and the bad infinity of natural life. The genus is preserved only by the decline and death of individuals: old age, illness and spontaneous death. In illness, the total organism is divided, not merely differentiated but broken up in its relation to the inorganic, to the inorganic *Potenz*. Entering into conflict with it, one of the systems or organs of the individual is separated from the whole, acquiring a sort of abnormal independence that harms the "fluidity" of the whole, and the circulation of its inner exchanges. The cause of this is an external aggression coming from the inorganic, a heterogeneous "stimulation" (*Erregung*). One very learned appendix goes back to Herodotus and the aphorisms of Heraclitus on fever; it puts to work all the medical knowledge of the age, gives the latest on syphilis, deals with the "third type" of illnesses, those of the soul, which are proper to man (the *Encyclopedia* offers a discourse on madness and refers to Pinel), can be born of fear or displeasure and can go all the way to death.

The process of the cure is the illness itself. As for the treatise on the remedy, it comfortably exceeds the treatise on the ailment. Like the illness, the remedy is an *Erregung*, an external and aggressive stimulation. It always remains difficult to assimilate, as the other of the organism. It is a counter-stimulant designed to "sublate" the first aggression. It must be analyzed under the category of digestion: it is by definition hard to digest, "intolerable." A medicament is not digested more or less easily, it is never digested, *qua* absolute other of the organism. This limit is that of the speculative dialectic of digestion and interiorization. The higher one rises in the differentiating hierarchy of animality, the more what is digestible can be heterogeneous to the organism, the more the organism is capable of assimilating foreign bodies or differentiated organic totalities. Conversely, at the bottom of the ladder, in vegetable life or animal life incapable of "difference in itself", what is digestible can only be homogeneous, homogeneous to itself, homogeneous in itself: water for plants, mother's milk (a predigested element) for nurslings. The more differentiation increases, the more the stimulus must be differentiated and heterogeneous in itself for the organism to tolerate it. It can be homogeneous with the organism only in proportion to an equal degree of

I said softly, in my state of fatigue: 'I'm going to pray for your mamma.'"

He makes himself as supple as possible, he ties himself in knots, *E tu, lenta ginestra*.

The line dividing in two doesn't only encircle the neck cut by the guillotine; it recuts the edge of the (cop) cordon that separates him, that detaches him moreover from what remains of his mother to whom he was nevertheless tied. She delimits the scaffold.

Remains—the mother.

However, two pages

example of the reading advice that I erase the whole time: since I don't stop decapitating metalanguage or rather sticking its head back in the text, only to pull it out again regularly, long enough to take a breath, one who reads "page" must bring together everything that lies on it. For example: "A while ago, in my cell, the two pimps said: 'We're making the pages.' They meant they were going to make the beds, but a kind of luminous idea transformed me there, with my legs spread apart, into a husky guard or palace groom who 'makes' a palace page just as a young man makes a chick.
To hear this boasting made Divine swoon with pleasure, as when she disentangled—it seemed to her that she was unbuttoning a fly, that her hand, already inside, was pulling up the shirt—certain pig-latin words from their extra syllables, like finery or drag: edbay, allbay."

later, in the penultimate

heterogeneity: thus mother's milk, like water, would be difficult to tolerate for the adult. That is what Hegel says. Quite logically, this leads to meat eating for humans. And even to anthropophagy: this is conceptually required by speculative idealism. It even culminates in it at the opening of *Sa*.

Medicines (at least allopathic medicines: a note allows for homeopathy, and for hypochondria—Hegel was an expert—for depression, for hypnosis, for restorative sleep, etc.) are differentiated foodstuffs, but totally indigestible, negative and foreign.

They are poisons. "In so far as they are *negative* stimuli, medicaments are poisons (*Gifte*)." One presents to the organism which has, in illness, as it were "alienated" itself, something, in the form of the remedy, that is foreign to it, from outside (*als ein ihm äußerliches Fremdes*). Faced with this indigestible, "intolerable" stimulant, the organism pulls itself together, reappropriates itself, begins a "process" that allows it to regain possession of its "feeling of self" and of its "subjectivity." So the pharmaceutical intervention works only to the extent that it is rejected, as it were. If he cannot vomit out the pharmaceutical poison, and thereby get hold of what is proper to him, the sick man dies.

Are we to conclude from this that every death of natural life is violent, that it gives in to war or illness? That there is no natural death of natural life?

There is a natural death; it is inevitable for natural life since it happens in finite individual totalities. These are inadequate to the universal genus and die because of that. Death is this inadequation of the individual to generality; it is *classification* itself, the inequality to self of life. In this sense, death also takes on the figure of abstraction, it is only an abstraction but this abstraction is a "power," a force at work in a process from which it cannot be abstracted.

Inadequation—classification and abstraction—of the generic syllogism: it has been demonstrated that it put into motion sexual difference and copulation. These latter therefore inhabit the same space, they have the same possibility and the same limit as natural death. And if "inadequation to the universal" is the "originary illness" (*ursprüngliche Krankheit*) of the individual, one ought to be able to say as much of sexual difference. And if inadequation with respect to the universal is for the individual its "inborn seed of death" (*Keim des Todes*), one must understand the same of

sentence of the book, "the rest is unutterable [*indicible*]."

Remaining [*reste*] is always said of the mother.

Who always wants to hold in her gaze the detachment that is leaving. "I realize that I loved my Colony with my flesh just as, when it was reported that the Germans were preparing to leave, France realized, in losing the rigidity they had imposed on her, that she had loved them. She squeezed her buttocks. She begged the supplanter to remain inside her. 'Stay [*reste*] a while,' she cried. Thus, Touraine was no longer fecundated."

"These papers are their graves. But I shall transmit their names far down the ages. This name, alone, will remain in the future, divested of its object. . . . If I take leave of this book, I take leave of what can be related. The rest is unutterable. I say no more and walk barefoot."

Very close to the end again, "Stay there! (SAÏD [the son] *hesitates again, then leaves.*) Fire!" and "THE MOTHER leaves last." She is always last to leave like the closest epiphany. "*Finally, there she is behind the last screen, that is, the one nearest the audience, and, tearing this last sheet of paper, appears: it is* THE MOTHER."

The mother would offer for analysis the term of a regression, a signified of last resort, only if you knew what the mother names or means, what she is pregnant with. Now you could know that only after exhausting all the rest, all the objects, all the names that the text puts in her

sexual difference, and not only by "metaphor," by some figure whose meaning would be made complete by the word "death." *Seed of death* is all but tautologous. Deep within the seed, as it circulates in the gap of sexual difference, that is to say as finite seed, death is prescribed, seeded in the seed. An infinite seed, spirit or God engendering itself or naturally inseminating itself, does not tolerate sexual difference. It disseminates only as a feint. *In this feint,* it is immortal. *Like* the Phoenix.

Reason in History specifies the limits that should be put on the Phoenix's wingspan: it is only an "image" of spirit, an analogy drawn from the "natural life" of the body and what is more an "oriental image." With the image of the Phoenix and the idea of metempsychosis, Hegel thinks oriental "metaphysics" has reached its summit. For the Westerner, on the contrary, spirit is admittedly younger in its resurrection, but it stands higher and in a clearer glory (*erhöht, verklärt*). It "enjoys itself" and "in the enjoyment of its activity it has only to do with itself."

So: seed; finite seed of sexual difference, seed of death—is it a metaphor of the infinite seed? Or the other way round? The value of "metaphor" would be powerless to decide this if it were not itself reconstructed on the basis of this question.

"The sublation of the inadequation," of sexual difference and death is the return to self of lost spirit, spirit lost for a time, for time, in nature. In order to fulfil this "destiny," natural life "kills itself." Suicide is natural, it is the operation of spirit in nature. Spirit is understood as suicide, that's where it begins to resonate for itself, where it becomes an object for itself, self-consciousness. That is where spirit calls itself—spirit—recalls itself to itself. Just as the male sex activates itself by coming out of the envelope that held it enclosed in the woman, spirit comes out of the "dead envelope" that was still constraining it in nature: "*Über diesem Tode der Natur, aus dieser toten Hülle geht eine schönere Natur, geht der Geist hervor.*" *Hülle* is envelope, veil, mask, skin, sheath. And spirit, "the more beautiful nature," is therefore the elevation of a cadaver, a sort of collapsed erection, the glorious ascension of "remains": dialectic of nature.

Such is the "concept of the philosophy of nature": the liberation of the concept that wants to gather itself by itself after having organized the suicide of nature, i.e. of its double, its "mirror" (*Spiegel*), its "reflection" (*Reflex*). This latter captivated it but also dispersed it in its image, in a sort of polymorphy that had to be reduced. The Proteus had to be strictly subjugated (*diesen*

place (galley, gallery, executioner, flowers of every kind are merely some *examples*). As long as you haven't spelled down to the last detail each of those names and each of those things, there will remain something of the mother

I am (following) the mother. The text. The mother is behind—everything I am, do, seem—the mother follows. Because she follows absolutely, she always survives—future that will have never been presentable—what she has engendered, attending, impassive, fascinating and provocative, the burial of that whose death she foresaw. The logic of obsequence. Such is the grand genetic scene: the secuting mother [*mère sécutrice*] denounces the son, then allows him to die—transforming him thereby into a daughter—abandons her, and as a result has her die, then, divine whore that she is, simulates suicide.

See, further along, this stony calculus [*calcul*] of the mother.

In short what she wants, she first of all: take back the—her—knell from the son, masturbate her own nipple, sound by herself the—her own—tocsin (what her son desires instead of her). And remain, or get out last, when everybody else is out of time. What can a mother do better than that?
But while she is there, representing and detaching herself, you can always kill yourself signing, she transforms your act into a sin in all languages, your text into *ersatz,* your paraph into a fake. She holds your hand and you always countersign.

Subject of the denunciation: I call myself my mother who calls herself (in) me. Give, accuse. Dative, accusative. I bear my mother's name, I am (following) my mother's name, I call my mother to me, I call my mother for me, I call my mother in me, recall myself to my mother. In all cases I decline the same subjugation.

The mother's calculus—which I am (following): Oh, if my mother could attend to me at my burial

that you won't have exhausted. Since there is no object and therefore no knowledge that does

Proteus zu bezwingen). Nature will have asked for nothing other than this: "The purpose of nature is to extinguish itself, and to break through its rind of immediate and sensuous being, to consume itself like a Phoenix in order to emerge from this externality rejuvenated as spirit."

The rhapsodic multiplicity of these figures foregrounds nature, precisely. The spiritual unity of the concept must do them violence in order to liberate itself from them. This operation, "the operation of spirit is philosophy."

We have still not encountered the family. At least not the human family, the one that, for the sake of a convenience that is more and more problematic, we might still be tempted to call the family *properly speaking*: neither the infinite Holy Family, nor the natural cell of the finite living being.

The analysis of the human family now seems accessible: on the way out of nature, when spirit gathers itself, becomes an object for itself in consciousness. The first philosophy of spirit, in Jena, inscribes the first determination of the human family in a theory of consciousness. The organizing concepts of this are therefore those of *Potenz* and *Mitte,* power and mid-term, middle, center. The family is the third *Potenz,* the last one, that of consciousness. It is fulfilled in *Sittlichkeit* and in the spirit of a people.

As return to itself of spirit, consciousness is the simple and immediate opposite of itself. It is that of which it is conscious, i.e. its opposite. Both active and passive, identifying with its own opposite, it separates itself from itself as from its object. But it binds itself as the strict unity of its own separation: "and on the other hand (*das andre Mal*), [consciousness] is the opposite of this sundering, the absolute union (*Einssein*) of the difference, the union of the difference both in being and sublated." As such, the two opposites *and* the movement of opposition, what is different *and* the difference, consciousness is *Mitte,* mediation, milieu, medium.

This granted, each "power" of consciousness will have the determination of a milieu. And since consciousness is the sublation of nature into spirit, each of these milieus

not concern the mother, the proposition of absolute knowing—"*it is the* THE MOTHER"—forms a tautological screen, or even the hymen that tears itself. Once the screen is analyzed, one keeps (care of) nothing. The *para* falls in the wind or remains suspended in farts.

Rain has dispersed the spectators, sent running in all directions. What is going on here in the end? Citing, reciting *genêt* page after page? Interpreting it, performing it, like a piece of music? Who is being made fun of? What is being proposed? Frills? An anthology? By what right? And the complete text is to remain hidden from us?

Not even an anthology. Pieces of anthology. As an invitation, if possible, to rebind [*relier*], in any case to reread [*relire*]. Back and front, taking it from every angle.

Nevertheless, all the pieces can't, naturally, be bound together.

The object of the present work, also its style, is the *bit* [morceau].

Which is always detached, as its name indicates, and just so you don't forget, by the teeth.

The object of the present work (tailor's code) is what of a bite [*morsure*] sticks in the throat: the bit [*mors*].

retains in itself a sublated natural determination. It corresponds each time to the idealization of a natural milieu and consciousness is the milieu of ideality in general, and therefore of universality in general. It is the ether: an absolutely welcoming transparency offering no resistance. The ether is not natural like air, but it is not purely spiritual. It is the milieu in which spirit relates to itself, repeats itself by traversing nature like wind.

Consciousness idealizes nature by negating it; it produces itself *through* what it negates (or sublates). Through: traversal and transgression leave in the ideal medium the analogical mark of the natural medium. So there is a power and a medium corresponding to the air: memory and language; then to the earth: labor and tools. In the case of the family, third power, there is an essential supplementary complication: the medium through which my family is produced is no longer *inorganic* like air or earth. It is not simply external to the ideal medium. More than one consequence will flow from this.

How does the family come to air and earth, i.e. to language and memory, to labor and tools?

Homogeneous and fluid, air allows transparency and resonance, seeing and hearing. Theoretico-phonic medium. The first power of consciousness is "pure theoretical existence." It is determined and retained as such in memory, i.e. without any solid support. Obviously we are talking about pure living memory. It would be purely evanescent without language which provides it with products that are stable but still entirely inner and spontaneous. But because of this interiority and this spontaneity, language is a product that erases itself in time. In it theoretical consciousness disappears also. It cannot *posit itself*, cannot exist as theoretical consciousness. To do so, it must therefore go outside itself, pass again into its opposite, negate its own theoricity, its *air*. It can posit itself as theoretical consciousness only by becoming practical consciousness, through the earthy element. Labor is at that point linked to memory, as tool and product of labor it is linked to the linguistic product of memory. Just as language was both the effect and the organ of memory, the tool (*Werkzeug*) serves the labor from which it proceeds. In both cases, an activity gives rise to the production of a permanence, a relatively subsistent element.

The family presupposes the two preceding powers;

To the extent that it can't, naturally, be bound (hardbound).

At best grafted it still can be.

The graft that is sewn, the substitution of the supplementary signet "constitutes" the text; its necessary heterogeneity, its endless network of lines to be tapped *en allo* requiring that the piece that gets reported back be accounted for.

To read—its walking function with a prosthesis. Whose sound isn't, as one might believe, dissonant, on the contrary. It works, walks and sings with parentheses

("Parenthesis. n. 1. Group of words forming a distinct, separate sense from that of the sentence in which it is inserted. 'These long parentheses that break up the liaison between things' (Bouhours). 'One must avoid overlong parentheses, and place them so as not to unbalance the sentence, or to prevent the mind from perceiving the sequence of correlatives' (Dumarsais)."

"*Prosthesis*, n. Surgical term. Part of surgical therapy designed to replace by an artificial preparation an organ that has been removed in whole or part. . . . 2. In Ancient Greece, prosthesis altar, small altar on which everything required for a ritual sacrifice is prepared." *Littré*)

in the body.

but it also traverses the *organic* element, desire and sexual difference. The permanent product is the child and the family possessions (*Familiengut*). Family property finally raises inorganic nature (earth and air) to the ideality of a universal property guaranteed by juridical rationality. At which point the ether becomes absolute again and the family fulfils itself by disappearing, by negating its singularity in the spirit of the people.

Such is the general schema. Let's look more closely at the transition from the second to the last *Potenz*, namely the origin of the family.

In language, an invisible, sonorous, evanescent medium, theoretical consciousness erases itself, negates itself, is reduced to a punctual instant. Therefore theoretical freedom is negative and formal here. As it is but a point, it converts itself into its opposite. Its universality becomes a pure singularity, its freedom caprice or stubbornness (*Eigensinn*). The *proper meaning* of this stubborn freedom is death. In order to be sure of remaining with itself and of letting nothing go, theoretical consciousness gives up everything. It wants to escape from the death of the inorganic, from earth, but it remains in the air and dies all the more. The purity of life is death.

Practical consciousness is therefore both the negation and the positing of theoretical consciousness. This plays out in the passage from desire to labor.

Desire is theoretical but as such tormented by a contradiction that makes it practical.

For indeed, theoretical consciousness (death) has dealings only with the dead. In the opposition that constitutes it, its object, its opposite is not a consciousness, it is a—dead—thing that for its part does not stand opposite, does not itself enter into relation. It is in the relation without itself relating-to. Theoretical consciousness thus has the form of a contradiction, the form of a relation that relates to something that is not related, does not relate (itself) (*Widerspruch einer Beziehung auf ein absolut nicht Bezogenes*), which absolves itself of the relation.

This changes only with desire. Desire relates to a living thing, and thus to something that relates (itself). The negation of theoretical consciousness is therefore first of all desire. Desire necessarily implies the very thing it negates: theoretical consciousness, memory, and language.

One might be tempted to conclude from this that desire is proper to the speaking being. In fact Hegel does not refuse desire to the animal. So it is the passage from animal desire to human desire that presupposes theoretical consciousness and speech as such. As such, because there is

And if all this galleyslave labor had been exhausted in emitting (the word "emit" strikes me as interesting but insufficient, we should also say anoint, induce, enjoin, paste)

GL

I don't say the signifier GL, or the phoneme GL, or the grapheme GL. "Mark" would be better if one were to hear that word carefully, or open one's ears to it; not even "mark" then.

It is also imprudent to advance or set going *le* or *la* GL, to write it or articulate it in capitals. It has no identity, no sex, no gender, makes no sense; it is neither a definite whole or the detached part of some whole

gl remains gl

falls just right, a pebble into water—though not to be taken for an archi-gloss (because it is but a piece of a gloss, but not yet a gloss and hence, element detached from any gloss, much more and something other than the *Urlaut*), for consonants without vowels, "sounded" syllables, non-vocalizable letters, according to some basic drive of phonation, a voiceless voice stifling a sob

first sob or first burst of laughter, a full mouth challenges you to decide whether the agglutinations here stick to signifiers or signifieds. Whence the beauty of the thing and the sob that always requires some contraction of the gullet, constriction or tightening of the gob. The experience of the beautiful, or of what is called thus, can never be wr [*ne s'ec*] without *gl*. I call to the stand the expert in tongues and letters: "No sooner had this canvas leaped to my eyes, than I experienced what I have called elsewhere the aesthetic sob (that 'aesthetic' doesn't exactly please me now), well, call it a kind of spasm between the pharynx and the esophagus, and my eyes filled with tears." (Ponge)

or clot of

indeed also a theoretical attitude in the animal if the theoretical is the relation to the dead thing. In this respect, nothing is more theoretical than the animal. But neither the animal nor the theoretical can *posit themselves as such*. Following a robust tradition, the animal is supposedly incapable of both language and labor.

Hegel at least does not refuse desire to the animal. The animal even has the power to restrain or inhibit its desire. Simply, the structure of inhibition is different. It is true that the tendency to destroy the object (the desired) is inhibited (*sich hemmt*). The members of the opposition must be sublated (*als aufzuhebende*) and it is as such that they are "posited." Desire itself posits itself as "to be destroyed." It holds back on the destruction of what it desires, i.e. of what it desires to consume, destroy, annihilate. It wants to keep what it wants to lose. Desire is *of the Aufhebung*. Inhibition and sublation are inseparable, the effect of ideality that always ensues also belongs to the structure of animal desire in general.

So what distinguishes it from human desire? It's a matter of time. The moments of the operation are dissociated and external in the animal *Aufhebung*. Destruction and preservation are juxtaposed, are "held apart in time" (*in der Zeit auseinandergerückt*). Consumption and repression are not present at the same time, they do not occupy the same present. So there is no *present Aufhebung* for the animal, and *a fortiori* not in inorganic nature. It is the very definition of nature, and not one of its predicates among others. In this sense it is not absurd to say that there is no *Aufhebung* or dialectic of nature. At least the dialectic does not *present* itself in nature. It announces itself—already—in the mode of the not-yet. Nothing more dialectical than that, however.

There is animality when consumption and nonconsumption follow each other but do not gather themselves together. The animal as such (which is why it supposedly has no history and repeats itself without end), man *qua* animal consumes, then does not consume, destroys then does not destroy, desires to destroy then desires not to destroy, satiates himself then stops, stops then satiates himself and starts over again. This dissociation or this successivity is the very thing that human desire sublates. This time the inhibition inhabits consummation itself. Ideality, an effect of inhibition, *forms part* of the present of consummation. The *Aufhebung* produces itself in it *presently*, at the heart of enjoyment. "Human desire must be ideally canceled in its very sublation [*im Aufheben selbst*], it must be

milk in the throat, tickled laugh or gluey vomit of a gluttonous baby, the imperial flight of a bird of prey

"... he sees love swooping down on me—it is not mere rhetoric which requires the comparison—like a falcon ..." "I felt as if I were being carried by him. It was as if he were already on top of me and had screwed me, laying me out with all his weight and also drawing me to him as the eagle drew Ganymede, as he was to do that fourth night when, better prepared, I let him enter me deeply and he swooped down on me with his huge bulk (a whole sky falling on my back), his claws digging into my shoulders and his teeth biting the back of my neck. He was planted inside me, pushing into my soil and, above me, unfurling a bough and a leaden foliage." And further along, again in *The Thief's Journal*, Ganymede gets literally stolen: "Jupiter carries off Ganymede and screws him: I could have indulged in every kind of debauchery." The *gls* of the eagle are at the same time or alternately the aerial raising of the concept, absolute knowing that carries you off, and the heaviness of the signifier that crushes you or pushes into you. In *Funeral Rites* the (church of the) Trinity displays the eagle of the Reich. At the moment you are called, you are always in the process of getting screwed in contraband, such is philosophy

swooping down all of a sudden on the back of your neck, the sticky, frozen, cold piss name of an impassive Teutonic philosopher, with his well-known stammer, sometimes liquid and sometimes guttural and tetanic, with swollen or cooing goiter, everything that rings strange in the tympanic pit or canal, spit or paste on the soft palate, orgasm of the glottis or uvula, clitoral glue, abortion cloaca, spermchoke, rhythmic hiatus of an occlusion, staccatodance spasm of an eruptojaculation, syncopated valve of the tongue and lips, or a nail falling in the

sublated [*aufgehoben*] and the object must abide (*bleiben*) even when (*indem*) it is sublated."

Aufhebung thus sublates *itself* in present desire. Human desire: sublation of sublation, sublating presence of sublation, sublatance [*relevance*]. The truth of ideality presents itself as such in it.

Aufhebung is not something determinate, nor a formal structure whose undifferentiated generality applies at every moment. It is the history, the becoming of its own presentation, of its own differentiating determination, and it is subject to the law, to the same law as that of which it is the law: it gives itself first as immediate, then mediates itself by negating itself, etc. The fact that it is subject to the law of that of which it is the law is what gives Hegel's system a form that is so tricky and hard to grasp.

How does desire become labor? Why does it remain desire in the animal whereas it cannot fail to posit itself as labor in man?

In animal desire—which constitutes the animal as such—ideality is not internal to consummation, to satisfaction, but merely follows it: "the actual coming-to-pass of the sublation, the stilling [*Stillung*] of desire, is for the animal an immediate state of sublation without any ideality, without consciousness." (One could already conclude, against the clear interest of this obscure humanism, that the ideality, the consciousness, the humanity of desire is the supplementary mediatization of animal desire—neither more nor less). Insofar as it is no longer dealing with a dead object and preserving ideality spares the desired object, desire is no longer a merely theoretical operation. It is already a practical relation. Human desire is labor. In itself. This depends on the fact that inhibition in general structures it in the most inner and essential way. We must make room for the generality of this structure, and then wonder whether something like repression can figure in it as a species of the genus *Hemmung*, if the logic of repression is compatible with the general logic of inhibition and of sublation. If there were a decidable answer to this question it would not be just one word.

So Hegel must describe simultaneously the emergence of human desire and the emergence of the practical relation. There is no animal labor, and praxis is a "power" of consciousness. "The practical connection is a connection (*Beziehung*) of consciousness." This depends on the fact that in its very simplicity the annihilation of the object is an operation that inhibits itself in itself and opposes itself to itself

silence of the milky voice [*la voix lactée*] (I note in parentheses that from the beginning of this reading I haven't stopped thinking—as if it were my principal object—of the brands of milk for newborns known as Gloria and Gallia, of everything that can happen with porridge, of the potage of greedy nurslings, stuffed with or weaned from a cleaved breast, and there you have it, everything takes, congeals and falls into galalith).

Milk stone. A sort of galalith tombstone in synthetic mineral, a milky knock-off. A block of curdled milk. Galalith is plastic matter obtained by treating pure casein with formaldehyde. When Leila brings out all those objects from under her skirt in the "mother's house," lamp, shade, "bits of broken glass . . . or fragments . . . pieces of glass . . . shards . . . splinters," she is asked by The Mother: "You have everything there?" LEÏLA: Everything. THE MOTHER (*pointing to* LEÏLA*'s bulging belly*): And that? LEÏLA: That? THE MOTHER: What's that? LEÏLA (*laughing*): My latest little one. THE MOTHER (*also laughing*): Got it where? . . . No one saw you? All right, put it there. (*She points to a stool drawn on the screen in* trompe-l'oeil. *With a charcoal pencil that she has taken from her pocket* LEÏLA *draws, above the table, an alarm clock.*) . . . . It's very pretty. What is it? Real marble or imitation [*galalithe*]? LEÏLA (*with pride*): Imitation [*Galalithe*]."

(*ein in sich Gehemmtes und Entgegensetztes*). This is why desire is never satisfied and that is its very "practical" structure. "Desire does not come to its satisfaction in its nullification." Its object remains, not because it escapes annihilation, holds itself out of reach for it, but because it remains *in* its annihilation. *It remains insofar as it does not remain.* An operation of *mourning*: idealizing consummation. This relation is called labor. Practical consciousness *elaborates* in the place in which it annihilates and holds together the two opposed terms of the contradiction. In this sense labor is the middle term (*Mitte*) of the opposition intrinsic to desire.

In its turn this middle term posits itself, gives itself a permanence. Without this, it would collapse into a pure negativity, it would sink like a pure activity, carrying itself off of its own accord at each moment. In order to posit itself, labor must therefore pass into its opposite, fix itself outside itself in the resistance of the medium. This is the origin of the *tool* (*Werkzeug*), the *object* (producer and product) *of labor*. "Labor as such . . . is itself a thing (*Ding*). The *tool* is the existing rational middle, the existing universality, of the practical process."

What is such a thing (*Ding*)? What is the being-thing of this thing (*Ding*)? It is an existing universality because the *generality* of the tool prevents labor from being exhausted by the singular acts of an empirical subjectivity. Without the universal objectivity of the tool, labor would be a unilateral experience. It would destroy itself and carry itself off in the ineffable multiplicity of gestures. So the tool preserves labor from self-destruction, it is the sublating ideality of *praxis*, it is both active and passive: the remains of labor that enters into tradition, practical history. But practical history as a history of desire. Desire and labor disappear, with their objects, *qua empirical individuals.* One desires, one consumes, one works, it all passes and dies. *Qua* empirical individuals. Tradition (Hegel's word) is therefore what resists this loss and constitutes maintained ideality: not the finite and elaborated object but the instrument of labor that can be used again because of its general structure. It is endowed with an identity that is ideal, reproducible, perfectible, it gives rise to accumulation, etc. So one cannot desire without desiring to produce tools, i.e. instruments of production.

galalith

The word is detached, sounds all by itself. The thing also. It is an alarm clock. In the swollen belly there was this ringing object of plastic matter carrying in its own belly a little hammer, a mini-tocsin whose ringing can be triggered unexpectedly. Glug-glug/Tick-tock. All this galactic matter signals fake, not only because its substance is synthetic, but because this cheap bazaar object is merely drawn, and then in trompe-l'oeil, and on a screen. Interminable funeral [*obsèque*] of the thing itself. Before the representative of the law, The Mother takes on as it were the property of galalith, takes the alarm clock back into her belly. Then she mimes the gestures of her son in order to open the belly for him, that of the alarm clock. The gendarme observes the screen: "You were seen in a mirror, running away. . . . The clock was no longer there. (*A pause.*) Is that the one? THE MOTHER: No. The clock's always been there. . . . The clock's been there for ages. How would we wake up without it? Just imagine, one day, when he was very little, Saïd took it completely apart. Completely. Piece by piece, to see what was inside, and he put all the springs on a plate. He was still a tot, and just then I entered the house. That was long ago, as you can imagine. I was returning from the grocer's, and what did I see on the floor? . . . (*She mimes the scene.*) But really, like some kind of vermin ready to scamper away: little wheels, little stars, little nuts, little worms, little nails, gobs and gobs of thingum-bobs, little springs, sparrow's wings, cigarettes, bayonets, castanets [*des harengs saurs, clés à mollettes, cigarettes, trottinettes*]. . . ."

Now we have to take the hardest step: marriage.

A few lines—more enigmatic than ever—close the analysis of the second "*Potenz*" (the tool) and in short have to explain the appearance of the third (the family) in its first phase. So the point is to account for the production of marriage by the tool.

As always this movement has the form of a production by *positing*: objectivation, contradiction, interiorization, subjectivation, idealization, liberation, sublation. Marriage: sublation of the tool.

The tool is solid. Resisting consumption in this way, ensuring tradition, it exists by the same token as an external constraint. Elaborating desire does indeed give itself the tool, but only as a thing that is external and in a relation of heteronomy. It no longer freely, spontaneously, from within, forbids itself from consuming the other. Ideality is still in a certain dissociable outside. Freedom of consciousness does not assert itself fully in the inhibitory reserve.

Marriage is the sublation of that constraint, the interiorization of that exteriority, the consummation of the tool. Labor of desire without tool. The externality of the instrumental chain has just been defined: "The freedom of consciousness sublates this need and restricts the nullification in enjoyment, through [that freedom of consciousness] itself [*durch sich selbst*]; it makes the two sexes conscious of each other, into beings on their own account . . . in such a way that in the being-for-self of the other, each is him/herself."

This is the first time that the Jena philosophy of spirit touches on sexual desire. The philosophy of nature dealt with biological sexuality. As for desire, it had not yet been specified as sexual desire—it could just as well be about eating and drinking. So it is at the moment when the *Aufhebung*, within enjoyment, inhibits, holds back and sublates pleasure so as not to destroy the other and thereby destroy itself as enjoyment, limits in order to preserve, negates in order to enjoy, as if in fear one must not reach a *too good* that would run the risk of carrying away what is given in its very excess—it is at this furtive moment, very close and very far from itself, from its own present, barely phenomenal, between night and day—twilight—that Hegel determines desire as sexual desire. This secret of enjoyment that sacrifices itself, immolates itself to itself, albeit on the altar of enjoyment, so as not to destroy (itself), itself and the other, the one in the other, the one for the other—essential

The mechanism of the signifier, which also covers the flight of the other (Leila) can no more be stopped than can the ringing of the alarm clock. It will also have set off this disquieting trance of impossible partition: between signified and signifier, true and false, living and inanimate, piece and organic whole. All these little fetuses, penises, or clitorises at the same time dead and alive, screws and worms, swarming with neither head nor tail, passing on both head and tail in order to crawl between your fingers and get everywhere, fitting into one another in fake belly [*trompe ventre*]. Naturally the gendarme doesn't like galalith, he doesn't like what is *ersatz*, he is for the authentic and doesn't see a thing: "It's imitation marble [*galalithe*] or real marble, you can bet it's imitation. The stuff that's sold in the villages and at fairs and markets nowadays! Nothing's like it used to be."

They'd sell you anything these days.

If *gl* isn't sufficient for you, if it doesn't get you off at all, if you really don't give a fuck about it, if you want to give back *gl*, to me or to this galleyson nicknamed Gallien, make one more effort. Suppose what is being erected here more properly is still something shaped like an A, for putting one's head through and risking the blow. Not to add it to

un-enjoyment and im-potence—that's what Hegel calls love. The two sexes pass the one into the other, are the one for and in the other—which constitutes the ideal, the ideality of the ideal.

This latter has its "middle" [*milieu*] in marriage. Free inhibition in desire, the desire that "frees itself from its connection with enjoyment" is love; and the subsistence of love, its duration, its elementary milieu, is marriage. ". . . and the connection of the sexes comes to be one, in which in the being of the consciousness of either party, each is him/herself one with the other, in other words an ideal union. Desire thus frees itself from its connection to enjoyment, it comes to be an immediate union [*Einssein*] of both in the absolute being for self of both, i.e., it becomes *Love*; and the enjoyment is in this intuiting (*Anschauen*) of oneself in the being of the other consciousness. The connection itself becomes in the same way the being of both, and something that abides [*bleibende*] as much as they do, that is, it becomes *marriage*."

An addition in the *Philosophy of Right* will distinguish marriage from concubinage by the "repression" of the natural urge (the *Naturtrieb* is *zurückgedrängt* in it). Concubinage satisfies it, to the contrary.

We have come back to the syllogistic deduction of love and marriage as the immediate unity of the family.

Duration, what remains (*bleibt*) of this moment, which is to love what the tool is to labor, does not remain in peace. A new dialectical cycle gets started here, a new war begins to rage. The struggle to the death for recognition is here inscribed within the family syllogism. One difference between the Jena analysis and that of the *Philosophy of Right,* which is much fuller: the former includes, in the development concerning the child, an explication of the struggle to the death for recognition and possession.

Marriage is thus the first moment of the family, the most natural and the most immediate. It is monogamous: this is a constant implication, declared later in the *Philosophy of Right*: "Marriage, and essentially monogamy, is one of the absolute principles on which the *Sittlichkeit* of a community is based," or again "Marriage is essentially *monogamy*."

As free inclination of both sexes, it excludes any contract. Such an abstract juridical link could indeed link persons only to (dead) things, and could not engage two living

gl (the 's' once more fallen) but to write italic like

(*PARANTHESIS*)

Among all the sewing of the genetic text, six lines in parentheses and in italic.

Why do they fascinate?

What do they fascinate? Short of verifying later with the assistance of machines for reading and writing theses, cases of such an insertion (not really an insertion [*incise*], but it is at least monstrous both in size and beauty) seem rare. It isn't one of those *mises en abyme* by which the author pretends to intervene as author in a narrative to play at explaining to you what he is working at while all along having you swallow something that you can't see yet, that you don't even have the time to slow down and recognize. In these six lines, it seems to be a case of a simple shift of the *camera* that diverts the chronological storyline, a rather banal way of doing without parentheses and especially italics. So why?

freedoms. There can be empirical determinations toward marriage, "pathological" inclinations, but that is inessential.

No consideration on the empirical limitations of freedom can measure up to the essentiality of marriage. Therefore Hegel never takes into consideration Kant's whole pragmatic anthropology, everything in it that concerns conjugal agonistics, the struggle for mastery between husband and wife. The philosophy of spirit never says anything about the sexual difference between the spouses. Nothing could be more logical: everything should proceed as though the spouses were of the same sex, were both bisexual or asexual. The *Aufhebung* has operated.

War begins with the child. So any discourse on the inequality of the sexes in marriage would remain empirical, irrelevant, foreign to the essence of marriage. In the "Characteristic," the second part of his *Anthropology*, Kant analyses "the character of the female sex" in and out of marriage. He does so in terms of a struggle for domination, a complex struggle in which mastery passes from one sex to the other according to different domains and moments. Mastery is rarely to be found where one expects to find it. The inequality of the sexes is the condition of a harmonious union. Equality of strength would render one sex insufferable to the other. So the progress of culture should favor inequality for the protection and propagation of the species. In the service of natural teleology, culture produces and accentuates heterogeneity in the disproportion of the sexes. The man must be superior in his physical strength and his courage; the woman by—I quote—"her natural talent [*Naturgabe,* natural gift] for mastering his desire for her." This strange superiority of the woman is not natural. It depends on culture which thus privileges the woman since in nature all the superiority "is on the side of the man." If then culture transforms the natural situation by procuring some artificial superiority for the woman, a theory of culture—what Kant here calls anthropology—ought to have as its privileged, if not only, object, the status of femininity. Anthropology ought to be a theory of woman. ". . . the characteristic features of the female sex (*weibliche Eigentümlichkeit*), more than those of the male sex, are a topic of study for the philosopher."

Culture is not limited to the simple revelation of an enveloped feminine specificity.

It grafts. The relative superiority of the cultivated woman is a male graft: "In the crude state of nature (*in rohe Naturstände*) one can no more recognize these characteristic

I don't intend to account for it, not because I am keeping the reason for it to myself but because, being concerned with grafting in all cases and in all senses, the principle of reason is perhaps no longer current. At the least the reason for it can't be asked of the one writing.

The operation would therefore consist, for the moment, simply in shifting the graft of the paranthetic organ, not knowing whether it is bleeding or not, then, following the ablation and a certain treatment that does not at all consist in curing, in putting the whole back in place, sewing it back, in spite of its perhaps not being appeased in its restored constitution but instead tearing itself to shreds more than ever.

That presumes that it will be quoted at least twice.

A first time to extract

"*(Long afterward, when I ran into him in Antwerp, I spoke to Stilitano about the fake bunch hidden in his fly. He then told me that a Spanish whore used to wear a muslin rose pinned on at cunt level.*

'To replace her lost flower,' he said.)"

It's a cutting from *The Thief's Journal*. Which carried as headline [*portait à la une*] in two columns:

1. the effect: "clothing," uniform or adornment (like the shoes from the first sequence of *The Screens* or the gloves whose reversible fingers, name, occurrences and transformations orchestrate *The Maids* from the moment of the raising of the curtain on the raising of the curtain);

2. the stating of a law of oscillation and in-

features [specific to woman] than those of crab apples and wild pears, which reveal their diversity (*Mannigfaltigkeit*) only through grafting (*Pfropfen*) or inoculation (*Inokulieren*)." The graft transforms here only by deploying natural properties, which explains why the relative superiority it confers on the woman should appear to reverse the natural situation, but consists only in knowing how to submit to the man's inclination. "For culture does not introduce these feminine qualities," it merely produces them, brings them to light, "allows them to develop and become recognizable under favorable conditions."

Within this general anthropo-botanics, Kant analyzes the war of the sexes in marriage. The woman has a taste for domestic warfare, which the man flees; he "loves domestic peace" and happily submits to the government of the woman. "Woman wants to dominate (*herrschen*), man to be dominated (*beherrscht*) (especially before marriage)." As a consequence of culture, marriage liberates the woman and enslaves the man: "Woman becomes free by marriage; man loses his freedom by it."

This is a simulacrum of a reversal: the woman does not become the stronger, but culture makes her weakness into a lever. The possibility of inverting natural signs—femininity itself—forbids one from analyzing a feminine essence or nature. Femininity is the power to be other than one is, to make a weapon of one's weakness, to remain secret. Woman has a secret (*Geheimnis*), man is deprived of it. This is why he is easy to analyze (*der Mann ist leicht zu erforschen*). The analysis of woman is impossible, she does not reveal her secret, which does not prevent her from regularly revealing the secrets of others. Because she talks: the reign of culture as reign of woman is also the field of speech. Language only ever speaks this perversion of nature by culture—by woman. Woman's weapon is the tongue. It transforms the weakness of the slave into mastery through the tongue but already, always, by that perversion of discourse constituted by chatter, loquacity, verbosity, volubility (*Redseligkeit*). This is how she triumphs in domestic warfare and how she likes it, unlike the man who has other things to do out of the house. She triumphs by ruse, piling up all the rights: sheltered behind her husband (right of the stronger), she commands her master (right of the weaker). Art of the lever.

Through this law of perversion that displaces the primitive hierarchy, natural teleology continues to operate;

decision (as for example "What remains of a Rembrandt" whose "neither true nor false" or almost-false invites you to follow the tacking between the two columns) that remarks the incessantly instantaneous turning inside out of the flower: penis/vagina, castration/virginity, erection/fallout, natural organism/disarticulated artifact, whole proper body/fetishized piece, etc.

All the while that flowers—anthologic of the undecidable—are writing on and as a clothing artifice, they lean into italics, then fall into a note about the *affect* of indecision that interests us above all else here.

First sentence of the *Journal*: "Convicts' garb is striped pink and white."

A printed fabric is described thus, with lines and crossings-out, flower-colored stripes (the flower is immediately induced, by means of the "pink [*rose*] and white," in the second sentence), like a thief's journal that will have to be followed through every which way in order to cut in it or pick from it all the flowers.

Rose is also the first word of *The Screens*. Play emerges between color and flower, adjective and noun. It floats like women's clothing over the whole

the Rembrandt already reverberates the literal echo sent from the surface of *The Screens*. Laughter from The Mother: ". . . . (*She roars with laughter, and it is with roars of laughter that she says the following.*) Those are the truths . . . ha! . . . ha! . . . ha! ha! . . . that can't be demonstrated . . . ha! ha! (*Her laughter seems irrepressible.*) It's the truths that are false! . . . ha! ha! ha! ho! ho! ho! . . . ha! ha! (*She is bent double with laughter.*) It's the truths that you can't carry to their extremes . . . ho! ho! ho! ho! Oh! Oh! Ha! ha! Ho! ho! ho! . . . without seeing them die and without seeing yourself die of laughter, that you've got to exalt . . ."

Our Lady of the Flowers: "Don't complain about improbability. What's going to follow is false, and no one has to accept it as gospel truth. Truth is not my strong point. But 'one must lie in order to be true.' And even go beyond. What truth do I want to talk about? If it is really

it realizes its normal, normalizing designs, via ruses and detours. Kant's "description" stubbornly restores its intention.

Woman does indeed look like a "folly" of nature, the human folly of nature. But in seducing man, diverting him from his natural trajectory, she in the end accomplishes the wise design of nature. The divergence has been calculated for all time, the two sexes have been gently and implacably ordered toward this great purpose, without the subjects understanding it at all. This is why we cannot think female sexuality. Our categories, our aims, the forms of our consciousness are incapable of it, a little like anthropomorphic metaphors in a discourse on God. To gain access to the "characteristic of the female sex" one must follow not "what we *make* our end" but "what *nature's end* was in establishing womankind." The "foolishness of human beings" is a means in view of that end which is "wisdom" when we consider "the intention of nature." The principle of the characteristic does not therefore depend on "our choice" but on "a higher purpose": "preservation of the species," "cultivation of society and its refinement by womankind." Along what paths?

Having entrusted to woman a womb whose "fruit (*Liebesfrucht*)" allows the species to develop, nature took fright for the one in whom the "pledge" to propagate was deposited; she preserved her daughter, kept her sheltered, made her fearful and timid when faced with danger. She was granted man's protection. Woman's fear is nature's fear or life's fear for itself. Social refinement obeys the same purpose. To encourage it, nature has "made this sex man's ruler (*Beherrscher*)." This mastery was ensured by a moralization: not in the sense of morality, *Moralität*, but mores, *Sittsamkeit*, if not *Sittlichkeit*. *Sittsamkeit* is decency, honesty, modesty, reserve. Twice in two lines we see it opposed to morality (*Moralität*). With its ease of discourse and the play of mimicry, *Sittsamkeit* is even the mask of morality (one would render the text illegible if one translated *Sittsamkeit* as morality), the ruse which enslaves man. Man is at that point, because of his "own magnanimity," "imperceptibly fettered by a child." As modesty, decency, reserve, *Sittsamkeit* indeed serves as a veil or as "clothing (*Kleid*)" for an invisible morality. Woman is on the side of *Sittlichkeit* or *Sittsamkeit*, which Kant places below

true that I am a prisoner who plays (who plays for himself) scenes of the inner life, you will require nothing other than a game."

text. It hides the sex organs and announces it, although one doesn't know which article is involved. Pink [*le rose*] or rose [*la rose*]? The opening of *The Screens* suspends it for a time in an exclamation: "Rose! (*A pause.*) I say to you rose!"

"Convicts' garb is striped pink and white. Though it was at my heart's bidding that I chose the universe wherein I delight, I at least have the power of finding therein the meanings I wish to find: *there is a close relation between flowers and convicts*. The fragility and delicacy of the former are of the same nature as the brutal insensitivity of the latter.*"

The asterisk keeps the veil lifted.

The footnote reference won't make you fall and be paralyzed in the trap of an antonymy or an antinomy.

On the contrary, it says what provokes a movement that is infinite, shivering, quivering (the latter two words are rather studied, and are again movements, emotions of flowers).

Here is the note: "*My excitement [*émoi*] is the oscillation from one to the other."

Whose excitement? Author's? Narrator's? Who signs the footnote? Since excitement is the oscillation ("my excitement [*émoi*] is the oscillation"), the *I* is carried away, divided, sidelined in the trait that relates it to anything at all. Undecidable for its part also in its signature.

In two pages the consequences have been drawn, always with the detachment of grand style, that is to say giving the appearance of being busy with something else. Drawn like a veil that marries,

morality. Hegel will reverse the relation of *Moralität* to *Sittlichkeit.* There is a chiasmus here that cannot be maintained within the limits of an "anthropology."

How does (female) perversion place itself in the service of the teleology hidden in marriage? And how does this teleological problem reproduce the chiasmus?

In the state of nature, in the Kantian sense, man's polygamy is pretty much natural. The paradigmatic structure looks like that of the harem. Man naturally desires all women and not one woman, deals only with instances of femininity. He does not love, he loves any woman. Woman is a kind of whore. *Conversely,* in the state of culture, woman does not abandon herself to man's pleasure outside marriage, monogamous marriage; but she desires all men and thus becomes, in act or in intention, a whore. Kantian man thus is always only dealing with the whore and if one asked this categorical pornographer which he preferred, the whore or the virgin, he would reply the virgin, well knowing that nature, who is leading him here, sees to it that at the limit this comes down to the same thing. A situation that cannot have no relation to what Hegel will analyze as beautiful soul and unhappy consciousness.

In both cases, natural polygamy and historical monogamy, it is always the place of the man that determines the concept. Monogamy is one man and one woman; polygamy is again one man and many women. Woman is never polygamous, either in Kantian nature or in Kantian culture. Such is the appearance: in truth the woman always has everything, both in monogamy and in polygamy. In the harem, for example, there is no true multiplicity and man loses at every turn. The women wage war on each other to restore the monogamous relation and so that one of them can have all of the man, at least potentially. To the extent that they all have him, none of them is deprived, and one of them also ends up ruling over him. Described in this way, the harem belongs neither to nature nor to culture. Polygamy cannot be thought within this opposition. In nature there is no true marriage; in true culture, marriage is monogamy. Kant qualifies as "barbarian" this unclassifiable phenomenon, this society that is no longer natural and is not yet moral. On the basis of this "perversion" we need to interrogate the opposition of concepts from which polygamy escapes—the polygamy of man Kant is talking about, that of woman about which he says nothing.

In the harem, woman is no longer the "domestic

hides, and lets show through the form of all the chains. Those of convicts but also those linking the rhetoric of veils to the stealing away of truth, castration, erection, nomination. The veil is remarked there, folded over, recut around flowers that are at once flowers of rhetoric and stagings—putting it into question—of rhetoric. For example, immediately following the asterisk that keeps the veil lifted: "Should I have to portray a convict—or a criminal—I shall so bedeck him with flowers that, as he disappears beneath them, he will himself become a flower, a gigantic and a new one."

Under the necklace, the garland, the crown made from artificial flowers, under the poetic parade or adornment, one promises *at the same time* to provoke stifling, the embalmed disappearance beneath funeral rites, and to make burst out the erect phallus. It is here not a matter of choice, disjunction, accumulation. My excitement is the oscillation. The game (erection tombfalls) is announced as a mortuary ceremony burying the other under flowers but in the same swoop giving him a hard-on under the figures of rhetoric and veils or sails of every kind.

All that for nothing, without any actual insemination. The anther in play encloses pollen before fecundation (it surrounds the style and forms one of two parts of the stamen).

animal" she must have been in nature; she begins to fight and plot to enchain man's drive or capture his desire. The harem is a prison, an enclosure (*Zwinger*), but woman already knows how to establish her mastery in it. Man knows no rest amidst the busy competition of women.

Such is the "barbarian constitution" of oriental polygamy, neither natural nor civilized. In the monogamy of (bourgeois) civil society, so long as the culture is not very developed, the man punishes the woman if she threatens to give him a rival. But when civilization (*Zivilisierung*) becomes refined to the point of decadence, when it permits "gallantry" (the fact of a married woman having lovers) and turns it into a fashion that makes jealousy ridiculous, then the female character "reveals itself." The perversion of gallantry reveals the true nature of woman, her profound design: "by extending favors toward men, woman lays claim to freedom and, at the same time, to the conquest of the entire male sex." This conquest, takeover, theft (*Eroberung*) of the man by the woman is not simply condemned by Kant. In his analysis of female perversion we can read the complex system of phallogocentrism. But this system is always precarious and neutralizes itself, *contains* what contradicts it. Here for example, Kant ceaselessly erases the moralizing connotation that seems, however, so huge: he often specifies that one must not let oneself be taken in by the illusions of consciousness or intention. In female perversion, in its cultural, symbolic, verbal ruses—this all goes via woman's language, Kant must read the text of love in the language of woman who herself knows how to bind virile energy—we must recognize a hidden natural process, a wisdom of nature. In spite of strong and ridiculous appearances, Kant's discourse would not be in the end the moral disqualification of a monstrosity.

But we must recognize that this last proposition immediately reverses itself. If Kant does not produce the discourse of anti-female morality, this is because he moralizes through and through his recourse to nature, to the providential wisdom of she who watches over the perversion. Nature is good, she is a good woman, i.e. in truth—through her productive force, her reason, her profound *logos* that dominates all female chatter, her imperturbable and always victorious logic, her educative resources—a father. The good woman is a father, the father is a good woman, and simply this is what is speaking through the mere women who intend to appropriate it.

"My adventure, never governed by rebellion or a feeling of injustice, will merely be one long mating [*pariade*], burdened and complicated by a heavy, strange, erotic ceremonial (figurative ceremonies leading to jail and anticipating it)."

The text of the *Journal* and the convicts' costume will be cut from the same cloth, the same flowery fabric: naked, veiled, hairy, eriopetal flowers (all that is very loaded, no? too rich and in bad taste, as the gendarme or grand bourgeois might say, but also like the ceremony projected above).

One has to be able to die laughing while practicing queer inversion: "Desiring to hymn them, I use what is offered to me by the form of the most exquisite natural sensibility, which is already aroused by the garb of convicts.

the point is always to circle the absent word, letting it echo as if in the hollow of a bell, producing emptiness in the center of the space reserved for it, without ever writing, ever pronouncing what you are however being constrained to hear, on one stage or the other, and which, as a result, for not being mastered in an act, strikes all the harder. Something recognized in its effects. There is no warding off this mode of writing, since you are never shown the weapon, since one pretends to hide it out of modesty. Immodesty is often the repression of a fear: one shows one's hand in panic in order to provoke a general disarming.
Always apotropaic show [*monstration*]. The obscene is on the contrary modest, hardbinding the bit whose cortege you are slowly following.
"Parade" seems to describe it correctly—given the context—rather than mating [*pariade*]. Parade in the double hardbind of the word (ornament for adornment and protection—umbrella [*parapluie*], screen [*paravent*], parachute, etc.). One could even bet [*parier*] it's a typo. But a more open context (a few pages later) also gives their chance to pair and partridges. The mating season [*la pariade*] is the time when partridges pair up by breaking with the group, excluding themselves. Among partridges, this is the closest detachment: "It was therefore natural for me to imagine what his penis would be if he smeared it for my benefit with so fine a substance, with that precious cobweb, a fabric that I secretly called the veil of the palate. He wore an old grey cap with a broken visor. When he tossed it on the floor of our room, it suddenly became the carcass of a poor partridge with a clipped wing."

The text *presents itself* in this way as

Natural reserve: if, in bourgeois monogamous marriage, the woman wants to appropriate the whole of the opposite sex, this is because the man (husband or father) is finite; he dies, sometimes young, almost always before the woman, who then remains alone, young, widowed. And she will then have had to be prepared for this mourning, knowing herself to be always threatened, on the way to lacking a man. She is interested in sex as a provision, following the maternal advice of nature. "This inclination, though it indeed stands in ill repute under the name of coquetry, is nevertheless not without a real basis of justification. For a young wife is always in danger of becoming a widow, and this causes her to extend her charms over all men whose fortunate circumstances make them marriageable; so that, should this situation occur, she would not be lacking in suitors."

This hidden teleology justifies all the dissymmetries and all the inequalities of development that Kant thinks he can describe under the heading of sexual difference.

The woman wants to be a man; the man never wants to be a woman. "When refined luxury [*Luxus*] has reached a high level, the woman appears demure [*sittsam*] only by compulsion [*Zwang*] and makes no secret of wishing that she might rather be a man, so that she could give her inclinations larger and freer latitude [*Spielraum*]; no man, however, would want to be a woman." Kant does not expand on this last proposition, at the end of a paragraph. It goes without saying that this has never been heard of and never will be. Even if perchance one thought one had encountered such an aberration, what would it mean? What would it mean for a man to want to be a woman, given that the woman wants to be a man to the extent that she cultivates herself? It would mean, with only an apparent detour, wanting to be a man, wanting to be—i.e. remain—a man.

Is it so simple? Does Kant say that the woman wants to be a man? More precisely, he says that in certain situations she would like to take on manly attributes in order to realize her womanly designs: to be better placed to have all men. She pretends to want to be a man or to be man so as to "give latitude" to her inclinations. Everything is reversed: either the man who wants to be only a man wants to be a woman insofar as the woman wants to be a man; so he wants to be a woman in order to remain what he is. Or else the man who wants to be a woman wants only to be a woman since the woman wants to be a man only to succeed in her womanly designs. Namely man. Etc.

This all happens very fast in the masculine penumbra

The material evokes by its roughness, over and above its colors, certain flowers whose petals are slightly fuzzy, whose detail is sufficient for me to associate the idea of strength and shame with what is most naturally precious and fragile. This association, which tells me things about myself, would not suggest itself to another mind; mine cannot avoid it. Thus I offered my tenderness to the convicts; I wanted to call them by charming names, to designate their crimes with, for modesty's sake, the subtlest metaphor (beneath whose veil I couldn't ignore the murderer's rich musculature, the violence of his sexual organ). Is it not by the following image that I prefer to imagine them in Guiana: the strongest, with a horn, the "hardest," veiled by mosquito netting? And each flower within me leaves behind so solemn a sadness that all of them must signify sorrow, death. Thus I sought love as it pertained to the penal colony."

Function of the prison colony. Of Guiana, whose end is approaching. Guiana's dying days are announced loud and clear in the first pages of the *Journal*.

Function of the prison colony: it is the place of what we shall henceforth call *antherection*—the time of a countered erection, recut by its contrary, in place of the flower. Enanthiosis.

The recutting overlaps itself indefinitely.

commentary on the absent word that he delimits, envelops, serves, surrounds with his attentions. The text *presents itself* as metalanguage of the language that isn't presented. But it is simply a case of parading. And whoever comes after that to exhibit the active holes in the other and to pronounce the unpronounced—parade again as metalanguage—simulates presentation, leaves behind blisters or bells or airstreams in his body, encircles and excludes still other words, etc. The death throes of metalanguage are therefore structurally interminable. But as effort and as effect. Metalanguage is the life of language: it always flounders like a bird caught in a subtle glue (trap).

[*le pénombre*] in which desire itself is bound, if any such thing exists.

In fact, even if she really wanted, which is not the case, the woman could never be a man. The male attributes with which she adorns herself are only ever fake, signifiers without signification, fetishes. For show [*de la montre*]. A watch [*une montre*] not set to the movement of the sun. To illustrate the fact that the woman can never appropriate the male attribute—for example or by substitution science, culture, the book—Kant denounces a sort of travesty: "As concerns scholarly women: they use their *books* somewhat like their *watch*, that is, they carry one so that it will be seen that they have one; though it is usually not running or not set by the sun." The choice of paradigm confirms once again that one cannot think "genius" without the unconscious.

The endless dissymmetry between the sexes is accentuated when it comes to the taboo of virginity. The woman does not desire that the man have been a virgin or continent before his marriage. She doesn't even ask herself any question about this. For the man the question is "infinitely" important. Kant does not say that he requires virginity, nor even that he desires it, but that the question is for him the most serious one. Perhaps he can love only virginity, perhaps he never can, perhaps his desire is born of the overlapping of virginity with its contrary. Everything is played out in the space of a sign which is almost nothing and is necessarily described in the subtlety of nuances and word plays: the man is patient (*duldend*), the woman tolerant (*geduldig*), and they do not suffer, do not behave in the same way in what they suffer (*dulden*). The man is sensitive (*empfindsam*), sentimental, the woman is impressionable (*empfindlich*), excitable, touchy, ticklish. The man's economy tends to *acquire,* the woman's to *economize*. The man is jealous when he is in love, the woman is jealous also when she is not in love.

This cultural theory of the difference of the sexes in marriage has no possible place in Hegel's philosophy of spirit. Love and marriage belong to the element of the freedom of consciousness and presuppose the *Aufhebung* of sexual difference. The war described by pragmatic anthropology can take place in it *in fact*, but only to the extent that the partners are not *true* spouses, that the essence of marriage is not fulfilled. In that case one remains at the level of the sex life

Whence the effect of capitalization but also of unlimited effusion. If erection is inhabited by contraband, by what produces it by cutting it, if it is therefore in advance, already, *antherection*, there can and must be a castration of castration, an antherection of antherection, and so on ad infinitum.

The *Journal* opens with the castration of antherection. In a single stroke the whole antherection of the text is set in motion, but not quickly, like a long procession, a long theory chased from the prison colony since its closing.

For if prison is explicitly defined as a castration, the closing of the prison is experienced as a castration of castration, a "punishment of punishment," decapitation of the scaffold ("the heir of kings feels a like emptiness if the republic deprives him of his anointment"), the fall of a crowned head, that is to say here of a bowed head, the convict having made his crown from the very thing that made him bow his head: "The end of the penal colony prevents us from attaining with our living minds the mythical underground regions. Our most dramatic movement has been clipped away: our exodus, the embarkation, the procession on the sea, which was performed with bowed head. The return, this same procession in reverse, is without meaning. Within me the destruction of the colony corresponds to a kind of punishment of punishment: I am castrated, I am shorn of my infamy. Unconcerned about beheading our dreams of

of empirical nature, before the emergence of *Sittlichkeit*. What Kant has described is on that view basically a structure of empirical, "pragmatic" accidents that do not come under the pure concept of marriage or deviate from it through vice or perversity. Kant was not able to think, did not begin by thinking the concept of marriage. Once this has been posited, Hegel wants on the contrary to deduce its development and not its regression. Yet again, Kant supposedly remained with that non-dialectical conjunction between an empiricism and a formalism denounced in the article on natural law. If one does not proceed from the essential unity of marriage, one accumulates and one abstracts descriptive features in a disorderly way, one yokes together empirical violence and contractual formalism.

One must think the speculative dialectic of marriage: the being-one (*Einssein*) of the spouses, the consciousness of the *one* in that of the other, such is the *milieu* of the exchange. Sexual opposition is sublated in it. *Qua* middle or mediation, this milieu has two sides: the one whereby the two spouses recognize each other and sublate their difference; the other, whereby this consciousness must be, *qua* milieu, opposed to theirs and carry its sublation.

This is the child. "It is the child in which they recognize themselves as one, as being in one consciousness, and precisely therein sublated, and they intuit in the child their own coming sublation." They thus "produce their own death." To think this death, one must bring in the milieu of consciousness and think childhood as consciousness. The natural child, *qua* living animal, does not bear the death of its progenitors. The death of the parents therefore *forms* the consciousness of the child.

This is education. Empirico-formalism cannot think education because it cannot think the necessary death of the parents in the child. Kant does however speak of the death of the parents. It will be said that this is still about empirical death: the preference of the father for the daughter, of the mother for the son, and especially for the most insolent and unruly son, are again explained by the possibility of widowhood. The child of the opposite sex is supposed to be the better support in old age. And yet this derisorily empirical explanation does discover the essential affect—mourning—that relates one of the parents to the child of the other sex on the basis of the death of the spouse. The mother loves the son according to the death of the father, the father loves the daughter who succeeds the mother. As regards empiricism, is one not thus going further than

their glories, they awaken us before

the alarm always rings to set off an abortive interruption. Like the galalith alarm clock that emerges from the belly like the clapper of this bell: "In the evenings . . . We wanted to sleep together a whole night long, coiled up and entangled in each other until the morning, but as that was impossible we invented one-hour nights, while above us, in the dormitory that was woven with tackle to which the hammocks were attached, the night-light which burned like a lantern, the surge of sleeping, the steel of the cigarette-lighter striking the flint (we would say: 'Listen to the alarm bell'), the whisper of a youngster [*gars*], the moan of a jerk [*cloche*] whom the big shots called 'a poor martyr,' and the exhalations of the night, made us castaways of a dream. Then we would unglue our mouths: it was the alarm awakening us [*le réveil*] . . ." You can check how the word *gars* often echoes in proximity to some sort of *cloche*. And there are many of them. Also follow the flint, or firestone.

The separation, comma, between arousal [*émoi*] and *moi*, upon awakening, is equal to lifting off [*décoller*] (detachment of the neck [*cou*] and what sticks [*colle*]), and decollation is equal to a sublimating idealization that raises back up what is detached. Indecision, oscillation, the trembling vibration whereby ideality is announced, is always called *frisson*, quivering, etc. "That shudder, as it were, also enhanced my happiness, for it made our trembling kiss seem to take wing, to be idealized. . . . he had been on the alert [*en éveil*] all the time and that he had not been roused during the embrace, for on hearing the sound he would have had slight difficulty, despite his quick reflexes, in shaking off the excitement [*émoi*], and I [*moi*], who was stuck to him, would have detected that slight twinge, that unsticking of a subtle glue." (*Miracle of the Rose*)

our time. The home prisons have their power: it is not the same."

Hegel's deduction of the death of the parents, which appears rather undifferentiated and abstract from the sexual point of view? Chiasmus again: the speculative dialectic thinks this death in its structural necessity, it *thinks* it, as it thinks the erasure of the sexual difference that an empiricism puts forward.

What is education? The death of the parents, the formation of the consciousness of the child, the *Aufhebung* of the child's unconsciousness in the form of ideality. "In education the *unconscious unity* of the child is sublated." We must not rush to identify this idealizing sublation with a "repression" of the "unconscious." But one cannot avoid the question of such a translation. Education (*Erziehung*) and culture (*Bildung*) violently delimit a matter through the form that contains it. This violent form is ideal, it goes via the agencies of language and labor, voice and tool. Like all formation, all imposition of form, it is on the side of the male, here of the father, and since it bears the death of the parents, it operates especially against the father. But the death of the father is merely the real death of the mother, and corresponds to the idealization of the father. The father is not simply annihilated in it. Sublating education internalizes him. Because death is a sublation, the parents, far from being lost or scattered without return "intuit in his evolution their own passing into sublation." They keep their own disappearance in it, regard their child as their own death, and, so regarding it [*la regardant*], they retard it [*la retardent*], appropriate it, they maintain in the monumental presence of their seed—in the name—the living sign that they are dead, not that *they are dead* but that *dead they are*, which is something different. Ideality is death, true, but is being dead—this is the whole question of dissemination—is it *being* dead or being *dead*? The ever so slight difference of emphasis, conceptually imperceptible, the internal fragility of each attribute produces the oscillation between the presence of being as death and the death of being as presence. So long as the parents are present to their death in the formation of the child, so long as one keeps the sign or the seme of what is no longer, were it only ash consumed in the masculine penumbra of the early morning, enjoyment remains of the very thing that is, even of what is dead as what is no longer. But if death is the being of what is no longer, the no-longer-being, then death is nothing—in any case not death. One's own death, when contemplated in one's child, is the death one negates, the death that *is*, i.e. negated. When one says "death is," one is saying "death

Supplementary antherection: that of the mainland prison is going to be substituted for that of Guiana.

Castrated by the first, the other gets more beautifully hard: "it is not the same. It is minor. It has none of that elegant, slightly bowed grace. The atmosphere there is so heavy that you have to drag yourself about. You creep along. The home prisons are more stiffly erect, more darkly and more severely; the slow, solemn

> to put to the test the logic of antherection, the time of erection that can no longer stop abridging its stigma and resembles no other present—it is what presents; to verify everywhere the internal antagonism doubling each column, for example the prison ("slow . . . agony of the penal colony"); to see what matters in that concerning the-deconstruction-of-ontology, etc., I propose trying in general to replace the verb "to be" [*être*] with the verb "to get a hard-on [*bander*]."
>
> And conjugate a little.
>
> Then, have brought back into it activity, transitivity, the object supplement. Pronouns. The forename, etc.
>
> In that way one will perhaps be introduced, in another style, to the metaphysics, grammar and etymology of "to be," to the question of *casus* (πτωσις) and *declinatio* (εγχλισις).
> And what leans or winks (—) between the two (sides of the) neck (—) [*Et du clin* (—) *entre les deux col* (—)]

agony of the penal colony was a more perfect blossoming of abjection."

It remains, to say nothing more, that the place of antherection, what gets hard and in which it gets hard—a necessarily enclosed and guarded place—is, whatever name you give to it (Guiana, galley or Colony), always lived in like a detached province of the mother. "When talking about the

is negated," death is not insofar as it is *posited.* Such is the Hegelian *thesis*: philosophy, the pos(it)ing of death.

The child—sublation of loss. This loss, work of form on matter, putting into form of the unconscious, economic process, production, exchange, is amortized. *Aufhebung* is the amortization of death. It is the concept of economy in general in speculative dialectics.

Economy: law of the family, of the family house, of possession. The economic act renders familiar, proper, intimate, private. The meaning of property in general is gathered in the *oikeios*. Whatever the exportation or generalizing expropriation of the concept of economy, it never breaks the umbilical cord that ties it to the family. Or rather yes, it always breaks it, but this break is the *deduction* of the family; it belongs to the family process inasmuch as it comprises a cutting agency. *Aufhebung*, economic law of the absolute reappropriation of absolute loss, is a familial concept.

And therefore a political concept. The political is opposed to the familial in fulfilling it. So political economy is not a region of general onto-logics, it is coextensive with it. The more so as in Hegelian systematics there is never a simple hierarchical relationship between genus and species: each part represents the whole, each region is capable of everything.

Ideality, a production of *Aufhebung*, is therefore an onto-economic "concept." The *eidos*, the general form of philosophy, is properly familial. It is produced as *oikos*: house, habitation, apartment, chamber, residence, temple, tomb, (bee)hive, goods, family, race, etc. If there is a common seme to all that, it is keeping the proper: it retains, inhibits, consigns absolute loss or consumes it only the better to see it come back to itself, even in the repetition of death. Spirit is the other name of this repetition.

Such is the cost of the child: "In his education the *unconscious unity* of the child is sublated [*hebt sich auf*], it articulates itself inwardly (*gliedert sich in sich*), it becomes cultured *consciousness* (*gebildeten* Bewußtsein); the consciousness of the parents is its matter (*Materie*), at the cost of which (*auf deren Kosten*) it is formed; they are for the child an unknown, obscure presentiment of himself; they sublate his simple and compact (*gedrungen*) state of self-containment; what they give him they shed themselves; they die in him; for what they give him is their own consciousness."

If one were to cut here, education could be a loss without return, a gift without counter-gift, without exchange.

Colony I sometimes refer to it as 'The Old Lady' or 'The Battleaxe.' These two expressions would probably not have sufficed to make me identify Mettray with a woman, but, in addition to the fact that they usually designate a mother, they occurred to me, in connection with the Colony, at a time when I was weary of my orphaned solitude and when my soul yearned for a mother."

This mother's breast steals away from all names, but also steals them all, it is before all names,

like death, the mother fascinates on the basis of the absolute of an *already*. The fascination produces the excess of zeal. In other words, jealousy. Jealousy is always excessive because it fusses over a past that will never have been present and that can never therefore present itself or let one hope for presentation, presenting. One is never jealous faced with a present scene—albeit the worst imaginable—or a future one, at least inasmuch as it seems pregnant with a potential theater. Zeal only lets loose with a whip from the absolute past. *Madame Edwarda* would be ridiculously inoffensive and defuse itself, making a spectacle of its apotrope, *to the extent that it were to open onto a present experience*. It only manages to be terrible by stuffing into itself a past, an absolute already: by giving to be read, not to be seen. But it is not enough to get out of the "book" to be brought to light and to interrupt reading.

One is therefore jealous only of the mother or of death. Never of a man or woman as such.

One is jealous, then, only of a signet [*seing*], or, what comes down to the same thing, of an *already* [déjà].

But in truth the exchange has happened. The other consciousness, that of the child, in which the parents lose theirs, is their own consciousness. The other and the proper are not opposed, or rather they are opposed, but the opposition is what permits, not what interrupts, the specular, imaginal or speculative circulation of the proper. The proper posits itself by opposing itself in the other, by de-separating itself from itself. The unity of the specular and the speculative can be seen in the parents' possibility of looking at, contemplating their own disappearance sublated in the mirror of the child; of the child in formation, as becoming-conscious; in the material unconscious they would see nothing, not even their own death, the death in which they are kept, not even death, then, or only death. *Die Eltern schauen in seinem Werden ihr Aufgehoben-werden an:* "the parents intuit in the child their own coming sublation."

The child's consciousness does not come into the world as into a material and inorganic exteriority. The world is already elaborated when education begins, it is a culture penetrated, informed by the "knowledge of the parents." What initially stands opposite the child as and in place of inorganic nature is inherited knowledge, already a certain ideality. So the child is raised in the "contradiction" between the real world and the ideal world. The process of education consists in sublating this contradiction. That is possible only with the (sublating) disappearance of the family itself, since the family is the place of this contradiction: it is the passage to the spirit of the people.

This is where the struggle to the death for recognition comes in. It is most often known in the form given to it by *The Phenomenology of Spirit*. But before that, three texts had dealt with it: the *System of Ethical Life*, probably very slightly earlier than the Jena *Philosophy of Spirit,* the Jena *Realphilosophie*, at about the same time as *The Phenomenology of Spirit*, and the *Philosophy of Spirit.* This latter is the only one to explicate this struggle within a problematic of the family.

In it, the struggle does not oppose, as has been thought, heads of families. The text gives no sign of this. Once the family is constituted, as a power of consciousness, the struggle can break out only between consciousnesses, and not between empirical individuals. From this point of view, the gap between the Jena text and the *Phenomenology* shrinks. If the latter comes to the family moment after the dialectic of the master and the slave, this is because the family

That is why metaphysics, which is jealous, will never be able to take account in its language, in the language of presence, of jealousy.

That is why the mother (whatever forename or pronoun one gives it) is situated beyond sexual opposition. It especially isn't a woman. She allows herself simply to be represented, detached, by a sex.

That is why the thief distinguishes between the maternal and the feminine. And he distinguishes it in what you would call a man: "... not by a man's fist but by having crashed against the glass walls which cut us off from your world—[his physical appearance] evokes for me now, though it might not have done so in the past, the prison of which he seems to me the most significant, the most illustrious representative. I was summoned to him, hastened toward him, and it is now, in my desperation, that I dare to be engulfed within him. The maternal element I perceived in him was not feminine. Men sometimes hail each other as follows:

'Well, Old Gal?'

'Hi, you Hen!'

'Is that you, Wench?'

This usage belongs to the world of poverty and crime. Of punished crime, which bears upon itself—or within itself—the mark of a faded brand. (I speak of it as of a flower, preferably as of a lily, when the brand was the *fleur de lis*.) ... La Guyane is a feminine noun. Guiana contains all those males who are called tough. ... I aspire to Guiana. ... She is kindly [*bonne*]." Just below: "I call the Virgin Mother and Guiana the Comforters of the Afflicted."

Guillotine is also a feminine noun

is interrogated in it following a very particular guiding thread: the passage from the ancient family and city to Roman law and formal morality. Which is why—another architectonic phenomenon that is disconcerting at first blush—in the *Phenomenology* the moment of "morality" and formal law follows that of the family, whereas the opposite happens in the *Philosophy of Right*. There, the Greek is inscribed in a general problematic of the history of the family. So there is here no "evolution of Hegel's thought."

At the point we have reached, the struggle to death for recognition opposes consciousnesses, but consciousnesses that the family process has constituted into totalities. The individual who gets into war is a family-individual. One cannot understand the essence of consciousness without passing through the familial *Potenz*. One cannot describe a phenomenology of spirit, i.e. according to the subtitle, an "experience of consciousness" without recognizing in it the onto-economical labor of the family. There is no pure consciousness, no transcendental ego into which the familial nucleus can be reduced. This is the place for the principle of a critique of transcendental consciousness as a formal *I think* (thinking is always said of a member of the family), but also of concrete transcendental consciousness in the style of Husserlian phenomenology. Not only is there no monadic consciousness, no sphere of the proper belonging of the ego, but it is impossible to "reduce" the family structure as a vulgar empirico-anthropological addition to transcendental intersubjectivity. This latter would be abstract and formal—constituted and derived—if one did not recognize in it the family structure as one of its essential structures, with all the powers Hegel implies: memory, language, desire, labor, marriage, property of goods, education, etc.

Consciousness relates to itself, gathers itself into a totality, becomes for itself—becomes conscious—only in the family. "The *totality of consciousness* is in the family the totality as an evolution into being *for self;* the individual intuits himself in the other." Consciousness posits itself for itself only via the detour of another consciousness that itself posits itself as the same and as the other. So there are here, standing face to face, two totalities. Singular totalities because they also make two: absolute, insoluble and unlivable contradiction. The relation can only be violent. The two

it is regularly forenamed: Guiana, Colony, here more precisely, perhaps more silently *Galley* buoyed by the waters: "And everything that one associates only with women: tenderness, slightly nauseating whiffs from the open mouth, deep bosom heaving like a swell, unexpected punishment, in short everything that makes a mother a mother."

If one were to stumble across the sea mother's forename one would perhaps see that she shines, she does, and keeps vigil deep into the night, illuminating the galley that she bears along at full sail. "You can see a woman's ample bosom rising and falling. The priest's belly swelled out in like manner. . . . I endowed the Colony with all these disturbing and ridiculous attributes of womankind, until there was established in my mind not the physical image of a woman but rather a soul-to-soul bond which exists only between mother and son and which my undeceivable soul recognized. . . . Little by little the veils fell away from her. The mother materialized. In the cell, I returned for good to her throbbing breast and had real dialogues with her, and perhaps these transformations [*avatars*] which made Mettray my mother added an incestuous feeling to my love for Divers, sprung from the same breast as I."

Is effected, then, a substitution, an enchained detachment. The Colonies, Jails, Prisons form this chain of chains that are all detached (that is to say chained one to the other and linked to what

consciousnesses structurally need one another but can get themselves recognized only by suppressing, or at least by sublating, the singularity of the other—which excludes it. A pure singularity can recognize another singularity only by suppressing itself or by suppressing the other *qua* singularity. Contradiction—although not explicated here in this form—opposes more precisely knowing (the *kennen* in the *erkennen*) which can deal only with universal ideality, and the singularity of the totality "consciousness": being-in-the-family.

The struggle to the death that is then unleashed between two stances seems in its exterminating violence to be more pitilessly concrete than in the later texts. But two conditions contain it, two conditions whose concepts must be carefully calibrated.

1. Death, "the demonstration that ends only with death," destroys the singularity, it goes after what remains singular in the other family-consciousness. This is not about death simply put, but the annihilation of the characteristics of singularity, of any mark of empiricity. The name, for example: is it the stake that goes down or the stake that is saved in this war?

It will be said: what remains when one suppresses the whole of empiricity? Nothing, nothing present or existent. Of course. But what is present, what *is* as such when there is only singularity? Nothing. One fights to the death, in every case for nothing—that is no doubt the point hidden in the shadow of Hegel's discourse. By definition, this point cannot be stated as such, as discourse is precisely what makes the universal pass as something, makes one believe that something remains when every singularity has been swallowed up. Medusa's face watching over Hegel's text in the masculine penumbra that links desire to death, that reads desire as desire for death.

We have not replied to the question: is the proper name of a family or of an individual who is *classified* in the family a pure singularity? No. Is it a pure ideality? No.

2. Second strict conceptual condition: the death of singularity is always an *Aufhebung*. The widespread translation of *Aufhebung* as *suppression* erases precisely this: that death suppresses pure and simple suppression, death without phrase, death without name. "It is absolutely necessary that the totality which consciousness has reached in the family recognizes itself as the totality it is in another such totality of consciousness; in this cognition, each is for the other immediately an absolute singular (*ein absolut*

mandates or hardbinds them) from the breast, the good breast, from the mythical cell where one finds again "for good" her breast.

But once it detaches (itself), the breast falls and is no longer simply good, her breast "for good." It is poisoned, gets aggressive, castrates castration. But since the first good breast was already an *avatar*, its fall brought the annunciation of all the others. Downfall can only deteriorate, history can only get worse, all the way to the Apocalypse.

"The Bishop replied: . . . Our Lord said: 'Suffer little children to come unto me. Who could be so hardhearted as not to heed that appeal of the divine child and to prefer the black . . . breast . . .'" (*Miracle of the Rose*)

Is effected, then, a substitution: the black antherection of the mainland prisons that succeeds—like a detachment or damned procession—the bright antherection of the penal colony. The homespun brown clothing of the mainland prison ["So that now the home jails, bloated with evil males, are black with them, as with blood that has been shot through with carbonic gas. (I have written "black." The outfit of the convicts—captives, captivity, even prisoners, words too noble to name us—forces the word upon me: the outfit is made of brown homespun). It is toward them that my desire will turn. I am aware that there is often a semblance of the burlesque. . . . a brown homespun beret. They strike poses of wretched humility. (If they are beaten, something within them must nevertheless stiffen. . . .)"] is substituted, detaching itself from it, for the "striped pink and white" costume of Guiana. One column and one fabric, one style also, replaces the other. Somber cutting and castration of the sun of castration, "I secretly recompose, within me and for myself alone, a colony more vicious than that of Guiana.

Einzelner). Each posits himself (*setzt sich*) in the consciousness of the other, sublates (*hebt auf*) the singularity of the other, or each [posits] the other in his consciousness as an absolute singularity of consciousness."

A consciousness can be posited as such only in another consciousness: to see itself, to know itself, to have itself recognized. Once the other consciousness recognizes "mine," it departs from its empirical singularity. I have to provoke it to this, and the radical departure from empirical singularity has no other name than death. Putting to death here implies the whole chain of essential concepts of the speculative dialectic (sublation, positing as passage into the opposite, ideality as product of negativity, etc.).

The destruction of singularity must leave no remainder, no empirical or singular remainder. It must be total and infinite. If they come to desire to be loved, recognized by the consciousness of the other, the subjects must accept bearing or suffering (reciprocity here is the rule) a wound, an infinite injury ("the injury (*Verletzung*) of one of its singularities is thus infinite"). The outrage, offence, violation (*Beleidigung*), collision (*Kollision*) ends only with death. As it is mutual (*gegenseitige*), the project of mastery, of getting-onseself-recognized, must by the same token engage infinite desire in a risk of absolute non-mastery: the subject must admit to himself that he no longer dominates his relation to the other. That is where he desires. He posits his desire only by risking death.

Total and real violence: language is of course implicated in this but in this business it's not just talk. The war is not waged by trading signifiers, especially not linguistic signifiers. With names perhaps, but is the proper name a linguistic signifier? Hegel insists on this: the struggle for recognition does not find its element in language. It is played out between bodies, of course, but also economic forces, goods, real possessions, especially those of the family. The linguistic element implies an ideality that can only be the *effect* of the destruction of empirical singularities, an effect and not a milieu of the struggle. In the *practical* war between the singular forces, the wounds must effect actual expropriations. They must tear away from the other the use of his body, his language, literally dislodge him from his possessions. The field of the word does not suffice for this: "Speech, declarations, promising are not this recognition, for speech is only an ideal middle (*ideale Mitte*); it vanishes as soon as it appears, it is not an abiding (*bleibendes*), real recognition." The insistence

I add that the home prisons can be said to be 'in the shade.' The colony is in the sun."

Antherection of style *en abyme*. One-armed Stilitano, who also dominates the scene of the *Journal*, implants and repeats, in his body, the substitution that both castrates and gives a hard-on—harder, stiffer, darker. In terms of arboriculture this is literally seed-tree cutting [*coupe sombre*]: "When a limb has been removed, the remaining one grows stronger. I had hoped that the vigor of the arm which Stilitano had lost might be concentrated in his penis. For a long time I imagined a solid member, like a blackjack, capable of the most outrageous impudence, though what first intrigued me was what Stilitano allowed me to know of it: the mere crease, though curiously precise in the left leg of his blue denim trousers. This detail might have haunted my dreams less had Stilitano not constantly put his left hand on it, and had he not, like ladies making a curtsey, indicated the crease by delicately pinching the cloth with his nails."

economy of the abyss and of the center. The *mise en abyme* can always fill in the abyss by positing it, by saturating it to infinity with its own representation. The motif of the *mise en abyme* could, here and there, play that role of appeasement, within a certain formalism. Whence its success. Like that of decentering; if the abyss were in the center and if you were to distance yourself by taking the center away with you (while keeping yourself in it)

"The remaining one grows stronger," the more it remains the stiffer it gets. Remainder equals hardon. In all events, play with replacing remaining

is heavily marked: linguistic idealism, linguisticism can always resurge—the temptation is too great—so as to edulcorate or scar over the injury, to make one forget that the milieu of the carnage is not ideal but "actual": "Neither can prove this to the other through words, assurances, threats, or promises; for language is only the ideal existence of consciousness, and here there are actual [consciousnesses], i.e. they are absolutely opposed absolute beings for themselves in opposition; and their relation is strictly a practical one, it is itself actual, the middle of their recognition must itself be actual. *Hence they must injure one another.* The fact that each posits himself as exclusive totality in the singularity of his existence must become actual; the offence [*Beleidigung*: the outrage, the violation, the insult] is necessary."

Without this offence, no consciousness, no desire, no relation to the other could *posit itself*. But this effraction that comes to wound the proper of the other does not come down to a singular initiative, to the decision of a freedom. It is engendered by a contradiction that inhabits the proper itself. We are dealing here—since Hegel insists especially on the possession of things rather than of the body proper—with a contradiction in the thing itself. It is contradictory that a thing (*Ding*) be proper to someone or some people. "In particular each must be disturbed in his possession (*Besitze*), for in possession there lies the [following] contradiction: . . ." An external thing, a thing, a universal reality of the earth, essentially exposed to all, cannot, without essential contradiction, remain in the power of a singularity. The contradiction must be resolved. It can be resolved only by the violent and total expropriation of the singularity. But if this injury were the redistribution of bits of property, if a singular reappropriation were to ensue, the same contradiction would persist. The only possible end is therefore the putting to death of the singularity as such, of the possession of the proper in general. In what is said here of the body in general, of the thing of the earth, of everything that is exposed to the light, how are we to mark the exception of the body proper? *Qua* visibility and availability at least, it is worked over by the same contradiction, the stake of the same putting to death.

And yet death does not resolve the contradiction. Saying "on the contrary" would be too simple and unilateral. We must again speak of sublation: *Aufhebung* is indeed the contradiction of contradiction and non-contradiction, and

with getting hard, remainder with hardbinding. You will begin to think what an event or case is, let's say rather an occurrent. We must not simplify the logic of antherection. It doesn't erect *against* or *despite* castration, *in spite of* the wound or infirmity, by castrating castration. It gets hard, castration. The infirmity itself bandages itself by hardbinding. It is what, as one still says today in old parlance, *produces* the erection: a prosthesis that no event of castration will have preceded. The structure of prosthesis belongs to intumescence. Nothing stays standing otherwise.

occurrent in botany means "partitions that all converge toward a fictive central axis" (*Littré*)

That's the stance of the pegleg in *Our Lady of the Flowers*. Listen: "rattled like scrap iron," "the miracle . . . blazed forth." "Closed skylight," "icy sky," "catastrophic horror." Yet the miracle is "radiant as the solution of a mathematical problem, frighteningly exact." "What was one supposed to think [*que fallait-il penser*]?" he wondered earlier.

The pegleg. It is exhibited, like every prosthesis, every epithesis, every erection, every simulacrum, every apotrope, every parade, every masquerade, coquettishly. "The little hoodlum pulled back the covers daintily and asked:

'Will you help me off with my leg?'

He had a wooden leg which was fastened to a stump below the knee by a system of straps and buckles."

also the unity of that contradiction. Unity and contradiction are here, strictly, the same.

I can indeed endanger another's life—in its singularity—only by risking my own. Positing oneself (*sich setzen*) as a consciousness presupposes exposure to death, engagement, putting into play or wagering. "When I go for his death, I expose myself to death [*setze ich mich selbst dem Tode aus*], I wager my own life (*wage ich mein eignes Leben*)." This putting (into play, into a wager) must, like any investment, be amortized and produce a profit; it works toward my recognition by the other, toward the positing of my living consciousness, freedom, mastery. Now because death is on the cards, in that I must *actually* run that risk, I might always lose the profit of the operation: if I die but also if I live. Life cannot last in the incessant imminence of death. So I lose every time. A supreme contradiction that Hegel brings out with fewer concessions than in the *Phenomenology*.

I lose every time, on both accounts. Recognize, with cheerful cruelty, with all possible enjoyment, that none of this is actually viable, that in any case it will all end very badly, and that yet, on the cutting edge of this blade, thinner and more elusive than any thing, a limit so flimsy in its inexistence that no dialectical concept can grasp it, master it, speak it, a desire is stirring. Dancing, losing its name. A desire and a pleasure that have no sense. No philosopheme is ready to make its bed here. Above all not that of desire, pleasure or sense in Hegel's onto-logic. What is more, no concept. What must be put into play here without amortization, is the concept that always wants to grasp something. Of this edge, this blade the instant before it falls and cuts, there is no possible philosophical statement that does not lose what it is trying to retain, and that does not lose it precisely by retaining it. Nothing more to be said about it than what was said in Jena. The blow against the other is the fatal contradiction of a suicide. "When I go for his death, I expose myself to death, I wager my own life; I perpetrate the contradiction of wanting to affirm (*behaupten*) the singularity of my being and my property; and this affirmation passes over into its contrary, that I offer up (*aufopfere*) everything I possess, and the very possibility of all possession and enjoyment, my life itself; in that I posit myself

The counting, frighteningly exact, lets surplus value show through; not that of what has to be compensated—the one limb deficit—but of the prosthesis that stands erect all by itself. The stance of the pegleg, like that of a stone colossus, won't involve rest anymore. It does without a subject, survives its bearer and puts him out of reach of any state of lack. It keeps vigil while he sleeps. When Culafroy, whose "infirmity" inspired in him as much repulsion as did "reptiles," overcomes his disgust by means of a "sublime effort," and clasps the wooden leg to his chest, "it was now a live limb, an individual, like an arm or leg detached from the trunk by a surgical operation. The peg spent the night standing up, a night of vigil, leaning in a corner against the wall." Disturbing stance. However, the lame man dreams: oranges in one hand, cutlass in the other, "the scepter and the golden globe."

In the same way that *The Thief's Journal* leaves, proceeds from Guiana, is expressed like an exit from Guiana ("that region of myself, which is Guiana"), so *gl* begins to spurt [*gicler*], dribble, drip: from the stylite's mouth or cock, the tube of vaseline, the suckling's esophagus. Sperm, saliva, mucus, clotted spit, tears of milk, jellied vomit, all those white and heavy substances will slip one into the other, agglutinate, agglomerate, spread out *at the edge* of all figures and flow through all canals.

as totality of singularity, I sublate myself as totality of singularity."

If I did not commit myself absolutely in this contradiction of the concept, I would not raise myself above life, I would not be rational. If I committed myself partially, I would be a *slave*—the word already appears. The contra*diction* can only get sharpened up. It is not only of the concept or in the statement but with them: "This recognition of the *singularity of the totality thus brings the nothing of death in its train* [. . .] This recognition of the singular is thus [an] absolute internal contradiction; the recognition is just the being of consciousness as a totality in another consciousness, but as far as it is actually achieved, it cancels the other consciousness, and thereby the recognition is sublated too; it is not realized, but rather ceases to be, just when it is (*indem es ist*). Yet (*zugleich*) consciousness only is the gaining of recognition from another at the same time as it only is as absolute numerical unity, and that is what it must be recognized as; but that is to say it must go for the other's death, and for its own; and it only *is* in the actuality of death."

There are many propositions of this type. They entail the equivalence or the absolute continuity of murder and suicide. I affect myself specularly with that with which I affect the other. The almost undecidable suspense we were talking about—hanged man's rope between life and death or the unstable balance of a tightrope walker—leaves each consciousness to an absolute solitude in the very instance of recognition. But this suicidal solitude leaves two lives—and the other—in play. Imagine rather two bodies on the edge of a cliff, gripping onto each other: it is impossible that the one that pushes the other not be *attracted* by the void. He desires this fall, his desire is the push of this fall, it holds itself back in it as though to himself in the process of falling, reaches for it without knowing which of the two can keep the other—i.e. see him dead. There is no other definition of suicide. In the Jena *Realphilosophie*, in the chapter on *The struggle for recognition* (*Der Kampf des Anerkennens*): "To him as consciousness it appears that in this he must intend the death of the other, although it is his own death that is at issue—suicide (*Selbstmord*), in that he exposes himself to danger."

Let's not forget that it is singularities that the suspense of *Aufhebung* is thus holding in the air in the contradiction or the absolute equivalence of the opposites,

The word "globs [*glaviaux*]" will be pronounced only later, after being invisibly assimilated and deglutinized, after elaboration and agglutination to "gladiolus."

But even before being presented in the text and opening out right next to the flower, it animates, by means of its circumscribed energetic absence, the description of spit. The description is caught in a veil. "Stilitano was big and strong. His gait was both supple and heavy, brisk and slow, sinuous; he was nimble. A large part of his power over me—and over the whores of the Barrio Chino—lay in the spittle he passed from one cheek to the other, and which he would sometimes draw out in front of his mouth like a veil. 'But where does he get that spit,' I would ask myself, 'where does he bring it up from? Mine will never have the unctuousness or color of his. It will be merely spun glassware, transparent and fragile.' It was therefore natural for me to imagine what his penis would be if he smeared it for my benefit with so fine a substance, with that precious cobweb, a tissue which I secretly called the veil of the palate [*palais*]."

Our Lady of the Flowers has float over "the Court [*Palais*], which you are not to confuse with any other," a sort of veil, the muslin wing. The glossing seems therefore to resonate in every direction under the vaults of a *palais*. Sense is made by the gluetrap of a dicethrow [*la glu de l'aléa fait sens*]. All the causes deploy their discourses, their effects, their substance throughout veils and sails [*voiles*] of every kind, through spiderwebs or canvas pants [*toiles d'araignée ou de pantalon*]. The tongue makes every word slide over its moist surface. Further along (about twenty pages) the *toile-voile*-spit agglomeration comes together again, but by thickening, as it were, in other contents.

i.e. just as much in indifference. In the absolute tightening of singularity, to give is to take, to give a present is to steal, to love is to strike dead. Difference of degree falls as much as does opposition: "Every form between absolute singulars is a neutral one [*gleichgültige*: equivalent, indifferent], for it makes no difference [formally] whether one makes another a gift (*beschenken*), or one robs him (*als ihn berauben*) and puts him to the sword (*totzuschlagen*); and there is no boundary between the least and the greatest outrage."

One can come out of indifference, i.e. absolute contradiction, the infinite outflowing of the one into the other, only by sublating the singularity into the universal that determines, marks the opposition, the hierarchy, etc. Once sublated, the singular totality becomes a universal totality, absolute spirit. It still exists as a singular totality—"family," "possession," "enjoyment"—but relates to itself only in an ideal mode and "proves itself in its self-sacrifice." Through this sacrifice, it sees itself, has itself recognized in another consciousness, that of the people. It is "saved" at the same time as it is lost *qua* singularity. It allows what singularizes it in the banal sense to dissolve, renounces its "stubbornness" ("his singular freedom is only his stubbornness [*Eigensinn*, proper sense, own sense, sense of property], his death") in order to present itself in the "absolute substance" as spirit of the people.

It has thus erected itself into its opposite.

"Singularity is absolute singularity, it is infinity, the immediate contrary of itself, the essence of spirit, which is to have infinity within itself in an infinite way so that the antithesis immediately cancels itself."

From this point on, through the passage to the spirit of the people as absolute spirit, death, suicide and losing with every move are amortized in the political: at the end of the operation, absolute spirit chalks up a profit in every case, including that of death.

As we still need to take account of the structural discrepancies and architectonic chiasmuses, I open without more

Its constraint appears more formally.

one can always, although it is never indispensable, turn reference inside out like a glove. Pretending to describe this or that, veils or webs, of saliva for example, the text veils itself by unveiling itself, and describes, with the same exhibitionist modesty, its own texture. That is how—of what—I compose myself, of what fabric, of what stream of saliva. But that reference to self must remain suspended, like Stilitano's gob of spit, for without that the text becomes the single object of a univocal description: naivety of a formalist textualism that veers immediately into the contrary (substantialist, thetic, semanticist) of what it claims to be. The suspension of the veil or spit, the time of elaboration of excrement is thus *also* the indecision between the two senses of reference. Its being ajar, its hiatus.
Description of the man with style: "Rapid as my glance at him was, I had time to take in Stilitano's superb muscularity and to see, between his lips, rolling in his half-open mouth, a white, heavy blob of spit, thick as a white worm [inverted image, or, conversely, counterproof of the "spun glassware, transparent and fragile" of the spit of the author, just over twenty pages earlier], which he shifted about, stretching it from top to bottom until it veiled his mouth."
Much further along, in the *Journal*, concerning the gladiolated stylite: "I used to wonder what could possibly be hidden behind that veil of saliva, what the meaning was of the unctuousness and whiteness of his spittle, which was not sickly but, on the contrary, thrillingly vigorous, able to stir up orgies of energy." The gaze descends, in little spasms [*secousses*], then comes back up and contemplates still the same structure: "between his lips . . . . He stood barefoot in the dust. His legs were contained in a pair of worn and shabby faded blue denim trousers. The sleeves of his green shirt were rolled up, one of them above a hand amputated at the wrist, slightly shrunken, where the resewn skin still revealed a pale pink [*rose*] scar."

"Rose! (A pause.) I say to you rose!"

It is hardly worthwhile recalling here that the "veil of the palate" adds another quality to the question of truth.

ado the *Phenomenology of Spirit* in the middle: passage from consciousness, from self-consciousness and reason to *spirit*. Its first formation is, precisely, true spirit as *Sittlichkeit*. In it spirit is defined as "ethical life of a people."

Hegel's text remaining to be read, I re-form its ellipsis around two focal points: burial, and the bond between brother and sister.

So Antigone organizes the scene and is our guide in this abrupt passage.

We again find the dissymmetrical opposition between the singular and the universal. With death between the two of them. More precisely, the two terms of the opposition are not the singular and the universal but the *law* of singularity and the *law* of universality. The opposition is determined between these forms of universality that laws are (*Gesetz der Einzelheit, gesetz der Allgemeinheit*) since it is working within the ethical realm which is the realm of law.

This great opposition (law of singularity/ law of universality) puts in order a whole series of other couples: divine law/ human law, family/city, woman/man, night/day, etc. (The) *human* law is the law of *day* because it is known, public, visible, *universal*; it rules not the family but the *city*, the government, war; and it is made by *man* (*vir*). Human law is the law of man. Divine law is the law of woman, it hides itself, does not offer itself in this openness of manifestation (*Offenbarkeit*) that produces man. It is nocturnal and more natural than the law of universality, just as the family is more natural than the city. Once again, the family appears as the most *natural* degree of the ethical community. Natural, divine, feminine, nocturnal, familial, such is the predicative system, the law of singularity. In it—this is said more especially, here, of the family—the concept is "unconscious." The Penates are opposed to the people, to absolute spirit, to the labor that produces universality. The proper aim of the family, of the woman who represents it, strictly, is the singular as such.

At which point the contradiction reappears: in its essentiality, singularity can only disappear, it can only posit itself *as such* in death. So if the family has singularity as its proper object, it can only busy itself *around death*. Death is its essential object. The family has as its destination the cult of the dead, it must devote itself to the organization of burial. "Therefore the action, which embraces the entire existence of blood relations, has as its object and content

Just like the muslin wing (death), the membrane partition called the soft palate [*voile du palais*], attached on its upper side to the edge of the roof of the mouth [*voûte*], has a lower edge that *floats* freely over the back of the tongue. Its two side edges (it is quadrilateral) are called pillars. In the middle of this floating side, at the entrance to the gullet, there hangs the fleshy appendage called the uvula, like a small grape. The text is spat out. It is like a discourse whose units mold themselves in the manner of an excrement or secretion. And since we are here concerned with a glottic gesture, the work of the tongue upon itself, its element is the saliva that also glues one unit to another. Association is a sort of gluey continuity, never reasoning or symbolic appeal; sense is made by the glue of chance, and progress has for rhythm *little staccato jerks*, clutching and suction, veneering—in every sense—and slippery penetration. Into the embouchure or along the column.

uvula [*luette*] is sometimes said to derive from uvette, "with agglutination of the article—*l'uvette, luette*," and hence from *uva*, grape and uvula

". . . secretly called the veil of the palate. He wore an old cap with a broken visor. When he tossed it on the floor of our room, it suddenly became the carcass of a poor partridge with a clipped wing . . ."

Mating is dreamed, then, between two *voiles*

the individual—not the citizen, for he does not belong to the family, nor does it have the individual who is to become a citizen and is supposed to *cease* counting as *this individual*—but rather, it has the individual who as *this* individual belongs to the family, and who as a *universal* being is exempted from his sensuous, i.e., individual actuality. The action no longer concerns the *living* but rather the *dead*; it concerns the one who, out of the long progression [*Reihe,* series] of his scattered existence, is condensed [*zusammen gefaßt*: is gathered] into *one* completed shape (*vollendete* eine *Gestaltung*) and who has been elevated out of the unrest of contingent life into the motionlessness of simple universality.—Because he is only *actual* and *substantial* as a citizen, the individual, taken not as a citizen but as belonging to the family, is merely the *unreal* shadow who lacks any core at all [*marklose,* without marrow]."

The family, as the natural moment of ethics, has only a singular, essentially singular, object, i.e. one which, without gaining access to the universal legality of the city, is stripped of every empirical character. This pure singularity, stripped but incapable of passing to universality, is the dead one—more precisely the name of the dead one—the cadaver, the shade without force, the negation of the living being-there insofar as it has *not yet* given rise to the life of the citizen. Already dead (*qua* empirical existence), not yet living (*qua* ideal universality). If the family's thing is pure singularity, one belongs to a family only by busying oneself around the dead: washing the corpse, institution of death, vigil, monumentalization, archive, heritage, genealogy, classification of proper names, engraving on tombs, burial, sepulcher, funereal chant, etc.

The family does not yet know the labor that is productive of universality in the city, only the labor of mourning.

If the family figures mourning, the economy of the dead, the law of the *oikos* (*tomb*), if the house, the place where death keeps itself by and from itself [*la mort d'elle-même se garde*], forms a theater or a funeral rite, if the woman takes care of the representation of it, it falls to married femininity to manage, strictly, a cadaver. When a man *binds himself* to a woman, even in secret (marriage does not, according to Hegel, depend on a formal contract), the point is always to entrust her with one's death. Every calculation, every ruse and act of blackmail can be wrapped in this offer of a pure singularity (which is lost and preserved in the name). Entrust death to her, the guardianship of a marrowless body, give to the woman responsibility for erecting its sepulcher after having

of different sexes. The veil [*le voile*] of the palate has scarcely been named when already, in little jerks, the text is raised like a sail [*une voile*], at first rolled then floating and stretched, receiving and giving movement (". . . what meaning would there be in the sight that staggers me when, in a harbor, I see a sail, little by little, by fits and starts [*par saccades, à petits coups*], spreading out and with difficulty rising on the mast of a ship, hesitantly at first, then resolutely, if these movements were not the very symbol of the movements of my love for Stilitano? I met him in Barcelona.")

the *little spasms* mark the very rhythm of *gl,* the barely stifled emotionalizing of the text, the anguishing stricture of antherection, its staccato force of penetration, through cuts and thrusts, what is efficacious in its repeated failing, ". . . our yielding to the illusion that the finished melody was well worth the loss of precious air. By small, successive spasms we have slowly but surely turned the play into something insipid. Successive spasms in order to make certain we would have a success which, to my mind, is in the final analysis a failure." (*Letters to Roger Blin*).

And the spit smeared on the slippery mast, the quill dipped in very fluid stickiness, very quickly becomes vaseline. And even, without having to force things, vaseline with gomenol.

Coming up all of a sudden, but in a very elaborate form, the "tube of vaseline" that, in 1932—two pages away—a policeman takes out of the pocket of the narrator (the word is more and more comical; it transforms everything into an *ex cathedra* discourse, into an eternal seminar, built on the presumption that there is *something* in the author's pocket, *which* that author is recounting to us: event, object, history, sense, all

buried the rigid cadaver (unction, bands, etc.), thus maintaining it in a living, monumental, interminable surrection. In her: under the earth, but the night of the subterranean world is woman, as Hegel specifies. Freud will also have shown the other side of this desire: the fear of being trapped in the maternal womb is represented in the anxiety of being buried alive.

What is a cadaver? What is it to make a present of a cadaver?

Pure singularity: neither the empirical individual destroyed, decomposed, analyzed by death, nor the universal rationality of the citizen, of the living subject. What I make into a present for the woman, in exchange for funeral rites, is my absolutely proper body, the essence of my singularity. The woman receives it in the night, however long or short it be. But what she receives, *qua* pure singularity, immediately passes over into its opposite. The female sepulcher keeps nothing, unless there be an instance—for example the so-called proper name—that tries to stay standing, to stretch out between the contraries or the equivalents even as they cancel each other out.

The erection of the sepulcher is said to be the feminine work. Against what does it stand out? And what is the woman keeping in this way, by following the dead man, surviving him, keeping vigil over him? Why is she a woman in doing these things? And why does the name she surrounds with her care not come from elsewhere to be engraved on the stela or the slab? Why is it inscribed there as though for the first time?

We know the old humanist and metaphysical theme: burial is proper to man. Among the most tenacious obscurantist residues, there is this terrified misrecognition of everything one would like to refuse to "animality": with the *logos*, burial and a few other complications. Hegel also thought that burial is proper to man. The familial and feminine operation of mourning transforms the living being into consciousness and wrests its singularity from nature. It prevents the corpse from returning to nature. By embalming it, burying it, binding it in bands of cloth, of language and writing, by raising the stela she raises it to the universality of spirit. Spirit disengages itself from the decomposition of the corpse, it delivers itself from it and rises thanks to burial. It is sublating repetition.

Is it simply a question of fighting in this way against material decomposition, against a simple dissociation that makes the organic return to the inorganic? Is the force against which the funeral rite works, which goes by the name

within range of knowledge. So try it with the tube of vaseline)

"I was dismayed when, one evening, while searching me after a raid—I am speaking of a scene which preceded the one with which this book begins—the astonished detective took from my pocket, among other things, a tube of Vaseline. We dared joke about it since it contained mentholated vaseline [*vaseline goménolée*]. . . . It concerned a tube of vaseline, one of whose ends was partially rolled up. Which amounts to saying that it had been put to use. Amidst the elegant objects taken from the pockets of the men who had been picked up in the raid, it was the very sign of abjection, of that which is concealed with the greatest of care, but yet the sign of a secret grace which was soon to save me from contempt. . . . But lo and behold! that dirty, wretched object whose purpose seemed to the world—to that concentrated delegation of the world which is the police . . . utterly vile, became extremely precious to me. Unlike many objects which my tenderness singles out, this one was not at all haloed; it remained on the table, a little grey leaden tube of vaseline, broken and livid, whose astonishing discreteness, and its essential correspondence with all the commonplace things in the record office of a prison (the bench, the inkwell, the regulations, the scales, the odor), would, through the general indifference, have distressed me, had not the very content of the tube made me think, by bringing to mind an oil lamp (perhaps because of its unctuous character), of a night light beside a coffin." Tombfalling, the spurt [*jet*], the jaculations immediately change signs. The object is abject ("the very sign of abjection"), the object falls "amidst the elegant objects taken from the pockets . . ." (*elegant* is regularly association with *gallant*, with *glove* [gant], and turns inside out, immediately inverting its value) but picks itself up by that very means, by means of its very fall: it sublates *out of* its fall. The fall it picks itself up from is that which exalts it. That holds for all cases. Its knell is a *coup de grâce* ("yet the sign of a secret grace"). In its form, the *gomenolated* object is certainly not "haloed," but the secret of the sticky, milky substance, that is expressed out of it—which shines, it does, like gold—fills with marvel, illuminates a catafalque, a crypt, the tomb that it lays low

before the beginning of the book. Is it said in the book?

of death, a mechanical and anonymous exteriority, physical, non-conscious? Such an analysis would be trite. The feminine operation of burial does not oppose the exteriority of a non-conscious matter: it represses an unconscious desire. The family wants to prevent the dead one from being "destroyed" and the sepulcher violated *by this desire*. Such a remark forms the systematic opening of this analysis onto later problematics concerning the labor of mourning, anthropophagy, cannibalism, all the processes of incorporation and introjection. Hegel does not determine the unconscious desires against which the dead man/person must be preserved. The (consanguineous) family interrupts the abstract material work of nature and "takes" destruction "upon itself" (*über sich nimmt*). "He who is dead, by having his *being* set free from his *doing*, that is, his negative oneness, is empty individuality, merely a passive *being for others*, and is left to the mercy of every lower singularity devoid of reason and to the forces of abstract matter, both of which are now more powerful than he, that is, the former lower creatures for the sake of the life that they have and the latter forces of matter for the sake of their negative nature. The family keeps the dead away from those dishonoring activities of unconscious desires [*bewußtloser Begierde*] and abstract beings, and in place of them, it puts their own activities; it weds their kin to the womb of the earth (*vermählt den Verwandten dem Schoße der Erde*), to the elemental, imperishable individuality. The family thereby makes the dead into a member of a polity which to a greater degree overwhelms and keeps in check (*gebunden hält*) the powers of the particular elements of matter and the lower living creatures (*Lebendigkeiten*) which sought to be set free from him and to destroy him."

Enter Antigone. Oedipus's daughter protests against (the) human law in the name of (unwritten) divine or family law. She demands a burial. For a brother, the only "irreplaceable" relative. She could, she says, have replaced a dead husband, a dead son and, given that fact, left them to rot on the ground so as not to go against the laws of the city. But she cannot hope for another brother. Her song rises at the moment when Creon gives the order to lock

The hymn that is dedicated to it, transforming it necessarily into an "oil lamp" (*elaion*) or into a "night light beside a coffin," is suspended throughout a long parenthesis that itself impregnates another large, teeming, gluey and fatty paranthesis of *gl*s.

The tube of vaseline, this "little object" in fact induces into the text the appearance of a mother, the apparently unexpected intervention of a maternal image ("the following image cuts in"). This mother is a thief. Also the figure of a substitutive and phallic mother (moon-fish). Wish to cover her with flowers and kisses (kill-adore-fuck-embalm-make hard), to drool and vomit on her, not directly onto her breast (or it falls, for since the cradle weaning has been achieved, the executioner has grown old) but into her pubic hair or her hands, which must have (should have [*auraient dû*], that can be said only in English) caused the tube to be expressed and to have fucked the baby's ass: the *gl* that spreads out is cut, starts again, flows everywhere, oozes from every orifice, drowns all the figures, fulfills all the functions, excludes, solicits, gathers all the pieces, gets lost and disseminated. The place of passage isn't yet named; it is muslin.

". . . had not the very content of the tube made me think, by bringing to mind an oil lamp (perhaps because of its unctuous character), of a night light beside a coffin.

her in a "rock tomb" so she may live or die in it without seeing the sun.

> Ὦ τύμβος, ὦ νυμφεῖον, ὦ κατασχαφὲς
> ὄιχεσις αἰείφρουροσ
> O tomb, o marriage chamber, o subterranean dwelling,
> My prison forever . . ."

Where does Antigone's desire lead?

The two functions of burial relieve [*relèvent*] the dead one of his death, preventing him from being destroyed—eaten—by matter, nature, the being-outside-itself of spirit but also by the probably cannibalistic violence of the unconscious desires of the survivors. Which means essentially women, since women, *qua* guardians of burial and of the family, are always in a position of survival. The law of singularity (divine, feminine, familial, natural, nocturnal) as it were protects itself from itself, against itself. And by the same token against the other, human law (virile, political, spiritual, diurnal). The two laws fight each other and change places across differences of strata, stages or levels (*Stufen*). The law of the human community, a manifest law, a law from above, a solar law, works through the rule of a government (*Regierung*). In government effective spirit gathers and reflects itself. The community relates to itself in it as in a head, a place of individuality or indivisibility. The head holds together, from the top, the scattered members of the community. But the present and real existence (*Realität* or *Dasein*) of the community remains the family. It organizes its existence in relative independence: personal independence, independence of property (*Eigentum*) always linked to the family, personal right and right of things (*dingliche Recht*) which ensures possession and use of things, work aiming at acquisition and enjoyment. But if the government—the head—authorizes and organizes this family right, element and natural being-there of the community, it is also threatened by it. The family puts the head in danger. For the family risks installing itself, sinking into its private interest, into its right of possession and enjoyment. At the head, the government must therefore become the enemy of the very thing it is ruling, it must repress the family not as natural singularity but in the juridical system

(In describing it, I recreate the little object, but the following image cuts in: beneath a lamppost, in a street of the city where I am writing, the pallid face of a little old woman, a round, flat little face, like the moon, very pale; I cannot tell whether it was sad and hypocritical. She approached me, told me she was very poor and asked for a little money. The gentleness of that moon-fish face told me at once: the old woman had just got out of prison.

'She's a thief,' I said to myself. As I walked away from her, a kind of intense reverie, living deep within me and not at the edge of my mind, led me to think that it was perhaps my mother whom I had just met. I know nothing of her who abandoned me in the cradle, but I hoped it was that old thief who begged at night."

The lunar, maternal star activates the text from inside (pointedly, acutely, "within me") in a way that is at once beneficent and maleficent: this fish fresh out of prison is thus a rather stupid animal at the very moment when it gives such pleasure, "round . . . like the moon," empty like a begging hole, asking to be covered, filled, impregnated; a poor piggy bank asking me "for a little money," and to whom, still within parantheses, I respond.

as always, semantic necessity, giving rise to a hermeneutics, a semiotics, even a psychoanalytics, remains undecidably suspended on the chance of an agglutination said to be formal or signifying. The lifting [*vol*] of that suspense, and its necessity, derails semanticism as much as it does formalism. *Thief* [voleuse] catches *nightlight* [veilleuse] in flight [*au vol*] and attaches it a little lower down in *old thief* [vieille voleuse]. Marvelous writing. Incredibly precious

"'What if it were she?' I thought as I walked away from the old woman. 'Oh! If it were, I would cover her with flowers, with gladioluses

proper to it: war of the government of the city against the family, law of the day against law of the night, human law against divine law, law of man against law of woman. This war is not one war among others, it is *war itself*. Because the only, or at least the best way of preventing the family from dissolving the city is indeed to drag the community into war against another city. The government—the virile head exposed to the sun—thus violates the woman or the family. It reminds her that her master is death, violent death, the struggle for recognition, the name, the phenomenon of spirit. "In order not to let them become rooted and rigidly fixed within this activity of isolating themselves, an activity which would otherwise let the whole come undone and the spirit within it fade away, the government must from time to time (*von Zeit zu Zeit*) shake them to their core by means of war. As a result, it infringes on their established order, violates (*verletzen*) their right to self-sufficiency and throws them into disarray. By the labor the government imposes on them, those individuals, who have become more and more absorbed in their own lives and who thereby tend to tear themselves loose from the whole in striving after inviolable *being-for-itself* and personal security, are made to feel the power of their lord and master, namely, death. By way of this dissolution of the form of durable existence, spirit wards off its descent (*Versinken*) out of ethical life and into merely natural existence, and it sustains and elevates the self of its consciousness into *freedom* and into its *force*."

This should happen only *from time to time*. Intermittence—jerking rhythm—is an essential rule. If there were only war, the natural being-there of the community would be destroyed, and destroyed by its own human law, by the very principle of universality. The family, the natural being-there of the community, must therefore also resist war and oppose it with its "force of preservation." It *must* resist what it *must* do: twice *must*: two forces of law stand up one in the other and one against the other. The community can live only in their dialectical opposition. The absolute triumph of the one or the other would send it to oblivion. Each law is therefore a law of death.

The "force of preservation," in the service of the law of singularity, is the woman; it is the family insofar as it is represented in femininity. It is the divine law of the subterranean realm. Like the law of man, the law of woman involves differences of strata and is worked over by an internal opposition.

and roses, and with kisses! I would weep with tenderness over those moon-fish eyes, over that round, foolish face!' 'And why,' I went on, 'why weep over it?' It did not take my mind long to replace these customary marks of tenderness by some other gesture, even the vilest and most contemptible, which I empowered to mean as much as the kisses, or the tears, or the flowers.

'I'd be glad to slobber over her,' I thought, overflowing with love. (Does the word *glaïeul* [gladiolus] mentioned above bring into play *glaviaux* [gobs of spit])? To slobber over her hair or vomit into her hands. But I would adore that thief who is my mother.)"

Function of the paranthesis: time of writing. At the moment when, at present [*présentement*], I am writing, "in a street of the city where I am writing," I open the paranthesis to describe, comment, remark on the narrative, the other time that is being narrated. That fiction of the "at present" of writing opens a paranthesis in the paranthesis—and it is not by chance, each paranthesis of an at present is pregnant with another—in order to comment on the choice of words and the agglutination of *gl*s: "(Does the word *glaïeul* mentioned above bring into play *gla-*

"spat into my mouth.
An almost unconscious movement of deglutition made me swallow the gob [*glaviaud*]. [The spelling of this word, which has never belonged to the language [*langue*], which is made to be detached from it like a fatty gob of word [*molardon*], remains uncertain, plastic, elastic finally, and

The two laws do not confront each other like two volumes or two full surfaces, identical to each other, homogeneous in themselves. Each is fissured, cut into on the inside, and already so by the work of the other in it. For example, the logic of the human law commanded that one absolutely not do what it absolutely commanded one to do: wage war. It had to take into account, register the calculus of the opposing law. The same goes for the law of the family.

Hegel examines here the elementary structures of kinship. His classification appears limited: he does not justify his historical, sociological, ethnological model, namely the Greek Western family. Within it, he considers only a limited number of elements and relations: husband/wife, parents/children, brother/sister. No grandparents, no uncles or aunts, no cousins male or female, no possible plurality of brothers and sisters, this latter relationship always remaining singular.

Three relations are thus held to be primitive and irreducible. They are organized in a three-level hierarchy. It seems that one rises within it by appeasing or even strictly annulling sexual desire. Between husband and wife, the relation of recognition is the most natural and the most immediate. It dispenses with a third party. Specular and sensory like the natural desire that in principle marriage does not repress. The parents/children relation implies a mediation: what was only an image (*Bild*) and an anticipatory representation (*Vorstellung*) of spirit in (natural and immediate) conjugal desire becomes actuality of spirit. That's progress. But both relations have a common limit. In both cases we are dealing with a transitory and unequal *piety*. The mutual piety of the spouses remains sensory and natural; it loses itself, does not return to itself as spirit. Natural desire, as such, is destined to to lose itself, to be incapable of reflecting itself in its naturality. If it did so, it would no longer be what it reflects—natural. In the mutual piety of parents and children, some natural contingency cannot be reduced. The relation here is still affected by a remainder of non-return. This only apparently contradicts the movement of narcissistic and sublating reappropriation the general logic of which orchestrates everything. The sublation takes place, precisely, only to the extent that the family gets outside itself in order to constitute itself, destroys its formal economy, its self-identity, its tautology: to the extent that it posits itself, because the thesis (*Setzung*) is always sublating. So how is it with this non-return that must precisely be posited, sublimated, suspended or sublated?

The piety of the parents for the children is affected with an original emotion: namely that one's own actuality is

lactic. In *Our Lady*, it's *glaviots:* "I envy you your glory. You would have done me in, as they say in jail, just as you did in the Mexican. During your months in the cell, you would have tenderly spat heavy oysters [*glaviots*] from your throat and nose on my memory." In *Miracle of the Rose*, it's also *glavios:* "When the big shots wanted to needle a jerk or an available chicken, or a bleater (squealer), they would go looking for him . . . [and] spit oysters [*glavios*] and frightful insults in his face." "Deloffre [global event] spat in my eyes. The seven of them took their turn, in fact several times, including Divers. I received the spit in my distended mouth, which fatigue failed to close. Yet a trifle would have sufficed for the ghastly game to be transformed into a courtly one and for me to be covered not with spit but with roses that had been tossed at me. For as the gestures were the same, it would not have been hard for destiny to change everything." (*Miracle of the Rose*)

As always, this is a violent, parodic, radiographic, profound, implacably ridiculous interpretation of Golgotha. A galalith Golgotha, staged by Matthew, and elsewhere by John: "and they bowed their knees before Him, and mocked Him, saying, Hail, King of the Jews! And they spat upon Him, and took the reed, and smote Him on the head." It would have taken so little . . .

"it would not have been hard for destiny to change everything: the game is organized . . . youngsters make the gesture of hurling . . . it would cost them no more to hurl happiness. We were in the middle of the most flowery park in France. I waited for roses. I prayed God to alter his intention just a little, to make a false movement so that the children, ceasing to hate me, would love me. They would have gone on with the game . . . but with their hands full of flowers, for it would have taken so little for love to enter Van Roy's heart instead of hate. . . . They moved closer and closer until they were very near me, and their aim got worse and worse."

That is to say, better and better: "I saw them spread their legs and draw back, like an archer stringing a bow [*qui bande l'arc*], and make a slight forward movement as the gob spirted. I was hit in the face

exiled into the other—the child; that one's own for-oneself is in another "without return." The consciousness of the child does not come back to me, does not return to me the consciousness I entrusted to it. Here there is no *Zurückerhalten*: the word designates return, recovery of funds, return reception of an outlay, amortization. The actuality of the child is foreign (*fremde*) because it is proper (*eigene*), proper to itself. The seed does not return to the source, no longer circulates. Likewise, the piety of the children for the parents is marked by the same cut. The child knows that it attains being-for-self by separating itself from its starting-point. "Separation from the origin" (*Trennung von dem Ursprung*) in which the source "dries up."

The *Realphilosophie* nevertheless analyzes this drying up as a sublation of the origin: the child is *der sich aufhebende Ursprung*. The contradiction is not here a formal effect of philosophical discourse but the essence of sublation.

Another apparent paradox: the limit of the conjugal relation is the contrary of the genealogical limit. There, the return is merely specular (and thus immediate, natural and sensory); here, it is mediacy in expansion, outpouring, pouring out without return of what flows from the source. These two relations, still too natural, and dissymmetrical, are carried off in the transitory (*Übergehen*), imbalance and inequality (*Ungleichheit*). This is because desire lets itself be drawn into seminal outpouring.

Whence the infinite superiority of the relation between brother and sister. A familial bond, yes, since blood speaks in it, but the only one that absolutely suspends all desire. No desire surfaces in consciousness—Hegel is analyzing consciousnesses here—whereas consciousness was, in the other relations, essentially desiring. No desire, then, between two singularities of the opposite sex, an "unmixed relationship (*unvermischte Verhältnis*)." The brother and sister "do not desire each other." The for-self of the one does not depend on the other. These are, it would seem, the only consciousnesses in the Hegelian universe that relate to one another without going to war. Given the generality of the struggle for recognition in the relation between consciousnesses, one would be tempted to conclude that in the end *there is no* brother/sister bond, there is no brother and sister. If such a relation is unique and arrives at a sort of rest (*Ruhe*) and balance (*Gleichgewicht*) refused to all others, this is because the brother and the sister do not receive from the other their for-self and nevertheless are constituted as "free individualities." The

and was soon slimier than a prickhead under the discharge. I was then invested with a deep gravity."

No longer his mother but his mother, no longer the bad mother, whom one cannot erect, but the phallus ejaculating on the cross, the right [*droite*], that is to say normal mother, rightangled, the very one who has shone, in Galilee, from the very beginning, whose upright sex gleams, dribbles with sperm. But the best is the worst (it took so little), the most serious: "I was then invested with deep gravity. I was no longer the adulterous woman being stoned. I was the object of an amorous rite. I wanted them to spit more and thicker slime. Deloffre was the first to realize what was happening. He pointed to a particular part of my tight-fitting pants and cried out:

"Hey! Aim at his pussy! It's making him shiny wet, the slut [*ça le fait reluire, la morue*]!"

There were seven of them spitting at him, like the archangels whose names you know. Their bow gets taut and the mother is among them: it is a man, a man of God. Gleam, shine, appear, be present, grow (*phuein*)—get hard. The ark or the galley. In the beginning, *en archè*, it will have been hardbound. And the archangel who bears the name of the man of God, "in the sixth month the angel Gabriel was sent from God unto a city of Galilee" to announce to an espoused virgin that a babe would soon "leap in her womb" and be "filled with the Holy Ghost."

"The Tightrope Walker": "But when the Angel is announced, stand alone to receive him."

viaux?)" The other present (further up) in the paranthesis is already a past, it has resonated by having been proffered higher up than the others and it is the height of its being pronounced that controls by echoing [*arrésonne*], calls forth the word *glaviaux*, calls out from *glaïeul* to *glaviaux*.

for-selves recognize each other without dependency, desire each other no more than they tear each other apart.

Is it impossible? Is it in contradiction with the whole system? Are we still in the natural sphere of *Sittlichkeit* (the family) once sexual difference seems to be suspended, once desire absents itself along with the opposite of desire in a sort of fidelity without love? But then why brother/sister and not brother*s* or sister*s*? Because in truth we still need there to be a sexual difference, a sexual difference posited as such and yet without desire. Femininity must be represented in this "relation without desire" (*begierdeloser Beziehung*) since it is the familial, the law of singularity. But this representation must here go to the highest degree of naturality, to the point where femininity, remaining feminine, detaches itself from natural desire, deprives itself of pleasure and, in so doing, foresees better than ever the essence of *Sittlichkeit* of which the family is only the first stage, the first anticipation. Femininity raises itself to that point *better* as sister, *less well* as wife, mother or daughter. "The feminine (*das Weibliche*), as the sister, hence has the highest intimation of the ethical essence (*des sittlichen Wesens*)." If it does not go beyond intimation, this is not because of being a sister, but because of remaining feminine. She rises higher than the mother, the daughter or the wife, but *qua* feminine, caught up in the naturality of sexual difference, can only have a presentiment of ethical spirituality. *Qua* sister, she stands suspended between a desire she does not feel, that she feels she does not feel, and a law that is universal (non-familial: human, political, etc.) which remains foreign to her. The fact that she is of the same blood as her brother seems to suffice to exclude desire. Appendix to the *Philosophy of Right:* "The brother-sister relation—a *non-sexual* relation (*Geschwister—ein* Geschlechtloses *Verhältnis*)." As we are dealing only with the monogamous family, the brother and sister are not uterine brother-sister but consanguineous, in the technical sense that metaphysics gives this word, attributing blood only to the father. So there is here a relation of consanguinity that breaks with (desiring) naturality.

Antigone is not named as such in the passage but the whole analysis is fascinated by the essential figure of this sister who never becomes citizen, wife, or mother. Dead before being able to marry, she fixes, grasps, freezes, transfigures herself in this figure of eternal sister carrying off with her her womanly desire.

Hegel thinks this is very good, very calming. Not explicitly in the *Phenomenology,* but in the *Aesthetics.* There

But the agglutination does not only find its consistence in the signifying paste (*gl* degenerated as *son* or *sa*), it sticks to sense: flower-spit analogy for that with which one covers what one loves (seeing dead), passage from flower to spit, from phallus to sperm, from gladiolus (sword of justice, virgin's dagger) to seminal ooze, etc. But that double series, which we could track for quite some distance, interests us and makes a text only to the extent of a remainder of *gl*

re-elaborate, account taken of this remainder, a thinking of *mimesis:* without imitation (of a represented, identifiable, prerequisite and repeated object), without repetition (of a thing, an event, a referent, a signified), without signification (of a sense or a signifier). Logic of a disconcerting stricture: its simulacres and phantasms defying the terms of every analysis but it renders a rigorous account of interminability.

For example (the unicity of the example is destroyed by itself, immediately elaborating the power of a generalizing organ), at the very moment when we might claim to grasp in it, within a determinate text, the work of an idiom, linked to a chain of proper names and singular empirico-signifying configurations, *glas* also names *classification,* that is to say the inscription within networks of generalities interwoven *ad infinitum,* in genealogies of a structure such that the intersections, coupling, shunting, detours and forks never simply derive from a semantic law or formal law. No absolute idiom, no signature. The effect of idiom or signature only relaunches, makes resound, the clang.

The clang is—therefore—the knell of some idiom, some signature.

Of the absolute progenitor [*aïeul*].

Hence one never finds it here or there, in the unique configuration of a text. It always lends itself, affects itself or steals itself. At the moment you think you are reading it here, commenting or deciphering this text, you are commented on, deciphered, observed by another: what has remained.

he writes, "But to the sister, the brother is an essence itself, which is both motionless and the same as her (*das ruhige gleiche Wesen überhaupt*), and her recognition in him is pure and unmixed with any natural relation. The indifference of individuality (*die Gleichgültigkeit der Einzelheit*) and its ethical contingency is thus not present [*vorhanden*] in this relationship."

An example unique in the system: a recognition that is not natural and yet (which) goes via no conflict, no injury, no violation: absolute uniqueness, yet universal and without natural singularity, without immediacy; a symmetrical relation that needs no reconciliation to be appeased, which knows nothing of the horizon of warfare, infinite wound, contradiction, negativity. Is that the inconceivable itself? What the greater logic cannot assimilate? Why is this the very thing that affords Hegel this feeling of infinite peace he confides in us? Very near the end, in the *Aesthetics*: "Of all the masterpieces of the classical and the modern world—and I know nearly all of them and you should and can—the *Antigone* seems to me to be the most magnificent (*vortrefflichste*) and satisfying (*befriedigendste*) work of art of this kind."

A strange declaration: as in the *Phenomenology*, it speaks of peacefulness but in the tone of a personal confidence. This is quite rare: one can count the statements in the first person, the allusions to personal reading, pieces of advice, the cases of "it seems to me." What is going on? And why does this happen when the body of the system should be tensing up in a phenomenon of rejection? This graft appears to have an unassimilable structure.

This remark in confidence sounds the more strangely for the fact that it closes a most "Hegelian" paragraph. War rages in it. The carnage in Sophocles' play is laid out. The fall or final elevation receives from this its whole force of displacement, the occult strangeness of its being an aside. Hegel has just analyzed the difference between epic reconciliation and tragic reconciliation. Tragedy is still war unleashed in order to sublate the unilaterality of individual consciousness. Individuals enter into a struggle in order to assert themselves as totalities in their concrete "presence", in such a way that they are themselves "in the power of what they are fighting." The "injury" (*Verletzen*) they inflict on others must honor what corresponds to "their own existence." "For example, Antigone lives under the political authority of Creon; she is herself the daughter of a King and the fiancée of Haemon, so that she ought to pay obedience to the royal command.

There is—always—already—more than one—clang.

One has to read *glas* as "singular plural" (fall of gold [*or*] in the double session). It has its shattering in itself, it immediately affects itself from this literal damage and echoes off it.

No genetic singularity. I am not here writing (on) any singular text, any inimitable signature. It is known that paternity is always attributed at the end of proceedings, in the form of a judgment. Which means in the form of a generality. But the mother? Especially one who does without a father? Can one not hold out hope for a genealogy that is pure, purely singular, immediately idiomatic? Doesn't what is proper belong in the end to the mother?

No more than the knell that she sets clanging. The mother is a thief and beggar. She appropriates everything but that is because she possesses nothing of her own [*en propre*]. She gives/takes for loving/hating but is nothing. Here again the galactic law is at work, but to resist it, the work of dialectical, phenomenological, ontological law.

For example (but the singularity of the example allows itself to straightaway be carried off into textual chains articulated ad infinitum), the semantic concatenation is as powerless as the formal concatenation when it comes to circumscribing, without remainder, the scene of the old beggar woman.

Or, for example, completely different, the same, Mallarmé's "Aumône [Alms]." Suppose that, from a long time back, for a long time, here and elsewhere, without knowing it, you were doing nothing other than deciphering it, this "poem," letter by letter, syllable by syllable, word by word, line by line, in every sense, in its general form, its relation to Mallarmé's "corpus," to the French language, other languages, the history of past literature and that still to come, its other versions, the infinite constraints and opening of what is so naively called a context: what would that give?

But Creon too, as father and husband, should have respected the sacred tie of blood and not ordered anything against its pious observance. So there is immanent in both Antigone and Creon something that in their own way they attack, so that they are gripped and shattered by something that belongs to the circle of their own actual being (*Kreise ihres eigenen Daseins*). Antigone suffers death before enjoying the bridal dance, but Creon too is punished by the voluntary deaths of his son and his wife, incurred, the one on account of Antigone's fate, the other because of Haemon's death. Of all the masterpieces of the classical and the modern world—and I know nearly all of them and you should and can—the *Antigone* seems to me to be the most magnificent and satisfying work of art of this kind."

An effect of focalization, in a text, around an impossible place. Fascination with a figure that cannot be taken in by the system. Vertiginous insistence on something unclassifiable. And what if the unassimilable, the absolutely undigestible played a role in the system that is fundamental, abyssal rather, the abyss playing a quasi

for anyone getting impatient about seeing nothing coming from that side, we should here name Christiane, Hegel's sister, or Nanette, "a girl put up in the family house." If we are to believe a comment of Bourgeois's, she "had inspired in Hegel a feeling that was perhaps at first amorous, but that the letters from Frankfurt to Nanette Endel reveal to be a feeling of sincere friendship." I do not know of what name Nanette is the diminutive form. Nana could always play the sister. In the Phrygian legend of Attis, Nana is a sort of Holy Virgin. Zeus disseminates in a dream, and lets his sperm fall on the rock. Agdistis, the hermaphrodite, is born of it. The other gods take hold of it and castrate it. From the bloody amputated member there grows an almond tree. Nana, daughter of the river-god Sangarios, picks a milk-almond, inserts it into herself and gives birth to Attes, a very beautiful boy who was subsequently loved by Agdistis, the hermaphrodite become a woman (according to another version, he had his member cut off by Dionysos).

Did Hegel know how to dance? The question is more obscure than one might think. Like Rousseau in any case—but do people dance in Rousseau?—he liked balls and this he confides in Nanette: "I like balls a lot; they are the merriest thing in our sad times." The *Critique of Judgment* also talks about dancing: an example of purposiveness for a lawn surrounded by trees, in a forest.
Quoting the letters is not to be confused with various so-called "biographical" operations referring to "the author's life." They have a separate status, not just because their stuff is writing, but because they engage with what we are here tracking interminably under the name "signatory." Consider that I quote this or that letter to

Prends ce sac, Mendiant ! tu ne le cajolas
Sénile nourrisson d'une tétine avare
Afin de pièce à pièce en égoutter ton glas.

Tire du métal cher quelque péché bizarre
Et, vaste comme nous, les poings pleins, le baisons
Souffles-y qu'il se torde ! une ardente fanfare.

Église avec l'encens que toutes ces maisons
Sur les murs quand berceur d'une bleue éclaircie
Le tabac sans parler roule les oraisons,

Et l'opium puissant brise la pharmacie !
Robes et peau, veux-tu lacérer le satin
Et boire en la salive heureuse l'inertie,

Par les cafés princiers attendre le matin ?
Les plafonds enrichis de nymphes et de voiles,
On jette, au mendiant de la vitre, un festin.

Et quand tu sors, vieux dieu, grelottant sous tes
toiles
D'emballage, l'aurore est un lac de vin d'or
Et tu jures avoir au gosier les étoiles !

Faute de supputer l'éclat de ton trésor,
Tu peux du moins t'orner d'une plume, à complies
Servir un cierge au saint en qui tu crois encor.

Ne t'imagine pas que je dis des folies.
La terre s'ouvre vieille à qui crève la faim.
Je hais une autre aumône et veux que tu m'oublies

Et surtout ne va pas, frère, acheter du pain.

If one asks oneself further questions about the identity of this poem, the system of its constraints and the force of its motivations (over-motivations or over-determinations we would say rather, to mark the *fold,* and to note that in this work it is not a matter of accumulating riches, effects of *over-employment*), it is not to be forgotten that we have here only the fourth draft of a poem in the process of formation ("Haine du pauvre," 1862; "A un mendiant," 1864; "A un pauvre," 1866; "Aumône, 1887). It will always be possible to treat the "definitive" call to a halt as empirically random. If we were only to let ourselves be fascinated by the "word" *glas,* we would remark first of all that it appears only from the second version on

I. Ta guenille nocturne étalant par ses trous
Les rousseurs de ses poils et de ta peau, je l'aime
Vieux spectre, et c'est pourquoi je te jette vingt sous

II. Pauvre, voici cent sous . . . Longtemps tu cajolas,
—Ce vice te manquait,—le songe d'être avare ?
Ne les enfouis pas pour qu'on te sonne le glas

III. Prends le sac. Mendiant. Longtemps tu cajolas
—Ce vice te manquait—le songe d'être avare ?
N'enfouis pas ton or pour qu'il te sonne le glas

Nanette, or to his fiancée Marie only to recall in passing that the signature most often skipped its vowels to be abbreviated, semitically, as HGL.

"Frankfurt am Main, February 9, 1797

My dear sweet Nanette

Meine liebe sanfte Nanette!

How much I am obliged (*verbunden*) to you, my gentle dear Nanette, for having insisted on writing to me as soon as possible, and for . . . being good enough to compensate me (*ersetzen*) occasionally by written conversation for the loss of your company. Indeed an imperious fate grudgingly (*neidisch*) restricts me to this alone. But it is conquered by my power of imagination, which makes good (*meine Einbildungskraft bezwingt es und ersetzt das*) what fate has withheld: the sound of your voice (*den Ton ihrer Stimme*), the soft glance of your eyes, and all else of which life (*alles übrige Leben*) boasts over written words. I have written more extensively to my sister of my situation, and to you I can only say that nothing remains for me to desire but the possibility of hearing from time to time in the evening an account *of soeur Jaqueline,* etc. [Jacqueline Arnauld, Mère Angélique, about whom Nanette, a practicing Catholic, must have talked to Hegel.] . . . Upon mature reflection I have decided not to try to improve anything in these people [of the town], but on the contrary to howl with the wolves. I have decided to preserve abstinence *à la* Alexis for the day my star for once leads me to Kamchatka or the Eskimos, and only then to raise my hopes of being able by my example to help these nations resist many sorts of luxury—such as the wearing of taffeta bodices, a host of rings, and such things.

I am surrounded on all sides by objects which remind me of you. Next to my bed hangs the lovely watch chain (*porte-montre*); over my little table hangs—according to my servant's arrangement—the most darling small pouch for my toothpicks (*guisdents*). Each *"ist"* reminds me of your pronunciation. In Swabia I was still saying *"ischt."* But ever since inhaling Palatine air I hiss only fine *"ists."*

How anybody, especially the Privy Councillor, could have the idea of calling you roguish I do not understand at all. Against that charge brashly invoke my own testimony. Who will say of water that it is hard, of a lamb that it is impatient, of a brook that it flows upward, or of a tree that it grows downward! There is also a Catholic church here. . . . As soon as I learn that there is a high mass I will go to perform my religious duties and to lift my soul in prayer to any beautiful image of the Virgin Mary (*Marienbild*) . . ."

"Frankfurt am Main, March 22, 1797

. . . I only hope this letter finds you still in Stuttgart, and serves in my place. . . . Because of your departure from our house, you appear to become even more separated

The final version (the knell no longer "tolls")

Prends ce sac, Mendiant! Tu ne le cajoles
Sénile nourisson d'une tétine avare
Afin de pièce à pièce en égoutter ton glas.

carries to its highest degree of pertinence, that is to say of contiguity (contact, suction, aspiration), *glas* inasmuch as it touches on the breast, for the astonishment or disgust of whomsoever would still be wondering (arbitrarily or motivatedly) which lactiferous form to recognize in the tocsin (in the word? thing? sense?). In its highest degree of pertinence but without reducing the plays of unsticking that the suction cup requires. Granted, the first three versions form a more homogeneous series on the surface. But "Haine du pauvre" works on the fleece

("Ta guenille nocturne étalant par ses trous
Les rousseurs de ses poils et de ta peau, je l'aime,
. . .
Et ne vas pas drapant ta lésine en poëme.
. . .
Mets à nu ta vieillesse et que ta gueuse joue,
Lèche, et de mes vingt sous chatouille la vertu,
A bas ! . . .–les deux genoux ! . . .—la barbe dans la boue!

of a cutlass [*coutelas*] that seems to rhyme with the first lines of the three subsequent poems (*cajolas*). It is the only rhyme with *las* and the last line of "Haine du pauvre."

Throw of the dice? Of gold? silver? copper?

Que veut cette médaille idiote, ris-tu?
L'argent brilla, le cuivre un jour se vert-de-grise,
Et je suis un peu dévot et je suis fort têtu,

Choisis.—Jetée ? alors, voici ma pièce prise.
Serre-là dans tes doigts et pense que tu l'as
Parce que j'en tiens trop, ou par simple méprise.

C'est le prix, si tu n'as pas peur, d'un coutelas.

from me. I can imagine the sadness your departure will cause my sister.... But do charge my sister with letting me know right away the news you will give her.... I remember having traveled through Memmingen and having come upon a nice fertile region which is in particular completely sown with hop gardens. On the banks of the Iller you will surely find nice parts. Your spiritual nourishment is surely also well provided for. I remember having been in a Franciscan monastery. I do not know whether I should say that I fear the good seed which the young Protestant clergy in Stuttgart has sprinkled into your soul may risk being choked off there, or rather that such weeds may come to be rooted out there [Matthew, Mark, Luke]. At least you must sincerely procure a rosary, prepare longer for confession, pay more respect and reverence to the saints in word and deed, etc.

Your sincere friend,
Hgl."

"Frankfurt am Main, July 2, 1979

This being, dearest friend, the first time in a long while that I have again taken pen in hand to write anyone at all a letter, let it be to pay a most oppressive debt.... The recollection of those days passed in the country even now ever drives me out of Frankfurt. And so as I reconciled myself there in the arms of nature with myself and with men, I thus often flee here to this faithful mother, separating myself again with her from the men with whom I live in peace, preserving myself under her auspices from their influence, forestalling an alliance (*Bund*) with them.... What my sister and the people in Stuttgart generally are doing I have no idea.... As soon as you stopped holding me to piety, it was all over. I never more than pass by churches. According to your letter, in church attendance at Memmingen you find not only no consolation for itself, but also cause for sorrow and regret in the miserable sustenance being handed out to the two-legged believers."

"July 17

I had written this far some time ago, and would have left this sheet lying around for still some time if a higher power, my guardian spirit, had not suddenly awakened me from my lethargy. My patron himself, the blessed Saint Alexis, called out to me in symbols on the day of his celebration: Wake up, you who sleep, arise from the dead; only in friendship is life and light!

Since I feel myself too unworthy to approach this Saint, he could easily regard this lack of reverence and service—which has its source in the very feeling of my baseness—as sinful negligence. He could thus deprive me of his clemency and grace. Fortune has accordingly bestowed upon me a mediator between saints and human beings who represents me before him, and through whom the Saint allows his grace to flow toward me.

No more fleece in the subsequent versions: smooth, naked face, no beard. The "senile old man suckling on a [miserly] teat" is born with the so-called "definitive" version, the fourth. "Miserly [*avare*]" and *glas* were already there, so the rhyme hasn't been disturbed. A necessity has slowly been imposed—from piece to piece—in the formation of the poem, right up to the term of what one might be tempted to call a gestation. We won't give in to that naturalist and teleological reading, but will hold on to the hypothesis of a necessity in the forward march—the market—of over-employs.

Just for one moment, attributing to it one single employ, the "piece by piece [*pièce à pièce*]" of "expensive metal [*métal cher*]" falls drop by drop from the "purse [*sac*]" of the "miserly teat [*tétine avare*]": (the) knell tolls in proximity to (the) teat. (The) teat resounds and resonates. The possibility of adding the article in parentheses presumes that interval and that passage (rhythm of the suction cup) between usages (between, if you insist, its use as signifier, as signified, as referent). It is a matter of ceding to the necessity that associates in the maximum of usages and over-usages the greatest number of marks, as for example the *tétine* that resounds [*retentit*] in a knell. Who ever heard such a thing? That particular tintinnabulum?

The fact that each version *also* works through another version—and that must also be able to be said of the "first"—always confers a supplementary fold or use on the whole scene, impressing onto all its referential movements a sort of lateral torsion. The poem is always also the active "translation" of another poem that resonates in it. A little as though each time, "within" Mallarmé's "corpus," between Mallarmé and Mallarmé, there were reproduced the operation of "Bells."

I accept with all due respect one of the significant symbols—the ecclesiastical collar—along with what he thereby wished to recall to me. I will guard both as a precious treasure, a relic, and take great care not to profane them by usage and application. The other, more beautiful, human symbol—the wreath that unites parted friends—I wish to make the companion of my life. The flowers are of course dry, and life has vanished from them. But what on earth is a living thing if the spirit of man does not breathe life into it? What is speechless but that to which man does not lend his speech? This little wreath will always lisp to me: "There lives somewhere a small black-eyed being—a dove nonetheless—who is your friend." And as proof that I gladly allow the small wreath to tell me this, I will occasionally leave a visiting card with my address, as is now the fashion in the world. One drives up, makes someone's mouth water as if he were now to get much to hear, and then simply leaves a card.

Farewell! I am going to bathe in the Main. The waves which will cool me perhaps you yourself saw flowing by Obbach.

Your friend
Hgl.
(still, as ever, *magister* in the address)"

"Frankfurt am Main, November 13, 1797

For a long time, dearest friend, I have had an almanac on my desk that was meant for you, and that I am finally sending. I only hope it will not have lost the appeal of novelty for you because of my delay. Yet this story can be always reread from time to time. In any case, only the pleasure of repeated viewing is decisive in the beauty of a work of art—the fact that one gladly returns to it. . . . I do not know why I always fall into general reflections. But you will forgive a man who once was a Master, and who drags himself around with this title and its accessories as with a thorn in the flesh from an angel of Satan [2 Cor 12:7]. You will still remember our way and manner from Stuttgart. I have every reason to assume that longer association with you would have liberated me more and granted me a greater capacity for merrymaking (*eines frohen Spiels*).

"Frankfurt am Main, May 25, 1798

Dear Nanette,

Do not spare me. Tear me to pieces, tell me yourself how irresponsible my negligence is. You do nothing but exercise justice. Burden me with hearing masses, with telling beads, with as many rosaries as you like, I have deserved it all. Just do not do me the injustice of believing I have not appreciated the value of your gift. You consecrated it in memory. To know good pure souls among human beings, to preserve their image in one's heart, and to live in one's faith in them—this is the best treasure a

"Les cloches" (1872) "translates," or transposes, echoes rather "The Bells." It indeed reproduces the grand semantic organization of Poe's poem (silver bells, golden bells, bronze bells, iron bells), as well as the greatest possible number of thematic motifs, based on a calculation, losses and gains, redistributions of usage that analysis, that is to say decomposition or reduction to elements, would not be able to exhaustively account for. Not only—right here—because of the richness or subtlety of the machinations, but, as a matter of principle, by reason of the generative transformation that feigns imitation and transposes the text into another system. The greatest correspondence is attained only in the most different element, in a completely different organization of resources (quantity, quality, rhyme).

For example, it must be admitted that *mimesis* is recharged and operates from one text to the other, from each text to its theme or reference, without the words resembling the things originally, and without their immediately resembling one another. Nevertheless, resemblance is reconstituted, superimposed or superimprinted through and thanks to differential or relational structures. The content wears out in this process, sometimes almost to the point of disappearing; disappearing as *quality*, as *quantity*, but more rarely as *rhythm* (the point would be, from "The Double Session" on, to rethink the value of rhythm and to introduce it so as to reelaborate the graphics of mimesis. In "The Economic Problem of Masochism," stumbling over the logic of quantity and quality, Freud looks—as a very vague hypothesis—into rhythm). Poe's rhymes are not preserved, of course, but the beating of a rhythm is—on all scales, as much as possible—whatever its support or material surface be. Moreover the word "rhyme" ("Runic rhyme"), is itself regularly replaced by the word *rythme* (Runic rhythm, rhythm of ancient, secret, difficult writing).

A few exemplary echoes—just the most striking—among so many subtle, or stifled other ones:

"How they tinkle, tinkle, tinkle,
In the icy air of night!"
Comme elle tinte, tinte, tinte, dans le glacial air de nuit

person can gain. . . . But why have you, loose child, added a butterfly to a gift offered to memory? Do you not feel the contradiction? (*Fühlen Sie nicht den Widerspruch?*) A butterfly flutters from one flower to another without recognizing the soul of either. The fleeting theft of a few sweets is the butterfly's pleasure, but it has no sense (*Anschauung*) of what is immortal. With a base soul, memory is only a soulless impression (*seelenlose Eindruck*) on the brain, the mark (*Abdruck*) on a material that always remains different from the imprint (*Gepräge*) it possesses and never becomes one with it.
I hear that your Babet is married. My sister no doubt attended the wedding. There must have been much merrymaking. We would have surely also danced a lot—like the evening before my departure. I have turned in circles ever since (*Ich habe seitdem mich immer so im Kreise gedreht*). Have you not had any balls in Memmingen? I very much like balls (*Ich bin der Bälle sehr gut*). It is the happiest thing there is in our sorrowful times. . . .
I am sending this letter to my sister for handling since I do not know where you are. . . ."

Thirteen years later—Jena and the *Phenomenology* in the meantime—here, for Marie (one of the three) the fiancée, a poem in ten quatrains, "The Phoenix." For example:

Come to mountain tops with me.
    From clouds below tear yourself free;
Here in the clear air may we stand.
    In Light's colorless womb (*In des Lichtes farbelosem Schoss*) take my hand.

What opinion (*Meinung*) has in sense (*Sinn*) injected
    From truth and madness equally collected
Has as a lifeless mist (*leblosen Nebel*) lifted,
    By the breath of life, of love, evicted.

The valley below of narrow nothingness (*des Engen Nichts*),
    Of vain exertion repaid in an exertion endless,
With dulled senses to desire bound (*an die Begier gebunden*)
    There your heart never has been found.

. . .

See the altar here atop mountains,
    On which Phoenix dies in a flaming fountain,
Only to rise in youth everlasting—
    This fruit of its ashes endlessly winning.

Phoenix's brooding, turned back on itself alone.
    Was now preserved as merely its own (*Hatte sich zu eigen es gespart*).
The point of its existence shall vanish (*Nun soll seines Daseins Punkt zerrinnen*),
    And the pain of sacrifice weigh on it in anguish.

. . .

Keeping time, time, time,
In a sort of Runic rhyme
To the tintinnabulation that so musically wells
From the bells, bells, bells, bells,
Bells, bells, bells—
From the jingling and the tinkling of the bells.

allant, elle, d'accord (d'accord, d'accord) *en une sorte de rythme runique, avec la "tintinnabulisation" qui surgit si musicalement des cloches* (des cloches, cloches, cloches, cloches, cloches, cloches)*, du cliquetis et du tintement des cloches.*

. . .

—how it tells
Of the rapture that impels
To the swinging and the ringing
Of the bells, bells, bells,
Of the bells, bells, bells, bells,
Bells, bells, bells—
To the rhyming and the chiming of the bells!

qu'il dit le ravissement qui porte au branle et à la sonnerie des cloches (cloches, cloches—des cloches, cloches, cloches, cloches)*, au rythme et au carillon des cloches !*

. . .
In a clamorous appealing to the mercy of the fire—

dans une clameur d'appel à la merci du feu

. . .
By the side of the pale-faced moon.
Oh, the bells, bells, bells!
What a tale their terror tells
Of Despair!
How they clang, and clash, and roar!
What a horror they outpour
On the bosom of the palpitating air!

aux côtés de la lune à la face pâle. Oh ! les cloches (cloches, cloches)*, quelle histoire dit leur terreur—ce Désespoir ! Qu'elles frappent et choquent, et rugissent ! Quelle horreur elles versent sur le sein de l'air palpitant ! encore l'ouïe sait-elle, pleinement par le tintouin et le vacarme, comment tourbillonne et s'épanche le danger ; encore l'ouïe dit-elle, distinctement, dans le vacarme et la querelle, comment s'abat*

But the feeling of striving immortal
Pushes (*Treibt's*) him beyond his selfs narrow portal.
May his earthly nature quake
In names this striving comes awake.

Narrow bands (*enge Binden*) dividing us, fall away!
Sacrifice alone is the heart's true way
I expand myself to you, as you to me.
May what isolates us go up in fire, cease to be.

. . .

Once the spirit atop free mountains has flown (*Tritt*),
It holds back nothing of its own (*Er behält vom Eignen nichts zurück*).
Living to see myself in you, and you to see yourself in me,
In the enjoyment of celestial bliss shall we be (*So genießen wir der Himmel Glück*)."

(April 13, 1811)

Four days later, another poem:

You are mine! A heart as yours I may call mine.
In your look (*in Deinem Blick*) may I divine
Love's look returned (*Wiederblick*), oh bliss,
Oh highest happiness (*o höchstes Glück*)!

Yet the poverty of words I address,
Whose power love enchanted to express—
A love which from within presses with force
O'er to the heart—is frustrated in its course.

"I could envy. Nightingale,
Your throat's power (*Deiner Kehle Macht*), making mine pale.
Yet, spitefully, Nature has merely lent
The language of sorrow an instrument so eloquent!

Yet if Nature did not grant the lips
Expression in speech of love's bliss,

For lovers' bond (Bunde) it has given with just finesse
These lips a token of greater tenderness.
Souls touch in the kiss—more profound than speech.
My heart overflows into yours, within mutual reach."

The next day, a letter to Niethammer.

". . . I learn that if you remain you can be more active on behalf of the university system than in your situation thus far. Since the matter is still pending, my letter would really seem doubly superfluous. But I have a more precise motive for writing: namely, my bond (*Verbindung*) with a good and very dear girl. My happiness (*Glück*) has in part been made contingent on my faculty appointment at the University. Since the day before yesterday I have

ou s'enfle le danger, à l'abattement ou à l'enflure dans la colère des cloches, dans la clameur et l'éclat des cloches !

Yet the ear, it fully knows,
By the twanging
And the clanging,
How the danger ebbs and flows;
Yet the ear distinctly tells,
In the jangling,
And the wrangling,
How the danger sinks and swells,
By the sinking or the swelling in the anger of the bells—
Of the bells—
Of the bells, bells, bells, bells,
Bells, bells, bells—
In the clamor and the clangor of the bells!

Hear the tolling of the bells—
Iron bells!

What a world of solemn thought their monody compels!
In the silence of the night,
How we shiver with affright
At the melancholy meaning of their tone!
For every sound that floats
From the rust within their throats
Is a groan.

Entendez le glas des cloches—cloches de fer ! Quel monde de pensée solennelle comporte leur monodie ! Dans le silence de la nuit que nous frémissons de l'effroi ! à la mélancolique menace de leur ton. Car chaque son qui flotte, hors la rouille en leur gorge—est un gémissement.

And the people—ah, the people—
They that dwell up in the steeple,
All alone,
And who tolling, tolling, tolling
In that muffled monotone,
Feel a glory in so rolling
On the human heart a stone—
They are neither man nor woman—
They are neither brute nor human—
They are Ghouls;

*Et le peuple—le peuple—ceux qui demeurent haut dans le clocher, tous seuls, qui sonnant (*sonnant, sonnant*) dans cette mélancolie voilée, sentent une gloire à ainsi rouler sur le cœur humain une pierre—ils ne sont ni homme ni femme—ils ne sont ni brute ni humain—ils sont des Goules : et leur roi, ce l'est, qui sonne ; et il roule (*roule—roule*), roule un Péan hors des cloches ! Et son sein content se gonfle de ce Péan des cloches ! et il danse, et il danse, et il hurle :*

been certain of calling this dear heart mine. I know I have your warm wishes for my happiness. I have told her moreover that I would first write to you and the best of women. Her name is Marie von Tucher.... I spare myself a description of how happy I feel. Supply (*supplieren Sie*) the image of it from your own memory and present.... But do not as yet tell anybody anything of this. Due to the external conditions and her father, we cannot yet talk aloud of it. At most Roth and his wife may be told, but they should likewise keep it in confidence...."

Niethammer is waiting for a decision from the King about him, he is slow to respond, excuses himself but expresses his disagreement as to the procedure: "If I have understood your letter right, you warn to delay not only concluding your marriage, but even publicly announcing the engagement you have made, until your nomination at Erlangen is done. In no way can I approve that. Your nomination is, according to my information, so little in doubt that I cannot question it even in the case of me abandoning my post. . . . To speak to you frankly, I consider this as a timidity as unfortunate as unjustified on your part. At a time when even kings themselves are no longer expected to prove their ancestry to win the right to court royal daughters, at a time when the personal merit and rank one has acquired on one's own without ancestry ennobles more than all proofs of hereditary nobility, there is nothing to fear from public opinion in a union such as yours.... So do not allow such idle worries—not to speak of a certain vanity on your part, which so ill befits a philosopher—keep you from concluding your marriage as soon as possible.
But I have still another reason that makes it my duty to advise you against this delay. Permission for marriage, that in your capacity as civil servant you must receive directly from His Majesty the King: you will obtain it much more easily as rector at Nuremberg than in the capacity of professor at Erlangen. The reason is very simple. The principal viewpoint considered when the matter concerns granting permission to marry is the pension assured the widow, according to the practice generally in use for all servants of the State, which poses each time the question of the funds from which the said pension must be taken. Now this question is far easier to resolve for institutions already having a regular budget than for the University of Erlangen, which does not yet have any regular funds at its disposal . . ."

Hegel is, as always, slow to respond:

"It is your letter's wealth of gratifying content, my dear friend, which has kept me silent for so long, and my head is still so filled with it that I can hardly put it into the usual language of a letter. Your staying on at your present post, the altered circumstances in which you are doing so, your anticipated arrival at the wedding reception, the reception itself—everything is so intertwined that it will be difficult at first to pick up a thread from such

*allant d'accord (*d'accord, d'accord*) en une sorte de rythme runique, avec le tressaut des cloches—(*des cloches, cloches, cloches*) avec le sanglot des cloches ; allant d'accord (*d'accord, d'accord*) dans le glas (le glas, le glas) en un heureux rythme runique, avec le roulis des cloches—(*des cloches, cloches, cloches*) avec la sonnerie des cloches—(*des cloches, cloches, cloches, cloches, cloches—cloches, cloches, cloches*)—le geignement et le gémissement des cloches.*

And their king it is who tolls;
And he rolls, rolls, rolls,
Rolls
A pæan from the bells!
And his merry bosom swells
With the pæan of the bells!
And he dances, and he yells;
Keeping time, time, time,
In a sort of Runic rhyme,
To the pæan of the bells—
Of the bells:
Keeping time, time, time,
In a sort of Runic rhyme,
To the throbbing of the bells—
Of the bells, bells, bells—
To the sobbing of the bells;
Keeping time, time, time,
As he knells, knells, knells,
In a happy Runic rhyme,
To the rolling of the bells—
Of the bells, bells, bells—
To the tolling of the bells—
Of the bells, bells, bells, bells,
Bells, bells, bells—
To the moaning and the groaning of the bells.

What one would be tempted to isolate as galactic segment (moon, tocsin, a breast that swells, heaves or palpitates—twice—pouring out, etc.) does not even constitute a semantic or thematic chain, whether apparent or hidden. That chain is carried off

a tissue. To be sure, I see my Marie unwind many a ball of yarn, and I help her all the more diligently to look for the ends, inasmuch as completion of the trousseau and acceleration of preparations for the wedding depend on such things. For, as you know, women want to have such important matters in order from one end to the other, and do not take to the suggestion that something like that might equally be done afterwards. But I notice that these threads have taken me right to the heart of the matter, and thus continue to say that the necessary arrangements will in any case not be in place before fall. So now it is only a question of having her father—for the rest of the family has agreed—give his assurance that, even if I am to be still a gymnasium rector, the wedding will take place in the fall. The excellent explanations which you have handed on to me have not gone unused. One objective reason, namely the greater difficulty of obtaining Royal authorization from Erlangen, I have not been able to use for all it is worth. For as you know, even fanatics and liars can persuade others only inasmuch as they have persuaded themselves of the reasons to be used. But undoubtedly I can go to Erlangen only if the university is organized, in which case funding will also be taken care of, and thus funding for the widow's pension as well. You moreover know people here in Nuremberg. If all imaginable reasons counsel these people from Nuremberg to buy a horse, their first deliberations always bring them to the point of buying—for the time being—a packet of horsehair. But since the rest of the nag adheres to this hair, the whole animal must likewise little by little be drawn into the stable. Disclosure of the engagement came about by itself. Marie's father introduced me to her grandfather. He who first says A now goes on through the entire alphabet. We thus comport ourselves as engaged before the entire world. You know anyway that one who has founded one's cause on the goodness of women, especially in such matters, has not built on sand. . . . There has already been so much talk about Erlangen that our union has come to be completely fused with the city in our imagination, much as man and wife. The improvement of my economic situation is necessary due to my lack of means because my Marie, whose grandfather is still alive and whose father still has seven children apart from herself, can obtain an annual sum of only 100 florins beyond the dowry. . . .

Your sincere friend Hgl"

From the summer that follows, just before the marriage, there are again two letters to Marie.

"Nuremberg, summer 1811

Dear Marie,

I have written to you in thought almost all night long! What was at issue in my thoughts was not this or that isolated matter between us, but rather, inevitably, the whole thought: are we thus going to make ourselves

into indecision through the suspended swinging or beating, the oscillation of the clapper (the "true" impossible theme of the piece) being remarked or reverberating in the neither-nor of the ghouls (between man and woman, human and inhuman, language and non-language, etc.). Semantic sense is struck by the rhythm of its other, exposing itself there, open, offered in its very hiatus.

That other, which one might be tempted to isolate as a concatenation of signifiers, of identities with arbitrary elements, is endlessly reused according to a mimetics that does not relate to a real sound, to a full content, but indeed, as the transposition shows, to relational rhythmic structures without any invariant content or ultimate element.

There is indeed the appearance of a simple nucleus around which everything seems to agglomerate: *gl, cl, kl, tl, fl,* and, restricting oneself to lexical counting—which is more than insufficient for reading rhythm—one can surely pick up *tinKLe, oversprinKLe, jinGLing, turTLe, GLoats, starTLed, CLamorous, CLang, CLash, janGLing, wranGLing, CLamor, CLangor, FLoats, GLory, CLoches, GLacial, CLigner, CLiquetis, FLotte, enFLe, CLameur, éCLat, GLas, GLoire, gonFLe, sanGLot,* whose two-letter combinations recompose their attraction elsewhere in the poem, at a distance, according to numerous complex plays. That appearance of a nucleus is moreover more baldly seen, better read and remarked when the two versions—Poe's and Mallarmé's—are put in relief. That does not mean that there is an absolute nucleus and dominant center, for the rhythm is tied not only to words, and especially not to the proximity of contact between two letters. Nevertheless, unaware of "Les Cloches," Fónagy remains deaf to the +L (consonant + L) effect, not only in the translations where it doesn't occur but even in the German one where it does: "The main purpose of *translation* in prose is to translate, to carry over the message from the original to the target language by substituting the form *a* of the original language by form *b* of the target language. . . .

unhappy (*unglücklich*)? From the depth of my soul came the reply: This cannot, ought no, and must not be. It shall not be! (*Dies kann, dies soll, und darf nicht sein—Es wird nicht sein!*)
However, what I have long told you is to me summed up in the conclusion that marriage is essentially a religious bond (*Band*). To be complete, love requires a still higher moment than that in which it consists merely in and for itself. What perfect satisfaction—i.e., being entirely happy (*glücklich sein*)—means can only be completed by religion and the sense of duty; for only therein do all particularizations of the temporal self (*Selbst*) step aside, particularizations which in actuality could cause trouble. Such total satisfaction by itself remains imperfect and cannot be taken as ultimate, though it should constitute what is called earthly happiness.
I have before me the draft of the lines which I added to your letter to my sister. My postscript, to which you certainly attached too much importance, is missing. I was thus reminded of exactly what occasioned the frame of mind in which I wrote that postscript even while recopying the draft. Had we not talked the evening before and definitely agreed that we prefer to call what we were certain to attain together satisfaction (*Zufriedenheit*)? And did we not say: "There is a blessed (*selige*) satisfaction which, all illusion aside, is more than all that is called being happy." As I wrote the words now before me, whose meaning is so dear to me "You may see from it how happy I can be with her for the rest of my life, and how happy winning such love, which I scarcely still hoped for in this world, has already made me" I added, as if this happy sensation of mine and its expression had been excessive over against what we had already said: ". . . insofar as happiness belongs to my life's destiny (*Bestimmung*)." I do not think this should have hurt you! I remind you, dear Marie, that your deeper sense, the formation of what is higher in you, has taught you as well that in nonsuperficial natures every sensation of happiness is connected with a sensation of melancholy. Furthermore, I remind you of your promise to heal me of any disbelief in satisfaction that might remain in my nature, i.e., to reconcile my true inner self with the way I too frequently am toward and for the actual. I equally remind you that this point of view gives a higher dimension to your destiny, that I credit you with strength for it, that this strength must lie in our love. Distinguishing (*Unterscheidung*) your love for me and mine for you, if I may be so emphatically explicit, would separate our love: this love is solely ours, merely this unity, this bond (*Band*). Turn away from reflection within this distinction (*Unterschied*), allow us to hold fast to this One (*diesem Einen*) that can alone be my strength as well, my new love of life. Let this trust be the basis for everything, and then all will be truly well.
Oh, how much more I could still write—about my perhaps hypochondriacal pedantry, which led me to insist

Contrary to this procedure the translator of poems carries over certain features of form *a* of the original into form *b* of the target language. The silvery tinkling of the bells in the icy air of night in the poem of Edgar Allan Poe is reflected also in the Hungarian and German and Italian translations by the prevailing *i* sounds and the sequences *ng, nk, nt, nd,* and the chains of nasal sounds:

ng, nk, nt, nd.

How they *tin*kle, *tin*kle, *tin*kle
In the icy air of night . . .

Hall*d*, m*in*d, pen*dül*, kon*dul*, cse*ndül* . . .
(Mihály Babits)

W*i*e s*i*r kl*ing*en, kl*ing*en, kl*ing*en,
Zw*ink*ernd s*i*ch zum Reigen schl*ing*en . . .
(Th. Etzel)

Come *tint*innano, *tint*innano, *tint*innano
D*i* una cr*i*stall*i*na del*i*z*i*a
(Frederico Olivero)"

If one wanted to reduce still further the apparent nucleus of the + L effect (gl, cl, kl, tl, fl, pl, etc.), one would then isolate the L. Now, it is concerning L that Fónagy, following a rich analysis (so rich that it cannot decide on any determinate result), has to conclude, quite correctly (but what then does his project become?), that a determination, hence a motivation, hence a univocal semantics, is impossible: "The complex character of the consonant L reminds us of a hardly surprising but important truth. There is no simple and exclusive correspondence between a drive and a given sound." The drive to motivate always finds what both feeds and frustrates it. Its result necessarily contradicts it because the drive itself, of itself, separates into two columns. One could demonstrate that essential division of the so-called Cratylist motif in *English Words,* for they necessarily submit to the law of antherection and dissemination. Examples:
"G (while not being the letter that governs the greatest number of words) has its importance, signifying in the first place a simple aspiration toward a point to which the breath leads it: that this guttural sound, always hard as an initial letter, be followed by a vowel or

so greatly on the distinction between satisfaction and happiness (*Glück*), a distinction which is once again so useless; or about how I have sworn to you and myself that your happiness (*Glück*) shall be my dearest possession. There is still much that passes away, is forgotten, and remedied merely by not being evoked.

One more thing: I have long doubted whether I should write to you, since everything written or spoken again depends solely on explanation; or, since I feared explanation, which once embarked upon is so dangerous. But I have overcome this fear and have the highest hope that your heart will know how to receive these words.

Farewell until, dear Marie, we see each other today again untroubled. I would still like only to be able to tell you this: what feeling, how very much—my existence as much as it is—lies for me in the words: *dear Marie*.

Your Wilhelm"

"Nuremberg . . .

. . . I have hurt you by a few things I said. This causes me pain. I have hurt *you* by seeming to censure moral views I can only repudiate, as if they were principles of *your* own thought and action. About this I now *say* to *you* only that I reject these views in part inasmuch as they abolish the difference between what the heart likes—i.e., what pleases it—and duty; or rather inasmuch as they completely eliminate duty and destroy morality (*Moralität*). But likewise—and this is the most important matter between us—please believe me when I tell *you* that I do not attribute these views, insofar as they have this consequence, to you, to your self; that I view them as lying merely within your reflection (*Reflexion*); that you do not think, know, or gain an overview of them in their logical connection; that they serve you as a way of excusing others. To justify (*rechtfertigen*) is something else, for what one may excuse in others is not therefore considered permissible in oneself. Yet what one can justify is right for everyone, and thus for ourselves as well.

With regard to myself and my manner of explanation, do not forget that if I condemn maxims (*Maximen*), I too easily lose consciousness of the way in which they are actual in determinate individuals—in you, for instance. Nor should you forget that such maxims appear before my eyes too earnestly in their universality, in their logical consequences, extended results, and applications. Far from taking these things to be entailed for you, you give them no thought. At the same time you yourself know that, even though character and the maxims governing insight are different, what maxims govern insight and judgment is not unimportant (*gleichgültig*). Yet I know just as well that maxims, when they contradict character, are still less important in the case of women than men. Lastly, you know that there are evil men who torture

consonant. Add to that that desire, satisfied by L, expresses with said liquid, joy, light, etc., and that from the idea of slipping one moves also to that of an increase through vegetal growth or by any other mode; finally, with R, there appears to be a seizing of the object desired with L, or the need to crush or grind it. L. . . . This letter sometimes seems powerless to express through itself something other than an appetite not followed by any result."

In observing just the principle and logic (not the empirical approximations within a given language, English) one can state at least this: L, here satisfying desire, allowing the seizure of its object, marks—like G—in the first place an aspiration, or an appetite, an unsatisfied desire. The object—of desire: an—unsatisfied—desire for an object. The problematic of "Bases pulsionnelles de la phonation" omits above all an essential relay: the effect of the proper name. If Fónagy *is right* not to provide an overhasty response (so even though he quotes Mallarmé—"With the tired finger will you press the breast / By which the woman flows in sibylline whiteness [*Avec le doigt fané presseras-tu le sein / Par qui coule en blancheur sibylline la femme*]"—in the middle of his analysis of M, of L, referring to milk, "the archetype of any liquid serving as nourishment," and "probably figuring as the secret link which associates the L sound with the term 'liquid,' with the color white and with the sensation of a liquid that flows sweetly in poetry," then to "mama," etc., he proposes no relation with the name of Mallarmé. Nor with the name of Poe, on the same page: "artificial sucking which releases some MOE or POE, associated with nourishment and the mother. MOE and POE are supposed to be 'synonyms' at this stage of development"), he appears to miss a decisive structural articulation that prevents him from even anticipating the theoretical locus of the question

that belongs neither to one nor to the other, making them adhere somewhere one to the other; opening them both together, putting them to work like a sort of general *suction cup*.

their wives merely so that their behavior, along with their patience and love, may be constantly tested. I do not believe that I am that evil. Yet although no harm ought ever be done to such a dear human being as you, I could almost be free of regret for having hurt you. For through the deeper insight into your being that I have thus gained I feel the intimacy and depth of my love for you have increased. So be consoled that what may have been unkind and harsh in my replies will all vanish through the fact that I feel and recognize ever more deeply how thoroughly lovable, loving, and full of love *you* are.
I have to go lecture (*Ich muß in die Lektion*). Farewell, dearest, dearest, most lovely Marie.

Your Wilhelm"

After the marriage, he writes to Niethammer, to whom he had confided that he loved Marie also because of her resemblance with "the best of women" (Niethammer's wife):

". . . On the whole—apart from a few modifications still to be desired—I have now reached my earthly goal. For what more does one want in this world than a post and a dear wife! Those are the principal articles (*Hauptartikel*) one has to strive for as an individual. The rest (*Das Uebrige*) no longer make up chapters in themselves (*eignen Kapitel*) but perhaps only paragraphs or remarks (*Anmerkungen*). There is really not much more I wish to tell—or have to tell—about the weeks of my married life thus far. . . .
. . . I learned . . . that you had showed a little more hope than when Roth left of further upgrading the University of Erlangen this fall, and that you no longer found yourself obliged to send Ludwig elsewhere, i.e., to Heidelberg.
Heidelberg, however, brings me to Fries and his *Logic*. Stein's bookstore knew nothing of a copy ordered for you but let on that it would receive a copy in three weeks. I have since received one from another bookstore. But my feeling in connection with it is one of sadness. I do not know whether as a married man I am mellowing, but I feel sadness that in the name of philosophy such a shallow man attains the honorable position he holds in the world, and that he even permits himself to inject such scribblings with a tone of importance. On such occasions one can become angry that there is no public voice to speak with integrity in such matters, for certain circles and persons would greatly benefit from it. I have known Fries for a long time. I know that he has gone beyond the Kantian philosophy by interpreting it in the most superficial manner, by earnestly watering it down ever more, making it ever more shallow. The paragraphs of his *Logic* and the accompanying explanations are printed in separate volumes. The first volume of paragraphs is spiritless, completely shallow, threadbare, trivial, devoid of the least intimation of scientific coherence. The explanations are likewise totally shallow, devoid of spirit, threadbare, trivial, the most slovenly disconnected explanatory lecture-hall twaddle, such as only a truly empty-headed individual in his hour of diges-

The suction cup is adoration. Adoration is always that of the Holy Virgin, of the Galilean mother in which one is conceived without a father and whom one desires as closely as possible to the Spanish whore. The Holy Virgin is included [*comprise*] —compressed [*comprimée*], imprisoned, wrapped, hardbound—in the tube of vaseline, which she expresses, or which expresses her just as much.

the tube is (hardbinds) both the Virgin and Christ; vaseline is (hardbinds) the latter coming out of the former like a cock [*verge*] or sperm, his mother spat out. He spits himself from inside his mother, at least that's how it looks. They are (hardbind) both of them adored and exposed. The Roman soldiers are (hardbind) there in legion, like an armored and compact phalanx, "strong, handsome, husky." "Lying on the table, it was a banner telling the invisible legions of my triumph over the police. I was in a cell. I knew that all night long my tube of vaseline would be exposed to the scorn—the contrary of a Perpetual Adoration—of a group of strong, handsome, husky policeman. So strong that if the weakest of them barely squeezed his fingers together, there would shoot forth, first with a slight fart, brief and dirty, a ribbon of gum which would continue to emerge in a ridiculous silence. Nevertheless, I was sure that this puny and most humble object would hold its own against them; by its mere presence it would be able to exasperate all the police in the world; it would draw upon itself contempt, hatred, white and dumb rages."
For a reading of these pages from the point of view of existential psychoanalysis, see what *Saint-Genet* says of such a "'constellation' of images" and the passage from one "theme" to another

The pendulum movement that brings with it all these "objects," themselves split, between one value and the opposing one, is also a movement of the tongue, mouth, glottis. Adoration is first of all the effect of an *inversion* of sense. Demonstration:

1. agglutinate: "(. . . But I would adore that thief who is my mother.)" Next paragraph: "I knew that all night long my tube of vaseline would be exposed to the scorn—the contrary [*inverse*] of a

tion could ever come up with (*das saloppste erläuternde unzusammenhängendste Kathedergewäsche, das nur ein Plattkopf in der Verdauungsstunde von sich geben kann*). I prefer to say nothing more specific about his miserable thought. The main discovery, for the sake of which he has written his whole system, is that logic rests on anthropological foundations and completely depends on them; that Kant, like Aristotle before him, was deeply steeped in the prejudice of the autonomy of logic, but that they were of course right about it not being based on empirical psychology, for nothing indeed can be demonstrated from experience. Yet it is still alleged to rest on anthropological foundations, and it is moreover claimed that there is a difference between demonstration and deduction. *Logic* can be deduced, and indeed can be deduced from anthropological presuppositions based on experience. So babbles on this individual about his fundamental concept. His pure general logic in his system starts out "the first means employed by the understanding in its process of *thinking* are concepts," as if chewing and swallowing food were a mere means of eating, and as if the undemanding still did much else besides thinking. This is the sort of shallow slovenliness (*Salopperie*) with which this man babbles on—encompassing everything from A through Z twice over—if I am not mistaken, without the least precision even in matters known to everyone, such as definitions of the faculty of imagination, of memory, and so on. I heard that his lectures were not well attended because by the time one had understood a single word, he had already sputtered out (*herausgesprudelt*) twelve more. I find this quite believable. For his shallowness drives him to pour out twelve new words on top of each word he utters, so that he may drown in himself the feeling of the misery of his thoughts, and likewise drown the students in such verbiage that they become incapable of holding onto or noting any thought whatsoever. It has been said that the higher authorities have talked of calling Fries to Erlangen to have textbooks fabricated by him. Apart from the fact that I might ultimately have reason to be quite happy about this, since perhaps a slot might thereby open up for me in Heidelberg, one would have to be curious about a university in which, next to Fries, our friend Heller is called to teach philology and aesthetics, in which—as has been assured—Graser is called upon for philosophy of education, our local secretary Kiefhaber for diplomacy, the former librarian Mr. von Aretin for the humanities, and Harl for finance and public administration (*Polizeiwissenschaft*).

I hope to be able to bring out my work on logic by next Easter. My psychology will follow later. It might not be ill-advised for the authorities to wait upon further treatments of logic before sanctioning and publicly introducing for instructional purposes the old logical shambles which already in and for themselves have become flat and threadbare, but which in Fries's hands have been completely trampled and washed away like some old last-remaining, used-up paper towel. No professor at a classical or modern gymnasium in the Kingdom of Bavaria can be in such misery as to cling to such shal-

Perpetual Adoration—of a group of strong, handsome, husky policemen."

2. slide along the bars, they are mine, jump from one to the other: "The tube of vaseline / whose destination is well known to you, summoned up the face of her who, during a reverie that moved through the dark alleys of the city / was the most cherished of mothers."

We're seeing a sort of rhetorical (metaphorico-metonymic, etc., if you press the executioner) rip-off in a tube [*entubage*]: the Holy Mary tube of vaseline, glottis, clitoris, or exposed Christ (the Lord's anointed) must be celebrated by the tongue ("I would like to hymn it [the tube or ribbon of gum] with the newest words in the French language"). It must be adored, like the holy mother, and kissed, loved "by some other gesture, even the vilest and most contemptible." Like the Virgin Mary and before her, already, behind her, the Immaculate Conception.

nearly a hundred pages further along: "There I met handsome criminals, violent and somber, swearing in a savage language in which the oaths are the finest in the world.
'I fuck the Mother of God in the ass!'
'I fuck the wall!'"

The hymn that is raised to the tube comes from the throat. Everything that is beautiful "provokes, and in our throat reveals, song." Everything that "makes us sing," even a "night light beside a coffin"

"Aesthetic sob" again

lowness. By fall my own labors for the lecture hall may likewise result in a more popular and easily accessible form, displaying more of the tone expected both of a general textbook and of gymnasium instruction. For I feel every year more inclined to make myself accessible, especially since my marriage. At the same time, I am every year more persuaded that there might be almost too much philosophical instruction in the gymnasium. That one hour is being dropped on account of religion helps some. In the meantime there is still almost too much of a good thing. I realize, of course, that the highest authorities have decreed that instruction should consist, in part or predominantly, in practical exercises. Yet I have no clear representation as to how one could engage in practical exercises in speculative thinking. Practical exercises in abstract thinking are already extremely difficult, while due to its manifoldness empirical thinking is most dispersive. The situation is much like learning to read: one cannot start right off reading entire words as some super-clever pedagogues have wished to do, but must start with what is abstract, with individual letters. So in thinking, in logic, the most abstract is really the easiest of all, for it is completely simple, pure, and uncompounded. Only gradually, as those simple sounds have penetrated as distinct from one another, can one proceed to mental exercises in what is sensory or concrete. I just now recall that a few days ago I read an excellent lead article for a third public school curriculum, which succeeds previous ones as the third just as Christ the Lord joined the buyers and sellers as the third man in the Temple. Explanations of such excellence I call truly classical. Thank goodness simple common sense and an actual earnest will to learn something are finally to be allowed to break through. As I see from the newspapers, Mr. von Zentner is back. Thus the decision about Erlangen can probably be expected soon—namely, that it has once again been postponed . . .

Your Hgl"

transcendental role, allowing there to be formed above it something like an effluvium, a dream of appeasement? Is it not always an element excluded from the system that ensures the space of possibility of the system? The transcendental has always been, strictly, a transcategorial, something that could not be received, shaped, finished in any of the categories internal to the system. The vomit of the system. And what if the sister, the brother/sister relation here represented the transcendental position, ex-position?

In the figure of the sister, femininity has the highest presentiment of the ethical essence but does not reach consciousness: the law of the family remains unconscious, locked up, in the lower darkness, with divine power. The

or treachery, is related to beauty, and all beauty provokes a movement in the back of the throat. The (French) tongue must therefore celebrate, sing the praises of the little tube of vaseline.

The celebration is supposed to take place at Christmas. Strange association. It runs invisibly under the page. The French tongue, and the narrator, give several *coups de gl* ("brilliance [*éclat*]," "hoarfrost [*verglas*]", "calamity [*calamité*]", "frost [*gel*]," "glory [*gloire*]," etc.). Immediately following the hymn to the funereal tube, the preferred glans—of the one-armed man—takes action, its thrusts smeared with almost testamentary unguents and chrisms.

At present: "Now as I write, I muse on my lovers. I would like them to be smeared with my vaseline, with that soft, slightly mentholated substance; I would like their muscles to bathe in that delicate transparence without which their dearest attributes are less lovely.

When a limb has been removed, the remaining one is said to grow stronger. I had hoped that the vigor of the arm which Stilitano had lost might be concentrated in his penis. . . . In order to do justice to the one-armed Stilitano I shall wait a few pages. Let it be known from the start that he was devoid of any Christian virtue. All his brilliance, all his power, had their source between his legs. His penis, and that which completes it, the whole apparatus, was so beautiful that the only thing I can call it is a generative organ. One might have thought he was dead . . ."

sister goes further or higher than the daughter. *Qua* daughter, she loses her parents with an ethical quietude and a natural emotion. Like all children, she attains her being-for-self in losing her parents. From then on she no longer needs her parents. Mortal or dead, they provoke her only to a natural, merely natural, positive relation. Which is no longer the case with the brother. With the brother (let's not speak of her sister, as she has not come up: Hegel presupposes that she would not have a sexual relation with her sister; nor with her brother, but in that case the non-desire is not the without-desire of a non-sexual relation, but a desire suspended in sexual difference), the sister sets in motion a positive, but non-natural, relation of recognition. She depends on him in her for-herself.

The sister goes further or higher than the mother and the wife. These latter, as such, are still mired in nature by the "pleasure" they take. The sister, *qua* sister, takes none. And then their singularity is negative: it can be *replaced*. The value of *replaceability* operates discreetly but decisively in this analysis judged to be disconcerting by more than one commentator. The replaceable or the replacer (*Ersatz*) seems at first to be opposed to the singular. It thus implies a certain universalization initiated by the repetition of the *Ersetzen*. Wife and mother are on one side rooted in singularity, but on another side the singular that occupies them takes on a certain contingency and "can be replaced" (*ersetzt werden kann*). If desire and pleasure are, for wife or mother, singular, the fact remains that in the ethical home, in the "house of ethicity" (*im Hause der Sittlichkeit*), this singularity offers itself up to substitution. Without which there is perhaps family but not ethical family. This latter requires that the wife be dealing no longer with this husband here, this child here, but with "a husband or children in general (*ein Mann, Kinder überhaupt*)." When they die, she can replace them. This possibility ensures the ethical structure of the relation to the other members, its access to ideality, conceptuality, etc. The wife always marries something of a concept (the man), she always conceives something of the order of concepts (the children). In general. "These female relationships are grounded not on sentiment but on the universal." This feature is determined in this context as an inferiority. The sister, for her part, remains in singularity, but a singular singularity: purely universal at the same stroke, without cutting herself from the natural bond of consanguinity.

So the woman (mother-wife) is posited in the opening

Periodically, parodically, the precious inversion of the object in an anonymous, anachronic style.

But then, without any obvious transition, with a quick jolt, following an invisible nocturnal elaboration, you are taken from Stilitano's scarcely Christian fly to the passion of and for Salvador (the Savior), who "took care of me." This passion lives in humiliating poverty. The word and signs of "poverty" accumulate for these two pages. But "poverty made us erect," just as the sick person "gets an erection" when he has scabies or leprosy and "scratches himself." The scene is invaded by lice. Not invaded from outside, but occupied like a familiar, if not natural place: "lice, our pets [*familiers*].

the *topos* of the louse [*pou*] is not just the pubic fleece, place of the exposed/dissimulated limit between presence and absence of penis or hole (truth is a lousy concept). It is also, for the same reasons, the neck [*cou*]. A scene from the *Journal,* written to glorify Stilitano's ass (his "solemn posterior", which was a "Station [*Reposoir*]") follows the movement of a louse on his collar, next to Stilitano's neck. The louse finds there "its domain—its space rather." This time the louse is unique, but its name is lost and found again, chased over the surface of the text, taking over all the objects and inhabiting many words at once. All that is observed, narrated in the *annal* style, from Stilitano's "behind," in the course of a game of poker ("*poker . . . s'apporta* [blew in] . . . *posa* [placed] . . . *postérieur . . . croupe* [rump] . . . *postérieur . . . Reposoir . . . poker . . . col* [collar] . . . *pou* [louse] . . . *col . . . pou . . . col . . . Cologne . . . cou* [neck] . . . *coupés* [cut] . . . *pou . . . col . . . col . . . cou*"). The text is indeed a fleece. Note that the word ass [*cul*] has not (no more than has the word *coup*) been written. Its hole is simply circumscribed—like a louse—between collar and neck. *Miracle of the Rose,* poem: "To the glory of the trusty [*prévôt*]: . . . When the men who are being punished see him marching in front of them, they slyly say of his round and not very mobile buttocks: 'They gabble.'
And then, that last stroke [*coup*], that finishing stroke [*coup de grâce*], his neck [*cou*]."

of an *Ersatz*. But so is the man (father-husband). Where is the difference? What is specific about female "conceptuality"?

Its immediacy. To be understood politically. Foreign to the city as such, the woman retains an immediate relation to the universal. She remains stuck in the natural, in sensibility. The man to the contrary dissociates and mediates *qua* member of the city, *qua* political actor. He thus possesses "the force of the self-conscious universal." *Qua* political force he mediates and negotiates his right to desire. To a desire he does not lose whereas the woman can lose it in immediate universality: she can dream of anyone in place of anyone. By negotiating and mediating his right to desire, the man keeps his freedom, his mastery, his power of substitution. Substitution means something else here, it is not immediate and undifferentiated. The man can take, leave, take back. The man "buys (*erkauft*: buys himself) the right to desire (*Recht der Begierde*) and thus preserves his freedom with respect to this desire." That is the dissymmetry: her politico-sexual status deprives the woman of the right to desire and of her freedom as to desire. If she has a desire, she has no right to it. The man who leaves the house and goes into the "bourgeoisie" (*Bürgerlichkeit*), into civil society, has the right to desire but also the freedom to dominate that desire. To say that he *buys* is not to say what the price he pays is, what political mediation hides by way of expense or unproductive investment. A desire the right to which one buys, over which one can be sure of having mastery and freedom—is that a desire? Is it so good? Who gains by this deal? And who makes this deal happen?

You can always send off to the sister the one who asks the transcendental question of the conditions of possibility of your own discourse.

one of the rare letters from Christiane Hegel to her brother, dated Stuttgart, January 15, 1799: "Last night, a little before midnight, our father died peacefully. I cannot write more.
Your Christiane."

The greater logic is there to suspend the choice and prevent you from deciding between the transcendental sister and the empirical sister. Far from barring the process, the brother/sister relation is another moment to get through. To get the family outside itself. Once again it marks the reconciliatory transition, the passage of divine law and human law (the) one into the other. At least that is what the *Phenomenology of Spirit* means to say. But where do you get that for a sister the brother

The lice inhabited us." The lice don't inhabit a house but a body, and in the body, the pubic fleece, place of antherection. They are sought out, at night, by candlelight, in the seams of Salvador's trousers. The miniscule animal is crosscut even more by the logic of antherection: prosperity/poverty, shame/glory, savage/tamed, improper/proper: "We liked to know—and feel—that the translucent bugs were swarming; though not tamed, they were so much a part of us that a third person's louse disgusted us. . . . The lice were the only sign of our prosperity, of the very underside of prosperity, but it was logical that by making our state perform an operation which justified it, we were, by the same token, justifying the sign of this state. . . . the lice were precious. They were both our shame and our glory."

In extreme poverty [*dèche*], in the creche illuminated by the opening of a fly, one sleeps with the savior, that is to say with a sort of beggar (like the Spanish thiefwoman), but also, the glans by the same token turned inside out, with the Virgin Mary who erects in what comes out of her, completely immaculately conceived like her, by her who was conceived without sin, before any sinning, already.

Here is the passage from the one-armed man

is irreplaceable? More irreplaceable than a husband, a son, a daughter, a father or a mother? What is the axiomatic value of this assertion? Empirically, it seems false. One can always have another brother. What is more, Hegel is not here not speaking the language of empiricity; his propositions are structural, they are stating the legality of a typical figure. So where did he get that a brother cannot be replaced? From the mouth of Antigone, of course. She is not named but she dictates the statements. And what does she say, Sophocles' Antigone?

She recalls that she is leaving life "last of them all" after having "washed and dressed" all the bodies of the family, after having offered them "drink-offerings at their graves," after "tending" Polyneices' corpse. She complains about being ill-paid but congratulates herself on having been right to render these funeral honors, to have been right [*avoir eu raison*] with all those who have reason [*qui ont la raison*], with all sensible people. If she had had children or if it were her husband's body that was rotting, she would have obeyed the law of the city. She could have had other children with another husband. "But when father and mother are hidden in Hades, no brother could ever bloom for me again."

So the brother is irreplaceable—not the mother, the only member of the family who is *naturally* exempt from all substitution. But the brother is irreplaceable only in a highly determinate empirical situation, determined by the factual death of Antigone's parents. Shall we say that Hegel has transformed into a structural and paradigmatic legality an empirical situation described in a particular text from the history of tragedy? And that for the needs of an obscure cause—or sister?

Unless the contingency can be reduced. What if being an orphan were a structure of the unconscious? Antigone's parents are not parents among others. She is the daughter of Oedipus and, according to most of the versions taken as inspiration by the classical authors, of Jocasta, her incestuous grandmother. Hegel never speaks of this *extra* generation, as if it were external to the elementary structures of kinship. The model he is interrogating is perhaps not as empirical as one might imagine. But it does not have the universal clarity he gives it. It stands, like the name, between the two. Like

to the savior who comes back to the mother like her phallus: "One might have thought he was dead, for he rarely, and slowly, got excited: he kept watch. He generated [*élaborait*] in the darkness of a well-buttoned fly, though buttoned by only one hand, the luminosity with which its bearer will be aglow.

My relations with Salvador lasted six months. . . . The lice inhabited us. . . . It was good that, in the depths of such wretchedness, I was the lover of the poorest and homeliest. . . . Yet, light and brilliance being necessary to our lives, a sunbeam did cross the pane and its filth and penetrate the dimness; we had the hoarfrost, the silver thaw, for these elements, though they may spell calamity, evoke joys whose sign, detached in our room,

strange occurrence of the word *élaborait.* Frequent, unusual usage. Labor of the truth, labor of conception. Here what is elaborated is a "luminosity." Further down, it will be the child. Here, what is elaborated is destined to *show* itself and to shine like beauty ("the luminosity with which its bearer will be aglow [*dont resplendira son porteur*]"). Further down, what is going to emerge from the womb after being elaborated there will *show itself* [se montrera] only as a "monster," but by the same token in order to be erected ("to love this monster, to love the ugliness that had come out of her belly in which it had been elaborated, and to erect it devotedly"). In both occurrences—in others as well—the elaboration takes place under a surface, a star, a layer of skin. Light and life, timepiece [*montre*]—or alarm clock—and monster work inside a pocket, under a sheath. One imagines them rather than see them move, adjust, swell, topple. I, for example, have often used the word "elaborate" to describe—here—textual labor. No doubt because it proceeds like this monstrous light: same movement, same place, same "object." But especially because it was necessary to extract from within the elaborated text the instrument of reading or of writing, the *style* with which to treat it; with which to *write*, that is to say fold the metalanguage. But the fold itself—the usage—of metalanguage is irreducible. Like a pouch, a cyst that reforms endlessly. By generalizing, by systematizing for example the recourse to the word "elaborate" I make of it a sort of concept, a rule, a law whose extension dominates—relatively—the text from which I nevertheless extract it. It barely covers it, it incubates it for a limited time. The cystic metalanguage—sewn pocket—

being an orphan. One more proof, if it were needed, that nothing is less an-oedipal, or even anti-oedipal, than an orphan unconscious.

Nothing should be able to survive the death of Antigone. Nothing more should ever follow, come out of her, after her. Her death notice should ring out the absolute end of history. Icy transparency, virgin, sterile. Without desire and without labor.

An end of history without *Sa*. *Sa* cannot come back to a sister. To a father, a mother, a son, perhaps, not to a sister.

And yet everything almost stopped, in mid-step, on a step, stumbled or lost its footing.

Like Hegel, we have been fascinated by Antigone, by this incredible relation, this powerful liaison without desire, this immense impossible desire that could not live, able only to overturn, paralyze or exceed a system and a history, interrupt the life of the concept, take its breath away or, what comes down to the same thing, support it from the outside or the underneath of a crypt.

A crypt—we might have said something transcendental or repressed, unthought or excluded—that organizes the ground to which it does not belong.

What the speculative dialectic means-to-say, is that the crypt can still be incorporated into the system. The transcendental or the repressed, the unthought or the excluded must be assimilated by the corpus, internalized as moments, idealized in the very negativity of their work. The halt forms merely a stasis in the introjection of spirit.

Antigone is a moment to get through, a terrible and divine moment, for the brother and for the sister. The two laws (divine and human, subterranean and diurnal, feminine and masculine, familial and political, etc.) are going to pass the one into the other, allow themselves to be mediated and become the one for the other. Count the one for the other.

The brother/sister relation is a limit. The family as such finds its own limit (*Grenze*) here, is circumscribed within it. Without that limit, the family would not be determined, would not be what it is. Nor with that limit. The

was adequate for us: all we knew of Christmas and New Year's festivities was what always accompanies them and what makes them dearer to merrymakers: frost. . . . Poverty made us erect. All across Spain we carried a secret, veiled magnificence unmixed with arrogance. . . . Thus developed my talent for giving a sublime meaning to so beggarly an appearance. (I am not yet speaking of literary talent.) It proved to have been a very useful discipline for me and still enables me to smile tenderly at the humblest among the dregs, whether human or material, including vomit, including the saliva I let drool on my mother's face, including your excrement. I shall preserve within me the idea of myself as beggar.

I wanted to be like that woman who, at home, hidden away from people, sheltered her daughter, a kind of hideous, misshapen monster, stupid and white. When the mother gave birth, her despair was probably such that it became the very essence of her life. She decided to love

describes, envelops, guards and regards the labor of the text that it was big with. I have elaborated elaboration. But all that must remain under the sheath. In the unlikely event that one wishes to take more pleasure in it. Must remain under the sheath like the show monsters [*mon(s)tres*] of language. It must be left to the imagination under the pocket that is swollen and worked on by all the movements (fragmenting [*morcellement*], gathering, cutting, agglutinating); the clang of language must be left to be silently elaborated. If you show naively, like a cocky virgin lad anxious in case his tube is misjudged, everything you can do with language (cut, recompose, displace, agglutinate, etc.), it'll all misfire. It's like premature ejaculation. No time even to get hard. And then you think and want to have it thought that you are the master of this labor of language: it isn't elaborated any more, it doesn't hardbind any more. And finally it remains intact, unaffected, uninfected. There is more enjoyment to be had—but of course one may always want to deprive (oneself) of that or wean off it—by making like the fish remained whole, still living, in the netting, all the more mobile, slippery, elusive for feeling threatened

limit being what it is—in Hegel—it is not what it is, it is crossed as soon as it is reached. With the brother/sister relation the family is exceeded by itself. "It dissolves and moves outside of itself." The family is resolved on this limit, at the very moment when what enters into it gets outside itself, both sensibly and insensibly, like a point in a null and infinite, interminable time. Antigone *herself* is just this [*c'est ça*], and the family, which is Antigone herself, is this, this pure passage, this trance that does not retain itself. It is retained, rather, according to the sublation, only by being lost. To sublate a limit is to keep it but to keep (a limit) is here to lose it. To keep what gets lost is to lack. The logic of *Aufhebung* turns at every moment into its absolute opposite. Absolute appropriation is absolute expropriation. Onto-logic can always be reread or rewritten as a logic of loss or expenditure without reserve.

This possibility vacillates or is cut short in the sepulcher. What is a stony monument, that is the question. But the stone in it shakes the *what is? What is?* is, like every question in general, engaged in the process of reappropriation that the stone threatens. The question-form of the question is turned to stone [*médusée*] in advance.

And yet there is stone. What does *there is* mean once we subtract what there is from the *it is,* from *this is*, from the ostension of any presence? Speaking of the process of propriation (*Ereignis*), Heidegger liberates the *es gibt* in *es gibt Sein*, from the all-powerful precession of being. Let us wager that the value of the *gift* (*Gabe*), foreign to the *there is,* will have pre-occupied everything.

So the brother leaves. If he isn't dead. The one who is not dead. The one who lives *qua brother*. He leaves. He is "the aspect in terms of which the family's spirit becomes that of individuality, an individuality which turns towards others and makes its transition into the consciousness of universality." The brother breaks with the singular bond that held him to the family and for example to Antigone. He goes off toward the city, he abandons the immediate, elementary, unconscious, negative form of *Sittlichkeit*, in order to become a citizen, a man of the human law. He will concern himself with politics.

What does Antigone do? If she does not die, she marries. In any case she remains, she continues to stand guard for the family. After the departure of the brother towards the "human law," "the sister becomes, or the wife remains, the overseer [*Vorstand*] of the household and the guardian of

this monster, to love the ugliness that had come out of her belly in which it had been elaborated, and to erect it devotedly. Within herself she ordained an altar where she preserved the idea of Monster. With devoted care, with hands gentle despite the callus . . ."

To protect oneself from the scaffolding being put up here—this is the most sane, most natural reflex—one will protest: sometimes against these over-lengthy quotations that should have been cut; sometimes, on the contrary (or else at the same time) against these samplings [*prélèvements*], selections, sections, ellipses, stitchings, detachments. Detachments of the sign, of course, (it didn't escape you, above, that what was detached, and as always, detached in our room, was a sign, "sign, detached in our room." That's where someone is stealing). For the sign to detach of course signifies that it is cut from its place of emission and from where it naturally belongs; but the separation is never perfect, difference is never consummated. The bloody detachment is also—repetition—delegation, mandate, delay, relay. Adherence. The detached remains stuck thereby, by the glue of differance, by the a. The a of gl agglutinates the different detachings. The scaffold of A is gluey.

So one will protest: you cut too much, you

the divine law." That is what the sister becomes or the wife *remains* [*bleibt*]. "In this way, both the sexes overcome [*überwinden*] their natural essence [*natürliches Wesen*], and they emerge in their ethical significance [*sittlichen Bedeutung*] as diverse individuals [*als Verschiedenheiten*] who divide between them [*unter sich teilen*] the two distinctions [*Unterschiede*] which ethical substance gives itself."

Sexual difference is *overcome* when the brother leaves, and the other (sister and wife) remains. There is no longer any sexual difference *qua natural difference*. "The sexes overcome their natural difference." Once it has been overcome, sexual difference will have been merely a natural diversity. The opposition between difference and qualitative diversity is a hinge of the Greater Logic. Diversity is a moment of difference, an indifferent difference, an external difference without opposition. So long as the two moments of difference (identity and difference since identity differs, *qua* identity) only relate to themselves and not to the other, so long as identity is not opposed to difference nor difference to identity, there is diversity. So diversity is a moment both of difference and of identity, it being very explicitly understood that difference is the whole *and* its own moment. So that is also true of sexual difference: it is identity, identity is difference, itself the whole and its own moment.

By overcoming natural difference *as diversity* of the sexes, one passes to difference *as opposition*. In *Sittlichkeit,* sexual difference finally becomes a true opposition: what it was moreover *called,* destined to be. The determinateness of the opposition (the opposition *qua* determinate—*bestimmte*) corresponds to determination as vocation, destination (*Bestimmung*) of sexual difference. *Difference* is much too general and indeterminate a concept, we must follow the determining process of sexual difference, distinguish at least between difference as diversity and difference as opposition, both also being differences as identities.

When the brother leaves, "this moment loses both the indeterminateness [*Unbestimmtheit*] which it still had there and the contingent diversity of aptitudes and capacities." What is lost is the natural diversity of the sexes and (the) difference without opposition. What is gained against this contingency, this natural multiplicity, is difference determined into opposition, *sexual contradiction*. This moment

stick together too much, you quote too much and too little. The two charges are well known; they pertain to the logic that is under scrutiny here.

For those who all the same wouldn't consider *gl* a satisfactory response—because they first expected it to be a response—those to whom *gl* says nothing—because they first believed that *gl* was not saying nothing—those who, hoping, one wonders, for what repast, continue to drool standing still, let's suggest that the theoretical question, which is surely (metalanguage—always reconstituting itself—in the best spot) elaborated by that intervention, there is no other possible word today, submitted in advance to the censorship of the remainder in the ideological field, will produce, that's how it has to be said, the following thesis: every thesis is (hardbinds) a prosthesis; what is offered for reading is offered for reading by means of quotations (necessarily truncated, cuttings, repetitions, suctions, sections, suspensions, sewing, grafting, faking, organs without a proper body, a proper body covered with blows, traversed by lice).

"is now the determinate opposition of the two sexes [*der bestimmte Gegensatz der zwei Geschlechter*], whose naturalness at the same time takes on the significance of their ethical destinies [*ihrer sittlichen Bestimmung*]."

Sexual difference has only just appeared. It has only just become determinate in appearing as such, *in positing itself*, i.e. by opening itself to negativity and by becoming an opposition. By beginning then to sublimate itself. If difference was destined to opposition, there was not yet sexual difference between Antigone and her brother. Their relation was not as strange as one might have thought, nor (was) the absence of desire between them.

What is the position of desire in this passage from difference-diversity to difference-opposition? Is there already desire in the former? Must one wait for opposition or contradiction to see it emerge? There is no reply to a question posed in this form. The concept of desire is no more homogeneous and univocal than is that of difference. Just as there is not a sexual difference in general but a dialectical process of sexual difference that passes for example from diversity to opposition, there is not first of all *a desire in general* which, from diversity to opposition, *determines itself*, conforms to its teleological calling (*Bestimmung*), posits itself more and more as desire. By departing from nature, negating it in itself, sublating, sublimating, idealizing, it becomes more and more desiring. Human desire is, then, more desiring than animal desire; masculine desire is more desiring than feminine desire which remains closer to nature. More desiring, it is therefore more unsatisfied and insatiable. But this proposition is only valid to the provisional, relative, limited extent to which femininity has not yet acceded to properly ethical opposition. Once she does accede to this, the woman is in the same position as the man (beyond nature), except as to degree. By the same token, if there is more sublimation in the man, desire (natural, originary, etc.) is also more inhibited, less (naturally) free than with the woman. Freer also for the same reason, with a spiritual freedom.

The (sexual) opposition that has just appeared is not absolute. Its contradiction does not make the unity of the ethical substance explode. On the contrary, it constitutes its becoming. This becoming is constructed according to the opposition of the sexes, in other words according to the opposition of the two laws. "The distinction between the sexes and their ethical content nonetheless remains (*bleibt*) within the unity of the substance, and the distinction's movement is precisely the constant coming to be (*das bleibende Werden*) of that substance."

That is how a text gets infatuated [*s'entiche*]. With another. It doesn't happen without profits and losses for the organism undergoing the graft after getting itself picked up.

Which happened globally to the mother. To the global mother. Hardly had she, devoutly, erected when the grand discourse on thievery came up.

The pieces that I cut and sew in the text designated by the one denominated Genet must not either destroy its form or break the rhythm of its breathing (don't say its unity, the question being posed here asks what *a* text *alone* [un *texte* un] could be and whether such a thing exists any more than a unicorn), nor must it recompose

"*Enticher*, verb. 1. To begin to spoil, corrupt. Used in this sense only as past participle. 2. Dressmaking term. When placing patterns over fabric for cutting, *on entiche* when one of the patterns catches a small corner of the fabric of the pattern placed next to it; that involves encroaching upon—with the idea of saving fabric—what is meant for another piece required for the whole. 3. Fig. Spoil by means of something false or morally bad. 4. *S'enticher*, reflexive verb. To become infatuated. He was totally absorbed [*s'était entiché*] by that vice. To be infatuated with a person. He fell for an actress [*s'enticha d'une comédienne*] and married her." (From the *Littré*, which adds regarding etymology: "Diez and Scheler derive it from German *anstecken*, infect with a contagion; but one cannot conceive of how the 's' would have disappeared. The proper form is entecher, composed of *en* (1st sense) and Old French *teche*, which is the same as *tache* ['stain']; *entecher* or enticher is thus identical to *entacher*. *Entecher*, *enticher* must not be confused with the old verb *enticier*, to excite, noun form: *enticement*, instigation."

It will perhaps be considered that I use the dictionary a great deal. I try to do that as signatory of a corrupting text [*texte entichant*] (that is to say in a genetic style) that doesn't hesitate to provoke a poetics based on Larousse: in *Querelle*, "Under the word 'pederast,' Larousse entry: 'In the quarters of one of them was found a large quantity of artificial flowers, garlands and wreaths, intended, without any doubt, for use as decorations and ornaments in their grand orgies.'"

One still cannot conceive of how the 's' would have disappeared

Neither of the two laws posits itself alone in itself and for itself. "In its living movement, human law originates from the divine law, the law which is validly in force on earth originates from the law of the underworld, the conscious law originates from the unconscious law, mediation originates from immediacy, and all equally return to that from whence they came."

In the end the diaphanous law of consciousness (man) and the obscure law of the unconscious (woman) must be identified in the depths of their opposition. But in that case they appear in the light, the law of laws. The opposition of midnight and midday is resolved at midday. Such is the *truth* of a sexual revolution the general necessity of which was prescribed by *The Difference Between Fichte's and Schelling's System of Philosophy*. In the obstinacy of its common sense, of its health, human understanding wants to keep the terms of the opposition shielded from each other (consciousness/ unconsciousness, light/ matter). Speculation, i.e. sublation of opposition, scares it. It fears the destructive character of its operation. In fact, paradoxically, it is afraid because it does not know how far speculation destroys. If it could grasp the extent (*Umfang*) of that destruction (*Vernichten*), it would be reassured; it could no longer consider speculation to be an adverse power (*Gegnerin*). For destruction is also a power "of the highest synthesis of consciousness and unconsciousness," it requires a "destruction of consciousness itself." Speculative reason (*Vernunft*) then sinks (*versenkt*) with its knowledge and its reflection of absolute identity. It throws itself into its "own abyss" (*eigenen Abgrund*) and "in this night of mere reflection and of the calculating intellect, in this night which is the noonday of life, common sense and speculation can meet one another."

There is still no purely human family. The value "family" still stands out against a theological horizon or background. What we saw in the space of Christian infinitism is here confirmed on a Greek model. The theological ahuman is also to be found on the side of the natural ahuman. The limit of the human thus cannot be located, (is) always disappearing. Insofar as it remains still too natural, the family comes under divine law. If the Greek model places the divine on the side of the subterranean sepulcher, the Judeo-Christian paradigm, celestial and sublime, is opposed to this only inasmuch as it really produces religion: the rotting of the Christic corpse will have strung things out.

The union of opposites, of man and woman, has the

or seize its integrity in one of the formal or semantic nets that we have made as if to throw and throw out again countless times: just that, in order to show or rather pull along beyond any manifestation, the net operates only to the extent that it is indebted to a remainder. It holds only remainders, monumental remains, and lets the rest tombfall. And from this remainder that isn't, that makes text, the fall, the case, the discounted remainder erects [*échafaude*] all the writing machines. The rest is all head to tail, no question of bringing it on a platter.

Even if we were able to reconstitute, piece by piece, the emblem or signature of a proper name, it would only be to extract—like someone buried alive extracted from a tomb—the very thing that neither Genet nor I would have ever managed to sign, to reattach to the lines of a paraph, and that as a result speaks of that fact. We do not comprehend here the text denominated (by) Genet, it is not exhausted in the pouch that I cut, sew, and retie. The text is what pierces it, waylays [*harponne*] it and takes it into its purview; but it is also what sees it escape, diverting its trajectory toward quarters unknown. This text (or clang) is no more summed up in a reading of Genet—which forms neither the example nor essence of it, neither its case nor truth—than it lets itself be gathered or oriented by,

form of a syllogistic copulation. More precisely, this syllogistic copulation unites two syllogisms in one and thus produces the ethical realm. One of the extremes, universal spirit, conscious of itself, is linked to its other, unconscious spirit, by the mediation of man, the individuality of man. The divine law has its individuality in woman, the unconscious spirit of the singular has its being-there there; woman is the milieu (*Mitte*), the means whereby the spirit emerges from its inactuality, passes from unconscious to conscious. The union of man and woman joints the two laws or the two syllogisms. Of the two movements—that of woman who plunges into the subterranean, into danger and trial by death, that of man who rises towards the light—that union makes a single movement, traversed by a single motive force.

As though two moving bodies each endowed with its own principle of automotion, setting off from opposites places, crossed paths or met up during a circular trajectory, fell still, and from the collision formed a single vehicle on an infinite circle. What then is done, and is never again undone, remains unrepresentable or unimaginable. This is what Hegel calls *Wirklichkeit*, the operation of actuality, and the power of the syllogism.

The copulation of these two "opposing movements" appeases nothing. No reconciliation at all. Tragedy begins here, and the opposition continues to rage in *Sittlichkeit*. Once the preceding syllogism has taken place, action has not yet happened, no operation (*Handlung*) has been actual in the city. Just when the point is to act, operate, effectuate, the contradiction re-emerges, this time in the form of fault or crime. Tragic carnage: murder no longer proceeds from a voluntary decision, it is inscribed as a fatality in the structure of the operation. The ethical substance may well unite the two laws, the operation always falls to a singular individual. It therefore reawakens the scission, the opposition of the divine and the human, of woman and man. Each on one side, Antigone and Creon hear or read only one law, miss and betray the other.

Any operation is *a priori* guilty. "Innocence amounts to non-action [*Nichttun*], like the being of a stone and not even like that of a child."

Ethical action therefore comprises in itself the moment of crime, it is moral by dint of murder—or of playing one law against the other. This is why the unconscious cannot be reduced. No operation can be carried out in the light of consciousness without having structurally to restrain

among others, my paraph. And everything in it that insists on the singular form of the signature, of this one or that one, retains a totally abnormal value. It falls under no rule and does not provide any. The operation must each time be singular, and risk its chance uniquely.

Granted, of course, that there is signature.

Knowing-being—suspended among several *clin*s—clinical, clinamen, *clinanth*—and several *col*s— . . .

Things would be different were the signature to be merely a clang effect, stated otherwise a classification, the network of more than one name. Then, this operation would somehow be exemplary and normative, even scientific, yes, but so timidly preliminary: a barely annunciated conception.

The labor of reconstituting the glorious and integral corpus of a property, in the authentic signature without organ, although tireless, will not always have failed, *in the end* (will have the aura of signet): what sets it moving, its first thief, *volens nolens*, what makes writing, is what separates and sows, disperses signacutting and signasewing. What desingularizes, deseals, disinitials, opens the eyes by blinding.

(will we say repress, encircle, suppress, push into the shadows, un-think, not-know?) the other law. The unconscious is constituted, in the order of *Sittlichkeit*, by this double articulation of the law: one can never know what one is doing on both sides at once, on the side of the human law and on the side of the divine law, i.e. on the man's side or the woman's side.

The other counts.

Oedipus is summoned to appear as the example of this general necessity.

There is no unconscious without operation. Operation is action, certainly, but taking account of a law, of one law *or* another (human or divine), and therefore of one law *and* another, of the opposition of the two laws. In other words of sexual opposition. No unconscious without sexual opposition (more or less than sexual difference).

The law commands one to act in reality. But the unconscious exists, so to speak, only insofar as the action, which cannot obey both laws at once, is guilty. Guilt—relation to the unknown or the unconscious of the other law—takes on its relief, the irreversible existence that comes from the fault, only if it enters into relation with the other of consciousness that has remained, precisely, unconscious. Which appears trite: the crime is irreversible once committed. It is less trite that the crime be necessarily and structurally unconscious, not present to itself, unknown to its "author" at the moment it is committed. This does not lighten the guilt, which remains entire (there is here no involuntary manslaughter, no "no-one is voluntarily bad"). The crime is unconscious and that is why it remains entire and irreversible. Its fatal necessity is inscribed in the divided structure of *Sittlichkeit*. No unconscious without operation, no operation without law, no law without double law, without opposition, therefore without crime (with respect to the other law), no innocent ("Rousseauian") unconscious. It is as impossible to reduce the operation as it is to efface the crime (Mallarmé says this very clearly in his way, with the same words). But if there is always crime without knowing, and if we care to bear in mind that crime without knowing does not take place, then there is never crime.

Oedipus—then: "Hence, actuality keeps concealed within itself (*in sich verborgen*) this other aspect which is alien to knowledge and which does not show itself to consciousness as it is in and for itself—which neither shows the son that the man insulting him and whom he strikes dead is his father, nor shows him that the queen whom he takes as his wife is his mother. In this

Hardly had the mother erected, devoutly, than the discourse celebrated theft.

Is it by chance that the father then enters the scene. Under his name, one could say, or almost, he who appeared so absent until now, unactualized. Is it by chance that that movement leads toward the hymn to the proper name. That that hymn couldn't care less about the official record. And that Genêt dons in all seriousness a circumflex like a royal crown. A floral corolla also since the accent deforms the emblem and allows the vegetal to be read in place of the animal?

Step by step, the father comes back into the saga of thieving, between the erection of the mother and that of the circumflex. Rape of the law, law of theft, morality. "I [born of an unknown father: "My mother's name was Gabrielle Genet. My father remains unknown."] try to charm them by moral acts, chiefly by charity." "Them" refers to "unknown powers."

Then he explains how he, Genet, gives up his seat to the elderly, stands aside to let them pass, helps blind men cross the street.

The old man and the blind man, sole examples chosen.

The circumflex (we'll name in this way what distinguishes it from the author and rises higher than he) breaks in [*crochette*] and takes the creche away toward the crossroads:

way, a power that shuns the daylight [*lichtscheue*: fearing the light, photophobic] preys on ethical selfconsciousness, a power which bursts forth only (*erst*) after the deed is done and when it has taken the deed in its grip. This is so because the completed deed is the sublated opposition between the knowing self and the actuality confronting it. The agent can deny (*verleugnen*) neither the crime nor his guilt."

So the operation sublates the opposition between the self who knows and the actuality it does not know, between the conscious and the unconscious. But the sublation does not lift the guilt, it does not wash clean of the crime. There is here an *after* effect that resists endlessly. The crime has taken place, the guilt remains. Even if the agent did not know he was killing or whom he was killing. More than elsewhere the unconscious here appears set against simple nonconsciousness. Perhaps we could draw authority from this to set the *Aufhebung* apart from Hegel's intended meaning—Hegel who in a moment is going to re-correlate it with the teleology of consciousness. The few lines that comment on Oedipus' operation already announce the reappropriation, the becoming-conscious of the unconsciousness that renders the foreign proper and reunifies the elements of the scission. Like *Antigone*, *Oedipus at Colonus* ends in the calm equality of death, in the final appeasement. Even though, along with comic laughter, its "perversity" is welling up.

"The agent can deny neither the crime nor his guilt.—The deed consists in setting the unmoved into motion, which thereby brings forth what had been shuttered up as mere possibility, and it links (*verknüpfen*) the unconscious to the conscious and the nonexistent to being." The unconscious is thus a possible consciousness, a virtual truth. "In this truth, therefore, the deed

"*Finally*, more beautiful than this rather external sort of denouement [the *Philoctetus*'s deus ex machina] is an inner reconciliation which, because of its subjective character, already borders on our modern treatment. The most perfect classical example of this that we have before us is the eternally marvellous *Oedipus at Colonus*. Oedipus has murdered his father, taken the Theban throne, and mounted the marriage-bed with his mother. These unconsciously committed crimes do not make him unhappy; but of old he had solved a riddle and now he forcibly extracts [from the oracle] a knowledge of his own dark fate and acquires the dreadful realization that it has been accomplished in himself. With this solution of the riddle in his own person he has lost his happiness as Adam did when he came to the knowledge of good and evil. The seer now, he blinds himself, resigns the throne, exiles himself from Thebes, just as Adam and Eve were driven from Paradise, and wanders away a helpless old man." After preferring the voice of his Erinnye to that of his son, after having thus overcome the internal division, appeased, reconciled the split (*Zwiespalt*) in himself, Oedipus then undergoes a sort of glorification, radiance, illumination in death (*Verklärung im Tode*). This luminous glory

the antherection of Mary-Jocasta, who gives to the text its Greek ration. The old man and blind man have to cross in the middle of the intersection. Naming Oedipus here doesn't mean semanticizing, inflating each textual atom with sense; on the contrary it is to deflate what has had for the last while to be called the Oedipal myth as a semantic mirage.

The circumflex here gives its Greek guarantee: "The nervousness provoked by fear, and sometimes by anxiety, makes for a state akin to religious moods. At such times I tend to see omens in the slightest accidents. Things become signs of chance. I want to charm the unknown powers upon which the success of the adventure seems to me to depend. I try to charm them by moral acts, chiefly by charity. I give more readily and more freely to beggars, I give my seat to old people, I stand to let them pass, I help blind men cross the street, and so on. In this way, I seem to recognize that over the act of stealing rules a god to whom moral actions are agreeable. These attempts to throw out a net, on the chance that this god of whom I know nothing will be caught in it, exhaust me, disturb me and also favor the religious state. To the act of stealing they communicate the gravity of a ritual act."

That ritual, this passage in the text that initiates you, leads you by the hand to the fictive position of the proper name, multiplying over some fifteen pages—as if nothing were going on—the paternal associations, even alliances.

to give one's hand to Oedipus. To give Oedipus a helping hand. Is that to come to his rescue? Who could? From where? Why? Would need to wait and see. The archangels, on the contrary, spit in his face. With as much acuteness as gravity the circumflex brought to our attention what happens when they don't aim straight, "It's making him shiny wet, the slut [*ça le fait reluire, la morue*]!"

is spiritual, his blind eyes become glorious [*verklärt*], they become light [*wird hell*]. It is in particular because of this glory, this transfiguration of the body (Oedipus' bones become the ramparts of the city that welcomes him) that it was possible for people to find a Christic harmony here. "But the Christian religious reconciliation is a transfiguration of the soul [*Verklärung der Seele*] which bathes [*gebadet*] in the spring of eternal salvation. . . ." It makes the heart into the "grave of the heart" [*Grabe des Herzens*]. In exchange for complaint or accusation [*Anklagen*], it is the body that expiates the earthly fault in order to accede to a purely spiritual beatitude. "On the other hand, the transfiguration of Oedipus always still remains the Greek transfer of consciousness from the strife of ethical powers, and the violations involved, into the unity and harmony of the entire ethical order itself. What is further implied in this reconciliation is *subjective* satisfaction, and this enables us to make the transition (*Übergang*) to the sphere of *comedy*, the opposite of tragedy." In the "reversal" of (the) tragic "plasticity," comedy will liberate the "perversity" (*Verkehrtheit*) of the subjective principle. But what perverted the plasticity of ancient tragedy will be the very mainspring of modern tragedy.

comes to light—as that in which the conscious is combined (*verbunden*) with the unconscious and in which what is one's own (*das Eigene*) is combined with what is alien. It comes to light as the estranged essence (*entzweite Wesen*), whose other aspect consciousness also experiences as its own, namely, as a power violated [*verletzte*] by it and thereby roused to hostility."

The analysis of an absolutely unconscious crime, which gets its meaning as crime only after the blow, reintroduces the teleological temporality of self-presence, of consciousness. This movement is accentuated: if it is true that an operation is guilty *a priori*, even in its unconscious, the fault is more "pure," more purely guilty, when it is conscious and known in advance to be so. As in the previous case, the operation is structurally criminal, there is no innocent operation in that one appeals to one law against another. But the crime is more *purely* ethical when the opposition of one law to the other becomes conscious, when the operation is liberated and deliberated. In that case one is indeed in the order of universality—law against law—even if it is in the name of the law of singularity that one commits the crime. As the scene of the crime opens between two laws (singularity/universality, woman/man), is read both ways [*sur les deux tableaux*], there is no murder that is not the (ethical) effect of sexual opposition. All crime is a sexual and familial operation.

Given all this, Oedipus is a crude murderer, half innocent, in any case impure, since he did not know what he was doing. The pure crime, the one that corresponds to the most "complete" ethical consciousness, is the one committed by his daughter, a little orphan consciousness. This time Antigone is named. She knew what she was doing and she here becomes the best example of ethical consciousness. "It can be that the right which lay in reserve

See even this in fact: between Mary-Jocasta's legs, thanks to what is ejaculated by some tube of vaseline or other signifying substance, one could equalize, without deciding either way, the mother and the father and vice versa. Equalize, by pruning or unloading [*Egaler, en élaguant ou en larguant*], endlessly finding again always one in the other. The place of the son slips there, once more.

The rite of passage aims at reconstituting in the father's abode the law of the house—economy—as presence and as total presence. Theft is absolute knowing. The executioner threatens but in the place of the cradle, from where one observes and elaborates. The scene of theft is prepared by the insistent description of the nocturnal. The theft occurs while families—"people"—are sleeping. The ritual act "will really be performed in the heart of darkness, to which is added that it may be rather at night, while people are asleep, in a place that is closed and perhaps itself masked in black." Then, patiently repeated, the acts of unearthing, ransacking, exposure of a "defenseless body," etc.

Following the rule of economy, I comment only on the presence, the gathering of self to oneself, the *parousia* in the father's abode, at the return of the prodigal son: ". . . the prudence, the whispering voice, the alert ear, the invisible, nervous

is not on hand in its distinctive shape for the acting *consciousness* but is only on hand *in itself*, that is, in the inner guilt of the decision and the action." This is the case with Oedipus. "However, ethical consciousness is more complete (*vollständiger*) and its guilt purer (*reiner*) if it both *knows* the law *beforehand* and the power against which it takes an opposing stance, and it takes them to be violence and wrong [only a law can be unjust but the injustice of a law is necessarily a non-juridical contingency], to be an ethical contingency, and then, like Antigone, knowingly (*wissentlich*) commits the crime . . . , ethical consciousness must recognize its opposite as its own. It must acknowledge its guilt: '*Because we suffer, we acknowledge that we have erred*' (*Antigone*)."

Everything stops here and yet nothing stops. The course is interminable even if at every step one might fall (absolutely) still in the final ambush. Antigone accedes to the purity of crime. But ethical plenitude is not accomplished in crime. The crime is pure *qua* crime because it reveals more purely the split, the opposition of laws that constitutes ethics. But this constitution is achieved only when its negativity, which is essential, is totally sublated. No doubt Antigone's "knowledge" of the crime has worked towards this, it indeed corresponds to the birth of ethical consciousness, to the ethical disposition (*Gesinnung*), its sense. But Antigone remains half way up the climb, at the level of "disposition": in any case, caught between two laws, she disobeys. She falls back. Powerless in her action, she returns to the abyss (*zu Grunde*), towards hell and the subterranean world that is her fundamental place, her proper place. She is the figure of the fall (*Untergang*), of decline, she walks downwards and drags her whole family with her, even Hemon who was waiting for her and kills himself on her dead body. All individuality is "consumed" in guilt. The victory of one law or another is always a catastrophe for *Sittlichkeit*, since it opens in it a *colpos* in which everything is regularly swallowed up, or rather each bank of which collapses in turn. So, for *Sittlichkeit* to be accomplished, the swallowing up has to be swallowed up and the collapse must collapse. Equilibrium (*Gleichgewicht*) between the two laws will be attained when absolute right, reconciling objective right and subjective right, swallows up the two opposites, makes their incessant fall fall. Such will be the appeasing victory of "destiny": "It is in the

presence of the accomplice and the understanding of his slightest sign, all concentrate our being within us, compress us, make of us a very ball of presence, which so well explains Guy's remark:

'You feel yourself living.'

But within myself, this total presence, which is transformed into a bomb of what seems to me terrific power imparts to the act a gravity, a terminal oneness—the burglary, while being performed, is always the last, not that you think you are not going to perform another after that one—you don't think—but because such a gathering of self cannot take place (not in life, for to push it further would be to pass out of life); and this oneness of an act which develops" does not, as in Hegelian gathering at home with oneself, have the form of some oak tree following the case of the acorn; but what comes down to the same thing remains, in parentheses, an anthological blossoming: "this oneness of an act which develops (the rose its corolla) into conscious gestures, sure of their efficacy, of their fragility and yet of the violence which they give to the act, here too confers upon it the value of a religious rite."

a break-in [*cambriolage*], as the word indicates, is always effected into a room [*chambre*] or family abode, here a dark room. It is always the last, that is to say there never was one previously that counted. It is therefore the first, the most primitive. The obscure economy of the chamber [*camera*] as archeo-eschatology. Finally, if you detach the liaison (*gl*), in the beginning would have been theft. Everything would have begun by ending, on the eve of the *obsequent* "funeral mime" ("That Strange Word . . ."). Strange mode and logic of *obsequence*

The religious act, the *anthic* theft, the gathering of the flower, are dedicated to the one—singular individual—who has lost his member at the foot of a tree where it will grow no more. Stilitano was in fact first to have "the benefit of such homage."

equal subjection (*gleichen Unterwerfung*) of both sides that absolute right is first achieved, and ethical substance, as the negative power that devours [engulfs, swallows, *verschlingt*] both sides has emerged. That is, *fate*, omnipotent and just, has come on the scene."

Laughter of the sister. As if she knew that one cannot carry out these movements of swallowing up to their extremes. But the laughter is also that of the mother. This muted laugh does not burst out immediately, and later in the scene the derision is amplified by an echoing (*repercussion*) without origin.

Scarcely has it been accomplished than the ethical essence begins to dissolve. Once again two laws oppose each other, but they are represented by two individuals of the same sex. By Antigone's two brothers. Eteocles and Polyneices combat each other, the one inside the community, to defend it, the other to attack it from without. Antigone's brother is unique only according to the feminine law of the familial community. If Antigone declares only one brother, the one she chooses in identifying or uniting with him, it is the one who combats the city, Polyneices. It is on Polyneices' body that she throws a handful of earth as a sign of burial. Antigone is also the brother-enemy of Eteocles.

The two brothers have killed each other.

How is that possible?

A scandalized question traverses the text. How, when it comes down to it, is a brother possible? How can one have two sons? How can one be the father of two phalluses, the one erected against the other? How can one have a brother? How can two beings of the same sex cohabit in a family? i.e.—the question is less easy than people think—in the ethical realm? Of course, in the natural realm of animality, it is possible. Two males can, for example, belong to the same litter. But precisely they are not brothers. Brothers are not possible in nature.

But nor are they possible in culture. So fraternity must be lodged between nature and culture. A figure of monstrosity: passing into culture it must disappear violently.

"I think it was by him that I was initiated, that is, my obsession with his body kept me from flinching. To his beauty, to his tranquil immodesty, I dedicated my first thefts. To the singularity too of that splendid cripple whose hand, cut off at the wrist, was rotting away somewhere, under a chestnut tree, so he told me, in a forest of Central Europe. During the theft, my body is exposed. I know that it is sparkling with all my gestures. The world is attentive to all my movements, but it wants to trip me up. I shall pay dearly for a mistake, but if there is a mistake and I catch it in time, it seems to me that there will be joy in the Father's dwelling. Or, I fall . . ."

I/tomb/fall. The play of antherection by which I am born to my name presumes that in more than one stroke I tread on flowers and forge a path through the virgin thicket of erianthus toward the primal scene, that I fake and filch the genealogy. ". . . the Father's dwelling. Or, I fall, and there is woe upon woe and then prison. But then it's the savages; inevitably the convict who risked 'the Getaway' will meet them by means of the procedure briefly described above in my inner adventure. If, going through the virgin forest, he comes upon a placer guarded by ancient tribes, he will either be killed by them or saved.

Two brothers, standing up to each other, can only kill each other.

Qua brothers. Which is the death of Antigone, not without her laughing about it as she is the last one to leave.

At the moment (indeed) when the (educated) young man leaves his family to become a citizen, he tears himself free from the law of the family, from its whole system, from natural and immediate ethics. And yet he still keeps an attachment to it precisely to the extent that he has a brother. The figure of two brothers can only be contingent. Because of this contingency (*Zufälligkeit zweier Bruder*), naturality remains. And yet this irrational, inconceivable contingency —parents should never conceive two sons, at least if they want them to live—is strange or anxiety-producing only insofar as it is not entirely natural, as would no doubt be the case for two sisters, and certainly for two cats. But brothers are neither sisters nor cats because males are male insofar as they lay claim to rational universality, to law and right: "two brothers with equal rights [*mit gleichem Rechte*] to take possession of the polity." One cannot conceive that two identical and complete individualities—who thus do not complete each other—should lay claim equally to one and the same thing, namely a law of universality. The government (*Regierung*), a universal force of law embodied in a "simple soul" or in the "self of the spirit of the people", "does not tolerate a dualism of individuality [*Zweiheit der Individualität*]." No right of the elder or other privilege of that type can resolve this problem. Being born first is, just like the simple duality, a natural fact that ethical rationality cannot take into account. There is no way out other than death. As the brothers both have reason, have good reason, *qua* men, and as there cannot be two of them—two foundations, two discourses, two *logoi*, two accounts, two reasons, two heads—they are both wrong. It all ends very badly: "their equal right (*gleiches Recht*) to the power of the state shatters both of them, each of whom is equally in the wrong (*gleiches Unrecht*)."

They must each fall on, and fell, the other [*s'abattre l'un (sur) l'autre*].

But, once again, they die *as singularities*; the community, attacked and defended by two emptied-out singularities, "maintains itself," constructs itself on the basis of the death of the brothers. *Qua* brothers: but the *"qua"* disappears in

It is by a long, long road that I choose to go back to primitive life. What I need first is condemnation by my race."

Enter Grandad [*Pépé*]. Pépé then occupies the whole space, bifurcating—separating—from this sentence the para(gra)ph that declines the signature and official status, toward which we are heading down a very long path.

Isn't Pépé, name of father or grandfather, also the diminutive for Joseph, the excluded father (unactualized in himself) of what was immaculately conceived? His name strikes the circumflex, no less than its devirilized characters. "'Pépé,' I said to myself, 'his name is Pépé.' And I left, for I had just noticed his delicate, almost feminine little hand. . . .

'My name is Pépé,' and he held out his hand. . . .

'He's a girl,' I thought, summoning up that image of his slender hand, and I felt that his company would bore me."

The encounter with this sort of smooth-faced figure had been elaborated, once more, by an opposition between black and white ("black wool"/"white wool," "black sheet [*drap noir*]" of a stolen woolen cape and "nuptial scene" between two legionnaires, "couple both veiled with tulle and dressed in a parade uniform") and, in the middle, the removal of oppositions—toward

its very appearing. "Individuality, which *in its being-for-itself* is linked to a danger to the whole, has expelled itself from the polity and has been dissolved within itself." The community honors the one who defends it; the government for its part punishes him by depriving him of burial, abandoning his body to the "dogs" and to the "birds." In so doing, the

Christiane Hegel—also—had two brothers. So the man we call Hegel had a single sister and a single brother (Georg Ludwig, an officer in the Wurtemberg army, who dies in 1812, after the *Phenomenology of Spirit,* during the Russian campaign. We know nothing of his burial. He bore the father's forenames.) The same year (first volume of the *Greater Logic*), comes the birth and the death of Hegel's daughter, Susanna Maria (suffocating catarrh), who did not, then, know her two brothers, born in 1813 and 1814, Karl and Emmanuel. After the birth of the latter, Hegel writes to Niethammer:

"Dear friend and godfather,

At the baptism I stood proxy for you. I took care to behave negatively during the ceremony, so as not to place myself between your godfathership and its effects upon him, but rather to allow everything to flow smoothly and properly without hindrance. His name, about which you inquire, is Thomas Immanuel Christian; we have taken 'Christian' from my sister, 'Thomas' from Seebeck, while 'Immanuel'—the name by which he is known—has been taken from you. He shall be known as 'Christian' because he is baptized a Christian; his name is also 'Thomas' because he shall pass over to the other extreme of unbelief. But by virtue of his middle name these extremes shall be fused in friendship and philosophy, and shall be moderated and equalized as the point of indifference (*Indifferenzpunkt*)-in-the-other.
So far the child has not belied the blessing he has received. He is thriving, thank goodness. Although my wife is not breast-feeding, she is likewise healthy . . ."

Reply from Niethammer (in English riveter, riveting hammer):

". . . May he not be inclined too much toward Thomas and find the point of indifference without sinking into the indifference and without ending, so to speak, in *Inani El*! With regard to the name Christian, I will confidently leave that to the spirit of my co-godmother whose name he bears, so that he does not become a Christian weak of spirit, but a Christian with a strong spirit, as is fitting to the one that begins with Thomas! May the race of weak individuals without courage, who play the comedy of Christianity with cross, blood, death, humiliation, self-degradation. etc., be abhorrent for him all his life, as it is for his godfather!"

undecidable suspense—by the crane movement of the circumflex: "'Really, when you pick up a client, it's *you* who ought to pay *him*,' he told me. . . . that very evening I brought back the cape of a custom's officer. . . . black sheet of his woolen cape. I wrapped myself up in it in order to return to the hotel, and I knew the happiness of the equivocal, not yet the joy of betrayal, though the insidious confusion which would make me deny fundamental oppositions was already forming."

So Joseph "is" (hardbinds) a girl, more or less, in erection ("From the opening emerged a solid neck, as broad as his head. When he turned it without moving his chest, an enormous tendon stood out [*bandait*]"), the circumflex an old blind Oedipus who climbs the road to Calvary supported by his daughter, but his daughter is his father whose scepter or sword or gladiolus he stands in for. No Oedipus walking without *gl*. He is thus the phallus of his father who is at the same time his mother and daughter. Never saw such cavorting [*Qu'est-ce que ça cavale*].

His other eponym (the "co-godmother"), the aunt, Hegel's sister, Christiane, commits suicide in 1832 shortly after her brother's death. She had been committed in 1820 to the lunatic asylum at Zwiefalten, then treated by Schelling's brother. Her "nervous troubles" begin in 1814 (after the death of Georg Ludwig, when Marie Hegel is pregnant with her first boy):

"Nuremberg, April 9, 1811

Your condition as described in your letter received yesterday, dear sister, touches me and my wife very deeply. There is no question as to what is to be done. If your current illness is such that a trip is enough for your diversion and recovery, by all means visit us. . . . My wife will be delivering this fall, and if you could lend her a hand your presence would be doubly advantageous. . . . We can set you up in a small room of your own, a type of garret-room, which is of course heatable.
Above all put your mind at rest. . . . Seek your reward for your efforts in part in the vocation (*Bestimmung*) you have had to follow thus far due to your economic situation, but also in the work itself, in the physical and spiritual welfare of the children committed to your care [Christiane was governess in the house of Count von Berlichingen]. . . . For the rest consult yourself and the doctor about what is to be done for your well-being."

In November 1815, in a draft of a letter from Christiane to Hegel:

". . . I have disturbed the order of your house and am sorry about that, but not the peace of your house, and that comforts me . . .

Christiane then settles near her cousin, the pastor Göriz. Hegel: ". . . Greet cousin Goriz along with his wife and sister. It is a particular relief for me to know that you have in him such a true and genuine friend and counsellor. Have total confidence in him, and subject your thoughts to his well-intended advice and insights. The most important thing for a human being is to free oneself of one's idle thoughts, and to find this liberation and at once the satisfaction of one's mind in a fruitful activity for a noble cause—an activity you have found under your friend's guidance. Add to this the remembrance of, even from afar,

Your ever-faithful brother,
Wilhelm"

"I . . . likewise learn from your letters that you are continuing with the useful occupation and activity of teaching which you had begun. The success of your undertaking truly pleases me, first because you thus have a further source of income, and second because your occupation is both beneficial to health and—through the consciousness of being useful to others—satisfying to the heart. . . . On the whole, as I said, you will find in the confidence you have found among the inhabitants of Aalen as in your beneficial activity both support and sat-

Oedipus already lodges "within himself" his derision, his parody, his simulacrum, and, like what never belongs to him, whatever *finds him* reversed. Like all flowers. From the very beginning (oracle and good news), the anthoedipus has been in the wings, and it arrives with every season like a flower. It is spat out behind a reseda. That is how Stilitano takes him by the hand and leads him up the speaking staircase. The stairway always leads to death: up to the top and by stages, flight by flight, held up by another. Oedipus and Christ met on a staircase.

What is going on here, must it be repeated, is *steps* [marches].

Stilitano says "follow me." Scandal of the stumblingblock not to be tripped over.

"'Follow me,' he said. 'And stop talking. The staircase speaks [*est bavard*].'"

Gently he led me from step to step. I no longer knew where we were going. A wondrously supple athlete was leading me about in the night. A more ancient and more Greek Antigone was making me scale a dark, steep Calvary. My hand was confident, and I was ashamed to stumble at times against a rock or root, or to lose my footing.

Under a tragic sky, I will have traveled through the most beautiful landscapes in the world once Stilitano took my hand in the night. What sort of fluid was this that passed from him into me, giving me such a charge [*décharge*]?"

Climbing the stairs, "scal[ing toward] Calvary," is as glorious as the ascension of the body onto the scaffold (one mounts the scaffold: "death on the scaffold which is our glory") and the two robbers are agreed that they will play all the characters at

isfaction of heart and conscience. And this motive must always be foremost in our commissions and omissions. I am sending you in advance the interest due on 300 florins capital along with a small supplement. . . ."

Two years later, three letters to cousin Göriz to ask him to act "in my name as a brother" when what a man can dread worst, the "hardest" and "most unfortunate" experience, occurs.

"Berlin, March 19, 1820

I am, dear cousin, much obliged to you for procuring and sending my certificate of baptism. I have thus incurred a monetary debt to you as well. I would, of course, like to pay you in person, and am sure you would be willing to bear with me until I visit my old fatherland. The only problem is that this might take too long, and that too much interest might accumulate. You can settle accounts through my sister.

I am also grateful to you for the sad notification you give me of my sister's unfortunate condition. My activities kept me from replying earlier in this regard. Yesterday I finished my lectures, but even today I do not know what I am to say of this. The news has moved me deeply. Of all the things that can affect a human being, this is the hardest (*das Harteste*) to take. She recovered quickly, however, from the earlier attack that befell her when she was still in Mr. von Berlichingen's household, although she admittedly retained an unhappy, irritated mood from that experience. Is it not possible that this relapse is connected with her current age, and that the change in the female constitution—which in her case is only now appearing, though normally it should probably have happened already a few years ago—has had such an effect! You still describe her problem chiefly as hysteria, which was likewise the case then.

The only consolation I can have in this is knowing that she enjoys your loving supervision and, as you have assured me already in your letter, that she does not want for anything. I must likewise appeal to your kind attentions and judgment to decide what further is to be done for her, and what provision and treatment are to be arranged. Since it is in the first instance the physical condition of hysteria which effects such a release [*Entbindung* is also delivery, childbirth] of the inner passions, there might still be hope for her recovery through your loving care combined with medical treatment. Because she probably retains awareness of her surrounding actual environment despite her confused frame of mind, your care is what is most beneficial for her deranged mind, which requires the respect and deference which she will have for you in order to be controlled.

I give you once more my heartfelt thanks for all your kindness and love in this sad situation. I may still ask you for news of her from time to time, and of changes in her condition.

Please remember me cordially to your family. My wife and children, thank God, are well. I learned only from your greetings, however, that you have remarried. I have received no news from my sister in more than a year. So

once. Father Oedipus (Mary-Jochrist) is led by the hand, of her child, son or daughter, granted, toward the bedroom, hotel room, simulacrum of the family room and of the temple, which they explore in the night like thieves. The staircase speaks and orders the whole space. "Hardly had I touched him than the staircase changed: he was master of the world"; he, Stilitano, and not the staircase. But Stilitano is master inasmuch as he holds up (on) the staircase. The glorious one-armed man forms a sort of truncated, castrated column around which the staircase twists, like a plant. Occurrent always around a fictive column.

Another stairway scene. This time the holy family altar house [*hôtel*] is one-eyed [*borgne*]. It's a parenthesis: "(Sometimes at night I meet a youngster and go with him to his room. At the foot of the stairs, for my trade lives in shady hotels [*hotels borgnes*], he takes me by the hand. He guides me as skillfully as did Stilitano.)"

What sticks to the body of the truncated column, along the twisting staircase, is indeed a father become son. Of his father, no doubt, of who else?

However it's okay in his steps [*sa marche*]: ". . . He guides me as skillfully as did Stilitano.)

'Watch out.'

He mumbled these words,

as is known, at least since Jacob, every time one dreams of a sexual act it symbolically represents climbing up [*escalade*] or tumbling down [*dégringolade*].

"Steps, ladders or staircases, or, as the case may be, walking up or down them, are representations of the sexual act" (*Traumdeutung*).

The stairs, then, speak. They are sonorous (wooden). Like the walls of a hotel, like its partitions [*galandages*] (he really likes the word and his whole literature could be said to form a galanthus; the galanthus is a *fleur de lait*).

please accept my warm congratulations. May all the love you have given be returned to you in this marriage.

Your sincere cousin and friend,
Hegel"

Berlin, May 13, 1820

Dear cousin,

At the beginning of April, I informed you in a letter of the reports reaching me from Jaxthausen of my sister's illness, and also asked you for your further assistance in this matter. According to further letters from Jaxthausen, the appointment of a guardian to oversee her financial and personal well-being seems necessary. She is indeed in Neustadt, and as she herself writes no doubt has very good accommodations. But she has already found aspects of her present situation which lead her to wish a change. From my present distance I find myself obliged to address myself to others to accomplish what I cannot do myself. And in whom could I have greater confidence than in you, my old friend and cousin! What my sister needs is the sort of friend you have always been to her to manage her financial affairs and advise as to her situation—but at once a friend who has legal authority over her in handling such matters. I likewise need a friend who is closer by to tell me what steps I must take from a legal standpoint. Privy Councillor Count von Berlichingen of course suggests to me the Orphans' Court in Stuttgart, which is responsible for ratification of a guardianship and which exercises ultimate supervisory authority. But I cannot personally arrange for such prior legal guardianship from here, and thus can immediately accomplish the necessary steps only by proxy. So I address my request to you in this unfortunate affair—which is indeed the most unfortunate (*unglücklichsten*) that can befall men—to intercede and initiate the necessary steps. If a formal authorization is necessary from me beyond the fact that I hereby authorize you in this letter, I would make it over to you upon some indication from you. But my authorization for establishment of a guardianship over my sister also of necessity depends on the medical attestations and testimonies of others regarding her condition and behavior, which I will have to ask you to procure yourself, and which you either already have or can quickly get. The sort of guardianship you already have at once for itself implies the more specific authorization to apply for further legal authority. I have written today to Dr. Uhland in Neustadt, who is her doctor and who has provided for her accommodation. I have asked him to establish contact with you, in part with regard to the expenses of her stay there, since so far you have handled her financial affairs. Because her own means will not be sufficient to procure decent accommodations—the contract for room and board there amounts to 300 florins a year—I have promised a supplement of 100 to 150 florins. I should really settle accounts with you first regarding this side of the question. According to what you indicated earlier, in Aalen she was no doubt able to get by with what she had. In Neustadt she now longs to return to Aalen, but the only question is whether she can remain or be left there. On the other hand, I have asked

which were too sweet for me. Because of the position of our arms I was pressed against his body. For a moment I felt the movement of his mobile buttocks. Out of respect I moved a little to the side. We mounted, narrowly limited by a fragile wall which must have contained the sleep of the whores, thieves, pimps and beggars of the hotel. I was a child being carefully led by his father. (Today I am a father led to love by his child.)"

Today, in parentheses, is the *at present* of the writing: I am a father. But "I was a child" in the preceding sentence, outside of parentheses, belongs to the time of the narrative according to which, a page earlier, or one flight lower, the child was old Oedipus held up by his daughter (Stilitanantigone) to whom he gave a "confident hand." Who is giving whom a helping hand [*coup de main*] in this story? To whom does the hand revert? What is the sense of its trembling? Who emits *gl*, the fluid discharge?

Stilitano, son and daughter column father, one-armed stylist, always uses as a hook the circumflex that lends him a hand around places where he elaborates his luminosity. The circumflex then

"Separated by a thin wall from Armand, sleeping with Robert, I suffered at not being in the place of either one of them or at not being with them or at not being one of them. I envied them, but I felt no hatred. I went up the wooden staircase very carefully, for it was squeaky and rickety and almost all the partitions [*galandages*] were wooden."

Insatiable jealousy, for oneself, already (I miss, I miss myself): tear down the walls, the divisions [*clivages*], the partitions in order to occupy all the places at once, be loved in place of the other, put an end to the worst suffering (be jealous of not being jealous enough, of not even being able to reappropriate jealousy as one's suffering, hurt, one's very own), swallow oneself, touch oneself [*s'attoucher*], deliver oneself [*s'accoucher*], give birth to oneself and give oneself one's own (breast), then get hard enough to die, masturbate finally or fuck oneself by flowing out [*en s'écoulant*]: *je m'ec*, I fuck myself in the a [*je m'enc*]

Dr. Uhland to inform you of her condition, which will determine whether she could remain in private life or must be placed in the care of a public institution. From all that I have been told and that you have already found out yourself, an authority exercising legal power over her is indispensable to keep her quiet and submissive in private life. The other solution, a public institution, can even more clearly be decided only by a formal and official guardian.
I thus ask you to act in my name as a brother. It is most reassuring for me to be able to see you represent me in this sacred concern.
The mail is about to leave, and so I close with the warmest of farewells.

Your cousin,
Hegel"

"Berlin, June 17, 1820

Dear cousin,

Following kind notification from you at the end of last month, I am sending you first the enclosed draft for 300 florins to pay off the sum which I still owed my sister. It has just occurred to me that I should have added interest for you, but this can be done later. A remittance to Stuttgart could not be made. But from what I hear drafts for Frankfurt are sought after in Stuttgart, and you will perhaps be able to sell it yourself in Aalen. Secondly, I am also sending a statement authorizing you to assume the guardianship you have kindly offered to undertake. This authorization can take effect, however, only if tutelage is legally granted and acknowledged. You will know best what is to be done in this regard, and will kindly take care of it.
This formality of guardianship moreover bears on what I will be able and willing to do further for my sister's care. If she acknowledges the tutelage or allows it to be exercised willingly, well and good. But if her actions remain at her own discretion, there is no way I could consent to expenditures in support of her extravagances (*Extravaganzen*)—here is where the requested supervision of all her household effects is in order—and the costs they occasion even if I had more money available than I in fact have. Such assurance is available only through a court order by which her conduct is no longer abandoned to a willfulness on her part that refuses all good advice. The doctor in Zwiefalten likewise has absolute need of such authorization over her conduct in order to undertake treatment. Though he is indeed charging a little too much in relation to the cost of board. So my express request to you is still to take the preliminary steps in your or my name at the Orphans' Court in Stuttgart.
In thanking you in advance for your friendship in this matter, I at once ask you to express to your mother, brothers, and sisters—and especially the postal secretary—my cordial gratitude for the many troubles they have taken. I hope someday to have the opportunity of returning the favor to you and your family. Farewell.

Your faithful cousin,
Hegel

Please hand over the enclosed brief letter to my sister."

becomes his phallus, the detached member that grows back after rotting at the foot of a tree. "By remaining inaccessible, he became the epitome of those whom I have named and who stagger me. I was therefore chaste. At times, he was so cruel as to require that I button the waistband of his trousers, and my hand would tremble. He pretended not to see anything and was amused. (I shall speak later of the character of my hands and of the meaning of this trembling. It is not without reason that in India sacred or disgusting persons and objects are said to be Untouchable.) . . . Stilitano was happy to have me at his beck and call and he introduced me to his friends as his right arm. Now, it was his right hand that had been amputated. I would repeat to myself delightedly that I certainly was his right arm; I was the one who took the place of the strongest limb."

Ten or so lines after that, slicing royally through that development, without any other apparent elaboration, at the moment when Stilitano leaves the scene opened by "follow me," the circumflex opens another scene, its own, that of the accent thereby announced: here is who I am, where and how I was born, how I gave myself a name, baptized myself (John baptized Christ); I call myself by name, I listen to myself, I nickname myself

On page 3 of this letter, the following proxy:

"By these presents I give full powers to my cousin, Dean M. Göriz—since my sister Christiane Hegel, according to all the information received, is found suffering from mental illness, to act in my name in the affairs that concern her, and I establish him her guardian, as far as that depends on me.

G. W. F. Hegel
Professor of Philosophy
at the Royal University
of this city.
Berlin, June 17, 1820"

A year later, Christiane leaves the mental home at Zwiefalten:

"Berlin, August 12, 1821

My dear sister,

It has pleased me deeply to learn from your letter of June of the fortunate restoration of your health, and of the strengthening and recovered possession of your mind. I only wish this were the only sentiment with which your letter left me. Most of all, I could only wish that the painful and bitter feelings it awakened in me might merely have concerned the past, and not refer to the present and future. For from the strengthening of your spirit and mind it is to be hoped that you may overcome the past, the memory of your sufferings, the feeling of having suffered the injustice and insults of others. I may at least draw your attention first to the fact that above all you ought to work within yourself to put this past behind you, and to concern yourself with your present frame of mind and behavior toward others. The more you can subdue and remove such memories from your present—both your inner present and your outer present over against others—the sounder of health your mind will become, and the friendlier your relation to others, and their relation to you. In your letter to me you found it necessary for your self-justification to return to so much that is painful. Naturally you needed to convince me of the evil treatment you have received. But consider yourself generally convinced that the repetition in recollection of this past will only be detrimental to the complete restoration of your health. What most justifies you toward others is your sensible present behavior. Justification stemming from past treatment toward you, since it inevitably assumes the form of reproaches, turns away the affection of those before whom you wanted to justify yourself far more than it is able to win them over to you. My advice for your health may principally consist in encouraging you to allow your recollection of suffered injustice to dissolve and disappear. But take this matter to be of the greatest importance.

I of course had to expect you to write to your brother of the circumstances that contributed to making you so unhappy. But I shall thus have as little as possible cause to want to justify others or myself here and there against you, and to stir up in you and bring before you again

flower (baptism is a second birth), I am born once more, I give birth to myself as a flower. The race having been condemned, the circumflex is consecrated by opening the mouth and sticking out the tongue—the syllable drags a little; the circumflex raises and places itself as crowned head.

The flower of rhetoric organizing this antitrope, this metonymy simulating autonymy, is what I baptize "anthonymy." One could just as well say "anthonomasia." Antonomasia is a "sort of synecdoche consisting in taking a common noun for a proper name, or a proper name for a common noun" (Littré).

"I went back to the hotel and told Stilitano about it. He said he would attend to the matter and then left."

"I was born in Paris on December 19, 1910. As a ward of the *Assistance Publique*, it was impossible for me to know anything about my official status [*état civil*]. When I was twenty-one, I obtained a birth certificate. My mother's name was Gabrielle Genet. My father remains unknown. I came into the world at 22 Rue D'Assas.

what you are rather to consider as over and done with. So I will touch just briefly on a few points which may be of interest with respect to the future. After all you have written to me about it, it is evident you can no longer enter into a relationship with Dean Göriz. It seems increasingly clear to me that this relationship has been the cause of your illness. I see from what you still write about the idea of returning to the estate of Count von Berlichingen that—as is only natural—you have merely an imperfect representation of the effect which your behavior during your illness has had on others, and can even less grasp their behavior regarding yourself. But this makes the challenge to unburden yourself of the representations you have of these matters simply all the greater. I of course am no longer in correspondence with the Count.

I must mention two things about my own behavior. I wrote to you in Neustadt, asking you in the letter above all to direct your soul to the thought of God, and to receive into your mind (*Gemüt*) strength and consolation from this higher love. I have also written to you about this in a letter to Zwiefalten. But I feel you have replied in a way I had not expected, though what I said could not have come more deeply from my heart. In short, after this letter I immediately received news from you that you want to leave Neustadt, where my second letter thus no longer reached you. I wrote to Stuttgart right away, receiving the reply that you had already left from there as well. Thus neither my exhortation nor the assistance which, at my request, my friends perhaps might have given you could reach you any longer. Whether this letter will still find you in Zwiefalten or Stuttgart I do not know. As for the other matter of giving you evidence of my concern by advancing some money, you know that I scraped up the 300 florins which I still owed, and have sent them to our cousin the Dean. I have likewise committed myself to support you in the future as much as my circumstances permit. The reimbursement of that capital has of course hampered me ever since. However, as soon as I know where you will be staying I will make an effort to contribute to it. I must regret you have not wished to retain Zwiefalten as your further place of residence—once more in view of the expenses of a trip, and of the transportation of your luggage. After all that has happened to you in Aalen, and after the impression you made during your illness, you can no longer return there. But I would have thought a small town to provide the most advantageous opportunity for you—if only because the cost of living is less. But why do you not mention at all the intention of occupying yourself again with teaching, which you did successfully and, from what you write to me, with the grateful appreciation of people of Aalen? This would provide you with a more secure subsidy than what you can expect from the assistance of others. Such a purpose, by which you can render service to others, will be the most certain means of preserving your mental and thus physical health. I can never regret enough that you gave up such a situation in Aalen, and have put yourself in a situation of dependence on people on whom you thought you could rely, which has in all probability been the cause of your illness. But once you

'I'll find out something about my origin,' I said to myself, and went to the Rue d'Assas. Number 22 was occupied by the Maternity Hospital. They refused to give me any information. I was brought up in the Morvan by peasants. Whenever I come across *genêt* (broom) blossoms on the heaths—especially at twilight on my way back from a visit to the ruins of Tiffauges where Gilles de Rais lived—I feel a deep sense of kinship with them. I regard them solemnly, with tenderness. My emotion seems ordained by all nature. I am alone in the world, and I am not sure that I am not the king—perhaps the sprite—of these flowers. They render homage as I pass, bow without bowing, but recognize me. They know that I am their living, moving, agile representative, conqueror of the wind. They are my natural emblem, but through them I have roots in that French soil which is fed by the powdered bones of the children and youths screwed, murdered, and burned by Gilles de Rais.

Through that thorny plant of the Cevennes,[1] I take part in the criminal adventures of Vacher. Thus, through her whose name I bear, the vegetal kingdom is my familiar. I can regard all flowers without pity; they are members of my family. If, through them, I rejoin the nether realms—though it is to the bracken and their marshes, to the algae, that I should like to descend—I withdraw further from men.[2]

1. The very day he met me, Jean Cocteau called me his 'Spanish *genêt*' (*genêt d'Espagne*—rush-leaved broom). He did not know what that country had made of me.

2. Botanists know a variety of *genêt* they call winged-broom (*genêt ailé*)."

resolve to rely on yourself, you will be most securely sheltered, both inwardly and outwardly—but on yourself at once means on a frame of mind directed toward something Higher. As for teaching, I as well earn my living from it, and honor myself with it just as it honors me in the eyes of others. How this can be accomplished for you again your friends will be able to advise on the spot. But I implore you to accept the good advice of others. At least you may believe me when I say that you have spurned and severely undercut the well-intentioned sentiment of others in your regard by not accepting their advice and assistance in your own best interest, and by not allowing yourself to be restrained from what has become and has been harmful to you.
Accept these brotherly admonitions as they have come from my heart. May peace be in your heart!
I must still briefly report on myself, wife, and children. The latter will make themselves heard on their own. We thank God that we find ourselves in better health this summer than last winter, when I felt poorly and when my wife was still sicker and weaker. Of my external situation there would be much to say. As satisfied as I am with it, a position in a great state is different. In my field this situation cannot always be free of apprehension and anxiousness for me—whether founded or unfounded. Farewell for now, dear sister.

Your brother,
Wilhelm"

Six years later, still from Berlin (1827).

"My dear sister,
. . . I have learned from your letter of the mishap with my bust; it is to be sure breakable . . ."
(The bottom half of the letter is missing.)

Four years later (the year of his death).

". . . A copper engraving of me, of which you wished two copies, can no longer be found. But since I have not only been engraved and sculpted but now imprinted on a medal as well, I shall send you two such medals instead. I would already have done so had I only known how. Sending them by mail would cost more than the medals themselves. I thus prefer to await a favorable occasion. . . .
". . . We are presently and—we hope—forever safe from all the current unrest. But these are still anxious times, in which everything that previously was taken to be solid and secure seems to totter . . ."

The medal offered to Hegel by his students carries on its reverse side a celestial genius, standing, and flanked by a woman on his right. She is holding a cross of which the genius will take possession. On the other side, a philosopher sitting in front of a column. Above the column, the owl taking flight at the end of history. The philosopher is writing in a book open on his knees.
Around the same time, Hegel is made Knight of the Order of the Red Eagle, 3rd class, for services rendered to science and in his capacity as a professor. The red eagle is

winged phallus, "winged prick" of *Miracle*. In the course of *Funeral Rites*, J.D.'s mother (the good one) follows his body, "to go to the cemetery . . . she put the veil behind her by simply turning that fantastically winged hat around her head." "The horse that was drawing the hearse was weary," she was wanting to avoid "the jaunty posture of a very proud lady," "she herself was the dead person"

This name of a flower will therefore be a cryptogram or cryptonym. It isn't proper because it is common. On the one hand,

antonomasia. This alienation, already, even before I come back to myself, walks the streets with my proper name, *classifying* [classe] it in the "natural" world, freezing [*glace*] the appellation in an exterior thing, in its name or in its form. My signature trails behind [*traîne*]. Dereliction, endless wandering [*errance*]. Equivalent among things, but absolutely alone. It will have *gelled* [pris] following a great variety of paths. One would have to analyze that systematically. For example, in the case of the broom [*genêt*], the emblem is constituted quite easily and close to consciousness—that is why this reading is very preliminary—to the extent that it works through a whole nominal form. The horse or flower are not on the outside like Giacometti's dog: the latter is detached—but also, like every signature, pulls on its leash—following a very different track. Reread "curled into a ball": "Its rigid horizontality perfectly reproduced the shape a cat keeps, even when it is curled up [*en boule*].
As I am surprised that there is an animal—it's the only one among his figures:
HIM: It's me. One day I saw myself in the street like that. I was the dog.
If it was first chosen as a sign of misery and solitude, it seems to me that this dog is drawn as a harmonious signature, the curve of the spine answering the curve of the paw, but this signature is also the supreme magnification of solitude."

The emblem and coat of arms open and close (noise

not Napoleon's eagle, the only one before which speculative idealism knelt. As before "the spirit of the times" which advances like "a closely drawn armored phalanx moving irresistibly, and as imperceptibly as the sun." One letter to Niethammer (July 15, 1816) is overflowing with scorn for those "ants, fleas and woodlice" who claim to oppose it and who are not even worthy, as it is said in the Gospel, to untie his shoelaces: "They can perhaps reach the shoelaces of this colossus, and smear on a bit of boot wax or mud, but they cannot untie the laces. Much less can they remove these shoes of gods-which ... have elastic soles or are even themselves seven-league boots—once the colossus pulls on.... To edify the entire bustling zealous assemblage, one can even stand there and help daub on the cobbler's wax that is supposed to bring the giant to a standstill. For one's own amusement, one can even lend a hand...." The same year (1831), Victor Cousin becomes an officer in the Order of the Légion d'Honneur, itself instituted by the Empire (the other eagle). He announces it to Hegel: "Here I am, my dear friend; let us chat a moment as though we were still both stretched out on your sofa three hundred leagues from unwelcome intruders and business dealings. As I had just about told you, they have made me a Counsellor of State, and an officer of the Légion d'honneur; it's a little more relief without much more work. But as for the political career, I repeat that I do not wish to enter it. Even being a député tempts me scarcely at all and I remain faithful to philosophy. My place on the Council of Public Instruction is agreeable to me only for the services it allows me to render to philosophy; and between us I can say that over the past year I have rendered it some quite considerable ones. I constituted the Ecole normale, in other words our true philosophical seminary, I have renewed the teaching personnel; I have made rules, instituted competitions: in short given administratively your dear studies a strong push forward. That is why I entered the Council; the day I no longer have this useful influence on the study of philosophy is the day I shall retire and limit myself to serving philosophy with my lectures and my books. So be in no doubt, dear Hegel, that my soul is entirely devoted to philosophy. That is the refrain of the poem of my poor life, as I told you; politics fills only episodes."

To sneak in the whole Cousin/Hegel correspondence or their whole relationship (it's about getting penetrated and even fecundated in the name of France, by the aquiline concept):

"... How are you? How is the good Madame Hegel? And your children? Your soul is at peace, Hegel. Mine is sick. I spend my life missing my prison [Cousin had been arrested in Dresden for "participation in German revolutionary actions," of which Hegel had always believed him to be innocent. But his incontestable "liberalism" had made the accusation plausible, as it had motivated the suspension of his teaching at the Sorbonne and at the École normale, which was closed, moreover, in 1820.] But I do not forget that I am not alone with you, all alone, at night, on your settee; and it is not at a distance of 300 leagues that we can chat intimately ..." (December 13, 1825) ...

and stricture of the valve) the staccato effusion from a wound. The whole of "The Studio" works on that wound. The signature is a wound and there is no other origin to the work of art. "Beauty has no other origin than a wound, unique, different for each person, hidden or visible, that everyone keeps in himself, that he preserves and to which he withdraws when he wants to leave the world for a temporary, but profound solitude. . . . Giacometti's art seems to me to want to discover that secret wound of every being, and even of every object, so that it can illumine them." And without any apparent transition—a double-line blank space—we get the paragraph on Osiris in the "crypt of the Louvre." The hidden wound of the signature, the bleeding cryptogram, is the fragmentation of Osiris. But the economy of the signature never interrupts its work. It finds in the remainder of infirmity a supplemental apotrope, a sort of reseda. In the way that Stilitano gets a little harder for being one-armed. In the way of Querelle's squint. Oedipus will have never walked and worked so well since his recent (if that can be said) accident. Oedipus is in a class, but because limping adds class, confers a more or less proper name. Claudication: classification. To the floored tightrope walker: "I would even go so far as to advise him to limp." "He (Giacometti) resumes walking, limping. He tells me he was very happy when he found out that his operation—after an accident—would leave him lame. That is why I chance this: his statues still give me the impression that they are taking refuge, finally, in some secret infirmity that grants them solitude." The "secret wound" is also the "innermost core [*for intérieur*]" of the tightrope walker, what "he will inflate, fill."

The studio opens onto all the brothels where the lame one stalks the virgin reserved since one night before any past, "his fingers climb and descend like a gardener's trimming or grafting a climbing rose bush."

"I want to get myself trained, Hegel; so I need both for my conduct and my publication austere opinions, and I expect them from you . . . . There are four points in this little text: 1. Method. 2. Application to consciousness or Psychology. 3. Passage from Psychology to ontology. 4. Some sketches of a historical system. Let something good fall from your good head on these four points. Be all the more pitiless that, determined to be useful to my country, I will always permit myself to modify according to need and the state, as it is, of this poor country, the instructions from my masters in Germany. . . . The point is not to create here in a greenhouse an artificial interest for foreign speculations; no, the point is to implant in the country's innards fecund seeds that develop naturally there, according to the native virtues of the soil; the point is to impress on France a French movement that thereafter moves on its own. . . . I will regulate the strength of the wind according to that of the poor lamb; but as for me, not a lamb, I ask the wind to blow with all its might. I feel I have a back strong enough to support it; I ask pity only for France. Hegel, tell me the truth, and then I will pass on to my country what it will be able to understand." (August 1, 1826). ". . . As for me. I have made my decision. No, I do not wish to enter into business: my career is philosophy, teaching, public instruction. I have declared so once and for all to my friends, and I shall maintain my resolution. I have started in my country a philosophical movement that is not without importance; in time I wish to attach my name to it, and that is my entire ambition. That's the ambition I have; I have no other. With time I wish to strengthen, enlarge, improve my situation in public instruction, but only in public instruction. What do you say to that, Hegel?— Consequently, all I have asked from the new administration is that I be restored to my Chair, but with a more solid title than that of deputy professor. . . . That is how I am neither deputy nor titular, but adjunct, which is better than one, less than the other, and gives me independence and unmovability. . . . I need, even for here, a little success in Germany. So, Hegel, see if it would be impossible that Proclus, Plato, Descartes or the *Fragments* might obtain in your *Journal* the honors of a small article. By you, my Lord, would be too much; but have M. Gans or the excellent Hotho write a few pages about it. . . . I attach to your copy another for whoever would accept to make a little announcement about it in your Journal or elsewhere, for example, if possible . . ." (7 April 1828). "My lectures have just ended, and I hasten to write to you, my very dear Hegel. Between us, they had a little success; they had the honor of being stenographed, and they are out and about. Have they come to Berlin, to you? In doubt, I send you a complete copy, on condition, Lord, that you tell me what you think. . . . Three thousand copies of my lectures have been sold. Now here's the other side of the coin. There has been a real insurrection of all the materialists and industrialists. The old ruins of the Condillac school have risen up, recognizing their old adversary. In the absence of good reasons, accusations and insults have not been wanting. But I am not the kind of

To notice the cynical character of the paraph one has to see the photograph of the sculptor, face on, at the beginning of the book (each trait falls from it, as

from a beaten dog); but even more so the signature of the other. Without believing in chance or whether this was such a good thing to do, they have reproduced this signature, in a bad book, beside a photo of the author: he is carrying, upright, the cane that he has had so much trouble detaching himself from for the last several years.

The signature is a snapshot. Rights to reproduce refused

on the other, it isn't proper because it also leads back to lower domains, to wetlands, or even to the bottom of the sea. Above the sea is the galley, its flanks heavy, but buoyed by it. At the bottom of the sea, algae. The galley is moreover covered in algae ("velvet algae," "azure algae," etc.).

man to trouble myself much about all that. On another side, theology has had me under close surveillance and looks at me with an anxious eye. It does not consider me an enemy but a suspect. I have tried to give it no pretext; but the supremacy of Reason and Philosophy! . . ." (August 15, 1828)

universal merely "brushes" the "pure summit of its pyramid" at the moment it wins its victory over the rebellious principle of singularity and over divine law. The fact is that the continuous struggle of "conscious spirit" with "unconscious spirit" has not come to an end. The unconscious has not been destroyed, only "wounded," hurt, offended. "The revealed spirit has the roots of its force in the underworld (*Unterwelt*); the people's self-reassuring *certainty* possesses the *truth* of its oath which binds them all into one (*die* Warheit *ihres Alle in Eins bindenden Eides*), only in the mute unconscious substance of all, in the waters of forgetfulness. The achievement of public spirit is thereby transformed into its opposite, and the public spirit experiences that its supreme right is supreme wrong and that its victory is to an even greater degree its own downfall (*sein eigener Untergang*). For that reason, the dead whose right is infringed knows how to find instruments for his vengeance which are as actual and forceful as the power that injured him."

The dead one continues to act, then, the *dead one is wounded,* he re-enters the fray from the mute and unconscious substance into which they tried to push him down, reduce him, compress him. The return of the dead one, the revenge of the suppressed gains depth in wild nature: the birds and the dogs eat pieces of the body abandoned without burial, on the surface of the earth, and go on to "sully" with them the altars of other communities. The dead body in pieces drools, bleeds and spits on the places of worship. "These powers rise up in hostility and destroy the polity that has dishonored and disrupted its own force, the piety of the family."

Those the community has killed, in order to maintain itself, are again, under the name of brothers, women—representatives of the family. The human law, the law of the rational community which is instituted against the private law of the family, always suppresses femininity, stands against it, hems it in, presses and compresses it. But masculine power has a limit—an essential and eternal limit: the weapon, no doubt powerless, the all-powerful weapon of powerlessness, the inalienable blow struck by the woman is *irony*. The woman, "internal enemy of the polity," can always burst out laughing at the last moment: she knows, in

The alga is a cryptogam, one of those plants that conceal their

other metonymy of that "thief who is my mother"; here one has to read Genette, "Metonymy in Proust," allowing to develop, abyssally, far out to sea, an infinite work, running through, dredging languages or lagoons that—in all senses, false or true—hollow out there, literally, the threat of engulfing everything: ". . . or again, [there is the] much more complex network of analogies and adjacencies that is woven into this other passage from *The Fugitive,* where the narrator recalls his visits, in the company of his mother, to the San Marco Baptistry: 'The time has now come for me when, on remembering the baptistery, facing the waters of the Jordan where St John immersed Christ while the gondola awaited us by the Piazzetta, I cannot remain indifferent to the fact that there was by my side in this cool twilight a woman clothed in mourning, whose respectful but enthusiastic fervour matched that of the elderly woman who can be seen in Venice in Carpaccio's *St Ursula,* and that nothing can ever again remove this red-cheeked, sad-eyed woman, in her black veils, from the softly lit sanctuary of St Mark's, where I am certain to find her, because I have reserved a place there in perpetuity, alongside the mosaics, for her, for my mother': mosaic of baptism 'in relation to the site,' in which the Jordan presents something like a second baptistery *en abyme* within the first; echo of the waters of lagoon in front of the Piazza in those of the Jordan, the icy cold that strikes visitors like baptismal water, woman in mourning like the one in Carpaccio's painting close by, that painting itself offering Venice *en abyme* in Venice, the priestly immobility of the maternal image in the memory of the 'sanctuary,' as in one of the mosaics facing the narrator, and, by the same token, suggestion of an analogy between the narrator's mother and the mother of Christ. . . . But the most spectacular example is clearly Part I of *Sodom and Gomorrah,* that thirty-page piece that is entirely constructed along the parallel between the 'Jupien-Charlus conjunction' and the pollination by a bumblebee of the Duchess's orchid: a parallel carefully prepared, managed, sustained, and reactivated from page to page throughout the episode (and the discursive commentary that it inspires), and whose symbolic function endlessly feeds, as it were, on the relation

tears and in death, how to pervert the power that suppresses her. The power of irony—the ironic position, rather—depends—syllogistically—on the fact that the master produces and proceeds from what he suppresses, needs it and returns to it. Antigone is Cybele, the Mother-goddess who precedes and follows the whole process. She is present at every catastrophe, every fall, every carnage, remains invulnerable to them. Even her death does not affect her.

at first blush at least, one might find it strange to see the figure of Cybele come up in "The Spirit of Judaism," in the place of the infinite God facing which there are only beings who are stony, without life, without right, without love for themselves. In a note: "The priests of Cybele, the sublime godhead that is all that is, was, and is to be, and their veils no mortal has unveiled—her priests were castrated (*verschnitten*), unmanned in body and spirit (*an Leib und Geist entmannt*)." The logic of this comparison is now confirmed

Everything remains to her. She is to be followed.

"Thus, in its universal existence, that is, the polity, human law *is* within its activity itself the manliness of the polity and *is* within its actual activity the government, and it *moves* itself and *sustains* itself by absorbing into itself the isolation of the Penates, that is, their self-sufficient individualization into different families over which women preside and which keeps them dissolved (*aufgelöst erhalt*) within the continuity of its fluidity. However, the family is at the same time (*zugleich*) its elemental unit, and its universal energizing ground is individual consciousness. Since the polity gives itself durable existence only by disrupting familial happiness and by dissolving self-consciousness in the universal, it creates an internal enemy for itself in what it suppresses (*erzeugt es sich an dem, was es unterdrückt*), which is at the same time essential to it, that is, it creates an enemy in the feminine itself. By intrigue, the feminine—the polity's eternal irony—changes the government's universal purpose into a private purpose, transforms its universal activity into this determinate individual's work, and it inverts the state's universal property into the family's possession and ornament (*Putz*). In this way, the feminine turns to ridicule the solemn wisdom of maturity, which, being dead to individuality—dead to pleasure and enjoyment as well as to actual activity—only thinks of and is concerned for the universal. The feminine turns this mature wisdom into an object of ridicule for immature, high-spirited youths and into an object of contempt for those youths' enthusiasm. As such, she elevates the force of youth into the status of what is validly in force—she elevates the force of the son, born to his mother

of contiguity that has been established in the Hôtel de Guermantes courtyard (unity of place) at the moment when the insect and the Baron enter it together (unity of time), buzzing in unison. It isn't therefore enough for the miraculous encounter (at least judged to be so by the hero) of two homosexuals to be 'like' the miraculous encounter between a bee and an orchid, or for Charlus to enter 'humming *like* a great bumble-bee,' or for Jupien to be immobilized under his gaze so as to be 'taking root . . . *like* a plant,' etc.; it is also necessary that the two encounters take place 'at the same instant,' and in the same place, for then analogy no longer seems a sort of secondary, and perhaps illusory effect of *concomitance*."

sex organs. Like ferns, which propagate in general by dispersing their spores. Whether they can be noticed on the surface or not, the text is full of them. The "ferns" of "The Man Condemned to Death" are "rigid." Certain arborescent ferns unfold their fronds several meters above the ground. Cryptogams obviously don't have flowers.

Antheridium is the name for the male organ of most cryptogams.

The association of algae with ferns in anthonomasia would therefore be a dream desiring vegetative cryptogamy (I move to the side, "I withdraw further from men") under a floral phaneronymy. Phanerogams are traditionally the opposite of cryptogams. And among the former, which show their sex organs, and make

as her master, and what counts is the force of the brother as one in whom the sister finds a man as an equal with herself, the man through whom the daughter, freed from her own non-self-sufficiency, achieves the enjoyment and the dignity of womanhood (*Frauenschaft*). —However, the polity can only sustain itself by suppressing (*durch Unterdrückung*) this spirit of individuality, and because that spirit is an essential moment, the polity likewise creates it (*erzeugt*) by its repressive stance towards it as a hostile principle." Repression therefore produces the very thing—the singularity of the unconscious, the irony of femininity—that it represses as its "essential moment." It traps itself, and gets glued up in its essence. Whence the eternal burst of laughter of the unconscious—or of woman, the exclamation that infinitely harasses, questions, turns to ridicule, makes fun of the essence, of the truth (of man).

Thus the family collapses, "is swallowed up," "falls into the abyss." It devours itself. But do not rush to see in this the end of phallocentrism, of idealism, of metaphysics. The destruction of the family constitutes a stage in the advent of the *Bürgerlichkeit* (civil and bourgeois society) and of universal property. A moment of infinite reappropriation, the most reassuring metaphysical normality of idealism, of interiorizing idealization. Cunning of reason or eternal irony of woman, each able to take itself for the other and *play the other*. If God is (probably) a man in the speculative dialectic, the deity of God—the irony that divides him and unhinges him—the infinite restlessness of his essence is (if possible) woman.

You have come back, without ever having left it, to the middle of *The Philosophy of Right*. And yet everything here seems to set off again in the other direction. Antigone, for example, had before her abstract right, formal morality, etc. Now she has them behind her. What was *to come* (from the

flowers, gymnosperms bare their seeds whereas angiosperms enclose them within a vase, a vessel, a reservoir. Gymnosperms, it seems, appear halfway between vascular cryptogams (ferns, for example) and angiosperms. In the case of vascular cryptogams the spore engenders a prothallus separate from the mother plant. Germination takes place on it. The fertilized ovule of an angiosperm, on the other hand, remains on the mother plant, and the seed is sheltered by the fruit.

Cryptography makes use of phanerogamy, then, in order to lead the proper astray. What is thus improper is the flower's name, the accent on *genêt* that is barely pronounced. The circumflex with which it is adorned is a sort of head or fake headpiece. It is sewn in the place of a wound that is living and that signs.

The sewing of the fake hairpiece, the *ersatz*, substitute, is left to be cut through, three pages further along, by the episode of the bunch of grapes (cellulose and cotton wool) that Stilitano had stuck inside his pants.

Between anthonymy and the bunch of grapes scene, halt in front of a room apparently pinned onto or brought back into the fabric of the text: an image in the tapestry.

It begins thus after a fictive break in the narrative:

"I had just broken with the army, had just shattered the bonds of friendship.

The tapestry known as 'Lady with the Unicorn' excited me for reasons which I shall not attempt to go into here. But when I crossed the border

Roman world to Kant) in the phenomenology of spirit will have been *past* in the philosophy of right (i.e. in the encyclopedia system). Antigone serves twice, opens on both sides, but remains in the same place: law of the family, first moment of *Sittlichkeit.* She is even mentioned at the first moment of the first moment: monogamous marriage. But this time the tragic (because immediate) opposition of the two laws, of Antigone and Creon, has a different paradigmatic value; it is not the example of the dissolution of ethics *into* its negative (abstract right, etc.) but of the constitution of ethics *against* its negative. Simultaneous effects of chiasmus and circle, of encircled chiasmus.

The first of the three parts (marriage) of the first of the three sections (the family) of the third part (*Sittlichkeit*) recalls the Antigone of the *Phenomenology:*

"The *natural* determinacy of the two sexes acquires an *intellectual* and *ethical* significance by virtue of its rationality. This significance is determined by the difference into which the ethical substantiality, as the concept in itself, divides itself up in order that its vitality (*Lebendigkeit*) may thereby achieve a concrete unity.

§166. The *one* is therefore spirituality which divides itself up (*sich Entzweiende*) into personal self-sufficiency with being *for itself* and the knowledge and volition of *free universality,* i.e. into the self-consciousness of conceptual thought and the volition of the objective and ultimate end. And the *other* is spirituality which maintains itself in unity as knowledge and volition of the substantial in the form of concrete *individuality* and *feeling.* In its external relations, the former is powerful and active, the latter passive and subjective. Man, therefore has his actual substantial life in the state, in learning (*Wissenschaft*), etc., and otherwise in work and struggle with the external world and with himself, so that it is only through his division that he fights his way to self-sufficient unity with himself. In the family, he has a peaceful intuition of this unity, and an emotive and subjective ethical life. *Woman*, however, has her substantial vocation in the family, and her ethical disposition consists in this *piety.*

In one of the most sublime presentations of piety—the *Antigone* of Sophocles—this quality is therefore declared to be primarily the law of woman, and it is presented as the law

from Czechoslovakia into Poland, it was noon, in the summer. Its ideal line ran through a field of ripe rye, the blondness of which was as blond as the hair of young Poles; it had the somewhat buttery softness of Poland, about which I knew that in the course of history it was more sinned against than sinning."

The motif of the limit, of the frontier, of the dividing line runs through the whole sequence. From one mother the other.

The affect of passage: the exceptional emotion born from penetration. Penetration is the crossing of a limit, that is to say of a *step* [marche] separating two opposite places. Which nevertheless continue naturally, like Czechoslovakia and Poland, resembling each other, looking at each other, but separated by a frontier that is all the more mysterious, excluded from the crossing, for being abstract, legal, ideal: "I crossed the border from Czechoslovakia into Poland, it was noon, in the summer. Its ideal line . . . ," that is to say invisible, artificial, non-existent, that is transgressed without seeing it, with a single step, in an instant on the edge, like noon, no, that isn't crossed in the present but is going to be crossed, has been crossed: "Fear, and the kind of emotion that I always feel when I cross a border, conjured up at noon, beneath a leaden sun, the first fairyland. . . . The crossing of borders and the excitement [*émotion*] it arouses in me were to enable me to apprehend directly the essence of the nation I was entering."

of emotive and subjective substantiality, of inwardness which has not yet been fully actualized, as the law of the ancient

the divine law, the woman's recourse is always already there. The absolute already: the woman's side. Antigone insists: the advantage of unwritten laws is that, as they are not instituted by men, they have been forever engraved in the heart, one cannot determine the event of their origin.
Ou gar ti nun ge kachthes all'aie potel zē tauta, koudeis oiden ex otou phanē
Reason in History also relies on this. But it does so in order to see in it the sign of a profound rationality (at work from the threshold of ethics, even if the law of the woman—of the already—opposes its rationality to that of the man). "Sophocles' Antigone says: 'The divine commands are not of yesterday, nor of today; no, they live eternally, and no one could say whence they came.'?" The "eternal irony" of woman will never let itself be touched behind the absolute retrenchment of this already, higher up than the origin, older than birth, present at death.
Like irony, the woman is both a *moment to get through* and the very *form* of *Sa*. Double mark and double place. Irony (another architectonic index) defines the "extreme point" of subjectivity (at the end of the second part of the *Philosophy of Right*, at the moment of the "passage" from *Moralität* to *Sittlichkeit*) but it already has, *qua form* of absolute subjectivity, the infinite power of *Sa*. In the experience of irony (that must be determined against Plato and against the Romantics), "You in fact honestly accept a law as existing in and for itself; I too am with this law and within it (*dabei und darin*), but I go further than you, for I am also beyond (*ich bin auch darüber hinaus*) this law and can do *this or that* (so oder so) as I please. It is not the thing (*Sache*) which is excellent, it is I who am excellent and master of both law and thing [Hegel adds by hand: Virtuosity, Genius, master of ethics]; I *merely play* (nur spielt) with them as with my own caprice, and in this ironic consciousness in which I let the highest of things perish, I *merely enjoy myself* (nur mich genieße).' —In this shape (*Gestalt*), subjectivity is not only *empty* of all ethical *content* in the way of rights, duties, and laws, and is accordingly evil (evil, in fact, of an inherently wholly universal kind); in addition, its form (*Form*) is that of *subjective* emptiness, in that it knows itself as this emptiness of all content and, in this knowledge, knows *itself* as the absolute."

Absolute woman, irony, evil verge on and mimic *Sa*—for the form

gods and of the chthonic realm as an eternal law of which no one knows whence it came, and in opposition to the public law, the law of the state—an opposition of the highest order in ethics and therefore in tragedy, and one which is individualized in femininity and masculinity in the same play"; cf. *Phenomenology of Spirit*, §§443–75.

What is it to cross from Czechoslovakia into Poland?

The passage across the march between two (within a naturally continuous element: two lands, two seas separated by a name or a law) arouses a unique affect, then, an "emotion" (twice in the same passage). At the beginning of the *Journal*, the same word, or almost: "My excitement [*émoi*] is the oscillation from one to the other," the undecided suspense between two opposite but continuous significations, between Czechoslovakia and Poland. Here being agitated [*l'émoi*] is also *being moved between*. At the pinpoint instant, ungraspable but revolutionary (noon) when I enter (when I crossed the border from Czechoslovakia into Poland) and when I push myself, into new ground, a new power, a new law, the opposition is removed, the limit suspended, inside and outside pass one into the other.

Like the law and the outlaw that overlap reciprocally in the same passage, within the interval of a few pages: "Though the blue woolen cape I had stolen from the customs officer had already afforded me a kind of presentiment of a conclusion wherein law and outlaw merge, one lurking beneath the other but feeling,

Addition

"Plant, animal—

Individuality not divided in two.

In itself difference, division into two and universality.

Science, art, poetry.

Wherever women and young people rule in the State, the State rots . . .

Women may well be educated, but they are not made for the higher sciences, for philosophy and certain artistic productions which require a universal element. Women may have insights (*Einfälle*), taste, and delicacy, but they do not possess the ideal. The difference between man and woman is the difference between animal and plant. . . .

§167. Marriage is essentially *monogamy* . . ."

How does monogamy intervene in the chain, or rather in the system opposing the two chains of laws, the masculine and the feminine? Is it only a matter of a homogeneous relation between two forces that are unequal but of the same nature? In an open field in which shadow would just be a degree of light? Unconsciousness a virtual consciousness? In short: can one think repression according to the dialectic? Does the heterogeneity of all the restrictions, of all the counter-forces of striction (*Hemmung, Unterdrückung, Zwingen, Bezwingung, zurückdrängen, Zurücksetzung*) always define species of general negativity, forms of *Aufhebung,* conditions of sublation? Repression—what is today imagined, still very confusedly, under this word—could occupy several places with respect to these re-strictions: 1. Within the series, the class, the genus, the type; 2. Outside: no longer like a case or a species but as a quite different type; 3. Outside inside, like a transcategorial or a transcendental of all possible re-striction.

Can one think repression according to the dialectic? The answer is necessarily affirmative: if thinking means what thinking has always meant in the history of thought. And if thought is what forms the question in general, what imposes the questioning form of the question, the copulation question/response. This latter has an ontological, i.e. dialectical, "destination." If one asks "*what is* repression?," "*what is* the re-stricture of repression?" in other words "how to *think* it?", the reply is Dialectic.

with a touch of nostalgia, the virtue of its opposite, to Stilitano it would offer an adventure less spiritual or subtle but more deeply involved in daily life, better utilized. It will not yet be a question of treason. Stilitano was a power. His egotism sharply marked out his natural frontiers. (Stilitano was a power to *me*.)"

However, we are reading—"The tapestry known as 'Lady with the Unicorn,' which "excited me for reasons which I shall not attempt to go into here." We are advancing inside a representation, or we are rather penetrating without advancing, without pushing deeper, on the surface of an image pinned or sewn into the general weave of the text. But every penetration, inasmuch as, with a step, it crosses a line that is merely ideal, suspends the opposition, does not find itself confronted with a substance that is really opposable. Given that it suspends and traverses, penetration is only ever that of an image: "apprehend directly the essence of the nation I was entering. I would penetrate less into a country than to the interior of an image. Naturally I wished to possess it, but also by acting upon it. The military apparatus being that which best denotes it, that was what I hoped to tamper with."

Apparatus was earlier the word for Stilitano's "generative organ," there where his "luminosity," his phanerogamy is developed.

So one penetrates or penetrates oneself with a representation [*on (se) pénètre donc (d') une représentation*]. Sewn into the text or faced with the text, looking at it rather impassively, severely (like the remains of the Rembrandt, for example, but there are so many others).

But to say that re-stricture—under its name "repression"—remains today a confused imagination, is perhaps only to designate, with respect to philosophy, what does not allow itself to be *thought* nor even interrogated with a question. The question is already stricturing, being encircled, girdled.

In other words: what about the prohibition of incest? What relation does it have to the constitution of each chain of legality? With the opposition of the two chains?

One might interrogate from this point of view the concept of marriage, the first moment of the family syllogism. Can a certain scansion of reading bring out in it, at least hypothetically, the feature that links the double concatenation to the forbidding of incest? What relation is there between monogamy, the prohibition of incest, and the appearance of the value of objectivity (activity, virility, differentiation, reason, freedom, etc.) which forms the value of opposition in general? A slight syncope urges the question: what can the relation to the object possibly have to do with the prohibition of incest?

The principle of objectivity is privileged from the start in the deduction of marriage. Or rather, it is not privileged, it is privilege itself, the very excellence of the "point of departure" in the inaugural act of marriage, once one analyzes it as an operation of *Sittlichkeit,* of ethics, what has often been translated as "objective morality."

How does one get married? There can be two "points of departure" for conjugality—the subjective and the objective. In the class of subjective points of departure, depending on a particular, empirical, more or less contingent motivation, there are two possibilities: 1. The "particular inclination" of two individuals who meet by chance; 2. The "foresight" of the parents who arrange things. At this moment in the text, the marriage "arranged" by the parents is classified in the "subjective" category since it appears to depend on the singular initiative of empirical individuals—the parents. In both of these cases freedom goes missing.

The right "point of departure" is objective, and depends on a "free consent" (*freie Einwillung*), independent both with respect to contingent (amorous) inclination

The sewing of what you will call *the penitrate* [le pénètre] (signifier to be dug through every which way) is crosscut here more than once.

First, a pictorial text, representative, iconic, the tapestry, is applied over a narrative or discursive text: one piece playing inside the other as for example in *The Maids.*

Next, the piece is this time less improperly *sewn*: we have fabric [*étoffe*] (literal sense) stuck onto a weave [*tissu*] (figurative sense).

Finally, the content, if one can say that, of this representative abyss, in this passage from noon to gold [*or*] (one should pick up the buttery sliding of all the signifiers into *or*), it is the penitrate of the lady, the grafting of a penis (a phallus) that hesitates being, and hesitates being what it is at home with her, on the

and with respect to the particular will of the parents. In free consent, two subjects fuse into one, rid themselves of their natural predicates, or at least subordinate them in order to become a single free person. In this marriage, one becomes a person [*personne:* no-one], i.e. freedom. No doubt *natural* freedom is a "limitation of self" (*Selbstbeschränkung*), but the fierce set formed by the system of conjugal constraints produces by the same token the "liberation" of the person and allows that person to gain access to a "substantial self-consciousness." In this way the person unbinds both from the contingent attachments of love and the authority of the preceding generations.

To get married is to respond to a destination, an objective vocation (*objektive Bestimmung*) and to ethical duty, in the order of objective morality (*sittliche Pflicht*). Whoever does not marry either remains at the stage of the animal naturality of desire, or of the formal subjectivity of "*Moralität.*" One accedes to ethics and politics only on condition of being married. That being said, a long note specifies that the "point of departure" is by nature "contingent." It depends on the "culture of reflection" (*Bildung der Reflexion*).

This remark discreetly introduces the decision that breaks the equilibrium or the indifference. To illustrate the "two extremes" of the point of departure, it places parental intervention on the side of objectivity, and therefore of freedom, and no longer, as in the body of the text, on the side of subjectivity: "[There are here two extremes:] At one extreme, the initial step is taken by well-intentioned parents [*wohlgesinnten*: a crucial qualification; the parents are well-intentioned when they wish that the purpose of marriage—in particular, freedom—be realized; so they intervene in order to ensure freedom. Just like all "good intentions," the most effective, then, the ones that ensure the most sublime mastery], and when the persons destined (*bestimmt*) to be united in love get to know each other as destined partners, a mutual inclination results."

In this case, the well-intentioned parents arrange destiny: not that they fabricate destiny, rather they make themselves arrange for it, enter into its views and its ways, have a preview (*Vorsorge*) of what calls (*bestimmt*) their children one toward the other; and then love does not fail to be born—it was on the program. We must not simplify these statements, nor reduce their historical scope: it is not just about a psychological deliberation in the mind of a father/mother, but

head of a fabulous animal: "the most gentle and most terrible."

The word being homed in on is perhaps CHIMERA. Dissimulated like an animal, agile, lively, discernible within the vegetation, it has to be tracked down, flushed out.

The unicorn, the universal antidote, thus repairs all the tears and all the stitchings. It isn't natural, has no natural place, perhaps doesn't even take place, a frontier that is instantaneously crossed between two weaves, two texts, two sexes. That oscillation is my excitation [*émoi*]. I am almost (barely) the lady with the unicorn and the lady with the unicorn is (almost) for me, I am the lady and the unicorn. My mother has given birth to the unicorn and I give birth to it in turn by crossing the line. I give birth to myself and write myself from that fact. In plainsong. I listen to myself.

"*Unicorn,* n. . . . they [unicorn horns] are taken to be a universal counter-poison. . . . 'it is the finest, the proudest, most terrible, and at the same time most gentle animal that ornaments the earth.' Voltaire" (*Littré*). *Thief's Journal,* concerning the one-armed man: "It was no longer even the memory of him that I carried away with me but rather the idea of a fabulous creature, the origin and pretext of all desires, terrifying and gentle, remote and close to the point of containing me . . ."

That's where—here—I rye or eagle myself [*je seigle ou m'aigle*].

I am first of all "squatting on the edge," then there is the birthing and identification: "I remained a long time squatting at the edge, intently

also a social class calculus and a probability of a meeting that works out. That is the objective extreme. The other extreme: inclination appears first (*zuerst erscheint*) in the persons *qua* "infinitely particularized" in their "infinite singularity." One might wonder how infinite singularity can give rise to any kind of ethical categoriality, to conjugality for example, how one can pass from one stage to the other. Or conversely, how an objective motivation can one day give birth to a singular affect. Yet both things happen and it is this inconceivable fact, unintelligible to the understanding, that the speculative dialectic intends to account for: one can get married on the basis of an infinitely unique passion and conversely one can love on the basis of a marriage. What is unintelligible—not inconceivable—is conception, the birth of the concept on the basis of pure singularity, the engendering of the singular (infinite determination) on the basis of the concept, the becoming-object of the subject, the becoming-subject of the object. That's history, what makes history, (hi)stories, marriage in general.

At a stroke, objectivity gets the upper hand and the symmetry is broken. We said: "the point of departure" is contingent, indifferent; now we are saying: the first extreme is better. Parental arrangement—a particular case of objective beginnings—is better than singular inclination. Not absolutely, but from the ethical point of view: it is more ethical (*sittlich*), it is a better way, a more objective-moral way (*der sittlichere Weg*).

This breaking of symmetry is reacting to romanticism, to the so-called first "philosophy of love and life," to historical, literary, dramatic romanticism, dominated by the subjective principle and the value of infinite singularity.

The interest of the condemnation is that it accuses the cold and not the hot: romantic love, the lure of the false infinite, hides a deathly cold beneath the ardent discourse of passion. Those who say they love each other on the basis of the infinite singularity of subjectivity are only getting themselves worked up—they do not love each other. Their subjective infinite is not really infinite. The infinite in itself must also be objective and it is not satisfied with the secrecy of absolute singularity. "In the latter extreme, it is *infinitely particular* distinctness which asserts its claims; this is associated with the subjective principle of the modern world." This principle, foreign to the ancient world, proper to Christianity and Romanticism, rules over "*Moralität*" and shows up

wondering what lay hidden in the field. What if I crossed it? Were customs officers hidden in the rye? Invisible hares must have been running through it. I was uneasy. At noon, beneath a pure sky, all nature was offering me a puzzle, and offering it to me blandly.

'If something happens,' I said to myself, 'it will be the appearance of a unicorn. Such a moment and such a place can only produce a unicorn.'

Fear, and the kind of emotion I always feel when I cross a border, conjured up at noon, beneath a leaden sun, the first fairyland. I ventured forth into that golden sea as one enters the water. I went through the rye standing up. I advanced slowly, surely, with the certainty of being the heraldic character for whom a natural blazon has been formed: azure, field of gold, sun, forests. This imagery, of which I was a part, was complicated by the Polish imagery.

'In this noonday sky the white eagle should soar invisible!'"

enter the water, adore the mother's coat of arms. During the anthonomasia, earlier, of the broom [*genêt*], cryptonym of the mother: "I should like to descend" toward nether realms, marshes and algae

"When I got to the birches, I was in Poland. An enchantment of another order was about to be offered me. The 'Lady with the Unicorn' is to me the lofty expression of this crossing the line at noontide."

the eagle appears beneath a leaden sky. You'll have noticed that he always comes to swoop down (on you), fall upon you or float over you. It's a phallic sun, a lead coffin, heavy stiff excrement that

everywhere in historical modernity ("Political constitution," "History of art, history of sciences and philosophy"). Everywhere it imprints the mark of a reflection that is abstract and fixed in opposition. Whence the blandness and coldness of modern dramatic representation: stubborn falsification of the infinite, narcissistic assertion drawing all its force from what it negates or denies, that signifies itself with all the more apparent passion for not experiencing what it says and scarcely even pretending to believe in it. "But in those modern dramas and other artistic presentations in which love between the sexes is the basic interest, we encounter a pervasive element of frostiness (*das Element von durchdringender Frostigkeit*) which is brought into the heat of the passion such works portray . . ." What can be of "infinite importance" for passion is not at all important "in itself."

It follows from this demonstration that there is no infinite love without marriage, no marriage that does not proceed from parental objectivity, representing *Sittlichkeit,* law, universality, rational society, etc. No marriage that is not decided by parental authority, whatever the form of its intervention: crude or elegant, immediate or represented, brutal or cunning, conscious or unconscious.

How is this essential objectivity of marriage constituted? And since it is the first staging of *Sittlichkeit* in general, how does this latter get involved with it? How, according to what *act,* does it become *more than* the subjectivity of sentiment?

The reply is difficult: no value will here be accorded to contract. So it will be necessary to find a form of objectifying engagement that does not come down to the contractual type. Moreover, the speculative dialectic always takes the form of a general critique of the contract, or at least of contractual formality, of contract in the strict sense.

The contractual signature falls under abstract right, and only ever concerns one thing, the possession or disposal of a thing external to persons. Is the seal on the contract itself not in the end a thing, a remainder between persons, drawing its effectiveness from that status? But the union, the identification of the spouses forms one single person; and for the engagement of persons one toward another as such, without a third party and without a thing, no contract can intervene. There may well be "marriage contracts" bearing on goods, income, pensions, and other similar things (although the

There follows the "ghost of Vacher" who cut the throats of children. During the anthonomasia the ghost was that of Gilles de Rais, who screwed, murdered and burned them.

The flight of the eagle had been pre-elaborated by a whole gleaning of rye ("Its ideal line ran through a field of ripe rye. . . . the rye field was bounded. . . . hidden in the rye. . . . I went through the rye standing up," etc.). But it isn't the word "rye" that produces the superscript number for this footnote: "The first line of verse which to my amazement I found myself composing was the following: 'Harvester of stolen breath [*souffles coupés*].' I am reminded of it by what I have written above."

I forget, in a way, everything I write, no doubt

falls down and pushes into you from behind, just like, coming from higher up, Ganymede's eagle (or the angel Gabriel flying to make you pregnant from behind. He announced the birth not only of Jesus to Mary but also of John to Zacharias: "thy wife Elisabeth shall bear thee a son, and thou shalt call his name John" (Luke). That was John the Baptist, about whom some wondered whether it might not be Christ (his cousin, more or less) whom he baptized. Both, then, were announced by Gabriel but only one of them was imprisoned then decapitated: a wish that Herodias whispered to her little girl. "And he went and beheaded him in the prison, And brought his head in a charger, and gave it to the damsel: and the damsel gave it to the mother." Mark) Like the signifying material tombfalls

Philosophy of Right does not literally refer to them), but there is no *marriage* contract, no contract *of* marriage. Such a contract inspires horror. And for the one who thinks marriage under the category of contract, it's better to remain single: "*Marriage* cannot therefore be subsumed under the concept of contract; this subsumption—which can only be described as disgraceful—is proposed in Kant's *Metaphysical Elements of the Theory of Right.*" No contract once the formal and the concrete unite in speculative marriage: whence the immediately consequent condemnation of so-called Platonic marriage and monastic life which separate the sensory from the spiritual and the natural from the divine.

So then, failing a signed contract, what becomes of the objectifying engagement of marriage? The *Philosophy of Right* allows for there to be an act of language, the production of a sign, the existence of a sort of formal declaration. But such an attestation is not said to bind the two spouses the one to the other (between them, there could not be an objectifying sign, a seal or a legible contract), but to give rise to marriage for the community, for the rest of the family. The fact remains that only such a sign of attestation gives marriage its actuality, its ethical reality. From this (ethical) point of view, one is only ever *married*: one never marries (since this act does not take place for the two persons who make only one), but one is married by others, for others and in the element of language, the most spiritual of all the elements. What does not pass via others and language cannot be called marriage. In a purely dual relation, if such a thing existed, no marriage, not even a secret one, could find its place. But as monogamous marriage (without contract), the only one that can be admitted here, ought to be limited to the dual relation, marriage is in every case impossible. Or else it is possible only after the fact and never as an act.

"Just as the stipulation of a contract in itself contains the genuine transfer of property, so also do the solemn declaration (*feierliche Erklärung*) of consent to the ethical bond (*sittlichen Bande*) of marriage and its recognition and confirmation by the family and community constitute the formal (*förmliche*) *conclusion* and *actuality* of marriage. (That the *church* plays a part in this connection is a further determination which cannot be discussed here.) It is accordingly only after this ceremony has *first taken place,* as the completion of the *substantial* [aspect of marriage] by means of the *sign*—i.e. by means of language as the most

also, in a different way, what I read. Except for this or that sentence, or phrase, seemingly secondary, one whose seeming little importance does not in any case justify this sort of resonance, this obsessive echoing that keeps itself, detached, so long after the increasingly rapid engulfing of all the rest. That is where (coagulation of sense, form, rhythm) one must put one's finger on the compulsional matrix of writing, its organizing affect. I have never retained "by heart," in what I have written, anything more, more or less, than these few words on the basis of which I'm here probably falling for the genetic "first line" and certain others. Here they are: "the epigraph and the breathless recumbence of his discourse [*l'exergue et le gisant essouflé de son discours*]" and "as waiting block. And cornering as one may, by chance or recurrence, receive it from certain trademarks [*en pierre d'attente. Et d'angle comme on pourra, par chance ou recurrence, le recevoir de quelques marques déposées*]." Without a comma after cornering. The corner [*angle*] is always, for me, a tomb edge. And I hear this word, *angle*, its *gl*, in the back of my throat as what both cut and breathes in me all the rest.

I was forgetting. The first line that I published: "pond glue milk of my drowned death [*glu de l'étang lait de ma mort noyée*]."

Harvester of stolen breaths. The other, "sent from God," "whose name was John" had come to say "In the beginning was the Word."

spiritual existence of the spiritual (see § 78)—that this bond (*Verbindung*) has been ethically constituted. The sensuous moment which pertains to natural life is thereby put in its ethical context as an accidental consequence."

The linguistic sign, element of sublimating spiritualization, precisely sublates the sensory formality of the operation. In it the signifier is raised and fulfilled. If one confused marriage with the "external formality" of the declaration, one would understand nothing of its living spirituality. One would remain at the level of the sensory exterior which, as always, forms a system with formalism. To remain with the formality of the signature is to believe that marriage (or divorce) depends on it, to deny the ethics of love and return to animal sexuality. Now, in what does the ethics of love that satisfies no bourgeois or civil prescription (*bürgerliche Gebot*) consist?

It consists in "that higher suppression and subordination of mere natural drive (*die höhere Hemmung und Zurücksetzung des bloßen Naturtriebs*)." To hold fast to the contractual formality of the signifier is to allow oneself to be held back by instinct or give free—unrestricted—play to nature: the complicity of formalism and empiricism is confirmed again.

The essence of marriage appears in this active and sublimating inhibition which raises while abasing, which goes without the impulse, exercises on it a downward pressure to allow the higher to burst through: but by the same token, because marriage ensures entry into *Sittlichkeit*, this same movement of restriction produces ethical objectivity in general, its truth as objectivity. The emergence of the object in its truth here presupposes that the natural impulse be compressed, tightly held in strict bonds, dissimulated, violently veiled under these impediments.

Where does this truth (the violent imposition of the veil) appear in quasi-originary fashion?

In shame [*pudeur*]. The truth (of marriage) is shame. No accident, its being named here. The spiritual is produced under the veil that forbids one to appear naked. Shame (*Scham*), chastity (*Keuschheit* or *Zucht*), the truth of sex, finds its destination in marriage. More precisely, shame, which is *still natural*, is spiritually fulfilled in the conjugal bond. "Although such an opinion [*Meinung*—formalist, contractualist, naturalist] claims to impart the highest conception of the freedom, inwardness, and perfection of love, it in fact denies [or disavows: *leugnet*] the ethical character (*Sittliche*) of love, that higher suppression and subordination of

He shows up to sound the knell of the breath, to cu

after developing the radiographic negative of testamentary chrisms and wrappings [*bandelettes*] (why anointing and binding in the two testaments?), after getting seriously into, analyzing the relics, having them reveal their colors in a sort of reactive bath, why not look into them for John's remains? The Gospel and Apocalypse violently broken up, fragmented, redistributed, with blanks, displaced accents, lines jumped or out of order, as though they were coming to us across a faulty teleprinter, a wiretap in an extra busy telephone exchange: "The light shineth in the darkness; and the darkness comprehended it not. . . . glory as of the only begotten son of the Father, full of grace and truth. John bare witness of him, and cried, saying, This was he of whom I spake, He that cometh after me is preferred before me: for he was before me. . . . The world is turned inside out like a glove. It happens that I am the glove, and that I finally realize that on Judgment day it will be with my own voice that God will call me: 'Jean, Jean!' . . . And they which were sent were of the Pharisees. And they asked him, and said unto him, Why baptizest thou then, if thou be not that Christ, nor Elias, nor that prophet? John answered them, saying, I baptize with water, but there standeth one among you, whom ye know not; He it is, who coming after me is preferred before me, whose shoe's latchet I am not worthy to unloose. . . . After me cometh a man which is preferred before me: for he was before me. . . . How can a man be born when he is old? can he enter the second time into his mother's womb, and be born? . . . The Son can do nothing of himself, but what he seeth the Father do. . . . For as the Father raiseth up the dead, and quickeneth them; even so the Son quickeneth whom he will. . . . Ye sent unto John, and he bare witness unto the truth. . . . He was a burning and a shining light: and ye were willing for a season to rejoice in his light. But I have greater witness than that of John. . . . Search the scriptures; for in them ye think ye have eternal life: and they are they which testify of me. And ye will not come to me, that ye might have life. . . . And when they were filled, he said unto his disciples, Gather up the fragments that remain, that nothing be lost. . . . as the scripture hath said, out of his belly shall flow rivers of living water. . . . Art thou also of Galilee? Search, and look: for out of Galilee ariseth no prophet. . . . We be not born of fornication; we have one father . . . . Jesus made clay, and

mere natural drive which is already naturally present in *shame* and which the more determinate spiritual consciousness raises to *chastity* and *decency.*"

An addition opposes this conjugal bond to "concubinage" which "is chiefly concerned with the satisfaction of the natural drive, whereas this drive is repressed (*zurückgedrängt*) within marriage."

Conjugal "repression" gives access to a chastity that was only announced in nature. That is the semantic content of a statement that still remains to be modalized, valorized. That things *happen this way*, or rather *must* happen this way, does not yet allow one to decide if it is good or bad, if they *must*, in the sense of (motor, efficient, material) constraint or of teleological necessity, or of moral prescription. In short, can one ask whether repression is good or bad? Or else is there between repression and value-opposition a link that renders derisory in advance any question about the *value* of repression? *A fortiori* a whole modern preaching that mounts the pulpit to condemn repression (or else to reduce it verbally to a mythology) with as much theoretical inanity as edifying blandness?

"Repression: that's bad." Who's talking about what?

Hegel also condemns "repression": in the name of the freedom of spiritual consciousness, etc. But—for the same reason—he prescribes the "repression" of animal drives, which makes possible spiritual liberation, etc. One repression for another, a restriction for an erection, press down on one side so it goes up on the other. Repression—here sublation—is not on one side or the other, to left or right: it "is" the relation between the two accounts, the two registers, the two operations of this economy.

The philosopher of *Sa* is teaching morality here, of course, which obliges him to take repression most rigorously into account. But can one not regularly transform the at least apparently prescriptive mode of his discourse into a descriptive mode? And if this possibility offers itself regularly, does it not belong to the very structure of the text? When Hegel says that marriage is not limited to signifying formality and therefore to sensory nature, that it rises by accomplishing the repression of the natural drive, when he points out the link between elevation, spirit, objective morality, objectivity, etc., on the one hand, and the repression or inhibition of natural drives on the other, is he

anointed mine eyes. . . . I am the door: by me if any man enter in, he shall be saved. . . . It was that Mary which anointed the Lord with ointment, and wiped his feet with her hair. . . . And he that was dead came forth, bound hand and foot with graveclothes; and his face was bound about with a napkin. . . . Then Jesus six days before the Passover came to Bethany, where was Lazarus which had been dead, whom he raised from the dead. There they made him a supper; and Martha served: but Lazarus was one of them that sat at the table with him. Then took Mary a pound of ointment of spikenard, very costly, anointed the feet of Jesus, and wiped his feet with her hair: and the house was filled with the odour of the ointment. Then saith one of his disciples, Judas Iscariot, Simon's son, who should betray him, Why was not this ointment sold for three hundred pence, and given to the poor? This he said, not that he cared for the poor; but because he was a thief, and had the bag, and bare what was put therein. Then said Jesus, Let her alone: against the day of my burying hath she kept this. . . . Now there was leaning on Jesus's bosom one of his disciples, whom Jesus loved. . . . He then lying on Jesus' breast saith unto him, Lord, who is it? Jesus answered, he it is, to whom I shall give a sop, when I have dipped it. And when he had dipped the sop, he gave it to Judas Iscariot. . . . Pilate saith unto him, What is truth? . . . Pilate answered, What I have written I have written. . . . Then they took the body of Jesus, and wound it in linen clothes [*bandelettes*] with the spices, as the manner of the Jews is to bury. . . . The first day of the week cometh Mary Magdalene early . . . and seeth the stone taken away from the sepulcher. . . . And [Peter] stooping down, and looking in, saw the linen clothes lying; yet went he not in. Then cometh Simon Peter following him, and went into the sepulcher, and seeth the linen clothes lie. And the napkin, that was about his head, not lying with the linen clothes, but wrapped together in a place by itself. . . . For as yet they knew not the scripture, that he must rise again from the dead. . . . As soon as they were come to land, they saw a fire of coals there, and fish laid thereon, and bread. Jesus saith unto them, Bring of the fish which ye have now caught. . . . I am Alpha and Omega . . . What thou seest, write in a book. . . . Write the things which thou hast seen, and the things which are, and the things which shall be hereafter. . . . we will fight against them with the sword of my mouth. . . . To him that overcometh will I give to eat of the hidden manna, and I will give him a white stone, and in the stone a new name written, which no man knoweth saving he that receiveth it. . . . Who is worthy to open the book, and to loose the seals thereof? . . . And the heaven departed as a scroll when it is rolled together. . . . There are mornings when all men experience with fatigue a flush of tenderness

prescribing or is he describing? Is he content to say *how it is* (because *well, that's how it happens* and has always happened?). Or else is he implying that *it is well that that is how it happens*?

We are dealing with a norm, a prescription. But what is it to describe a norm, a prescription? A simple play of quotation marks can transform a prescriptive statement into a descriptive statement; and the mere textuality of a statement makes possible a placing in quotation marks. Given this, taking writing rigorously into account can cause the oppositions accepted up until now to vacillate—for example between prescription and description. One will always be able to treat a discourse that is metaphysical (or develops metaphysics) as though it were content to describe metaphysics, its norms and its effects. It would be easy to show that with classical (ontological and constative) philosophical statements; it suffices, to complete the demonstration, to take into account the difficulties into which citationality, quotation marks and the signature put the theory of the performative.

"*You must*" rise-repress-sublimate, accede to chastity in marriage. To understand this proposition [*which says that you must*—] is to think according to the speculative dialectic, simultaneously sublate the sensibility and the understanding which are equally shameless. So one can think the tauto-heterological proposition of the speculative dialectic only in marriage. And only in Christian-monogamous marriage. One can and one must. ". . . consciousness emerges from its naturalness and subjectivity to concentrate on the thought of the substantial. Instead of further reserving to itself the contingency and arbitrariness of sensuous inclination, it removes the marriage bond from this arbitrariness and, pledging itself to the Penates, makes it over to the substantial; it thereby reduces the sensuous moment to a merely *conditional* one—conditioned, that is, by the true and ethical character of the relationship, and by the recognition of the marriage bond as an ethical one. It is impertinence and its ally, the understanding, which cannot grasp the speculative nature of the substantial relationship; but both the uncorrupted ethical emotions and the legislations of Christian peoples are in keeping with this speculative nature."

When it "leaves its naturality," monogamous conjugal consciousness escapes indecency; which might make one think that indecency is natural and that it suffices to leave nature to cover it up. And yet indecency presupposes the understanding, the formal relation to the concept and to the law. It is not only sensory, natural, inferior, an object baser than another; its baseness is the object of an interdiction, a

that gives them a hard-on. One day at dawn I found myself placing my lips lovingly, though for no reason at all, on the icy banister of the Rue Berthe; another time, kissing my hand; still another time, bursting with emotion, I wanted to swallow myself by opening my mouth very wide and turning it over my head so that it would take in my whole body, and then the Universe, until all that would remain of me would be a ball of eaten thing which little by little would be annihilated: that is how I see the end of the world. . . . And I John saw these things and heard them." As his name indicates: the apocalyptic, in other words the capital unveiling reveals in naked truth hunger for the self. In *Funeral Rites,* remember, within the space of a page: "Jean was taken away from me. . . . Jean needed a compensation. . . . the inner revelation of my friendship for Jean. . . . I was hungry for Jean." That is what's called a colossal compensation. Absolute phantasm of having oneself knowing absolutely [*s'avoir absolu*] in one's most mourned glory: engulfing oneself so as to be at-home-with-oneself, making a mouthful of oneself, being-becoming (in a word hardbinding) one's own bit

t, reap, glean every exhalation. Then to bind them, in the middle of a song, as bouquet, sheaf [*gerbe*]. Sheaf is always used for something that has been cut.

He is in any case amazed to have formed this line. He perhaps invented it to put it there but its necessity would only be all the more confirmed.

The rare force of the text comes from your not being able to catch it by surprise (and so limit it to) saying *this is that*, or, what comes down to the same thing, this has a relation of apophantic or apocalyptic unveiling, a determinable semiotic or rhetorical relation to that, this is the subject, this isn't the subject, this is the same, this is

repression whose counter-force (of law) does not have the form of a distance taken from nature, of a mere rising above animality in the ontological hierarchy, of a negativity homogeneous with all the other forms of negativity. But nothing is ever homogeneous in the different breaks, stances or leaps of the speculative dialectic. Is this heterogeneity of the interdiction heterogeneous with respect to the *general* (and therefore homogeneous) heterogeneity of the ontological system? Can one ever speak of a *general heterogeneity*? Does the repression that forbids merely introduce an extra inflection [*flexion*] in heterogeneity (a reflection of alterity)? Or else a heterogeneity that no longer allows itself to be internalized in a reflection?

The concept of general heterogeneity being as *impossible* as its opposite, such a question cannot be *posed*. The posing of the question is the cancellation of the question.

The *text* (of "Hegel") is offered, open, to both responses, both interpretations. It is text, or rather textualizes itself to the extent that it gives purchase and gives weight to both readings, i.e. lets itself be struck with indeterminacy by the impossible concept, divides in two.

The paragraph concerning the prohibition of incest is both the example of this and its hinge. The example and the hinge of the system. It is contradictory in itself, with a contradiction of which one cannot say whether it operates *within* or *against*. The "opposition" plays twice over, and with it every conceptual determination. An index: the prohibition of incest breaks with nature and *this is why* it is more in conformity with nature. What appears as formal incoherence, denegation or "rationalization" denounces at the same time, critically, but unbeknownst to it, the absence of a concept of nature, reason or freedom, and posits, but unbeknownst to itself, the necessity of accounting for the "obscure feelings." Thus: "Furthermore, since marriage arises out of the *free surrender* by both sexes of their personalities, which are infinitely unique to themselves, it must not be concluded within the *naturally identical* circle of people who are acquainted and familiar with each other in every detail—a circle in which the individuals do not have a distinct personality of their own in relation to one another—but must take place [between people] from separate families and personalities of different origin (*ursprünglich verschiedener*). Marriage between *blood relations* is therefore at variance with the concept of marriage as an ethical act of freedom rather than an association (*Verbindung*) based on immediate natural existence and its

the other, this text, this corpus here. It is always a question of still something other. A rare force. At the outside, none. One should say the power [*puissance*] of the text. In the way that one would speak of the musculature of a tongue. But also of a mathematical development. But also of the enveloping of what remains as potential [*en puissance*]. At the outside, none. Non-existing because it remains infinitely potential. To be condemned to potential and to remain there.

What I wanted to write is POTENCE of the text.

I'm exposing myself there, I lean that way a lot.

Anyway, the scene will end badly. He is going to hold a murderous grudge against me, I know from experience the law of this process. He'll hold a murderous grudge against me for all sorts of reasons that I won't undertake to enumerate. And in every case. If I support or valorize his text, he'll find in that a type of approbation, even a masterly, academic, paternal or maternal appropriation. It's as

drives, and hence it is also at variance with genuine natural feeling (*somit auch wahrhafter natürlicher Empfindung zuwider*).

If marriage itself is regarded as an arbitrary contract and as grounded not in natural law but merely in the natural sexual drive, and if external reasons for monogamy have been derived even from the physical relation between numbers of men and women, and obscure feelings (*dunkle Gefühle*) have been cited as the only reason for prohibiting marriage between blood relations, such arguments are based on the common notion of a state of nature and of the naturalness of right, and on the absence of the concept of rationality and freedom."

Dialectic of nature: it produces the incest prohibition by breaking with itself but this break with itself is in its nature, in the nature of nature. Formally, this gives an argumentation in kettle form: one must interrupt conaturality and forbid incest [here it's essentially about brother and sister; a note to the same paragraph says that the brother/sister relation is a-sexual (*geschlechtloses*)] *and* that prohibition is in nature. Whence in the note the empirico-genetic argumentation grounding shame in nature and alleging the notorious weakness or fragility of the offspring of consanginous marriages: "it is well known that reproduction within a family of animals produces more feeble offspring."

Interdiction and prohibition are thus supposed to be

in the margin of the speculative remark—this is also the place of Kierkegaard and of what falls to one side, after the fact, in the *Post-Scriptum to the Philosophical Fragments*: "Does explaining something mean to *annul* it? I do know that the word *aufheben* has various, indeed opposite, meanings in the German language. It has often been noted that the word can mean both *tollere* [annul, annihilate] and *conservare* [preserve]. I am not aware that the Danish word *ophæve* [annul] allows any such equivocation, but I do know that our German-Danish philosophers use it like the German word. Whether it is a good quality in a word to have opposite meanings, I do not know, but anyone who wants to express himself with precision usually avoids the use of such a word in decisive places. There is a simple folk saying that humorously denotes the impossible: to have one's mouth full of crackers and to whistle at the same time. Speculative thought accomplishes a tour de force somewhat like that by using a word that also denotes the very opposite. In order to denote very clearly that speculation knows nothing of any decision, it itself uses an ambiguous word in order

if I were stealing his erection. His death: "And the picture showing the execution of a convict in Cayenne made me say: 'He stole my death'" (*Miracle of the Rose*). And if, what is more, I exposit like a professor the Greater Logic of this operation I only make things worse. If I didn't valorize, didn't "magnify" his knell (but what have I done at the end of the day?), the ringer would give even less of a shit. Anyway, the signatory reminded Roger Blin about a mislaid letter in which he confided that his books and plays were written against himself. But he adds: "And if I do not succeed in exposing myself through the text alone, then you have to help me. Against myself." Elsewhere, that his actors had to show him, himself, naked. So I am in any case judged and condemned, that's what he was always trying to do: if I write for his text, I write against him, if I write for him, I write against his text. That friendship is irreconcilable.

Anyway he'll throw it all up at me, he won't read it, won't be able to read it.

Am I really writing *for him*? What would I like to do to him? do to his "work?" Ruin it by erecting it, perhaps.

to denote the kind of understanding that is speculative understanding. Upon closer inspection, the confusion becomes more evident. *Aufheben* in the sense of *tollere* means to annihilate; in the sense of *conservare*, it means to preserve (*bevare*) in altogether unaltered condition, to do nothing at all to what is being preserved. If the government dissolves (*ophæve*) a political society, it abolishes it; if a man keeps or preserves something for me, it is of particular importance to me that he make no change whatever in it. Neither of these meanings is the philosophical *aufheben*. So speculation annuls (*aufhebt*) all difficulty and then leaves me with the difficulty of understanding just what it is doing with this *aufheben*. But now let this *aufheben* mean reducing something to a relative factor, which it does mean when what is decisive, the paradox, is reduced to a relative factor, which means that there is no paradox, no decision, since the paradox and the decisive are what they are just because of their unyielding resistance. Whether speculative thought is in the right is a different question . . ."]

thinkable—as effects of sublation. The *Aufhebung* is supposed to dominate this process.

And what if *Aufhebung* were a Christian mother?

Writing now: "complete lack of awareness about the seemingly *formal*, but really *vital* question: how do we now stand as regards the Hegelian *dialectic*?" Or again: "critical settling of accounts with the mother . . . the Hegelian dialectic," we appear to be brusquely opening the archive of a problem in a very particular place. The third of the *Manuscripts of 1844* reproaches the German criticism of Hegel with allowing itself to be foreseen, caught up, informed by the very logic it claims to be criticizing. This is said to be the case with Bruno Bauer's *Das entdeckte Christentum*. The critique (of a logic) that reproduces in itself (the logic of) what it is criticizing will always be—don't forget this lesson—an idealist antic. "After all these delightful antics of moribund idealism in the guise of criticism (i.e., of Young-Hegelianism)—even now it has not expressed the suspicion that the time was ripe for a critical settling of accounts with the mother of Young-Hegelianism—the Hegelian dialectic—and even had [nothing] to say about its critical attitude towards the Feuerbachian dialectic."

At that date, Feuerbach was considered to be the only "serious" critic of the Hegelian dialectic, "the true conqueror of the old philosophy." Precisely because he attacked what the *Aufhebung* permitted: the profound identity, thanks to the play of the *already* and the *not-yet*, of representation and presence, of the future perfect of truth, between true religion and speculative philosophy.

So that it is longer read? so that it is read only on this basis, from the moment that I consign and countersign it?

But he himself? he himself wanted to calculate ruin. "And the ruin! I almost forgot the ruin. The ruin of the teeth cultivated with Warda's needle, and the total shambles of the play itself. I mean it: when the public leaves the theater I want them to carry the well-known taste of ashes and an odor of decay in their mouths. And yet I want the play to have the consistency of flint [*silex*], not of a scooter [*solex*]."

He is impregnable because he doublehardbinds: for galalith against natural milk but for nature against fakery.

there are always moreover of what is leftover [*il y a toujours du reste*] two overlapping functions. The word hardbinds double: transitively and intransitively, nominally and verbally. In every gender. Remains always a more or less cavalier bit

Mourning milk.

His tombfalling [*sa tombe*], he loves only that.

"Feuerbach's great achievement is: (1) The proof that philosophy is nothing else but religion rendered into thoughts and thinkingly expounded, and that it has therefore likewise to be condemned as another form and manner of existence of the estrangement of the essence of man." And indeed, Feuerbach: "*Speculative philosophy* is the *rational* or *theoretical* elaboration and dissolution of the God that, for religion, is other-worldly and nonobjective. . . . The *essence* of speculative philosophy is nothing other than the *rationalized, realized, actualized essence of God.* Speculative philosophy is the *true, consistent, rational* theology."

Marx goes on to exposit Feuerbach's critical movement in its most effective instance: putting into question the *Aufhebung* and the negation of the negation. The absolutely positive, the critique of religion or of the Holy Family must not pass via the negation of the negation, via Hegelian *Aufhebung,* supposing there is any other. The speculative unity, the age-old complicity of philosophy and religion—the former being the truth and essence of the latter, the latter the representation of the former—their homogeneity or their homology, is the process of sublation. Feuerbach was able to oppose "the negation of the negation from the point of view of the positive relation inherent in it as the true and only positive." The Third Manuscript continues: "Feuerbach explains the Hegelian dialectic (and thereby justifies starting out from the positive, from sense-certainty) as follows:

Hegel sets out from the alienation of Substance (in Logic, from the Infinite, the abstractly universal)—from the absolute and fixed abstraction; which means, put popularly, that he sets out from religion and theology.

Secondly, he sublates the infinite, and establishes the actual, sensuous, real, finite, particular (philosophy—sublation of religion and theology).

Thirdly, he again sublates the positive and restores the abstraction, the infinite—Restoration of religion and theology.

Feuerbach thus conceives the negation of the negation only as a contradiction of philosophy with itself—as the philosophy which affirms theology (the transcendent, etc.) after having denied it, and which it therefore affirms in opposition to itself.

The position or self-affirmation and self-confirmation contained in the negation of the negation is taken to be a position which is not yet sure of itself which is therefore

For it to fall [*que ça tombe*] into ruins

he loves what is fake [*le toc*], but not just any kind, a thingamajig, but whose lack of value, defying economics, is priceless, the most naturally in the world. That goes for literature, the *ersatz* in literature. Worst is best, but don't be mistaken, the worst is not the least good. The best, don't be mistaken. You have to really know your fake.

Is what I am writing a sort of popular novel? He says that he likes that: "I continue my reading of cheap novels. It satisfies my love of hoodlums dressed up as gentlemen. Also my taste for imposture, my taste for the sham [*le toc*], which could very well make me write on my visiting cards: 'Jean Genet, bogus Count of Tillancourt.' . . . I read these works which are idiotic to the sense of reason, but my reason is not concerned with a book from which poisoned, feathered phrases swoop down on me. The hand that launches them sketches, as it nails them somewhere, the dim outline of a Jean who recognizes himself, dares not move, awaiting the one that, aimed at his heart in earnest, will leave him panting. I am madly in love (as I love prison) with that close print, compact as a pile of rubbish, crammed with acts as bloody as linens, as the fetuses of dead cats, and I do not know whether it is stiffly erect pricks which are transformed into tough knights or knights into vertical pricks." (*Our Lady of the Flowers*)

but like a stone, a flint stone, a silex, even an unscratchable diamond. For it to fall into dust but like a gravestone, so natural that it is recomposed in the very earth, and still harder. He petrifies himself [*se méduse lui-même*].

burdened with its opposite, which is doubtful of itself and therefore in need of proof. . . .

Let us take a look at the Hegelian system. One must begin with Hegel's *Phenomenology*, the true point of origin and the secret of the Hegelian philosophy."

Just as the positive "doubts," needs to be sure of the contrary with which it affects itself, so the young Hegelians need their "mother," Hegelian logic; they stand in a "lack of awareness about the relationship of modern criticism to the Hegelian philosophy as a whole and especially to the Hegelian dialectic."

Hegelian dialectic, mother of critique, is first of all, like all mothers, a daughter: of Christianity, in any case of Christian theology. It ceaselessly comes back to it as to its *lap*. *Aufhebung* is a Christian daughter-mother [*fille-mère,*

"God is God only through the fact that he overcomes and negates matter; that is, the negation of God. And according to Hegel, it is only the negation of the negation that constitutes the true positing. And so in the end, we are back to whence we had started—in the lap of Christian theology. Thus, already in the most central principle of Hegel's philosophy we come across the principle and result of his philosophy of religion to the effect that philosophy, far from abolishing the dogmas of theology, only restores and mediates them through the negation of rationalism. The secret of Hegel's dialectic lies ultimately in this alone, that it negates theology through philosophy in order then to negate philosophy through theology. Both the beginning and the end are constituted by theology; philosophy stands in the middle as the negation of the first positedness, but the negation of the negation is again theology. At first everything is overthrown, but then everything is reinstated in its old place, as in Descartes. The Hegelian philosophy is the last grand attempt to restore a lost and defunct Christianity through philosophy, and, of course, as is characteristic of the modern era, by *identifying* the *negation* of Christianity *with Christianity itself*. The much-extolled speculative identity of spirit and matter, of the infinite and the finite, of the divine and the human is nothing more than the wretched contradiction of the modern era having reached its zenith in metaphysics. It is the identity of belief and unbelief, theology and philosophy, religion and atheism, Christianity and paganism. This contradiction escapes the eye and is obfuscated in Hegel only through the fact that the negation of God, or atheism, is turned by him into an objective *(objectiven)* determination of God; God is determined as a process, and atheism as a moment within this process. But a belief that has been reconstructed out of unbelief is as little true belief—because it is always afflicted with its contrary—as the God who has been reconstructed out of his negation is a true God; he is rather a self-contradictory, an atheistic God."

How can one petrify oneself? It must be understood that *he* isn't *himself* before petrifying himself. He comes to himself on the basis of petrification [*depuis la méduse*]. Being oneself is being petrified and consequently being-petrified constitutes itself, that is to say defends itself, makes itself hard, and is elaborated only by being petrified by itself, eating-petrifying itself, making of itself a bit that lets go of itself. Sure of itself. No *logic* is more powerful than that apotropics. No absolutely general economy, no pure exposure or expenditure: a more or less firm stricture.

His petrification [*sa méduse*], always.

Bite of self.

"Thus lifted, raised, with body erect, he reaches the bench of the accused, facing a special court clad in scarlet, which is the blood that has been shed, the blood in person, demanding vengeance and getting it. It is perhaps this gift of producing a miracle by a mere stab of the knife that astonishes the mob, alarms it, rouses it and makes it jealous of such glory. The murderer makes blood speak. He argues with it, tries to compound with the miracle. The murderer creates the Criminal Court and its machinery. In view of this, one thinks of the birth of Chrysaor and Pegasus, who sprang from the blood of Medusa."

"Because guards don't make a move when a deadly battle rages, you think they're brutes and you're right. I like to think they were petrified [*médusés*] by a wrathful spectacle, the grandeur of which was beyond them. What was their petty existence compared to the radiant life of the children? For

unmarried mother]. Or else: the daughter-mother, the Holy Christian mother is called *Aufhebung*. She—sublation—is the contradiction and the satisfaction of Christian desire or what the *Third Manuscript* calls "critical Christ": desire for maternity *and* virginity. *The Essence of Christianity* establishes an equivalence between the categories of miracle, imagination and sublation. The transformation of water into wine, of wine into blood, transubstantiation, the resurrection especially are operations of *Aufhebung*: what is destroyed is preserved, what dies can be reborn. Admirable and miraculous, *Aufhebung* is the productive imagination. In the same way the dogma of the Virgin Mary has its contradiction lifted or washed away [*lever ou laver*] by an *Aufhebung* that suspends what it keeps or regards what it lifts. "Here we have the key to the contradiction in Catholicism, that at the same

"But as the Resurrection, which terminates the sacred history—a history (*Geschichte*) that does not have the signification of a mere recounted history (*Historie*), but of the truth itself—is a realised wish, so also is that which commences it, namely, the supernatural birth, though this has relation not so much to an immediately personal interest as to a particular subjective feeling (*Gefühl*).

The more man alienates himself from Nature (*sich der Natur entfremdet*), the more subjective, i.e., supernatural or antinatural, is his view (*Anschauung*) of things, the greater the horror he has of Nature, or at least of those natural things and processes which displease his imagination, which affect him disagreeably. The free, objective man doubtless finds things repugnant and distasteful in Nature, but he regards them as natural, inevitable results, and under this conviction he overcomes his feeling as a merely subjective and untrue one. On the contrary, the subjective man, who lives fixed only in the feelings and imagination, regards these things with a quite peculiar aversion. He has the eye of that unhappy foundling, who even in looking at the loveliest flower could pay attention only to the little 'black beetle' which crawled over it, and who by this perversity of perception had his enjoyment in the sight of flowers always embittered. Moreover, the subjective man makes his feelings the measure, the standard of what *ought to be*. That which does not please him, which offends his transcendental, supernatural, or antinatural feelings, ought *not to be*. Even if that which pleases him cannot exist without being associated with that which displeases him, the subjective man is not guided by the wearisome laws of logic and physics, but by the self-will of the imagination; hence he drops what is disagreeable in a fact, and holds fast alone what is agreeable. Thus the idea of the pure, unpolluted Virgin pleases him; still he is also pleased with the idea of the Mother, but only of the Mother who suffers no inconveniences, who already carries the infant on her arms.

Stone, stele, recumbent statue, patently agglomerated concretion: I am my mother's stone [*calcul*].

I counterhardbind for her with the smuggled remainder I make myself a gift (of) [*Je contrebande pour elle du reste dont je me fais cadeau*].

I don't know whether I have tried to understand him. But if he were to think that I had understood him, he wouldn't tolerate it, or rather he would like not to tolerate it. What a scene. He wouldn't tolerate what he, himself, likes to do. He would already feel hoodwinked. Like a column, in a cemetery, eaten by ivy, a parasite arriving too late.

I have introduced myself as third party, between his mother and him. I have given him up. I've made blood speak.

Not interested. I am not however going to take his mother from him, or teach her to him, and the rest.

I am looking for the right metaphor for the enterprise I am pursuing here. I'd like to describe my gesture, the posture of my body behind this machine.

the colonists were all noble, even the jerks, since they were of the sacred race, if not of the sacred caste." Separation [*écart*] of race, trace of separation [*trace d'écart*], interminable caste struggle, it's a case of reading, the castrated one [*la castrée*] (is—hardbinds—tombfalls) in the bag [*sac*]. To be "petrified" in front of "pants," a belt, or fly: that scene is reinforced in the *Journal*, the word "fascinated" also; and in *Funeral Rites*, which again names Medusa and her son Chrysaor, he of the golden sword who, along with his brother Pegasus, the winged horse, came out of the neck of the Gorgon at the moment when Perseus sliced off her head. He was born brandishing his weapon

In the inmost essence of his spirit, his belief, Virginity is in and for (it)self his highest moral concept, the *cornu copiae* of his supranaturalistic feelings and ideas, his personified sense of honour and of shame before common nature. Nevertheless, there stirs in his bosom a *natural* feeling also, the compassionate feeling of maternal love. What then is to be done in this difficulty of the heart, in this conflict (*Zwiespalt*) between a natural and a supernatural or antinatural feeling? The supranaturalist must unite (*verbinden*) the two, must comprise in one and the same subject two properties which exclude each other. Oh, what a plenitude of agreeable, sweet, supersensual, sensual emotions lies in this combination!

Here we have the key to the contradiction in Catholicism, that at the same time marriage is holy and celibacy is holy. This simply realises, as a *practical contradiction,* the *dogmatic contradiction* of the *virgin Mother* or the mother Virgin. But this wondrous union of virginity and maternity, contradicting Nature and reason, but in the highest degree accordant with the feelings and imagination, is no product of Catholicism; it lies already in the twofold part which marriage plays in the Bible, especially in the view of the Apostle Paul. The supernatural conception of Christ is an essential doctrine of Christianity, a doctrine which expresses its inmost dogmatic essence, and which rests on the same foundation as all other miracles and articles of faith. As death, which the philosopher, the man of science (*Naturforscher*), the free objective thinker in general, accepts as a natural necessity, and as indeed all the limits of nature, which are impediments to feeling, but to reason are rational laws, were repugnant to the Christians, and were set aside by them through the supposed agency of miraculous power; so, necessarily, they had an equal repugnance to the natural process of generation, and relieved [*aufheben* came to correct *negieren* in a third version] it by miracle. The supernatural birth is not less welcome than the Resurrection to all, namely, to all believers; for the conception of Mary, not polluted by male sperm, which constitutes the contagium [contagious poison, *ansteckende Gift*] peculiar to original sin, was the first act of purification of mankind, soiled by sin, i.e., by Nature. Only because the God-man was not infected with original sin, could he, the pure one, purify mankind in the eyes of God, to whom the natural process of generation was an abomination, because he himself is nothing else but *supernatural feeling* (Gemüt).

Even the arid Protestant orthodoxy, so arbitrary in its criticism, regarded the conception or the God-producing Virgin as a great, adorable, amazing, holy mystery or faith, transcending reason. But with the Protestants, who reduced and limited the speciality of the Christian to the domain of faith, and with whom, in life, it was allowable to be a man, even this mystery had only a *dogmatic, and no longer a practical significance*; they did not allow it to interfere with their desire of marriage. With the Catholics, and with all the old, uncompromising, uncritical Christians, that which was a mystery of *faith* was a *mystery of life, of morality.* Catholic morality

What he would have the most difficulty tolerating would be my assuring myself or others of mastery over his text. By procuring—they say—the rule of production or the generative grammar of all his utterances.

No risk of that. We are a long way away from that; this, I repeat, is barely preliminary, and will remain that way. No more names. One has to return to his text, which oversees this one as it plays out.

I am therefore looking for the right movement. Have I constructed something like the matrix of his text? On the basis of which one could read it, that is to say re-produce it?

No, I see instead (although it's still perhaps a matrix or grammar) a sort of dredging machine [*machine à draguer*]. From inside my hidden, enclosed, little glass crane's cabin, I manipulate the levers and from a distance—as I saw done at Les Saintes-Maries-de-la-Mer at Easter—I plunge a steel mouth into the water. And then I scrape the bottom, picking up stones and weed that I bring back up to drop on the earth while the water rapidly drains from the bucket.

And I start over, scraping, rasping, dredging the bottom of the sea.

I can hardly hear the sound of the water from inside my little enclosure.

The *matrix dentata* [*matrice dentée*] pulls out only what it can: seaweed, stones. Pieces, because it bites. Detached ones. But what is left [*le reste*] drains through its teeth, between its lips. The sea can't be taken. It reforms always.

It remains. There, equal, calm. Intact, impassive, still virgin.

But then I'm not going to surprise his text

> is Christian, mystical; Protestant morality was already, in its very beginning, *rationalistic*. Protestant morality is and was a carnal mingling of the Christian with the man, the natural, political, civil, social man, or whatever else he may be called in distinction from the Christian; Catholic morality cherished in its heart the mystery of the unpolluted virginity. Catholic morality was the *Mater dolorosa;* Protestant morality a comely matron blessed with children. . . . Just because the mystery of the *Virgo Deipara* had with the Protestants a place only in theory, or rather in dogma, but no longer in life [first edition: praxis], they declared that it was impossible to express oneself with sufficient care and reserve concerning it, and that it ought not to be made an object of speculation. That which is denied [*negiert*, then *verneint*] in practice has no true basis and durability in man, is a mere spectre of imagination; and hence it is hidden, withdrawn from the understanding. Ghosts do not brook daylight.
> Even the later doctrine (which, however, had been already enunciated in a letter to St. Bernard, who rejects it), that Mary herself was conceived without taint of original sin, is by no means a *'strange school-bred doctrine,'* as it is called by a modern historian. It comes much more from a natural consequence and a pious, thankful attitude toward the mother of God. That which gives birth to a miracle, which brings forth God, must itself be of miraculous divine origin and essence. How could Mary have had the honour of being overshadowed by the Holy Spirit if she had not been from the first pure? Could the Holy Spirit take up his abode in a body soiled by original sin! If the principle of Christianity, the holy and miraculous birth of the Saviour, does not appear strange to you, do not think strange the naive, simplistic, well-meaning inferences of Catholicism!"

time marriage is holy and celibacy is holy. This simply realizes, as a *practical contradiction*, the *dogmatic contradiction* of the *virgin Mother* or the mother Virgin."

The *Theses on Feuerbach* and *The German Ideology* criticize the philosophy of religion and the "intuitive" or sensualist materialism of Feuerbach who "does not conceive sensuousness as practical activity." The Fourth Thesis delimits Feuerbach's critique of religion as mere theoretical critique. A theoretical critique leaves its object in place, touches neither the terrain nor the structure whose elements it combines. In making of religion the alienated essence of man, in bringing the religious world down to the terrestrial world one changes nothing in the latter, in the anthropological basis of the critique, in the human family alienated—specularly—in the Holy Family. The operation remains speculative, it retains an old concept of family and religion. The internal structure

with a matrix dentata. He writes, describes only that: matrix dentata. It is *his* object.

Can an object include what it is the object of, that is the question that was posed at Les Saintes-Maries-de-la-Mer at Easter. The remains of the Rembrandt was no doubt ready to reply—oh yes—to that question.

Yes, by virtue of the stricture that interests and constrains us, the transcendental matrix always lets fall the remainder of the text.

He petrifies himself. Well played. He is said to be, known to be generous, detached, spendthrift. He keeps nothing with him. Neither goods, nor works, especially not. But they already have their depository for perpetuity in all national and international libraries, across worldwide theatrality, the contract is signed, author's royalties are returned or caused to return.

He makes a gift of/to himself. Infinite present.

He keeps nothing with him, neither goods, nor works, nor himself: no absolute having

of the concept and of reality has not been transformed—one has merely analyzed a representation, in all the senses of that word. So long as one believes one knows what a family in general is, i.e. here a human family, one does not analyze the process of alienation or of projection of the human family into the heavenly family, the contradiction that constitutes and produces this process. One does not understand why or how one would change that state of things. Now a purely theoretical critique of the family cannot alone transform the object called family, the self-evidence of which seems to go without saying. The same goes for religion *qua* familial production. "Feuerbach starts out from the fact of religious self-alienation (*Faktum der religiösen Selbstentfremdung*), of the duplication (*Verdopplung*) of the world into a religious world and a secular (*weltliche*) one. His work consists in resolving the religious world into its secular basis. But that the secular basis lifts off from itself (*sich abhebt*) and establishes itself as an independent realm in the clouds can only be explained by the self-tearing (*Sichselbstzerrissenheit*) and intrinsic contradictoriness (*Sichselbstwidersprechen*) of this secular basis. The latter must, therefore, itself be both understood in its contradiction and revolutionized in practice. Thus, for instance, once the earthly family is discovered to be the secret *(Geheimnis)* of the Holy Family, the former must then itself be destroyed in theory and in practice."

This problematic will have been developed in the camera obscura of ideology: grappling with the question of fetishism and truth (unveiled thought), of the status of *analogy* in the Marxist or psychoanalytic critique of religion.

Reconstitution of a column: we are interested in the continuous quality—or the already [*déjà*]—of a fetish-value. To ground *or* destroy religion (the familial production) always comes down to wanting to reduce fetishism. This latter, just because it unites against it founders and destroyers, must somewhere constitute the opposing unity: the unveiling of

as being at home with oneself. He has no place. He slips away and squanders. But he's perhaps the most consequential miser in all the annals of literature. He is above his work: the latter, able in this way to be cut away and to fall from him, is not equal to him. He rises above the rest. The most consequential miser: he carries on him only cash and something (a passport) to confirm his signet. According to the latest report he had forgotten, he told me, that Gabrielle was in the *Journal*. It is about amassing an absolute treasure, exempt from all evaluation. Priceless. Advice to the tightrope walker: "A lot, a whole lot of dough! A load of it! A vile amount! And then to let it pile up in a corner of your shack, never touching it, wiping your ass with your finger. As night approaches, to wake up, tear yourself away from this evil, and in the evening, dance on the wire.

the consequence, here: avoid having to have oneself knowing [*éviter, d'avoir pour s'avoir*], in order to be without its tombfalling, without its being cut from oneself. Don't spend money, don't put it in the bank, don't even put it in circulation, destroy it by dint of keeping it next to you. Money is already the sublime being-home-with-oneself of excrement. Excrement is what I can most easily keep. Absolute value, without value, equivalent of every value. Not in any case to be deposited, then: another way of cancelling it in its own contradiction. "... but who am I to talk, since I piss in the sink, I forget turds that I leave in old newspapers in the wardrobes of hotel rooms, and I don't have the guts to leave my money in my room for an hour. I walk with it, I steal with it, I sleep with it." (*Funeral Rites*)

I say to him again:

—You will have to work to become famous . . .

—Why?

—To hurt.

—Do I have to earn so much dough?

—Indispensable."

the column, the erection of the thing itself, the rejection of the substitute. The same desire works on the Christian mother, her ancestors and her descendants. So long as one criticizes fetishism—for or against religion, for or against the family—will one have touched the economy of metaphysics, the philosophy-of-religion?

Is it by chance that the father then enters the stage?

Already—Kant defined religion within the limits of reason alone by opening the question of fetishism to that of the Papa (*παπα*) and the cunning, violent, manipulative appropriation of the priests. The teleological horizon of the "true and unique religion" is the disappearance of the fetish.

Now still in the name of the father, Hegel basically reproaches Kant with still remaining at the level of the fetish

how does speculative dialectics stand with respect to the fetish? In its strictly religious sense (the one spoken of by the President des Brosses), the fetishistic type is, according to *Reason in History,* African. It belongs more precisely to inner Africa. Which is to say, *if we extract the logical schema* of the analysis, to an unconscious which cannot be dialectized as such, has no history, stands stubbornly on the threshold of the historico-dialectical process. But this non-dialecticity, this ahistoricity can always be interpreted as negativity, the resistance proper to the dialectical economy, and thenceforth interned in the speculative process. A certain undecidability of the fetish leaves us oscillating between a dialectic (of the undecidable and the dialectic) or an undecidability (between the dialectic and the undecidable). *If we extract the logical schema:* because Hegel's concrete description of the Negro might confuse it a little. This description is composed on the basis of Ritter's *Geography* and missionary narratives. Hegel recognizes the difficulty: to speak of the African one would have to abandon all our "categories" and yet they always intervene "surreptitiously." Having taken this precaution, the discourse of *Reason in History* gets moving: Africa "properly speaking" has no history "properly speaking." The Negro has reached neither consciousness nor objectivity properly speaking, he is the man who does not distinguish between "himself as an individual and his essential universality," he is "man in his immediate existence," "man in the raw state," "barbaric," "savage." "We cannot properly feel ourselves into his nature, no more than into that of a *dog*, or of a Greek as he kneels before the statue of Zeus." So we must try to gain access, not by feeling, but by thought, into this state of "self-unconsciousness" and of "innocence." In order to analyze the "general representation of the African subject," we must turn to his religion. Now it is constructed on the opposition of man and nature, the latter allowing itself to be dominated by the former. A strange interpretation: we have just been told that the negro is conflated with nature and in a moment we are going to be told that nature dominates him. The threatening power of the natural elements constrains him to use *magic.*

What is his class situation—objectively, in actuality? Yes, he is everywhere things are blowing up. He no longer inhabits the Judeo-Christian West. But—objectively, in actuality—the cord? The leash?

He knows that one keeps only what one loses. Himself. One doesn't lose only what one doesn't keep, one loses what one keeps. The other thing (the other band, the other sign, etc.) is lost because you renounce it. But the one you keep is lost because you renounce the other. And the gap between the two is nothing. However, it's what you have to occupy. The consequent miser analyzes the gap. Then he shuttles between the two.

one doesn't touch on clanging, then, without touching on class. Nor on the economy of antherection without class struggle. But the coded, civilized discourse on class struggle, for foreclosing the question of the clang (everything forged in it, everything it echoes off, in particular the expropriation of the name everywhere that it extends) is missing at least one revolution. And what is a revolution that doesn't take on the proper name? But, by the same token, what is *the* revolution if the proper name (effect of *glassification*)—*already*—antherects itself, *begins,* then, by falling into ruin? When it comes to revolutions

Shuttle [*navette*] is the word.

First of all it's what I was looking for earlier—when a gondola came across a galley—the grammatical back-and-forth between tongue [*langue*] and lagoon (*lacuna*).

One would have to use punch cards to know whether the word *navette* appears, as such

He believes that in so doing, by fantastic all-powerfulness —"the Negroes' power over nature is merely an imaginary power, an illusory authority"—he can gain real efficacy over the elements. "They do not turn to any higher power, for they believe that they can accomplish their aims by their own efforts. To prepare themselves for their work, they work themselves into a state of frenzy; by means of singing, convulsive dancing, and intoxicating roots or potions, they reach a state or extreme trance in which they proceed to issue their commands. If they do not succeed after prolonged efforts, they decree that some of the onlookers—who are their own dearest relations—should be slaughtered, and these are then devoured by their fellows. In short, man considers himself the highest commanding authority. The priest will often spend several days in this frenzied condition, slaughtering human beings, drinking their blood, and giving it to the onlookers to drink." Are we not far from the other Supper scene [*l'autre Cène*]?

Fetishism corresponds to the *second moment* of African religions. The Negro gives himself an intuition and a representation of his power, an "image" ("animal, tree, stone, wooden image"). But this "fetish" is not "objective," it merely represents, without opposing it, the arbitrariness (*Willkür*) of negro subjectivity. The fetishist remains "master of his image." This is written down on the debit side (arbitrariness, imagination, whim) rather than the credit side (freedom, autonomy of consciousness, etc.) of the negro. The fact that he manipulates the fetish, that he rises above it, if only because he knows how to produce it and "depose" it at will, change it when it does not serve him (Hegel makes much of this), "tie it up or beat it" when the harvest is poor, the fact that he lends it an ambivalent meaning, that he exalts and/or abases it—all this proves that the negro does not rise above the level of the arbitrary. The cult of the dead itself—elsewhere considered the inaugural stage of ethics—is corrupted by fetishism: "They resort to them [the deceased] in the same way as to fetishes, offering them sacrifices and conjuring them up; but where this proves unsuccessful, they punish the departed ancestor himself, casting his bones away and desecrating him. On the other hand, they believe that the dead avenge themselves if their needs are not satisfied. . . . The power of the dead over the living is indeed recognized, but held in no great respect; for the Negroes issue commands to their dead and cast spells upon them. In this way, the substance always remains in the power of the subject. Such is the religion of the Africans, and it does not extend any further." But if this being-subject of substance is devalorized for once, that is because this subject (arbitrary, capricious, imaginary) is not that of consciousness.

The negro is not even a man because he despises man. Whence—firstly—his anthropophagy. Hegel here accumulates two contradictory accusations: whereas for man there is never pure instinct (human flesh is not meat), for the negro it is meat and nothing more. And yet he does not consider it essentially as food. He does not even kill in order to eat: "the eating of human flesh is quite compatible with the African principle; to the sensuous (*sinnlichen*) Negro, human flesh is purely an object of the senses, like all flesh. It is not used primarily as food; but at

(as such, without which one would need a machine with such fine teeth and so many of them, which surely doesn't yet exist; a text like this one is only a slightly more evolved, slightly more subtle mechanical reader. Each word cited gives you an index card or grid that you can walk through the text. It is accompanied by a schema that you must be able to verify with each occurrent) in the so-called "complete works."

The word—*la navette*—is indispensable. It had to have been there. First because it is a term from church and everything here is plotted against a church. It's a small metal container in the shape of a boat (*navis*, *navetta*). Incense is kept in it.

Next, the weaver's shuttle. Made to run. Back and forth wefted along a chain. The weft is in the shuttle. You see everything that could have been done with that. Isn't elaboration a weaver's movement?

We were nevertheless wary of the textile metaphor. That's because it still retains—for example on the side of the fleece—a sort of virtue of naturality, originarity, properness. At least it's still more natural, originary, and proper than that of sewing. The latter still happens to an artifact.

the difficulty of principle is that there is no *unity* of occurrence: fixed form, identifiable theme, element determinable as such. *Anthemes* only, scattered throughout, gathered in every place. If, for example, the machine were to select only words or themes, it could collect them in a net about five and a half pages long—"The Fisherman of Le Suquet"—which I could pretend to be commenting on, to encompass within an interminable commentary without ever quoting it. You need only go to it, you'll find in it all of this lexicon, this whole thematics, but that remains *another* text

festivals. . . ." Whence—secondly—slavery: "the Negroes see nothing improper about it," and "slavery has awakened more humanity among the Negroes." Doubtless "the essence of man is freedom, but he must first become mature before he can be free. Thus it is more fitting and correct that slavery should be eliminated gradually than that it should be abolished at once." Meantime, the contempt of negroes for human life continues to show up in the ease with which they "they allow themselves to be shot down in thousands in their wars with the Europeans," the absence of family feeling (hence absence of ethical law, of constitution, of state) which comes from their unbridled polygamy (Hegel never tires of citing the King of Dahomey's 3,333 wives; the fact seems almost as scandalous to him as the rule of a woman over the Dschaks). Africa properly speaking "has no history in the true sense of the word." "And such events as have occurred in it—i.e. in its northern region—belong to the Asiatic and European world." When the African unconscious enters history, it dialectizes itself and becomes conscious, begins to Europeanize itself, engages its arbitrariness in the teleological decision of spiritual economy, welcomes into it the labor of the negative, submits to the empire of speculative idealism. To the eagle.

What is it to speculate when it comes to the fetish? For such a question, the heading without heading is undecidability. In spite of all the variations to which it can be subjected, the concept of fetish comprises an invariable predicate: it is a substitute—for the thing itself *qua* center and source of being, origin of presence, the thing itself par excellence, God or the principle, the archon, what occupies the function of center in a system, for example the phallus in a certain fantasmatic organization. If the fetish substitutes itself for the thing itself in its manifest presence, in its truth, there should no longer be any fetish as soon as there is truth, presentation of the thing itself in its essence. According to this minimal conceptual determination, the fetish is opposed to the presence of the thing itself, to the truth, signified truth of which the fetish is a substitutive signifier (given which every fetish is a signifier, even if every signifier is not necessarily a fetish), truth of a signifier that is "privileged," transcendental, fundamental, central, signifier of signifiers, no longer belonging to the series. Some thing—the thing— is no longer itself a substitute, there is some non-substitute—that's what constructs the concept of fetish. If there were no thing, the concept of fetish would lose its invariable nucleus. What we call fetishism would have to be analyzed in a quite different space. If what has always been called "fetish," in all critical discourses, implies the reference to a non-substitutive thing, there ought to be somewhere—and that's the truth of the fetish, the relation of the fetish to the truth—a decidable value of the fetish, a decidable opposition of the fetish to the non-fetish. This space of truth, the opposition of the *Ersatz* to the non-*Ersatz*, the space of good sense, of sense itself, apparently constrains all treatises on fetishism. And yet—here is the heading without heading—there might perhaps be, in particular in Freud, the means, not to explode but to reconstruct on the basis of its generalization a "concept" of the fetish that can no longer be contained in the space of truth, in the opposition *Ersatz*/non-*Ersatz* or in opposition

Now, it is sewing that is in action [*s'agit*] here.

Which puts, which he puts in play—theatrically—in pieces.

For, it must be insisted, the seams don't hold at all costs. They must not be here, for example, unfailingly solid. That's why it's working the whole time. At sewing up [*coudre*] the wound, coming to blows [*en découdre*], sewing back up, forcing to sew, preventing from sewing. Other italics in parentheses, waiting for us further along: "(*I kept myself from learning to sew.*)"

So sewing *betrays*, it exhibits what it should hide, *dissimulacrums* what it signals.

The Lady with the Unicorn has barely faded into the tapestry when, two pages further along, the purest miser grabs your sleeve to whisper what he thinks of "theft," "treason" and "dialectics."

at all. To say that there might be the means to construct such a "concept" (but what is a concept that escapes opposition, which is determined outside opposition; what is an undecidable concept?), is to imply that the structure of the text, Freud's text in particular, comprises statements that are heterogeneous, not contradictory but of a singular heterogeneity: the heterogeneity that for example relates in a text (but can one then speak of *a* text, of one and the same textual corpus?) decidable statements to undecidable statements. In the essay on *Fetishism*, after having recalled the case of the *Glanz auf der Nase* of the Englishman who had "forgotten" his mother tongue (shine: *Glanz:* glance—on the nose), Freud recognizes that he runs the risk of disappointing when he says that the fetish is a "penis substitute (*Penisersatz*)" and, "more plainly," "the substitute (*Ersatz*) for the woman's (the mother's) phallus that the little boy once believed in and—for reasons familiar to us—does not wish to give up." Whence, from the point of view of the representation and not of the affect, the *Verleugnung*, the "disavowal" that protects the infant against the threat of castration and maintains his initial belief (*Glauben*) intact. The fetish stands up here like a "monument," a "*stigma indelebile*," a "sign of triumph." This monumental erection of a supplementary column is a compromise solution, a counterweight solution to balance the "conflict" between the "weight" (*Gewicht*) of the "undesired perception" and the "force of the counter-wish" (*Gegenwunsch*). It sometimes allows the fetishist to bypass his homosexuality: thus supplemented, the woman becomes a "tolerable" sexual object. All of that proceeding from the spectacle of the woman's two legs, seen from below with, at the center of the two standing legs, between them, the fleece.

After these determinate, decidable statements, Freud in this short six-page article launches a development that seems to follow their consequences and which yet perhaps does not do this so simply. To do so, he says he is taking a "purely speculative path." One can interrogate the status of the speculative by recalling that the step *Beyond the Pleasure Principle* also advances, as Freud insists, down a "speculative" path. Here, he comes to recognize "the divided attitude of fetishists (*zwiespältige Einstellung des Fetichisten*)" and the oscillation of the subject between two possibilities. Then, to give some weight to the speculative hypothesis he offers a "description." A description of refined cases, "very subtle instances (*ganz raffinierten Fällen*)." But if such cases exist, and especially if one claims the authority to recognize them under the category of fetishism, one must be able to account for them. The category must be able to welcome them, extend into them and comprehend them.

In these very refined cases, then, the structure, the construction (*Aufbau*) of the fetish rests *at the same time* on disavowal and on affirmation (*Behauptung*), assertion or assumption of castration. This at-the-same-time, this by-the-same-token of two opposites, of two opposed operations, forbids us from deciding in the undecidable. It constitutes an economy of the undecidable: not that the undecidable here interrupts the efficacy of the economic principle. It places itself in the service of a general economy the field of which must then be opened up. There is an economic *speculation* on the undecid-

"For I am so poor, and I have already been accused of so many thefts, that when I leave a room too quietly on tiptoe, holding my breath, I am not sure, even now, that I am not carrying off with me the holes in the curtains or hangings."

All the examples are cut out like that. Look at the holes if you can.

Then he has you kneel in front of a vegetal fetish. This one is not even sewn. Just pinned onto the fabric. With—lots of swaddling in all that—a safety pin. Here is the "operation," doing its business still very close to Stilitano's "natural frontiers":

". . . excluded . . . I dared not ask for further details.

'Get started!'

With a gesture of his lively hand, he motioned to me that he wanted to undress. As on other evenings, I got down on my knees to unhook the bunch of grapes.

able. It is not dialectical but plays with the dialectic. The feint consists in pretending to lose, to castrate oneself, to kill oneself in order to cut it off. But the feint does not cut it. One loses on both sides, in both registers, from knowing how to play both sides. It is on this condition that the economy becomes general. A fetishism also spreads out without limit, within which it will be necessary to delimit the contours of a *strict* fetishism: the one in which metaphysics itself always operates.—Far from generalizing the *Ersatz* or the simulacrum, strict fetishism takes an *Ersatz* for *the thing itself.* —It desires (only) the thing itself and the *Sa* of the thing itself.

Why *general* fetishism? Once the economy of the undecidable ensures the greatest solidity of the fetish, as Freud recognizes, its lesser consistency already presupposes some link with opposing interests. The measure of solidity or consistency would thus be the ligament between the contraries, this double tie (*doppelt geknüpft*) and the undecidable mobility of the fetish, its power of excess with respect to opposition (true/non-true, substitute/non-substitute, disavowal/affirmation, etc.). The argument of the *girdle* organizes the heading without heading of this discourse: "In very subtle cases both the disavowal and the affirmation of the castration have found their way into the construction of the fetish itself. This was so in the case of a man whose fetish was an athletic support-girdle which could also be worn as bathing drawers. This piece of clothing covered up the genitals entirely and concealed the distinction between them. Analysis showed that it signified that women were castrated and that they were not castrated; and it also allowed of the hypothesis that men were castrated, for all these possibilities could equally well (*gleich gut*) be concealed behind the girdle—the earliest rudiment of which in his childhood had been the fig-leaf on a statue. A fetish of this sort, doubly derived from contrary ideas, is of course especially solid." Same thing with the *coupeur de nattes* whose act "reconciles (*vereinigt*) two mutually incompatible affirmations."

(a word that *Lessons on the Philosophy of History* refer to its Portuguese origin, *feitiço*).

It's about jealousy.

The (Kantian) precept according to which "we can know nothing of God" is a prejudice of the times, with which one needs to break if one wants to inaugurate a philosophy of religion. Which must be Christian—Hegel does not put that into question. But he draws from this a diametrically opposed conclusion: if in piety the point is to please God the Father and take pleasure in the law (Kant), to seek perfection for this purpose, how would that be possible if we were locked into the phenomenon and left God beyond knowledge (theoretical knowledge, which Hegel here does not want to distinguish from the practical relation)? According to the formalizable law of a chiasmus, Hegel is basically reproaching Kant with being unfaithful to reason and

Inside his trousers was pinned one of those imitation bunches [*une de ces grappes postiches*] of thin cellulose grapes [*grains*] stuffed with cotton wool. (They are as big as greengage plums; elegant Spanish women of the period wore them on their loose-brimmed, straw sun bonnets.) Whenever some queer at the Criolla, excited by the swelling, put his hand on Stilitano's basket, his horrified fingers would encounter this object, which they feared might be a bunch of his real treasure, a branch of it on which there hung comically too much fruit.

The Criolla was not only a fairy joint. Some boys in dresses danced there, but women did too. Whores brought their pimps and clients. Stilitano would have made a lot of money were it not that he spat on queers. He despised them. He was amused at their annoyance about his grapes. The game lasted a few days. So I unhooked the bunch, which was fastened to his blue trousers by a safety pin, but, instead of putting it on the mantelpiece as usual and laughing (for we would burst out laughing and joke during the operation), I could not restrain myself from keeping it in my cupped hands and laying my cheek against it. Stilitano's face above me turned hideous.

'Drop it, you bitch!'

In order to open the fly, I had squatted on my haunches, but Stilitano's rage, had my usual fervor been insufficient, made me fall to my knees. That was the position I used to take mentally in spite of myself. I stopped moving. Stilitano struck me with his two feet and his one fist. I could have got away. I stayed there.

Christianity, just as Kant reproaches those who believe they know God (which will have been the case with Hegel) for degrading religion into religious folly, prideful delirium or fetishism: "This [Kantian] stand-point must, judged by its *content,* be considered as the last stage of the degradation of man in which at the same time he is all the more arrogant inasmuch as he has proved to himself that this degradation is the highest possible state and his true destination." In spite of the interest of this formalism which declares that we can know everything except the true, "this standpoint and this result are diametrically opposed to the whole of Christian religion." Revelation is revelation. A revealed religion is a religion in which God reveals himself. He does not hide in it, does not reserve himself in it, does not preserve himself in it. The Christian religion is true, because it is the religion of truth, of manifestation and revelation.

In the Encyclopedia, the third moment of the philosophy of spirit (absolute spirit that reconciles objective spirit and subjective spirit in art, revealed religion and philosophy), each synthesis is the truth of the previous synthesis: revealed religion is the truth of art (*die schöne Kunst*). This latter comprises its own religion, which is but a stage in the liberation of spirit and has its destination in "true religion," truth of past art, of what art will have been. In the fine arts, the content of the idea was limited by sensory immediacy, and did not manifest itself in the universality of an infinite form. With *true* religion (the true religion, the Christian religion, the religion of the infinite God), sensory, finite and immediate intuition passes into the infinite of a knowledge that, *qua* infinite, no longer has any exteriority, therefore knows itself, becomes present to itself. A presence (*Dasein*) that therefore knows itself since it is infinite and has no outside, a truth that announces itself to itself, resonates and reflects itself in its own element: the manifest, the revealed, *das Offenbaren*. If one wishes to think revelation in its essence, what revealing means-to-say in revealed-religion, one must think this *Offenbaren*: not as a finite subject would think a revelation coming to it from God (abstract moment), but as the infinite revelation of God revealing itself in its infinity: revelation itself or the revelation of revelation, un-veiling as the unveiling of the veil itself. Claiming to think absolute, true and revealed religion while maintaining, as does Kant, the limits of a finite subjectivity, is to *forbid* oneself from thinking what one says one is thinking, is not to think what one is already thinking,

'The key's in the door,' I thought. Through the fork of the legs that were kicking me furiously I saw it sticking out of the lock, and I would have liked to turn it with a double turn so as to be locked in alone with my executioner. I made no attempt to understand the reason for his anger, which was so disproportionate to its cause, for my mind was unconcerned with psychological motives. As for Stilitano, from that day on he stopped wearing the bunch of grapes. Toward morning, having entered the room earlier than he, I waited for him. In the silence, I heard the mysterious rustling of the sheet of yellow newspaper that replaced the missing windowpane.

'That's subtle,' I said to myself.

I was discovering a lot of new words. In the silence of the room and of my heart, in the waiting for Stilitano, this slight noise disturbed me, for before I came to understand its meaning there elapsed a brief second of anxiety. Who—or what—is calling such fleeting attention to itself in a poor man's room?

'It's a newspaper printed in Spanish,' I said to myself again. 'It's only natural that I don't understand the sound it's making.'

Then I really felt I was in exile, and my nervousness was going to make me permeable to what—for want of other words—I shall call poetry.

The bunch of grapes on the mantelpiece nauseated me. One night Stilitano got up to throw in into the toilet. During the time he had worn it, it had not marred his beauty. On the contrary, in the evening, slightly encumbering his legs, it had given them a slight bend and his step a slightly rounded and gentle constraint and when he walked near me, in front or behind,

is to chatter—in the infidelity, the idolatry, the formalist abstraction of the understanding. "It lies essentially in the notion of religion—the religion i.e. whose content is absolute spirit—that it be *revealed* (*geoffenbart*), and, what is more, revealed by *God*." As infinite, this revelation can no longer be contained in a determinate historical event, as is usually imagined. The movement of manifestation of infinite truth merges with the history of spirit, progressive revelation and reappropriation of the divine absolute. "The history of religions coincides with world-history." Absolute presence (*Dasein*) is knowledge (*Wissen*), it has itself and knows itself as absolute substance that manifests itself to itself, determines itself (*das Selbstbestimmende ist*). The being of God is absolutely present, manifest, *there* (*da*). It is the very act of manifesting itself, of being *there*. The there, the *Da* does not supervene upon it, it is *Da*, the manifest(ing) of manifestation (*schlechthin Manifestieren*).

Now the Christian religion is the only one in history that expressly named itself revealed religion. It calls itself the revealed (*ausdrücklich die geoffenbarte heisst*). No other religion is absolutely true—not by dint of being false—but by dint of not being the truth, of not having made of the truth (of unveiling) of manifestation, of the open (and openable) its proper essence. Given this, to claim to ground Christianity in reason and yet make of the non-manifestation, the being-hidden of God the principle of this religion, is (Kant) to understand nothing about revelation.

Kant is Jewish: he believes in a jealous, envious God who hides and guards his *Da*. This is an all the more serious failing for a philosopher in that Plato already, and Aristotle, had condemned the hypothesis of a miserly and hidden God. They had objected to Nemesis, an equalizing power (*gleichmachende Macht*) conceived by abstract understanding, that God is not "jealous" (*neidisch*). Nemesis: on the one hand the figure of the law, of distributive, equalizing, formal, homogenous, at bottom indifferent justice, a dead and deadly operation of the understanding that abases grandeur and destroys the sublime. Kant's God, a power of death, would have no living generosity, primarily because of his zeal to fold his *Da* back into himself.

But Nemesis is not only for the Greeks distributive justice and *nomos* (division), it is also resentment faced with injustice, then envy, jealousy, shame [*pudeur*] too, and punishment. This whole chain of significations links law to jealousy or resentment, and by the same token a certain Greek,

I felt a delicious agitation because my hands had prepared it. I still think it was by the insidious power of these grapes that I grew attached to Stilitano. . . . I shall prudently refrain from comment upon this mysterious wearing of the bunch of grapes; yet it pleases me to see in Stilitano a queer who hates himself.

'He wants to baffle and hurt, to disgust the very people who desire him,' I say to myself when I think of him. As I ponder it more carefully, I am more disturbed by the idea—which I find pregnant with meaning—that Stilitano had bought a fake wound [*une plaie postiche*] for that most noble spot (I know that he was magnificently hung) in order to save his lopped-off hand from scorn. Thus, by means of a very crude subterfuge here I am talking again about beggars and their misfortunes. Behind a real or sham physical ailment which draws attention to itself and is thereby forgotten is hidden a more secret malady of the soul.

I list the secret wounds:
decayed teeth,
foul breath,
a hand cut off,
smelly feet, etc. . . .
to conceal them and to kindle our pride we had
a hand cut off,
a gouged eye,

bunches of grapes hung to hardbind the eye.

"They cling to loyalty as do others to virility. At noon, on a heavy, broad-rumped, hairy-legged nag that was still wearing its brass and leather harness, Harcamone, riding side-saddle with his legs dangling to the left, crossed the Big Square on his way back from cartage or work in the fields. He had the audacity to hook at the edge of his tilted cap, near his ear and almost covering his left eye with a trembling mauve leucoma, two huge bunches of lilac. He must have been quite sure of his integrity. In the Colony, he alone could coyly adorn himself with flowers. He was a true male." (*Miracle of the Rose*)

"First I took the girl to my room. No one saw her going up. She wanted my lilacs.

MAURICE: What?

a certain Jew and a certain Kant. In each case we are dealing with a divinity whose justice is unjust, vengeful, finite, negating, cruel, castrating, fearful. The figure of a father who would not wish that his offspring resemble him. Now jealousy (*phthonos*), says the *Phaedrus*, cannot be a divine attribute. It stands "outside the divine choir": this at the moment when, in the myth of the procession of souls, Zeus takes off on his winged chariot, followed by an army of gods and demons, whereas Hestia remains alone in the house of the gods (*Estia en theôn oikô, monè*). The *Timaeus* interprets non-jealousy, in the father/son or generator/generated relation, as the desire for resemblance: the god wants what he produces to resemble him. "He was good, and in him that is good no envy (*phthonos*) ariseth ever concerning anything; and being devoid of envy He desired that all should be, so far as possible, like unto Himself." From its opening, the *Philosophy of Religion* also draws an argument from *analogy*: "Christ says, 'Be perfect as your heavenly Father is perfect.' This lofty demand is to the wisdom of our time an empty sound." To resemble God, one must know him and think him, see him reveal himself here, *da*, and not ignore him in an incomprehensible beyond. A father cannot hide himself, he cannot reserve his *Da*. The non-jealousy of the generator (which these discourses do not distinguish from the father: the father has the signification of the generator in any case) does not belong to him as a psychological character, one feature among others. It is not an attribute: generator-being excludes envy. A father cannot be jealous *qua* father, since he gives birth. He is good (*agathos*) insofar as he gives rise to *genesis*, brings to the light of day, gives birth and form. Those who say that God is jealous are liars, Greeks, Jews, or Kantians. Liars or poets but poets are liars (Aristotle, before Nietzsche, had recalled the proverb) who understand nothing of the difference between day and night.

Freud is surprised when Kant compares the moral law within us to the spectacle of the celestial vault above our heads. This is not only because he was breathing in the mists of Königsberg whose veils the sun does not penetrate. The law, the father, the God one must please is a God one cannot know, a nocturnal God: jealous, hiding his *Da*, moral and castrating, allowing himself to be seen, like the galactic structure, only by twinkling, blinking against a background of darkness—lit by a sun one cannot see.

a peg leg, etc.

We are fallen during the time we bear the marks of the fall, and to be aware of the imposture is of little avail. Using only the pride imposed by poverty, we aroused pity by cultivating the most repulsive wounds."

Why cut here?

If we weren't reading, we ourselves would be imprudent enough to comment on the wearing of the bunch of grapes. We would impose on this piece new words, in any case words that are foreign to it. Before all the plagues of Egypt one imagines the doctors nodding their heads and chanting: castration, fetishism, castration of the mother, fetishism, castration, castration I tell you, still more castration.

GREEN EYES: I had a bunch of lilacs between my teeth. The girl followed me. She was magnetized. . . . Then, she wanted to scream because I was hurting her. I choked her. I thought that once she was dead I'd be able to bring her back to life."

It's thus what's fake, detachable, that seduces, fascinates, attaches the detachable. That is at the origin of "what—for want of other words—I shall call poetry." It is what can "baffle and hurt . . . disgust [*je m'ec*] the very people who desire it."

Don't look for more shuttle style words. And ask yourself why you don't need them. And what is poetry, here named for lack of other words, if it prescribes, inscribes and comprises and overflows in advance, swallowing it into its abyss, the hermeneutic doctoral discourse?

Now the tradition to which Hegel is appealing—here—is a solar and diurnal tradition, a tradition of *agathon*, of the good god who engenders, gives form and visibility. Unity of the values of life and truth, unveiling to sight. Goodness and absence of jealousy does not consist merely in giving birth, in producing life but also in giving to be seen, producing oneself. The value of jealousy (*Neid*) allows one to merge a problematic of life and a problematic of truth as productivity. The essence of God cannot be jealousy because the essence, namely the energy of presence, the *Da,* cannot hide itself. The essence is not jealous, jealousy is not essential, or else it is only the negative of essentiality. In pure essentiality, jealousy is totally sublated. Hegel recognizes, it is true, that there has been, that there will have been negativity in God (restlessness, anger that gets him outside himself, etc., torment, originary torsion: *Qual Quelle*; as though he began *by* castrating himself *in order to* erect his *Da*, or *by* having an erection *in order to* cut himself back; as if in this simulacrum he was turning himself to stone (*se médusait*), or rather came to himself, to his *Dasein* via the medusa. The sea-nettle, the acaleph, the drifting medusa are called, as Hegel does not say, *Qualle*); what he says of absolute religion and of the non-jealous God is valid only at the end of a process of reappropriation of the absolute by itself. Before the end, there is finitude and therefore jealousy. But jealousy of self. Who could God be jealous of, except himself, therefore of his own son? Nemesis, Judaism, Kantianism are necessary, but abstract moments of this infinite process. In *Sa,* jealousy no longer has a place. It always comes from the night of the unconscious, from the unknown, from the other. Pure sight sublates all jealousy. Not seeing what one sees, seeing what one cannot see and what cannot present itself—such is the operation of jealousy. It is always dealing with trace, never with perception. Seen from the vantage of *Sa,* the thinking of the trace would thus be a jealous thinking (finite, filial, servile, ignorant, lying, poetic). A tradition since Aristotle's *Metaphysics*: "For this reason its acquisition might justly be supposed to be beyond human power, since in many respects human nature is servile; in which case, as Simonides says, 'God alone can have this privilege,' and man should only seek the knowledge which is within his reach. Indeed if the poets are right and the Deity is by nature jealous (*pephukè phthonein to theion*), it is probable that in this

That's subtle, I tell myself. The author who narrates himself cannot, he says, lock himself in with his executioner's key (the universal key, the mother's phallus, they say, nodding their heads). Lock himself in with the key of his cradling executioner who replaces his wound by another, by a detachable object that is the very thing that nauseates and attaches by means of its insidious power.

The key: "sticking out of the lock."

What remained of a Rembrandt torn into small quite regular squares and tossed in the shitcan. The strange word *écoeurement* [being nauseated].

In the room—impossible to lock oneself in with the executioner who lets you see the key between the fork of his legs—a draught, missing windowpane. The latter is replaced, it too. But by what? by a particular and determinable object? If we were imprudent enough to comment, and if we were to be concerned with psychological motives, we would predict it with certainty. One could make a thesis out of it.

case He would be particularly jealous, and all those who excel in knowledge unfortunate. But it is impossible for the Deity to be jealous (indeed, as the proverb says, 'poets tell many a lie (*polla pseudontai aoidoi*)'), nor must we suppose that any other form of knowledge is more precious than this; for what is most divine is most precious. Now there are two ways only in which it can be divine. A science is divine if it is peculiarly the possession of God, or if it is concerned with divine matters. And this science alone fulfils both these conditions; for (a) all believe that God is one of the causes and a kind of principle, and (b) God is the sole or chief possessor of this sort of knowledge."

A question of filiation. Speculative staging. Legend. Kant is trying to withdraw his discourse from the authority of psychoanalysis: "The whole genealogy of morals described by psychoanalysis (parental situation, law of the father, castration, etc.) is perhaps valid in a field of phenomenal empiricity, for particular mores, a given determinate culture, empirical relations between sensory fathers and sons, finite psychological determinations, non-universal religions, idolatries and fetishisms. Is Freud not condemned to a crude analogism—that he must indeed admit to himself—when he writes in the Introduction to *Totem and Taboo*: "The difference [between the explanation of the totem and that of Taboo] is related to the fact that taboos still exist among us. Though expressed in a negative form and directed towards another subject-matter, they do not differ in their psychological nature from Kant's 'categorical imperative,' which operates in a compulsive fashion and rejects any conscious motives." Freud is not wary enough of analogy, against which he warns us, for example in *The Future of an Illusion*. He says: taboo, for us, today, is the Categorical Imperative, except for these small differences, which he basically does not want to take into account: 1. The taboo is negative, the IC [*Impératif Catégorique*] is positive ("although conceived negatively"); 2. The objects of the one and the other are different ("bearing on different objects"); 3. The identity is only valid from a psychological point of view ("they do not differ in their psychological nature from the categorical imperative"); 4. Taboo acts

What replaces the missing windowpane is only a newspaper [*journal*], not *The Thief's Journal*, larger than this whole scene, which is a part of it, infinitely larger, and which is also printed, in a certain way, in Spanish. No, a newspaper like any other, whose thief complains about not understanding its meaning, pleases himself with it also, enjoying till he comes, in the anguish of the room, from hearing only this unidentifiable noise nevertheless Spanish like his name. This piece is a page detached from the journal of a thief, prepared by the hands of the author, too prudent to comment on anything other than his text, which is always concerned with something else in respect of which nothing greater can be thought.

Here again I do nothing, can do nothing other than quote, as you have perhaps just noticed: simply displace the syntactic arrangement around a physical wound, real or sham, that draws attention to and causes the other to be forgotten.

I have discovered many new words and yet I always come back to the same ones for want of others.

by constraint and unconscious motivation, the IC presents itself at least as the very manifestation of the autonomy of consciousness, or freedom and will. Setting aside these four differences, I agree with Freud: my IC is his taboo: "it does not differ." To the extent that the IC is negative—which it is not; that it has the same object—which it does not; that it is psychological, empirico-phenomenal—which it is not; that it has a heteronomic structure—which it does not, it would indeed be nothing other than what to which Freud assimilates it under the name "taboo." But never could a process of idealization and interiorization moving from negative to positive, from one object to another, from unconscious to conscious, from constraint to autonomy, from the psychological to what presents itself as non-psychological and non-phenomenal—never could such a process account for the properly infinite leap that produces the object of pure morality.

True religion—the pure morals that ought to ground it—breaks with all finite determinations, criticizes fetishism, anthropomorphism and all sensory representations, in short all phenomenal religion organized according to a relation to the father or the law *qua* finite objects. Once the law, God the father, etc., are no longer finite objects—i.e. as soon as they are no longer (present), do not appear—the principle of the psychoanalytic genealogy of religion and morals becomes null and void."

Hegel ("the obscure philosophy of Hegel," as Freud calls it) sets the merry-go-round spinning again. It is the circular repetition of the debate, its vicious circle that is still interesting: "Freud is right when he talks about Kantian morality and religion; they remain within finitude, sensory representation, psychologism, fetishism, (the) relations of jealousy between the hidden, invisible father and the impotent son, [Kantian thought] does not manage to reach a thought

unless, after a deconstructive displacement of all the oppositions banked on by Kant's discourse, in order to make an analogical process impossible in it (sensible/intelligible, phenomenal/noumenal, intuitus derivativus/intuitus imaginarius, etc.), unless psychoanalytical discourse determines—in Kant's logic—the sensitive spot: the point of sensibility where the two terms of the opposition touch and do without the leap. For example, *respect* for the moral law which belongs neither to the rational order of the law nor to the order of psychological phenomena; or again the *interest* of reason and in general the whole schematism of the transcendental imagination which, lifting the opposition, *suspends the leap*. There is also a Kantian analogism.
The age is unanimous about this: to leap is good. But we always have to ask why and over what we are in such a hurry to leap

What is poetry? What hardbinds this text, seduces and disturbs doctoral discourse, introduces a gap [*écart*] (a "Big Square [*Carré*]") into the room where the patient undresses, lies down, finally says nothing, instead makes the master stutter. Some days later, the master sends a manuscript with a dedication to the writer-patient: with my admiration. It's great, isn't it? That's a bit like what you are doing, no? The writer doesn't respond. He is above all not virginal enough to say that he occupies the place of the other.

The text is bunched.

Whence the permeable, seduced, on-one's-knees nervousness of whomever wishes to take it, comprehend it, appropriate it for themself.

There is treatment of *ersatz* there, in a language foreign to what one puts and adds in its place.

The thesis (position, proposition, *Satz*) protects what it replaces, however.

Yet we have here a contemporary (that fact matters a great deal), who should have been prepared by everything—if not by his own clang—to read this scene, who gets flustered, no longer wants to see, says the opposite of what he means, goes to war, climbs up on his high horse.

The *ersatz*, he says, isn't good.

it all comes down to sponging off an amputee's hook [*vivre au crochet d'un manchot*]; the bunch [*grappe*], the grapnel form a sort a sort of hooked matrix. "*Grappe*. Etym. Picard and Champ. *crape;* Provenç. *grapa,* hook; Span. *grapo,* hook; Ital. *grappo,* hook; Low Lat. *grapa, grappa,* in Quicherat's *Addenda;* from Old High Germ. *chrapfo,* hook, modern Germ. *Krappen;* comp. Cymric *crap.* One thus said *la grappe* because it had something hooked, hooked onto." (*Littré*)

of the infinite and of the true religion, it stays within the limits of sensory (fetishistic, anthropomorphic) religion or, what comes to the same thing, within the limits of a formal religion of the understanding. Now psychoanalysis can account for the genealogy of such a religion, but not of a religion of the concept or of speculative reason that, for its part, sets out from the infinite, etc., etc., etc."

Kant: "Upping the analogical ante! Complicity of *Schwärmerei,* religious folly and fetishism (God present in sensory finitude). Erasure of Christianity, infidelity, neopaganism. The speculative dialectic is more than ever subject to psychoanalytic jurisdiction. Confusionism, misrecognition of the specificity of the religious that gets dissolved into philosophy whereas my essay on religion within the limits of reason alone operates in that respect a more complex movement in its relation to Scripture, etc."

Hegel: "But in it you speak of a progress of reason. I am not proposing a formal and tautological identification of the philosophical object and the religious object, but an identification that is concrete, historical, heterological, laborious, dialectical. I account—effectively—for the shameful teleology that leaves its stigmata on your work. I do—with no jealousy, of course, especially not that—what you ought to have done. My critique pays homage to a filiation, etc."

The identity of philosophy and religion concludes a historical syllogism, a history, Hegel specifies, whose *internal* meaning must be understood. The analogy put forward tells us at the same time everything we must not be interested in if we want to accede to the meaning of painting (and to—internal—meaning in general): an external history is blind to the truth of

Freud (one foot on the merry-go-round): "What happens when two philosophical systems (erect, upright, non-twisted paranoid manias) confront or persecute each other and reproach one another with understanding nothing about religion (about erect, upright, non-twisted obsessional neurosis)? What happens when two philosophical systems laying claim to truth claim to have in their possession *both* the truth of neurosis and that of paranoia, paranoia that psychoanalysis claims to know well, for its part, what it is: since it knows that they are, the one the exaggeration or the caricature (*Zerrbild*) of religion, the other of philosophy?" How can they talk to each other and each claim that the truth of the one is in the other, and the whole of one in the whole of the other? Will I get out of this merry-go-round with the diagnosis that philosophy equals "overestimation of verbal magic"?
Good luck with that [*voire*].
And what is the third one doing meantime, the artist or the hysteric? And which holds the truth of the other

Hard-to-explain alliance with Sartre. And yet: "Sartre himself noted a curious difficulty at the basis of Genet's work. Genet, the writer, has neither the power to *communicate* with his readers nor the intention of doing so. The elaboration [clearly not done on purpose] of his work has the sense of a negation of those who read it. Sartre saw, though he drew no conclusions, that in these conditions the work was not entirely a work, but an *ersatz,* half way from the major *communication* at which literature aims. Literature is communication: it goes out from a sovereign author who addresses sovereign humanity, beyond the servitude of the isolated reader. . . .

an author

Not only has Genet no intention of communicating when he writes, but, whatever his intention may be, in that a caricature or an *ersatz* of communication would be established, the author refuses his readers this fundamental similitude which the vigor of his work might risk revealing. . . .

the caricature, the *ersatz,* isn't good, it's false. He likes the original edition, the seal, the signet of the authentic. Not the false, the true. He doesn't like galalith. It is surely galalith, nothing is like before

the vigor of his work

Genet himself never doubts his weakness. To create a work of literature can only be, I believe, a *sovereign operation.* This is true in the sense in which the work requires its author to go beyond the pauper within himself who is not on the level of these sovereign moments. . . .

produce literary work

the work asks the author to surpass the poor person in himself, one not up to the task . . . yes

religion. "A blind person can deal with the frame, the canvas, the varnish of a picture; can know the history of painters, the fate of a picture, its price, into what hands it has fallen, and can see nothing of the picture itself. What obstructs religion in our epoch is that science has not been reconciled with it. Between the two is found a barrier . . ."

The identity of philosophy and religion finds its ultimate mediation in the philosophy of religion. Philosophy is the truth (the philosophy) of religion and religion already represents (the name of) philosophy: "Thus religion and philosophy are one"; "Philosophy is only explicating *itself* when it explicates religion and when it explicates itself it is explicating religion."

The places where this unity is produced as such are par excellence the transitions to *Sa,* the circular passages from *Sa* to *Sa* (end of the encyclopedia: cycle of *paideia,* of the absolute spirit of God who instructs himself, engenders himself like his own son and then enjoys himself speculatively; end of the phenomenology of spirit, of the phenomenon or the self-revelation of spirit, passage from absolute religion to *Sa*).

In any case religion saves by/from itself [*la religion sauve d'elle-même*].

Absolute religion is not yet what it already is: *Sa.* Absolute religion (the essence of Christianity, religion of the essence) is already what it is not yet: *Sa* which itself is already no longer what it still is, absolute religion.

The already-there of the not-yet, the already-no-longer of the still cannot be understood [*ne peuvent pas s'entendre*].

Ne peuvent pas s'entendre—in several senses:

1. The *absolute* already-there-of-the-not-yet passeth understanding, comes under reason, constitutes what reason sublates absolutely. The *true* relation between philosophy and religion (or family) is not commensurate with the finite-formal understanding but with infinite-concrete reason.

2. The *absolute* already-there-of-the-not-yet (or the already-no-longer-of-the-still) passes what is supposedly given to be heard in the time of voice or hearing. Unheard-of relation to the extent that the *absolute* already-there of the not-yet or the already-no-longer-of-the-still no longer belong to time, i.e. to pure insensible-sensibility. They describe an eternal or intemporal circle. Hegel determines their translation into a temporal grammar, into the syntax of the adverbs of time and of negation as a fall of meaning

Not that we should stop when we read: '. . . I wrote to make money.' Genet's 'work as a writer'

and why wouldn't we stop there? Who said it wasn't appropriate to write for money? Who could have said that? That money is evil? What indeed? And why not wonder how one was able to write that? Who? for whom? why?

"I am listening to myself" in Greek equals "I am my first client."

Critique of Judgment: "Art is also distinguished from handicraft: the first is called liberal, the second can also be called remunerative art. . . . beautiful art must be free art in a double sense: it must not be a matter of remuneration, a labor whose magnitude can be judged, enforced, or paid for in accordance with a determinate standard; but also while the mind is certainly occupied, it must feel itself to be satisfied and stimulated (independently of remuneration) without looking beyond to another end."

By whom, and in what, then, is the "author" paid? fed? By a (liberal) economic entity, represented by a (liberal) editorial market, a ministry of (liberal) culture, indeed by Frederick the Great, poet and liberal monarch.

Unless he were to steal? Is that worse than or other than writing "for money?" Does it mean changing systems? In any case, the liberal esthete doesn't like it. But one sees again how next to nothing is needed for the motif of pure expenditure and extra-circulation to get reinscribed in the exchange of a restricted economy (here, liberal). But what happens when some little nothing is all that is needed? The risk (comforting corruptibility also) inhabits risk. The master can always live in the same house as the sovereign

into the body, an outside of the circle immediately drawn back into the circle, a sort of false tangent of the adverb to the verb, of the tense of the verb to the verb.

Now *absolute* philosophy or religion must account for this fall and this strange modification of the verb. The absolute reason of absolute (revealed, Christian, etc.) religion comprehends its own fall into body and time. Absolute privilege of Christianity, absolute essence of religion: determine oneself on the basis of one's fall (*Sa-tombfall*) and one's absolute sublation.

This absolute circle that draws and sublates its tangents, that produces both the deportation and the concentration of its other, is a family circle.

This statement requires the support neither of witticism [*le mot d'esprit*] nor of familialism. Unless we specify that the circle is that of the word "spirit" [*le mot d'esprit*], of its *economy,* of the property law of spirit which is at home in language, in the word in which it falls and which it sublates.

If one hears Hegel, if one understands (from within the picture) the meaning of what his text means-to-say, one cannot reduce the *absolute* already-there of the not-yet or the (absolute) already-no-longer of the still to what one believes one knows, familiarly, of the family. What Hegel means-to-say, is that the absolute meaning of the absolute family, the being-familial of the family, delivers itself up only in the passage between absolute religion and the *Sa*, in the penultimate chapter of the phenomenology of spirit: from the absolute of the already-there of the not-yet or the still of the already-no-longer. To abridge this syntagm and de-temporalize it, let us simplify it into *pas-là* (the being-there (*da*) of the *pas* which being there is not, *not there*). So one cannot reduce the *pas-là* to the circle of a family about which we would already, familiarly, know what it is and want it means-to-say. On the contrary, one can accede to the absolute essence of the family only by thinking the absolute of the *pas-là.* To think the family one must think absolutely the being of the already-there of the not-yet or the still of the already-no-longer. This familial between can be read inside and outside—at its limit—the phenomenology of spirit, at the hinge [*charnière*] of the penultimate and last chapters.

in a crenellation, unheard-of lure of a *Sa:* the Christic carcass, with a few others, in sublime decomposition. In terms of falconry, of course, the hunter disposes and bloods [*acharne*] the lure in a trap called a *charnière*

Indeed: in absolute religion, the division into two (*Entzweiung*) is *not yet* absolutely overcome by reconciliation. One opposition (*Entgegensetzung*) remains, and it is determined in an anticipatory representation (*Vorstellung*). Final limit of the absolutely true, absolute, revealed religion: it remains

is one of those most worthy of attention. Genet himself is eager to be sovereign. But he has not seen that sovereignty involves the *élan* of the heart, it requires loyalty, because it is given in communication. . . .

of those most worthy of attention

Genet is lacking in heart. And loyalty

GENET'S FAILURE

Genet's indifference to communication is at the origin of a certain fact: his *récits* are interesting, but not *enthralling*. There is nothing colder, less touching, under the glittering parade of words, than the famous passage in which Genet recounts Harcamone's death. It has the beauty of a piece of jewelry: it is too rich and in somewhat cold bad taste. . . . The scholar who imposes titles on people demonstrates the same stupidity as Genet, who wrote these lines

"Genet's failure." What a title. Magic, animistic, fearful denunciation. What effect is he after? But wasn't "failure" something Genet calculated? He repeats as much all the time; he wanted to succeed at failure. And so, by the simple provocation of his text he constructs a scene that obliges the other to take off his mask, trip over his tongue, get flustered, say what he supposedly didn't want to say, should not have said. It's that, (Genet) the text that entraps, hounds, reads the reader, the judgment, the critique. Like Rembrandt. Paradigmatic scene

for bad taste, see a little further along

at the level of *Vorstellung*. The essential predicate of this representation is the exteriority of what presents or announces itself in it. It posits in front of itself, it has a relation to an object that is pre-sent, goes ahead only insofar as it remains external. The unity of object and subject is not yet accomplished presently, actually; the reconciliation between the subject and the object, the inside and the outside, is left waiting. It is represented, but represented reconciliation is not actual reconciliation. There is nothing fortuitous in this representative exteriority's being, at the same time, time. If in the absolute religion of the absolute family there is already some not-yet or a not-yet of the already (of *Sa*), this is quite simply, so to speak, because there is—still—time. Religion is representative because it needs time.

And if we take account of the fact that *Sa*, as is said in the chapter that is named for it, is both a suppression pure and simple (*Tilgen*) and a sublation (*Aufhebung*) of time, we get a sense of the extraordinary difficulty, if not the impossibility, of this thinking of *Sa* in its time.

This scarcely existent limit, crossed as soon as it is posited, is already not what it still is and doesn't even give us the time to think its time. It is what presents itself, scarcely, between absolute religion and *Sa*.

Now, it describes an absolute family scene. Elliptically. It is the very ellipsis in the family circle: this latter is inscribed in an ellipsis in which what is missing (ellipsis) has to do with the fact that the family cannot manage to center itself. It has a double focus [*foyer*]. This ellipsis is time—the truth of space—between the last two chapters (the last two "times" or beats) of the phenomenology of spirit: "Since this unity of essence (*Wesen*) and self (*Selbst*) has *in itself* been achieved, consciousness also still (*noch*) has this *representational thought* (Vorstellung) of its reconciliation, but as a representation."

The reconciliation between being and the same, between the being itself of being and the very-being of being [*entre l'être lui-même de l'être et l'être-même de l'être*] is produced, granted, in revealed religion, but there it puts itself forward as an object for the consciousness that *has* this representation, which has it *before* it. The reconciliation has happened and yet it *has not yet* taken place, it *is not present*, only represented or present as remaining ahead, distanced, to come, present as not-yet-there and not as presence of the present. But as this reconciliation of being and the same (reconciliation itself) is absolute presence, absolute parousia, we have to say that in

concerning when he travelled through Spain [quote about "the palace

> among other constructions of the same kind, one would have to circulate through all the palaces, in the labyrinth, yes, through all the palaces (Palais de Justice in *Our Lady*, palace of the Grandee in Spain, where we are, the "veil of [Stilitano's] palate [*palais*] . . . that precious cobweb" where the *gl*s are elaborated. One would then notice—by spending some time there and by putting one's tongue to work somewhat—that the *palais* is precisely what I am talking about. A lot [*Beaucoup*]. I slang, I jargon, I give the impression of inventing new words, a new lexicon. An *argot* only, a *jargon*. Both of them come out of the back of the throat, they sojourn, for a time, like a gargle, deep in the gullet, making one clear the throat and spit.
>
> *Argot* is an argot word. Like all argot words. Littré doesn't mention that. To use slang [*argotiser*] is to work against the lexicon. But by arguing, elaborating, alleging from inside its corpus. Argot is a very old word, rooted in language and literature. Like jargon. And yet its usage is first of all *argotic*, limited to a gang or a school.

of which I speak (for it has no other name)"]. The interesting aspect of Jean Genet's work does not reside in its poetic power, but in the lesson we can learn from its weaknesses. . . . There is, I don't know what, a fragile, cold, friable quality in Genet's writing, which does not necessarily prevent us from admiring it, but which makes us hesitate to agree with him."

I don't know what. Critique of "I don't know what." I don't know what of fr

the heart really isn't in it

What, in spite of everything, makes one recognize here a text by Bataille? In spite of everything, in spite of "The Language of Flowers," in spite of (?) "*Le glas*," in spite of what, following the general logic of his

religion, in absolute revelation, presence is present as representation. Consciousness has the representation of this presence and this reconciliation but as it is only a representation of what is outside it (before or behind, it comes to the same thing here), this representation remains external to it. Consciousness represents unity to itself but is not there yet. That is, moreover, why it has the structure of a consciousness, and the phenomenology of spirit, science of the experience of consciousness, finds its necessary limit in this representation.

So absolute religion still retains some negativity, it remains in conflict, scission, restlessness. The critique of previous religions or philosophies of religion is somewhat disqualified by this: they were always being reproached with not getting past division, with not reaching reconciliation.

Hegel does indeed determine as reconciliation the unity of being and the self-same: with forgiveness, rapprochement and expiation. This psycho-anthropological figure of Christianity is illuminated in return by its ontological meaning. What consciousness is seeking beyond this scission is an appeasement (*Befriedigung*) through forgiveness. This gives to the apparently metaphorical family structure its weightiness of gravity, sin and guilt: "[Consciousness] achieves appeasement by *externally* adding (*außerlich hinzufügt*) to its pure negativity the positive meaning of the unity of itself with essence; its appeasement thus itself remains (*bleibt also*) burdened with the opposition of an other-worldly beyond (*mit dem Gegensatze eines Jenseits*)." The fact of representation, the *Vor-stellen*, forms an opposite (*Gegensatz*), an object (*Gegenstand*) which, like all objects, is opposed to consciousness. Because it still has an object, a desire or a nostalgia, absolute religious consciousness remains in opposition, scission. Reconciliation remains a beyond. The temporal motif (movement of transcendence, relation to a past or future non-presence, de-presentation) is the truth of a metaphorically spatial motif (the "far off," the non-proximate, non-proper). The familial proper has not yet, in the absolute family, recovered its identity or its proximity with itself. The family has not yet reconciled with itself, is not yet absolutely absolved. This dehiscence of the familial proper forms an ellipsis that distances the religious focus from the philosophical focus, Christianity from *Sa*. And if we consider that philosophy—*Sa*—is the myth of

"**Knell**
In my voluptuous bell
[*Dans ma cloche voluptueuse*]
the bronze of death dances
[*le bronze de la mort danse*]
the clapper-cock rings out
[*le battant d'une pine sonne*]
a long libidinous swing
[*un long branle libidineux*]"

Elaborations.

"**Sky**

1. The bronze of love rings out
[*Le bronze de l'amour sonne*]
The red clapper of your cock
[*Le battant rouge de ta pine*]
in the bell of my cunt
[*dans la cloche de mon con*]

2. The bald clapper of your knell
[*Le battant chauve de ton glas*]
in the cunt's (crossed out: my vagina's,
my urine's) bell
[*dans la cloche du con*]
the bronze of love rings out
[*le bronze de l'amour sonne*]
its long voluptuous swing
[*le long branle voluptueux*]

3. The bronze of love dances
[*Le bronze de l'amour danse*]
its long voluptuous swing
[*le long branle voluptueux*]
and the bald clapper of the knell
[*et le battant chauve du glas*]
rings and rings and rings and rings
[*sonne et sonne et sonne et sonne*]
in my libidinous bell
[*dans ma cloche libidineuse*]

4. In my libidinous bell
[*Dans ma cloche libidineuse*]
the bronze of death rings out
[*le bronze de la mort sonne*]
the clapper-prick dances
[*le battant de la verge danse*]
its long voluptuous swing
[*le long branle voluptueux*]"

G. Bataille

thinking (simulacrum, sovereignty as untenable

absolute reappropriation, of a self-presence absolutely absolved and recentered, then the absolute of revealed religion would have a *critical* effect on *Sa*. We'd have to stay on the (other) shore, that of religion and the family, in order to resist the lure of *Sa*. Combinatory hypothesis.

Religion saves by/from itself.

Family time: there is time only of the family. Time passes only in the family. The opposition of the already, the not-yet, the already-no longer, all that forms the time of not being present (*pas-là*), everything that constitutes time as the *Dasein* of a concept that is not there [*(n')est pas là*], the being-there of the not-there (one step more—*pas-pas-là*—or less), is a family scene.

"Its appeasement thus itself remains burdened with the opposition of an other-worldly beyond. Its own reconciliation (*seine eigene Versöhnung*) therefore enters into its consciousness as something *remote* (*als ein* Fernes), something far away in the *future*, just as (*wie*) the reconciliation which the other *self* achieved appears as something remote in the *past*." So there is an analogy (*wie*) between one's own reconciliation to come and the past reconciliation, between the past and the future, a circular analogy between the end of the world or the last judgment and the incarnation of God in Christ. An analogy too between this situation and the trinitarian family structure in general; and then, in it between the individual family and the family as universal community: "Just as (*so wie*) the *individual* divine man has a father existing-*in-itself* (ansich*seienden* Vater) and merely an *actual* mother (*und nur eine* wirkliche *Mutter*), so too the universal divine man, the religious community (*Gemeinde*), has as its father its *own activity and knowledge* (*ihr* eigenes Tun *und* Wissen) , but for its mother it has *eternal love,* which it merely *feels* (*nur* fühlt) but does not *intuit* in its consciousness as an actual immediate *object* (Gegenstand). Its reconciliation exists thereby within its heart, but it is still estranged (*noch entzweit*) from its consciousness, and its actuality is still fractured (*noch gebrochen*)."

The *noch* and the *nur* that give these statements their rhythm (only this, still that, there remains this, there remains that) clearly mark the—temporal and structural—limit that holds absolute religion back in opposition and separates it absolutely from *Sa*: a limit that is scarcely visible, however, an almost nothing that separates the present out from its representation, and separates it out from it in its very (re) presentation.

A series of equivalent oppositions: father/mother (but these are not terms, rather relations already: relation to the father, relation to the mother, described from a third

limit, transgression, expenditure, etc.) should have led him to a different reading? If what must be called the sententious academism of this edifying discourse is not completely accidental, if there is in it a logical effect of blindness, of denying, of negatively inverting (as when one says—and here this is not, simply, a figure of speech—that neurosis is the negative of perversion), then it is perhaps because the system permits it. Everything can, at any moment, swerve toward the most strictly policed, sinister, moral and ridiculously reactive sermonizing. As unstable, inaccessible limit, sovereignty and its whole system (simulacrum, expropriation, loss, major laughter, etc.) along with it is always in the process of tipping over into metaphysics (truth, authenticity, propriety, mastery). It can always be read in the code that it overthrows, that it does more than overthrow but also must overthrow. In order for the metaphysical reading to be imposed some little nothing is all it takes, some logical or linguistic or discursive nothing: the *affect* of an intolerable identification (what is he afraid of? what is he incapable of?) provokes an interpretative decision. The negative then comes back on stage. Decision is here not an act of sovereign freedom. It is a position. One that cannot *see itself*, cannot stand the very picture of itself inverted. But one that, as a result, lets itself be observed, signed, assigned, affected from the place of Rembrandt.

beyond all the discursive combinatories, versions and inversions, all the logico-linguistic exchanges and cancellations, what perhaps brings an interpretation, the fact of a text, to a definitive end is affect. But it is classified, is affected also by its reverse side, and that false opposition also falls, must be known

Remember, it is he who is reading you.

term, the product of the operation, the son), in itself/for itself, knowing/feeling (love, heart). How do they operate? The singular divine man—Christ—has a father in himself, with whom he does not have an actual relation. Only his relation to his mother is actual. We don't have to ask what the name of his father is: be it Joseph or the Holy Spirit, they are not actual because they did not intervene actually, so to speak, with warm earthy seed, in the conception. In the religious moment of religion, the son has a father but the latter remains beyond phenomenal actuality, invisible. The father is in-himself but does not present himself. The son cannot interiorize in actuality, actually have for himself what of the father is in-himself. And which remains absent, transcendent, hidden, separated, severe, *pas-là.* Paternal generosity and goodness are merely represented, are not presented nor assimilated.

This unfinishedness then affects the reconciliation, in the son, of the father and the mother. Jesus too suffers from the divorce of his parents. The father (knowledge) is cut off from actuality, the mother (affect) is too natural and severed from knowledge.

Here is the place of Gabriel, the problematic place of an Annunciation.

She makes the child without knowing, without an actual father. The father is an object but a non-present object, the mother is present (phenomemom) but is not an object for consciousness, presents herself only to the heart. There is reconciliation with the mother, but in natural, sensory, worldly immediacy. Reconciliation with reason, the reconciliation of the heart and reason, of the for-itself and the in-itself is not yet accomplished.

The opposition of father and mother is equivalent to all the other oppositions in the series. Equivalent, then, to *opposition itself* insofar as it constitutes the structure of representation. What holds short of *Sa* while already touching on it, the null and infinite difference would be sexual difference *as opposition*: what *Sa* will have sublated [*relevé*], and which therefore until then comes under it [*relève d'elle*].

And if it sublates difference, opposition, then conceptuality itself is homosexual. It begins to be so when sexual difference*s* (in the plural) are erased and are determined as difference (in the singular).

In his time the doctors came up to him and didn't recognize him.

How to take hold of the bunch?
Do the grapes of this fakery form a fetish?

Let's appose here the question of the fetish. A question of style. Of pastiche, Gadda would say. Or Warda. Stilitano's question—antherection of the column—posed, inverted, out of the sublime cold of ice: "He [Stilitano] became the representation of a glacier. I would have liked to offer myself to the most bestial of negroes, to the most flat-nosed and most powerful face, so that within me, having no room for anything but sexuality, my love for Stilitano might be further stylized."

"At Stilitano's feet all was as bounding of fawns. Robert twined his garlands about him. The cripple was the column, the other the wisteria."

For that, propose to the stylite (whose "frigidity," "modesty," "symbol of chastity" has just been noted) that he crossdress.

"'Would you like me to dress up as a woman?' I murmured."

The style in question, the fakery held in place

This determination of sexual difference as opposition, as an opposition engaged in the whole process of opposition (*Entgegensetzung*) in general, of objectivity (*Gegenständlichkeit*) and representation (*Vorstellen*), entertains an essential historical and systematic relation with the Immaculate Conception: if not with the dogma concerning the birth of Mary, at least with its premise or conclusion—the virginity of the mother. Indispensable to Hegel's argumentation, to the speculative dialectic and to absolute idealism, it rules over what we could call *Sa's approach.*

As soon as one determines difference as opposition, one can no longer avoid the phantasm (word to be determined) of the *IC*: namely a phantasm of infinite mastery over both sides of the relation of opposition. The virgin-mother does without the actual father, both in order to come and in order to conceive. The father in himself, the real author, the subject of conception and even of the annunciation, passes over the woman, passes over that which he only passes, without touching her. All the oppositions that are linked around that one (active/passive, reason/heart, beyond/this world, etc.) have for cause and effect the immaculate maintenance of each of the terms, their independence and consequently their absolute mastery. An absolute mastery they have conferred on them phantasmatically at the very moment they are overturned and subordinated. It is when the virgin has the in-itself of the conceiving act withdrawn from her that she actually does without the father, etc. The phantasm is denounced and delimited as such on the basis of the *Sa* that makes the moment of absolute religion appear as a simple representation (*Vorstellen*).

Can the current concept of "phantasm" dominate this discourse in a relevant way? In fact it is determined by it, on the basis of it. For example, the effect of mastery produced by the determination of difference as opposition (and all the way to the value of mastery itself), of sexual difference as sexual opposition, each term of which would be sure of being dominant and having absolute autonomy in the *IC,* would be phantasmatic: the effect—the son (rather than the daughter), is mine, all mine. The *failure* of such a desire for a return to self, on the circle of double virginity, would be the limit of the phantasm, it determines the phantasm as such, at the end of the phenomenology of spirit. The phantasm is the phenomenon. The words indicate as much.

by a safety pin, is it a fetish?

That form of questioning presupposes already that one at least knows a fetish to be something. Here, apparently, yes, it is a fetish: substitute for the penis adored by the child who doesn't want to give up the phallus of the mother, monumental erection of the triumph over the threat of castration, denial, compromise, etc. Isn't all that completely recognizable?

What the stylite procures is not however the substitute for a penis with which he is well and powerfully endowed, but already for a "fake wound" (a fake *coup,* and a wound always comes suddenly from a blow [*d'un coup*] as the word indicates) as much as for a fetish member, for remarking-compensating

one column here—so think the other over there. One rises when the other descends, but isn't the level just about constant, "just about," only because you have nothing to do with measuring the two heterogeneous columns. No common measure at the very moment when you think you are engaging/disengaging, manipulating, orchestrating, raising or lowering the musical liquid by playing the pedals. The columns play with you, threatening to collapse one upon the other and leave you no way out.

No clang without some machinery being interposed.

That isn't handled like a quill.

No more than it can be measured by its logic, no organon is capable of its music. But doesn't the organologist think he can recognize his object: the machine has adapted to all the progress of Western technology (bellows, acoustics, electronics); it does without breath, divides the body, gears down, powerfully supplants the organist's gestures, comprising in turn a *body and a face* (the case and its show pipes), a *respiratory system* (bellows, wind chest), a *muscular system* (manual keyboards, pedal boards, wind chest valve, horizontal

But does one ever encounter such a failure? Where? Who can speak of it? What is it to fail in a case of absolute phantasm? The value of failure is feeble and confused. In the face of what would the phantasm of the *IC* have failed? In the face of "reality"? But measured by the potency of the greater logic that thinks the truth of the *IC,* this notion of "reality" also remains very confusedly empirical. Who would dare to say that the phantasm of the *IC* has not succeeded? Two thousand years, at least, of Europe, from Christ to *Sa,* not to speak of the retroactive effects, the representations, the effects of borders and their overflow, of everything one could call imperialism or the colonialisms and neo-colonialisms of the *IC.* Will we say, in order to determine the *IC* as a phantasm, that it is not *true*, that that's not how it happens, that it is only a myth? That would be pretty silly, and the silliness would still claim the authority of "sexual experience." But yes, that is how it happens and what the greater logic shows impeccably—that's the word—is that not only is this myth true, but that it gives the measure of truth itself, the revelation of truth, the truth of truth. So the (absolute) phantasm of the *IC* as absolute phantasm is the (absolute) truth. Truth is the phantasm itself. The *IC,* sexual difference as opposition (thesis against thesis), the absolute family circle would be the general equivalence of truth and phantasm. Homosexual *enantiosis*.

Is not this difference determined as contradiction or as opposition precisely religion (representation) resolved in *Sa?* Does *Sa* not permit us, precisely, to think the limit of this limit, to make this limit appear as such, to *see* the phantasm in its truth? Is not *Sa*, the resolution of absolute difference, the reconciliation of the in-itself and the for-itself, of the father and the mother, the very *Sa* of the phantasm?

Inasmuch as it effects the passage from representation to presence and produces the truth (present to itself in knowledge) of the absolute phantasm, inasmuch as it is the truth of the absolute phantasm, its unveiled essence (*Wesen: Gewesenheit:* the phantasm having-been), *Sa* is the final accomplishment of the phantasm, the being-with-itself of the *logos*. The absolute phantasm: *Sa*. But do not conclude from this: *Sa* is only—the phantasm, the truth of truth is still *only* phantasmatic. Once *Sa* accedes to itself, everything that is equivalent to it is infinite. One can no longer say of an infinite phantasm that it *is only*. The discourse of *Sa* disqualifies the *only*.

rollers and vertical rods), a *nervous and cerebral* system (console) with draw knobs corresponding to stops, combination pedals and couplings between one keyboard and another and between keyboards and pedals and sometimes fixed and free combinations of programmed registrations, a *vocal* system (ranks of pipes—as many as three thousand—reed and flue pipes). A flue pipe has a *foot;* air enters it and strikes the *languid,* and passing through the space between the languid and lower lip, then strikes the upper lip, causing air to vibrate inside the pipe. Pitch is determined by the length of the air column in the body; but a pipe that is stopped (drone) produces the effect of a pipe twice as long. A reed pipe comprises a tongue (thin brass blade that strikes the shallot, the copper tube closed at one end and protruding at the other through the lead block into the body of the resonator). An iron tuning wire, is adjusted with a tuning knife to regulate the length of the tongue and hence the pitch.

And taking into account the "swell" division [*récit*], the "shutters" [*jalousies*] of the "expressive division," the "full chorus [*plein-jeu*]," the "grand jeu," classic, double manuals [*bi-claviculation*], baroque or romantic organs, could one not reconstitute an organigraphical model, a new *De organographia*

Ja dieses vielstimmige liebliche Werck begreifft alles das in sich / was etwa in der Music erdacht vnd componiret werden kan / vud gibt so einen rechten natürlichen klang/laut vnd thon von sich/nicht anders als ein gantzer Chor voller Musicanten, do mancherley Melodeyen/von junger Knaben vnd grosser Männer Stimmen gehöret werden. In summa die Orgel hat vnd begreifft alle andere Instrumenta musica, groß vnd klein/wie die Nahmen haben mögen / alleine in sich. Wiltu eine Trummel/Trummet/Posaun/Zincken/Blockflöt/Querpfeiffen/Pommern/ Schalmeyen/Dolzian/Racketten/Sordounen/Krumphörner/Geigen/Leyern/ etc. hören/so kanstu dieses alles/vnd noch viel andere wunderliche liebligkeiten mehr in diesem künstlichem Werck haben: Also daß/wenn du dieses Instrument hast vnd hörest / du nicht anderst denckest/du habest vnd hörest die andern Instrumenta alle miteinander.

Michael Praetorius «De Organographia» Wolfenbüttel 1619,

which would be like the absolute knowing of clang?

But absolute knowing, like the "shutter," is but a piece of the machinery, an effect of working

another substitute for castration,

Such would be the bar (opposition and tiller) of religion/philosophy. Between them, the sails of the *IC,* of virginity or of truth, for spirit to blow into.

(Absolute) knowledge, truth (of the) phantasm (of) philosophy—(absolute) religion; this proposition draws no limit, it is the infinite proposition of the hetero-tautological speculative dialectic. Infinite circle of auto-insemination that draws the *paideia* of any seminar into its phantasm. What can there be outside an absolute phantasm? What can one still add to it? Why and how could one desire to get out of it?

We have to give ourselves the time. The time that remains.

The time that remains—for the seminar of *Sa*—is nothing.

Everything that is, all [the] time, is precomprehended, strictly, in the circle of *Sa*, which always comes back to itself, presupposes its beginning and reaches it only at the end (*in sich zurückgehende Kreis, der seinen Anfang voraussetzt und ihn nur im Ende erreicht*).

Try to *think* (but this word already holds us back in the circle) a remainder of *time* (but time already engages us in the circle), which would not be, which would not come under a present, a mode of being or presence and that would consequently fall outside the circle of (the) *Sa,* would not fall out of it as *its* negative, ready to get back on the tangent so as to remain bonded to the circle and let itself be drawn back by it. The remainder, moreover, would not fall out of it at all. All that falls indeed still comes under *Sa.*

So it would be about a suspended remainder.

his missing hand, etc. Moreover, he often cuts himself ("Stilitano used to cut himself, his fingertips were finely gashed, his nail was black and crushed, but this heightened his beauty.")

Is the undecidable not the undeniable.

In remarking his supplementary castration, Stilitano seems to affirm himself just as much as a male as he does as a modest woman or as a "queer who hates himself." Just a little further along, hymn to his "solemn behind," his "rump," his "*Reposoir.*"

Once the thing itself, in its unveiled truth, is already found to be involved in the unveiling itself, in the play of supplementary difference, then the fetish no longer has any rigorously decidable status. Knell of phallogocentrism.

After announcing the general laws and describing the essential structure of fetishism, the doctor reports, as if in an appendix, certain "very subtle cases (*In ganz raffinierten Fällen*)" where the fetish divides into two contrary positions (*zwiespältige Einstellung*).

That is the argument of the girdle [*gaine*] (*Gürtel*).

A little before that one had taken—as in *Beyond the Pleasure Principle*, and each time that the logic of the unconscious forces *both* the empirical

Which would not be: neither presence, nor substance, nor essence. In general, we think that what remains is permanent, substantial, subsistent. Here the remainder would not remain in this sense.

We also think that the remainder is the residue of an operation (subtraction or division), a waste, a piece of refuse that falls or stays. Here the remainder would, rather, provoke the operation. The remainder would not remain in either of these two senses. So why this word, why keep a "remainder" that does not correspond to the remainders of traditional semantics? Will we say that it retains a metaphorical relation with this semantics? That would still mean reappropriating it to metaphysical circulation. What remains of the "remainder" when one breaks it into pieces in this way? Whence the *rule* of its being broken into pieces? Must one still seek to determine a regularity when one breaks into pieces what remains of the remainder? A strictly angular question. The remainder here suspends itself.

Let's give ourselves the time of this suspense. For the moment time will be merely the suspense between the regularity and the irregularity of the pieces of what remains.

The question of time is indecipherable in the *Sa* chapter: in it is both annulled and sublated, suspended between annulation (*Tilgen*) and sublation (*Aufhebung*), the latter running the risk of getting lost in the ring that risks being sublated in the circle.

Does time remain in *Sa*? Such is, for the question, the structure of the annular. Does time remain and if it remains, does it remain in *Sa*? *What is it to remain?* is no longer even the question: if remaining is something, remaining annuls itself in the circle. *What does remaining mean* is no longer even the question, for everything that means-to-say belongs to the circulation of *Sa*. So how to get out of the ring, and is it a matter of getting out or of gripping it (thinking it) as closely as possible?

If one thinks what the *logos* means-to-say, if one fills with thought the words of the phenomenology of spirit and the logic, for example, there is no way to get out of the absolute circle. That is in any case what the discourse of *Sa* means-to-say. If one believes or claims (*meint*) to be getting out, it's pure verbalism: one is not thinking what one says, one is not conceiving the signification of the words which then remain empty.

The best example—and thus the essential example—

and the metaphysical *at the same time*—"quite a speculative" path. The very subtle case was that of a pubic corset ("suspensory belt") (*Schamgürtel*) also worn as bathing drawers (*Schwimmhose*), which totally hid the genitals and hence the difference between sex organs (*Unterschied der Genitalien*). It gave the appearance *just as much* "that a woman is castrated [as] that she is not castrated," and beyond that (*überdies*) "it even allows of a supposition (*Annahme*) that a man may be castrated. . . . Naturally, a fetish of this kind constructed out of two opposing ideas is capable of great tenacity (*Ein solcher Fetisch, aus Gegensätzen doppelt geknüpft, hält natürlich besonders gut*)." If the fetish is all the more solid, has all the more consistency and economic resistance for being doubly linked to contraries, its law is shown in the very subtle case and in the appendix.

Consistency, resistance, remaindering [*restance*] of the fetish is proportionate to its undecidable link to contraries. The fetish—in general—therefore begins to exist only inasmuch as it begins to be linked to contraries. This double link, this double ligament thus defines its most subtle structure. One must draw from that all the consequences. The economy

instead of quoting other "cases" (Schreber again) or other contracts (Christoph Haitzmann's double pact—red and black—and the devil with breasts): "This may not be an original thought with me, but let me restate it anyway, that the patron saint of actors is Tiresias, because of his dual nature . . . For seven years a man's clothing, for seven more a woman's. . . . his femininity followed in close pursuit of his virility, the one or the other being constantly asserted, with the result that he never had any rest, I mean any specific place where he could rest." (*Letters to Roger Blin*)

The Tightrope Walker, the bleeding headless sheath [*le sanglant de gaine*]: "And your costume? At once chaste and provocative. It is the skintight body stocking of the Circus, in blood-red jersey. It outlines your musculature exactly, it sheathes you, it gloves you, but from the collar—open in a circle, cut clean, as if the executioner were going to behead you tonight—from the collar to your hip, a sash, also red, but from which float panels—fringed with gold."

of this is the Trinity. This latter is thought only if one does not remain at the level of the formality of the arithmetical three, the empty signification of the three. And the trinity is bound up with the circular structure which can neither be assimilated nor let the remainder drop.

Given this, but by dint of no longer having the "question" form, the question of the remainder of time, the question of the three, and the question of the semantic void are elaborated together. The *Sa* fills up on meaning in the remainderless unity of a triangulo-circular structure.

So what happens when one does not read Hegel's text, or when one reads it *badly*? What happens if one immobilizes oneself in representation, in empty signification? Or if one strays from [*s'écarte*] the three, the *écart*, as its name indicates, cutting the text into squares or raising it to its square power, dividing it into more or less regular quarters, exalting it (to the contrary or by that very fact) or revering its charter, unless it deals it out like playing cards. How is it with the text as remainder—a set of pieces that no longer proceed from the whole and will never quite form one. This is no longer a question.

For example, when the temporal adverb (*still*) describes the approach of *Sa,* can it be read, semantically accomplished, on the basis of the absolute concept? Or without it? In the first case, it disappears, loses its temporal sense, is in a sense not read. In the other case, it is deprived of absolute conceptuality and cannot really be understood. It is still not read. In both cases it is read on condition of not being read. Because *reading* has been defined simultaneously as semantic filling and as remainder of semantic void.

How—for example—to read the anointed of the Lord in the text, on the threshold of *Sa*, at the end of the penultimate chapter of the phenomenology of spirit? How to read the adverb of the *logos*? We have understood that he has a father in-himself but an only actual mother whose eternal love he *feels* in his heart. "Its reconciliation exists thereby within its heart, but it is still estranged (*noch entzweit*) from its consciousness, and its actuality is still fractured (*noch gebrochen*). What enters into its consciousness as the *in-itself*, that is, the aspect of *pure mediation*, is the reconciliation which lies in the otherworldly beyond, but what appears as the *present* [as now: *als* gegenwärtig], as the aspect of *immediacy* and of *existence* (*Dasein*) is the world, which still (*noch*) has to await its transfiguration. The world is indeed *in itself* reconciled with the essence (*Wesen*); and it is indeed known of that essence that it no longer takes cognizance of the object as self-alienated,

of the fetish is more powerful than that of the truth—which is decidable—of the thing itself, or than a discourse deciding castration (*pro aut contra*). The fetish is not opposable.

It oscillates like the clapper of a truth that rings hollow [*qui cloche*].

Like the tongue [*batail*] in the throat, in other words in the chasm of a bell.

I do what I don't say, pretty much, I never say what I do.

For example, everything is going on as though I were first working to name, but also to found a bell. To have it both ring out and disappear in its nomenclature, to have it raised to the top of some tower and from there, unhooking it with a burst of laughter, have it founder, there you have what I say I do. I de-scribe.

Batail is first of all an old name for a bell clapper. Set in motion by the swing it hits the bowl (*panse*, also *pans*) like a sort of interior hammer. Not far from the curve [*faussure*], the place where the bell's shape begins to widen, to flare out. One also speaks of the *faussure* (or *faulsure*) of a tower.

but knows it as the same as itself in its love. However, for self- consciousness, this immediate presence (*diese unmittelbare Gegenwart*) does not yet (*noch nicht*) have spiritual shape. The spirit of the religious community is within its immediate consciousness still separated from its religious consciousness, which indeed declares (*zwar es ausspricht*) that *in itself* these two are not supposed to be separated, but that they have become an *in-itself* which is not realized, that is, which has not yet (*noch nicht*) become an equally absolute being-for-itself."

What can follow that does not already precede—subsequently—this penultimate not yet? In the *Sa* chapter, the last, then, what remains of time, i.e. of not-yet, is reduced, but suspended between sublation (*Aufhebung*) and annulation (*Tilgen*). To what "time" does the "text" of *Sa,* on *Sa* belong, then, the time of its repetition, of its legibility—full or empty? Who reads it? Who writes it? Who frames it? Who signs it?

"*Time* is the *concept* itself that *exists there* (*der* da ist) and is represented (*sich vorstellt*) to consciousness as empty intuition. Consequently, spirit necessarily appears (*erscheint*) in time, and it appears in time as long as (*so lange* (!)) it does not *grasp* its pure concept, which is to say, as long as it does not annul (*tilgt*) time [*tilgen*: to destroy, to annihilate, to erase, to abolish, to cancel, for example a debt: *eine Schuld tilgen*: to cancel or amortize a debt, a fault; *eine Rente tilgen*: to pay off a rent]. Time is the pure self (*Selbst*) *externally* intuited by the self but not *grasped* [conceptually] by the self; time is the merely intuited concept. Since [*indem*: while and inasmuch as] this concept grasps itself, it sublates its temporal form (*hebt er seine Zeitform auf*), comprehends the act of intuiting (*begreift das Anschauen*), and is intuition which has been conceptually grasped and is itself intuition which is comprehending. —Time thus appears as the destiny and necessity of the spirit inasmuch as it is not yet consummated within itself."

The *Da* of the concept (time) thus marks its incompleteness, its inner failing, the semantic void that keeps it in movement. Time is always of this vacancy with which

In the taking turns [*tour à tour*] in all genders of the fetish—which I defer—the splay of a *falsure*, neither this nor that, or even neither true nor false. But the operation is not negative, it affirms with a yes without limit, immense, prodigious, inaudible. And it constructs a sort of solid crossbeam to suspend the bell in the middle of the two towers. The headstock itself, sturdy horizontal wooden beam on which the bell is suspended, ends in two yokes [*tourillons*]. Wood, impassive matter, but, already, artifact. Forgotten, unperceived, deadening [amortissant] all resonance. Wooden. The beam [*madrier*]. She is, already, the *madrier*.

I write myself on that. On the headstock, between the two.

I hear myself saying, from afar, everything I write. I imitate it myself, I edit myself, I apostrophize all the top verbs. I deafen them.

Headstock pendulum, the fetish oscillates—

Sa affects itself. For it affects itself by itself; *Sa* empties itself with a view to determining itself, *it gives itself time*. It imposes a gap in signing itself. The *Da* of *Sa* is none other than the movement of signification.

The philosophy of religion, working in the name of God, does indeed distinguish two significations of signification. In it one wonders, when it comes to God, what the word *signify* (*bedeuten*) itself means. It signifies two "things"—opposite and symmetrical—which have in common a specific vacuum between signification (*Bedeutung*) and representation (*Vorstellung*). Sometimes we have the representation and we miss the concept, the plenitude of signification (for example when we ask ourselves "what the term 'God' signifies"). Conversely it happens that we have the signification without representation and what we then demand is an example (*Beispiel*) that "plays beside the essence" of substantial thought. But this double signification always signifies that thought gives of itself—examples, plays itself exemplarily.

The fact remains that in this play the meaningful gap always allows a text to function on empty. The concept can always not come back to itself in a text. The triangle or the circle can remain open when *Sa* arrives at the text. The text would then be what *Sa* cannot always give itself, what happens [*arrive*] to it rather than it arriving at itself in it.

The *Sa* interprets the event as one of its moments; as its own negative in the form of naturality, representation, empty signification. These negative values are regularly associated among themselves, for example in the first moment of the concept of absolute religion (first of three of the last of three moments of revealed religion). It is a reading of the Trinity according to John by the phenomenology of spirit:

"Spirit, represented (*vorgestellt*) initially as substance within the *element of pure thought*, is immediately thereby the simple, eternal selfsame *essence* (*sich selbst gleiche ewige* Wesen); however, its meaning is not this abstract *meaning* (Bedeutung) of essence but rather that of absolute spirit. Yet spirit is this, namely, not to be a meaning, not to be the inner, but rather to be the actual (*Wirkliche*). Hence, the simple eternal essence would be spirit merely in terms of empty words (*leeren Worte*) if were to remain within representational thought (*Vorstellung*) and the expression (*Ausdruck*) of

like the clapper of a truth that tilts, that *cl*—

The undeniable is the uncastratable.

That doesn't mean that there is no castration but that this *there is* has no place to take. The fact that one [*il y a qu'on*] cannot come down in favor of one or the other of the two contrary functions recognized in the fetish, no more than can one choose between the thing itself and its supplement. No more than one can between two sexes.

The tongue remains in the sheath [*la langue reste dans la gaine*],

the argument of the girdle thus envelops everything that, like a glove or flower, can be turned inside out in every way, or upside down without losing a certain form. That alone allows more aponeurotic effects of the tongue. For poetics, one profits again by playing the *Littré*, taking from it *dissemence*. Under *gaine*, it notes:
"1. Sheath for a knife or sharp, slicing instrument. Scissors in their *gaîne*.
Seafaring term: broad seam around sails to strengthen them before sewing the selvedge. Wind vane sheath, band of cloth attaching the wind vane to its shaft. *Gaîne de flamme*, cloth sheath in which one places a torch shaft. *Gaîne de pavillon*, band of cloth sewn to fit the whole width of a flag. 2. Architectural term: type of support, larger on top than on bottom, on which one places a bust; named thus probably because

simple eternal essence. However, because it is an abstraction, simple essence is in fact the *negative in itself*; namely, it is the negativity of thought, that is, negativity as it exists within the *essence* in itself, i.e., it is the absolute difference (*Unterschied*) from itself, that is, it is its pure becoming-other. As *essence*, it exists merely in itself, that is, for us, but since this purity is the abstraction itself, that is, negativity, it is *for itself*, that is, it is the *self* (*das* Selbst), the *concept*. —It is thus *objective* (gegenständlich), and since representational thought apprehends and expresses as an *event* (*als ein* Geschehen) what has just been expressed as the *necessity* of the concept, it will be said that the eternal essence in its own eyes *creates* an other (*sich ein Anderes* erzeugt). However, in this otherness, it has likewise immediately returned (*zurückgekehrt*) into itself again, for the distinction is the distinction *in itself*, i.e., the distinction is immediately distinguished merely from itself, and it is thus the unity returned into itself.

There are therefore three moments to be distinguished: *Essence*; *being-for-itself* which is the otherness of essence and for which essence is; and *being-for-itself* which is self-knowledge in an *other*. The essence intuits merely itself in its being-for-itself; in this self-emptying (*Entäußerung*), it is merely at one with itself (*bei sich)*, the being-for-itself which excludes itself from the essence. It is the *essence's knowledge of itself*, the word (*Wort*), which, when spoken (*ausgesprochen*), empties itself from the speaker and leaves him behind as emptied and hollowed out (*ausgeleert zurückläßt*), but which is likewise immediately heard, and it is only this hearing-of-itself which is the existence of the word (*und nur dieses Sichselbstvernehmen ist das Dasein des Wortes*). In that way, the distinctions which are made are likewise immediately dissolved just as they are made, and they are likewise immediately made just as they are dissolved, and the true and the actual are this very movement circling around within itself (*in sich kreisende Bewegung*).

This movement within itself expresses the absolute essence as *spirit*. The absolute essence which is not grasped as spirit is merely the abstract void, in the same way that spirit, when it is not grasped as this movement, is merely an empty word. Since its *moments* are grasped in their purity, they are restless concepts (*ruhelosen Begriffe*), which only exist in that they are in themselves their own opposite and that they are

the half-figure seems to emerge from a sheath; named *termes* when the sheath and the bust are a single piece. Place busts on their *gaînes*. 3. Botanical term: lower part of certain leaves covering the twig and as it were replacing the petiole. If the edges adhere the *gaîne* is full; if not, it is said to be split. 4. Anatomical term: Name given to certain parts serving as envelopes for other parts, used especially for an aponeurosis enveloping a fleshy mass. Entomological term: In sucking insects, tube enclosing the apparatus that the insect uses for sucking. In hymenoptera, the tube in which the labrum and proboscis are enclosed. 5. *Gaîne de chauffe*, referring, in a furnace, or a heat ventilator, to the apparatus that conducts air from the heating chamber to the area to be heated. Proverb: he who strikes with a knife will die from the sheath [*qui frappera du couteau mourra de la gaîne*], proverb based on "he who lives by the sword dies by the sword." NB: The Academy, which adds a circumflex to *gaîne* and *gaînier*, does not add one to the composite forms *dégainer, engainer, rengainer*. That is an irregularity that fruitlessly complicates the spelling. Etym. Wallon, *vaimm;* Hainaut, *waine* ; from Lat. *vagina*, gaîne. *Gaîne* is one of the examples where the Latin *v* changes to *g*. The ancient form must have been *gaaine*, representing *vagīna;* but if one finds *gaine* earlier than the 14th century it would have to be presumed that at the origin the Latin accent had been displaced, and one would have said *vagīna*."

Question of the circumflex: a "fruitless" complication in spelling.

What does the sheath suit?

motionless in the whole. However, the religious community's representational thought (*Vorstellen*) is not this *comprehending* thought. Rather, it has the content without its necessity and, instead of the form of the concept, it brings the natural relationships of father and son into the realm of pure consciousness."

Earlier, already dealing with the "actual mother" and the father "being in himself," these relations were presented as "drawn from natural generation." Religion, *qua* religion, never absolutely gets beyond representation or nature. Both the figure of natural representation (for example that of the fall, the son, etc.) and arithmetical formality (for example counting the moments) must be sublated in the concept. The death of Christ marks both the destruction of his natural being and the end of the abstraction of the divine essence. God himself is dead but the knowledge of his death produces that "spiritualization" through which "the substance has become subject" at the moment when abstraction and cadaverous cold (*Leblosigkeit*) rise to the warm and glorious light of life. The triumphal moment of mourning.

At the corner of the phenomenology of spirit and the (greater logic's) *Sa,* at the hinge, the tomb of the Son.

"I called her Mag, when I had to call her something. And I called her Mag because for me, without my knowing why, the letter g abolished the syllable Ma, and as it were spat on it, better than any other letter would have done. And at the same time I satisfied a deep and doubtless unacknowledged need, the need to have a Ma, that is a mother, and to proclaim it, audibly. For before you sag mag, you say ma, inevitably. And da, in my part of the world, means father. Besides, for me the question did not arise, at the period I'm worming into now, I mean the question of whether to call her Ma, Mag or the Countess Caca, she having for countless years been as deaf as a post."

"It is significant that in order to replace *Mag* by some name or other Molloy chooses by chance the title 'Countess Caca,' as if the nickname *Mag* were a condensation of *Mama* and *caca,* with a softening of K into G. The G could at the same time contain an allusion to the contraction of the pharynx that accompanies the refusal of food.

In this connection, Dr. Ilse Barande has pointed out to me that a passive homosexual American patient who spoke very good French, regularly pronounced *vaguin* instead of *vagin.* He introduced an occlusive, a hard, sharp sound, one that interrupts breathing, to replace the fricative Ž (GE), a sliding, fluid sound. The supplementary velar occlusive could in that case reflect a phantasm of the *vagina dentata.*" Fonagy

The remainder of time is undecided between three and more-than-three, fulfillment or the voiding of signification. *Sa* suffers this indecision. It tries to get its rhythm back and to find in it something like a return of the seasons.

One could just as well speak—the two words are related—of the Saturnalia of *Sa.* Festivals in honor of Saturn: the Italic god had been identified with Kronos (an empty play on words and there was time—that one would

what is it not to read Hegel or to read Hegel badly, Hegel or rather the *Sa* text? Is this negativity comprehended and at work in the *Sa* text? To admit that, one has first to read it and read it well. But what recourse would the *Sa* text have and before what authority could it bring this prior non-reading or bad reading, or all the seductions, drifts, perversions, neither real nor fictitious, neither true nor false, that would draw it outside itself without submitting to its jurisdiction? It is impossible to *know* if such a feint is possible. Rather one can only *know* it to be impossible, if knowledge presupposes the hierarchized opposition of the true and the false, the infinite and the finite. A finite feint cannot withdraw from the infinite authority of the *Sa.*

It will perhaps be considered that I use the *Littré* a great deal. I use it [*je m'en sers*], that's the word I'm looking for. Not trust it, play with it. Genetically. The etymologist's phantasm has been sent packing elsewhere, long ago, that of the word is on its last legs; and for poetics, if anyone still cared about that today, to have simply commented, illustrated with trips to the dictionary, lexicons and encyclopedias, *that strange word* [l'étrange mot d'].

What would not understanding (Hegel) the *Sa* text mean? If it is a finite failing, then it is comprehended in advance in the text. If it is an infinite fault or lack, we would have to say that *Sa* does not think itself, does not speak itself, does not write itself, does not read itself, does not know itself, which no longer means anything, by definition. *Sa* always ends up being full of itself, heavy with itself.

The hypothesis of a bad reading, here, therefore has no place. It does not even take place. We have to let it drop, in the margin or as an exergue, like a remainder about which we don't know whether it *works*, in view of or in the service of whom or what. Like this note from the *Post-Script* to the *Philosophical Fragments*, crumbs of crumbs beneath the stage:

"Similarly Hegel also is supposed to have died with the words that no one understood him except one person, who misunderstood him. . . . In the first place, Hegel's statement has the flaw that it is a direct statement and thus is totally inadequate for such a misunderstanding, and this sufficiently shows that Hegel did not exist artistically in the illusiveness of double-reflection. Next, it has the flaw that Hegel's communication in the seventeen whole volumes is direct communication, so that if he has not found anyone who has understood him, it is all the worse for Hegel. It would be a different matter with Socrates, for instance, who artistically arranged his entire mode of communication so as to be misunderstood. Regarded as a dramatic utterance at the moment of death, Hegel's statement is best regarded as delirium, as thoughtlessness on the part of one who, now in death, wants to take paths he had never taken in life. If Hegel as a thinker is one of a kind, then there is indeed no one with whom he can be compared, and if there should nevertheless be someone with whom he could be compared, so much is certain, that he would have absolutely nothing in common with Socrates." Elsewhere: "Presumably, this continuous progress has also given rise to the misunderstanding that it takes a devil of a fellow in speculative thought to free himself from Hegelianism. Far from it; only sound common sense is needed, a pithy sense of the comic, a little Greek ataraxia. Apart from logic, and also somewhat in logic because of an ambiguous light that Hegel has not excluded, Hegel and Hegelianism are a venture in the comic. By now, the late Hegel has presumably met his

come here to celebrate as *Sa*). He supposedly took refuge in Italy after his son had dethroned and thrown him from the top of Mount Olympus. He had himself sliced off his father's testicles with the help of his mother, Gaia. It was again Gaia, already her, who put the sickle in the hands of the son. And perhaps her, again, who allied herself with Zeus, her grandson, against Kronos, her son, and made him swallow a pharmakon that caused him to vomit up all the children he had eaten. So Saturn is supposedly an ousted father to whom the Latin period had left the memory of a mythical golden age. He became the god of agriculture and more precisely, armed with a sickle and a billhook, he would preside over the pruning of vines. Like Dionysus-Bacchus, he was closely associated with wine. He was also considered to be the god of the underworld.

So the saturnalia corresponded to the rhythm of the *season*, a word which no doubt comes, like Saturn, from *sata*, the fruits of the earth, and seeding, from *serere,* to sow, or from *satus,* son. Sowing is a

Consider the title, the false title, the apostrophe that suspends and diverts the strange word. The way it works is unusual. One expects the word *urbanism,* as in the first sentence ("That strange word 'urbanism'"). And indeed urbanism provides the apparent theme of these nine pages. But through a movement of erection (also the theme of the piece), that is to say a movement of theatrical and funerary overturning, the writing obliquely describes the title itself: namely the word, and that it is strange. And it doesn't omit, as is often the case, the always oblique aspect of erection ("in a cemetery, or quite close to the crematorium furnace, to the stiff, tilting [*oblique*], phallic chimney").

As for the strangeness of the word, here is the end of the text that this very clang has never stopped accompanying, escorting or preceding; or betraying: "Where? Rome, I read, had—but perhaps my memory deceives me—a funeral mime. His role? Preceding the procession, he was supposed to mime the most important deeds that made up the life of the dead man when he—the dead man—was alive. Improvise gestures, attitudes?

Words. Lived I don't know how, the French language hides and reveals a war that words make, enemy brothers, one tearing itself away from the other or becoming infatuated with it. If tradition and treason were born from one single original gesture and diverge so that each can live its individual life, how is it that they are linked in their distortion all through language?"

What is given, delivered by *traditio,* here, thanks to the gift of language and of style, is at the same time an example and an essence, an event and a rule. *Traditio* is an example of the *traditio* of language, it gives the gift and betrays the treason. Tongue proceed by tradition and treason. That is how the word is a word.

master in the deceased Socrates, who undoubtedly has something to laugh about, that is, if Hegel has remained unchanged. Yes, there Socrates has found a man worth talking with and especially worth asking (something Socrates intended to do with all the dead) in Socratic fashion whether or not he knows something. Socrates must have changed considerably if he would be even remotely impressed if Hegel were to begin to reel off paragraphs and promise that everything would become clear at the end."

season, *serere* supposedly has the same semantic origin as *semen, seminare*. The Greek ancestor could be *saô* (to winnow). During the saturnalia, order was inverted, law was transgressed: a time of debauchery, of license, of drunkenness, a spasmodic revolution during which, says an anachronistic treatise on mythology, "the social classes were topsy-turvy," the masters becoming the slaves of their slaves, whom they served at table. The evil trick of the seasons coming to throw the history of spirit out of joint, the saturnalia of *Sa* would then be intimately bound up with a malfunctioning of the *seminarium*.

Play with the four of the seasons: this play, the sickness of *Sa,* opens it with a *gap* that no longer allows it to be sure of being able to reappropriate itself in the Trinitarian circle. This seasonal sickness neither destroys nor absolutely paralyzes the infinite concept. If it merely formed its negative, it would confirm it again dialectically. Rather it puts it out of joint, jams it, makes it seize up inconceivably. Claws it [*le griffe*] with writing also. The etymon of *Begriff* is waiting there.

As soon as it is seized [*saisi*] by writing, the concept is done [*cuit*]. Thus perhaps are the saturnalia of *Sa* unleashed, the drunkenness, satiety, the "Bacchic inebriation (*Taumel*)" with which the true is possessed, sparing no "member" (*Glied*), but about this delirium it would no longer be certain whether *Sa* introduces itself to itself, announces it at the beginning of the phenomenology of spirit to awake from its revels at the end, once a momentary inebriation has passed, the time of a part(y) (of itself).

Because one might be tempted to reduce *Sa*'s drunkenness [*cuite*] to a typical phase—essential, certainly, but very determinate—of the phenomenology. Does it not give its rhythm to the whole phenomenology of religion? In its three beats, natural religion, aesthetic religion, revealed or absolute religion?

An external index: one passes for example from the religion of flowers, then of *raw* animality (natural religion) to an "overflowing divine inebriation" (*unbefestigte Taumel des Gottes*) which has to calm down by making itself an object in

"Lived no more poorly than any other, yet this language, like others, allows words to mount [*se chevauchent*] each other like animals in heat, and what comes out of our mouth is an orgy of words that mate, innocently or not, and that give French discourse the salubrious air of a forested country where all the wandering animals are coupled. Writing in such a language—or speaking it—one says nothing. One just allows a torrent of beings, or, if you like, of ambiguous words, like the beasts of the Fable, to mill about some more, to mingle and mix, in the midst of vegetation that is itself distracted, patterned by its mixture of pollen, by its random grafts, by its sprouts, its cuttings.
If anyone expects that by means of such a proliferation—or luxuriance—of monsters he can handle a coherent discourse, he is mistaken; at best he breeds larval and sly swarms similar to the processions of processionary caterpillars, which exchange their sperm to give birth to a grotesque progeny without any progress, without importance, come hither from Greek, Saxon, Levantine, Bedouin, Latin, Gaelic, from a wandering Chinese, from three vagabond Mongolians, and which speak not to say anything, but, by mating, to reveal a verbal orgy whose meaning is lost, not in the night of time, but in the infinity of tender or brutal mutations.
And the funeral mime?
And the Theater in the cemetery?
Before burying the dead man . . ."

There I'm cutting it off, go see for yourself what the dead man becomes in the course of the celebration. When "the celebration is over," it's back to words, which, without seeming to, are allowed to be hardbound, covered with flowers along the length of the funeral procession. Strange death. "When one is clever, one can pretend to know what is going on, one can pretend to think that words do not move, that their meaning is fixed, or that it moves thanks to us, who—one claims to believe, if one modifies their appearance a little—voluntarily become gods. Whereas I, facing this enraged herd caged in the dictionary, I know that I have said nothing and that I will never say anything: and the words don't give a fuck. . . .

the living work of art of aesthetic religion. This drunkenness will have made one pass from flower to fruit and to wine, to fermented fruit, the Bacchic moment of aesthetic religion: not-yet but already the bread and wine, flesh and blood of the Christian supper. This phenomenological banquet is set up at the center of the center: in the middle of aesthetic religion which itself occupies a mediating position between natural religion and revealed (absolute) religion. It happens at sundown: "This *pathos* is on its own the essence of the *sunrise* (des Aufgangs), but which has henceforth *turned inward* (in sich *untergegangen*) and *within itself* become the *sunset*; self-consciousness and thereby existence and actuality has its sunset, its downfall (*Untergang*), in itself.—Here it has run its course through the movement of its actualization. Reducing itself from its pure essentiality into an objective force of nature and into the expressions of this force, it is an existence for the other, for the self by which it is consumed (*verzehrt wird*). The silent essence of self-less nature (*selbstlosen Natur*) attains in its fruits (*Frucht*) the level where it, nature, in preparing itself and in being digested, offers itself up (*darbietet*) to self-like life (*dem selbstischen Leben*); it is in its utility, that is, in its being able to serve as food and drink, that it attains its highest perfection. This is so because in that kind of utility, it has the possibility of a higher existence, and it comes into contact with spiritual existence. —In its metamorphosis, the spirit of the earth (*Erdgeist*) has in part developed and become a silently powerful (*stillkräftigen*) substance, and in part it has become spiritual ferment (*geistigen Gärung*). As the former, it progressively develops itself into the feminine principle of nurturance (*weiblichen Prinzipe der Ernährung*), and as the latter into the masculine principle of the self-impelling force (*sich treibenden Kraft*) of self-conscious existence."

Enjoyment here enjoys manifestation, the phenomenon, the light, the luminous essence (*Lichtwesen*) insofar as it emerges. There is a "mystery" there, but what is "mystic" does not depend on some dissimulation (*Verborgenheit*) or some intimate secret (*Geheimnis*) of knowledge. What is mystical is the revelation, the manifestation of self uniting with the essence that becomes "consumable," "object of a desire." This is the moment of the cult: "What through the cult has thereby been revealed to self-conscious spirit within itself is the *simple* essence. This is in part as the movement of that essence's departing from its nocturnal concealment (*nächtlichen Verborgenheit*) and moving up into consciousness,

So, for the great parade before the burial of the corpse, if the funeral mime wants to make the dead man live and die again, he will have to discover, and dare to say them, those dialectophage words that in front of the audience will devour the life and death of the dead man."

beats under the sheath, cavorting there, cutting, cracking, reforming, absenting, gluing, detaching, separating, alleging, delegating, arguing, tending, getting hard.

The bit flashes itself but benefits from a gain in strength only by holding back the turbulence swollen under the fabric.

Desirable if impregnable, or close to being (so).

Toilette at every instant of the bit, bandaged, hardbound, verified, mummified.

It would be too easy otherwise.

gl remains under the sheath.

Of all the fragmenting [*morcellements*], of all the reagglutinations without which *skisis* could not even *be produced*—*gl* would be, would hardbind the transcendental accomplice [*compère*] of *skzz*, the *originarilie* [l'originaire-ment], like galalith, synthetic, which closes opens the sluice, stops the flow at the very instant when with a gentle explosion it forces the lock—of all the proliferating wounds, bites, breaks, sutures, edgings and grafts that *gl* took advantage of, there appeared, infinitive scene, at the end of the operation, only the oiled, smooth surface, neither wrinkled nor scarred, the calm sea of the letterhead. The title displays, plus a sign of fatigue, the appeased, glorious integrity of a whole word, the verbal body of *glas*. Interposed before the disseminating mark, the vowel is no longer seen, no longer scaffolds. It sings the bit or has it sing for its supper.

which is to be its silently nurturing substance; it is in part as the movement of its equally losing itself again in the night of the underworld, in the self, and that of lingering above that underworld only with silent maternal yearning. —However, the sheer impulse (*lautere Trieb*) is the multiply-named (*vielnamige*) luminous essence of the sunrise and its tumultuous life, which, having equally been emptied of its abstract being, has at first entered into the objective existence of the fruits of the earth, and then, surrendering itself to self-consciousness, has attained there its genuine actuality – it now roams about as a throng of madly rapturous women (*als ein Haufen schwärmender Weiber*), the unrestrained (*ungebändigte*) revel of nature in a self-conscious shape."

Such a delirium manifests only immediate spirit, the spirit of nature: bread and wine, Ceres and Bacchus. The higher gods, themselves conscious of themselves, have not yet appeared. Now self-consciousness presupposes the *sacrifice* of spirit. What already announces itself in nature, in the sacrifice of bread and wine, is not yet what it announces, "the mystery of the flesh and the blood."

The seasons, the seizure of the concept, the saturnalia, the passage from flower to fruit, from fruit to wine, from wine to blood, the spiritual fermentation that introduces one sex into the other, so many therms: phenomena of warming or rather of reheating. Opposition of the raw and the cooked, of the cold and the hot, passage from one opposite into the other, spirit reappropriates itself by warming itself up again, taking itself back from nature. It had gotten lost there, chilled, alienated; this is not said by metaphor: the tropes here are produced by (the) spiritual fermentation. Warming *signifies* life in general, organic life and spiritual life, the consummation of life. Natural life is destroyed to

to Aulic Councilor Forster:
"Lagrime Christi!
From this we can now clearly see that the tears the Lord has shed over the abuses of Catholicism have been not only salt water but bottles of liquid fire.
And now you wish generously out of friendship to help me prepare the flow of Latin prose that I must now work up, and are going to do so by drawing on this same fire. For this I must first of all thank you. And if this poor vessel which is to distill the fiery substance does not spoil it, my amply tortured audience shall thank you for the warmth emanating from me to them.

B. $\frac{22}{6}$ 30 Yours, Hegel"

"If you, dear friend, still have a sufficient supply of *Lagrimae Christi* to pour me another half dozen bottles, I will be much obliged—and indeed invigorated!—for you to put aside for me such an amount. Could you perhaps send some immediately along with the bearer of this note?
My best compliments to your equally dear wife.

Yours Hgl $\frac{3}{10}$ 30."

That's where (one has) to put the accent in the case where one wishes to understand something about writing, to decipher or decircumcise that text that one tolls.

There is there—taking into account the bit and the sublingual drool, the caesura and the agglutination—no sign, no language, no noun, and especially not any "primitive word" in the Cratylic sense; nor moreover is there some transcendental privilege accorded an elementary couple at which the analytic regression would finally stop, nor even—since no being or sense is represented there—is there a mimeme.

Remains that: the problem of *mimesis* has to be reelaborated here beyond the opposition between nature and law, motivation and arbitrariness, beyond all the ontological couples that have rendered it, along with *Cratylus*, illegible.

gl wrenches "body," "sex," "voice," "writing" away from the logic of consciousness and representation that used to govern the debate. While remaining one effect of the bit among others, *gl* also remarks within it—whence, always, the interested-party transcendental effect—the angular cut of opposition, *both* the differential *skisis* *and* the continuous flow of the couple, *both* the distinction *and* the copulating unity (for example of arbitrariness and motivation). It is one of the de-terminant sluices—only one but as interested party—open closed to a rereading of *Cratylus*.

be sublated into spiritual life. Warming allows for assimilation, digestion, nutrition, interiorization, idealization—sublation. *Aufhebung* is a *fermentation* (*fervere*, *fermentum*) in nature and in natural religion, a *fervor* when religion internalizes or spiritualizes itself. In coming back to itself in warmth, producing itself as self-repetition, spirit rises, sublates itself and holds itself in sublime suspension above natural fermentation like gas or effluvium.

Whether it be about ferment or fervor, the tumultuous opposition of two "principles" is always at work: the feminine (night and natural silence of substance) and the masculine (light, *logos* of self-consciousness, becoming-subject of substance). This opposition, like opposition in general, will have been at one and the same time the manifestation of difference (as a consequence of that remainder of time in which the void of signification veers off [*s'écarte*]), *and* the process of its erasure or its reappropriation. As soon as difference is determined, it is determined as opposition, it manifests itself, certainly, but its manifestation is at the same time (this is the time of the same as erasure of the rest of time in the self (*Selbst*)) reduction of difference, of the remainder, of the gap [*écart*]. That's the thesis.

Religious animation, the history of religious manifestation, religion in the phenomenology of spirit describes this effort to assimilate the remainder, to cook, eat, swallow, internalize the remainder without leftovers. After fermentation, the banquet leftovers are reappropriated at Supper.

The concept of religion is filled out, determined, by opposing itself to itself then reconciling with itself: in three moments that accomplish absolute spirit. In a first moment, absolute spirit finds its actual existence in religion, but in a religion the concept of which remains yet empty and indeterminate. Religion here is *immediate* and *natural*. Spirit sees itself outside, apprehends itself as its own object in a natural and immediate figure. This is the moment of natural religion (sun, plant, animal, work of the artisan). Spirit loses itself and finds itself again in external, sensory and natural objects. The last of the three (the three and not the four, as the religion of plants or flowers does not form a stabilized structure, a true religion), the least natural, the work of the artisan ensures the mediation towards the next moment: aesthetic religion. In the first moment, in natural religion,

Socrates pretends to take sides. For example: "He further observed the liquid movement of λ, in the pronunciation of which the tongue (*glôtta*) slips (*olisthanei*), and in this he found the expression (*aphomoiōn ōnomasē*) of smoothness (*ta tē leia*), as in λειος (level), and in the word ολισθανειν (to slip) itself, λιπαρον (sleek), in the word κολλωδες (gluey), and the like; the heavier sound of γ detained (*antilambatenai ē tou gamma dynamis*) the slipping tongue (*olisthanouses tes glottes*), and the union of the two gave the notion of a glutinous clammy nature, as in γλισχρος, γλυκυς, γλοιωδες."

The enigma is thus that of the sphingtor, of what the sphigma has let through. Tighten (the text) so that it secretes, repress it with an antileptic (g), liquid antagonism makes coming flow out. No period following the *gl*, a comma and even then, *gl* remains open, unblocked, ready for every concubination, every collage. It's not an element, *gl* unblocks toward what is called an element (river mouth opening onto the sea for example).

It's not a word—*gl* hoists up language but doesn't keep it there, always letting it fall back down, not belonging to it—even less a name, barely a proforename [*proprénom*].

But may be the subject of annunciation.

The sciences, all of them, have to register here the dice throw. And the strength of chance [*aléa*], as clinamen—the other collar [*col*] that some double constrains.

spirit has not come back to itself, is not yet itself (*Selbst*). By negating the natural exteriority of the sensory thing in which it had lost itself, by consuming it, internalizing it, sublating it, it identifies itself, finds itself again, recognizes itself as such (*Selbst*). The second moment of religion is therefore that of the "figure of sublated naturality or of the *Selbst*." The moment of aesthetic religion: spirit contemplates itself in the object that it has itself produced, in its work. It no longer has consciousness only of the object (sun, plant, animal, etc.) but consciousness of itself. We have passed over from nature to art, as from consciousness to self-consciousness, from object to subjectivity. This last opposition, and the unilaterality of the two agencies, is sublated into absolute (revealed or manifest) religion. In this ultimate sublation, spirit reveals itself in its true figure but what sublates and reveals itself here (it suffices to think of what withdraws in this movement of the veil to see introduced, in the anagrammatical throw of the dice [*se relève/se révèle*], the fermentation of truth) still remains at the level of figural representation. "However, although spirit indeed achieves its true *shape* (*zu seiner wahren* Gestalt) in revealed religion, the very *shape* itself and the *representational thought* (Vorstellung) of it are still the aspect which has not been overcome (*unüberwundene Seite*). Spirit must pass over from that aspect into the *concept* in order to fully dissolve the form of objectivity within the concept, that is, the concept which likewise includes its opposite within itself." *Sa* has no figure, is not a figure, whereas absolute religion is still (true) figure and representation.

Whence the circle of this syllogistic chain: natural religion, the first moment of religion (immediate consciousness and sense certainty) comprises three moments of which the first (the first moment of the first moment) is also, like *Sa* at the other end, absence of figure, an unrepresentable moment. Figure withdraws at the beginning and the end of religion, before and after religion: the becoming of which literally describes a consummation of the figure, between two suns. Another jealousy of Hegel's God who begins and ends by making his own figural representation disappear in the fire. This jealousy, this *zelos* is not to be reduced to the passion of the Jewish God who never shows himself. Here God shows himself neither at the beginning nor at the end of time, but so as to show himself at all times through his figures and in an absolute light. It is true that he shows himself the better by not showing himself, since determinate figures precisely dissimulate him in their determination. Between

Everything is in training for making a big thing of chance. It can only ever fall advantageously and *encanker* [enchancrer] the necessary at the unlocatable instant when the proper name breaks into the tongue, destroys itself there in an explosion—dynamite—leaving something like a hole. Covered over very quickly: a parasitic vegetation and without memory.

Under the effect of the *obliquid*, erection is always spilling over in order to fall. Or even to invert itself.

gl protects against the *skisis* that *gl* produces.

Antherection is also the "feminine counterpart [*pendant*] of Stilitano's bunch of grapes." No more than does betrayal, crossdressing doesn't provide the theme of this narrative; it gives the "literary" operation its reach.

The feminine counterpart of the bunch of grapes is elaborated at the same time as is spoiled [*s'abîme*] the literary fetish, the "literary diversion" that "this journal" I am writing does not reduce to.

Immediately before the crossdressing sequence and following a linking or mounting of "rump" (Stilitano's) and cups, *coups*, collars [*cols*], lice [*poux*] and other now familiar antherianthems, we learn that Pépé has been arrested.

"'How long can they give him [*Qu'est-ce qu'il risque*]?'

'Life [*Perpétuité*].'

We made no other comment.

This journal is not a mere literary diversion."

the Jewish god and the Hegelian god, the problem of the remainder is played out in the form of an excess of zeal. Jealousy is between them.

In the first moment of natural religion, that of the luminous-essence (*Lichtwesen*), spirit is at first only its own concept. But this concept remains in abstract indetermination, has not yet deployed itself, manifested itself, produced itself. It still reserves itself "in the night of its essence (*die Nacht seines Wesens*)." In the first scission that unveils the secret (*Geheimnis*) of spirit, the latter relates to itself according to a "simple relation," without mediation or determination. The being "filled" (*erfüllte*) by this concept of spirit is indeterminate; it appears, appears to itself as such: pure light, simple determinability, pure milieu, ethereal transparency of manifestation in which nothing appears but the appearing, the pure light of the sun. This first figure of natural religion figures the absence of figure, a purely visible and therefore invisible sun, which allows seeing without showing itself or which shows itself without showing anything, consuming everything in its phenomenon: *die Gestalt der Gestaltlosigkeit*. This figure is "the pure, all-embracing and all-filling *luminous essence*," that of the rising or the orient (*Lichtwesen des Aufgangs*). As nothing shows itself here, the orient here immediately passes into its pure being-other, absolute shadow or occidentality. Analyzed as abstract subjectivity, this figure without figure, first moment of natural religion in the *Phenomenology of Spirit*, corresponds to the third moment of natural religion in the *Lectures on the Philosophy of Religion* ("Historically, cult of light is the perspective of the religion of the Parsis [founded by Zoroaster]. The cult has its existence in this religion. They do not adore the light under the form of the sun; their adoration is not, in the strict sense, a cult of nature; but the light directly signifies the Good").

Pure and without figure, this light burns everything. It burns itself in the burn-all that it is, leaves, of itself or anything, not a trace, not a mark, no sign of passage. Pure consummation, pure effusion of light without shadow, midday without contrary, without resistance, without obstacle, waves, downpourings, enflamed floods of light: "the movements of its own emptying, its creations in the unresisting elements of its otherness, are all castings of light (*Lichtgüsse*), and in their simplicity they are at the same time (*zugleich*) both its coming-to-be-for-itself and its return out of its existence, that is, the shapes of consuming streams of fire."

The louse stands out [*se détache*] on Stilitano's collar, which it assumes as its "domain," its "space." The collar is cut out within a whole panoply of semantic and formal variations. The turbulence of those associations calls forth the detachable collar [*faux col*], which doesn't arrive. In order to submit to the flexible but persistent force of writing, to its endless simulacrum, and re-emerge as false eyelashes on the other page. And sticking to fingers, to phalanges rather.

False eyelashes on one of the *mariconas* called Pedro. That's the moment when the remark "This journal is not a mere . . ." transits toward a young monkey jumping on the *maricona*'s shoulder. "His eyelashes remained stuck to my phalanges; they were false. I had just discovered the existence of fakes."

A last station in the procession toward the grand paranthesis.

The feminine counterpart of Stilitano's bunch of grapes is put in place, stitched into the text, only after the castration described by another column, also the monumentalization of the wound covered over with flowers.

It's the knell of a urinal.

Following the destruction of the little edifice the obsequent procession gets moving, like that of the inmates following the castration of Guiana. Beside the still smoking scar the queens come to place their flowers. The sepulcher is once more erected care of a delegation, a detachment of transvestites.

By very reason of this indifference—or rather this absence of opposition—the pure content of this being has no essence. The burn-all is "an essenceless byplay in this substance, which merely *rises* without *descending* into itself (*ein wesenloses Beiherspiel an dieser Substanz, die nur* aufgeht, *ohne in sich* niederzugehen), that is, without becoming a subject and consolidating its distinctions through the self (*Selbst*)."

A pure play without essence, a play that plays without limit, even though it is already destined to work in the service of essence and meaning. But as such, supposing one can say "as such" of something that is not some thing, this play is not yet working, it does not yet have an onto-theo-teleological horizon: artistic fire without being. The word itself (*Beiherspielen*) plays the example (*Beispiel*) beside the essence. Here the pure example plays to such an extent *beside* the essence, it stands to such an extent apart from the essence that it has no essence: pure example, without essence, without law. Therefore without example, like God of whom Hegel says he cannot be made into an example but because *he* merges with the pure essence, it too without example. The total burning—which takes place only once and yet is repeated *ad infinitum*—stands so well apart from any essential generality that it looks like the pure difference of an absolute accident. Play and pure difference, that's the secret of an imperceptible burn-all, the torrent of fire that enflames itself. Carrying itself off, pure difference is different from itself, therefore indifferent. The pure play of difference is nothing, it does not *relate* even to its own burning. The light darkens before even becoming subject. To become subject, the sun must indeed decline. Subjectivity is always produced in a movement of occidentalization. Now here the sun does not set—or else it sets immediately, it knows no decline, no trajectory that brings it back to itself, no season, season in the sense of cycle, only a pure season, in the sense of seminal effusion without return. This difference without subject, this play without work, this example without essence, deprived of self (*Selbst*), is also a sort of signifier without signified, the waste of an adornment without body proper, total absence of propriety, of truth, of meaning, a scarcely manifest deployment of forms that immediately destroy themselves. It is a One both infinitely multiple and absolutely different, different from itself, a One without self, the other without self that means nothing, whose language is absolutely empty, like an event that never arrives at itself.

Blank, as always, between two antherections, an interior margin between two supplementary columns that seem detached one from the other: "Stilitano stepped back slowly, protected by his outstretched st [*moi*]

you can always look for the subject.
Nothing ever gets hardbound, it seems, other than a stump.
A truncated wrist that grows back stronger.
Funeral Rites: "His hands were in his pockets. He was heavy and yet light, for each of his angles was imprecise. He looked like a walking willow, each stump of which is lightened and thinned by an aigrette of young branches. He had a revolver."
"A posture of Erik's: his thumb was in the space between his two fly buttons. Like Napoleon, who used to hook his thumb on his vest. A sick man fearing the rush of blood to his bandaged hand."
Miracle of the Rose: "Another of Harcamone's embellishments: his hand swathed in white. . . . A trifle would injure him. Perhaps there was nothing wrong with him and he feigned injuries! Yards of white gauze were wound around his hand. . . . Those dressings made him cruel, him the gentlest of angels. . . . Like lots of tough guys, he wore on his right wrist a broad leather band . . . a 'wrist-support [*poignet de force*],' but it had become an ornament, a symbol of manliness. It was laced on by a leather cord, at the bend of the elbow."
These angel's bandages resemble those used to swaddle babies after their circumcision. That is to say all the time. Gauze flannel and crape band. "And it came to pass, that on the eighth day they came to circumcise the child; and they called him Zacharias, after the name of his father. And his mother answered and said, Not *so;* but he shall be called John. And they said unto her, There is none of thy kindred that is called by this name. And they made signs to his father, how he would have him called. And he asked for a writing table, and wrote, saying, His name is John. And they marvelled all. And his mouth was opened immediately, and his tongue *loosed* . . ." Luke's narrative of the birth of John the Baptist.

What is needed here: to induce one's hands to bandage the column. The column is wounded,

"Its determinations [that of this pure being or of this play without essence] are merely attributes that do not progress up to the point of self-sufficiency (*Selbstständigkeit*); rather, they remain (*bleiben*) merely names of the many-named 'one' [empty names, then: there is not yet any meaning, time, or circle]. This 'one' is clothed with the manifold forces of existence and with the shapes of actuality as if they were selfless ornaments (*als mit einem selbstlosen Schmucke*). They are merely messengers of its power, and they lack any will of their own, any intuitions of its glory, and any voices in its praise."

How can the self and the for-itself appear? How could the sun of the burn-all get going on its course and its decline?

At first blush one cannot see how the situation could change, nor why the void of the concept would have to be filled.

How can anything remain from this consummation without limit to start the dialectical process and open history? Conversely, if the process begins, how would it reduce this pure differential consummation, this pure destruction that can proceed only from fire? How could solar expenditure produce a remainder—something that abides or exceeds itself? How would the purest of the pure, the worst of the worst [*le pur du pur, le pire du pire*], the panic fire of the burn-all grow any monument, even a crematory monument? Some stable, geometrical, solid form, for example a *pyramis* that retains a trace of the dead?

Pyramis is also a cake made with honey and flour. It was given as a reward for a sleepless night to whomever stayed awake. It was also a conical cake presented to the dead. The Greeks gave this name to Egyptian monuments, or so some believed, because of the word *pyr*, because flames end in a point, or because of this conical flour cake (soft or hard wheat, *pyros*).

If it destroys everything including its letter and its body, how can the burn-all keep a trace of itself and start a history in which it preserves itself by losing itself?

Here we experience the implacable force of meaning, of mediation, of the laborious negative. In order to be what it is, purity of play, of difference, of consummation, the burn-all must pass into its opposite: keep itself, keep its

it wouldn't be a column otherwise. It is truncated, marked, covered with scars and inscriptions. The Stylite wears an "enormous bandage," his arm is folded as if in a sling but "I knew that the hand was missing."

The scars are tattoos, words and designs incrusted in each column, notches mixing black ink and red blood in order to sign the contract in the skin and treat the text. The *gl* ceremony thus obeys, in its form, the "Order of Tattoos" whose institution is recounted in the *Miracle of the Rose*.

The tattoos also have the relief of brilliant, sharp stones like those that the Dayak of Borneo—I think—would stick into the surface of the penis after making an incision, so as to enhance the woman's enjoyment, or so they say.

Elsewhere *gl* pierces the tattoo of a silent, precious, brilliant antheme. "'Bye-bye, bugger.' He doesn't mean that he assumes the singer has a wild rose tattooed on his thigh or that his shoulder is branded with a *fleur de lis*; but that he hopes the child will be entered."

Our Lady of the Flowers will therefore have prescribed the clang form: "The great nocturnal occupation, admirably suited for enchanting the darkness, is tattooing. Thousands and thousands of little jabs with a fine needle prick the skin and draw blood, and figures that *you* would regard as most extravagant are flaunted in the most unexpected places. When the rabbi slowly unrolls the Torah, a mystery sends a shudder through the whole epidermis, as when one sees a colonist undressing. The grimacing of all that blue on a white skin imparts an obscure but potent glamor to the child who is covered with it, as a neutral [*indifférente*], pure column becomes sacred under the notches of the hieroglyphs. Like a totem pole. Sometimes the eyelids are marked, the armpits, the hollow of the groin, the buttocks, the penis, and even the soles of the feet. The signs were barbaric and as meaningful as the most barbaric signs: pansies, bows and arrows, hearts pierced and dripping blood, overlapping faces, stars, quarter-moons, lines, swallows, snakes, boats, triangular daggers and inscriptions, mottoes, warnings, a whole fearful and prophetic literature."

movement of loss, appear as what it is in its very disappearance. As soon as it appears, as soon as the fire shows itself, it remains, retains itself, loses itself as fire. Pure difference, different from itself, ceases to be what it is in order to remain what it is. This is the origin of history, the beginning of the decline, the setting of the sun, the passage to Western subjectivity. The fire becomes for-itself and is lost; still worse because better.

Then, instead of burning everything, people begin to love flowers. The religion of flowers follows the religion of the sun.

The erection of the pyramid keeps life—the dead one—to give rise to the for-itself of adoration. It has the signification of a sacrifice, of an offer whereby the burn-all annuls itself, opens the ring [*anneau*], tightens it again in the anniversary of the solar revolution by sacrificing it as burn-all, therefore by keeping itself. The sacrifice, the offer or the gift do not destroy the burn-all which is destroyed in them, they have it gain access to the for-itself, they monumentalize it. Placing the instant of consummation into historical orbit gives it the chance of the anniversary movement from orient to occident. Chance of substance, of remaining [*restance*] determined as substance. Last words of "Das Lichtwesen": "However, this swaying [tottering, tumultuous: *taumelnde*] life must [*muß;* why must it?] determine itself into *being-for-itself* and must give durable existence (*Bestehen*) to its vanishing shapes. *Immediate being*, in which it places itself over and against its consciousness, is itself the *negative* power that brings its distinctions to dissolution (*auflöst*). It is therefore in truth the *self* (Selbst), and spirit therefore passes over into it in order to know itself in the form of the self. Pure light scatters (*wirft auseinander*) its simplicity as an infinity of forms and exhibits itself as a sacrifice to being-for-itself so that the individual may wed himself to the durable existence in its substance."

The difference and the play of pure light, panic-stricken and pyromaniac dissemination, the burn-all offers itself as a holocaust to the for-itself, *gibt sich dem Fürsichsein zum Opfer*. It sacrifices itself but so as to remain, keep itself safe, bind itself to itself, strictly, become itself, for-itself, by itself. To sacrifice itself, it burns itself. The burning then burns itself and goes out, the fire dies down, the sun begins to decline, to cover the trajectory that will take it into Western interiority (the Westerner, as we know from elsewhere, bears

In Algeria, in the middle of a mosque that the colonizers allegedly transformed into a synagogue, the Torah is brought out from behind the curtains and carried around in the arms of a man or child, kissed or touched by the faithful as it passes by them. (The latter, as is well-known, are enveloped in a veil. Some carry it fully rolled up around the neck, like a cord, a scarf, or an unknotted tie. Others, more broadly arranged on the shoulders and bust, flowing down to the ground. Others—and all of them at particular moments—on the head. The veil is sometimes striped in blue and white, sometimes in black and white. Sometimes, but extremely rarely, as if by chance or choice, it is pure white. The dead person is enveloped in his tallith—that is the word for the veil—after having his body washed and all his orifices stopped.)

The Torah wears a robe and crown. Its two rolls are then separated like two legs, it is raised to arm's length and the rabbi's scepter roughly follows the standing text. The bands that were tied around it had been first undone and usually given into the care of a child. The latter, not understanding anything about these signs so full of meaning, had to climb up to the gallery where the women sat, the old women especially, and hand them the rumpled bands. The old women would roll them up like the crape swaddlings of infant children and the child would bring them back to the Tebah.

Meanwhile the body of the Torah was laid on a table, and the men would busy themselves, each of them taking turns with a passage according to the ritual, assisted by the rabbi. They would disappear upright into these movements of veils and phylacteries (*tefillin:* little cubes of skin or parchment containing sacred texts, they are attached to the forehead and the hand with small bands, straps rather, of black leather pulled very tight, like a tourniquet, around the head, arm, and middle finger, which loses all freedom of movement). Like all the gestures dedicated to the ritual, the passage—the more or less laborious reading of a piece of text—was first sold at auction (one of these onerous operations, the most theatrical as I saw it, consisted, as I was saying, in raising the two separated columns, bringing them at arm's length so as to present the text to the congregation of faithful from afar, as if they could read, learn, and even buy from such a

the sun in his heart). This sacrifice belongs, like its negative, to the *logic* of the burn-all, one could say the double register of its countable calculus. If you want to burn everything, you have also to consume the fire, avoid keeping it alive like a precious presence. So you must extinguish it, keep it in order to lose it (truly), or lose it in order to keep it (truly). The two processes are inseparable, one can read them in any direction, from right to left or from left to right, the sublation of the one has to take the other into consideration. Panic inversion, without limit: the word *holocaust* which as it happens translates *Opfer* is more appropriate to the text than Hegel's own word. In this sacrifice, everything (*holos*) is burnt (*caustos*) and the fire will be able to go out only if stoked.

We are here at this critical point of the anniversary where we can look at both sides of the revolution, towards the East or towards the West.

What is getting started here? What is at stake in this column?

Wagering, engaging, stakes, that's exactly what it's about. What is put into play in this holocaust of play itself?

This perhaps: the gift, the sacrifice, setting everything on fire or putting it all into play, are potentially ontological. They carry ontology and overrun it but cannot fail to give birth to it. Without the holocaust the dialectical movement and the history of being could not open, start out on the ring of their anniversary, annul themselves in producing the solar course from East to West. Before, if one could count with time here, before every thing, before every determinable being, there is, there was, there will have been the irruptive event of the gift. An event which no longer has any relation to what is commonly designated by this word. So we can no longer think donation on the basis of being, but "the contrary," we might say if this inversion were pertinent here at the point where we are not yet dealing with logic but the origin of logic. In *Zeit und Sein*, the gift of the *es gibt* is given to be thought before the *Sein* in *es gibt Sein* and displaces everything that is determined under the name *Ereignis,* often translated as *event.*

distance a book—the first—thick, dense, difficult, weighty, unaccented. That man had to be sturdy and rich, or else supported by his sons. If by chance, in the course of this movement, his veil were to slip off his shoulders, he would not be able to pull it back up, since his hands weren't free. One of his sons, among those who had bought him the honor, would devotedly do it in his place.) The sacred text then had to be rolled up and banded again. The song was never interrupted.

The children who observed the pomp of this ceremony, even more so those who were able to lend a helping hand, perhaps dream of it long after, as a way to put together all the pieces of their lives.

What am I doing here? Let's say that I am working at the origin of literature by miming it. Between the two. Read Jean Paul's *Life of Fibel,* for example, "first tome, containing the *Fata* of the same while in his mother's womb":

"Now be beside yourselves, you whole body of Literati!

And there were thirty-nine more entire volumes there touching the part of his life subsequent to his birth . . . . I easily bought of the Jewish Christian at the price current the privilege of extracting, that is of tearing away all this printed matter from the volumes, provided I spared the bindings. I was thus enabled in the following biography, to authenticate, as it were with Jewish oaths and *pièces justificatives,* chapters which had been abstracted from the abstracted leaves, by simply heading them: *Judas' Chapter.* That is to say, Judas is our Anabaptist Jew's Christian name; for he has exchanged his earlier Jewish name Judas, which was borne by Iscariot the traitor, for the Christian name of Jude [it's the same name in German], the Apostle, who, as is well known, appears in the New Testament with his very short Epistle of Saint Jude. Meanwhile this nominal assonance or milk brotherhood may well have contributed more than one imagines to keep the worthy Judas constantly thirsting afresh for baptismal water, because so soon as he had jumped out of basin so almost before he had dried himself, he lost himself again in his simultaneous Church of the two Judases and wanted to form a partnership of goods of the Old and New Covenants under the title of Judas & Co. [*et compagnie,* in French in the text]. And thus he could never get himself converted often enough." Perhaps what I am doing with you

ump [*gnon*], which was placed simply in front

How is the event of an anniversary possible now? What is given in an anniversary?

This, perhaps: the process of the gift (before exchange), a process which is not a process but a holocaust, a holocaust of the holocaust, *gets the history of being started* but does not belong to it. The gift *is not*, the holocaust *is not*, if at least *there is any*. But as soon as it burns (the fire is not a being) it must, burning itself, burn its operation of burning and begin to be. This reflection on, this reflection of, the holocaust gets history started, the dialectics of meaning, ontology, the speculative. The speculative is the reflection (*speculum*) of the holocaust of the holocaust, the fire reflected and refreshed by the mirror's glass. The dialectic of religion, the history of philosophy (etc.), is produced as the reflection-effect of a gift-blow in holocaust [*un coup de don en holocauste*].

But if the burning up is not yet philosophy (and the rest), it cannot, however, not give rise to philosophy, to dialectical speculation, to the ring of exchange, to the declining course, to the circulating revolution. There is here a *fatum* of the gift, and this necessity was spoken in the "must" (*muß*) that was indicating it to us earlier: *Taumeln,* vertigo, delirium *must* be determined as for-itself and take on consistency. Once this constraint, this striction of the "must" comes to press on the mad energy of a gift, what it provokes is necessarily a counter-gift, an exchange, in the space of debt. I give you—pure gift, without exchange, without return—but whether I like it or not, the gift is kept and thenceforth you must owe [*tu dois*]. For the gift to be kept you must owe. You must at least receive it, already know it, recognize it. Exchange has begun even if the counter-gift gives only the receiving of the gift. I give you without expecting anything in exchange, but this very renunciation, once it *appears*, forms the most powerful and most inner ligament. This link of the for-itself and the debt, this contracture of meaning, is already the cunning of dialectical reason at work as the negative in the holocaust. The gift can only be a sacrifice—such is the axiom of speculative reason. Even if it emerges "before" philosophy and religion, the gift has as its destination or determination, as *Bestimmung,* a return to self in philosophy, the truth of religion. Always *already*, it opens exchange, it enchains, it constructs its monuments, calculates, in double entries, expenses

of him. The absence of the hand was as real and effective as a royal attribute, as the hand of justice.

Those whom one of their number called the Carolinas paraded to the site of a demolished street urinal. During the 1933 riots, the insurgents tore out one of the dirtiest, but most beloved pissoirs. It was near the harbor and the barracks, and its sheet iron had been corroded by the hot urine of thousands of soldiers. When its ultimate death was certified, the Carolinas—not all, but a formally chosen delegation—in shawls, mantillas, silk dresses and fitted jackets, went to the site to place a bunch of red roses tied together with a crape veil. . . .

When they reached the harbor, they turned right, toward the barracks, and upon the rusty, stinking sheet iron of the pissoir that lay battered on the heap of dead scrap iron they placed the flowers.

I was not in the procession."

These roses placed by the transvestites on the side of a hole and on the vestigial site of a column within which were antherected other column-flowers, are here transplanted, sewn back onto the very place—one needs only go back a page—where the anthonym crossdresses.

After extracting, one quotes a second time, one stitches up all the same, and all that, once the weaver's loom is looked at right side up, is recut more or less, put back in place, the text takes time to be ready for hardbinding. Long paranthesis.

"When I arrived at Fontevrault, Harcamone had been in irons for ten days. He was dying, and that death was more beautiful than his life. The death-throes of certain monuments are even more meaningful than their period of glory. They blaze before going out."

The flower is grafted. Question of style and taste.

and receipts, the owing, the debit, the incomes and outgoings, how much it makes and how much remains.

The gift, the donation of the gift, the pure present therefore cannot be thought by the dialectic to which it nonetheless gives rise. The donation of the gift is understood here before the for-itself, before all subjectivity and all objectivity. But when *someone* gives *something* to *someone*, we have already long been in calculative dialectic and speculative idealization. I give *myself*, I make myself a present. To whom?

If one can speak of the gift in the language of philosophy or of the philosophy of religion, one *must say* that the holocaust, the pure gift, the cake of honey or of fire withhold themselves in giving themselves, only ever exchange themselves according to the ring. Gift for self. The prototype of the present is therefore the ring, the bangle or the necklace, the chain. The ring, the chain of anniversary annularity is not a present among others, it delivers the gift [*cadeau*] itself, the very *cadeau* of the self (*Selbst*) for itself, the *cadeau* for self. The *cadeau* names what makes itself present.

Cadeau means *chain*. According to Littré, the "strokes of the pen with which writing-masters decorated their examples," or again "large letters placed at the head of acts or chapters in cursive manuscripts." Or again "previously, a party given principally for women, a pleasure outing." Still according to Littré, the etymology refers to "*Catellus,* a little chain, from *catena*, because of the linked form of the strokes of the pen. [The grammarian Gilles] Ménage tells us that "giving presents [(*faire des*) *cadeaux*]" was said of giving specious but useless things, metaphorically compared to these writing-masters' strokes. From there one passes without difficulty to *cadeau* in the sense of diversion, party and, finally, present." I make myself (a) present. With a view to what?

The useless, the specious, the frivolous do not escape from this contractual concatenation, commit one to it on the contrary, immediately put the debt on it. Make oneself a present.

To give means to give a ring and to give a ring means to keep: keep the present. (I) give (you) therefore (I give you) a ring therefore (I) keep (you). I lose therefore I win. You have to put the personal pronouns in parentheses. Rethink this movement before the constitution of the *Selbst.* The annular movement re-strains general economy (taking account, i.e. not taking account of the loss) into circulating economy. Economic tightening, restriction, forms the ring of the same, of the return to self, of reappropriation. Economy restricts itself, sacrifice sacrifices itself. Striction no longer allows itself to be

"'Would you like me to dress up as a woman?' I murmured.

Would I have dared, supported by his powerful shoulder, to walk the street in a spangled skirt between the Calle Carmen and the Calle Medi-odia? Except for foreign sailors, no one would have been surprised, but neither Stilitano nor I would have known how to choose the dress or the hair-do, for taste is required. Perhaps that was what held us back. I still remembered the sighs of Pedro, with whom I had once teamed up, when he went to get dressed.

'When I see those rags hanging there, I get the blues! I feel as if I were going into a vestry to get ready to conduct a funeral. They've got a priestish smell, Like incense. Like urine. Look at them hanging! I wonder how I manage to get into those damned sausage skins.'

'Will I have to have things like that? Maybe I'll even have to sew and cut with my man's help. And wear a bow, or maybe several, in my hair.'

With horror I saw myself decked out in enormous bows, not of ribbons, but of sausage meat in the form of pricks.

'It'll be a drooping, dangling bow,' added a mocking inner voice. An old man's droopy ding-dong. A bow limp, or impish! And in what hair? In an artificial wig or in my own dirty, curly hair?

As for my dress, I knew it would be sober and that I would wear it with modesty, whereas what was needed to carry the thing off was a kind of wild extravagance. Nevertheless, I cherished the dream of sewing on a cloth rose. It would emboss the dress and would be the femi-

the stylite, on the contrary, "used to cut himself, his fingertips were finely gashed"

defined as an ontological category, nor even, quite simply, a category, albeit a trans-category, a transcendental. Striction—what is used to think the ontological or the transcendental—is thus *also* in the position of a transcendental trans-category, a transcendental of the transcendental. The more so in that it cannot not produce the "philosophical" effect it produces. There is no choice to be made here: each time a discourse is held *against* the transcendental, a matrix—striction itself—constrains the discourse to place the non-transcendental, the outside of the transcendental field, the excluded, into a structuring position. The matrix in question constitutes what is excluded as the transcendental of the transcendental, as simili-transcendental, as transcendental contra-band. The contra-band is *not yet* dialectical contradiction. It necessarily becomes it, certainly, but its not-yet is not-yet teleological anticipation, which means that it never becomes dialectical contradiction. It *remains* something other than what, necessarily, it is to become.

Such would be the (non-dialectical) law of (dialectical) stricture, of the bond, the ligature, the garrote, the *desmos* in general when it comes to tighten (*serrer*) to make be. Lock (*serrure*) of the dialectic.

One can follow, if one knows how to read in counterbend (a term here borrowed from heraldry), the spiraled enchainment of the circle of circles. And, logic of the anniversary, the imposition at the corner of the curve.

Where are we?

At the limit or the mediation between the first and second moments of natural religion, between the religion of pure luminous essence and that of plant or animal. This is also the passage to the for-itself. And, in the history of religion, the passage from sense-certainty to perception.

Why plant and animal, plant then animal? With the becoming for-self, the opposition is internalized. It no longer scatters, it holds itself back, folds itself back, tight against

nine counterpart of Stilitano's bunch of grapes.

(*Long afterward, when I ran into him in Antwerp, I spoke to Stilitano about the fake bunch hidden in his fly. He then told me that a Spanish whore used to wear a muslin rose pinned on at cunt level.*

'To replace her lost flower,' he said.)

. . .

'You'll have a toilette, Juan.'

I was sickened by this butcher's word (I was thinking that the toilette was also the greasy tissue enveloping the guts [*tripes*] in animal's bellies). . . .

The foot of a blond young man had got caught in the lace. I hardly had strength enough to mumble, 'Watch what you're doing.' The face of the clumsy young man, who was both smiling and excusing himself, was so pale that I blushed. Someone next to me said in a low voice, 'Excuse him, señora, he limps.'

'I won't have people limping on my dress!' screamed the beautiful actress who smoldered within me. But the people around us were laughing. 'I won't have people limping on my toilette!' I screamed to myself. Formulated within me, in my stomach, as it seemed to me, or in the intestines, which are enveloped by the 'toilette,' this phrase must have been expressed by a terrible glare. Furious and humiliated, I left under the laughter of the men and the Carolinas. I went straight to the sea and drowned the skirt, bodice, mantilla and fan. The whole city was joyous, drunk with the Carnival that was cut off from the earth and alone in the middle of the Ocean. I was poor and sad.

('Taste is required. . . .' I was already refusing to have any. I forbade myself to. Of course I would have shown a great deal of it. I knew that cultivating it would have—not sharpened me but—softened me. Stilitano himself was amazed that I was so uncouth. I wanted my fingers

itself, organically unified in the strict unity of multiplicity. No opposition can be formed without beginning to internalize itself. This organicity is already bound to itself in the plant, but life is represented in it only by anticipation. The actual war, as opposition internal to the living, is not yet raging. The plant, as such, lives in peace: substance, yes, and there was not yet substantiality in light, but peaceful substance, without the internal warfare that characterizes animality. Already life and the self, but not yet the war of desire. Life without desire—the plant is a kind of sister.

Hegel does not say the religion of plants, but the "religion of flowers," "the innocence of the religion of flowers." The plant is not the flower but it finds in the flower "its own self (*ihr eigenes Selbst*)." The *Encyclopedia* proposes a vast and minute deduction of "vegetable nature," of the flowering and fruiting (the becoming of the anther, the *stilus* (*Griffel*), the *stigma* (*Narbe,* scar), etc.), mostly based on *The Metamorphosis of Plants* (Goethe). The subjectivity of the plant is not yet for itself. The criterion for this is classical: it does not give itself its own place. The "objectivation" by which the vegetable relates to itself remains "entirely formal," is not "a true objectivity." Its differentiation remains external, associative, angular, closer to geometrical forms and the regularity of crystals. The process of its formation, the "*inner* process of the plant's *relation to itself*" is primarily a relation to the outside, an exteriorization, an extraneity, a relinquishment (*Entäußerung*); its growth is a hardening, a becoming-ligneous or even stoney (as in the case of the tabasheer, for example). The plant is pulled from itself, toward the outside, by the light. But the flower liberates a progress in the movement of reappropriation and subjectivation. A moment of sublation: the light no longer comes to provoke or drag from outside, on the contrary it engenders itself spontaneously from the inside of the plant. This passage is analogous to the one that sublates the external resonance of noise in the voice. The agency of the *Klang*. The *color* of the flower manifests this phenomenal self-determination of the plant. "The plant also brings forth (*gebiert*) its light as *its own self* in the *blossom*, in which the neutral color green is then further specified."

A whole theory of colors (here too reference to

to be stiff: *I kept myself from learning to sew.*)"

Between two parantheses in italics (one sews [*coud*], the other countersews), he who bears within him a terrible tragic actress who doesn't want limping in his dresses, the transvestite, then, renders Cesarianlike the *toilettes* that belong to him after the violent disemboweling [*étripage*] of giving birth. He drowns them in the sea, surrenders them to the sea. Rendering homage and vomiting: "sickened by this word . . ." And he needed the sea-mother, for that to happen close to her.

But the structure of crossdressing is still more twisted.

He doesn't go from earth to sea to render his *toilette*. He is already in the sea-mother, invested by her, like an island swamped on all sides or almost.

Almost: the ideal space of crossdressing is, of course, almost island [*presqu'île*]. Peninsula.

He becomes almost woman on a tongue of earth alone penetrating into the middle of the Ocean. Reverse side or other version of a lagoon.

Geography writes that between earth and sea; it procures your passage more or less gratis from Barcelona to Cadiz. Barcelona is beside the sea, Cadiz, which he decides to "get to [*gagner*]" is "built right on the water, though connected to the mainland by a very long jetty." Barcelona faces east, giving on to the Mediterranean, Cadiz toward the setting sun, in the Ocean.

A note had sufficed to justify the necessity of crossdressing: "In rereading this text I realized that I had situated in Barcelona a scene from my life that took place in Cadiz. The phrase 'alone in the middle of the Ocean' reminded me of that. In writing I

Goethe and passionately anti-Newtonian) is implied here. And the spontaneous production of chromatic light, the internalization of the process, the relation to self, the anthopoetic subjectivity of the plant—all of that is also described as the dialectic of a *Hemmung*, an inhibitory stricture. The introjection of the sun, the sublime digestion of the luminous essence will end in "the heart of the West": it begins in the flower.

The flower-religion is innocent to the extent that the war internal to animality is not yet raging there. The relation to self does not yet trigger war because it is merely *represented* in the flower. The flower-religion (like the flower) mimics and anticipates the true self, it is contained in this "selfless representation of the self (*selbstlose Vorstellung des Selbsts*)." The flower plays the "same," it does not have the potency [*puissance*] or it only has the potential [*puissance*] to accede to it. But as it has already begun to subjectivate the luminous essence and the plant, it no longer simply falls into dissociative exteriority. It is neither an object nor a subject, neither a non-self nor a self, neither a pure alterity with no self-relation nor a *Selbst*. Innocent, certainly, and therefore non-guilty [*non coupable:* uncuttable] but one declares its innocence (which one would not do for the sun or the plant) only to the extent that it is susceptible to guilt, guilty of being able to become guilty. Among all these opposites, the essence of the flower appears in its disappearance, it vacillates like all representative mediations but also is exempt from oppositional structure. It provides the example of any possible representation but the circular system of inter-representation allows us to make the flower the trope of any representational milieu or to say that all representation is anthomorphic. The flower cuts itself from itself and simultaneously places itself *en abîme*.

Adoring flowers, kneeling before them, is only possible on the threshold of guilt. The cult of animals—the totemism referred to by the *Phenomenology*—emerges on the contrary in war, guilt, struggle to the death. Finally relating to itself, animal life destroys itself in order to rise to spiritual life, it divides itself, opposes itself to itself in order to erect itself in spirit. History and politics begin, in hatred, warfare, murder, guilt, punishment. We have left behind peaceful nomenclature, taxonomic religion entirely taken up with classifying botanical varieties. This is also the passage from pantheism to polytheism, or even to monotheism. "This pantheism, which

therefore made the error of placing it in Barcelona, but a detail crept into its description that allowed me to resituate it in its correct place."

The fact of the tongue that slides its detail in here is "cut off from the earth and alone in the middle of the Ocean." But he also needed, under the name Cadiz, a "very long jetty."

This masquerade (he somewhere defines femininity by that word), carnival between two counter-pointed parantheses, thus looks at the same time toward East and West, earth and sea, sunrise and sunset. The whole world hardbinds and is incorporated in the transvestite, opposites of all genders, sun and fish on one side, sea and night on the other. "At the outermost point of Western soil, I suddenly had before me the synthesis of the Orient." The signs of Arabia in Spain, that couldn't happen anywhere else. The fish are "caught at night." "The sun would be rising when my fish were cooked. . . . I had gathered the fish on the wharves in the darkness. It was still dark when I reached my rocks. The coming of the sun overwhelmed me. I worshiped it [*je lui rendais un culte*]. A kind of sly intimacy developed between us. I honored it, though without, to be sure, any complicated ritual; it would not have occurred to me to ape the primitives, but I know that this star became my god. It was within my body that it rose, continued its curve and completed it. If I saw it in the sky of the astronomers, I did so because it was the bold projection there of the one I preserved within myself. Perhaps I even confused it in some obscure way with the vanished Stilitano."

is initially the *motionless* durable existence (*das* ruhige *Bestehen dieser Geisteratomen*) of these spiritual atoms, becomes a *hostile* movement within itself (feindseligen *Bewegung in sich selbst*)." This movement presupposes a repression of the earlier structure: an internal suppression, the effect of a force which is no longer natural and instinctual, one that places spirit in relation to the universality of the law, whence the origin of guilt. "The innocence of the *flower religion*, which is merely a selfless representation of the self (*selbstlose Vorstellung des Selbsts*), passes over into the seriousness of warring life, into the guilt of *animal religion*; the motionless being and the impotence of intuiting individuality passes over into destructive being-for-itself. —It does not help to have taken the *death of abstraction* away from the things of perception and to have elevated them into the essence of spiritual perception; the ensouling (*Beseelung*) of this spiritual realm has that death by virtue of the determinateness and the negativity in it which makes it encroach on the innocent indifference of that religion. It is by virtue of this determinateness and negativity that the dispersal into the diversity of the motionless shapes of plants becomes a hostile movement in which the hatred of their being-for-itself gradually wears itself out. —The *actual* self-consciousness within this dispersed spirit is a multitude of individualized and unsociable spirits of different peoples, who, in their hatred, battle with each other to the death and become conscious of determinate shapes of animals as their essence, for they themselves are nothing more than spirits of animals, that is, animal lives separate and cut off from each other, conscious of no universality." In the form and the name of the totemic animal, spirit calls to itself, reappropriates itself but still remains foreign to itself, does not return to itself, by itself. It is represented by a determinate, particular, finite species in which its proper (name) is exiled. Supplementary classification.

One structural analogy after another: after the passage from sense-certainty to perception, the dialectic of the master and the slave. It develops in the third moment of natural religion, that of the artisan (*Werkmeister*). Like every moment, this one announces (itself). Announced and announcing, it is represented in the prior moment, and becomes the representative of the later and higher moment: circle and spiral. But in the artisan moment, we also witness the return of the returning, the determinate birth of the round form, the curve, this particular line that nonetheless figures the totality of the process. This happens to the phallic column, according to Hegel's own example.

The one-armed man crosses through his body like a solar column, rising and setting there. The incorporation of all sexes at once—one is still banking on a banquet or last supper, the fish are eaten "almost always . . . without bread or salt"—supposes cutting and supplementing inside the double hardbind. But once thanks to the supplementary cutting (the grafted flower) there are two bands, a double undecidable sex is activated, sheathing both father and mother.

at the end of Stilitano is the fingernail [*ongle*]. All that is written with fingernails. "Stilitano used to cut himself, his fingertips were finely gashed, his nail was black and crushed, but this heightened his beauty. (The purple of sunsets, according to physicists, is the result of a greater thickness of air which is crossed only by short waves. At midday, when nothing is happening in the sky, an apparition of this kind would disturb us less; the wonder is that it occurs in the evening, at the most poignant time of day, when the sun *sets*, when it disappears to pursue a mysterious destiny, when perhaps it dies. The physical phenomenon that fills the sky with such pomp is possible only at the moment that most exalts the imagination: at the setting of the most brilliant of the heavenly bodies.)" In the *Miracle of the Rose*, when Harcamone appears, faces turn toward him "as sunflowers turn to the sun." Apotropaic virtue of the heliotrope: it is also a precious stone that has attributed to it the special capacity to render those who wear it invisible. For example invisible to the serpents of the *Inferno*. "*Tra questa cruda e tristissima copia / Correvan genti nude et spaventate / Senza sperar pertugio o elitropia* [Among this cruel and depressing swarm, ran people who were naked, terrified, with no hope of a hole or heliotrope]."

This economic operation (economy of undecidable death) *affects* the linguistic, the verbal, the semiotic, the rhetorical and the dialectical, it does not depend on them.

It affects as an affect or a transvestite would affect, it gets them going, reaches them, touches them, plays them, loses them, supports them; but it has there neither its place nor efficacity, neither its force nor remainder.

". . . with the vanished Stilitano.

I am indicating to you, in this way, the form that my sensibility took. Nature made me uneasy.

The ring, the bangle, the necklace, the chain of the *cadeau*, the anniversary circle of the speculative thus always turns around a phallic column, whether this latter alternates with a finger or an ankle, a waist or a neck. Everything that is found to be wrapped around a cylinder, that's the word, will have the size of the phallus.

Simultaneously, in the moment of the *Werkmeister* and according to an internal necessity, meaning begins to be filled with voice. Begins only: in this marvelous form, the resonance (*Klang*) produced by the mere falling of light on stone, the music of the Memnons at dawn.

Let's pick it up again. In the totemic war, the for-itself is "sublated," destroyed and preserved. It avoids death pure and simple by holding onto itself in an object that survives the act of its production, survives being consumed by the producing self. At which point spirit manifests itself as artisan. The artist is only announced and represented here, just as the aesthetic religion is represented in the natural religion of the artisan. Spirit appears to itself as artisan and its operation (*Tun*) makes it again lose consciousness. It produces itself as object, does not take itself back, does not entirely recognize itself. This object is not yet compared to the honey cake but to the *pyramis* the example of which comes soon. Right from the first lines, the operation is nonetheless compared, following a figure become traditional, to the instinctive work of bees constructing their combs (*ein instinktartiges Arbeiten, wie die Bienen ihre Zellen bauen*). The pyramid rises immediately. But we notice a lack in it—and therefore a representation of what will appear only a little later: the curve, roundness, curvilinearity which can be produced only by living spirit. Cold, formal and deathly, the understanding proceeds geometrically, cuts and arrests angular forms. Artisanal religion is the history of a rounded angle, the passage from pyramid to column, from mathematics or calculation to the incommensurable grace of spirit. And this passage is a *filling*. The round and curvilinear form is fuller of spirit. "The first form, because it is the immediate one, is the abstract form of the understanding, and the work (*Werk*) is not yet in itself brought to fruition (*erfüllt*) by spirit. The crystals of the pyramids and of the obelisks, simple combinations of straight lines with even surfaces and equal relations of parts

My love for Stilitano, the roar with which he burst upon my wretchedness, and any number of other things, delivered me to the elements. But they are malicious. In order to tame them I wanted to contain them. I refused to deny them cruelty; quite the contrary, I congratulated them for having as much as they had; I flattered them.

As an operation of this kind cannot succeed by means of dialectics, I had recourse to magic, that is, to a kind of deliberate *predisposition*, an intuitive complicity with nature. Language would have been of no help to me. It was then that things and circumstances became maternal to me, though alert within them, like the sting of a bee, was the point of my pride. (Maternal: that is, whose essential element is femininity. In writing this I do not want to make any Mazdean allusion: I merely point out that my sensibility required that it be surrounded by a feminine order. It could do so inasmuch as it could avail itself of masculine qualities: hardness, cruelty, indifference.)" The reader is then asked not to be "duped" by words, which

this time, on the other hand, but it's so that you have no fixed point to rest on, femininity is the essential element of maternity. But it is only a sermon [*prédication*]. And the play of the copula is subtle. Like that of the couple in general. In fact, in the case of such a pair, why does one say "a couple?" "At the top of a slope, a pair [*un couple* (*ou une couple?*)] of colonists, outlined against the sky; a thigh swelling out a pair of canvas trousers; the toughs and their open flies from which there escaped, in whiffs that turned your stomach, the scent of tea-roses and wisteria fading into evening." Repetition—constraining argument, for pleasure—of the sheath, four lines lower down, "Harcamone as a child, swathed in princely poverty; the bugle opening in his sleep . . . ." Since then, Harcamone, who "was unable to have a calendar" erected "his destiny, as one erects a tower," "unique and solitary." Must one speak of a pleasure that would be born from stricture

in which the incommensurability of roundness is abolished (*an denen die Inkommensurabilität des Runden vertilgt ist*), are the works of this artisan of rigorous form (*der strengen Form*). On account of the bare intelligibility (*Verständigkeit*) of the form, the form is not its meaning (*Bedeutung*) in itself, not the spiritual self. Those works therefore either only receive spirit into themselves as an alien, isolated spirit which has forsaken its living permeation (*Durchdringung*) with actuality, and which, being itself dead, comes to reside in these lifeless crystals. —Or they relate themselves externally to spirit as something which exists there externally and not as spirit itself—to spirit as the light rising in the east, which casts its meaning on them (*als auf das aufgehende Licht, das seine Bedeutung auf sie wirft*)."

We must constantly refer to the philosophy of nature which dictates this interpretation of natural religion. And in the philosophy of nature, to the relations of space and time, light and sound in their long and minute deduction. For example during the rehearsal of the "birth of sound," so "difficult to grasp" (*Die Geburt des Klanges ist schwer zu fassen*), the act by which strings, pipes and bars vibrate is described as a "an alternating transition from the straight line to the arc." In the process of subjective idealization punctuated by trembling (*Erzittern*) and vibration (*Schwingen*), the difference between nature and spirit corresponds to the difference between what does not resonate of itself—bodies (*Die Körper klingen noch nicht aus sich selbst*)—and what resonates of itself. This is the history of the *Klang* that reappropriates itself to the point of resounding *with itself*. For "the *Klang* properly speaking (*eigentliche*)" is pure reverberation (*Nachhallen*), "the unhindered inner vibration of a body which is freely determined by the nature of its cohesion." The flux that purely and simply flows does not resonate (*Das bloß Flüssige ist nicht klingend*). In it the impression is freely communicated to the whole but this communication depends on the total absence of form, on the total lack (*Mangel*) of internal determination. Air and water do not resonate spontaneously, even if one accords them the ability to communicate the *Klang*. By contrast, the *Klang* itself presupposes the identity of determination, it is itself a form: "Pure *Klang* requires compact continuity and homogeneity of matter, and so metals—especially precious metals—and glass (*Glas*), give out a clear sound (*diesen klaren Klang*), a property developed by smelting."

fail to retain even the "pale reflection" of "defunct" states. What is defunct is a "pretext-subject," neither the object nor the truth of the journal. And one needs to distinguish between what I "say" and the "interpretation" by which I work on the defunct and play dead.

or sheaths of every sort? Some pages earlier: "The word pleasure isn't quite right [*ne colle pas*]."

So that goes on between blow-cut [*coupture*] and counter-blowcut. Always at the outside limit, of course, of the good taste "required" when one whispers in the ear of virgins or is at work in a library.

But why does he also stop himself from learning to sew, since he does it so well?

It's here that the argument of the girdle is necessarily contradicted—in its domestic logic, to begin—by a parergon that is never, as is known, internal or external. Whence the interest and the difficulty of the text. Always one letter extra and less.

The muslin rose [*rose d'étamine*] "replaces"—that's the word—the lost flower. Muslin replaces the natural rose that replaces virginity. The detachments linked without chains, the blowcut supplements are relayed indefinitely and mix up—such is the fault of taste, which always concerns a sex, wherever one puts it—all genders.

So, *étamine*. *L'étamine*—the whore's rose, cock given in homage to Mary and taboo of the hymen given back to the petal—names not only the light cloth that nuns sometimes use for a veil or through which one filters fine liquor. It is also the male sexual organ (*stamen*) of plants, according to the shuttle—that's the word—that runs back and forth between the codes of textiles and

If on the other hand a bell (*Glocke*) is cracked or scratched (*einen Riss bekommen hat*), one hears no longer only the pure swaying of the *Klang*, but the noise (*Geräusch*) of matter forming an obstacle, grinding, breaking, harming the equality of the form. Flat stones, slabs (*Steinplatten*) also produce a *Klang* even though they are hard, insensible, cold, brittle (*spröde*).

In the "singing of men" the external excitation and the vocal timbre are "homogeneous." It is in the voice alone that "the subjectivity or the independence of the form is present." The violin does not *resonate* (*tönt nicht nach*) like the voice, it merely *sounds* (*sie tönt nur*) for as long as the tightened strings are rubbed.

So the process of the *Klang* secures the passage from noise to voice. The *Encyclopedia* description repeats, in its general features, the description from the Jena *Philosophy of Nature*. There, the *Klang* was already recognized as this singular repercussion of interiority in exteriority. Sonority in general (*Der Ton*), in the continuity of earthly bodies, has two and only two forms: noise (*Geräusch*) and resonance (*Klang*). Noise expresses only immediate, *external* continuity, constraint, friction (*Reibung*). *Klang*, on the contrary, expresses its *internal* continuity, especially in the case of metal and glass (*Glas*). But in spite of this difference (outside/inside), both of them, noise and *Klang*, are only set going by a percussion *come from outside* (*nur außerlich angeschlagen*). This is what distinguishes them from *sense* (*Sinn*), for example the sense of hearing; what also distinguishes them from the voice, and above all from the echoing internal couple formed by voice and hearing. The voice is active hearing (*das tätige Gehör*), hearing is the receptive voice, conceiving, as one says of a woman (*die empfangene Stimme*). Through this couple the sensibility of the individual takes itself up again in itself, gathers itself, comes back to itself, contracts, passes a contract with itself (*sich in sich zurücknimmt*) and constitutes itself as universal.

It is here in the philosophy of nature that, in the *Encyclopedia*, heat (the element of fermentation and then of fervor) is deduced, and deduced, however strange it may appear, from the *Klang*. For the common way of seeing things, sound and heat have nothing in common and "it can appear striking" (*es kann frappant scheinen*) to compare them. *Klang* is the alternation (*Wechsel*) of the reciprocal exteriority of the parts of matter, of their *Außereinandersein*, *and*

botany. Arranged around the style and its stigma, the stamens usually form a thread, or filaments (*stamina*). Above the thread is a connective joined to four pollen sacs (microsporangia) that "elaborate and disperse the grains of pollen": the anther. It may be introrse, extrorse or lateral, depending on the orientation of the pollen sacs. That is the case for bisexual flowers, where the stamens constitute the androecia whereas the carpels (ovary, ovules and style) form the gynoecia. The latter is sometimes enclosed in the receptacle (epigynous flowers).

The flower is hypogynous when the ovary dominates the rest of the flower. Sometimes, the threads of the stamens stick together in one or more "fraternities," or even become concrescent with the petals (which sometimes extend themselves into spurs that bear the nectar glands) or with the gynoecia. That is the case for orchids.

In the case of unisexual flowers the fertilizing parts are similar. The general tendency is for floral systems to be unisexual. That goes hand in hand with the so-called natural selection that renders allogamy possible or indispensable: sexual

contiguous with a column of smoke (textual effluvium) here is another muslin rose [*rose d'étamine*]: "So here she is [Divine], having decided to return, lifted by a column of smoke, to her garret, on the door of which is nailed a huge discolored muslin rose" (*Our Lady of the Flowers*).
One says "abortive stamen" for a stamen having no anther. Abortive flower: "one that falls without leaving any trace of fertilization."

the pollen of the Orchidaceae is said to be "agglutinated," that of the Rosaceae, "sticky [*collant*]": it attaches itself to the bodies of animals attracted by the pollen or by the nectar secreted in certain glands. For example, by means of its form, color, and velvety texture, the bee orchid attracts bumblebees that, thinking they are fertilizing these fake bees, ensure the reproduction of the orchid by shuttling from one bee [*d'une avette*] to the other or rather from the form of a bee to the other

of its negation, its being-negated. This negation, as always, produces ideality, but an abstract ideality. The alternation is immediately the negation of specific exteriority and therefore the real identity of cohesion and specific weight—which Hegel calls heat. "The generation of heat in sonorous bodies (*klingende Körper*) and in those which are struck (*geschlagenen*) or rubbed together, is the manifestation of heat originating with sound in conformity with its Notion." There too there is a process of *Aufhebung* of materiality. Putting the body into vibration (*Erschütterung*) is not only "sublation of the present matter in an ideal mode," but a "real sublation" through heat. Heat is the sublation of the rigidity of the body (*Aufheben seiner Rigidität*). "Sound and heat are thus directly related; heat is the consummation (*Vollendung*) of *Klang*. . . . If, for example, a bell (*Glocke*) is struck (*geschlagen*) it gets hot; and this heat is not external to it. . . . Not only the musician gets warm, his instruments do also."

From the dead geometrical form—rectilinear and planar—artisanship rises to "animated roundness." It is first of all a mix, the mediation of a "blending" (*Vermischung*) that announces the "free architecture" of aesthetic religion.

What characterizes this anticipation of artistic spirit? The hieroglyphic limit of a language insufficiently filled with signification.

This limit also depends on a spatialization of language. It was already marked in the fact that sound remains external, produced by light, when the sunbeam comes to strike the stone. It falls on a monument, certainly, on a stone modeled by spirit, but which remains stone: white in Egypt, black in Mecca. The limit of language is determined from a certain void of signification. A sensory remainder prevents the three-stroke motor from running smoothly [*tourner rond*]. But it is merely promising a new anniversary.

What the artisan gives a "more animated form" to is

products are transported from one individual to another, genotypes intermingle or are reorganized, and pollen, protected from harsh weather by an impermeable sheath, is able to be dispersed by the wind or by animal organisms.

No more than for the flower is there, then, a univocal semantic or morphological definition for the stamen; simply, as modern anthological science recognizes, a functional or syntactic definition.

The stamen separates from itself and bursts its sheath [*gaine*], at the risk of disseminating its pollen. This always existing risk affects not only the androecia but also the gynoecia. An argument must be drawn from the fact that the seed [*graine*] can always burst or remain in dormancy [*en dormance*].

It's when it comes to the seed, the fertilized ovule, that one can properly speak of dissemination (in angiosperms or gymnosperms). The seeds are sometimes projected in all directions when the fruit bursts. More often, they escape through slits or holes opened in its wall, and wind or animals disperse them. Germination occurs immediately only when light and humidity permit. Otherwise, ripe seeds remain in a dormant state within an exterior milieu for weeks or months. Such dormancy may be true or false: true if the seed that has just been separated from the mother plant isn't mature or if its growth is inhibited by substances that are gradually reabsorbed; false if the inhibition resides in the thickness of the tegumental sheath and prevents the penetration of air and water. When it isn't

a habitation (*Behausung*). His art remains utilitarian, he merely anticipates and represents the art of the artist. He has nonetheless progressed from an inanimate naturality to a beginning of life and a prefiguration of self (*Selbst*).

How did he get there? By having matter vegetate, by bringing it to a sort of arborescence and efflorescence. The life of plants no longer forms the object of a cult. The flower becomes usable: as an ornament. The *Aesthetics* describes at length the organic figures that are closest to nature when they have just left that nature, when plant and tree launch themselves up into stone structures. Straight up towards the sky, like a "stem," both supple and rigid (*ein Stamm, ein schwanker Stengel*), a light and powerful creeper, sustained erection of a trunk. "The tree trunk already carries, as such, its own crown, the stalk the ear, the stem its flower." Columns derive from the most varied forms of plants (*Pflanzenbildungen*), such as lotuses, or onion bulbs. "Then out of this pedestal the slender stem rises up," or climbs by clinging round (*verschlungen*) like a twisted column and "the capital again is a flower-like separation of leaves and branches (*blumenartiges Auseinandergehen von Blättern und Zweigen*)." But the imitation of vegetable nature is not "servile," the plant forms are subjected to an architectonic stylization (circle, straight line, regularity of figures): this is the moment of the *arabesque*, the root of "free architecture."

Then the plant becomes animal-like. The artisan has recourse to (the) "animal form" (*Tiergestalt*). Twisted, deformed vegetable forms look like animal bodies. Through the rigidity for which the arabesque has been reproached, the for-itself is constituted.

Recognizing *his* work, the artisan sublates this animal form. This latter is indeed "*aufgehobene*" when it becomes language: first in the form of what is most primitive and subordinate, servile in language, namely a non-phonetic writing: "the animal shape is at the same time both sublated and becomes the hieroglyph of another meaning, the hieroglyph of a thought." The animal form becomes sign or writing when the human face appears in the dwelling, work of the artisan. The specificity of this moment is indicated in the Egyptian representations by the hieroglyphic mixture of animal figures and human figures.

The hieroglyph has torn itself free of painting—it does

dormant the seed swells and nourishes itself by digesting the prothallus (in gymnosperms) or albumen (in angiosperms with exalbuminous seeds). The embryo of the albuminous seed contains within itself all the reserves that it will consume.

Wailing [*vagir*] finally.

Good or bad, the thief's wailing (not the author's or narrator's—the subject isn't there, nor is the question—let's say the *sfeignctor*'s) attempts incessantly to resheath, to emparaph the seed [*semence*], to ensign the dissemination, numb the sperm with his signature, reappropriate the genealogy, reconstitute the gilded monument of his (seminary) ownness, digest, knock back without remainder his own blank check, to be son—not daughter, take note—of himself.

There needs to be an executioner and a cradle here (let's call it a mess tin [*gamelle*],

having oneself know [*s'avoir*] what one's name is. Mess tin: his forename always echoes close by. His forename, which?
Whose? The author's? the narrator's? the narratee's? the hero's? the colossus's? And of which text? "He brings with him his blankets, mess tin, cup, wooden spoon, and his story. At his first words I stop him. He keeps on talking, but I am no longer there.

not show a thing. By expressing a thought it announces language but its mute writing has not got there yet. What it lacks is a self that stands there as such, carrying outward what it is within, expressing an "inner meaning." "It lacks language," the tongue, speech (*Sprache*).

What is *Sprache* (tongue or language)? It is an externalization that presents; it gives the there, the *Da-sein*, to the inner meaning; but in order thus to put itself forth into presence it must first allow itself to be filled, filled up, fulfilled, swollen, curved out, *rounded* by the meaning that penetrates it. It is "the element (*Element*) in which the fulfilling sense (*der erfüllende Sinn selbst*) is there on hand (*vorhanden ist*)."

This element is called the voice: spontaneous production outwards of an inner meaning that then fills with presence the form of its emission. Spontaneity, the production of self by self gives the voice. Sound, for its part, resonates on the basis of the blow given from outside, it is not emitted. Sound announces and represents the voice but holds it back too, too external or too internal.

This moment of half-voice sculpts its paradigm in the statue of Memnon, son of the dawn adored by the Ethiopians and the Egyptians. The "colossal sounding statue" (*kolossale Klangstatue*) resounded under the first rays of the sun. The light striking the block provokes a kind of voice, it extracts, evokes a voice that is not yet one, even when Memnon (*tönend und stimmegebend*) thanks "with his voice" the faithful who come to offer him sacrifices. Even if the work no longer has an animal figure, the human face that presents itself is *tonlose*, noisy but mute: "Hence, the work [of the artisan], even when it is wholly purified of what is animalistic and even when it bears in it the shape of self-consciousness alone, is still the soundless shape that needs the rays of the rising sun in order to have a sound, which, although produced by the light, is also just *Klang* and not language, and which merely points to an external, and not to the inner, self."

The *Klang* of the stony block *is not yet* the voice that it is *already*: neither in nor out of language, a mediation *or* an excluded third. In the *Aesthetics,* the decipherment of Memnon follows the reading of the phallic columns. The Orient, Egypt, Greece devoted a cult to the general vitality (*allgemeine Lebenskraft*) of nature. It was addressed to the representation of animal "organs of reproduction" which were exhibited and considered sacred.

'What's your name?'
'Jean.'
That's enough. Like me and like the dead child for whom I am writing, his name is Jean. Besides, what would it matter if he were less handsome, but I have a run of bad luck. Jean there. Jean here. When I tell someone that I love him, I wonder whether I am not telling it to myself. I am no longer here, because I am again trying to relive the few times he let me caress him. I dared all and, in order to tame him, I allowed him to have the superiority of the male over me; his member was as solid as a man's, and his adolescent face was gentleness itself, so that when, lying on my bed, in my room, straight and motionless, he discharged into my mouth, he lost nothing of his virginal chastity. It is another Jean, here, who is telling me his story. I am no longer alone, but I am thereby more alone than ever. I mean that the solitude of prison gave me the freedom to be with the hundred Jean Genets glimpsed in a hundred passers-by, for I am quite like Darling, who also stole the Darlings whom a thoughtless gesture let escape from all the strangers he had brushed against; but this new Jean brings into me—as a folding fan draws in the designs on the gauze—brings in I know not what." (*Our Lady of the Flowers*)

There is always another Jean, eponym and nickname, nomothete or epithet of the "first," one doubling the other (the whole clan [*parentèle*]).

What is the epithet finally

with a little leftover mush), the angel to

This is especially the case with the phallus or the *lingam* (hieratic representation of the phallus in India; the word designates mark and genus—class—*and* the phallus). Herodotus, often quoted, recalls that for the Dionysia, "instead of phalli the Egyptians have invented other images, a cubit long, pulled by a thread." Phallophoric women pull the thread and the sex always rises up (*sich immer hebt*), almost as tall as the rest of the body.

In India more than elsewhere (the) phallic representation is architectural: enormous columns and towers of stone broader at the base than at the summit. They begin by adoring them for themselves then start making openings (*Öffnungen*), holes, incisions, excavations (*Aushölungen*) in which were inserted images of the gods. The gods appear there. The same practice is found in the hermetic columns of Greece. The legendary representation of gods, images, idols, altars came along to be inscribed like tattooing on the smooth surface of these rigid columns.

Now the origin of this process of excavation, its *Ausgangspunkt*, are columns without holes (*unausgehölten Phallus-Saülen*). The incisions supposedly supervened on columns that were originally untouched. These latter are moreover quite rare and tend rapidly to disappear.

The columns are later transformed into high and narrow habitations—pagodas—separated into shell and kernel. Herodotus also mentioned male columns that included, as ornament or decoration, signs of the female organ. He saw them only in Syria, and attributed them to Sesostris and interpreted them, according to Hegel, as a Greek, a true Greek, in the Greek sense: he transformed their "natural significance" into an "ethical (*sittliche*) significance." "In the countries where the people were brave in battle against Sesostris during his wars, he erected columns on which he inscribed his own name and country and how he had here reduced these peoples to subjection; where, on the contrary, they submitted without a struggle he added to this inscription on the pillar a female *pudendum* to indicate that they had been cowardly and unwarlike." The properly Greek interpretation, in the Greek sense (*im grieschischem Sinne*) thus deciphers the ethical in the natural and this passage from nature to *Sittlichkeit* merges with the phallocentric

hardbind the son (*gamelle* or *gargamelle* sounds more like it), talc, if not vaseline on the tips of fingers to avoid irritation in the folds or on the edges of orifices, the glorious aura of a milky voice bursting with sperm, as could always be contemplated, a song—that is to say an accent—circumflex to cover the head.

Will he have rained more pleasingly [*Aura-t-il plu?*]

Will he have ejaculated into the galaxy?

"Botanists know a variety of *genêt* which they call winged-broom (*genêt-ailé*)." She describes its flight in the *Journal*:

"As the theft was indestructible I decided to make it the origin of a state of moral perfection.

'It's cowardly, weak, dirty, low . . . (I shall define it only with words expressing shame). None of the elements composing it leaves me a chance to magnify it. Yet I do not deny this most monstrous of my sons. I want to fill the world with its loathsome progeny.'

hierarchization. It associates positive ethical values, and even sense itself, with virility.

This is where the statues of Memnon rise up. Obelisks had marked the transition. They have the symbolic value of sunbeams. They themselves represent rays of light, gold ingots or helioidal sex-organs. Egyptian letters sometimes came to be engraved in the petrified light of the obelisk. Heliogravure, like at Heliopolis where Mithra, god of the Medes and the Persians, lets himself be entreated by a dream to build obelisks, "stone sunbeams" (*Sonnenstrahlen in Stein*) and to have letters, "said to be Egyptian," engraved on them (*Buchstaben darauf einzugraben*).

At Thebes, the great statues of Memnon did not speak, although they had a human face. Some were monolithic (Strabo had seen some), others formed of two seated colossi.

How does language come to the column? From an inner sun. Meantime, the column must be weaned from the sensory sun. This latter must be negated and the stone do without daylight. The phallus is then blinded, loses the outside, the light, form, *eidos*. The white stone becomes black. The *Behausen*—the habitacle as phallus—gains the essential interiority of the *Selbst* only by plunging into night, elaborating its language in the black formless stone.

This is the Kabba, the black stone of Mecca: no remainders—everything is scraped, retrieved, inscribed, sublated.

A still negative interiority, covering over of the white stone, "inner cover": "Standing over and against this external shape [Memnon] is the other shape, which announces that it has in it an *inner*. The nature returning back into its essence deposes its living, individualizing, self-disorienting diversity in all its movement, and it lowers it into an inessential casing (*unwesentlichen Gehäuse*) which is the *covering of the inner* (Decke des inneren). This inner is at first still the simple darkness, the unmoved, the black formless stone."

The artisan is caught in this driving contradiction between the system of the white stone (lost and sublated) and that of the black stone that sublates the other only to lose again the true interiority by missing the voice. So the two presentations (*Darstellungen*) of the inside and the outside must be united or reconciled. How is the artisan to elaborate this contradiction?

But I cannot go into detail about this period of my life. My memory would like to forget it, would like to dim its contours, powder it with talcum, offer it a formula comparable to the milk bath which the elegants of the sixteenth century called *a bath of modesty*.

I got my mess-tin filled with leftover soup and went off to eat in a corner. I preserved within me, my head under my wing, the memory of a sublime and debased Stilitano. I was proud of his strength and was strong in his complicity with the police. All day long I was sad, though sober. A kind of dissatisfaction inflated each of my acts, including the most simple. I would have liked a visible, dazzling glory to be manifest in my fingertips, would have liked my potency to lift me from the earth, to explode within me and dissolve me, to shower me to the four winds, I would have rained all over the world. My powder, my pollen

pollen is always threatened, exposed to the risk of being lost or destroyed. The thief notes as much when he returns to Czechoslovakia. He has just climbed some stairs, this time those of the chief of police: "During the questioning (Why did I want to go to Czechoslovakia? What was I doing there?) I was all atremble lest my ruse be discovered. At that moment I experienced the anxious joy, fragile as the pollen on hazel blossoms, the golden morning joy of the murderer who escapes."

And pollen is not only fragile, as if fleeing from the law, it has a relation to yellow, it falls from yellow as what falls [*il tombe du jaune*], here from a musician's powder puff: "One feels that the yellow will powder them with its pollen" (*Miracle of the Rose*).

We're not going to develop here the theory of pollen and dissemence. From the beginning we've been following another theory: the logic of

Enigmatically.

We must distinguish here between the enigmatic and the oracular. In aesthetic religion the oracle will be the analogon of the enigma, its vocalized twin.

The artisan resolves the contradiction by producing enigmas that combine the two contraries, nature and consciousness, inside and outside, light and dark. It's a witticism [*mot d'esprit*]: difficult to decipher, nocturnal in its form, addressed also to the unconscious , profound wisdom incapable of giving its reasons, a sort of cryptogram that the Egyptians themselves, if we are to believe the *Aesthetics*, do not understand. The producer of the enigma can be irresponsible, blind to what is written by his hand: "The artisan thus combines both of them in his blending of the natural and self-conscious shapes. These ambiguous essences are riddles to themselves, that is, are the conscious wrestling with what lacks consciousness, the simple inner with the multiply shaped outer, the darkness of thought paired with the clarity of expression. Now these ambiguous essences break out into the language of a deeper, but scarcely comprehensible, wisdom."

The first language properly speaking is therefore "double" (*zweideutig*), enigmatic, it plays the contraries between conscious and unconscious, on two scenes at once.

The paradigm here is furnished by the Egyptian religion. The philosophy of religion interprets it as a "religion of the enigma," of darkness, of animal masks, of the walled-off unconscious. The Egyptian spirit lacks that unveiled transparency that characterizes the Greek. Its veil *represents by anticipation* the Greek unveiling. The representation is therefore a veil, the veil a representation. "The most important presentation *(Hauptdarstellung)* by which the essence of this combat [between the conscious and the unconscious, the clear and the obscure, etc.] is made completely accessible to intuition *(anschaulich)* is the image of the goddess at Sais (Neith) who was presented *(dargestellt)* veiled *(verschleiert).* It is symbolized therein and in the inscription in her temple—'I am what was, is, and shall be; my veil has been lifted by no mortal'—expressly declared that nature is a being-differentiated in (it)self, namely, an other opposed to its manifestation but which immediately offers itself, an enigma."

The veil does not symbolize the enigma. The enigma is the structure of the veil suspended between the contraries.

Does Hegel then make a witticism, is he playing

obsequence and of the apotropaic umbrella under the "four wind" downpour. One has always to get back to it but after indispensable detours and barely calculable delays. I am always (following) the dead one. Who sets my pace.

The galaxy doesn't figure the element that my sperm must touch ("my powder, my pollen, would have touched the stars"), it is itself a disseminal element. One has also to understand, then, how a certain abbé in *Our Lady of the Flowers* "ejaculated a seed [*semence*] of constellations."

The detours of theory, concerning text, unconscious, and obsequence, seem interminable. Each narrative pose, for example here, in what might resemble a bad popular novel, inscribes the theory in literature. The text grips each character, each name, forename, nickname, it hardbinds them by bending them to its own rhythm, to its own desire: pretext and payoff for a narrator who, like the abbé in question, crossdresses and comes over their dying, even their suicide: "Ernestine's final gesture might have been performed quickly, but, like Culafroy in fact, she is serving a text she knows nothing about, a text I am composing whose *dénouement* will occur when the time is ripe. Ernestine is perfectly aware of how ridiculously literary her act is, but that she has to submit to cheap literature makes her even more touching in her own eyes and ours."

wickedly, in the Egyptian manner, with the signifiers? Quoting the end of the inscription of the temple of Neith in Lower Egypt, he deciphers it into German-Greek so as to read in it the whole course of the sun that sets in the West and calls itself back within itself. The story of this *Erinnerung* is a family story. The spiritual sun is both the son and the father of the sensory sun, the same and the circular converse of the one that basically lit the Republic. Here, to announce the hermeneutic and teleological resolution of the enigma in the Greek (aesthetic) religion, then in the Christian (revealed) religion: "It [nature] . . . has an inner element, something that is hidden (*ein Inneres, Verborgenes*). But, it is stated further in this inscription, 'the fruit of my flesh is Helios'. This as yet hidden essence therefore expresses clearness, the sun, the becoming clear to oneself, the spiritual sun (*geistige Sonne*) as the *son* (*den Sohn*) who is born of her. It is this dearness which is attained to in the Greek and Jewish religions, in the former in art and in the beautiful human form, in the latter in objective thought. The *enigma* is solved; the Egyptian *Sphinx,* according to a deeply significant (*Bedeutungsvollen*) and admirable myth, was slain by a Greek, and thus the enigma has been solved. This means that the content is *man, free, self-knowing spirit.*"

The Oedipian resolution of the enigma tolls the end of natural religion in its last moment. Thought attains the clarity of its unveiled there (*Da-sein*), the artisan becomes a "laborer of spirit," conscious of his activity—an artist. The instinctive, quasi-animal elaboration is now an art.

An essentially Greek story, opened by the death of the Sphinx, the aesthetic religion also develops according to the ternary rhythm of a syllogism: the *abstract* work of art, the *living* work of art, the *spiritual* work of art. It is the same rhythm, with an analogous content, as that of natural religion (indeterminate abstraction of the luminous essence, life of plants and animals, spirituality), each of the three moments dividing in turn into three, according to a syllogistic structure that is infinitely self-representative and always abyssal. But is the abyss filled in or dug out by a "mise en abyme"? And then is digging taking a risk? And in view of what?

The abstract work of art maintains the figure of the gods in the block of the spatial thing. But in it the concept takes off the angular crystal of the understanding, the mix of inorganic and vegetable forms, imitation in general. The black stone is withdrawn from its animal mire,

Ernestine, Divine's mother, knows that he is going to die and that she must simulate her son's suicide: "'I'll say he killed himself.' Ernestine's logic, which is a stage logic, has no relationship with what is called verisimilitude, verisimilitude being the disavowal of unavowable reasons."

She sets the pace that's not to be followed.

In fact Ernestine is going to kill her son and "brood [*se couver*]" on a flagstone in the cemetery, on a "simple flagstone, slightly curved," like an egg [*oeuf*] or an *oeuvre*. She held the revolver like "a phallus in action," "big with murder, pregnant with a corpse." "This book aims to be only a small fragment of my inner life." Designs at the origin of *Funeral Rites:* the source is unique but the outflows or the columns double. One has to pass from one signature to the other, one cannot put one's hand or tongue on both at once.

Such is the unique and double origin of murder. Of the unique and double murder.

Designs that never reduce to a single one, whence the division of the clang: *colpos*.

the figures represented are no longer natural essences but clear spirits, the ethical spirits of self-conscious peoples. So long as they are singular national figures, Athena for example, they still retain in themselves a certain natural thickness, a remainder of nature. This naturality must be sublated. But so long as the work does not belong to the element of language, so long as it extends in space, it remains and falls outside the domain of the artist. It opposes it. The totality of the work is cut, like a remainder, from its elaboration.

This caesura takes two contradictory and indissociable forms that constantly cross each other. On the one hand, the erasure, the omission of the artist: he is disinterested enough to declare that his work lives on its own, has life without him, carries off his signature. But in carrying it off it keeps it, and under this modernitarian thematic Hegel immediately detects on the other hand the cunning or the dissimulated, dissimulating underside, the hypocrisy of the other unilaterality. For the artist verifies that the work by being able in this way to cut itself off and fall away from him, *is not his equal,* that it has not produced an essence equal to its author (kein ihm gleiches *Wesen hervorbrachte*). The animation proper to the work, the admiration of its admirers, the offerings or even the sacrifices it provokes and which bring it to consciousness—the artist knows that all that is inferior to his work, to his elaboration, to his production, precisely because it *detaches itself* from it. By his retreat the artist then rises above his remains and by the same token retains it as a small part, a piece of himself. The omission, the inapparent nature of the signature simultaneously starts off an operation of mastery and the mastery of the operation. All of which must be recognized as the *deed* (*Tat*) of the artist in his indefatigable strategy. If the admirers "place themselves *beneath* it (*darunter setzen*) and recognize in it [their] *essence* which dominates them, he knows himself to be master over that essence."

Hegel to an autograph hunter: "Had the wish of adding something from my hand as well to a collection of handwriting samples reached me directly, I would have requested some kind of content to be dictated to me. I cannot now make this request in writing, for this very act would render the request superfluous. So allow the superfluity of having submitted the request and thereby at once annihilated it suffice. Berlin, July 6, 1827. H."

In order to scar over this cut between elaboration and work, between the author and his remains, in order—therefore—to think it, the work must *remain present* to the artist, without falling from him like a truncated thing in space, like an admirable excrement over which the master sits on the throne, forgetting himself. The

The mother remains after killing because she no longer knows where to give suck. Flower drawings: "The old hallucination of my childhood obtruded itself, and I can render it only by the following image: still flowers that do not mingle, though they have a single source, rush into his mouth, which they spread and fill. One of the soldiers made a slight noise" (*Funeral Rites*).

gl: the stricture of the orifice—bottleneck [*goulot d'étranglement*]—then informs a block of casein, a belch, a fart, a remainder for making in any case one's tomb.

But it's always the mother: one knows now that that word no longer means anything other than what follows, obsequences, remains after killing what she has given birth to. It has just been verified for *Our Lady of the Flowers.* It can be done with *Funeral Rites.* I've often asked the question: what does *here* mean for a text and in a language in general. What is the *here now* of a clang?

Of a remainder?
Of a remainder that would no longer be that of any operation, neither relic nor residue.

The response from *Funeral Rites* accuses the remainder of the mother of committing the murder. Let's stop near here: "faded flowers. . . . Young! No doubt about it, I said to myself, it's here . . . I stopped there. The uttering of 'here' and, even if only mentally, of the words meant to follow, 'that he was killed,' gave to my pain a physical precision that aggravated it. The words were too cruel. Then I said to myself that the words were words and did not in any way change the facts.

element of art will therefore no longer be a thing in space without consciousness—it will be time and voice. Even if—and to the extent that—time is the truth of the space it sublates. The work must find time to become consciousness present to itself. The stone must begin to speak: "The work of art thus demands another element of its existence (*Dasein*); it demands that the god have another way of coming to light (*Hervogang*) other than that in which, in the depths of his creative night, the god descends into the very opposite (*in das Gegenteil*—its contrary piece—*herabfällt*), into externality, that is, into the determination of a *thing* lacking self-consciousness. This higher element is *language* (Sprache) —an existence (*Dasein*) which is immediately self-conscious existence (*Existenz*). Just as *individual* self-consciousness exists there (*da ist*) within language, it likewise immediately exists there as a *universal* contagion (*Ansteckung*)." The soul then exists "as soul."

The *hymn* is this presence of the universal to the singular, of the inside to the outside, of the production to the work, of the god to his animated figure. Religious song, the fervent flux of the religious voice gathers the singularities into the same element of fire and water (*die Andacht, in allen angezündet, ist der geistige Strom*). It flows and consumes all remainders.

And yet, contrary to habit, it is a question of a remainder after the hymn, and it is the object of a longer and more awkward development. This is about the *oracle*: it relates to the time of speech as the enigma to the space of writing. Simple and universal, oracular propositions come from outside the community (as opposed to the hymn, an experience of inner communion). They are sublime but their universality easily turns to triviality, especially in the first period of the oracle, that of natural religion and the luminous essence. In becoming for-itself, the oracle comes back to universal truths in a language *proper* to the community: this is for example the "certain and unwritten law" of Antigone, the law of the gods that speaks in the hearts of the citizens. This sublation of the "natural" oracle suspends luck, chance, the throw of the dice in language. The natural and spontaneous oracle is the fortuitous case where language happens upon the universal truth. Whence a sort of division

I forced myself to say over and over, inwardly, with the irritating repetitiveness of a saw [*scie*], Here [*I-ci*], He-re, He-re, He-re. My mind was being sharpened at the spot designated by 'Here.' I was no longer even witnessing a drama. No drama could have taken place in an area too narrow for any presence. 'He-re, He-re, He-re, He-re. That he was killed [*qu'on l'a tué*], that he was killed, that he was killed, cunt killed him [*con l'a tué*], cunt killed him . . .' and I mentally composed the following epitaph: 'Here cunt killed him.'"

Remains here or clang unstoppable.

That some double constrain(t)s [*Que quelque double entrave*].

Following Divine's death, the funeral is, then, arranged by the abbé who concentrates all desires on himself. He is a transvestite who knows his way around breaking, entering, and gutting. All the words follow in silence until the complete dispersion of theory and of the said seminary. Crumbling, defrocking, make-up powder and flowers.

"In the rain, this black cortege, bespangled with multicolored faces and blended with the scent of flowers and rouge, followed the hearse. The flat round umbrellas, undulating above the ambulating procession, held it suspended between heaven and earth. . . . The hearse had wings on its axles. The abbé emerged first into the rain singing the *dies irae*. He tucked up his cassock and cope, as he had been taught to do at the seminary when the weather was bad. . . . Bear in mind that the abbé was young. You could tell that under his funereal vestments he had the lithe body of a passionate athlete. Which means, in short, that he was in travesty [*portait le travesti*].

in two of the oracle: proper language and foreign language. Socrates, for example, seeks in himself the voice of philosophy but he lets the foreign speech of his daemon whisper to him unnecessary advice, contingent precepts, tell his fortune, converse with him about the opportuneness of a trip, etc. "So too the universal consciousness takes its knowledge about the contingent from birds or trees or the fermenting earth, whose vapor takes away from self-consciousness all its deliberateness. For what is contingent is the impulsive, the alien, and ethical consciousness thus also lets itself, for example, with a roll of the dice [*wie durch ein Würfeln*], determine itself in an impulsive and alien manner about these things." The oracle as such, before the internal and unwritten law, is linked to fate (*Los*). *Das Orakel oder Los.*

The petroglyph remains outside consciousness. Its opposite, the hymn, disappears immediately, like the voice, at the very moment of its production. Like time, it is no longer *there* as soon as, immediately, once it is *there,* insofar as it is *there* (*wie die Zeit, unmittelbar nicht mehr da, indem sie da ist*). The *Da* posits itself insofar as it withdraws. In its counter-time. Abstract art is made of this double unilaterality: spatial non-movement and temporal movement, double loss of the divine figure, plastic art and lyrical art.

This double loss is sublated in the *cult*. In it the divine essence descends from its beyond down to consciousness. The cult is initially abstract, it is announced in the fervor of the hymn which is limited to being its representation: inner, secretive, inactual. This is the moment of inner purification when the soul does not know that it is evil. It purifies its surface with water and covers it with white linens. But the cult must not be secret, it must give rise to actual gestures and operations: sacrifice and enjoyment, the cunning of enjoyment in sacrifice. The action of the cult, its manipulation (*Handlung*) begins with the abandonment (*Hingabe*), renunciation of possession and enjoyment, without apparent profit. But the sacrifice takes back with one hand what it gives with the other and the accounts must be kept with double entries. What one sacrifices goes up "in smoke" (*in Rauch*) like the effluvium of a consuming or a decomposition. But it is kept in the sublimity of its essence, like a spirit. The animal sacrificed becomes the sign of a god, the consumed fruits *are* Ceres and Bacchus living. The sacrifice reappropriates the enjoyment for itself but the "cunning" of enjoyment carries itself off, it consumes itself: "the result in *enjoyment* is itself robbed of its

In the church—the whole funeral service having been merely the 'do this in memory of me'—approaching the altar on tiptoe, in silence, he had picked the lock of the tabernacle, parted the veil like someone who at midnight parts the double curtains of an alcove, held his breath, seized the ciborium with the caution of an ungloved burglar, and finally, having broken it, swallowed a questionable host." Explore the corpus, make the inventory of all the tabernacles more or less emptied of sense, the "secret dwelling-place" of *Miracle,* "where the captain of the galley stands," receptacles with locks picked, broken into, gutted, cracked open. It's also, in *Our Lady of the Flowers,* the name of a nightclub: "All the queens of *The Tavernacle* and the neighboring bars . . ."

While he sings, transported into a fantastic Hungary (country of Huns and Geldings [*Hongres*]), the face of a young foreigner suddenly appears, an extinguished butt in his mouth.

The butt is in his mouth like a word [*mot*] or a bit [*mors*]. Exquisite.

Slang tongue, cut object almost letting its ash fall while one sucks it still, the gloss gives the abbé a hard-on: "The word 'butt [*mégot*]' and the taste of the sucked tobacco made the abbé's spine stiffen and draw back with three short jerks, the vibrations of which reverberated through all his muscles and on to infinity, which shuddered and ejaculated a seed of constellations."

would have touched the stars. I loved Stilitano. But loving him in the rocky dryness of this land, under an irrevocable sun, exhausted me, rimmed my eyelids with fire. Weeping a little would have deflated me. Or talking a lot, at great length, brilliantly, before an attentive and respectful audience. I was alone and friendless."

existence (*das Resultat im* Genusse *sich selbst seines Daseins beraubt*)."

The end of enjoyment is the end of enjoyment: endpoint. The snag with enjoyment, its chance and its loss, is that it must sacrifice itself to be there, to give itself its *there*, to touch on its *Da-sein*. *Telos* of enjoyment equals death, it would be the endpoint were there not, for the indefatigable desire of the speculative dialectic, another extra turn, rings still to be fulfilled and anniversaries to celebrate.

The opposition of sacrifice and enjoyment is sublated in labor, but in the enjoyment of labor, in the enjoyment of the durable products of the elaboration that defers enjoyment. The dwelling and the ornament of the gods, this whole material no longer has the naturality of statues. And it is elaborated by man who reappropriates the enjoyment of it in the festival. The places and objects of the cult, the altars, the temples, etc., are like the hard bone that remains from the sacrifices and the consummated enjoyment, certainly, but they occupy the place of labor in the city. The human producer here shares with the god all the enjoyments of the festival. "At the festivals, the people likewise adorn both their own dwellings and garments along with their own performances with graceful items. In this manner, they receive from a grateful god (*dankbaren Gotte*) a reciprocation (*Erwiderung*) for their gifts, and they receive the proofs of his favor, within which through their labors the people united themselves (*verband*) with the god. This unity with the god takes place not in a hope and a later actualization (*späten Wirklichkeit*); rather, in showing him the honor and in the offering (*Darbringung*) of alms, the people immediately have the enjoyment of their own wealth and adornment."

It is the festival of labor and the labor of the festival in the Greek city. The sacrifice reappropriates the enjoyment lost by labor in the cult; and the cult is an exchange of labor with the god who renders to the workers the *immediate* enjoyment of the products they had renounced, with no apparent hope of return. The god repays the workers for the sacrifice of surplus-value. Gift against gift: I give you or sacrifice to you this, which takes on more value for being sacrificed, an object of useless ornament, a lost piece of jewelry. The gratitude of the addressee returns the enjoyment; and the festival, this festival at least, far from opening a pure and impossible disseminal expenditure, strictly organizes the circulation of

What I feared, naturally, has come about. Already. The same stage. Today, here, now, I am abandoned, me, on the immense esplanade, the debris of [*le débris de*]

His hour unction death rattle extreme grimace slab basilica rises for the royal stiff his mother who dies wanting herself to close his eyelids.

Canopy of the eye rolled backward.

How does he do it? He is ready. He has always had his corpse about him, in his pocket, in a matchbox. To hand. It lights up on its own. It should. He feels himself standing in the way of his death—he the little one living, that is—of the sublime, beyond measure, outsized superelevation of his colossus. He is only a detail of his double, unless it be the other way around.

Always more, with a bit, than with the whole of the other. Hungry end of the drive [*Faim de la pulsion*].

enjoyment in the cult. *Telos* of the cult, speculate the enjoyment of God and just do it.

following the phenomenological gallery ("This coming-to-be exhibits (*stellt . . . dar*) a languid movement and succession of spirits, a gallery of pictures (*eine Galerie von Bildern*) . . .") from station to station, one comes back towards the *IC* and *Sa*, having passed "the Calvary of absolute spirit." One finds there again, very close to the "Calvary,"—to be looked at from both sides—the "certainty of its throne" (*Gewißheit seines Throns*).
It suffices, in short, scarcely, to wait.
All this will have been projected, torn to pieces, closed, nailed, fallen, risen again [*relevé*: sublated], repeated, around Easter. The circle of the phenomenological gallery is reproduced and encircled in the greater *Logic* and the *Encyclopedia*. What is the difference between two editions of the same circle? Hegel who has just learned of "the rapid sale of the second edition"of the *Encyclopedia*, confides his worries to Winter, in 1827. He asks him "to commit . . . to the prompt payment of the royalty. For the original eighteen sheets in the first edition we settled upon two-thirds of the 25 Florin royalty. For the additional number of sheets we reverted to this original royalty, and for the further eighteen sheets of the second edition we agreed on 22 Florins per sheet. In this agreement I reserved for myself the royalties of the first edition for the additional material contained in any new edition. . . . Whether, and by how much, this number of sheets might still be increased in the contemplated new edition I cannot yet say, since the task catches me by surprise, and since I have not yet had a chance to run through the text with this in mind. In general, however, I do not foresee undertaking any significant change or expansion. The printing remains fixed as before at a thousand copies, with eighteen complimentary author's copies, twelve on vellum and six on writing paper.
Since I have been notified so late of the need for a new edition—Mr. Oswald's letter is dated July 13—the manuscript may be sent off later than you probably would wish. Seeing how my work has since piled up, I cannot yet say anything definite on when it will be. I shall do my best, however, to enable the edition to appear by Easter."

We are in the Dionysian circle. The third moment of abstract art, the religion inscribed in it, is already the most abstract phase of the following moment, the living work of art. Through its syllogism, a language process is busy on the sublation of the remainder.

The first, unilateral moment, is the Bacchic delirium, the *Taumel*, the overflowing inebriation during which the god makes himself present. The rising luminous essence unveils itself as what it is. Enjoyment is the mystery of this revelation. For the mystical does not reside in the dissimulation of a secret (*Geheimnis*) or an unknown. But what is bared here still belongs to immediate spirit, to spirit-nature. The mystery of the bread and the wine *is not yet* what it is, *already*, that of flesh and blood. Dionysos must therefore pass into his opposite, calm down in order to exist, not let himself be eaten and drunk by "the horde of exalted women."

So he does gymnastics.

He is ready. How does he do it? so unprotected, stark naked. So many missing letters. No A tolls in his name; above all no R, not even one. No G either, no more than a consonant, an A or U to come to harden, stiffen, arrest or angle. To engrave. To prevent groaning, moaning, wailing. He is all alone, without any of the right letters, she has kept them all for herself, for her forename. The I, he also lacks that; L, he doesn't even have that.

Let fall, without ado, none at all, completely naked, just enough for speculating—without image, without knowing—on his name. Without what else [*sans quoi*].

Mourning milk signed and sealed (coacted, pressed, squeezed, hidden, coagulated, curdled).

I'm beginning to get jealous of his mother who could change phallus ad infinitum without being detailed. Godbecoming [*dieuvenue*] hypothesis father in itself for not being there.

Apollo is not named, it is true; but the opposite, the other side, the contrary stance into which the Dionysiac must pass in order to "calm down by becoming an object (*sich zum Gegenstande beruhigen*)," stands like the body erect in Greek gymnastics, beautiful *Körperlichkeit.* The figure of man is cultivated instead of the sculptural column of the divinity. The divine allows itself to be reappropriated in the human: exchange again of the two erections, the two institutions, putting into movement and recovery of life. Surplus-value of the contradiction that contracts (itself) with itself, makes a present to itself of the remainder [*se fait du reste cadeau*].

But once again, pendulum movement, everything gets fixed in the external objectivity that has been opposed to the Dionysian conflagration. So we have two opposed pieces that contradict each other in their respective unilaterality. The balance (*Gleichgewicht*) is ceaselessly broken. In delirium, the self (*Selbst*) loses consciousness; on the stadium, it is spirit that is outside itself.

Through the spiritual work of art—language through and through—the reconciliation is announced: synthesis of the aesthetic religion (abstraction, life, spirit). The syllogism of spiritual art (*epos*, tragedy, comedy) leads aesthetic religion to the revealed religion. Via comedy, then.

A time to perfect the resemblance between Dionysos and Christ.

Between the two (already) is elaborated in sum the origin of literature.

But it runs to its ruin, for having counted without

He, meanwhile, remains light, doesn't stop lightening up. How to live like that? Everything is blocked on the maternal account. Fallen due. So little would have been needed, an A, an R, a G, for it to set differently, to come to a halt elsewhere, to be anchored in different depths, claw or scratch another surface, yet the same. So that it no longer slides. Another contract with oneself, with one's funeral rite. Another legacy. To settle with, buy off the already of the absolute ancestor.

"*Vor der Sonne kamst du zur mir, dem Einsamsten.*

Wir sind Freunde von Anbeginn: uns ist Gram und Grauen und Grund gemeinsam: noch die Sonne ist uns gemeinsam.

Wir reden nicht zu einander, weil wir zu Vieles wissen -: wir schweigen uns an, wir lächeln uns unser Wissen zu.

. . . *was uns gemein ist, - das ungeheure unbegrenzte Ja-* . . ."

It's very arid on the immense esplanade, but the work has only just begun, here, from now on. From when it begins to write. It begins barely. Lacking only one piece now.

It's creaking. Rolling along laid tree trunks. Pulleys. The greased ropes tighten, you hear only them, and the breathing of slaves bent in two. Ready to pull. Whiplash crack of the overseer. Renewed bound force. The thing is oblique. It's at an angle, already, with the ground. Slowly bites into its own shadow, sure of itself. So little would have been needed, the least error in calculation, they say, if it falls, if it leans and inclines toward the bed of the other, the machine is still too simple, the mode of writing precapitalist.

What I feared, naturally, already, is happening again. Today, here, now, the debris of

posthumanities

CARY WOLFE, SERIES EDITOR

62 *Clang*
Jacques Derrida

61 *Radioactive Ghosts*
Gabriele Schwab

60 *Gaian Systems: Lynn Margulis, Neocybernetics, and the End of the Anthropocene*
Bruce Clarke

59 *The Probiotic Planet: Using Life to Manage Life*
Jamie Lorimer

58 *Individuation in Light of Notions of Form and Information Volume II. Supplemental Texts*
Gilbert Simondon

57 *Individuation in Light of Notions of Form and Information Volume I*
Gilbert Simondon

56 *Thinking Plant Animal Human: Encounters with Communities of Difference*
David Wood

55 *The Elements of Foucault*
Gregg Lambert

54 *Postcinematic Vision: The Coevolution of Moving-Image Media and the Spectator*
Roger F. Cook

53 *Bleak Joys: Aesthetics of Ecology and Impossibility*
Matthew Fuller and Olga Goriunova

52 *Variations on Media Thinking*
Siegfried Zielinski

51 *Aesthesis and Perceptronium: On the Entanglement of Sensation, Cognition, and Matter*
Alexander Wilson

50 *Anthropocene Poetics: Deep Time, Sacrifice Zones, and Extinction*
David Farrier

49 *Metaphysical Experiments: Physics and the Invention of the Universe*
Bjørn Ekeberg

48 *Dialogues on the Human Ape*
Laurent Dubreuil and Sue Savage-Rumbaugh

47 *Elements of a Philosophy of Technology: On the Evolutionary History of Culture*
Ernst Kapp

46 *Biology in the Grid: Graphic Design and the Envisioning of Life*
Phillip Thurtle

45 *Neurotechnology and the End of Finitude*
Michael Haworth

44 *Life: A Modern Invention*
Davide Tarizzo

43 *Bioaesthetics: Making Sense of Life in Science and the Arts*
Carsten Strathausen

42 *Creaturely Love: How Desire Makes Us More and Less Than Human*
Dominic Pettman

41 *Matters of Care: Speculative Ethics in More Than Human Worlds*
Maria Puig de la Bellacasa

40 *Of Sheep, Oranges, and Yeast: A Multispecies Impression*
Julian Yates

39 *Fuel: A Speculative Dictionary*
Karen Pinkus

38 *What Would Animals Say If We Asked the Right Questions?*
Vinciane Despret

37 *Manifestly Haraway*
Donna J. Haraway

36 *Neofinalism*
Raymond Ruyer

35 *Inanimation: Theories of Inorganic Life*
David Wills

34 *All Thoughts Are Equal: Laruelle and Nonhuman Philosophy*
John Ó Maoilearca

33 *Necromedia*
Marcel O'Gorman

32 *The Intellective Space: Thinking beyond Cognition*
Laurent Dubreuil

31 *Laruelle: Against the Digital*
Alexander R. Galloway

30 *The Universe of Things: On Speculative Realism*
Steven Shaviro

29 *Neocybernetics and Narrative*
Bruce Clarke

28 *Cinders*
Jacques Derrida

27 *Hyperobjects: Philosophy and Ecology after the End of the World*
Timothy Morton

26 *Humanesis: Sound and Technological Posthumanism*
David Cecchetto

25 *Artist Animal*
Steve Baker

24 *Without Offending Humans: A Critique of Animal Rights*
Élisabeth de Fontenay

23 *Vampyroteuthis Infernalis: A Treatise, with a Report by the Institut Scientifique de Recherche Paranaturaliste*
Vilém Flusser and Louis Bec

22 *Body Drift: Butler, Hayles, Haraway*
Arthur Kroker

21 *HumAnimal: Race, Law, Language*
Kalpana Rahita Seshadri

20 *Alien Phenomenology, or What It's Like to Be a Thing*
Ian Bogost

19 *CIFERAE: A Bestiary in Five Fingers*
Tom Tyler

18 *Improper Life: Technology and Biopolitics from Heidegger to Agamben*
Timothy C. Campbell

17 *Surface Encounters: Thinking with Animals and Art*
Ron Broglio

16 *Against Ecological Sovereignty: Ethics, Biopolitics, and Saving the Natural World*
Mick Smith

15 *Animal Stories: Narrating across Species Lines*
Susan McHugh

14 *Human Error: Species-Being and Media Machines*
Dominic Pettman

13 *Junkware*
Thierry Bardini

12 *A Foray into the Worlds of Animals and Humans,* with *A Theory of Meaning*
Jakob von Uexküll

11 *Insect Media: An Archaeology of Animals and Technology*
Jussi Parikka

10 *Cosmopolitics II*
Isabelle Stengers

9 *Cosmopolitics I*
Isabelle Stengers

8 *What Is Posthumanism?*
Cary Wolfe

7 *Political Affect: Connecting the Social and the Somatic*
John Protevi

6 *Animal Capital: Rendering Life in Biopolitical Times*
Nicole Shukin

5 *Dorsality: Thinking Back through Technology and Politics*
David Wills

4 *Bíos: Biopolitics and Philosophy*
Roberto Esposito

3 *When Species Meet*
Donna J. Haraway

2 *The Poetics of DNA*
Judith Roof

1 *The Parasite*
Michel Serres

Jacques Derrida (1930–2004) was a renowned French philosopher. He is associated with poststructuralism and postmodern theory and developed deconstruction as a form of semiotic analysis. He wrote more than sixty books, including *Of Grammatology* and *Writing and Difference.*

Geoffrey Bennington is Asa G. Candler Professor of Modern French Thought at Emory University. He is the author of many books in English and French, most recently *Scatter I: The Politics of Politics in Foucault, Heidegger, and Derrida*; *Scatter II: Politics in Deconstruction*; and *Kant on the Frontier: Philosophy, Politics, and the Ends of the Earth.* He is general editor, with Peggy Kamuf, of the English edition of *The Seminars of Jacques Derrida* and has translated several works by Derrida.

David Wills is professor of French and comparative literature at Brown University. He has written three books on the originary technicity of the human, including *Dorsality: Thinking Back through Technology and Politics* (Minnesota, 2008), as well as *Killing Times: The Temporal Technology of the Death Penalty*. He has translated various works by Jacques Derrida.